FOUNDATIONS OF PSYCHOLOGICAL THOUGHT

A History of Psychology

Edited by

BARBARA F. GENTILE
Simmons College

BENJAMIN O. MILLER
Salem State College

**SAGE**

Los Angeles • London • New Delhi • Singapore

For information:

SAGE Publications, Inc.
2455 Teller Road
Thousand Oaks, California 91320
E-mail: order@sagepub.com

SAGE Publications India Pvt. Ltd.
B 1/I 1 Mohan Cooperative Industrial Area
Mathura Road, New Delhi 110 044
India

SAGE Publications Ltd.
1 Oliver's Yard
55 City Road
London EC1Y 1SP
United Kingdom

SAGE Publications Asia-Pacific Pte. Ltd.
33 Pekin Street #02-01
Far East Square
Singapore 048763

Printed in the United States of America.

Library of Congress Cataloging-in-Publication Data

Foundations of psychological thought : a history of psychology/Barbara F. Gentile, Ben Miller, editors.
    p. cm.
Includes bibliographical references and index.
ISBN 978-0-7619-3077-8 (pbk. : alk. paper)
    1. Psychology—History. I. Gentile, Barbara F. II. Miller, Ben.
BF81.H564 2009
150.9—dc22   2008019311

This book is printed on acid-free paper.

08   09   10   11   12   10   9   8   7   6   5   4   3   2   1

Acquisitions Editors:	Cheri Dellelo, Erik Evans
Editorial Assistant:	Lara Grambling
Production Editor:	Karen Wiley
Typesetter:	C&M Digitals (P) Ltd.
Proofreader:	Susan Schon
Indexer:	Sheila Bodell
Cover Designer:	Gail Buschman
Marketing Manager:	Stephanie Adams

FOU   NS OF
PSYC   ICAL
THE   IT

not be issued
hour only, an

We dedicate this book to our colleague
Peter W. Castle, who always asks the right questions.

Contents

Acknowledgments ix

Introduction xi

PART I: THE MIND AND THE BODY 1

1.1 René Descartes (1596–1650)
The Passions of the Soul (1649) 5

1.2 William James (1842–1910)
Psychology (1892) 22

1.3 Wilhelm Wundt (1832–1920)
Outlines of Psychology (1897) 36

1.4 Alan Turing (1912–1954)
Computing Machinery and Intelligence (1950) 45

1.5 John Searle (b. 1932)
Minds, Brains, and Science (1984) 65

PART II: PERCEIVING 85

2.1 George Berkeley (1685–1753)
An Essay Towards a New Theory of Vision (1709) 94

2.2 Thomas Reid (1710–1796)
Essays on the Intellectual Powers of Man (1785) 113

2.3 Hermann von Helmholtz (1821–1894)
Treatise on Physiological Optics (1867) 136

2.4 J. J. Gibson (1904–1979)
The Perception of the Visual World (1950) 161

2.5 David Marr (1945–1980)

Visual Information Processing: The Structure
and Creation of Visual Representations (1980)   **180**

PART III: OPENING THE BLACK BOX   **203**

3.1 F. C. Donders (1818–1889)

On the Speed of Mental Processes (1868–1869)   **206**

3.2 E. B. Titchener (1867–1927)

An Outline of Psychology (1896)   **219**

3.3 Sigmund Freud (1856–1939)

Psychopathology of Everyday Life (1901)   **237**

3.4 Herbert Simon (1916–2001) and Kenneth Kotovsky (b. 1939)

Human Acquisition of Concepts for Sequential Patterns (1963)   **244**

3.5 B. F. Skinner (1904–1990)

About Behaviorism (1974)   **261**

3.6 Michael I. Posner (b. 1936), Steven F. Petersen (b. 1952), Peter T. Fox (b. 1951), and Marcus E. Raichle (b. 1937)

Localization of Cognitive Operations in the Human Brain (1988)   **279**

PART IV: NATIVISM AND EMPIRICISM—AKA HEREDITY AND ENVIRONMENT   **295**

4.1 René Descartes (1596–1650)

Notes Directed Against a Certain Programme (1648)   **300**

4.2 John Locke (1632–1704)

An Essay Concerning Human Understanding (1690)   **304**

4.3 Charles Darwin (1809–1882)

The Origin of Species (1859)   **320**

4.4 Hermann von Helmholtz (1821–1894)

The Facts of Perception (1878)   **337**

4.5 Sigmund Freud (1856–1939)

Instincts and Their Vicissitudes (1915)   **353**

4.6 John Watson (1878–1958)

What the Nursery Has to Say About Instincts (1926)   **370**

4.7 Keller Breland (1915–1965) and Marian Breland (1920–2001)

The Misbehavior of Organisms (1961) **391**

4.8 Noam Chomsky (b. 1928)

Language and Mind (1968) **401**

PART V: LEVELS OF EXPLANATION **423**

5.1 Max Wertheimer (1880–1943)

Laws of Organization in Perceptual Forms (1923) **427**

5.2 Ivan Petrovich Pavlov (1849–1936)

Conditioned Reflexes: An Investigation of the
Physiological Activity of the Cerebral Cortex (1927) **441**

5.3 Kurt Lewin (1890–1947)

Experiments in Social Space (1939) **454**

5.4 Edward Chace Tolman (1886–1959)

Cognitive Maps in Rats and Men (1948) **468**

5.5 Donald Hebb (1904–1985)

Organization of Behavior: A Neuropsychological Theory (1949) **483**

**5.6 Brenda Milner (b. 1918), Larry R. Squire (b. 1941),
and Eric R. Kandel (b. 1929)**

Cognitive Neuroscience and the Study of Memory (1998) **492**

PART VI: NORMAL AND ABNORMAL **513**

6.1 Benjamin Rush (1746–1813)

Medical Inquiries and Observations Upon
the Diseases of the Mind (1812) **517**

6.2 Henry J. Wegrocki (1909–1967)

A Critique of Cultural and Statistical Concepts of Abnormality (1939) **533**

6.3 Karen Horney (1885–1952)

Neurosis and Human Growth (1950) **544**

6.4 Evelyn Hooker (1907–1996)

The Adjustment of the Male Overt Homosexual (1957) **558**

6.5 Thomas S. Szasz (b. 1920)

The Myth of Mental Lllness (1960) **577**

6.6 Samuel B. Guze (1923–2000)

Biological Psychiatry: Is There Any Other Kind? (1989)   **589**

6.7 Corey L. M. Keyes (b. 1962)

*The Mental Health Continuum: From Languishing
to Flourishing in Life (2002)*   **601**

References   **619**

Index   **645**

About the Editors   **671**

Acknowledgments

We gratefully acknowledge many contributions to this book from many people. Our work would have been impossible without the expert assistance of the interlibrary loan offices at our respective institutions: Carol Demos and her staff at Simmons, and Martha-Jane Moreland and Becky LeMon at Salem State. We thank our friends and colleagues—Alec Bodkin, Peter Castle, Darlene Crone-Todd, Mindy Crowley, Patrick Drumm, Tim Eddy, Greg Feldman, Rachel Galli, Terry Lyons, Nadine Miller, Norman Miller, Diane Raymond, John Reeder, Geoff Turner, Maggie and Will Vaughan, Linda Watkins, and Al Yonas—who answered questions, read drafts, and made many helpful suggestions. At home, our families—Bob, Mike, and Jill Gentile, Sue Regan, Joseph and Jacob Miller—have sustained us, and at Sage, Jim Brace-Thompson, Cheri Dellelo, Erik Evans, Lara Grambling, and Karen Wiley have kept us pointed in the right direction and have been endlessly patient.

We would also like to thank the reviewers of earlier drafts, whose ideas and suggestions were of great value:

Susan T. Davis, University of Dayton

Laura Freberg, California Polytechnic State University, San Luis Obispo

James K. Horn, Saint Louis University

Roger Kreuz, University of Memphis

Robert Kugelmann, University of Dallas

Donald Polzella, University of Dayton

Roberto Refinetti, University of South Carolina

Dean Keith Simonton, University of California, Davis

William Tooke, State University of New York–Plattsburgh

Harry Whitaker, Northern Michigan University

Introduction

This book consists of 38 texts. They were written between 1648 and 2002, in Latin, French, Dutch, German, Russian, and English by philosophers, biologists, anthropologists, physicians, mathematicians, linguists, computer scientists, psychiatrists, physiologists, and psychologists. What they have in common—and the reason we have put them together between two covers—is that they provide a history of psychological thought.

WHAT IS PSYCHOLOGICAL THOUGHT?

The history of psychological thought is both more and less than the history of the field of psychology.

By *field of psychology* we mean the collection of people—teachers, students, researchers, practitioners—who identify their interests as psychology; the collection of academic and therapeutic disciplines that these people work in; the scientific, scholarly, and professional organizations they belong to; the books and journals they publish. The word *psychology* first appeared—in its Latin form *psychologia*—in Germany in the 16th century and gradually came into wider use in German, French, and English in the 18th century. Wilhelm Wundt established the first psychological laboratory at the University of Leipzig in 1879. Around the same time, William James began teaching the first psychology course at an American university (Harvard). James's student G. Stanley Hall earned the first American PhD for work in psychology in 1878 and founded the American Psychological Association in 1892. In short, psychology as an academic discipline, as a profession, as a livelihood is quite new.

By *psychological thought* we mean the questions that people have asked—and their attempts to answer those questions—about the mind. These days, a lot of the people who ask and try to answer questions about thinking, feeling, perceiving, knowing, remembering, understanding, communicating, and so on are psychologists, but interest in such questions has been around for a very long time. Just as psychological thought *precedes* psychology, we might also say that psychological thought *exceeds* psychology. Many of the people you will encounter in this book come from before psychology, and many others come from outside it—from philosophy, medicine, physiology, linguistics, computer science, mathematics. Psychology does not own the mind.

WHY READ ORIGINAL SOURCES?

The premise of this book is that it is worth our while to read original sources. There are many reasons, but in the present context three stand out.

Being There

"See Naples and die," say the Italians, meaning that when you have seen Naples you have had the best experience life has to offer. Notice they don't say, "See a picture of Naples and die." Being in Naples—or Paris or the Grand Canyon or the Bronx—is an experience that cannot be duplicated in pictures or words.

The importance of being there applies to most of life's pleasures. Looking at the Mona Lisa hanging in the Louvre is not the same as looking at a reproduction hanging on your wall, even if the reproduction is indistinguishable from the original. Reading *CliffsNotes* is not the same as reading Shakespeare. And so on.

We believe that a similar kind of being there is true for ideas. The understanding we get from secondary sources, useful as it is, is not *our* understanding. To have an understanding that we can call our own we must also read the original. No amount of reading *about* Aristotle's ideas, or Freud's or Darwin's, is the same as reading what Aristotle or Freud or Darwin actually said.

Getting It Right

There are a number of excellent histories of psychological thought. Learned and thoughtful scholars have spent years reading what people have had to say—in classical Greek, medieval Latin, Elizabethan English, and so on—about the mind over the last few thousand years. From this huge body of material they have abstracted what they consider to be the important ideas, significant discoveries, and historic trends. They have published the fruits of their labors, in clear modern English, for our convenience and edification. It is essential that we read these books.

For better or worse, however, the scholars don't always agree with one another. To make sense of it all we must, sooner or later, go to the source. When we do, we begin to see why scholars who have read the same texts have understood them differently, and we begin to understand them for ourselves.

If we had included every original source worth reading, we would not have called this book a reader. We would have called it a library. Our hope is that by reading this book you will acquire an appreciation for the breadth and depth of psychology's intellectual history and that you will learn how to read psychological ideas wherever you find them.

Being Fair

The explosion of science in the 19th and 20th centuries means that the average citizen of the 21st century knows a great deal more about some things than the sages and scholars of the 18th century and before. For example, it is hard not to chuckle when Descartes tells us that our nervous system runs on what he calls "animal spirits," fine particles that flow through the tube-like nerves. We moderns know that nerves conduct electrochemical impulses and that there are no animal spirits. But rather than congratulating ourselves on our superior understanding of neurophysiology, we must try to understand Descartes' theory in its context. We must try to see how, given what Descartes knew about anatomy and physiology, his theory was a reasonable conjecture. In reading him, we gain an appreciation of the struggle to understand our world and our mind, and we realize that the struggle is not over. Which of our favorite psychological theories will future students of history chuckle at?

ABOUT THE READINGS

By far the most challenging aspect of producing this book was keeping it portable. From the vast amount that has been written on psychological topics in modern times, we have selected 38 readings. We ought to explain how we did this.

Topics

We began by identifying enduring psychological questions. We found six that are intellectually and historically distinct from one another, and these topics provide the book's structure:

Part I, The Mind and the Body: Are minds and bodies different kinds of things, or are they different aspects of the same thing? In either case, how should we explain mental phenomena?

Part II, Perceiving: What does the mind know about the world, and how? What is the relation between the world and our perceptions of it?

Part III, Opening the Black Box: How can we objectively study something—the mind—whose principal attribute is subjectivity?

Part IV, Nativism and Empiricism: What characteristics and capabilities are common to all minds? In what ways do individual minds differ from one another? Where do these common characteristics and individual differences come from?

Part V, Levels of Explanation: What are the pros and cons of different levels of explanation—reductionist, holist, in between—as tools for understanding psychological phenomena?

Part VI, Normal and Abnormal: Why do we call some behaviors and personal characteristics normal and others abnormal?

We emphasize that the set of topics we have chosen is by no means the only way of organizing a book like this one.

Sources

For each topic, we identified a large number of relevant source texts and then gradually (and painfully) reduced the list for each topic to a manageable number. In this process our goal was to select texts that articulate important ideas or points of view. These texts are not the hit parade of intellectual history. We do not claim that they are the most important texts, nor that their authors are the most important thinkers. We have no illusion that these texts represent every historically important point of view, or that they present a picture of psychological thought that is comprehensive in any sense of that word. Indeed, there are some important readings (e.g., Fechner's *Psychophysics*) that we have, regretfully, left out because their style does not allow them to be shortened to a manageable length. Finally, these texts are not simply personal favorites of ours.

Just as our topics are not the only way to slice up the history of psychological thought, the texts we have chosen represent only one of many such collections, all equally good, useful, and important. It is inevitable that everyone who reads this book will be surprised by something we have included and disappointed by something we have excluded. This is not to say that the texts were chosen at random. In the introduction to each part, we have included a list of additional readings. Most of these are texts that we might/could/would have included in this book. Taken together, these lists constitute a second reader.

Editing

Once we had chosen the texts, we began to turn them into the readings that follow. Some readings are excerpts, or series of excerpts, from much longer source texts; others are shorter works from which we have removed material that is redundant or not germane to the topic for which we have selected that text. In some cases we have removed quite a bit, and in others very little, but most readings bear editorial scars. We have tried to wield the knife sparingly and carefully, so as not to alter the author's style or argument. Where we have removed something, we have left an ellipsis (. . .).

We have, on the whole, reproduced the texts as we found them, with a few exceptions. First, we have standardized the citations and references in all readings to follow the APA format. All references appear together at the end of the book. Second, authors, editors, translators, and typesetters are human, and we have corrected any obvious errors we have found (most of these have been in references). When in doubt, we have left things alone. Third, we have modernized spelling only when it seemed necessary to avoid confusion. Fourth, wherever possible we have supplied publication dates and references for works in press or otherwise not fully identified. Finally, we have in some cases renumbered footnotes and figures to reduce confusion.

Annotation

The notes we have added to the readings are intended to make the text more accessible and to enrich your understanding by providing context and connections. Thus we have added a note where there is

a familiar word or phrase used in an idiosyncratic, technical, or archaic sense

an unfamiliar word or phrase whose dictionary meaning may not improve your understanding of the reading

an obscure word or phrase that you are unlikely to find in a standard dictionary

a foreign word or expression

a difficult passage whose meaning is important to the reading as a whole

a reference or allusion to a historic person, or to a doctrine, argument, school of thought, or anything else that may be unfamiliar

an incomplete reference or allusion to a book or paper

an idea or argument whose connections to earlier or later ideas is not obvious, or that constitutes a rejection, extension, or correction of an earlier one, or about which someone later had something pithy or penetrating to say

All notes appear as sidebars or gray boxes, as close as possible to the subject of the note. If you do not want to be interrupted you can easily ignore them.

We hope our annotations will make these readings more accessible and rewarding. Nevertheless, there will be things you want to look up. In addition to a good English dictionary (e.g., the *American Heritage* dictionary), for more specialized terms we recommend the *Oxford Dictionary of Psychology* (Colman, 2003) and *The Penguin Dictionary of Philosophy* (Mautner, 2000).

Introductions

We have provided an introduction to each reading. Rather than pursuing consistency for consistency's sake—that is, providing the same categories of biographical information and the same level of detail about each author—we have tried to provide the background that the reader is least likely to have and most likely to need to get the full benefit of a given reading. In some cases, this means a fair amount of biographical information; in some cases, relatively little. In some cases, it means considerable historical, philosophical, or scientific context, and in others relatively little. In no case, however, have we summarized the reading. To do so would be inconsistent with at least two of the reasons we have given above for reading original sources, namely, (1) being there (you should get it from the horse's mouth, not from us), and (2) getting it right (our understanding of the text is not necessarily shared or endorsed by our colleagues).

TO THE INSTRUCTOR

We have not designed this book to be used in a specific way or for a specific course. The downside of this is that the book does not have the right-out-of-the-box compatibility with a traditional textbook that some instructors look for. The upside is that the book can be used on its own or as a supplement to another text. It can be used in history of psychology courses (traditional or otherwise), in other psychology courses concerned with the field as a whole, and in courses outside of psychology (e.g., philosophy, intellectual history, history of science). It can be used by students at different levels of training and preparation. It can be read from cover to cover, in either direction, or it can be assigned in bits and pieces.

We particularly want to emphasize that the chronological-within-topics organization of the readings should not present an obstacle to the instructor using one of the popular history of psychology texts, which are typically arranged chronologically in the early chapters and by school/system/specialty in the later ones. That is, any reading in this book can be safely extracted from its topical home and attached to a textbook chapter on the basis of either chronology or content. For example:

A typical chapter deals with philosophical positions taken in the 17th and 18th centuries that still shape the psychological landscape. Readings to accompany this chapter (or chapters) could be those from Descartes (1.1 & 4.1), Berkeley (2.1), Reid (2.2), and Locke (4.2).

A typical later chapter focuses on the 20th century emergence of cognitive psychology. Relevant readings are found in several sections of this book: Turing (1.4), Simon and Kotovsky (3.4), Chomsky (4.8), Wertheimer (5.1), and Tolman (5.4).

Part I

The Mind and the Body

What is the universe made of? In the 5th century BCE, the Greek philosopher Empedocles said that there are four kinds of things: earth, air, fire, and water. This set of basic substances seemed useful to the Greeks, who understood things like light and heat as manifestations of the element *fire;* bones and muscles as *earth;* and so on. There was one thing, however, that didn't seem to consist of any of the elements: mind. To some of the Greeks it seemed obvious that the mind was not made out of the *material* elements. If so, there had to be some other kind of substance, a substance that was not matter.

Over the years science has gradually broken earth, air, fire, and water into more fundamental things, and modern chemistry now recognizes 92 naturally occurring elements. We understand better than the Greeks did what kinds of things light and heat and bones and muscles are, but we have not made as much progress with what kind of thing the mind is. The mind doesn't seem to be made of carbon and hydrogen, or anything else in the periodic table, any more than it seemed to be made of earth, air, fire, and water. To some scientists and philosophers, this means that we have not yet reached the degree of sophistication needed to explain the mind in terms of material substances and material phenomena. To others, it means—as it did to some of the Greeks—that there must be another substance, an immaterial substance. The question of which of these points of view is better—the *mind-body* (or *mind-brain*) *problem*— is ancient but remains vitally important for psychology.

One of the most striking subjective facts of life is that we have thoughts, wishes, ideas, perceptions, memories, and so forth. Where do these things happen? In the head? Perhaps, but thought doesn't seem to happen in the head in the way that digestion happens in the stomach or that movement happens in the muscles. Accordingly, we have always had a special word: mind. But the question remains: What sort of thing is the mind? Is it a nonphysical substance, or is it a metaphor for physical processes that are too complex to understand as such?

Philosophers have struggled with the question whether the mind is material or immaterial since the beginning. Those who take the position that the mind—that thing that thinks, knows, imagines, loves, communicates, wishes, and so on—is something distinct from the brain, as it seems to be, are called *dualists,* reflecting their belief that the world consists of two kinds of substance—physical substance (body/brain) and mental substance (mind). Those who

1

take the position that there is only one kind of substance in the world are called *monists*. Monists who believe that the single substance in the world is mind are *idealists,* and those who believe there is only physical substance are *materialists.* In practice, idealist philosophies have attracted few followers, and the debate over mind and body has largely been between dualists and materialists.

With the emergence of psychology, the mind-body problem has taken on an applied significance. How we answer the question of what kind of a thing the mind is has important implications for the nature of psychological inquiry, theory, and practice. For example, dualists have difficulty explaining the effectiveness of psychotropic drugs. If mental illnesses are disorders of an immaterial mind, how do drugs administered to a material body alleviate (sometimes) the symptoms of those disorders? Conversely, materialists are challenged to explain the mind's ability, through its thoughts and moods, to alleviate (sometimes) the symptoms of bodily disorders. Other examples will appear in the readings that follow, but they all illustrate profound difficulties for both positions. Materialists have to explain how the brain can do all the things we call mind. Particularly difficult for materialists is the mind's apparent ability to control or influence the body, as in volition and choice. Dualists, on the other hand, have to specify the nature of the relation between mind and body: How does something immaterial (mind) create physical effects (behavior)?

What kinds of phenomena psychology can hope to explain, and how it can explain them, depends on whether we see the mind as a function—albeit a fantastically complex one—of the material brain, or as a function of some substance unlike any other known to science.

The readings in this section include both dualist and materialist views. Some selections explicitly address the mind-body problem; in others you will need to read between the lines. No philosopher is more strongly associated with dualism than Descartes, and no version of dualism has been more influential than his. Descartes offers at least two things that did not seem to concern earlier dualists such as Plato. First, Descartes offers *evidence* of mind-body dualism, in the form of a clever (and famous) argument. Second, he offers an *explanation* of the relation between mind and body, of how (and where) the two coordinate their respective activities.

James takes a rather pragmatic approach to the problem of mind and body, asking not so much *What kind of thing is the mind?* as *How should we talk about the mind?* Wundt answers this question very clearly: from a metaphysical point of view, mind is something the brain does, but we can talk about mind *as if* mental states cause other mental states. Wundt's position is very important for psychology.

If the mind is something that the brain does, and the brain is a kind of machine, then shouldn't it be possible to create another kind of machine—such as a computer—that has a mind? Turing, in the paper that should be thought of as the artificial intelligence manifesto, answers confidently in the affirmative. Searle, the most powerful and effective critic of artificial intelligence, answers equally confidently in the negative. The disagreement between Turing and Searle sheds interesting light on the mind-body problem.

In addition to the readings in Part I, several others touch on aspects of the relation of mind and brain, especially:

3.6   Posner et al.   Localization of cognitive operations in the human brain (1988)

5.7   Milner et al.   Cognitive neuroscience and the study of memory (1998)

ADDITIONAL READINGS

Plato   *Phaedo* (4th century BCE)

On the day of his execution, Socrates' description of the afterlife represents a simple and absolute dualism.

Aristotle   *On the soul* (*De anima*) (4th century BCE)

Aristotle takes a biological approach to the soul, which is found, in different degrees, in all forms of life.

Epicurus   *Letter to Herodotus* (4th–3rd century BCE)

Epicurus offers his disciple Herodotus a brief and energetic summary of his teaching, which derives from the atomistic philosophy of Democritus. Of particular interest is the atomists' materialist perspective on the mind.

Lucretius   *On the nature of the universe,* bk. 3 (55 BCE)

The Roman poet Lucretius was a follower of Epicurus, and in his poem he explains, at much greater length than Epicurus did, the Epicurean worldview, including its materialist concept of mind.

René Descartes   *Meditations* (1641)

The Meditations are the most developed statement of Descartes' philosophy; here he sets out, in more detail than in his other writings, the philosophical basis of mind-body dualism.

Thomas Hobbes   *De corpore* [*On the body*], part 4, ch. 25 (1655)
            Leviathan, ch. 1–3 (1651)

With respect to the nature of mind, Hobbes is one of the first modern materialists.

Baruch Spinoza   *Ethics* (1677)

Spinoza's "dual aspect" theory of mind and body has echoes in the positions of, among others, Wundt, James, and Searle.

Gottfried Wilhelm Leibniz   *Discourse on metaphysics* (1686)

Leibniz is a dualist but denies Descartes' claim that mind and body interact with one another.

Julien Offray de la Mettrie   *Man a machine* (1747)

La Mettrie embraces Descartes' mechanical explanation of the human body but insists (in opposition to Descartes) that the same mechanical explanation must extend to the mind.

John Stuart Mill   *A system of logic ratiocinative and inductive,* bk. 6, ch. 4 (1843)

Mill articulates an important and useful pragmatic perspective on the mind-body question.

Thomas Henry Huxley   *On the hypothesis that animals are automata, and its history* (1874)

Huxley attempts to revive Cartesian[1] mechanism in a much more biologically sophisticated form.

William James   *Are we automata?* (1879)

A response to Huxley's paper: James defends a commonsense view (much like Searle's) of consciousness and the mind-body relation and rejects both dualism and materialism. This paper appears, reworked and improved, in ch. 5 of *Principles of Psychology* (1890).

Gilbert Ryle   *The concept of mind* (esp. ch. 1) (1949)

A classic discussion of the mind-body problem from a monist perspective, and the source of the famous "ghost in the machine" critique of Cartesian dualism.

John von Neumann   *The computer and the brain* (1958)

Von Neumann, one of the inventors of the computer, is confident that the brain can be understood as a computer.

Karl Popper & John Eccles   *The self and its brain* (1977)

Popper, a philosopher, and Eccles, a neuroscientist, offer a detailed and sophisticated modern defense of Cartesian dualism.

John Eccles   *How the self controls its brain* (1994)

Eccles's dualism, updated in light of modern developments in neuroscience.

John Searle   *Minds, brains, and programs* (1980)

This extraordinarily influential and controversial paper is the original formulation of Searle's "Chinese room" argument. The same issue of the journal contains commentary by other scholars and Searle's responses.

Jerry Fodor   *The mind-body problem* (1981)

Fodor provides a thorough and very readable survey of the many theoretical positions that can be taken with respect to the mind-body problem.

Hans Moravec   *Mind children: The future of robot and human intelligence* (1988)

A discussion of machine minds that shows how far we had come in the 38 years since Turing's landmark paper.

Oliver Sacks   *Neurology and the soul* (1990)

A neurologist's reflections on mind and body from a clinical point of view.

Daniel Dennett   *Consciousness explained* (1991)

Dennett offers, among many other things, an interesting critique of Cartesian dualism, characterizing it as an obstacle to psychological progress.

Antonio Damasio   *Descartes' error* (1994)

A look at what modern neurobiology has to say about mind-body dualism.

---

[1] When, as he often did, Descartes wrote in Latin, his name was *Cartesius*, which has given us the adjectival form *Cartesian*.

René Descartes (1596–1650)
The Passions of the Soul (1649)

*Part First: Of the Passions in General, and
Incidentally of the Whole Nature of Man*

Descartes lived in a time when European civilization began to change rapidly, when many of the cultural and scientific foundations of the modern world were laid. Shakespeare, Cervantes, Monteverdi, and Molière; Galileo, Kepler, Bacon, and Hobbes were a few of Descartes' contemporaries. European powers were expanding rapidly overseas. Most significant, perhaps, for understanding Descartes is the fact that this was a time when science was beginning to show its power to explore the mysteries of the natural world and when the Church was beginning to lose its power to control those mysteries. As an example, consider the earth and the sun.

In 1500 the geocentric (earth at the center) universe was not only the scientific state of the art, it was the dogma of the Roman Catholic church. In the early 16th century, the Polish astronomer Nicolas Copernicus convinced himself that the geocentric description of the world was incorrect and proposed a heliocentric (sun at the center) description. Early in the 17th century, the German astronomer Johannes Kepler improved Copernicus's system by replacing his circular planetary orbits with elliptical ones. The Copernican system was gaining ground, and in 1616 the Church banned it. In 1632 Galileo published a work for the lay reader supporting the Copernican system; in 1633 he was tried by the Inquisition, forced to recant his belief in the heliocentric theory, and put under house arrest. (Luckily, his conviction was annulled in 1979 and the ban on the Copernican theory was lifted in 1992.)

Although it was unable to contain the Copernican system, the Church was still quite prepared to persecute heretics. This threat was not lost on Descartes, and as a result he delayed or refrained from publishing certain things and published others anonymously, even though

Source: Descartes, R. (1975). *The philosophical works of Descartes* (Vol. 1, E. S. Haldane & G. R. T. Ross, Trans.). London: Cambridge University Press. Reprinted with permission.

he lived much of his life in voluntary exile on Holland's Protestant soil. It is clear that Descartes had no wish to share Galileo's fate. Perhaps he might have done more had he been less cowed by the Church, but even so, Descartes' achievements are astonishing. His invention of analytic geometry assures his place among the great mathematicians, and while his philosophical contributions have not held up as well, his influence and historical significance cannot be overstated.

One of the boldest ideas in the history of philosophy is Descartes' suggestion that to know what is true, and only what is true, we should try to doubt everything we believe. That which can be doubted is not necessarily false, but that which cannot be doubted must be true. In his first published work, the *Discourse on the Method of Rightly Conducting the Reason and Seeking for Truth in the Sciences* (1637), Descartes applied this method of doubt to his own beliefs and arrived at a very important (and famous) result, summarized in the phrase usually translated as *I think, therefore I am.* This doesn't mean that thinking is the cause of existence; Descartes' point is that thinking is *evidence* of existence. Here is the argument:

> I had noticed long before, as I said just now, that in conduct one sometimes has to follow opinions that one knows to be most uncertain just as if they were indubitable; but since my present aim was to give myself up to the pursuit of truth alone, I thought I must do the very opposite, and reject as if absolutely false anything as to which I could imagine the least doubt, in order to see if I should not be left at the end believing something that was absolutely indubitable. So because our senses sometimes deceive us, I chose to suppose that nothing was such as they lead us to imagine. Because there are men who make mistakes in reasoning even as regards the simplest points of geometry and perpetrate fallacies, and seeing that I was as liable to error as anyone else, I rejected as false all the arguments I had so far taken for demonstrations. Finally, considering that the very same experiences [thoughts] as we have in waking life may occur also while we sleep, without there being at that time any truth in them, I decided to feign that everything that had entered my mind hitherto was no more true than the illusions of dreams. But immediately upon this I noticed that while I was trying to think everything false, it must needs be that I, who was thinking this, was something. And observing that this truth 'I am thinking, therefore I exist' was so solid and secure that the most extravagant suppositions of the sceptics could not overthrow it, I judged that I need not scruple to accept it as the first principle of philosophy that I was seeking. (Descartes 1954, Part 4)

The discovery that he can doubt everything but his own consciousness leads Descartes to divide the world into "thinking substance"—mind—and "extended substance"—body. One of the deepest issues raised by Descartes' distinction between mind and body was identified by Princess Elizabeth of Bohemia, Descartes' friend and philosophical correspondent. If the mind is an immaterial "thinking substance," she asked, how does the mind cause the body to move?

> For it seems that all determination of movement takes place by the propulsion of the thing moved, by the manner in which it is propelled by that which moves it, and by the qualification and shape of the surface of this latter. Contact is required for the first two conditions and extension for the third. You yourself entirely exclude extension from the

notion you have of mind, and a touching seems to me incompatible with an immaterial thing. (Descartes 1958, letter of May 16, 1643)

Descartes' reply begins as follows:

I can truthfully say that this question which your Highness proposes seems to me to be the question which above all others can most reasonably be raised, in sequel to [what I have said in] my published writings. For there are two things in the human soul upon which all the knowledge we can have of its nature depends, on the one hand that it thinks, and on the other that being united to the body it can act and suffer along with the body. I have said [in the *Meditations*] almost nothing of this latter, and have studiously set myself to expound only the former. The reason for my doing so is that inasmuch as my principal design was to prove the distinction subsisting between mind and body, the former could serve in this design, whereas the other, if dwelt on, would have been by no means helpful. But as your Highness is so clear-seeing that there is no concealing anything from her, I shall here endeavor to explain the manner in which I conceive the union of mind and body, and how the mind has the power of moving the body. (Descartes 1958, letter of May 31, 1643)

Descartes did not accomplish this endeavor to the princess's satisfaction in this letter, nor in the next. The effort led to *The Passions of the Soul,* a draft of which Descartes sent to Elizabeth in 1646. In 1647, alas, Descartes sent another copy of the draft to Queen Christina of Sweden, who invited Descartes to Stockholm in 1649, shortly before *The Passions* appeared in print. Descartes' life at court included philosophy lessons for the queen at five o'clock in the morning. After a few months of this regimen, Descartes died of pneumonia on February 11, 1650.

Nowhere in *The Passions* (or anywhere else) does Descartes succeed in explaining "the union of mind and body." Along the way, however, he has much to say about the functional distinction between what we call mind and what we call body, and he develops interesting and important ideas about the nature of the nervous system and about sensation and perception.

Descartes uses *passion* to refer not only to powerful emotion but also, and more importantly, to that which is received or undergone; *passion* is from the same root as *passive*.

For example, if A touches B, in Descartes' terminology A is the agent, B is the recipient, and the touch is both an action (for A) and a passion (for B).

1. That what in respect of a subject is passion, is in some other regard always action.

   . . . [To begin with, I consider that all that which occurs or that happens anew, is by the philoso-phers, generally speaking, termed a passion, in as   5
far as the subject to which it occurs is concerned, and an action in respect of him who causes it to occur. Thus although the agent and the recipient [patient] are frequently very different, the action and the passion are always one and the same   10
thing, although having different names, because of the two diverse subjects to which it may be related.

2. That in order to understand the passions of the soul its functions must be distinguished from those of body.

   Next I note also that we do not observe the existence of any subject which more imme-   15
diately acts upon our soul than the body to which it is joined, and that we must consequently consider that what in the soul is a passion is in the body commonly speaking an action; so that there is no better means of arriving at a knowl-edge of our passions than to examine the differ-   20
ence which exists between soul and body in order to know to which of the two we must attribute each one of the functions which are within us.

subject: As Descartes indicates in the previous paragraph, *subject* can refer to either the agent or recipient of an action. Here he means *agent*.

3. What rule we must follow to bring about this result.   25

   As to this we shall not find much difficulty if we realise that all that we experience as being in us, and that to observation may exist in wholly inanimate bodies, must be attributed to our body alone; and, on the other hand, that all that which is in us and which we cannot in any way conceive as possibly pertaining to a body, must be attributed to our soul.

4. That the heat and movement of the members proceed from the body, the thoughts from   30
the soul.

   Thus because we have no conception of the body as thinking in any way, we have reason to believe that every kind of thought which exists in us belongs to the soul; and because we do not doubt there being inanimate bodies which can move in as many as or in more diverse modes than can ours, and which have as much heat or more (experience demonstrates this   35
to us in flame, which of itself has much more heat and movement than any of our members),

we must believe that all the heat and all the movements which are in us pertain only to body, inasmuch as they do not depend on thought at all.

5. That it is an error to believe that the soul supplies the movement and heat to body.

By this means we shall avoid a very considerable error into which many have fallen; so much so that I am of opinion that this is the primary cause which has prevented our being able hitherto satisfactorily to explain the passions and the other properties of the soul. It arises from the fact that from observing that all dead bodies are devoid of heat and consequently of movement, it has been thought that it was the absence of soul which caused these movements and this heat to cease; and thus, without any reason, it was thought that our natural heat and all the movements of our body depend on the soul: while in fact we ought on the contrary to believe that the soul quits us on death only because this heat ceases, and the organs which serve to move the body disintegrate.

6. The difference that exists between a living body and a dead body.

In order, then, that we may avoid this error, let us consider that death never comes to pass by reason of the soul, but only because some one of the principal parts of the body decays; and we may judge that the body of a living man differs from that of a dead man just as does a watch or other automaton (i.e. a machine that moves of itself), when it is wound up and contains in itself the corporeal principle of those movements for which it is designed along with all that is requisite for its action, from the same watch or other machine when it is broken and when the principle of its movement ceases to act.

7. A brief explanation of the parts of the body and some of its functions.

In order to render this more intelligible, I shall here explain in a few words the whole method in which the bodily machine is composed. . . . We further know that all the movements of the members depend on the muscles, and that these muscles are so mutually related one to another that when the one is contracted it draws toward itself the part of the body to which it is attached, which causes the opposite muscle at the same time to become elongated; then if at another time it happens that this last contracts, it causes the former to become elongated and it draws back to itself the part to which they are attached. We know finally that all these movements of the muscles, as also all the senses, depend on the nerves, which resemble small filaments, or little tubes, which all proceed from the brain, and thus contain like it a certain very subtle air or wind which is called the animal spirits.

> Descartes' vagueness about the animal spirits is not surprising considering that they are purely hypothetical entities. They seem to be a fluid, consisting of extremely fine particles, distilled from the blood. *Animal* is used in the sense of "of the soul," and *spirit* comes from a root meaning "breath."

8. What is the principle of all these functions?

But it is not usually known in what way these animal spirits and these nerves contribute to the movements and to the senses, nor what is the corporeal principle which causes them   75 to act. That is why, although I have already made some mention of them in my other writings, I shall not here omit to say shortly that so long as we live there is a continual heat in our heart, which is a species of fire which the blood of the   80

> corporeal principle: that is, the part of the body that is ultimately responsible for movement

veins there maintains, and that this fire is the corporeal principle of all the movements of our members. . . .

10. How the animal spirits are produced in the brain.

But what is here most worthy of remark is that all the most animated and subtle portions   85 of the blood which the heat has rarefied in the heart, enter ceaselessly in large quantities into the cavities of the brain. And the reason which causes them to go there rather than else-

> subtle: very small; fine

where, is that all the blood which issues from the heart by the great artery takes its course in a straight line towards that place, and not being able to enter it in its entirety, because   90 there are only very narrow passages there, those of its parts which are the most agitated and the most subtle alone pass through, while the rest spreads abroad in all the other por- tions of the body. But these very subtle parts of the blood form the animal spirits; and for this end they have no need to experience any other change in the brain, unless it be that they are separated from the other less subtle portions of the blood; for what I here name   95 spirits are nothing but material bodies and their one peculiarity is that they are bodies of extreme minuteness and that they move very quickly like the particles of the flame which issues from a torch. Thus it is that they never remain at rest in any spot, and just as some of them enter into the cavities of the brain, others issue forth by the pores which are in its substance, which pores conduct them into the nerves, and from there into the   100 muscles, by means of which they move the body in all the different ways in which it can be moved.

11. How the movements of the muscles take place.

For the sole cause of all the movements of the members is that certain muscles con- tract, and that those opposite to them elongate, as has already been said; and the sole cause   105 of one muscle contracting rather than that set against it, is that there comes from the brain some additional amount of animal spirits, however little it may be, to it rather than to the other. Not that the spirits which proceed immediately from the brain suffice in themselves to move the muscles, but they determine the other spirits which are already in these two muscles, all to issue very quickly from the one of them and to pass into the other. By this   110 means that from which they issue becomes longer and more flaccid, and that into which they enter, being rapidly distended by them, contracts, and pulls the member to which it is attached. . . .

12.   How outside objects act upon the organs of the senses.

115   We have still to understand the reasons why the spirits do not flow always from the brain into the muscles in the same fashion, and why occasionally more flow towards some than towards others. For in addition to the action of the soul which is truly in our case one of these causes, as I shall subsequently explain, there are two others which depend only on the body, and of these we must speak. The first consists in the diversity of movements
120   which are excited in the organs of sense by their objects, and this I have already explained fully enough in the Dioptric; but in order that those who see this work may not be necessitated to read others, I shall here repeat that there are three things to consider in respect of
125   the nerves, i.e. first of all their marrow or interior substance, which extends in the form of little filaments from the brain, from which it originates, to the extremities of the other members to which these filaments are attached; secondly the membranes which surround them, and which, being conterminous with
130   those which envelop the brain, form the little tubes in which these little filaments are enclosed; and finally the animal spirits which, being carried by these same tubes from the brain to the muscles, are the reason of these filaments remaining there perfectly free and extended, so that the least thing that moves the part of the body to which the extremity of any one of them is attached, causes by that same means the part of the brain from
135   which it proceeds to move, just as when one draws one end of a cord the other end is made to move.

> *Dioptric: Optics;* published with the *Discourse on Method* in 1637. Much of the *Optics* is about vision and is of great psychological interest.

13.   That this action of outside objects may lead the spirits into the muscles in diverse ways.

      And I have explained in the Dioptric how all the objects of sight communicate themselves to us only through the fact that they move locally by the intermission of transpar-
140   ent bodies which are between them and us, the little filaments of the optic nerves which are at the back of our eyes, and then the parts of the brain from which these nerves proceed; I explained, I repeat, how they move them in as many diverse ways as the diversities which they cause us to see in things, and that it is not immediately the movements which occur in the eye, but those that occur in the brain which represent these objects to the
145   soul. To follow this example, it is easy to conceive how sounds, scents, tastes, heat, pain, hunger, thirst and generally speaking all objects of our other external senses as well as of our internal appetites, also excite some movement in our nerves which by their means pass to the brain; and in addition to the fact that these diverse movements of the brain cause

diverse perceptions to become evident to our soul, they can also without it cause the spir- 150
its to take their course towards certain muscles rather than towards others, and thus to
move our limbs, which I shall prove here by one example only. If someone quickly thrusts
his hand against our eyes as if to strike us, even though we know him to be our friend, that
he only does it in fun, and that he will take great care not to hurt us, we have all the same
trouble in preventing ourselves from closing
them; and this shows that it is not by the inter- 155
vention of our soul that they close, seeing that
it is against our will, which is its only, or at least
its principal activity; but it is because the
machine of our body is so formed that the
movement of this hand towards our eyes 160
excites another movement in our brain, which
conducts the animal spirits into the muscles
which cause the eyelids to close.

> Descartes conceived of bodies, but not minds, as machines because of the automatic quality of reflexes such as the one he is describing. The machine of our (human) body is no different from the machine of a dog's body or, for that matter, a fly's.

. . .

16. How all the members may be moved by the objects of the senses and by the animal
spirits without the aid of the soul. 165

We must finally remark that the machine of our body is so formed that all the changes
undergone by the movement of the spirits may cause them to open certain pores in the brain
more than others, and reciprocally that when some one of the pores is opened more or less
than usual (to however small a degree it may be) by the action of the nerves which are
employed by the senses, that changes something in the movement of the spirits and causes 170
them to be conducted into the muscles which serve to move the body in the way in which
it is usually moved when such an action takes
place. In this way all the movements which we
make without our will contributing thereto (as
frequently happens when we breathe, walk, eat, 175
and in fact perform all those actions which are

> *conformation of our members:* the arrangement of our limbs

common to us and to the brutes), only depend on the conformation of our members, and on
the course which the spirits, excited by the heat of the heart, follow naturally in the brain,
nerves, and muscles, just as the movements of a watch are produced simply by the strength
of the springs and the form of the wheels. 180

17. What the functions of the soul are.

After having thus considered all the functions which pertain to the body alone, it is
easy to recognise that there is nothing in us which we ought to attribute to our soul
excepting our thoughts, which are mainly of two sorts, the one being the actions of the
soul, and the other its passions. Those which I call its actions are all our desires, because 185

we find by experience that they proceed directly from our soul, and appear to depend on it alone: while, on the other hand, we may usually term one's passions all those kinds of perception or forms of knowledge which are found in us, because it is often not our soul which makes them what they are, and because it always receives them from the things
190   which are represented by them.

18. Of the Will.

Our desires, again, are of two sorts, of which the one consists of the actions of the soul which terminate in the soul itself, as when we desire to love God, or generally speaking, apply our thoughts to some object which is not material; and the other of the actions which
195   terminate in our body, as when from the simple fact that we have the desire to take a walk, it follows that our legs move and that we walk.

19. Of the Perceptions.

Our perceptions are also of two sorts, and the one have the soul as a cause and the other
200   the body. Those which have the soul as a cause are the perceptions of our desires, and of all the imaginations or other thoughts which depend on them. For it is certain that we cannot desire anything without perceiv-
205   ing by the same means that we desire it; and, although in regard to our soul it is an action to desire something, we may say that it is also one of its passions to perceive that it desires. Yet because this perception and this will are
210   really one and the same thing, the more noble always supplies the denomination, and thus we are not in the habit of calling it a passion, but only an action.

> To use Descartes' example, the desire to take a walk is an action of the soul; at the same time the soul's perception of that desire is a passion. In Descartes' view, actions are more noble than passions, so we refer to the desire to take a walk as an action (i.e., will) of the soul.

> *denomination:* name

20. Of the imaginations and other thoughts which are formed by the soul.
215   When our soul applies itself to imagine something which does not exist, as when it represents to itself an enchanted palace or a chimera, and also when it applies itself to consider something which is only intelligible and not imaginable, e.g. to consider its own nature, the perceptions which it has of these things depend principally on
220   the act of will which causes it to perceive them. That is why we usually consider them as actions rather than passions.

> *chimera* (ky-MERE-uh): fanciful or imaginary creature. The chimera was a fire-breathing monster of Greek mythology, depicted as a composite of several animals.

21. Of the imaginations which have the body only as a cause.

Amongst the perceptions which are caused by the body, the most part depend on the nerves; but there are also some which do not depend on them, and which we name imagina- 225 tions, such as those of which I have just spoken, from which they yet differ inasmuch as our will has no part in forming them; and this brings it to pass that they cannot be placed in the number of the actions of the soul. And they only proceed from the fact that the spirits being agitated in diverse ways and meeting with traces of diverse preceding impressions which have been effected in the brain, take their course there fortuitously by certain pores rather than by 230 others. Such are the illusions of our dreams, and also the day-dreams which we often have when awake, and when our thought wanders aim-lessly without applying itself to anything of its own accord. But, although some of these imagi-nations are the passions of the soul, taking this 235 word in its most correct and perfect significance, and since they may all be thus termed if we take it in a more general significance, yet, because they have not a cause of so notable and determinate a description as the perceptions which the soul receives by the intermission of the nerves, and because they appear to be only a shadow and a picture, we must, before we can distinguish them very well, consider the differ- 240 ence prevailing among these others.

> A modern version of this theory of dreams was proposed by Hobson (1988).

22. Of the difference which exists among the other perceptions.

All the perceptions which I have not yet explained come to the soul by the intermission of the nerves, and there is between them this difference, that we relate them in the one case to objects outside which strike our senses, in the other to our soul. 245

23. Of the perceptions which we relate to objects which are without us.

Those which we relate to the things which are without us, to wit to the objects of our senses, are caused, at least when our opinion is not false, by these objects which, exciting cer-tain movements in the organs of the external senses, excite them also in the brain by the intermission of the nerves, which cause the soul to perceive them. Thus when we see the 250 light of a torch, and hear the sound of a bell, this sound and this light are two different actions which, simply by the fact that they excite two different movements in certain of our nerves, and by these means in the brain, give two different sensations to the soul, which sensations we relate to the subjects which we suppose to be their causes in such a way that we think we see the torch itself and hear the bell, and do not perceive just the movements which pro- 255 ceed from them.

24. Of the perceptions which we relate to our body.

The perceptions which we relate to our body, or to some of its parts, are those which we have of hunger, thirst, and other natural appetites, to which we may unite pain, heat,

260 and the other affections which we perceive as though they were in our members, and not as in objects which are outside us; we may thus perceive at the same time and by the intermission of the same nerves, the cold of our hand and the heat of the flame to which it approaches; or, on the other hand, the heat of the hand and the cold of the air to which it is exposed, without there being any difference between the actions which cause us to feel

265 the heat or the cold which is in our hand, and those which make us perceive that which is without us, excepting that from the one of these actions following upon the other, we judge that the first is already in us, and what supervenes is not so yet, but is in the object which causes it.

25. Of the perceptions which we relate to our soul.

270 The perceptions which we relate solely to the soul are those whose effects we feel as though they were in the soul itself, and as to which we do not usually know any proximate cause to which we may relate them: such are the feelings of joy, anger, and other such sensations, which are sometimes excited in us by the objects which move our nerves and sometimes also by other causes. But, although all our perceptions, both those which we relate

275 to objects which are outside us, and those which we relate to the diverse affections of our body, are truly passions in respect of our soul, when we use this word in its most general significance, yet we are in the habit of restricting it to the signification of those alone which are related to soul itself; and it is only these last which I have here undertaken to explain under the name of the passions of the soul.

280 26. That the imaginations which only depend on the fortuitous movements of the spirits, may be passions just as truly as the perceptions which depend on the nerves.

It remains for us to notice here that all the same things which the soul perceives by the intermission of the nerves, may also be represented by the fortuitous course of the animal spirits, without there being any other difference excepting that the impressions

285 which come into the brain by the nerves are usually more lively or definite than those excited there by the spirits, which caused me to say in Article XXI that the former resemble the shadow or picture of the latter. We must also notice that it sometimes happens that this picture is so similar to the thing which it represents that we may be mistaken therein regarding the perceptions which relate to objects which are outside us, or at least

290 those which relate to certain parts of our body, but that we cannot be so deceived regarding the passions, inasmuch as they are so close to, and so entirely within our soul, that it is impossible for it to feel them without their being actually such as it feels them to be. Thus often when we sleep, and sometimes even when we are awake, we imagine certain things so forcibly, that we think we see them before us, or feel them in our body,

295 although they do not exist at all; but although we may be asleep, or dream, we cannot feel sad or moved by any other passion without its being very true that the soul actually has this passion within it.

27. The definition of the passions of the soul.

After having considered in what the passions of the soul differ from all its other thoughts, it seems to me that we may define them generally as the perceptions, feelings, or emotions of the soul which we relate specially to it, and which are caused, maintained, and fortified by some movement of the spirits.

300

28. Explanation of the first part of this definition.

We may call them perceptions when we make use of this word generally to signify all the thoughts which are not actions of the soul, or desires, but not when the term is used only to signify clear cognition; for experience shows us that those who are the most agitated by their passions, are not those who know them best; and that they are of the number of perceptions which the close alliance which exists between the soul and the body, renders confused and obscure. We may also call them feelings because they are received into the soul in the same way as are the objects of our outside senses, and are not otherwise known by it; but we can yet more accurately call them emotions of the soul, not only because the name may be attributed to all the changes which occur in it—that is, in all the diverse thoughts which come to it, but more especially because of all the kinds of thought which it may have, there are no others which so powerfully agitate and disturb it as do these passions.

305

310

315

29. Explanation of the second part.

I add that they particularly relate to the soul, in order to distinguish them from the other feelings which are related, the one to outside objects such as scents, sounds, and colours; the others to our body such as hunger, thirst, and pain. I also add that they are caused, maintained, and fortified by some movement of the spirits, in order to distinguish them from our desires, which we may call emotions of the soul which relate to it, but which are caused by itself; and also in order to explain their ultimate and most proximate cause, which plainly distinguishes them from the other feelings.

320

30. That the soul is united to all the portions of the body conjointly.

But in order to understand all these things more perfectly, we must know that the soul is really joined to the whole body, and that we cannot, properly speaking, say that it exists in any one of its parts to the exclusion of the others, because it is one and in some manner indivisible, owing to the disposition of its organs, which are so related to one another that when any one of them is removed, that renders the whole body defective; and because it is of a nature which has no relation to extension, nor dimensions, nor other properties of the matter of which the body is composed, but only to the whole conglomerate of its organs, as appears from the fact that we could not in any way conceive of the half or the third of a soul, nor of the space it occupies, and because it does not become smaller owing to the cutting off of some portion of the body, but separates itself from it entirely when the union of its assembled organs is dissolved.

325

330

335

31. That there is a small gland in the brain in which the soul exercises its functions more particularly than in the other parts.

small gland: This is the pineal gland, a small endocrine gland attached to the base of the brain. We now know that it secretes melatonin and is involved in circadian rhythms.

340 It is likewise necessary to know that although the soul is joined to the whole body, there is yet in that a certain part in which it exercises its functions more particularly than in all the others; and it is usually believed that this part is the brain, or possibly the heart: the brain, because it is with it that the organs of sense are connected, and the heart because it

345 is apparently in it that we experience the passions. But, in examining the matter with care, it seems as though I had clearly ascertained that the part of the body in which the soul exercises its functions immediately is in nowise the heart, nor the whole of the brain, but merely the most inward of all its parts, to wit, a certain very small gland which is situated in the middle of its substance and so suspended above the

350 duct whereby the animal spirits in its anterior cavities have communication with those in the posterior, that the slightest movements which take place in it may alter very greatly the course of these spirits; and reciprocally that the smallest

355 changes which occur in the course of the spirits may do much to change the movements of this gland.

duct: the third ventricle. The ventricles are openings in the brain filled with cerebrospinal fluid. Descartes supposed, not unreasonably, that the function of brain tissue was to regulate the flow of this fluid through the various nerves.

32. How we know that this gland is the main seat of the soul.

The reason which persuades me that the soul cannot have any other seat in all the body

360 than this gland wherein to exercise its functions immediately, is that I reflect that the other parts of our brain are all of them double, just as we have two eyes, two hands, two ears, and finally all the organs of our outside senses are double; and inasmuch as we have but one solitary and simple

365 thought of one particular thing at one and the same moment, it must necessarily be the case that there must somewhere be a place where the two images which come to us by the two eyes, where

It is true that the pineal gland is not "double" in Descartes' sense, but like the brain itself the pineal has a left side and a right side that are mirror images of one another.

the two other impressions which proceed from a single object by means of the double organs

370 of the other senses, can unite before arriving at the soul, in order that they may not represent to it two objects instead of one. And it is easy to apprehend how these images or other impressions might unite in this gland by the intermission of the spirits which fill the cavities of the brain: but there is no other place in the body where they can be thus united unless they are so in this gland.

. . .

34. How the soul and the body act on one another.   375

Let us then conceive here that the soul has its principal seat in the little gland which exists in the middle of the brain, from whence it radiates forth through all the remainder of the body by means of the animal spirits, nerves, and even the blood, which, participating in the impressions of the spirits, can carry them by the arteries into all the members. And recollecting what has been said above about the machine of our body, i.e.   380 that the little filaments of our nerves are so distributed in all its parts, that on the occasion of the diverse movements which are there excited by sensible objects, they open in diverse ways the pores of the brain, which causes the animal   385 spirits contained in these cavities to enter in diverse ways into the muscles, by which means they can move the members in all the different ways in which they are capable of being moved; and also that all the other causes which are capable of moving the spirits in diverse ways suffice to conduct them into diverse   390 muscles; let us here add that the small gland which is the main seat of the soul is so suspended between the cavities which contain the spirits that it can be moved by them in as many different ways as there are sensible diversities in the object, but that it may also be moved in diverse ways by the soul, whose nature is such that it receives in itself as many diverse impressions, that is to say, that it possesses as many diverse perceptions as   395 there are diverse movements in this gland. Reciprocally, likewise, the machine of the body is so formed that from the simple fact that this gland is diversely moved by the soul, or by such other cause, whatever it is, it thrusts the spirits which surround it towards the pores of the brain, which conduct them by the nerves into the muscles, by which means it causes them to move the limbs.   400

> The role assigned to the blood here would have been inconceivable before William Harvey established the circulation of the blood in 1628.

35. Example of the mode in which the impressions of the objects unite in the gland which is in the middle of the brain.

Thus, for example, if we see some animal approach us, the light reflected from its body depicts two images of it, one in each of our eyes, and these two images form two others, by means of the optic nerves, in the interior surface of the brain which faces its cavities; then   405 from there, by means of the animal spirits with which its cavities are filled, these images so radiate towards the little gland which is surrounded by these spirits, that the movement which forms each point of one of the images tends towards the same point of the gland towards which tends the movement which forms the point of the other image, which represents the same part of this animal. By this means the two images which are in the brain   410 form but one upon the gland, which, acting immediately upon the soul, causes it to see the form of this animal.

36. Example of the way in which the passions are excited in the soul.

415

And, besides that, if this figure is very strange and frightful—that is, if it has a close relationship with the things which have been formerly hurtful to the body, that excites the passion of apprehension in the soul and then that of courage, or else that of fear and consternation according to the particular temperament of the body or the strength of the soul, and according as we have to begin with been secured by defence or by flight against the hurtful things to which the present impression is related. For in certain

420

persons that disposes the brain in such a way that the spirits reflected from the image thus formed on the gland, proceed thence to take their places partly in the nerves which serve to turn the back and dispose the legs for flight, and partly in those which so increase or diminish the orifices of the heart, or at least which so agitate the other parts from whence the blood is sent to it, that this blood being there rarefied in a different man-

425

ner from usual, sends to the brain the spirits which are adapted for the maintenance and strengthening of the passion of fear, i.e. which are adapted to the holding open, or at least reopening, of the pores of the brain which conduct them into the same nerves. For from the fact alone that these spirits enter into these pores, they excite a particular movement in this gland which is instituted by nature in order to cause the soul to be sensible of this

430

passion; and because these pores are principally in relation with the little nerves which serve to contract or enlarge the orifices of the heart, that causes the soul to be sensible of it for the most part as in the heart.

. . .

41. The power of the soul in regard to the body.

435

But the will is so free in its nature, that it can never be constrained; and of the two sorts of thoughts which I have distinguished in the soul (of which the first are its actions, i.e. its desires, the others its passions, taking this word in its most general significance, which comprises all kinds of perceptions), the former are absolutely in its power, and can only be indirectly changed by the body, while on the other hand the latter depend absolutely on the actions which govern, and direct them, and they can only indirectly be

440

altered by the soul, excepting when it is itself their cause. And the whole action of the soul consists in this, that solely because it desires something, it causes the little gland to which it is closely united to move in the way requisite to produce the effect which relates to this desire.

42. How we find in the memory the things which we desire to remember.

445

Thus when the soul desires to recollect something, this desire causes the gland, by inclining successively to different sides, to thrust the spirits towards different parts of the brain until they come across that part where the traces left there by the object which we wish to recollect are found; for these traces are none other than the fact that the pores of the brain, by which the spirits have formerly followed their course because of the

presence of this object, have by that means acquired a greater facility than the others in   450
being once more opened by the animal spirits which come towards them in the same
way. Thus these spirits in coming in contact with these pores, enter into them more easily than into the others, by which means they excite a special movement in the gland
which represents the same object to the soul, and causes it to know that it is this which
it desired to remember.   455

43.   How the soul can imagine, be attentive, and move the body.

Thus when we desire to imagine something we have never seen, this desire has the
power of causing the gland to move in the manner requisite to drive the spirits towards
the pores of the brain by the opening of which pores this particular thing may be represented; thus when we wish to apply our attention for some time to the consideration of   460
one particular object, this desire holds the gland for the time being inclined to the same
side. Thus, finally, when we desire to walk or to move our body in some special way, this
desire causes the gland to thrust the spirits towards the muscles which serve to bring
about this result.

44.   That each desire is naturally united to some movement of the gland; but that, by inten-   465
tional effort or by custom, it may be united to others.

At the same time it is not always the desire to excite in us some movement, or bring
about some result which is able so to excite it, for this changes according as nature or custom have diversely united each movement of the gland to each particular thought. Thus,
for example, if we wish to adjust our eyes so that they may look at an object very far off, this   470
desire causes their pupils to enlarge; and if we wish to set them to look at an object very
near, this desire causes them to contract; but if we think only of enlarging the pupil of the
eye we may have the desire indeed, but we cannot for all that enlarge it, because nature has
not joined the movement of the gland which
serves to thrust forth the spirits towards the   475
optic nerve, in the manner requisite for enlarging or diminishing the pupil, with the desire to
enlarge or diminish it, but with that of looking at
objects which are far away or near. And when in
speaking we think only of the sense of what we   480
desire to say, that causes us to move the tongue and lips much more quickly and much
better than if we thought of moving them in all the many ways requisite to utter the same
words, inasmuch as the custom which we have acquired in learning to speak, caused us to
join the action of the soul (which, by the intermission of the gland can move the tongue and
lips), with the significance of words which follow these movements, rather than with the   485
movements themselves.

> The adjustment to the eye in this example
> should be in the shape of the lens rather
> than the size of the pupil, but this does not
> affect Descartes' argument.

FOR DISCUSSION

1. In #3 Descartes refers to "all that we experience as being in us, and that to observation may exist in wholly inanimate bodies." What are some examples?

2. What aspects of Descartes' account of the nervous system seem to agree with our current understanding?

3. In #17–26 Descartes divides our thoughts into actions and passions of the soul. He then divides each of these, and so on. Make a tree diagram to illustrate the classification of mental faculties contained in this passage.

4. How does Descartes account for the fact that we sometimes have perceptions of things that are not in fact present to our senses?

5. Using modern terminology, list the functions of the soul (mind) and the functions of the body (brain) according to Descartes.

6. What are the various functions of the pineal gland, both in Descartes' understanding and in the modern view?

William James (1842–1910)
Psychology (1892)

Chapter 12: The Self

As they approach adulthood, most humans face the need to make a living and must ask themselves *What choices do I have?* Only a small minority can instead ask themselves *What do I want to do with my life?* This enormous privilege can entail a period of doubt, ambivalence, conflict, despair, and so on, as a young person tries to sort out his talents, interests, obligations, and motivations. William James had a particularly rough time of it, enduring many reversals and a severe depression before he was through.

James's father had inherited a comfortable fortune, which enabled him to pursue the ideal education for William and his four younger siblings (who included Henry, the future novelist). Apparently he never found what he sought, for the family endlessly moved about, from school to school, from tutor to tutor, from place to place. Ironically, the James children wound up very well educated indeed—fluent in several languages, well and widely read, skilled in conversation and disputation—either in spite of or because of the family's unusual lifestyle. In his teens William showed artistic talent and briefly anticipated a career as a painter, but his father opposed this path. In 1861 James enrolled at Harvard to study chemistry, but his interest shifted to physiology, and then to medicine. In 1865 he put his medical studies on hold to accompany the Harvard biologist Louis Agassiz on an expedition to the Amazon to search for specimens that would refute Darwin's theory of evolution. Agassiz didn't get his evidence, and all James got was a case of smallpox.

In poor health and in despair over his future, James went to Germany to take the waters and to read the latest research in physiology. After 18 months James returned to Harvard, in slightly improved health, with a growing interest in the possibilities of a science concerned with the correspondence between brain activity and mental life. In 1869 he received his MD but had

---

Source: James, W. (1892). *Psychology*. New York: Holt. [This is the briefer version of his 1890 *Principles of Psychology*.]

no interest in practicing medicine. The following spring his depression was at its worst, and James suffered a sudden existential crisis, a horrifying conviction that his life was not his to determine and that he was at the mercy of some unknown and unknowable fate. At first James was devastated by his experience, but gradually he rehabilitated himself through the realization that what matters about free will is not whether it exists but whether we believe in it. "My first act of free will," James wrote, "shall be to believe in free will." James's recovery became complete when, in 1872, Harvard asked him to teach part of a new course in physiology. He accepted, and remained at Harvard for the rest of his life.

James's interests never stopped growing and shifting. The physiology in his lectures gradually gave way to psychology, which later gave way to philosophy. In 1875 James established a psychological laboratory at Harvard, though he himself lacked the experimental temperament.

In 1878 James contracted with the publisher Henry Holt to write a comprehensive textbook of psychology. He told Holt it would take 2 years, but in fact it took 12. In 1890 Holt finally published *The Principles of Psychology*, all 2 volumes, 28 chapters, and 1,377 pages of it, and we are all in debt to Holt for his patience. To describe *The Principles*, or simply *James*, as it is often referred to, as a comprehensive textbook is like describing *Don Quixote* as a Spanish novel. *The Principles* is not only a landmark—the first comprehensive treatment of psychology in English—but a masterpiece. Psychologists still read James, not for what he knew about psychology, but for the extraordinary depth and clarity of his experience of mental life and his gift for communicating that experience in vivid, stimulating prose. James was not a theorist or a systematizer so much as an enquiring observer. He does not try to sell us a unifying conception of psychology—he doesn't have one—but rather to show us what needs to be explained and how difficult it will be to do so.

The Principles was an immediate success, but even in the more leisurely 1890s it was a long book. Accordingly, in 1892 Holt published *Psychology: Briefer Course*, a slim 468-page abridgment. James frankly tells us in the preface that "About two fifths of the volume is either new or rewritten, the rest is 'scissors and paste.'" This sounds inauspicious, but in fact *Jimmy*, as the shorter book is affectionately known, is every bit as good as *James*. In the reading from *Jimmy* that follows, James discusses the nature of the self. When we think of the self, says James, we think of two different things. One is everything that is part of the self, part of who we are and of what pertains to us. The other is our sense of being a self, the thing that knows the parts of the self. James's discussion of self is not explicitly about the mind/body problem, but there is an important relation between the issue James discusses here and the mind/body problem.

The Me and the I.—Whatever I may be thinking of, I am always at the same time more or less aware of *myself*, of my *personal existence*. At the same time it is *I* who am aware; so that the total self of me, being as it were duplex, partly known and partly knower, partly object and partly subject, must have two aspects discriminated in it, of which for shortness we may call one the *Me* and the other the *I*. I call these 'discriminated aspects,' and not separate things, because   5
the identity of *I* with *me*, even in the very act of their discrimination, is perhaps the most ineradicable dictum of common-sense, and must not be undermined by our terminology here at the outset, whatever we may come to think of its validity at our inquiry's end.

I shall therefore treat successively of A) the self as known, or the *me*, the 'empirical ego' as it is   10
sometimes called; and of B) the self as knower, or the I, the 'pure ego' of certain authors.

A) THE SELF AS KNOWN

The Empirical Self or Me.—Between what a man calls *me* and what he simply calls *mine* the line is difficult to draw. We feel and act about   15
certain things that are ours very much as we feel and act about ourselves. Our fame, our children, the work of our hands, may be as dear to us as our bodies are, and arouse the same feelings and the same acts of reprisal if attacked.   20
And our bodies themselves, are they simply ours, or are they *us*? Certainly men have been ready to disown their very bodies and to regard them as mere vestures, or even as prisons of clay from which they should some day be glad   25
to escape.

We see then that we are dealing with a fluctuating material; the same object being sometimes treated as a part of me, at other times as simply mine, and then again as if I had nothing   30
to do with it at all. *In its widest possible sense, however, a man's Me is the sum total of all that he* CAN *call his*, not only his body and his psychic powers, but his clothes and his house, his wife and children, his ancestors and friends,   35
his reputation and works, his lands and horses, and yacht and bank-account. All these things give him the same emotions. If they wax and prosper, he feels triumphant; if they

---

pure ego: an important concept for Kant and for later German thinkers such as Fichte and Hegel. Evans put it this way:

> The seeming fruitlessness of the attempt to reach the self experientially has led some philosophers to the conclusion that the self must lie outside experience, and must be unknowable in itself. On this view our knowledge of the self is essentially inferential. We know of its existence only through its manifestations. We know what the self experiences and what it accomplishes, but what it is in itself remains forever a mystery. We call it the self, the mind, the ego, or the subject, but apart from dignifying it with a name, we cannot say what it is. Such, in essence, is the Pure Ego Theory of the self. (Evans, 1970, p. 29)

---

prisons of clay: A Christian phrase, evoking the idea that during life on earth the immortal soul is temporarily confined to the body; when the body dies the soul is freed. The idea itself predates Christianity, and is forcefully articulated by Socrates in Plato's *Phaedo*.

dwindle and die away, he feels cast down,—not necessarily in the same degree for each thing, but in much the same way for all. Under-standing the Me in this widest sense, we may begin by dividing the history of it into three parts, relating respectively to—

> *history:* James uses the word here not in its sense of *chronology* but in its sense of *account* or *inquiry*, as in *natural history.*

  a. Its constituents;

  b. The feelings and emotions they arouse,—*self-appreciation;*

  c. The act to which they prompt,—*self-seeking* and *self-preservation.*

a. The constituents of the Me may be divided into two classes, those which make up respectively—

The material me;

The social me; and

The spiritual me.

The Material Me.—The *body* is the innermost part of the material me in each of us; and cer-tain parts of the body seem more intimately ours than the rest. The clothes come next. The old saying that the human person is composed of three parts—soul, body and clothes—is more than a joke. We so appropriate our clothes and identify ourselves with them that there are few of us who, if asked to choose between having a beautiful body clad in raiment per-petually shabby and unclean, and having an ugly and blemished form always spotlessly attired, would not hesitate a moment before making a decisive reply. Next, our immediate family is a part of ourselves. Our father and mother, our wife and babes, are bone of our bone and flesh of our flesh. When they die, a part of our very selves is gone. If they do anything wrong, it is our shame. If they are insulted, our anger flashes forth as readily as if we stood in their place. Our home comes next. Its scenes are part of our life; its aspects awaken the ten-derest feelings of affection; and we do not easily forgive the stranger who, in visiting it, finds fault with its arrangements or treats it with contempt. All these different things are the objects of instinctive preferences coupled with the most important practical interests of life. We all have a blind impulse to watch over our body, to deck it with clothing of an ornamen-tal sort, to cherish parents, wife, and babes, and to find for ourselves a house of our own which we may live in and 'improve.'

An equally instinctive impulse drives us to collect property; and the collections thus made become, with different degrees of intimacy, parts of our empirical selves. The parts of our wealth most intimately ours are those which are saturated with our labor. There are few men who would not feel personally annihilated if a life-long construction of their hands or brains—say an entomological collection or an extensive work in manuscript—were suddenly swept away. . . .

The Social Me.—A man's social me is the recognition which he gets from his mates. We are not only gregarious animals, liking to be in sight of our fellows, but we have an innate propensity   75
to get ourselves noticed, and noticed favorably, by our kind. No more fiendish punishment could be devised, were such a thing physically possible, than that one should be turned loose in society and remain absolutely unnoticed by all the members thereof. If no one turned round when we entered, answered when we spoke, or minded what we did, but if every person we met 'cut us dead' and acted as if we were non-existing things, a kind of rage and impotent   80
despair would ere long well up in us, from which the cruellest bodily tortures would be a relief; for these would make us feel that, however bad might be our plight, we had not sunk to such a depth as to be unworthy of attention at all.

Properly speaking, *a man has as many social selves as there are individuals who recognize him* and carry an image of him in their mind. To wound any one of these his images is to wound him.   85
But as the individuals who carry the images fall naturally into classes, we may practically say that he has as many different social selves as there are distinct *groups* of persons about whose opinion he cares. He generally shows a different side of himself to each of these different groups. . . .

The Spiritual Me.—By the 'spiritual me' so far as it belongs to the empirical self, I mean no one of my passing states of consciousness. I mean rather the entire collection of my states of conscious-   90
ness, my psychic faculties and dispositions taken concretely. This collection can at any moment become an object to my thought at that moment and awaken emotions like those awakened by any of the other portions of the Me. When we *think of ourselves as thinkers,* all the other ingredients of our Me seem relatively external possessions. Even within the spiritual *Me* some ingredients seem more external than others. Our capacities for sensation, for example, are less intimate possessions,   95
so to speak, than our emotions and desires; our intellectual processes are less intimate than our volitional decisions. The more *active-feeling* states of consciousness are thus the more central portions of the spiritual Me. The very core and nucleus of our self, as we know it, the very sanctuary of our life, is the sense of activity which certain inner states possess. This sense of activity is often held to be a direct revelation of the living substance of our Soul. Whether this be so or not is an ulterior   100
question. I wish now only to lay down the peculiar *internality* of whatever states possess this quality of seeming to be active. It is as if they *went out to meet* all the other elements of our experience. In thus feeling about them probably all men agree.   105

> An *ulterior* question is one that is beyond the scope of the present discussion.

b. The feelings and emotions of self come after the constituents.

Self-appreciation.—This is of two sorts, *self-complacency* and *self-dissatisfaction.* 'Self-love' more properly belongs under the division *c,* of *acts,* since what men mean by that name is rather a set of motor tendencies than a kind of feeling properly so called.

Language has synonyms enough for both kinds of self-appreciation. Thus pride, conceit, van-   110
ity, self-esteem, arrogance, vainglory, on the one hand; and on the other modesty, humility, confusion, diffidence, shame, mortification, contrition, the sense of obloquy, and personal

despair. These two opposite classes of affection seem to be direct and elementary endowments of

115 our nature. Associationists would have it that they are, on the other hand, secondary phenomena arising from a rapid computation of the sensible pleasures or pains to which our prosperous or debased personal predicament is likely to lead,

120 the sum of the represented pleasures forming the self-satisfaction, and the sum of the represented pains forming the opposite feeling of shame.... [T]here is a certain average tone of self-feeling which each one of us carries about with him, and which is independent of the objective reasons we may have for satisfaction or discontent. ...

> *obloquy:* disrepute, disgrace

> *Affection* here means the state of being affected (by something), as in a sensation or feeling.

...

125 The emotions themselves of self-satisfaction and abasement are of a unique sort, each as worthy to be classed as a primitive emotional species as are, for example, rage or pain. Each has its own peculiar physiognomical expression. In self-satisfaction the extensor muscles are innervated, the eye is strong and glorious, the gait rolling and elastic, the nostril dilated, and a peculiar smile plays upon the lips. This whole complex of symptoms is seen in an exquisite way in

130 lunatic asylums, which always contain some patients who are literally mad with conceit, and whose fatuous expression and absurdly strutting or swaggering gait is in tragic contrast with their lack of any valuable personal quality. It is in these same castles of despair that we find the strongest examples of the opposite physiognomy, in good people who think they have committed

135 'the unpardonable sin' and are lost forever, who crouch and cringe and slink from notice, and are unable to speak aloud or look us in the eye.

> *unpardonable sin:* blasphemy; specifically, denying the divine origin of the miracles performed by Jesus

c. Self-seeking and self-preservation come next.

These words cover a large number of our fundamental instinctive impulses. We have those

140 of *bodily self-seeking,* those of *social self-seeking,* and those of *spiritual self-seeking.*

Bodily Self-seeking.—All the ordinary useful reflex actions and movements of alimentation and defence are acts of bodily self-preservation. Fear and anger prompt to acts that are useful in the

145 same way. Whilst if by self-seeking we mean the providing for the future as distinguished from maintaining the present, we must class both anger and fear, together with the hunting, the acquisitive, the home-constructing and the tool-constructing instincts, as impulses to self-seeking of the bodily kind. Really, however, these latter instincts, with amativeness, parental fondness, curiosity and emulation, seek not only the devel-

150 opment of the bodily Me, but that of the material Me in the widest possible sense of the word.

> *alimentation:* here, taking nourishment

> *amativeness:* amorousness

Our **social self-seeking**, in turn, is carried on directly through our amativeness and friendliness, our desire to please and attract notice and admiration, our emulation and jealousy, our love of glory, influence, and power, and indirectly through whichever of the material self-seeking impulses prove serviceable as means to social ends. That the direct social self-seeking impulses are probably pure instincts is easily seen. The noteworthy thing about the desire to be 'recognized' by others is that its strength has so little to do with the worth of the recognition computed in sensational or rational terms. We are crazy to get a visiting-list which shall be large, to be able to say when any one is mentioned, 'Oh! I know him well,' and to be bowed to in the street by half the people we meet. . . .

. . .

Under the head of **spiritual self-seeking** ought to be included every impulse towards psychic progress, whether intellectual, moral, or spiritual in the narrow sense of the term. It must be admitted, however, that much that commonly passes for spiritual self-seeking in this narrow sense is only material and social self-seeking beyond the grave. In the Mohammedan desire for paradise and the Christian aspiration not to be damned in hell, the materiality of the goods sought is undisguised. In the more positive and refined view of heaven, many of its goods, the fellowship of the saints and of our dead ones, and the presence of God, are but social goods of the most exalted kind. It is only the search of the redeemed inward nature, the spotlessness from sin, whether here or hereafter, that can count as spiritual self-seeking pure and undefined.

But this broad external review of the facts of the life of the Me will be incomplete without some account of the

Rivalry and Conflict of the Different Mes.—With most objects of desire, physical nature restricts our choice to but one of many represented goods, and even so it is here. I am often confronted by the necessity of standing by one of my empirical selves and relinquishing the rest. Not that I would not, if I could, be both handsome and fat and well dressed, and a great athlete, and make a million a year, be a wit, a *bon-vivant*, and a lady-killer, as well as a philosopher; a philanthropist, statesman, warrior, and African explorer, as well as a 'tone-poet' and saint. But the thing is simply impossible. The millionaire's work would run counter to the saint's; the *bon-vivant* and the philanthropist would trip each other up; the philosopher and the lady-killer could not well keep house in the same tenement of clay. Such different characters may conceivably at the outset of life be alike *possible* to a man. But to make any one of them actual, the rest must more or less be suppressed.

So we have the paradox of a man shamed to death because he is only the second pugilist or the second oarsman in the world. That he is able to beat the whole population of the globe minus one is nothing; he has 'pitted' himself to beat that one; and as long as he doesn't do that nothing else counts. He is to his own regard as if he were not, indeed he *is* not. Yonder puny fellow, however, whom every one can beat, suffers no chagrin about it, for he has long ago abandoned the attempt to 'carry that line,' as the merchants say, of self at all. With no attempt there can be no failure; with no failure, no humiliation. So our self-feeling in this world depends entirely on what we *back* ourselves to be and do. It is determined by the ratio of our actualities to our supposed potentialities;

190   a fraction of which our pretensions are the denominator and the numerator our success: thus,

$$\text{Self-esteem} = \frac{\text{Success}}{\text{Pretensions}}.$$

> By *pretensions* James means those characteristics and ambitions that we have chosen as part of our self.

195   Such a fraction may be increased as well by diminishing the denominator as by increasing the numerator. To give up pretensions is as blessed a relief as to get them gratified; and where disappointment is incessant and the struggle unending, this is what men will always do. . . .

. . .

B) THE SELF AS KNOWER

200   The I, or 'pure ego,' is a very much more difficult subject of inquiry than the Me. It is that which at any given moment *is* conscious, whereas the Me is only one of the things which it is conscious *of*. In other words, it is the *Thinker;* and the question immediately comes up, *what* is the thinker? Is it the passing state of consciousness itself, or is it something deeper and less mutable? The passing state we have seen to be the very embodiment of change. Yet each of us spontaneously considers that by 'I,' he means something always the same. This has led most

205   philosophers to postulate behind the passing state of consciousness a permanent Substance or

> *embodiment of change:* James is referring to the ever-changing stream of consciousness.

Agent whose modification or act it is. This Agent is the thinker; the 'state' is only its instrument or means. 'Soul,' 'transcendental Ego,' 'Spirit,' are so many names for this more permanent sort of Thinker. Not discriminating them just yet, let us proceed to define our idea of the passing

210   state of consciousness more clearly.

The Unity of the Passing Thought.—Already, in speaking of 'sensations,' from the point of view of Fechner's idea of measuring them, we saw that there was no ground for calling them compounds. But what is true of sensations cognizing simple qualities is also true of thoughts with complex objects composed of many parts. This proposition unfortunately runs counter

215   to a wide-spread prejudice, and will have to be defended at some length. Common-sense, and psychologists of almost every school, have agreed that whenever an object of thought contains many elements, the thought itself must be made up of just as many ideas, one idea for each element, all fused together in appearance, but really separate.

       "There can be no difficulty in admitting that association *does* form the ideas of an indefinite

220   number of individuals into one complex idea," says James Mill, "because it is an acknowledged fact. Have we not the idea of an army? And is not that precisely the ideas of an indefinite number of men formed into one idea?"

Similar quotations might be multiplied, and the reader's own first impressions probably would rally to their support. Suppose, for example, he thinks that "the pack of cards is on the table." If he begins to reflect, he is as likely as not to say: "Well, isn't that a thought of the pack of cards? Isn't it of the cards as included in the pack? Isn't it of the table? And of the legs of the table as well? Hasn't my thought, then, all these parts—one part for the pack and another for the table? And within the pack-part a part for each card, as within the table-part a part for each leg? And isn't each of these parts an idea? And can thought, then, be anything but an assemblage or pack of ideas, each answering to some element of what it knows?"

Plausible as such considerations may seem, it is astonishing how little force they have. In assuming a pack of ideas, each cognizant of some one element of the fact one has assumed, nothing has been assumed which knows the whole fact *at once.* The idea which, on the hypothesis [of] the pack of ideas, knows, *e.g.,* the ace of spades must be ignorant of the leg of the table, since to account for that knowledge another special idea is by the same hypothesis invoked; and so on with the rest of the ideas, all equally ignorant of each other's objects. And yet in the actual living human mind what knows the cards also knows the table, its legs, etc., for all these things are known in relation to each other and at once. Our notion of the abstract numbers eight, four, two is as truly one feeling of the mind as our notion of simple unity. Our idea of a couple is not a couple of ideas. "But," the reader may say, "is not the taste of lemonade composed of that of lemon *plus* that of sugar?" No! I reply, this is taking the combining of objects for that of feelings. The physical lemonade contains both the lemon and the sugar, but its taste does not contain their tastes; for if there are any two things which are certainly *not* present in the taste of lemonade, those are the pure lemon-sour on the one hand and the pure sugar-sweet on the other. These tastes are absent utterly. A taste somewhat *like* both of them is there, but that is a distinct state of mind altogether.

Distinct mental states cannot 'fuse.' But not only is the notion that our ideas are combinations of smaller ideas improbable, it is logically unintelligible; it leaves out the essential features of all the 'combinations' which we actually know.

All the 'combinations' which we actually know are EFFECTS, *wrought by the units said to be 'combined,'* UPON SOME ENTITY OTHER THAN THEMSELVES. Without this feature of a medium or vehicle, the notion of combination has no sense.

In other words, no possible number of entities (call them as you like, whether forces, material particles, or mental elements) can sum *themselves* together. Each remains, in the sum, what it always was; and the sum itself exists only *for a bystander* who happens to overlook the units and to apprehend the sum as such; or else it exists in the shape of some other effect on an entity external to the sum itself. . . .

In the parallelogram of forces, the 'forces' do not combine *themselves* into the diagonal resultant; a

parallelogram of forces: If forces F1 and F2 impinge simultaneously on an object ("body") O, the resultant force R in O can be represented this way:

Each force has a direction, represented by the direction of the arrow, and a magnitude, represented by the arrow's length.

265   *body* is needed on which they may impinge, to exhibit their resultant effect. No more do musical sounds combine *per se* into concords or discords. Concord and discord are names for their combined effects on that external medium, the *ear.*

...

Take a sentence of a dozen words, and take twelve men and tell to each one word. Then stand the men in a row or jam them in a bunch, and let each think of his word as intently as he
270   will: nowhere will there be a consciousness of the whole sentence. We talk, it is true, of the 'spirit of the age,' and the 'sentiment of the people,' and in various ways we hypostatize 'public opinion.' But we know this to be symbolic speech, and never dream that the spirit, opinion, or sentiment constitutes a consciousness other than, and additional to, that of the several individuals whom the words 'age,' 'people,' or 'public' denote. The private minds do not agglomerate into
275   a higher compound mind. . . .

The simplest thing, therefore, if we are to assume the existence of a stream of consciousness at all, would be to suppose that things that are known together are known in single pulses of that
280   stream. The things may be many, and may occasion many currents in the brain. But the psychic phenomenon correlative to these many currents is one integral 'state,' transitive or substantive (see p. 160), to which the many things appear.

> On p. 160 James says, "*Let us call the resting-places the 'substantive parts,' and the places of flight the 'transitive parts,' of the stream of thought.* It then appears that our thinking tends at all times towards some other substantive part than the one from which it has just been dislodged. And we may say that the main use of the transitive parts is to lead us from one substantive conclusion to another."

285   **The Soul as a Combining Medium.**—The spiritualists in philosophy have been prompt to see that things which are known together are known by one *something,* but that something, they say, is no mere passing thought, but a simple and permanent spiritual being on which many ideas combine their effects. It makes no difference in this connection whether this being be called
290   Soul, Ego, or Spirit, in either case its chief function is that of a combining medium. This is a different vehicle of knowledge from that in which we just said that the mystery of knowing things together might be most simply lodged. Which is the real knower, this permanent being, or our passing state? If we had other grounds, not yet considered, for admitting the Soul into our psychology, then getting there on those grounds, she might turn out to be the knower too. But if
295   there be no *other* grounds for admitting the Soul, we had better cling to our passing 'states' as the exclusive agents of knowledge; for we have to assume their existence anyhow in psychology, and the knowing of many things together is just as well accounted for when we call it one of their
300   functions as when we call it a reaction of the Soul.

> "It" is "the knowing of many things together."

Explained it is not by either conception, and has to figure in psychology as a datum that is ultimate.

But there are other alleged grounds for admitting the Soul into psychology, and the chief of them is

The Sense of Personal Identity.—In the last chapter it was stated that the thoughts which we   305
actually know to exist do not fly about loose, but seem each to belong to some one thinker and
not to another. Each thought, out of a multitude of other thoughts of which it may think, is able
to distinguish those which belong to it from those which do not. The former have a warmth and
intimacy about them of which the latter are completely devoid, and the result is a Me of yesterday,
judged to be in some peculiarly subtle sense the *same* with the I who now make the judg-   310
ment.—As a mere subjective phenomenon the judgment presents no special mystery. It
belongs to the great class of judgments of sameness; and there is nothing more remarkable in
making a judgment of sameness in the first person than in the second or the third. The intellectual operations seem essentially alike, whether I say 'I am the same as I was' or whether I say
'the pen is the same as it was, yesterday.' It is as easy to think this as to think the opposite and   315
say 'neither of us is the same.' The only question which we have to consider is whether it be a
right judgment. *Is the sameness predicated really there?*

Sameness in the Self as Known.—If in the sentence "I am the same that I was yesterday," we
take the 'I' broadly, it is evident that in many ways I am *not* the same. As a concrete Me, I am
somewhat different from what I was: then hungry, now full; then walking, now at rest; then   320
poorer, now richer; then younger, now older; etc. And yet in other ways I *am* the same, and we
may call these the essential ways. My name and profession and relations to the world are identical, my face, my faculties and store of memories, are practically indistinguishable, now and
then. Moreover the Me of now and the Me of then are *continuous:* the alterations were gradual and never affected the whole of me at once. So far, then, my personal identity is just like the   325
sameness predicated of any other aggregate thing. It is a conclusion grounded either on the
resemblance in essential respects, or on the continuity of the phenomena compared. And it
must not be taken to mean more than these grounds warrant, or treated as a sort of metaphysical or absolute Unity in which all differences are overwhelmed. The past and present
selves compared are the same just so far as they *are* the same, and no farther. They are the same   330
in *kind.* But this generic sameness coexists with generic differences just as real; and if from the
one point of view I am one self, from another I am quite as truly many. Similarly of the attribute
of continuity: it gives to the self the unity of mere connectedness, or unbrokenness, a perfectly
definite phenomenal thing—but it gives not a jot or tittle more.

Sameness in the Self as Knower.—But all this is said only of the Me, or Self as known. In the   335
judgment 'I am the same,' etc., the 'I' was taken broadly as the concrete person. Suppose, however, that we take it narrowly, as the *Thinker,* as *'that to which'* all the concrete determinations
of the Me belong and are known: does there not then appear an absolute identity at different
times? That something which at every moment goes out and knowingly appropriates the *Me*
of the past, and discards the non-me as foreign, is it not a permanent abiding principle of spir-   340
itual activity identical with itself wherever found?

   That it is such a principle is the reigning doctrine both of philosophy and common-sense,
and yet reflection finds it difficult to justify the idea. *If there were no passing states of consciousness,* then indeed we might suppose an abiding principle, absolutely one with itself,
to be the ceaseless thinker in each one of us. But if the states of consciousness be accorded as   345

realities, no such 'substantial' identity in the thinker need be supposed. Yesterday's and to-day's states of consciousnesses have no *substantial* identity, for when one is here the other is irrevocably dead and gone. But they have a *functional* identity, for both know the same objects, and so far as the by-gone me is one of those objects, they react upon it in an identical way, greeting it and calling it *mine*, and opposing it to all the other things they know. This functional identity seems really the only sort of identity in the thinker which the facts require us to suppose. Successive thinkers, numerically distinct, but all aware of the same past in the same way, form an adequate vehicle for all the experience of personal unity and sameness which we actually have. And

> *successive thinkers:* "I" am not the same thinker at a given moment as I am at the next moment; "we" are numerically distinct.

just such a train of successive thinkers is the stream of mental states (each with its complex object cognized and emotional and selective reaction thereupon) which psychology treated as a natural science has to assume.

The logical conclusion seems then to be that the states of consciousness are all that psychology needs to do her work with. Metaphysics or theology may prove the Soul to exist; but for psychology the hypothesis of such a substantial principle of unity is superfluous.

How the I appropriates the Me.—But *why* should each successive mental state appropriate the same past Me? I spoke a while ago of my own past experiences appearing to me with a 'warmth and intimacy' which the experiences thought of by me as having occurred to other people lack. This leads us to the answer sought. My present Me is felt with warmth and intimacy. The heavy warm mass of my body is there, and the nucleus of the 'spiritual me,' the *sense* of intimate activity . . . is there. We cannot realize our present self without simultaneously feeling one or other of these two things. Any other object of thought which brings these two things with it into consciousness will be thought with a warmth and an intimacy like those which cling to the present me.

Any *distant* object which fulfils this condition will be thought with such warmth and intimacy. But which distant objects *do* fulfil the condition, when represented?

Obviously those, and only those, which fulfilled it when they were alive. *Them* we shall still represent with the animal warmth upon them; to them may possibly still cling the flavor of the inner activity taken in the act. And by a natural consequence, we shall assimilate them to each other and to the warm and intimate self we now feel within us as we think, and separate them as a collection from whatever objects have not this mark, much as out of a herd of cattle let loose for the winter on some wide Western prairie the owner picks out and sorts together, when the round-up comes in the spring, all the beasts on which he finds his own particular brand. Well, just such objects are the past experiences which I now call mine. Other men's experiences, no matter how much I may know about them, never bear this vivid, this peculiar brand. . . .

And similarly in our waking hours, though each pulse of consciousness dies away and is replaced by another, yet that other, among the things it knows, knows its own predecessor, and finding it 'warm,' in the way we have described, greets it, saying: "Thou art *mine*, and part of the same self with me." Each later thought, knowing and including thus the thoughts that went before, is the final receptacle—and appropriating them is the final owner—of all that they contain and own. . . . It is this trick which the nascent thought has of immediately taking up the expiring

thought and 'adopting' it, which leads to the appropriation of most of the remoter constituents of the self. Who owns the last self owns the self before the last, for what possesses the possessor possesses the possessed. It is impossible to discover any *verifiable* features in personal identity   390
which this sketch does not contain, impossible to imagine how any transcendent principle of Unity (were such a principle there) could shape matters to any other result, or be known by any other fruit, than just this production of a stream of consciousness each successive part of which should know, and knowing, hug to itself and adopt, all those that went before,—thus standing as the *representative* of an entire past stream with which it is in no wise to be identified.   395

...

Review, and Psychological Conclusion.—To sum up this long chapter:—The consciousness of Self involves a stream of thought, each part of which as 'I' can remember those which went before, know the things they knew, and care paramountly for certain ones among them as *'Me,'* and *appropriate to these* the rest. This Me is an empirical aggregate of things objectively known. The *I* which knows them cannot itself be an aggregate; neither for psychological pur-   400
poses need it be an unchanging metaphysical entity like the Soul, or a principle like the transcendental Ego, viewed as 'out of time.' It is a *thought,* at each moment different from that of the last moment, but *appropriative* of the latter, together with all that the latter called its own. All the experiential facts find their place in this description, unencumbered with any hypothesis save that of the existence of passing thoughts or states of mind.   405

If passing thoughts be the directly verifiable existents which no school has hitherto doubted them to be, then they are the only 'Knower' of which Psychology, treated as a natural science, need take any account. The only pathway that I can discover for bringing in a more transcendental Thinker would be to deny that we have any such *direct* knowledge of the existence of our 'states of consciousness' as common-sense supposes us to possess. The existence of the 'states'   410
in question would then be a mere hypothesis, or one way of asserting that there *must be* a knower correlative to all this known; but the problem *who that knower is* would have become a metaphysical problem. With the question once stated in these terms, the notion either of a Spirit of the world which thinks through us, or that of a set of individual substantial souls, must be considered as *prima facie* on a par with our own 'psy-   415
chological' solution, and discussed impartially. I myself believe that room for much future inquiry lies in this direction. The 'states of mind' which every psychologist believes in are by no means

prima facie: "first face," i.e., first appearance; at first sight

Coon (2000) describes James as "extremely ambivalent about erasing the soul from the picture entirely. He periodically raised the soul only to bury it and then resurrect it again later" (p. 88). Coon concludes, "In the 20th century, psychologists effectively carried out the secularizing project that James initiated but could or would not complete."

420   clearly apprehensible, if distinguished from their objects. But to doubt them lies beyond the scope of our natural-science point of view. And in this book the provisional solution which we have reached must be the final word: the thoughts themselves are the thinkers.

For Discussion

1. Why are states of consciousness all that psychology "needs to do her work with" or "need take account of"?

2. What position on the mind/body question does James seem to be taking in his discussion of the self?

3. What happens to James's self when James is asleep?

4. James clearly wants to deal with the self as a psychological rather than metaphysical problem. What is the distinction?

5. What does James mean by the last phrase ("The thoughts themselves are the thinkers")?

Wilhelm Wundt (1832–1920)
Outlines of Psychology (1897)

Chapter 22. Psychical Causality and Its Laws

In 1908 Hermann Ebbinghaus famously said, "Psychology has a long past, yet its real history is short" (Ebbinghaus 1908/1973, p. 3). In the context of the short history, Wundt is often spoken of as a founder, as the "father of experimental psychology." Wundt was not the first to do psychological experiments (Fechner and Ebbinghaus, among others, preceded him), but Wundt established the first psychological laboratory (at Leipzig, in 1879), founded the first journal of experimental psychology (*Philosophische Studien* [Philosophical Studies], 1881), and trained the first generation of doctoral students in experimental psychology.

In the context of the long past, Wundt is better seen, with such figures as Fechner, Ebbinghaus, and James, as one of the 19th century visionaries who extracted psychological questions and theories from their ancestral home—philosophy and physiology—and set them on their own as a new science and as a distinct academic field.

Wilhelm Maximilian Wundt was trained in medicine at Tübingen and Heidelberg, but after practicing briefly he went to Berlin to study physiology with Johannes Müller and Émile du Bois-Reymond, two of the leading lights in the field. In 1858 Wundt returned to Heidelberg as a lecturer in physiology and soon became Hermann Helmholtz's assistant.

In the six years he spent with Helmholtz (2.3 & 4.4), Wundt's interests began to expand beyond the bounds of physiology proper. In 1862 he offered a course called "Psychology From the Standpoint of Natural Science" and began writing *Lectures on the Human and Animal Mind*. After leaving his position with Helmholtz, Wundt struggled to make a living by teaching and writing. The turning point in Wundt's career came in 1874, with the publication of *Principles of Physiological Psychology*. In the *Principles* Wundt showed how physiology and psychology could be combined in a new experimental science. The book was widely hailed, and in 1875 Wundt became a professor at Leipzig, where his colleagues included Weber and Fechner.

Source: Wundt, W. (1897). *Outlines of psychology* (C. H. Judd, Trans.). Leipzig: Engelmann.

Wundt remained at Leipzig until his retirement in 1917 and at his death left behind nearly 60,000 pages of published work. Years later, and in spite of his exalted status in the short history of psychology, few of those pages have been translated into English. In the present reading, Wundt addresses the mind-body question in the context of an explanation of psychology's place among the sciences.

§ 22. CONCEPT OF MIND

1. Every empirical science has, as its primary and characteristic subject of treatment, certain particular facts of experience whose nature and reciprocal relations it seeks to investigate. In solving these problems it is found to be necessary, if we are not to give up entirely the grouping of the facts under leading heads, to have *general supplementary concepts* that are not contained in experience itself, but are gained by a process of logical treatment of this experience. The most general supplementary concept of this kind that has found its place in all the empirical sciences, is the concept of *causality*. It comes from the necessity of thought that all our experiences shall be arranged according to reason and consequent, and that we shall remove, by means of *secondary* supplementary concepts and if need be by means of concepts of a hypothetical character, all contradictions that stand in the way of the establishment of a consistent interconnection of this kind. In this sense we may regard all the supplementary concepts that serve for the interpretation of any sphere of experience, as applications of the general principle of causation. They are justified in so far as they are required, or at least rendered probable, by this principle; they are unjustifiable so soon as they prove to be arbitrary fictions resulting from foreign motives, and contributing nothing to the interpretation of experience.

> *grouping . . . heads*: arranging natural phenomena in categories

2. In this sense the concept *matter* is a fundamental supplementary concept of natural science. In its most general significance it designates the permanent substratum assumed as existing in universal space, to whose activities we must attribute all natural phenomena. In this most general sense the concept matter is indispensable to every explanation of natural science. The attempt in recent times to raise *energy* to the position of a governing principle, does not succeed in doing away with the concept matter, but merely gives it a different content. This content, however, is given to the concept by means of a second supplementary concept, which relates to the *causal activity* of matter. The concept of matter that has been accepted in natural science up to the present time, is based upon the mechanical physics of Galileo, and uses as its secondary supplementary concept the concept of *force,* which is defined as the product of the mass and the momentary acceleration. A physics of energy would have to use everywhere instead of this the concept *energy*, which in the special form of mechanical energy is defined as half the product of the mass multiplied by the square of the velocity. Energy, however, must, just as well as force, have a position in objective space, and under certain particular conditions the points from which energy proceeds may, just as well as the points from which force proceeds, change their place in space, so that the concept of matter as a substratum contained in space, is retained in both cases. The only difference, and it is indeed an important one, is that when we use the concept force, we presuppose the

> A few years later, Einstein showed that matter and energy are two aspects of the same thing, but Wundt's point retains its force.

5

10

15

20

25

30

35

40   reducibility of all natural phenomena to forms of mechanical motion, while when we use the concept of energy, we attribute to matter not only the property of motion without a change in the form of energy, but also the property of the transformability of qualitatively different forms of energy into one another without a change in the quantity of the energy.

45   3. The concept of *mind* is a supplementary concept of psychology, in the same way that the concept matter is a supplementary concept of natural science. It too is indispensable in so far as we need a concept which shall express in a comprehensive way the totality of psychical experiences in an individual consciousness. The particular content of the concept, however, is in this case also entirely dependent on the secondary concepts that give a more detailed definition of psychical causality. In the definition of this content psychology shared at first the fortune of the natural sciences. Both the concept of mind and that of matter arose primarily not
50   so much from the need of explaining experience as from the effort to reach a systematic doctrine of the general interconnection of all things. But while the natural sciences have long since outgrown this mythological stage of speculative definition, and make use of some of the single ideas that originated at that time, only for the purpose of gaining definite starting-points for a strict methodical definition of their concepts, psychology has continued under the
55   control of the mythological, metaphysical concept of mind down to most modern times, and still remains, in part at least, under its control. This concept is not used as a general supplementary concept that serves primarily to gather together the psychical facts and only secondarily to give a causal interpretation of them, but it is employed as a means to satisfy so far
60   as possible the need of a general universal system, including both nature and the individual existence.

4. The *concept of a mind-substance* in its various forms is rooted in this mythological and metaphysical need. In its development there have not been wanting efforts to meet from this position, so far as possible, the demand for a psychological causal explanation, still, such
65   efforts have in all cases been afterthoughts; and it is perfectly obvious that psychological experience alone, independent of all foreign metaphysical motives, would never have led to a concept of mind-substance. This concept has beyond a
70   doubt exercised a harmful influence on the treatment of experience. The view, for example, that all the contents of psychical experience are ideas, and that these ideas are more or less permanent objects, would hardly be comprehensible without such presuppositions. That this concept is really foreign to psychology is further attested by the close interconnection in
75   which it stands to the concept of material substance. It is regarded either as identical with the latter, or else as distinct in nature, but still reducible in its most general formal characteristics to one of the particular forms of the concept matter, namely to the *atom*.

5. *Two* forms of the concept mind-substance may be distinguished. . . . The one is *materialistic* and regards psychical processes as the activities of matter or of certain material

> *mind-substance:* Descartes conceived of mind as being made of a special kind of substance, or "stuff," that is invisible and does not take up space and yet is capable of acting on the (physical) body. See 1.1.

spiritual nature: nonphysical; immaterial

complexes, such as the brain-elements. The other   80
is *spiritualistic* and looks upon these processes as
states and changes in an unextended and there-
fore indivisible and permanent being of a specifically spiritual nature. In this case matter is
thought of as made up of similar atoms of a lower order (monistic, or monadological spiritualism), or the mind-atom is regarded as specifically different from matter proper (dualistic   85
spiritualism).

In both its materialistic and spiritualistic forms, the concept mind-substance does nothing
for the interpretation of psychological experience. Materialism does away with psychology
entirely and puts in its place an imaginary brain-physiology of the future, or when it tries to give
positive theories, falls into doubtful and unreliable hypotheses of cerebral physiology. In thus   90
giving up psychology in any proper sense, this doctrine gives up entirely the attempt to furnish
any practical basis for the *mental sciences*. Spiritualism allows psychology as such to continue,
but subordinates actual experience to entirely arbitrary metaphysical hypotheses, through
which the unprejudiced observation of psychical processes is obstructed. This appears first
of all in the incorrect statement of the problem of psychology, with which the metaphysical   95
theories start. They regard inner and outer experience as totally heterogeneous, though in
some external way interacting, spheres.

6. It has been shown that the experience dealt with in the natural sciences and in psychology are nothing but components of *one* experience regarded from different points of view: in
the natural sciences as an interconnection of objective phenomena and, in consequence of the   100
abstraction from the knowing subject, as *mediate experience;* in psychology as *immediate and
underived experience.*

When this relation is once understood, the *concept of a mind-substance* immediately
gives place to the *concept of the actuality of mind* as a basis for the comprehension of psychical processes. Since the psychological treatment of experience is supplementary to that   105
of the natural sciences, in that it deals with the immediate reality of experience, it follows
naturally that there is no place in psychology for hypothetical supplementary concepts such
as are necessary in the natural sciences because of their concept of an object independent
of the subject. In this sense, the concept of the actuality of mind does not require any hypothetical determinants to define its particular contents, as the concept of matter does, but   110
quite to the contrary, it excludes such hypothetical elements from the first by defining the
nature of mind as the immediate reality of the processes themselves. Still, since one important component of these processes, namely the totality of ideational objects, is at the same
time the subject of consideration in the natural sciences, it necessarily follows that substance and actuality are concepts that refer to one and the same general experience, with   115
the difference that in each case this experience is looked at from a different point of view.
If we abstract from the knowing subject in our treatment of the world of experience, it
appears as a manifold of interacting substances; if, on the contrary, we regard it as the total
content of the experience of the subject including the subject itself, it appears as a manifold of interrelated occurrences. In the first case, phenomena are looked upon as *outer*   120

phenomena, in the sense that they would take place just the same, even if the knowing subject were not there at all, so that we may call the form of experience dealt with in the natural sciences *outer* experience. In the second case, on the contrary, all the contents of experience are regarded as belonging directly to the knowing subject, so that we may call

125 the psychological attitude towards experience that of *inner* experience. In this sense outer and inner experience are identical with mediate and immediate, or with objective and subjective forms of experience. They all serve to designate, not different spheres of experience, but different supplementary points of view in the consideration of an experience which is presented to us as an absolute unity.

130   7. That the method of treating experience employed in natural science should have reached its maturity before that employed in psychology, is easily comprehensible in view of the practical interest connected with the discovery of regular natural phenomena thought of as independent of the subject; and it was almost unavoidable that this prior-

ity of the natural sciences should, for a long

135 time, lead to a confusion of the two points of view. This did really occur as we see by the different psychological substance-concepts. It is for this reason that the reform in the fundamental position of psychology, which looks for

140 the characteristics of this science and for its problems, not in the specifically distinct nature of its sphere, but in its method of considering all the contents presented to us in experience in their immediate reality, unmodified by any

145 hypothetical supplementary concepts—this reform did not originate with psychology itself, but with the *single mental sciences.* The view of mental processes based upon the concept of actuality, was familiar in these sciences long

150 before it was accepted in psychology. This inadmissible difference between the fundamental position of psychology and the mental sciences is what has kept psychology until the present time from fulfilling its mission of serving as a

155 foundation for all the mental sciences.

single mental sciences: In his introduction, Wundt identifies these as follows:

> [P]hilology, history and political and social science, have as their subject matter, immediate experience as determined by the interaction of objects with knowing and acting subjects. None of the mental sciences employs the abstractions and hypothetical supplementary concepts of natural science; quite otherwise, they all accept ideas and the accompanying subjective activities as immediate reality. The effort is then made to explain the single components of this reality through their mutual interconnections. This method of psychological interpretation employed in *each of the special mental sciences*, must also be the mode of procedure in psychology itself, being the method required by the subject-matter of psychology, the immediate reality of experience. (p. 3)

    8. When the concept of actuality is adopted, a question upon which metaphysical systems of psychology have been long divided is immediately disposed of. This is the question of the *relation of body and mind.* So long as body and mind are both regarded as substances, this rela-

160 tion must remain an enigma, however the two concepts of substance may be defined. If they

like and *unlike* here mean same and different.

The first view is that of Leibniz; see his *New System of Nature* (1695) and his *Discourse on Metaphysics* (1686), §33. The second view belongs to Spinoza; see his *Ethics* (1665), Part 2.

are like substances, then the different contents of experience as dealt with in the natural sciences and in psychology can no longer be understood, and there is no alternative but to deny the independence of one of these forms of knowledge. If they are unlike substances, their connection is a continual miracle. If we start with the theory of the actuality of mind, we recognize the immediate reality of the phenomena in psychological experience. Our physiological concept of the bodily organism, on the other hand, is nothing but a part of this experience, which we gain, just as we do all the other empirical contents of the natural sciences, by assuming the existence of an object independent of the knowing subject. Certain components of mediate experience may correspond to certain components of immediate experience, without its being necessary, for this reason, to reduce the one to the other or to derive one from the other. In fact, such a derivation is absolutely impossible because of the totally different points of view adopted in the two cases. Still, the fact that we have here not different objects of experience, but different points of view in looking at a unitary experience, renders necessary the existence at every point of relations between the two. At the same time it must be remembered that there is an infinite number of objects that can be approached only mediately, through the method of the natural sciences: here belong all those phenomena that we are not obliged to regard as physiological substrata of psychical processes. On the other hand, there is just as large a number of important facts that are presented only immediately, or in psychological experience: these are all those contents of our subjective consciousness which do not have the character of ideational objects, that is, the character of contents which are directly referred to external objects.

9. As a result of this relation, it follows that there must be a necessary relation between all the facts that belong at the same time to 'both kinds' of experience, to the mediate experience of the natural sciences and to the immediate experience of psychology, for they are nothing but components of a single experience which is merely regarded in the two cases from different points of view. Since these facts belong to both spheres, there must be an elementary process on the physical side, corresponding to every such process on the psychical side. This general principle is known as the *principle of psycho-physical parallelism*. It has an empirico-psychological significance and is thus totally different from certain metaphysical principles that have sometimes been designated by the same name, but in reality have an entirely different meaning. These metaphysical principles are all based on the hypothesis of a psychical substance. They all seek to solve the problem of the interrelation of body and mind, either by assuming *two* real substances with attributes which are different, but parallel in their changes, or by assuming *one* substance with two distinct attributes that correspond in their modifications. In both these cases the metaphysical principle of parallelism is specific nature of spacial and temporal ideas, or of relating and comparing processes, because natural science purposely abstracts from all that is here

concerned. Then, too, there are two concepts that result from the psychical combinations, which, together with their related affective elements, lie entirely outside the sphere of experience to which the principle of parallelism applies. There

205 are the concepts of *value* and *end*. The forms of combination that we see in processes of fusion or in associative and apperceptive processes, as well as the values that they possess in the whole inter-connection of psychical development, can only be

210 understood through *psychological* analysis, in the same way that objective phenomena, such as those of weight, sound, light, heat, etc., or the processes of the nervous system, can be approached only by physical and physiological

215 analysis, that is, analysis that makes use of the sup-plementary substance-concepts of natural science based on the assumption that every physical process has a corresponding psychical process and vice versa; or on the assumption that the mental world is a mirroring of the bodily world, or that the bodily world is an objective realization of the

220 mental. This assumption is, however, entirely indemonstrable and arbitrary, and leads in its psy-chological application to an intellectualism con-tradictory to all experience. The psychological principle, on the other hand, as above formulated, starts with the assumption that there is only

225 *one* experience, which, however, as soon as it becomes the subject of scientific analysis, is, in some of its components, open to *two* different kinds of scientific treatment: to a mediate form of treatment, which investigates ideated objects in their objective relations to one another, and to an

230 *immediate* form, which investigates the same objects in their directly known character, and in their relations to all the other contents of the experience of the knowing subject. So far as there are objects to which both these forms of treat-ment are applicable, the psychological principle of parallelism requires, between the processes on the two sides, a relation at every point. This requirement is justified by the fact that both forms

235 of analysis are in these two cases really analyses of one and the same content of experience. On the other hand, from the very nature of the case, the psychological principle of parallelism can *not* apply to those contents of experience which are objects of natural-scientific analysis alone, or to those which go to make up the specific character of psychological experience. Among the latter we must reckon the characteristic *combinations* and *relations* of psychical elements and

240 compounds. To be sure, there are combinations of physical processes running parallel to these, in so far at least as a direct or indirect causal relation must exist between the physical processes whose regular coexistence or succession is indicated by a psychical interconnection, but the characteristic content of the psychical combination can, of course, in no way be a part of the

fusion: Wundt's term for the psychological combining of distinct elementary sensations, as distinct tones are combined in a chord; see *Outlines*, Part 2

association: the forming of connections between ideas as a result of similarity or temporal or spatial proximity between them

apperception: the process of making sense of a perception by integrating it with other relevant perceptions and knowledge

psychological principle: Wundt's psychophysical parallelism

ideated objects: objects represented as ideas; mediately known objects

causal relation between the physical processes. Thus, for example, the elements that enter into a spacial or temporal idea, stand in a regular relation of coexistence and succession in their phys-   245
iological substrata also; or the ideational elements that make up a process of relating or comparing psychical contents, have corresponding combinations of physiological excitation of some kind or other, which are repeated whenever these psychical processes take place. But the physiological processes can not contain anything of that which goes most of all to form the specific nature of spacial and temporal ideas, or of relating and comparing processes, because natural   250
science purposely abstracts from all that is here concerned. Then, too, there are two concepts that result from the psychical combinations, which, together with their related affective elements, lie entirely outside the sphere of experience to which the principle of parallelism applies. There are the concepts of *value* and *end*. The forms of combination that we see in processes of fusion or in associative and apperceptive processes, as well as the values that they possess in the   255
whole interconnection of psychical development, can only be understood through *psychological* analysis, in the same way that objective phenomena, such as those of weight, sound, light, heat, etc., or the processes of the nervous system, can be approached only by physical and physiological analysis, that is, analysis that makes use of the supplementary substance-concepts of natural science.   260

10. Thus, the principle of psycho-physical parallelism in the incontrovertible *empirico-psychological* significance above attributed to it, leads necessarily to the recognition of an *independent psychical causality*, which is related at all points with physical causality and can never come into contradiction with it, but is just as different from this physical causality as the point of view adopted in psychology, or that of immediate, subjective experience, is different from   265
the point of view taken in the natural sciences, or that of mediate, objective experience due to abstraction. And just as the nature of physical causality can be revealed to us only in the fundamental *laws of nature,* so the only way that we have of accounting for the characteristics of psychical causality is to abstract certain *fundamental laws of psychical phenomena* from the totality of psychical processes.   270

FOR DISCUSSION

1. What does Wundt mean by a "supplementary concept" (line 5)? What are some examples from other sciences?

2. How does Wundt classify the mind-body view of Descartes?

3. Why (and how) does Wundt distinguish between inner and outer experience?

4. Why (and how) does Wundt distinguish between mediate and immediate experience?

5. How do the natural sciences deal with the contents of experience? How is this different from the way psychology deals with them?

6. Is Wundt's psychophysical parallelism a monist or dualist solution to the mind-body problem?

Alan Turing (1912–1954)
Computing Machinery and Intelligence (1950)

The computer has become, along with automobiles and microwave ovens, part of the technological fabric of everyday life, but the capabilities of an ordinary desktop computer were the stuff of science fiction 50 years ago. The achievements of the engineers and programmers who created the hardware and software that we have come to rely on are indeed extraordinary, but before there was anything for engineers to build or for programmers to program, there had to be an idea. Turing was not the first or the only person responsible for the idea of the digital computer, but he was the first to conceive of the digital computer in an abstract form—as something that could be (and has been) made out of electric circuits, brass cogs, or tinkertoys—and the first to work out the logical properties, capabilities, and limitations, of digital computers.

Alan Turing was born in London and educated at Cambridge, where he studied mathematics. In 1937 he published a landmark paper in mathematical logic in which, among other things, Turing first described what he calls the *universal digital computer,* now usually referred to as a *Turing machine.* Imagine an indefinitely long roll of paper tape—though it could just as well be a roll of postage stamps or a strand of seaweed—marked off in squares. One square at a time, the machine can (a) read the symbol in that square, (b) erase the symbol in that square, or (c) write a new symbol in that square. The machine can also move the tape forward or backward to some other square. Turing showed mathematically that with the appropriate symbols on the tape such a machine can solve any problem that can be solved by following specified rules or instructions.

In 1937 there were no computers. In 1950 there were room-sized computers not much more powerful than a modern pocket calculator. An indication of Turing's brilliance is that even then he could articulate what is probably the most profound, difficult, and contentious question that can be asked about computers.

Source: Turing, A. M. (1950). Computing machinery and intelligence. *Mind, 59,* 433–460. Reprinted with permission.

1. THE IMITATION GAME

I propose to consider the question, 'Can machines think?' This should begin with definitions of the meaning of the terms 'machine' and 'think.' The definitions might be framed so as to reflect so far as possible the normal use of the words, but this attitude is dangerous. If the meaning of the words 'machine' and 'think' are to be found by examining how they are commonly used it is difficult to escape the conclusion that the meaning and the answer to the question, 'Can machines think?' is to be sought in a statistical survey such as a Gallup poll. But this is absurd. Instead of attempting such a definition I shall replace the question by another, which is closely related to it and is expressed in relatively unambiguous words. 5

The new form of the problem can be described in terms of a game which we call the 'imitation game.' It is played with three people, a man (A), a woman (B), and an interrogator (C) who may be of either sex. The interrogator stays in a room apart from the other two. The object of the game for the interrogator is to determine which of the other two is the man and which is the woman. He knows them by labels X and Y, and at the end of the game he says either 'X is A and Y is B' or 'X is B and Y is A.' The interrogator is allowed to put questions to A and B thus: 10

> C: Will X please tell me the length of his or her hair? Now suppose X is actually A, then A 15
> must answer. It is A's object in the game to try and cause C to make the wrong identification. His answer might therefore be
> 'My hair is shingled, and the longest strands are about nine inches long.'

In order that tones of voice may not help the interrogator the answers should be written, or better still, typewritten. The ideal arrangement is to have a teleprinter communicating between the two rooms. Alternatively the question and answers can be repeated by an intermediary. The object of the game for the third player (B) is to help the interrogator. The best strategy for her is probably to give truthful answers. She can add such things as 'I am the woman, don't listen to him!' to her answers, but it will avail nothing as the man can make similar remarks. 20

When a machine takes the part of A it is pretending to be a human, but not specifically a man. The interrogator's task is not to distinguish man from woman but to distinguish human from machine.

We now ask the question, 'What will happen when a machine takes the part of A in this game?' Will the interrogator decide wrongly as often when the game is played like this as he does when the game is played between a man and a woman? These questions replace our original, 'Can machines think?' 25 30

2. CRITIQUE OF THE NEW PROBLEM

As well as asking, 'What is the answer to this new form of the question,' one may ask, 'Is this new question a worthy one to investigate?' This latter question we investigate without further ado, thereby cutting short an infinite regress.

35   The new problem has the advantage of drawing a fairly sharp line between the physical and the intellectual capacities of a man. No engineer or chemist claims to be able to produce a material which is indistinguishable from the human skin. It is possible that at some time this might be done, but even supposing this invention available we should feel there was little point in trying to make a 'thinking machine' more human by dressing it up in such artificial

40   flesh. The form in which we have set the problem reflects this fact in the condition which prevents the interrogator from seeing or touching the other competitors, or hearing their voices. Some other advantages of the proposed criterion may be shown up by specimen questions and answers. Thus:

Q: Please write me a sonnet on the subject
45   of the Forth Bridge.

A: Count me out on this one. I never could
     write poetry.

Q: Add 34957 to 70764.

A: (Pause about 30 seconds and then give
50   as answer) 105621.

Q: Do you play chess?

A: Yes.

Q: I have K at my KI, and no other pieces.
     You have only K at K6 and R at RI. It is
55   your move. What do you play?

A: (After a pause of 15 seconds) R–R8 mate.

> The *Forth Rail Bridge* crosses the Firth of Forth, an arm of the North Sea, near Edinburgh. A major engineering achievement, the bridge is 1.5 miles long, built from steel, granite, and 8 million rivets. It was completed in 1890 and is still in use.

> This is a trivially simple chess problem.

The question and answer method seems to be suitable for introducing almost any one of the fields of human endeavour that we wish to include. We do not wish to penalise the machine for its inability to shine in beauty competitions, nor to penalise a man for losing in a

60   race against an aeroplane. The conditions of our game make these disabilities irrelevant. The 'witnesses' can brag, if they consider it advisable, as much as they please about their charms, strength or heroism, but the interrogator cannot demand practical demonstrations.

The game may perhaps be criticised on the ground that the odds are weighted too heavily against the machine. If the man were to try and pretend to be the machine he would clearly

65   make a very poor showing. He would be given away at once by slowness and inaccuracy in arithmetic. May not machines carry out something which ought to be described as thinking but which is very different from what a man does? This objection is a very strong one, but at least we can say that if, nevertheless, a machine can be constructed to play the imitation game satisfactorily, we need not be troubled by this objection.

70   It might be urged that when playing the 'imitation game' the best strategy for the machine may possibly be something other than imitation of the behaviour of a man. This may be, but I

think it is unlikely that there is any great effect of this kind. In any case there is no intention to investigate here the theory of the game, and it will be assumed that the best strategy is to try to provide answers that would naturally be given by a man.

. . .

In sections 3, 4, and 5, Turing explains what digital computers do and how they work. These ideas were new in 1950; few of Turing's contemporary readers would have seen or used a computer. Today the machines are ubiquitous, but Turing's abstract conception applies just as well to the very latest machine as it did to the very first. At the end of section 5, Turing reformulates his question.

It was suggested tentatively that the question, 'Can machines think?' should be replaced by 'Are there imaginable digital computers which would do well in the imitation game?' If we wish we can make this superficially more general and ask 'Are there discrete state machines which would do well?' But in view of the universality property we see that either of these questions is equivalent to this, 'Let us fix our attention on one particular digital computer C. Is it true that by modifying this computer to have an adequate storage, suitably increasing its speed of action, and providing it with an appropriate programme, C can be made to play satisfactorily the part of A in the imitation game, the part of B being taken by a man?' 80

6. CONTRARY VIEWS ON THE MAIN QUESTION

We may now consider the ground to have been cleared and we are ready to proceed to the debate on our question, 'Can machines think?' and the variant of it quoted at the end of the last section. We cannot altogether abandon the original form of the problem, for opinions will differ as to the appropriateness of the substitution and we must at least listen to what has to be said in this connexion. 85

It will simplify matters for the reader if I explain first my own beliefs in the matter. Consider first the more accurate form of the question. I believe that in about fifty years' time it will be possible to programme computers, with a storage capacity of about 10^9, to make them play the imitation game so well that an average interrogator will not have more than 70 per cent chance of making the right identification after five minutes of questioning. The original question, 'Can machines think?' I believe to be too meaningless to deserve discussion. Nevertheless I believe that at the end of the century the use of words and general educated opinion will have altered so much that one will be able to speak of machines 90

10^9, or one billion bits (a bit, or binary digit, is a storage element that can have the value 0 or 1) amounts to just over 119 megabytes, a small computer by modern standards.

75

100   thinking without expecting to be contradicted. I
believe further that no useful purpose is served by
concealing these beliefs. The popular view that scientists proceed inexorably from well-established
fact to well-established fact, never being influ-
105   enced by any unproved conjecture, is quite mistaken. Provided it is made clear which are proved

> A machine that could play the imitation
> game successfully, or "pass the Turing test,"
> was for many years a goal of many artificial
> intelligence researchers. There were, and
> are, many who believe this can't be done.

facts and which are conjectures, no harm can result. Conjectures are of great importance since
they suggest useful lines of research.

I now proceed to consider opinions opposed to my own.

110   (1) *The Theological Objection.* Thinking is a function of man's immortal soul. God has given
an immortal soul to every man and woman, but not to any other animal or to machines. Hence
no animal or machine can think.

I am unable to accept any part of this, but will attempt to reply in theological terms. I should
find the argument more convincing if animals were classed with men, for there is a greater dif-
115   ference, to my mind, between the typical animate and the inanimate than there is between man
and the other animals. The arbitrary character of the orthodox view becomes clearer if we consider how it might appear to a member of some other religious community. How do Christians
regard the Moslem view that women have no souls? But let us leave this point aside and return
to the main argument. It appears to me that the argument quoted above implies a serious
120   restriction of the omnipotence of the Almighty. It is admitted that there are certain things that
He cannot do such as making one equal to two,[1] but should we not believe that He has freedom
to confer a soul on an elephant if He sees fit? We might expect that He would only exercise this
power in conjunction with a mutation which provided the elephant with an appropriately
improved brain to minister to the needs of this soul. An argument of exactly similar form may
125   be made for the case of machines. It may seem different because it is more difficult to "swallow."
But this really only means that we think it would be less likely that He would consider the circumstances suitable for conferring a soul. The circumstances in question are discussed in the rest
of this paper. In attempting to construct such machines we should not be irreverently usurping
His power of creating souls, any more than we are in the procreation of children: rather we are,
130   in either case, instruments of His will providing mansions for the souls that He creates.

However, this is mere speculation. I am not very impressed with theological arguments
whatever they may be used to support. Such arguments have often been found unsatisfactory
in the past. In the time of Galileo it was argued that the texts, "And the sun stood still . . . and
hasted not to go down about a whole day" (Joshua x. 13) and "He laid the foundations of the
135   earth, that it should not move at any time" (Psalm cv. 5) were an adequate refutation of the

---

[1] Possibly this view is heretical. St. Thomas Aquinas (*Summa Theologica,* quoted by Bertrand Russell [1945],
p. 480) states that God cannot make a man to have no soul. But this may not be a real restriction on His powers, but only a result of the fact that men's souls are immortal, and therefore indestructible.

Copernican theory: that the Earth and other planets revolve around the sun

Copernican theory. With our present knowledge such an argument appears futile. When that knowledge was not available it made a quite different impression.

(2) *The 'Heads in the Sand' Objection.* "The consequences of machines thinking would be too   140
dreadful. Let us hope and believe that they cannot do so."

This argument is seldom expressed quite so openly as in the form above. But it affects most of us who think about it at all. We like to believe that Man is in some subtle way superior to the rest of creation. It is best if he can be shown to be *necessarily* superior, for then there is no danger of him losing his commanding position. The popularity of the theological argument is   145
clearly connected with this feeling. It is likely to be quite strong in intellectual people, since they value the power of thinking more highly than others, and are more inclined to base their belief in the superiority of Man on this power.

I do not think that this argument is sufficiently substantial to require refutation. Consolation would be more appropriate: perhaps this should be sought in the transmigration of souls.   150

(3) *The Mathematical Objection.* There are a number of results of mathematical logic which can be used to show that there are limitations to the powers of discrete-state machines. The best known of these results is known as Gödel's theorem, and shows that in any sufficiently powerful logical system statements can be formulated which can neither be proved nor disproved within the system, unless possibly the system itself is inconsistent. There are other, in   155
some respects similar, results due to *Church* (1936), *Kleene* (1935), *Rosser* and *Turing* (1937). The latter result is the most convenient to consider, since it refers directly to machines, whereas the others can only be used in a comparatively indirect argument: for instance if Gödel's theorem is to be used we need in addition to have some means of describing logical systems in terms of machines, and machines in terms of logical systems. The result in question refers to a type   160
of machine which is essentially a digital computer with an infinite capacity. It states that there are certain things that such a machine cannot do. If it is rigged up to give answers to questions as in the imitation game, there will be some questions to which it will either give a wrong answer, or fail to give an answer at all however much time is allowed for a reply. There may, of course, be many such questions, and questions which cannot be answered by one machine   165
may be satisfactorily answered by another. We are of course supposing for the present that the questions are of the kind to which an answer 'Yes' or 'No' is appropriate, rather than questions such as 'What do you think of Picasso?' The questions that we know the machines must fail on are of this type, "Consider the machine specified as follows. . . . Will this machine ever answer 'Yes' to any question?" The dots are to be replaced by a description of some machine in a stan-   170
dard form . . . When the machine described bears a certain comparatively simple relation to the machine which is under interrogation, it can be shown that the answer is either wrong or not forthcoming. This is the mathematical result: it is argued that it proves a disability of machines to which the human intellect is not subject.

The short answer to this argument is that although it is established that there are limitations   175
to the powers of any particular machine, it has only been stated, without any sort of proof, that

no such limitations apply to the human intellect. But I do not think this view can be dismissed quite so lightly. Whenever one of these machines is asked the appropriate critical question, and gives a definite answer, we know that this answer must be wrong, and this gives us a certain
180 feeling of superiority. Is this feeling illusory? It is no doubt quite genuine, but I do not think too much importance should be attached to it. We too often give wrong answers to questions ourselves to be justified in being very pleased at such evidence of fallibility on the part of the machines. Further, our superiority can only be felt on such an occasion in relation to the one machine over which we have scored our petty triumph. There would be no question of tri-
185 umphing simultaneously over *all* machines. In short, then, there might be men cleverer than any given machine, but then again there might be other machines cleverer again, and so on.

Those who hold to the mathematical argument would, I think, mostly be willing to accept the imitation game as a basis for discussion. Those who believe in the two previous objections would probably not be interested in any criteria.

190 (4) *The Argument from Consciousness.* This argument is very well expressed in *Professor Jefferson's* Lister Oration for 1949, from which I quote. "Not until a machine can write a sonnet or compose a concerto because of thoughts and emotions felt, and not by the chance fall of sym-

> Geoffrey Jefferson (1886–1961) was a prominent British neurosurgeon.

195 bols, could we agree that machine equals brain—that is, not only write it but know that it had written it. No mechanism could feel (and not merely artificially signal, an easy contrivance) pleasure at its successes, grief when its valves fuse, be warmed by flattery, be made miserable by its mistakes, be charmed by sex, be angry or depressed when it cannot get what it wants."

This argument appears to be a denial of the validity of our test. According to the most
200 extreme form of this view the only way by which one could be sure that a machine thinks is to *be* the machine and to feel oneself thinking. One could then describe these feelings to the world, but of course no one would be justified in taking any notice. Likewise according to this view the only way to know that a *man* thinks is to be
205 that particular man. It is in fact the solipsist point of view. It may be the most logical view to hold but it makes communication of ideas difficult. A is liable to believe 'A thinks but B does not' whilst B

> *solipsist:* one who holds the view that one can be certain of nothing except one's own existence and the contents of one's consciousness

believes 'B thinks but A does not.' Instead of arguing continually over this point it is usual to
210 have the polite convention that everyone thinks.

I am sure that Professor Jefferson does not wish to adopt the extreme and solipsist point of view. Probably he would be quite willing to accept the imitation game as a test. The game (with the player B omitted) is frequently used in practice under the
215 name of *viva voce* to discover whether some one really understands something or has 'learnt it parrot fashion.' Let us listen in to a part of such a *viva voce:*

> *viva voce:* Latin "with living voice," hence "by word of mouth." In British English a *viva voce* is an oral examination.

Interrogator: In the first line of your sonnet which reads 'Shall I compare thee to a summer's day,' would not 'a spring day' do as well or better?

Witness: It wouldn't scan.   220

Interrogator: How about 'a winter's day.' That would scan all right.

Witness: Yes, but nobody wants to be compared to a winter's day.

> Mr. Pickwick is a kindly and rotund gentleman, the beloved principal character of Dickens's *Pickwick Papers*.

Interrogator: Would you say Mr. Pickwick reminded you of Christmas?

Witness: In a way.   225

Interrogator: Yet Christmas is a winter's day, and I do not think Mr. Pickwick would mind the comparison.

Witness: I don't think you're serious. By a winter's day one means a typical winter's day, rather than a special one like Christmas.   230

And so on. What would Professor Jefferson say if the sonnet-writing machine was able to answer like this in the *viva voce?* I do not know whether he would regard the machine as 'merely artificially signalling' these answers, but if the answers were as satisfactory and sustained as in the above passage I do not think he would describe it as 'an easy contrivance.' This phrase is, I think, intended to cover such devices as the inclusion in the machine of a record of someone   235 reading a sonnet, with appropriate switching to turn it on from time to time.

In short then, I think that most of those who support the argument from consciousness could be persuaded to abandon it rather than be forced into the solipsist position. They will then probably be willing to accept our test.

I do not wish to give the impression that I think there is no mystery about consciousness.   240 There is, for instance, something of a paradox connected with any attempt to localise it. But I do not think these mysteries necessarily need to be solved before we can answer the question with which we are concerned in this paper.

(5)   *Arguments from Various Disabilities.* These arguments take the form, "I grant you that you can make machines do all the things you have mentioned but you will never be able to make   245 one to do X." Numerous features X are suggested in this connexion. I offer a selection:

Be kind, resourceful, beautiful, friendly, have initiative, have a sense of humour, tell right from wrong, make mistakes, fall in love, enjoy strawberries and cream, make some one fall in love with it, learn from experience, use words properly, be the subject of its own thought, have as much diversity of behaviour as a man, do something really new.   250

No support is usually offered for these statements. I believe they are mostly founded on the principle of scientific induction. A man has seen thousands of machines in his lifetime. From what he sees of them he draws a number of general conclusions. They are ugly, each is designed for a very

255 limited purpose, when required for a minutely different purpose they are useless, the variety of behaviour of any one of them is very small, etc., etc. Naturally he concludes that these are necessary properties of machines in general. Many of these limitations are associated with the very small storage capacity of most machines. (I am assuming that the idea of storage capacity is extended in some way to cover machines other than discrete-state machines. The exact definition does not matter as no mathematical accuracy is claimed in the present discussion.) A few years ago, when

260 very little had been heard of digital computers, it was possible to elicit much incredulity concerning them, if one mentioned their properties without describing their construction. That was presumably due to a similar application of the principle of scientific induction. These applications of the principle are of course largely unconscious. When a burnt child fears the fire and shows that he fears it by avoiding it, I should say that he was applying scientific induction. (I could of course

265 also describe his behaviour in many other ways.) The works and customs of mankind do not seem to be very suitable material to which to apply scientific induction. A very large part of space-time must be investigated, if reliable results are to be obtained. Otherwise we may (as most English children do) decide that everybody speaks English, and that it is silly to learn French.

There are, however, special remarks to be made about many of the disabilities that have been

270 mentioned. The inability to enjoy strawberries and cream may have struck the reader as frivolous. Possibly a machine might be made to enjoy this delicious dish, but any attempt to make one do so would be idiotic. What is important about this disability is that it contributes to some of the other disabilities, *e.g.* to the difficulty of the same kind of friendliness occurring between man and machine as between white man and white man, or between black man and black man.

275 The claim that "machines cannot make mistakes" seems a curious one. One is tempted to retort, "Are they any the worse for that?" But let us adopt a more sympathetic attitude, and try to see what is really meant. I think this criticism can be explained in terms of the imitation game. It is claimed that the interrogator could distinguish the machine from the man simply by setting them a number of problems in arithmetic. The machine would be unmasked because of its

280 deadly accuracy. The reply to this is simple. The machine (programmed for playing the game) would not attempt to give the *right* answers to the arithmetic problems. It would deliberately introduce mistakes in a manner calculated to confuse the interrogator. A mechanical fault would probably show itself through an unsuitable decision as to what sort of a mistake to make in the arithmetic. Even this interpretation of the criticism is not sufficiently sympathetic. But we can-

285 not afford the space to go into it much further. It seems to me that this criticism depends on a confusion between two kinds of mistake. We may call them 'errors of functioning' and 'errors of conclusion.' Errors of functioning are due to some mechanical or electrical fault which causes the machine to behave otherwise than it was designed to do. In philosophical discussions one likes to ignore the possibility of such errors; one is therefore discussing 'abstract machines.' These

290 abstract machines are mathematical fictions rather than physical objects. By definition they are incapable of errors of functioning. In this sense we can truly say that 'machines can never make mistakes.' Errors of conclusion can only arise when some meaning is attached to the output signals from the machine. The machine might, for instance, type out mathematical equations, or sentences in English. When a false proposition is typed we say that the machine has committed

an error of conclusion. There is clearly no reason at all for saying that a machine cannot make
this kind of mistake. It might do nothing but type out repeatedly '0=1.' To take a less perverse
example, it might have some method for drawing conclusions by scientific induction. We must
expect such a method to lead occasionally to erroneous results.

The claim that a machine cannot be the subject of its own thought can of course only be
answered if it can be shown that the machine has *some* thought with *some* subject matter.
Nevertheless, 'the subject matter of a machine's operations' does seem to mean something, at
least to the people who deal with it. If, for instance, the machine was trying to find a solution
of the equation $x^2 - 40x - 11 = 0$ one would be tempted to describe this equation as part of the
machine's subject matter at that moment. In this sort of sense a machine undoubtedly can be
its own subject matter. It may be used to help in making up its own programmes, or to predict
the effect of alterations in its own structure. By observing the results of its own behaviour it
can modify its own programmes so as to achieve some purpose more effectively. These are possibilities of the near future, rather than Utopian dreams.

The criticism that a machine cannot have much diversity of behaviour is just a way of
saying that it cannot have much storage capacity. Until fairly recently a storage capacity of even
a thousand digits was very rare.

The criticisms that we are considering here are often disguised forms of the argument from
consciousness. Usually if one maintains that a machine *can* do one of these things, and describes
the kind of method that the machine could use, one will not make much of an impression. It is
thought that the method (whatever it may be, for it must be mechanical) is really rather base.
Compare the parenthesis in Jefferson's statement quoted on p. 21.

(6) *Lady Lovelace's Objection.* Our most detailed information of Babbage's Analytical Engine comes from a memoir by *Lady Lovelace*. In it she states, "The Analytical Engine has no pretensions to *originate* anything. It can do *whatever we know how to order it* to perform" (her italics). This statement is quoted by *Hartree* (1949, p. 70) who adds: "This does not imply that it may not be possible to construct electronic equipment which will 'think for itself,' or in which, in biological terms, one could set up a conditioned reflex, which would serve as a basis for 'learning.' Whether this is possible in principle or not is a stimulating and

> The statement Turing refers to appears on p. 51 of this volume.

> Lady Lovelace was Augusta Ada Byron (1815–1852), the daughter of the poet, and a remarkable figure in the early development of computing machines. (The programming language *Ada* was named in her honor.) Lady L.'s interest in mathematics led to her extensive correspondence with Charles Babbage (1791–1871), whose Analytical Engine was arguably the first programmable computing machine. The Engine was a vast and immensely complex system of brass gears, shafts, dials, and so forth. Babbage, who occupied Isaac Newton's chair in mathematics at Cambridge, never raised the money to build the Engine.

295
300
305
310
315
320
325
330

335 exciting question, suggested by some of these recent developments. But it did not seem that the machines constructed or projected at the time had this property."

I am in thorough agreement with Hartree over this. It will be noticed that he does not assert that the machines in question had not got the property, but rather that the evidence available to Lady Lovelace did not encourage her to believe that they had it. It is quite possible that the machines in question had in a sense got this property. For sup-
340 pose that some discrete-state machine has the property. The Analytical Engine was a universal digital computer, so that, if its storage capacity and speed were adequate, it could by suitable programming be made to mimic the machine in question. Probably
345 this argument did not occur to the Countess or to Babbage. In any case there was no obligation on them to claim all that could be claimed.

> *discrete-state machine:* A machine whose elements can be in a finite number of distinct configurations, or states. Any universal digital computer is a discrete-state machine, but not all discrete-state machines are necessarily universal digital computers.

This whole question will be considered again under the heading of learning machines. A variant of Lady Lovelace's objection states that a machine can 'never do anything really new.' This
350 may be parried for a moment with the saw, 'There is nothing new under the sun.' Who can be certain that 'original work' that he has done was not simply the growth of the seed planted in him by teaching, or the effect of following well-known general principles. A better variant of the objection says that a machine can never 'take us by surprise.' This statement is a more direct challenge and can be met directly. Machines take me by surprise with great frequency. This is largely
355 because I do not do sufficient calculation to decide what to expect them to do, or rather because, although I do a calculation, I do it in a hurried, slipshod fashion, taking risks. Perhaps I say to myself, 'I suppose the voltage here ought to be the same as there: anyway let's assume it is.'

Naturally I am often wrong, and the result is a surprise for me for by the time the experiment is done these assumptions have been forgotten. These admissions lay me open to lectures on
360 the subject of my vicious ways, but do not throw any doubt on my credibility when I testify to the surprises I experience.

I do not expect this reply to silence my critic. He will probably say that such surprises are due to some creative mental act on my part, and reflect no credit on the machine. This leads us back to the argument from consciousness, and far from the idea of surprise. It is a line of argument
365 we must consider closed, but it is perhaps worth remarking that the appreciation of something as surprising requires as much of a 'creative mental act' whether the surprising event originates from a man, a book, a machine or anything else.

The view that machines cannot give rise to surprises is due, I believe, to a fallacy to which philosophers and mathematicians are particularly subject. This is the assumption that as soon
370 as a fact is presented to a mind all consequences of that fact spring into the mind simultaneously with it. It is a very useful assumption under many circumstances, but one too easily forgets that it is false. A natural consequence of doing so is that one then assumes that there is no virtue in the mere working out of consequences from data and general principles.

(7) *Argument from Continuity in the Nervous System.* The nervous system is certainly not a discrete-state machine. A small error in the information about the size of a nervous impulse impinging on a neuron, may make a large difference to the size of the outgoing impulse. It may be argued that, this being so, one cannot expect to be able to mimic the behaviour of the nervous system with a discrete-state system.

It is true that a discrete-state machine must be different from a continuous machine. But if we adhere to the conditions of the imitation game, the interrogator will not be able to take any advantage of this difference. The situation can be made clearer if we consider some other simpler continuous machine. A differential analyser will do very well. (A differential analyser is a certain kind of machine not of the discrete-state type used for some kinds of calculation.) Some of these provide their answers in a typed form, and so are suitable for taking part in the game. It would not be possible for a digital computer to predict exactly what answers the differential analyser would give to a problem, but it would be quite capable of giving the right sort of answer. For instance, if asked to give the value of π (actually about 3.1416) it would be reasonable to choose at random between the values 3.12, 3.13, 3.14, 3.15, 3.16 with the probabilities of 0.06, 0.15, 0.55, 0.19, 0.06 (say). Under these circumstances it would be very difficult for the interrogator to distinguish the differential analyser from the digital computer.

(8) *The Argument from Informality of Behaviour.* It is not possible to produce a set of rules purporting to describe what a man should do in every conceivable set of circumstances. One might for instance have a rule that one is to stop when one sees a red traffic light, and to go if one sees a green one, but what if by some fault both appear together? One may perhaps decide that it is safest to stop. But some further difficulty may well arise from this decision later. To attempt to provide rules of conduct to cover every eventuality, even those arising from traffic lights, appears to be impossible. With all this I agree.

From this it is argued that we cannot be machines. I shall try to reproduce the argument, but I fear I shall hardly do it justice. It seems to run something like this. 'If each man had a definite set of rules of conduct by which he regulated his life he would be no better than a machine. But there are no such rules, so men cannot be machines.' The undistributed middle is glaring. I do not think the argument is ever put quite like this, but I believe this is the argument used nevertheless. There may however be a certain confusion between 'rules of conduct' and 'laws of behaviour' to cloud the issue. By 'rules of conduct' I mean precepts such as 'Stop if you see red lights,' on which one can act, and of which one can be conscious. By 'laws of behaviour' I mean laws of nature as applied to a man's body such as 'if you pinch him he will squeak.' If we substitute 'laws of behaviour which regulate his life' for 'laws of conduct by which he regulates his life' in the argument quoted the undistributed middle is no longer insuperable. For we believe that it is not only true that being regulated by laws of behaviour implies being some sort of machine (though not necessarily a discrete-state machine), but that conversely being such a machine implies being regulated by such laws. However, we cannot so easily convince ourselves of the absence of complete laws of behaviour as of complete

415 rules of conduct. The only way we know of for finding such laws is scientific observation, and we certainly know of no circumstances under which we could say, 'We have searched enough. There are no such laws.'

420 We can demonstrate more forcibly that any such statement would be unjustified. For suppose we could be sure of finding such laws if they existed. Then given a discrete-state machine it should certainly be possible to discover by obser-
425 vation sufficient about it to predict its future behaviour, and this within a reasonable time, say a thousand years. But this does not seem to be the case. I have set up on the Manchester computer a small programme using only 1000 units of storage,
430 whereby the machine supplied with one sixteen figure number replies with another within two seconds. I would defy anyone to learn from these replies sufficient about the programme to be able to predict any replies to untried values.

435 (9) *The Argument from Extra-Sensory Perception.* I assume that the reader is familiar with the idea of extra-sensory perception, and the meaning of the four items of it, *viz.* telepathy, clairvoyance, pre-cognition and psycho-kinesis. These disturbing
440 phenomena seem to deny all our usual scientific ideas. How we should like to discredit them! Unfortunately the statistical evidence, at least for telepathy, is overwhelming. It is very difficult to rearrange one's ideas so as to fit these new facts in.
445 Once one has accepted them it does not seem a very big step to believe in ghosts and bogies. The idea that our bodies move simply according to the known laws of physics, together with some others not yet discovered but somewhat similar,
450 would be one of the first to go.

This argument is to my mind quite a strong one. One can say in reply that many scientific theories seem to remain workable in practice, in spite of clashing with E.S.P.; that in fact one can get along very nicely if one forgets about it. This is rather cold comfort, and one fears that thinking is just the kind of phenomenon where E.S.P.
455 may be especially relevant.

---

undistributed middle: A fallacious form of reasoning, such as the following:

1. All plumbers are human.
2. Joe is human.
3. Therefore, Joe is a plumber.

The conclusion (3) is invalid; Joe might be a plumber, but we cannot infer this from (1) and (2). Specifically, the middle term (human) is said to be *undistributed;* that is, neither premise (1 or 2) says anything about what humans are, so the fact that something is human tells us nothing about what else it is. Turing characterizes the argument from informality similarly:

1. All men with rules are machines.
2. There are no rules.
3. Therefore no men are machines.

Even if (2) is true, (3) is an invalid conclusion. Another example with the same form makes the fallacy more obvious:

1. All men who are clairvoyant are detectives.
2. There is no clairvoyance.
3. Therefore no men are detectives.

---

statistical evidence . . . overwhelming: Few psychologists or statisticians today would agree with this statement. In the 1930s and 1940s J. B. Rhine (1895–1980), who coined the term *extra-sensory perception,* produced a great deal of evidence of telepathy (e.g., Rhine, 1934, 1947), but his methods were questionable and his results not reproducible.

A more specific argument based on E.S.P. might run as follows: "Let us play the imitation game, using as witnesses a man who is good as a telepathic receiver, and a digital computer. The interrogator can ask such questions as 'What suit does the card in my right hand belong to?' The man by telepathy or clairvoyance gives the right answer 130 times out of 400 cards. The machine can only guess at random, and perhaps gets 104 right, so the interrogator makes the right identification." There is an interesting possibility which opens here. Suppose the digital computer contains a random number generator. Then it will be natural to use this to decide what answer to give. But then the random number generator will be subject to the psycho-kinetic powers of the interrogator. Perhaps this psycho-kinesis might cause the machine to guess right more often than would be expected on a probability calculation, so that the interrogator might still be unable to make the right identification. On the other hand, he might be able to guess right without any questioning, by clairvoyance. With E.S.P. anything may happen. 460

465

If telepathy is admitted it will be necessary to tighten our test up. The situation could be regarded as analogous to that which would occur if the interrogator were talking to himself and one of the competitors was listening with his ear to the wall. To put the competitors into a 'telepathy-proof room' would satisfy all requirements. 470

7. LEARNING MACHINES

The reader will have anticipated that I have no very convincing arguments of a positive nature to support my views. If I had I should not have taken such pains to point out the fallacies in contrary views. Such evidence as I have I shall now give.

Let us return for a moment to Lady Lovelace's objection, which stated that the machine can only do what we tell it to do. One could say that a man can 'inject' an idea into the machine, and that it will respond to a certain extent and then drop into quiescence, like a piano string struck by a hammer. Another simile would be an atomic pile of less than critical size: an injected idea is to correspond to a neutron entering the pile from without. Each such neutron will cause a certain disturbance which eventually dies away. If, however, the size of the pile is sufficiently increased, the disturbance caused by such an incoming neutron will very likely go on and on increasing until the whole pile is destroyed. Is there a corresponding phenomenon for minds, and 475

480

485

> The first self-sustaining nuclear chain reaction was achieved on December 2, 1942, at the University of Chicago using an *atomic pile,* a simple reactor consisting of alternating layers of uranium and graphite. Some of the neutrons spontaneously emitted by uranium atoms will cause *fission* (splitting) of other atoms; if there is enough uranium (a *critical* mass or size) the fission will sustain itself. (The role of the graphite is to absorb [some] neutrons, thus limiting the rate of the chain reaction; without this the pile would explode.)

is there one for machines? There does seem to be one for the human mind. The majority of them seem to be 'sub-critical,' *i.e.* to correspond in this analogy to piles of sub-critical size. An idea presented to such a mind will on average give rise to less than one idea in reply. A smallish proportion are super-critical. An idea presented to such a mind may give rise to a whole 'theory' 490

consisting of secondary, tertiary and more remote ideas. Animals minds seem to be very definitely
495   sub-critical. Adhering to this analogy we ask, 'Can a machine be made to be super-critical?'

The 'skin of an onion' analogy is also helpful. In considering the functions of the mind or the brain we find certain operations which we can explain in purely mechanical terms. This we say does not correspond to the real mind: it is a sort of skin which we must strip off if we are to find the real mind. But then in what remains we find a further skin to be stripped off, and so on.

500   Proceeding in this way do we ever come to the 'real' mind, or do we eventually come to the skin which has nothing in it? In the latter case the whole mind is mechanical. (It would not be a discrete-state machine however. We have discussed this.) These last two paragraphs do not claim to be convincing arguments. They should rather be described as 'recitations tending to produce belief.'

505   The only really satisfactory support that can be given for the view expressed at the beginning of § 6, will be that provided by waiting for the end of the century and then doing the experiment described. But what can we say in the meantime? What steps should be taken now if the experiment is to be successful?

As I have explained, the problem is mainly one
510   of programming. Advances in engineering will have to be made too, but it seems unlikely that these will not be adequate for the requirements. Estimates of the storage capacity of the brain vary from 10^{10} to 10^{15} binary digits. I incline to the lower
515   values and believe that only a very small fraction is used for the higher types of thinking. Most of it is probably used for the retention of visual impressions. I should be surprised if more than 10^9 was required for satisfactory playing of the imitation
520   game, at any rate against a blind man. (Note—The capacity of the *Encyclopaedia Britannica*, IIth edition, is 2×10^9.) A storage capacity of 10^7 would be a very practicable possibility even by present tech-

> *binary digits* are better known by the contraction *bits*. In the binary (base two) number system, each digit is either 0 or 1; thus the binary system is ideally suited to digital computers in which information is represented by devices (e.g., switches, transistors) with two possible values or states: off (0) or on (1).
>
> It is likely that Turing assumes that each synapse in the brain is a binary device, as Turing's range of 10^{10} (ten billion) to 10^{15} (one quadrillion) spans most estimates of the number of synapses in the brain.

niques. It is probably not necessary to increase the speed of operations of the machines at all.
525   Parts of modern machines which can be regarded as analogues of nerve cells work about a thousand times faster than the latter. This should provide a 'margin of safety' which could cover losses of speed arising in many ways. Our problem then is to find out how to programme these machines to play the game. At my present rate of working I produce about a thousand digits of programme a day, so that about sixty workers, working steadily through the fifty years might
530   accomplish the job, if nothing went into the waste-paper basket. Some more expeditious method seems desirable.

In the process of trying to imitate an adult human mind we are bound to think a good deal about the process which has brought it to the state that it is in. We may notice three components, (a) The initial state of the mind, say at birth, (b) The education to which it has been sub-
535   jected, (c) Other experience, not to be described as education, to which it has been subjected.

Instead of trying to produce a programme to simulate the adult mind, why not rather try to produce one which simulates the child's? If this were then subjected to an appropriate course of education one would obtain the adult brain. Presumably the child-brain is something like a note-book as one buys it from the stationers. Rather little mechanism, and lots of blank sheets. (Mechanism and writing are from our point of view almost synonymous.) Our hope is that there   540 is so little mechanism in the child-brain that something like it can be easily programmed. The amount of work in the education we can assume, as a first approximation, to be much the same as for the human child.

We have thus divided our problem into two parts. The child-programme and the education process. These two remain very closely connected. We cannot expect to find a good child-   545 machine at the first attempt. One must experiment with teaching one such machine and see how well it learns. One can then try another and see if it is better or worse. There is an obvious connection between this process and evolution, by the identifications

Structure of the child machine = Hereditary material

Changes of the child machine = Mutations   550

Natural selection = Judgment of the experimenter

One may hope, however, that this process will be more expeditious than evolution. The survival of the fittest is a slow method for measuring advantages. The experimenter, by the exercise of intelligence, should be able to speed it up. Equally important is the fact that   555 he is not restricted to random mutations. If he can trace a cause for some weakness he can probably think of the kind of mutation which will improve it.

> *intelligence:* Beyond the title, this is the only occurrence of the word in the entire paper.

It will not be possible to apply exactly the same teaching process to the machine as to a nor-   560 mal child. It will not, for instance, be provided with legs, so that it could not be asked to go out and fill the coal scuttle. Possibly it might not have eyes. But however well these deficiencies might be overcome by clever engineering, one could not send the creature to school without the other children making excessive fun of it. It must be given some tuition. We need not be too concerned about the legs, eyes, etc. The example of Miss *Helen Keller* shows that education   565 can take place provided that communication in both directions between teacher and pupil can take place by some means or other.

We normally associate punishments and rewards with the teaching process. Some simple child-machines can be constructed or programmed on this sort of principle. The machine has to be so constructed that events which shortly preceded the occurrence of a punishment-   570 signal are unlikely to be repeated, whereas a reward-signal increased the probability of repetition of the events which led up to it. These definitions do not presuppose any feelings on the part of the machine. I have done some experiments with one such child-machine, and

575 succeeded in teaching it a few things, but the teaching method was too unorthodox for the experiment to be considered really successful.

The use of punishments and rewards can at best be a part of the teaching process. Roughly speaking, if the teacher has no other means of communicating to the pupil, the amount of information which can reach him does not exceed the total number of rewards and punishments applied. By the time a child has learnt to repeat 580 'Casabianca' he would probably feel very sore indeed, if the text could only be discovered by a 'Twenty Questions' technique, every 'NO' taking the form of a blow. It is necessary therefore to have some other 'unemotional' channels of communi- 585 cation. If these are available it is possible to teach a

> The poem "Casabianca," by Felicia Hemans (1793–1835), which generations of schoolchildren memorized, begins, "The boy stood on the burning deck . . ."

machine by punishments and rewards to obey orders given in some language, *e.g.* a symbolic language. These orders are to be transmitted through the 'unemotional' channels. The use of this language will diminish greatly the number of punishments and rewards required.

Opinions may vary as to the complexity which is suitable in the child machine. One might 590 try to make it as simple as possible consistently with the general principles. Alternatively one might have a complete system of logical inference 'built in.'[2] In the latter case the store would be largely occupied with definitions and propositions. The propositions would have various kinds of status, *e.g.* well-established facts, conjectures, mathematically proved theorems, statements given by an authority, expressions having the logical form of proposition 595 but not belief-value. Certain propositions may be described as 'imperatives.' The machine should be so constructed that as soon as an imperative is classed as 'well-established' the appropriate action automatically takes place. To illustrate this, suppose the teacher says to the machine, 'Do your homework now.' This may cause "Teacher says 'Do your homework now'" to be included amongst the well-established facts. Another such fact might be, 600 "Everything that teacher says is true." Combining these may eventually lead to the imperative, 'Do your homework now,' being included amongst the well-established facts, and this, by the construction of the machine, will mean that the homework actually gets started, but the effect is very satisfactory. The processes of inference used by the machine need not be 605 such as would satisfy the most exacting logicians. There might for instance be no hierarchy of types. But this need not mean that type fallacies will occur, any more than we are bound to fall over unfenced cliffs. Suitable imperatives 610 (expressed *within* the systems, not forming part of the rules *of* the system) such as 'Do not use a

> *types:* In Bertrand Russell's theory of types (Russell, 1908), individual things are members of classes; these classes are in turn members of higher-level classes, and so on. Each level of this hierarchy is a *type*. No class is a member of itself, so any proposition asserting such self-membership is a fallacy.

---

[2] Or rather 'programmed in' for our child-machine will be programmed in a digital computer. But the logical system will not have to be learnt.

class unless it is a subclass of one which has been mentioned by teacher' can have a similar effect to 'Do not go too near the edge.'

The imperatives that can be obeyed by a machine that has no limbs are bound to be of a rather intellectual character, as in the example (doing homework) given above. Important amongst such imperatives will be ones which regulate the order in which the rules of the logical system concerned are to be applied. For at each stage when one is using a logical system, there is a very large number of alternative steps, any of which one is permitted to apply, so far as obedience to the rules of the logical system is concerned. These choices make the difference between a brilliant and a footling reasoner, not the difference between a sound and a fallacious one. Propositions leading to imperatives of this kind might be "When Socrates is mentioned, use the syllogism in Barbara" or " If one method has been proved to be quicker than another, do not use the slower method." Some of these may be 'given by authority,' but others may be produced by the machine itself, *e.g.* by scientific induction.

The idea of a learning machine may appear paradoxical to some readers. How can the rules of operation of the machine change? They should describe completely how the machine will react whatever its history might be, whatever changes it might undergo. The rules are thus quite time-invariant. This is quite true. The explanation of the paradox is that the rules which get changed in the learning process are of a rather less pretentious kind, claiming only an ephemeral validity. The reader may draw a parallel with the Constitution of the United States.

An important feature of a learning machine is that its teacher will often be very largely ignorant of quite what is going on inside, although he may still be able to some extent to predict his pupil's behaviour. This should apply most strongly to the later education of a machine arising from a child-machine of well-tried design (or programme). This is in clear contrast with normal procedure when using a machine to do computations: one's object is then to have a clear mental picture of the state of the machine at each moment in the computation. This object can only be achieved with a struggle. The view that 'the

615
620
625
630
635
640
645
650

Barbara: Medieval logicians used a mnemonic system to represent the forms of the valid syllogisms. The mnemonic *Barbara* represents this form:

All B are C.

All A are B.

Therefore all A are C.

Turing's reference to Socrates probably refers to a very common illustration of the Barbara form. If A stands for *Socrates* (or *thing called Socrates*), B for *human,* and C for *mortal,* we have the following syllogism in Barbara:

All humans are mortal.

Socrates is human.

Therefore Socrates is mortal.

Turing's parallel is the distinction between the articles of the constitution, on the one hand (the [relatively] unchanging rules), and laws adopted (and changed and abolished) by federal, state, and local governments, on the other.

machine can only do what we know how to order it to do,[3] appears strange in face of this. Most of the programmes which we can put into the machine will result in its doing something that we cannot make sense of at all, or which we regard as completely random behaviour. Intelligent behaviour presumably consists in a departure from the completely disciplined behaviour involved in computation, but a rather slight one, which does not give rise to random behaviour, or to pointless repetitive loops. Another important result of preparing our machine for its part in the imitation game by a process of teaching and learning is that 'human fallibility' is likely to be omitted in a rather natural way, *i.e.*, without special 'coaching.' . . . Processes that are learnt do not produce a hundred per cent certainty of result; if they did they could not be unlearnt.

It is probably wise to include a random element in a learning machine. A random element is rather useful when we are searching for a solution of some problem. Suppose for instance we wanted to find a number between 50 and 200 which was equal to the square of the sum of its digits, we might start at 51 then try 52 and go on until we got a number that worked. Alternatively we might choose numbers at random until we got a good one. This method has the advantage that it is unnecessary to keep track of the values that have been tried, but the disadvantage that one may try the same one twice, but this is not very important if there are several solutions. The systematic method has the disadvantage that there may be an enormous block without any solutions in the region which has to be investigated first. Now the learning process may be regarded as a search for a form of behaviour which will satisfy the teacher (or some other criterion). Since there is probably a very large number of satisfactory solutions the random method seems to be better than the systematic. It should be noticed that it is used in the analogous process of evolution. But there the systematic method is not possible. How could one keep track of the different genetical combinations that had been tried, so as to avoid trying them again?

We may hope that machines will eventually compete with men in all purely intellectual fields. But which are the best ones to start with? Even this is a difficult decision. Many people think that a very abstract activity, like the playing of chess, would be best. It can also be maintained that it is best to provide the machine with the best sense organs that money can buy, and then teach it to understand and speak English. This process could follow the normal teaching of a child. Things would be pointed out and named, etc. Again I do not know what the right answer is, but I think both approaches should be tried.

> There are now chess-playing programs that are roughly a match for the best human players. Understanding natural language (such as English), on the other hand, has turned out to be a colossally complex process that is—so far, at least—very difficult to capture in a computer program.

We can only see a short distance ahead, but we can see plenty there that needs to be done.

---

[3] Compare Lady Lovelace's statement (p. 450), which does not contain the word "only."

> The statement Turing refers to appears on p. 54 in this volume.

For Discussion

1. Is Turing a monist or a dualist?

2. Suppose a computer can pass the most stringent version of the Turing test (i.e., the imitation game) you care to propose. If so, what kind of thing is intelligence? What kind of thing is a mind?

3. Explain Turing's response to Professor Jefferson's criticism.

John Searle (b. 1932)
Minds, Brains, and Science (1984)

Chapter 1. The Mind-Body Problem

Chapter 2. Can Computers Think?

"**M**athematics," said Gauss, "is the queen of the sciences," but surely philosophy is their mother, and she works tirelessly to bring her children up right. Psychology's protracted adolescence, careening from one wild enthusiasm to the next, has always demanded a good deal of philosophical attention, though its effect is not always obvious. John Searle, a prominent and distinguished American philosopher, has spent a large part of his career trying to straighten out some basic psychological issues.

John Rogers Searle was born in Denver in 1932. He spent three years as an undergraduate at the University of Wisconsin and then went, as a Rhodes Scholar, to Oxford, where he earned his undergraduate and graduate degrees and began teaching. In 1959 he returned to the United States to teach at the University of California at Berkeley, where he has remained. His years at Oxford clearly shaped his thinking, but Searle's teaching and writing has a distinctly American style, blunt, confident, and unpretentious. Searle began his career working on problems of language and intentionality. In the 1970s he turned his attention to the new, exciting, and—in Searle's view—misguided field of artificial intelligence (AI). The AI perspective on mind—if it behaves like a mind, it's a mind—derives substantially from Alan Turing's 1950 paper, "Computing machinery and intelligence" (see 1.4), but Searle believes the Turing test is flawed and that it (along with much of psychology) rests on a basic and longstanding misunderstanding of the mind-body problem.

Source: Searle, J. R. (1984). *Minds, Brains, and Science*. Cambridge, MA: Harvard University Press. Copyright 1984 by John R. Searle. Reprinted with permission. [The informal tone (and British spelling) of these chapters reflects their origin in Searle's 1984 Reith Lectures, broadcast by the BBC.]

CHAPTER 1. THE MIND-BODY PROBLEM

For thousands of years, people have been trying to understand their relationship to the rest of the universe. For a variety of reasons many philosophers today are reluctant to tackle such big problems. Nonetheless, the problems remain, and in this book I am going to attack some of them.

At the moment, the biggest problem is this: We have a certain commonsense picture of ourselves as human beings which is very hard to square with our overall 'scientific' conception of the physical world. We think of ourselves as *conscious, free, mindful, rational* agents in a world that science tells us consists entirely of mindless, meaningless physical particles. Now, how can we square these two conceptions? How, for example, can it be the case that the world contains nothing but unconscious physical particles, and yet that it also contains consciousness? How can a mechanical universe contain intentionalistic human beings—that is, human beings that can represent the world to themselves? How, in short, can an essentially meaningless world contain meanings?

Such problems spill over into other more contemporary-sounding issues: How should we interpret recent work in computer science and artificial intelligence—work aimed at making intelligent machines? Specifically, does the digital computer give us the right picture of the human mind? And why is it that the social sciences in general have not given us insights into ourselves comparable to the insights that the natural sciences have given us into the rest of nature? What is the relation between the ordinary, commonsense explanations we accept of the way people behave and scientific modes of explanation?

In this first chapter, I want to plunge right into what many philosophers think of as the hardest problem of all: What is the relation of our minds to the rest of the universe? This, I am sure you will recognise, is the traditional mind-body or mind-brain problem. In its contemporary version it usually takes the form: how does the mind relate to the brain?

I believe that the mind-body problem has a rather simple solution, one that is consistent both with what we know about neurophysiology and with our commonsense conception of the nature of mental states—pains, beliefs, desires and so on. But before presenting that solution, I want to ask why the mind-body problem seems so intractable. Why do we still have in philosophy and psychology after all these centuries a 'mind-body problem' in a way that we do not have, say, a 'digestion-stomach problem'? Why does the mind seem more mysterious than other biological phenomena?

> *the right picture:* The ideas that became the digital computer emerged in the 1930s and 1940s, and with them came the idea that the computer might offer a useful model of the mind, or perhaps that the mind *is* essentially a computer. As computers spread, in the 1950s, this idea became the foundation of a wide range of research that can be referred to, loosely, under the heading of artificial intelligence. AI grew rapidly in the 1960s and 1970s, and with it the conviction that there is nothing uniquely or essentially human or biological about minds. It is this picture of mind as a program that can run on any kind of hardware that Searle questions.

5

10

15

20

25

30

35

40   I am convinced that part of the difficulty is that we persist in talking about a twentieth-century problem in an outmoded seventeenth-century vocabulary. When I was an undergraduate, I remember being dissatisfied with the choices that were apparently available in the philosophy of mind: you could be either a monist or a dualist. If you were a monist, you could be either a materialist or an idealist. If you were a materialist, you could be either a behaviourist or a physicalist. And so on. One of my aims in what follows is to try to break out of these tired old

45   categories. Notice that nobody feels he has to choose between monism and dualism where the 'digestion-stomach problem' is concerned. Why should it be any different with the 'mind-body problem'?

      But, vocabulary apart, there is still a problem or family of problems. Since Descartes, the mind-body problem has taken the following form: how can we account for the relationships

50   between two apparently completely different kinds of things? On the one hand, there are mental things, such as our thoughts and feelings; we think of them as subjective, conscious, and immaterial. On the other hand, there are physical things; we think of them as having mass, as extended in space, and as causally interacting with

55   other physical things. Most attempted solutions to the mind-body problem wind up by denying the existence of, or in some way downgrading the status of, one or the other of these types of things. Given the successes of the physical sciences, it is

60   not surprising that in our stage of intellectual development the temptation is to downgrade the status of mental entities. So, most of the recently fashionable materialist conceptions of the mind—such as behaviourism, functionalism, and physi-

65   calism—end up by denying, implicitly or explicitly, that there are any such things as minds as we ordinarily think of them. That is, they deny that we do really *intrinsically* have subjective, conscious, mental states and that they are as real and as irre-

70   ducible as anything else in the universe.

> *Behaviourism,* in this context, is the claim that all mental statements can be expressed as statements about behavior (or dispositions to behavior), with no subjective content whatsoever.
>
> *Functionalism* is the position that mental events are defined by their functions, by what they *do* rather than what they *feel* like.
>
> *Physicalism,* in its basic form, regards physical things and events as the only reality; therefore any meaningful statement is ultimately reducible (at least in principle) to a physical statement.
>
> See Fodor (1981) for a comprehensive and unusually lucid survey of these and many other mind-body -isms.

      Now, why do they do that? Why is it that so many theorists end up denying the intrinsically mental character of mental phenomena? If we can answer that question, I believe that we will understand why the mind-body problem has seemed so intractable for so long.

      There are four features of mental phenomena which have made them seem impossible to

75   fit into our 'scientific' conception of the world as made up of material things. And it is these four features that have made the mind-body problem really difficult. They are so embarrassing that they have led many thinkers in philosophy, psychology, and artificial intelligence to say strange and implausible things about the mind.

The most important of these features is consciousness. I, at the moment of writing this, and you, at the moment of reading it, are both conscious. It is just a plain fact about the world that it contains such conscious mental states and events, but it is hard to see how mere physical systems could have consciousness. How could such a thing occur? How, for example, could this grey and white gook inside my skull be conscious?

I think the existence of consciousness ought to seem amazing to us. It is easy enough to imagine a universe without it, but if you do, you will see that you have imagined a universe that is truly meaningless. Consciousness is the central fact of specifically human existence because without it all of the other specifically human aspects of our existence—language, love, humour, and so on—would be impossible. I believe it is, by the way, something of a scandal that contemporary discussions in philosophy and psychology have so little of interest to tell us about consciousness.

so little of interest: This state of affairs has improved somewhat in the last 20 years. See, for example, Baars, 1988; Baars, Banks, and Newman, 2003; Block, 1995; Crick, 1994; Dennett, 1991, 2001; Gray, 2004; Metzinger, 2000; and, of course, Searle, 1992.

atoms in the void: The reference is to Democritus's (4–3 century BCE) atomism, the earliest, simplest, and starkest formulation of the basic materialist point of view. See Epicurus (4–3 c. BCE/1940).

The second intractable feature of the mind is what philosophers and psychologists call 'intentionality,' the feature by which our mental states are directed at, or about, or refer to, or are of objects and states of affairs in the world other than themselves. 'Intentionality,' by the way, doesn't just refer to intentions, but also to beliefs, desires, hopes, fears, love, hate, lust, disgust, shame, pride, irritation, amusement, and all of those mental states (whether conscious or unconscious) that refer to, or are about, the world apart from the mind. Now the question about intentionality is much like the question about consciousness. How can this stuff inside my head be *about* anything? How can it *refer* to anything? After all, this stuff in the skull consists of 'atoms in the void,' just as all of the rest of material reality consists of atoms in the void. Now how, to put it crudely, can atoms in the void represent anything?

The third feature of the mind that seems difficult to accommodate within a scientific conception of reality is the subjectivity of mental states. This subjectivity is marked by such facts as that I can feel my pains, and you can't. I see the world from my point of view; you see it from your point of view. I am aware of myself and my internal mental states, as quite distinct from the selves and mental states of other people. Since the seventeenth century we have come to think of reality as something which must be equally accessible to all competent observers—that is, we think it must be objective. Now, how are we to accommodate the reality of *subjective* mental phenomena with the scientific conception of reality as totally *objective*?

Finally, there is a fourth problem, the problem of mental causation. We all suppose, as part of common sense, that our thoughts and feelings make a real difference to the way we behave, that they actually have some *causal* effect on the physical world. I decide, for example, to raise my arm and—lo and behold—my arm goes up. But if our thoughts and feelings are

120   truly mental, how can they affect anything physical? How could something mental make a physical difference? Are we supposed to think that our thoughts and feelings can somehow produce chemical effects on our brains and the rest of our nervous system? How could such a thing occur? Are we supposed to think that thoughts can wrap themselves around the axons or shake the dendrites or sneak inside the cell wall and attack the cell nucleus?

125   But unless some such connection takes place between the mind and the brain, aren't we just left with the view that the mind doesn't matter, that it is as unimportant causally as the froth on the wave is to the movement of the wave? I suppose if the froth were conscious, it might think to itself: 'What a tough job it is pulling these waves up on the beach and then pulling them out again, all day long!' But we know the froth doesn't make any important difference.

130   Why do we suppose our mental life is any more important than a froth on the wave of physical reality?

These four features, consciousness, intentionality, subjectivity, and mental causation are what make the mind-body problem seem so difficult. Yet, I want to say, they are all real features of our mental lives. Not every mental state has all of them. But any satisfactory account of the

135   mind and of mind-body relations must take account of all four features. If your theory ends up by denying any one of them, you know you must have made a mistake somewhere.

The first thesis I want to advance toward 'solving the mind-body problem' is this: Mental phenomena, all mental phenomena whether conscious or unconscious, visual or auditory, pains, tickles, itches, thoughts, indeed, all of our mental life, are caused by processes going on in the brain.

140   To get a feel for how this works, let's try to describe the causal processes in some detail for at least one kind of mental state. For example, let's consider pains. Of course, anything we say now may seem wonderfully quaint in a generation, as our knowledge of how the brain works increases. Still, the *form* of the explanation can remain valid even though the *details* are altered. On current views, pain signals are transmitted from sensory nerve endings to the spinal

145   cord by at least two types of fibres—there are Delta A fibres, which are specialised for prickling sensations, and C fibres, which are specialised for burning and aching sensations. In the spinal cord, they pass through a region called the tract of Lissauer and terminate on the neurons of the cord. As the signals go up the spine, they enter the brain by two separate pathways: the prickling pain pathway and the burning pain pathway. Both pathways go through the thala-

150   mus, but the prickling pain is more localised afterwards in the somato-sensory cortex, whereas the burning pain pathway transmits signals, not only upwards into the cortex, but also laterally into the hypothalamus and other regions at the base of the brain. Because of these differences, it is much easier for us to localise a prickling sensation—we can tell fairly accurately where someone is sticking a pin into our skin, for example—whereas burning and aching pains

155   can be more distressing because they activate more of the nervous system. The actual sensation of pain appears to be caused both by the stimulation of the basal regions of the brain, especially the thalamus, and the stimulation of the somato-sensory cortex.

Now for the purposes of this discussion, the point we need to hammer home is this: our sensations of pains are caused by a series of events that begin at free nerve endings and end in the

160   thalamus and in other regions of the brain. Indeed, as far as the actual sensations are concerned,

the events inside the central nervous system are quite sufficient to cause pains—we know this both from the phantom-limb pains felt by amputees and the pains caused by artificially stimulating relevant portions of the brain. I want to suggest that what is true of pain is true of mental phenomena generally. To put it crudely, and counting all of the central nervous system as part of the brain for our present discussion, everything that matters for our mental life, all of our   165
thoughts and feelings, are caused by processes inside the brain. As far as causing mental states is concerned, the crucial step is the one that goes on inside the head, not the external or peripheral stimulus. And the argument for this is simple. If the events outside the central nervous system occurred, but nothing happened in the brain, there would be no mental events. But if the right things happened in the brain, the mental events would occur even if there was no outside   170
stimulus. (And that, by the way, is the principle on which surgical anaesthesia works: the outside stimulus is prevented from having the relevant effects on the central nervous system.)

But if pains and other mental phenomena are caused by processes in the brain, one wants to know: what are pains? What are they really? Well, in the case of pains, the obvious answer is that they are unpleasant sorts of sensations. But that answer leaves us unsatisfied because   175
it doesn't tell us how pains fit into our overall conception of the world.

Once again, I think the answer to the question is obvious, but it will take some spelling out. To our first claim—that pains and other mental phenomena are caused by brain processes, we need to add a second claim:

> Pains and other mental phenomena just are features of the brain (and perhaps the rest   180
> of the central nervous system).

One of the primary aims of this chapter is to show how *both* of these propositions can be true together. How can it be both the case that brains cause minds and yet minds just are features of brains? I believe it is the failure to see how both these propositions can be true together that has blocked a solution to the mind-body problem for so long. There are different levels of   185
confusion that such a pair of ideas can generate. If mental and physical phenomena have cause and effect relationships, how can one be a feature of the other? Wouldn't that imply that the mind caused itself—the dreaded doctrine of *causa sui*? But at the bottom of our puzzlement is a misunderstanding of causation. It is tempting to think   190
that whenever A causes B there must be two discrete events, one identified as the cause, the other identified as the effect; that all causation functions in the same way as billiard balls hitting each other. This crude model of the causal relationships   195
between the brain and the mind inclines us to accept some kind of dualism; we are inclined to think that events in one material realm, the 'physical,' cause events in another insubstantial

---

causa sui: In Latin this means "self-caused" or "cause of itself." Searle seems to regard the phrase as an oxymoron, but in metaphysics it has had a slightly different meaning, as, for instance, in the first sentence of Spinoza's (1677/1955) *Ethics:* "By that which is *self-caused,* I mean that of which the essence involves existence, or that of which the nature is only conceivable as existent" (p. 45).

200   realm, the 'mental.' But that seems to me a mistake. And the way to remove the mistake is to get a more sophisticated concept of causation. To do this, I will turn away from the relations between mind and brain for a moment to observe some other sorts of causal relationships in nature. A common distinction in physics is between micro- and macro-properties of systems—the small and large scales. Consider, for example, the desk at which I am now sitting,
205   or the glass of water in front of me. Each object is composed of micro-particles. The micro-particles have features at the level of molecules and atoms as well as at the deeper level of sub-atomic particles. But each object also has certain properties such as the solidity of the table, the liquidity of the water, and the transparency of the glass, which are surface or global features of the physical systems. Many such surface or global properties can be causally explained by
210   the behaviour of elements at the micro-level. For example, the solidity of the table in front of me is explained by the lattice structure occupied by the molecules of which the table is composed. Similarly, the liquidity of the water is explained by the nature of the interactions between the H_2O molecules. Those macro-features are causally explained by the behaviour of elements at the micro-level.
215   I want to suggest that this provides a perfectly ordinary model for explaining the puzzling relationships between the mind and the brain. In the case of liquidity, solidity, and transparency, we have no difficulty at all in supposing that the surface features are *caused by* the behaviour of elements at the micro-level, and at the same time we accept that the surface phenomena *just are* features of the very systems in question. I think the clearest way of stating this
220   point is to say that the surface feature is both *caused by* the behaviour of microelements, and at the same time is *realised in* the system that is made up of the micro-elements. There is a cause and effect relationship, but at the same time the surface features are just higher level features of the very system whose behaviour at the micro-level causes those features.
        In objecting to this someone might say that liquidity, solidity, and so on are identical with features of the micro-structure. So, for example, we might just define solidity as the lattice struc-
225   ture of the molecular arrangement, just as heat often is identified with the mean kinetic energy of molecule movements. This point seems to me correct but not really an objection to the analysis that I am proposing. It is a characteristic of the progress of science that an expression that is originally defined in terms of surface features, features accessible to the senses, is
230   subsequently defined in terms of the micro-structure that causes the surface features. Thus, to take the example of solidity, the table in front of me is solid in the ordinary sense that it is rigid, it resists pressure, it supports books, it is not easily penetrable by most other objects such as other tables, and so on. Such is the commonsense notion of solidity. And in a scientific vein one can define solidity as whatever micro-structure causes these gross observable features. So one
235   can then say either that solidity just is the lattice structure of the system of molecules and that solidity so defined causes, for example, resistance to touch and pressure. Or one can say that solidity consists of such high level features as rigidity and resistance to touch and pressure and that it is caused by the behaviour of elements at the micro-level.
        If we apply these lessons to the study of the mind, it seems to me that there is no difficulty
240   in accounting for the relations of the mind to the brain in terms of the brain's functioning to

cause mental states. Just as the liquidity of the water is caused by the behaviour of elements at the micro-level, and yet at the same time it is a feature realised in the system of microelements, so in exactly that sense of 'caused by' and 'realised in' mental phenomena are caused by processes going on in the brain at the neuronal or modular level, and at the same time they are realised in the very system that consists of neurons. And just as we need the micro/macro distinction for any physical system, so for the same reasons we need the micro/macro distinction for the brain. And though we can say of a system of particles that it is 10°C or it is solid or it is liquid, we cannot say of any given particle that this particle is solid, this particle is liquid, this particle is 10°C. I can't for example reach into this glass of water, pull out a molecule and say: 'This one's wet.'

245

250

In exactly the same way, as far as we know anything at all about it, though we can say of a particular brain: 'This brain is conscious,' or: 'This brain is experiencing thirst or pain,' we can't say of any particular neuron in the brain: 'This neuron is in pain, this neuron is experiencing thirst.' To repeat this point, though there are enormous empirical mysteries about how the brain works in detail, there are no logical or philosophical or metaphysical obstacles to accounting for the relation between the mind and the brain in terms that are quite familiar to us from the rest of nature. Nothing is more common in nature than for surface features of a phenomenon to be both caused by and realised in a micro-structure, and those are exactly the relationships that are exhibited by the relation of mind to brain.

255

Let us now return to the four problems that I said faced any attempt to solve the mind-brain problem.

260

First, how is consciousness possible?

The best way to show how something is possible is to show how it actually exists. We have already given a sketch of how pains are actually caused by neurophysiological processes going on in the thalamus and the sensory cortex. Why is it then that many people feel dissatisfied with this sort of answer? I think that by pursuing an analogy with an earlier problem in the history of science we can dispel this sense of puzzlement. For a long time many biologists and philosophers thought it was impossible, in principle, to account for the existence of *life* on purely biological grounds. They thought that in addition to the biological processes some other element must be necessary, some *élan vital* must be postulated in order to lend life to what was otherwise dead and inert matter. It is hard today to realise how intense the dispute was between vitalism and mechanism even a generation ago, but today these issues are

265

270

275

> *élan vital:* In the philosophy of Henri Bergson (1859–1941), the "life-force," an explanation of biological phenomena that is not reducible to physics or chemistry. The view Searle is describing is *vitalism* and is not unique to Bergson.

no longer taken seriously. Why not? I think it is not so much because mechanism won and vitalism lost, but because we have come to understand better the biological character of the processes that are characteristic of living organisms. Once we understand how the features that are characteristic of living beings have a biological explanation, it no longer seems mysterious to us that matter should be alive. I think that exactly similar considerations should apply to our

280

discussions of consciousness. It should seem no more mysterious, in principle, that this hunk of matter, this grey and white oatmeal-textured substance of the brain, should be conscious than it seems mysterious that this other hunk of matter, this collection of nucleo-protein molecules

285   stuck onto a calcium frame, should be alive. The way, in short, to dispel the mystery is to understand the processes. We do not yet fully understand the processes, but we understand their general *character,* we understand that there are certain specific electrochemical activities going on among neurons or neuron-modules and perhaps other features of the brain and these processes cause consciousness.

290   Our second problem was, how can atoms in the void have intentionality? How can they be about something?

      As with our first question, the best way to show how something is possible is to show how it actually exists. So let's consider thirst. As far as we know anything about it, at least certain kinds of thirst are caused in the hypothalamus by sequences of nerve firings. These firings are

295   in turn caused by the action of angiotensin in the hypothalamus, and angiotensin, in turn, is synthesised by renin, which is secreted by the kidneys. Thirst, at least of these kinds, is caused by a series of events in the central nervous system, principally the hypothalamus, and it is realised in the hypothalamus. To be thirsty is to have, among other things, the desire to drink. Thirst is therefore an intentional state: it has content; its content determines under what con-

300   ditions it is satisfied, and it has all the rest of the features that are common to intentional states.

      As with the 'mysteries' of life and consciousness, the way to master the mystery of intentionality is to describe in as much detail as we can how the phenomena are caused by biological processes while being at the same time realised in biological systems. Visual and auditory experiences, tactile sensations, hunger, thirst, and sexual desire, are all caused by brain

305   processes and they are realised in the structure of the brain, and they are all intentional phenomena.

      I am not saying we should lose our sense of the mysteries of nature. On the contrary, the examples I have cited are all in a sense astounding. But I am saying that they are neither more nor less mysterious than other astounding features of the world, such as the existence of

310   gravitational attraction, the process of photosynthesis, or the size of the Milky Way.

      Our third problem: how do we accommodate the subjectivity of mental states within an objective conception of the real world?

      It seems to me a mistake to suppose that the definition of reality should exclude subjectivity. If 'science' is the name of the collection of objective and systematic truths we can state

315   about the world, then the existence of subjectivity is an objective scientific fact like any other. If a scientific account of the world attempts to describe how things are, then one of the features of the account will be the subjectivity of mental states, since it is just a plain fact about biological evolution that it has produced certain sorts of biological systems, namely human and certain animal brains, that have subjective features. My present state of consciousness is a fea-

320   ture of my brain, but its conscious aspects are accessible to me in a way that they are not accessible to you. And your present state of consciousness is a feature of your brain and its conscious aspects are accessible to you in a way that they are not accessible to me. Thus the existence of

subjectivity is an objective fact of biology. It is a persistent mistake to try to define 'science' in terms of certain features of existing scientific theories. But once this provincialism is perceived to be the prejudice it is, then any domain of facts whatever is a subject of systematic investi- 325 gation. So, for example, if God existed, then that fact would be a fact like any other. I do not know whether God exists, but I have no doubt at all that subjective mental states exist, because I am now in one and so are you. If the fact of subjectivity runs counter to a certain definition of 'science,' then it is the definition and not the fact which we will have to abandon.

Fourth, the problem of mental causation for our present purpose is to explain how mental 330 events can cause physical events. How, for example, could anything as 'weightless' and 'ethereal' as a thought give rise to an action?

The answer is that thoughts are not weightless and ethereal. When you have a thought, brain activity is actually going on.

Brain activity causes bodily movements by physiological processes. Now, because mental 335 states are features of the brain, they have two levels of description—a higher level in mental terms, and a lower level in physiological terms. The very same causal powers of the system can be described at either level.

Once again, we can use an analogy from physics to illustrate these relationships. Consider hammering a nail with a hammer. Both hammer and nail have a certain kind of solidity. 340 Hammers made of cottonwool or butter will be quite useless, and hammers made of water or steam are not hammers at all. Solidity is a real causal property of the hammer. But the solidity itself is caused by the behaviour of particles at the micro-level and it is realised in the system which consists of micro-elements. The existence of two causally real levels of description in the brain, one a macro-level of mental processes and the other a micro-level of neuronal processes 345 is exactly analogous to the existence of two causally real levels of description of the hammer. Consciousness, for example, is a real property of the brain that can cause things to happen. My conscious attempt to perform an action such as raising my arm causes the movement of the arm. At the higher level of description, the intention to raise my arm causes the movement of the arm. But at the lower level of description, a series of neuron firings starts a chain of events 350 that results in the contraction of the muscles. As with the case of hammering a nail, the same sequence of events has two levels of description. Both of them are causally real, and the higher level causal features are both caused by and realised in the structure of the lower level elements. 355

> *Both . . . causally real:* Searle is rejecting any kind of *epiphenomenalism,* the notion that the experience we call mind is a side-effect, or epiphenomenon, of the activity of the brain. All causality is in the brain; mental events seem causal only because they mesh so seamlessly with what the brain is doing.

To summarise: on my view, the mind and the body interact, but they are not two different things, since mental phenomena just are features of the brain. One way to characterise this position is to see it as an assertion of both physicalism and 360 mentalism. Suppose we define 'naive physicalism' to be the view that all that exists in the world are physical particles with their properties and relations. The power of the physical model of reality is so great that it is hard to see how we can

365 seriously challenge naive physicalism. And let us define 'naive mentalism' to be the view that mental phenomena really exist. There really are mental states; some of them are conscious; many have intentionality; they all have subjectivity; and many of them function causally in determining physical events in the world. The thesis of this first chapter can now be stated quite simply. Naive mentalism and naive physicalism are perfectly consistent with each other.
370 Indeed, as far as we know anything about how the world works, they are not only consistent, they are both true.

CHAPTER 2. CAN COMPUTERS THINK?

In the previous chapter, I provided at least the outlines of a solution to the so-called 'mind-body problem.' Though we do not know in detail how the brain functions, we do know enough to have an idea of the general relationships between brain processes and mental processes. Mental processes are caused by the behaviour of elements of the brain. At the same time, they
375 are realised in the structure that is made up of those elements. I think this answer is consistent with the standard biological approaches to biological phenomena. Indeed, it is a kind of commonsense answer to the question, given what we know about how the world works. However, it is very much a minority point of view. The prevailing view in philosophy, psychology, and artificial intelligence is one which emphasises the analogies between the functioning of the human
380 brain and the functioning of digital computers. According to the most extreme version of this view, the brain is just a digital computer and the mind is just a computer program. One could summarise this view—I call it 'strong artificial intelligence,' or 'strong AI'—by saying that the mind is to the brain, as the program is to the computer
385 hardware.

This view has the consequence that there is nothing essentially biological about the human mind. The brain just happens to be one of an indefinitely large number of different kinds of hardware
390 computers that could sustain the programs which make up human intelligence. On this view, any physical system whatever that had the right program with the right inputs and outputs would have a mind in exactly the same sense that you and I
395 have minds. So, for example, if you made a computer out of old beer cans powered by windmills; if it had the right program, it would have to have a mind. And the point is not that for all we know it might have thoughts and feelings, but rather that it must have thoughts and feelings, because that is all there is to having thoughts and feelings: implementing the right program.

Most people who hold this view think we have not yet designed programs which are
400 minds. But there is pretty much general agreement among them that it's only a matter of time

> *strong AI:* The view that thought is a strictly computational process and therefore can, in principle, be carried out by any suitable computing device (including the brain).
>
> *weak AI,* on the other hand, holds that any thought process can be simulated by a digital computer but distinguishes (as strong AI does not) between thought and simulation of thought.

until computer scientists and workers in artificial intelligence design the appropriate hardware and programs which will be the equivalent of human brains and minds. These will be artificial brains and minds which are in every way the equivalent of human brains and minds.

Many people outside of the field of artificial intelligence are quite amazed to discover that anybody could believe such a view as this. So, before criticising it, let me give you a few 405 examples of the things that people in this field have actually said. Herbert Simon of Carnegie-Mellon University says that we already have machines that can literally think. There is no question of waiting for some future machine, because existing digital computers already have thoughts in exactly the same sense that you and I do. Well, fancy that! Philosophers have been worried for centuries about whether or not a machine could think, and now we discover that 410 they already have such machines at Carnegie-Mellon. Simon's colleague Alan Newell claims that we have now discovered (and notice that Newell says 'discovered' and not 'hypothesised' or 'considered the possibility,' but we have *discovered*) that intelligence is just a matter of physical symbol manipulation; it has no essential connection with any specific kind of biological or physical wetware or hardware. Rather, any system whatever that is capable of manipulating 415 physical symbols in the right way is capable of intelligence in the same literal sense as human intelligence of human beings. Both Simon and Newell, to their credit, emphasise that there is nothing metaphorical about these claims; they mean them quite literally. Freeman Dyson is quoted as having said that computers have an advantage over the rest of us when it comes to evolution. Since consciousness is just a matter of formal processes, in computers these formal 420 processes can go on in substances that are much better able to survive in a universe that is cooling off than beings like ourselves made of our wet and messy materials. Marvin Minsky of MIT says that the next generation of computers will be so intelligent that we will 'be lucky if they are willing to keep us around the house as household pets.' My all-time favourite in the literature of exaggerated claims on behalf of the digital computer is from John McCarthy, the inventor of the 425 term 'artificial intelligence.' McCarthy says even 'machines as simple as thermostats can be said to have beliefs.' And indeed, according to him, almost any machine capable of problem-solving can be said to have beliefs. I admire McCarthy's courage. I once asked him: 'What beliefs does your thermostat have?' And he said: 'My thermostat has three beliefs—it's too hot in here, it's too cold in here, and it's just right in here.' As a philosopher, I like all these claims for a simple 430 reason. Unlike most philosophical theses, they are reasonably clear, and they admit of a simple and decisive refutation. It is this refutation that I am going to undertake in this chapter.

The nature of the refutation has nothing whatever to do with any particular stage of computer technology. It is important to emphasise this point because the temptation is always to think that the solution to our problems must wait on some as yet uncreated technological won- 435 der. But in fact, the nature of the refutation is completely independent of any state of technology. It has to do with the very definition of a digital computer, with what a digital computer is.

It is essential to our conception of a digital computer that its operations can be specified purely formally; that is, we specify the steps in the operation of the computer in terms of abstract symbols—sequences of zeroes and ones printed on a tape, for example. A typical com- 440 puter 'rule' will determine that when a machine is in a certain state and it has a certain symbol

on its tape, then it will perform a certain operation such as erasing the symbol or printing another symbol and then enter another state such as moving the tape one square to the left. But the symbols have no meaning; they have no semantic content; they are not about any-
445   thing. They have to be specified purely in terms of their formal or syntactical structure. The zeroes and ones, for example, are just numerals; they don't even stand for numbers. Indeed, it is this feature of digital computers that makes them so powerful. One and the same type of hardware, if it is appropriately designed, can be used to run an indefinite range of different
450   programs. And one and the same program can be run on an indefinite range of different types of hardwares.

> Searle is referring to the conceptual universal computing machine described by Turing (1937), often called a *Turing machine* (see 1.4).

But this feature of programs, that they are defined purely formally or syntactically, is fatal to the view that mental processes and program processes are identical. And the reason can be
455   stated quite simply. There is more to having a mind than having formal or syntactical processes. Our internal mental states, by definition, have certain sorts of contents. If I am thinking about Kansas City or wishing that I had a cold beer to drink or wondering if there will be a fall in interest rates, in each case my mental state has a certain mental content in addition to whatever formal features it might have. That is, even if my thoughts occur to me in strings of symbols, there
460   must be more to the thought than the abstract strings, because strings by themselves can't have any meaning. If my thoughts are to be *about* anything, then the strings must have a *meaning* which makes the thoughts about those things. In a word, the mind has more than a syntax, it has a semantics. The reason that no computer program can ever be a mind is simply that a computer program is only syntactical, and minds are more than syntactical. Minds are seman-
465   tical, in the sense that they have more than a formal structure, they have a content.

To illustrate this point I have designed a certain thought-experiment. Imagine that a bunch of computer programmers have written a program that will enable a computer to simulate the understanding of Chinese. So, for example, if the computer is given a question in Chinese, it will match the question against its memory, or data base, and produce appropriate answers to the
470   questions in Chinese. Suppose for the sake of argument that the computer's answers are as good as those of a native Chinese speaker. Now then, does the computer, on the basis of this, understand Chinese, does it literally understand

> *answers are as good:* The program passes the Turing test (see 1.4).

475   Chinese, in the way that Chinese speakers understand Chinese? Well, imagine that you are locked in a room, and in this room are several baskets full of Chinese symbols. Imagine that you (like me) do not understand a word of Chinese, but that you are given a rule book in English for manipulating these Chinese symbols. The rules specify the manipulations of the symbols purely formally, in terms of their syntax, not their semantics. So the rule might say: 'Take a squiggle-
480   squiggle sign out of basket number one and put it next to a squoggle-squoggle sign from basket number two.' Now suppose that some other Chinese symbols are passed into the room, and that you are given further rules for passing back Chinese symbols out of the room. Suppose that

unknown to you the symbols passed into the room are called 'questions' by the people outside the room, and the symbols you pass back out of the room are called 'answers to the questions.' Suppose, furthermore, that the programmers are so good at designing the programs and that you are so good at manipulating the symbols, that very soon your answers are indistinguishable from those of a native Chinese speaker. There you are locked in your room shuffling your Chinese symbols and passing out Chinese symbols in response to incoming Chinese symbols. On the basis of the situation as I have described it, there is no way you could learn any Chinese simply by manipulating these formal symbols. 485 490

Now the point of the story is simply this: by virtue of implementing a formal computer program from the point of view of an outside observer, you behave exactly as if you understood Chinese, but all the same you don't understand a word of Chinese. But if going through the appropriate computer program for understanding Chinese is not enough to give *you* an understanding of Chinese, then it is not enough to give *any other digital computer* an understanding of Chinese. And again, the reason for this can be stated quite simply. If you don't understand Chinese, then no other computer could understand Chinese because no digital computer, just by virtue of running a program, has anything that you don't have. All that the computer has, as you have, is a formal program for manipulating uninterpreted Chinese symbols. To repeat, a computer has a syntax, but no semantics. The whole point of the parable of the Chinese room is to remind us of a fact that we knew all along. Understanding a language, or indeed, having mental states at all, involves more than just having a bunch of formal symbols. It involves having an interpretation, or a meaning attached to those symbols. And a digital computer, as defined, cannot have more than just formal symbols because the operation of the computer, as I said earlier, is defined in terms of its ability to implement programs. And these programs are purely formally specifiable—that is, they have no semantic content. 495 500 505

We can see the force of this argument if we contrast what it is like to be asked and to answer questions in English, and to be asked and to answer questions in some language where we have no knowledge of any of the meanings of the words. Imagine that in the Chinese room you are also given questions in English about such things as your age or your life history, and that you answer these questions. What is the difference between the Chinese case and the English case? Well again, if like me you understand no Chinese and you do understand English, then the difference is obvious. You understand the questions in English because they are expressed in symbols whose meanings are known to you. Similarly, when you give the answers in English you are producing symbols which are meaningful to you. But in the case of the Chinese, you have none of that. In the case of the Chinese, you simply manipulate formal symbols according to a computer program, and you attach no meaning to any of the elements. 510 515 520

Various replies: There have been hundreds. The first were published with the original exposition of the Chinese room; see Searle (1980); others have been gathered by Preston and Bishop (2002). Searle still maintains that they are all inadequate.

Various replies have been suggested to this argument by workers in artificial intelligence and in psychology, as well as philosophy. They all have

525

something in common; they are all inadequate. And there is an obvious reason why they have to be inadequate, since the argument rests on a very simple logical truth, namely, syntax alone is not sufficient for semantics, and digital computers insofar as they are computers have, by definition, a syntax, alone.

I want to make this clear by considering a couple of the arguments that are often presented against me.

530

Some people attempt to answer the Chinese room example by saying that the whole system understands Chinese. The idea here is that though I, the person in the room manipulating the symbols do not understand Chinese, I am just the central processing unit of the computer system. They argue that it is the whole system, including the room, the baskets full of symbols and the ledgers containing the programs and perhaps other items as well, taken as a totality,

535

that understands Chinese. But this is subject to exactly the same objection I made before. There is no way that the system can get from the syntax to the semantics. I, as the central processing unit have no way of figuring out what any of these symbols means; but then neither does the whole system.

Another common response is to imagine that we put the Chinese understanding program

540

inside a robot. If the robot moved around and interacted causally with the world, wouldn't that be enough to guarantee that it understood Chinese? Once again the inexorability of the semantics-syntax distinction overcomes this manoeuvre. As long as we suppose that the robot has only a computer for a brain then, even though it might behave exactly as if it understood Chinese, it would still have no way of getting from the syntax to the semantics of Chinese.

545

You can see this if you imagine that I am the computer. Inside a room in the robot's skull I shuffle symbols without knowing that some of them come in to me from television cameras attached to the robot's head and others go out to move the robot's arms and legs. As long as all I have is a formal computer program, I have no way of attaching any meaning to any of the symbols. And the fact that the robot is engaged in causal interactions with the outside world

550

won't help me to attach any meaning to the symbols unless I have some way of finding out about that fact. Suppose the robot picks up a hamburger and this triggers the symbol for hamburger to come into the room. As long as all I have is the symbol with no knowledge of its causes or how it got there, I have no way of knowing what it means. The causal interactions between the robot and the rest of the world are irrelevant unless those causal interactions are

555

represented in some mind or other. But there is no way they can be if all that the so-called mind consists of is a set of purely formal, syntactical operations.

It is important to see exactly what is claimed and what is not claimed by my argument. Suppose we ask the question that I mentioned at the beginning: 'Could a machine think?' Well, in one sense, of course, we are all machines. We can construe the stuff inside our heads as a

560

meat machine. And of course, we can all think. So, in one sense of 'machine,' namely that sense in which a machine is just a physical system which is capable of performing certain kinds of operations, in that sense, we are all machines, and we can think. So, trivially, there are machines that can think. But that wasn't the question that bothered us. So let's try a different formulation of it. Could an artefact think? Could a man-made machine think? Well, once again, it

depends on the kind of artefact. Suppose we designed a machine that was molecule-for-   565
molecule indistinguishable from a human being. Well then, if you can duplicate the causes, you
can presumably duplicate the effects. So once again, the answer to that question is, in principle at least, trivially yes. If you could build a machine that had the same structure as a human
being, then presumably that machine would be able to think. Indeed, it would be a surrogate
human being. Well, let's try again.   570

> An interesting variant of the Turing test was raised by AI researcher Hans Moravec[1]:
>
> > You are in an operating room. A robot brain surgeon is in attendance. By your side is a poten-
> > tially human equivalent computer, dormant for lack of a program to run. Your skull, but not your
> > brain, is anesthetized. You are fully conscious. The surgeon opens your brain case and peers
> > inside. Its attention is directed at a small clump of about 100 neurons somewhere near the sur-
> > face. It determines the three-dimensional structure and chemical makeup of that clump non-
> > destructively with high resolution 3D NMR holography, phased array radio encephalography,
> > and ultrasonic radar. It writes a program that models the behavior of the clump, and starts it run-
> > ning on a small portion of the computer next to you. Fine connections are run from the edges
> > of the neuron assembly to the computer, providing the simulation with the same inputs as the
> > neurons. You and the surgeon check the accuracy of the simulation. After you are satisfied, tiny
> > relays are inserted between the edges of the clump and the rest of the brain. Initially these leave
> > the brain unchanged, but on command they can connect the simulation in place of the clump.
> > A button which activates the relays when pressed is placed in your hand. You press it, release
> > it, and press it again. There should be no difference. As soon as you are satisfied, the simulation
> > connection is established firmly, and the now unconnected clump of neurons is removed. The
> > process is repeated over and over for adjoining clumps, until the entire brain has been dealt
> > with. Occasionally several clump simulations are combined into a single equivalent but more
> > efficient program. Though you have not lost consciousness, or even your train of thought, your
> > mind (some would say soul) has been removed from the brain and transferred to a machine.
> >
> > In a final step your old body is disconnected. The computer is installed in a shiny new one,
> > in the style, color and material of your choice. You are no longer a cyborg halfbreed, your
> > metamorphosis is complete. (Moravec, 1986)
>
> That is, you are now a machine—specifically, a digital computer—and you are thinking.

The question isn't: 'Can a machine think?' or: 'Can an artefact think?' The question is: 'Can a
digital computer think?' But once again we have to be very careful in how we interpret the
question. From a mathematical point of view, anything whatever can be described *as if* it were
a digital computer. And that's because it can be described as instantiating or implementing a
computer program. In an utterly trivial sense, the pen that is on the desk in front of me can be   575

---

[1] Moravec, H. "Dualism From Reductionism" in *Proceedings of the International Symposium on AI and the Human Mind*, March 1–3, 1986. Reprinted by permission of Hans Moravec.

described as a digital computer. It just happens to have a very boring computer program. The program says: 'Stay there.' Now since in this sense, anything whatever is a digital computer, because anything whatever can be described as implementing a computer program, then once again, our question gets a trivial answer. Of course our brains are digital computers, since they
580   implement any number of computer programs. And of course our brains can think. So once again, there is a trivial answer to the question. But that wasn't really the question we were trying to ask. The question we wanted to ask is this: 'Can a digital computer, as defined, think?' That is to say: 'Is instantiating or implementing the right computer program with the right inputs and outputs, sufficient for, or constitutive of, thinking?' And to this question, unlike its
585   predecessors, the answer is clearly 'no.' And it is 'no' for the reason that we have spelled out, namely, the computer program is defined purely syntactically. But thinking is more than just a matter of manipulating meaningless symbols, it involves meaningful semantic contents. These semantic contents are what we mean by 'meaning.'

It is important to emphasise again that we are not talking about a particular stage of com-
590   puter technology. The argument has nothing to do with the forthcoming, amazing advances in computer science. It has nothing to do with the distinction between serial and parallel processes, or with the size of programs, or the speed of computer operations, or with computers that can interact causally with their environment, or even with the invention of robots. Technological progress is always grossly exaggerated, but even subtracting the exaggeration,
595   the development of computers has been quite remarkable, and we can reasonably expect that even more remarkable progress will be made in the future. No doubt we will be much better able to simulate human behaviour on computers than we can at present, and certainly much better than we have been able to in the past. The point I am making is that if we are talking about having mental states, having a mind, all of these simulations are simply irrelevant. It
600   doesn't matter how good the technology is, or how rapid the calculations made by the computer are. If it really is a computer, its operations have to be defined syntactically, whereas consciousness, thoughts, feelings, emotions, and all the rest of it involve more than a syntax. Those features, by definition, the computer is unable to *duplicate* however powerful may be its ability to *simulate*. The key distinction here is between duplication and simulation. And no simu-
605   lation by itself ever constitutes duplication.

What I have done so far is give a basis to the sense that those citations I began this talk with are really as preposterous as they seem. There is a puzzling question in this discussion though, and that is: 'Why would anybody ever have thought that computers could think or have feelings and emotions and all the rest of it?' After all, we can do computer simulations
610   of any process whatever that can be given a formal description. So, we can do a computer simulation of the flow of money in the British economy, or the pattern of power distribution in the Labour party. We can do computer simulation of rain storms in the home counties, or warehouse fires in East London. Now, in each of these cases, nobody supposes that the computer simulation is actually the real thing; no one supposes that a computer simulation
615   of a storm will leave us all wet, or a computer simulation of a fire is likely to burn the house down. Why on earth would anyone in his right mind suppose a computer simulation of mental processes actually had mental processes? I don't really know the answer to that,

since the idea seems to me, to put it frankly, quite crazy from the start. But I can make a couple of speculations.

First of all, where the mind is concerned, a lot of people are still tempted to some sort of behaviourism. They think if a system behaves as if it understood Chinese, then it really must understand Chinese. But we have already refuted this form of behaviourism with the Chinese room argument. Another assumption made by many people is that the mind is not a part of the biological world, it is not a part of the world of nature. The strong artificial intelligence view relies on that in its conception that the mind is purely formal; that somehow or other, it cannot be treated as a concrete product of biological processes like any other biological product. There is in these discussions, in short, a kind of residual dualism. AI partisans believe that the mind is more than a part of the natural biological world; they believe that the mind is purely formally specifiable. The paradox of this is that the AI literature is filled with fulminations against some view called 'dualism,' but in fact, the whole thesis of strong AI rests on a kind of dualism. It rests on a rejection of the idea that the mind is just a natural biological phenomenon in the world like any other.

I want to conclude this chapter by putting together the thesis of the last chapter and the thesis of this one. Both of these theses can be stated very simply. And indeed, I am going to state them with perhaps excessive crudeness. But if we put them together I think we get a quite powerful conception of the relations of minds, brains and computers. And the argument has a very simple logical structure, so you can see whether it is valid or invalid. The first premise is:

1. Brains cause minds.

Now, of course, that is really too crude. What we mean by that is that mental processes that we consider to constitute a mind are caused, entirely caused, by processes going on inside the brain. But let's be crude, let's just abbreviate that as three words—brains cause minds. And that is just a fact about how the world works. Now let's write proposition number two:

2. Syntax is not sufficient for semantics.

That proposition is a conceptual truth. It just articulates our distinction between the notion of what is purely formal and what has content. Now, to these two propositions—that brains cause minds and that syntax is not sufficient for semantics—let's add a third and a fourth:

3. Computer programs are entirely defined by their formal, or syntactical, structure.

That proposition, I take it, is true by definition; it is part of what we mean by the notion of a computer program.

4. Minds have mental contents; specifically, they have semantic contents.

And that, I take it, is just an obvious fact about how our minds work. My thoughts, and beliefs, and desires are about something, or they refer to something, or they concern states of affairs in the world; and they do that because their content directs them at these states of affairs in the world. Now, from these four premises, we can draw our first conclusion; and it follows obviously from premises 2, 3 and 4:

655   CONCLUSION 1. No computer program by itself is sufficient to give a system a mind. Programs, in short, are not minds, and they are not by themselves sufficient for having minds.

Now, that is a very powerful conclusion, because it means that the project of trying to create minds solely by designing programs is doomed from the start. And it is important to re-emphasise that this has nothing to do with any particular state of technology or any par-
660   ticular state of the complexity of the program. This is a purely formal, or logical, result from a set of axioms which are agreed to by all (or nearly all) of the disputants concerned. That is, even most of the hardcore enthusiasts for artificial intelligence agree that in fact, as a matter of biology, brain processes cause mental states, and they agree that programs are defined purely formally. But if you put these conclusions together with certain other things that we know, then
665   it follows immediately that the project of strong AI is incapable of fulfilment.

However, once we have got these axioms, let's see what else we can derive. Here is a second conclusion:

CONCLUSION 2. The way that brain functions cause minds cannot be solely in virtue of running a computer program.
670   And this second conclusion follows from conjoining the first premise together with our first conclusion. That is, from the fact that brains cause minds and that programs are not enough to do the job, it follows that the way that brains cause minds can't be solely by running a computer program. Now that also I think is an important result, because it has the consequence that the brain is not, or at least is not just, a digital computer. We saw earlier that anything can triv-
675   ially be described as if it were a digital computer, and brains are no exception. But the importance of this conclusion is that the computational properties of the brain are simply not enough to explain its functioning to produce mental states. And indeed, that ought to seem a commonsense scientific conclusion to us anyway because all it does is remind us of the fact that brains are biological engines; their biology matters. It is not, as several people in artificial
680   intelligence have claimed, just an irrelevant fact about the mind that it happens to be realised in human brains.

Now, from our first premise, we can also derive a third conclusion:

CONCLUSION 3. Anything else that caused minds would have to have causal powers at least equivalent to those of the brain.
685   And this third conclusion is a trivial consequence of our first premise. It is a bit like saying that if my petrol engine drives my car at seventy-five miles an hour, then any diesel engine that was capable of doing that would have to have a power output at least equivalent to that of my petrol engine. Of course, some other system might cause mental processes using entirely different chemical or biochemical features from those the brain in fact uses. It might turn out that
690   there are beings on other planets, or in other solar systems, that have mental states and use an

entirely different biochemistry from ours. Suppose that Martians arrived on earth and we concluded that they had mental states. But suppose that when their heads were opened up, it was discovered that all they had inside was green slime. Well still, the green slime, if it functioned to produce consciousness and all the rest of their mental life, would have to have causal powers equal to those of the human brain. But now, from our first conclusion, that programs are not enough, and our third conclusion, that any other system would have to have causal powers equal to the brain, conclusion four follows immediately: 695

CONCLUSION 4. For any artefact that we might build which had mental states equivalent to human mental states, the implementation of a computer program would not by itself be sufficient. Rather the artefact would have to have powers equivalent to the powers of the human brain. 700

The upshot of this discussion I believe is to remind us of something that we have known all along: namely, mental states are biological phenomena. Consciousness, intentionality, subjectivity and mental causation are all a part of our biological life history, along with growth, reproduction, the secretion of bile, and digestion.

FOR DISCUSSION

1. What is the difference between being *caused by* and being *realised in* a biological system?
2. Would Wundt agree with Searle's account of subjectivity?
3. Does Turing agree with Searle's distinction between *simulating* mind and *duplicating* mind?
4. How would we conclude that Martians have mental states?
5. Is Searle saying that mind is to body as digestion is to stomach? If so, what does this say about the nature of mind?

Part II
Perceiving

Take a look at this:

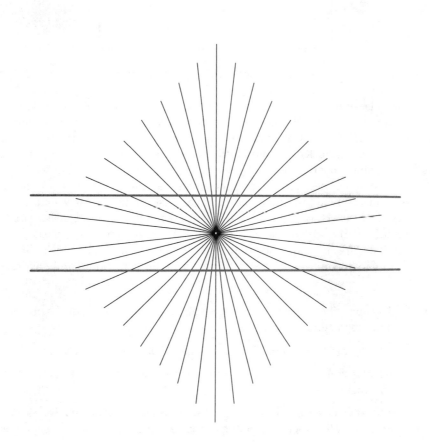

That is the Hering illusion, devised by the German physiologist Ewald Hering (1834–1918). The two horizontal lines are in fact straight and parallel to one another, but no matter how long and how carefully you look, they will appear slightly bowed. Check them with a ruler. You will see that they really are straight, but this will make no difference; they will still look bowed.

The obvious question that arises when we look at the Hering illusion, and at many others like it, is *Why do the straight lines not look straight?* This is indeed a fascinating question, but we want to ask something else. *Why is this interesting?* What is it about the illusion that captures our attention?

As is so often the case, an important clue comes from our choice of words. *Illusion* comes from the Latin *illudere,* to mock. Hering's figure is mocking us. We know that the two lines are straight, but try as we might we cannot see them that way. Some kind of trick is being played (*ludere,* to play) on our mind.

Notice that calling the above figure an illusion distinguishes it from other visual stimuli, such as this:

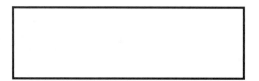

It looks like a rectangle, and if we check with square and straightedge we find that it is a rectangle. There is no trick, no illusion.

Or is there? Classifying our perceptions as illusory or nonillusory is possible in the two examples above because in both cases we can compare what we *see* with some independent knowledge of what *is.* But such examples are the exception rather than the rule. Most of the time we can't, or don't, check everything with drafting instruments to verify our perceptions. Suppose, for example, that the Hering figure and the rectangle were not printed on the page but painted in some inaccessible place—such as on the ceiling or high up on the side of a building. You can see them fine, but you cannot get close enough to the wall to check them with your tools. You see bowed lines in one figure, a rectangle in the other, but you have no independent information about what is really there. Therefore you have no basis for calling either one an illusion—or for denying that either is an illusion.

These examples illustrate the following points about our perceptions and their relation to the world:

1. Ordinarily our only source of information about the world—about the presumed cause of our perceptions—is our perceptions themselves.

2. Ordinarily, therefore, we cannot know whether *what we see* and *what is* are the same.

3. We speak of visual illusion only in those rare cases where we do know that what we see is not what is.

4. It follows that when we do not speak of illusion, we assume that what we see is what is. That is, we generally experience our perception as *veridical,* as coinciding with reality.

Every day we stake our very lives on the veridicality of our perceptions, and only very rarely do we have cause for regret. Paradoxically, the fact that perception works so well is one of the biggest obstacles to our understanding how it works.

It is probably fair to say that we now know more about how perception works than about any other "How?" question in psychology, but this is only because we have been at it for so long. Long before anyone had given much thought to our individual quirks and idiosyncrasies, long before we had unconscious urges, philosophers were deeply interested in questions about what we know about the world and how we know it. For this book we have chosen to focus on vision, which has the longest history, the richest literature, and, perhaps, the greatest importance for humans, but the general principles that are revealed in the study of vision also apply to hearing, smell, taste, and touch.

Visual perception is unimaginably rich and complex, and in many respects we have barely scratched its surface. We do, however, have a detailed understanding of the essential process by which the outside world makes contact with the inside world. Suppose, for example, you see a hawk soaring high above you. How does this happen? First, light from the sun falls on the hawk. Some of that light is absorbed by pigments in the bird's feathers, and the rest is reflected. Some of the reflected light heads toward you. As it passes through the cornea and lens of your eye it is focused, and an image of the hawk appears on the inside rear surface of the eye. [In optics, an *image* is not a perception but rather a pattern of light that has been focused by a lens and falls on a surface, such as the film in a camera or the screen in a movie theater.] This surface, the retina, contains specialized nerve cells that are sensitive to light, and they respond to the light from the hawk by emitting nerve impulses. The retina is where the outside world meets the nervous system; beyond the retina there is no light, no image, only nerve impulses. These impulses travel along the fibers of the optic nerve to various parts of the brain, where they somehow produce the experience we call vision; in this case, you see the hawk.

This sketch of the visual process reflects many important achievements in the history of visual science. It is useful to group these achievements according to three distinct questions about vision. The first question was raised by the ancient Greeks, so let us start there.

The Greeks' understanding of the senses began with touch, where they could clearly see the sensible object making direct contact with the sensory organ (the skin). They treated touch as the basic model of any sense and therefore developed theories of vision, hearing, smell, and taste that likewise depended on contact between the sensitive and the sensible. The first question about vision, therefore, was *How and where does contact take place between the visual sense and the object of vision?* The Greeks developed two kinds of answer to this question. *Extramission* theories held that the eye emits a visual ray, which makes contact with the visual object *at* the object. Conversely, *intramission* theories claimed that vision occurs when something from the object enters the eye; thus contact takes place somewhere in the eye. What that something might be was not at all obvious. One intramission theory, associated with the atomists, suggested that all visible objects give off faint physical emanations, or *eidola,* somewhat as a snake sheds its skin, which travel to the eye and there make contact (a kind of touch) with the visual sense.

From our 21st century vantage point, extramission and eidola theories may seem primitive and foolish, but consider what the Greeks had—or rather didn't have—to work with. Beare (1906) summarized their scientific situation rather bleakly:

They had, for example, to arrive at a theory of vision without a settled notion of the nature of light, or of the anatomical structure of eye or brain. . . . Physiology and anatomy, chemistry and physics, as yet undifferentiated, lay within the body of vague floating possibilities of knowledge studied by them under the name of Nature. For want of a microscope their examination of the parts of the sensory organs remained barren. They had no conception of the minuteness of the scale on which nature works in the accomplishment of sensory processes and in the formation of sensory organs. The retina, as well as the structure of the auditory apparatus, was wholly unknown to them. The nerve-system had not been discovered, and the notions formed of the mechanism of sensation and motion were hopelessly astray. (pp. 4–5)

Most of the items in Beare's list—particularly an understanding of optics, a detailed knowledge of the anatomy of the eye, and at least a vague notion of the nature of the nervous system—had to be developed before real progress in our understanding of vision was possible. Perhaps what the Greeks have to teach us is something they themselves did not appreciate, namely how easy it is to underestimate the complexity and subtlety of the mind's operations.

It was Ibn al-Haytham (c. 965–1039; known in the West as Alhacen or Alhazen) who finally, in the 11th century, resolved the intramission/extramission question, by means of careful geometric and optical reasoning showing that light enters the eye, not vice versa. (See Lindberg [1976] for a fascinating account of Alhazen's achievement.)

Even before Alhazen had established the intramission theory, there was much speculation about a second important question: Where in the eye does vision happen?

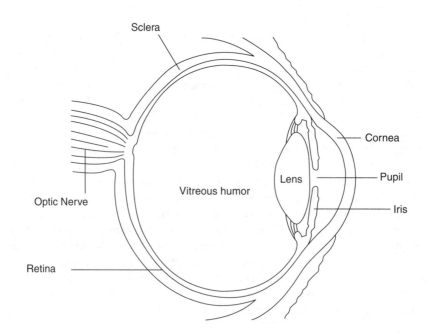

There were many possibilities. The Roman physician Galen (131–201) reasoned that it must be the "crystalline humor" (what we call the lens), because when a cataract forms between cornea and lens, vision suffers, and when the cataract is removed vision is restored. The Arab philosopher and scientist Al-Kindi (805–873) claimed that the power of vision lies in the cornea. Alhazen argued for the vitreous humor. The retina, however, was not suspected; at most, its role seemed to be to supply nourishment to the vitreous humor.

The question of the site of the visual sense remained unanswered until 1604, when the mathematician and astronomer Johannes Kepler (1571–1630) proved, geometrically and optically, that the sensitive part of the eye must be the retina. The proof is elaborate, but it boils down to this: Given what we know about the refraction of light and about the anatomy and optical properties of the eye, it must be the case that light entering the eye is refracted in such a way that an image of the distant scene (from which the light is reflected toward the eye) is formed on the retina.

I say that vision occurs when an image of the whole hemisphere of the world that is before the eye, and a little more, is set up at the white wall, tinged with red, of the concave surface of the retina. How this image or picture is joined together with the visual spirits that reside in the retina and in the nerve, and whether it is arraigned within by the spirits into the caverns of the cerebrum to the tribunal of the soul or of the visual faculty; whether the

> *arraigned*: called to account, here in the sense of *met and escorted*

visual faculty, like a magistrate given by the soul, descending from the headquarters of the cerebrum outside to the visual nerve itself and the retina, as to lower courts, might go forth to meet this image—this, I say, I leave to the natural philosophers to argue about. . . .

Vision thus occurs through a picture of the visible object at the white of the retina and the concave wall; and those things that are on the right outside, are depicted at the left side of the wall, the left at the right, the top at the bottom, the bottom at the top. Further, green things are depicted in the color green, and in general any object whatever is pictured in its own color within. The result of this is that if it were possible for this picture on the retina to remain while the retina was taken out into the light, while those things out in front that were giving it form were removed, and if some person were to possess sufficient keenness of vision, that person would recognize the exact configuration of the hemisphere in the compass of the retina, small as it is. Moreover, that proportion is preserved, such that when straight lines are drawn from the individual points of objects that can be viewed to some particular point within the compass of the eye, the individual parts within are depicted at very nearly the same angle at which the lines will have come together, so much so that not even the smallest points are left out. And to such an extent that the fineness of this picture within the eye of any person you please is as great as the acuteness of vision in that person. (Kepler, 1604/2000, pp. 180–182)[1]

The fact that the retinal image is upside-down and backward did not bother Kepler. He saw, correctly, that getting the image turned the right way is done—he had no idea how—somewhere beyond the retina, and that therefore it is not an optical process.

---

[1] Trans. by William H. Donahue. Reprinted with permission of Green Lion Press.

Alhazen's intramission theory and Kepler's retinal theory solved the optical problem of vision. Alhazen got the rays going in the right direction, and Kepler took the light as far as it would go. It was for others to figure out what happens beyond the retina, for here optics ends, and physiology and psychology take over. The Greeks imagined the percept to be a copy, in the mind, of the thing outside, and they had no reason to question this assumption. Kepler changed that by showing that the world doesn't get any farther than the eye. The brain/mind doesn't get an optical image; there is no movie screen inside your head, and no one there to see it. Instead, the brain receives from the eye a pattern of nerve impulses that somehow convey information about the world. Descartes makes this point in his *Optics:*

> [I]t is necessary to beware of assuming that in order to sense, the mind needs to perceive certain images transmitted by the objects to the brain, as our philosophers commonly suppose; or, at least, the nature of these images must be conceived quite otherwise than as they do. For, inasmuch as [the philosophers] do not consider anything about these images except that they must resemble the objects they represent, it is impossible for them to show us how they can be formed by these objects, received by the external sense organs, and transmitted by the nerves to the brain. And they have had no other reason for positing them except that, observing that a picture can easily stimulate our minds to conceive the object painted there, it seemed to them that in the same way, the mind should be stimulated by little pictures which form in our head to conceive of those objects that touch our senses; instead, we should consider that there are many other things besides pictures which can stimulate our thought, such as, for example, signs and words, which do not in any way resemble the things which they signify. . . . [A]bout the images that are formed in our brain . . . we must note that it is only a question of knowing how they can enable the mind to perceive all the diverse qualities of the objects to which they refer; not of [knowing] how the images themselves resemble their objects; just as when the blind man . . . touches some object with his cane, it is certain that these objects do not transmit anything to him except that, by making his cane move in different ways according to their different inherent qualities, they likewise and in the same way move the nerves of his hand, and then the places in his brain where these nerves originate. Thus his mind is caused to perceive as many different qualities in these bodies, as there are varieties in the movements that they cause in his brain. (Descartes, 1637/2001, pp. 89–90)[2]

Johannes Müller (1801–1858) brought the 19th century's rapidly expanding understanding of the structure and function of the nerves to bear on the question of what happens beyond Kepler's retinal image. He showed that it followed from that understanding that we are directly aware only of nerve activity, not of the causes of that activity.

> The senses, by virtue of the peculiar properties of their several nerves, make us acquainted with the states of our own body, and they also inform us of the qualities and changes of external nature, as far as these give rise to changes in the condition of the nerves. Sensation is a property common to all the senses; but the kind, *("modus,")*

---

[2] Excerpts reprinted from *Discourse on Methods, Optics, Geometry, and Meteorology*, trans. by Paul J. Oscamp. Reprinted with permission of Hackett Publishing Company, Inc. All rights reserved.

of sensation is different in each: thus we have the sensations of light, of sound, of taste, of smell, and of feeling or touch. . . . That which through the medium of our senses is actually perceived by the sensorium, is indeed merely a property or change of condition of our nerves; but the imagination and reason are ready to interpret the modifications in the state of the nerves produced by external influences as properties of the external bodies themselves. (Müller, 1838/1842, vol. 2, bk. 5, p. 1059)

Kepler may not have realized it, and in any case it didn't concern him, but it follows from the retinal theory that our visual awareness is not an awareness of the outside world but an awareness of the activity of our nervous system. This may seem a trivial distinction, but it means that there is a lot to explain about perception. If the central nervous system is the intermediary between the world and our knowledge of it, why does perception feel so seamless, why are we as accurate as we are, and why are we sometimes misled?

The readings that follow span nearly three centuries, but all of them are concerned, in one way or another, with explaining vision in the context of the retinal theory. Kepler showed that the optical image of the stimulus gets no closer to consciousness than the back of the eyeball, but if consciousness could somehow meet the optical image at the retina, vision would be a relatively simple thing. Berkeley presents a vivid and forceful argument that this is not the case. Reid is not concerned exclusively with vision, but the important distinction he makes between sensation and perception is consistent with Berkeley's position on what we know about the world through our sensations. Reid also deftly unravels the common confusion surrounding the distinction, first made by Galileo, between the primary and secondary properties of objects.

If Kepler left the question of how the soul goes forth to meet the retinal image for the natural philosophers to argue about, it was Helmholtz who picked up the challenge. Using a blend of physiological evidence and philosophical reasoning, Helmholtz set visual science on the path toward an explanation of the extraordinary things the visual system does to turn the retinal image into a conscious perception. Above all, Helmholtz showed that these visual processes are unconscious and thus helped set the stage for the adoption of unconscious processes in other branches of psychology.

The 20th century brought new approaches to vision, but they did not make Helmholtz obsolete. Unlike Helmholtz, Gibson was almost exclusively concerned with the aspect of vision that Reid would have called perception (as opposed to sensation). This allowed him to focus his investigations on determining the physical characteristics (or, more specifically, the optical expressions of those characteristics) that allow us to see objects, depth, and motion in a visual scene. Marr's approach could not have been more different. Marr insisted that to understand vision we must have an account of the problems that the visual system is, in effect, solving in order to turn the simple two-dimensional retinal image into the complex three-dimensional perceptions that we experience.

In addition to the readings in Part II, several others deal substantially with aspects of perception:

3.6   Posner et al.   Localization of cognitive operations in the human brain (1988)

4.4   Helmholtz   The facts of perception (1878)

5.1   Wertheimer   Laws of organization in perceptual forms (1923)

ADDITIONAL READINGS

Aristotle   *On the soul [De anima]* (esp. bk. 3)

   Sense and sensibilia [De sensu] (4th century BCE)

Aristotle raises many important scientific questions about what the senses are, how they work, what they are sensitive to, and what a sensation is. His answers are "wrong" but fascinating.

Epicurus   *Letter to Herodotus* (4th–3rd century BCE)

Epicurus explains the atomists' eidola theory of perception, by which faint copies of external objects impinge on the body's sense organs.

Ibn al-Haytham (Alhazen)   *Optics* (11th century)

Alhazen describes the optical experiments by which he established that vision occurs when light enters the eye (the intramission theory).

Johannes Kepler   *Optics* (ch. 5, "On the means of vision") (1604)

Kepler produces an elaborate argument to show that the locus of vision in the eye must be the retina. He sharply distinguishes between the optical problems of vision, which he has solved in a basic way, and the physiological and psychological problems of vision, which he leaves for others.

Galileo Galilei   *The assayer* (1623)

Galileo introduces the distinction, vital to the modern understanding of sensation, between primary and secondary qualities of objects.

Johannes Müller   *Elements of physiology* (1842)

Müller propounds the doctrine of specific nerve energies, which treats sensation as the experience of receptor activity, not of the (external) stimulus.

Gustav Fechner   *Elements of psychophysics* (1860)

Fechner's interest in perception is slightly different from that of the other authors represented in this section. He is concerned not directly with how we perceive things, but with the question of how we can study the quantitative relation between the (physical) magnitudes of stimuli and the (psychological) magnitudes of sensations.

Haldan Hartline & Floyd Ratliff (1957)   *Inhibitory interaction of receptor units in the eye of Limulus*

The discovery of lateral inhibition, the retinal mechanism that creates edges and calls them to the attention of higher parts of the visual system.

Eleanor J. Gibson   *Principles of perceptual learning and development* (1969)

This landmark book looks at research on perceptual learning, much of it done by Gibson herself. She looks at both the processes of perceptual development in childhood and at perceptual learning throughout our lives.

James J. Gibson *The ecological approach to visual perception* (1979)

Gibson's ecological approach tries to understand vision in its natural context. He is particularly interested in how the organization of the visual world itself facilitates our perception of it.

Eleanor J. Gibson & Anne Pick *An ecological approach to perceptual learning and development* (2000)

Gibson & Pick approach perceptual learning and development in the context of the framework developed by J. J. Gibson (above). They look at the fit between an organism and its environment and at the affordances the physical world provides.

2.1

George Berkeley (1685–1753)
An Essay Towards a New Theory of Vision (1709)

More than 250 years after Berkeley's death, philosophers still argue about him. Some say that Berkeley is an *idealist,* someone who believes that only ideas exist. No stars, no frogs, no galoshes—only the ideas of these things, and minds to entertain them. Others describe him as a *phenomenalist,* which, from a psychological point of view, is a much more interesting way to read Berkeley. Phenomenalism is the view that all we know—and all we *can* know—about the world outside the mind is what we take in through our senses. Berkeley puts it succinctly: *esse est percipi*—to be is to be perceived. A famous pair of limericks (the first by Ronald Knox, the second anonymous) satirically summarize Berkeley's position:

There was a young man who said, "God

Must think it exceedingly odd

If he finds that this tree

Continues to be

When there's no one about in the Quad."

Dear Sir: Your astonishment's odd:

I am always about in the Quad.

And that's why the tree

Will continue to be,

Since observed by Yours faithfully, GOD.

Source: *The Works of George Berkeley, Bishop of Cloyne*, Vol. 1. A. A. Luce and T. E. Jessop (Eds.). London: Nelson, 1948. [The practice of numbering paragraphs was common in Berkeley's time.]

For our purposes it matters less whether the tree continues to exist when it is not perceived than that our *knowledge* of the tree's existence depends on our seeing it. To say, *There is a tree in the quad* when we are not in the quad amounts to saying *If I go into the quad now I will have the sensations that I call "tree."*

Berkeley was born in Kilkenny, Ireland, to a well-off family with English roots. At the age of 15 he entered Trinity College (in Dublin), where he found a very stimulating and cosmopolitan intellectual environment. Berkeley graduated in 1704 and was ordained in the Anglican church in 1707. By age 30 he had written his three major philosophical works: *An Essay Towards a New Theory of Vision* (1709/1948), *A Treatise Concerning the Principles of Human Knowledge* (1710/1949b), and *Three Dialogues Between Hylas and Philonous* (1713/1949a). All are still widely read.

In 1724 the Church made Berkeley the dean of Derry, but it appears that he never occupied the deanery. In 1722 Berkeley had conceived the project of establishing a college in Bermuda for the education of both native and colonial Americans. He devoted most of a decade to the project, including three years (1728–1732) spent in Newport, Rhode Island, waiting for King George II to send the money he had promised. It never came, and Berkeley gave up. Having done such a good job as dean, in 1734 the Church appointed him bishop of Cloyne, a post he held for the rest of his life.

Berkeley was a genuine philosopher, but he was also a genuine clergyman, and as such was alarmed by the atheistic tendencies of two increasingly popular philosophical positions. One was materialism, the view that there are only material things in the world and that all phenomena have material causes, and the other was skepticism, the view that certain knowledge— knowledge of which we can (rightly) be certain—is unattainable. The "new" in Berkeley's title reflects his apparent aim of offering an alternative to these views. His philosophical position, accurately summarized in the above limericks, is that the world consists of perceptions and perceiving minds, including that of God. In this world certain knowledge is possible because perceptions are caused not by unknowable material forces but by God. Berkeley may not have changed any skeptic's or materialist's mind, but what he had to say about vision—and about sensation and perception generally—was indeed new and important.

1 My design is to shew the manner wherein we perceive by sight the distance, magnitude, and situation of objects. Also to consider the difference there is betwixt the ideas of sight and touch, and whether there be any idea common to both senses.

> *fund:* the deepest or lowest part (from Latin *fundus,* bottom, as in *fundamental*). *Fundus* refers to the back, inner lining of the eye, of which the most salient part is the retina.

2 It is, I think, agreed by all that distance, of itself and immediately, cannot be seen. For distance being a line directed end-wise to the eye, it projects only one point in the fund of the eye, which point remains invariably the same, whether the distance be longer or shorter.   5

3 I find it also acknowledged that the estimate we make of the distance of objects con-   10
siderably remote is rather an act of judgment grounded on experience than of sense. For example, when I perceive a great number of intermediate objects, such as houses, fields, rivers, and the like, which I have experienced to take up a considerable space, I thence form a judgment or conclusion that the object I see beyond them is at a great distance. Again, when an object appears faint and small, which at a near distance I have experienced to make a vigorous   15
and large appearance, I instantly conclude it to be far off: And this, 'tis evident, is the result of experience; without which, from the faintness and littleness I should not have inferred any thing concerning the distance of objects.

4 But when an object is placed at so near a distance as that the interval between the eyes bears any sensible proportion to it, the opinion of speculative men is that the two optic axes   20

> See our Figure 1 (at the end of the reading) for an illustration.

(the fancy that we see only with one eye at once being exploded) concurring at the object do there make an angle, by means of which, according as it is greater or lesser, the object is perceived to be nearer or farther off.   25

5 Betwixt which and the foregoing manner of estimating distance there is this remarkable difference: That whereas there was no apparent, necessary connexion between small distance and a large and strong appearance, or between great distance and a little and faint appearance, there appears a very necessary connexion between an obtuse angle and near distance, and an acute angle and farther distance. It does not in the least depend upon experience, but may be   30
evidently known by any one before he had experienced it, that the nearer the concurrence of the optic axes, the greater the angle, and the remoter their concurrence is, the lesser will be the angle comprehended by them.

6 There is another way mentioned by optic writers, whereby they will have us judge of those distances, in respect of which the breadth of the pupil hath any sensible bigness: And   35
that is the greater or lesser divergency of the rays, which issuing from the visible point do fall on the pupil, that point being judged nearest which is seen by most diverging rays, and that

remoter which is seen by less diverging rays: And so on, the apparent distance still increasing, as the divergency of the rays decreases, till at

40 length it becomes infinite, when the rays that fall on the pupil are to sense parallel. And after this manner it is said we perceive distance when we look only with one eye.

> See our Figure 2 (at the end of the reading) for an illustration.

7 In this case also it is plain we are not beholding to experience: It being a certain, neces-
45 sary truth that the nearer the direct rays falling on the eye approach to a parallelism, the farther off is the point of their intersection, or the visible point from whence they flow.

8 Now though the accounts here given of perceiving near distance by sight are received for true, and accordingly made use of in determining the apparent places of objects, they do nevertheless seem very unsatisfactory: And that for these following reasons.

50 9 It is evident that when the mind perceives any idea, not immediately and of it self, it must be by the means of some other idea. Thus, for instance, the passions which are in the mind of another are of themselves to me invisible. I may nevertheless perceive them by sight, though not immediately, yet by means of the colours they produce in the countenance. We often see shame or fear in the looks of a man, by perceiving the changes of his countenance to red or pale.

55 10 Moreover it is evident that no idea which is not it self perceived can be the means of perceiving any other idea. If I do not perceive the redness or paleness of a man's face them-selves, it is impossible I should perceive by them the passions which are in his mind.

11 Now from sect. 2 it is plain that distance is in its own nature imperceptible, and yet it is perceived by sight. It remains, therefore, that it be brought into view by means of some other
60 idea that is it self immediately perceived in the act of vision.

12 But those lines and angles, by means whereof some men pretend to explain the per-ception of distance, are themselves not at all perceived, nor are they in truth ever thought of by those unskillful in optics. I appeal to any one's experience whether upon sight of an object he computes its distance by the bigness of the angle made by the meeting of the two optic
65 axes? Or whether he ever thinks of the greater or lesser divergency of the rays, which arrive from any point to his pupil? Every one is himself the best judge of what he perceives, and what not. In vain shall any man tell me that I perceive certain lines and angles which introduce into my mind the various ideas of distance, so long as I my self am conscious of no such thing.

13 Since, therefore, those angles and lines are not themselves perceived by sight, it follows
70 from sect. 10 that the mind doth not by them judge of the distance of objects.

14 The truth of this assertion will be yet farther evident to any one that considers those lines and angles have no real existence in nature, being only an hypothesis framed by the mathematicians, and by them introduced into optics, that they might treat of that science in a geometrical way.

15 The last reason I shall give for rejecting that doctrine is, that though we should grant the real existence of those optic angles, etc., and that it was possible for the mind to perceive them, yet these principles would not be found sufficient to explain the phenomena of distance, as shall be shewn hereafter.   75

16 Now, it being already shewn that distance is suggested to the mind by the mediation of some other idea which is it self perceived in the act of seeing, it remains that we inquire what ideas or sensations there be that attend vision, unto which we may suppose the ideas of distance   80 are connected, and by which they are introduced into the mind. And *first,* It is certain by experience that when we look at a near object with both eyes, according as it approaches or recedes from us, we alter the disposition of our eyes, by lessening or widening the interval between the pupils. This disposition or turn of the eyes is   85 attended with a sensation, which seems to me to be that which in this case brings the idea of greater or lesser distance into the mind.

> *disposition of our eyes:* the way they are being used; here, the degree of convergence between the optic axes

17 Not that there is any natural or necessary connexion between the sensation we perceive by the turn of the eyes and greater or lesser distance,   90 but because the mind has by constant experience found the different sensations corresponding to the different dispositions of the eyes to be attended each with a different degree of distance in the object, there has grown an habitual or customary connexion between those two sorts of ideas, so that the mind no sooner perceives the sensation arising from the different turn it gives the eyes, in order to bring the pupils nearer or farther asunder, but it withal per-   95 ceives the different idea of distance which was wont to be connected with that sensation; just as upon hearing a certain sound, the idea is immediately suggested to the understanding which custom had united with it.

18 Nor do I see how I can easily be mistaken in this matter. I know evidently that distance is not perceived of it self. That by consequence it must be perceived by means of some other   100 idea which is immediately perceived, and varies with the different degrees of distance. I know also that the sensation arising from the turn of the eyes is of it self immediately perceived, and various degrees thereof are connected with different distances, which never fail to accompany them into my mind, when I view an object distinctly with both eyes, whose distance is so small that in respect of it the interval between the eyes has any considerable magnitude.   105

19 I know it is a received opinion that by altering the disposition of the eyes the mind perceives whether the angle of the optic axes or the lateral angles comprehended between the interval of the eyes and the optic axes are made greater or lesser; and that accordingly by a kind of natural geometry it judges the point of their intersection to be nearer or farther off. But that this is not true I am convinced by my own experience, since I am not conscious that   110 I make any such use of the perception I have by the turn of my eyes. And for me to make those judgments, and draw those conclusions from it, without knowing that I do so, seems altogether incomprehensible.

20 From all which it follows that the judgment we make of the distance of an object, viewed
115 with both eyes, is entirely the result of experience. If we had not constantly found certain sensations arising from the various disposition of the eyes, attended with certain degrees of distance, we should never make those sudden judgments from them concerning the distance of objects; no more than we would pretend to judge of a man's thoughts by his pronouncing words we had never heard before.

120 21 *Secondly,* An object placed at a certain distance from the eye, to which the breadth of the pupil bears a considerable proportion, being made to approach, is seen more confusedly: And the nearer it is brought the more confused appearance it makes. And this being found constantly to
125 be so, there ariseth in the mind an habitual connexion between the several degrees of confusion and distance; the greater confusion still implying the lesser distance, and the lesser confusion the greater distance of the object.

more confusedly: less sharply focused

22 This confused appearance of the object doth therefore seem to be the medium whereby the mind judgeth of distance in those cases wherein the most approved writers of optics will
130 have it judge by the different divergency with which the rays flowing from the radiating point fall on the pupil. No man, I believe, will pretend to see or feel those imaginary angles that the rays are supposed to form according to their various inclinations on his eye. But he cannot choose seeing whether the object appear more or less confused. It is therefore a manifest consequence from what hath been demonstrated that instead of the greater or lesser divergency
135 of the rays, the mind makes use of the greater or lesser confusedness of the appearance, thereby to determine the apparent place of an object.

23 Nor doth it avail to say there is not any necessary connexion between confused vision and distance, great or small. For I ask any man what necessary connexion he sees between the redness of a blush and shame? And yet no sooner shall he behold that colour to arise in the face
140 of another, but it brings into his mind the idea of that passion which hath been observed to accompany it.

24 What seems to have misled the writers of optics in this matter is that they imagine men judge of distance as they do of a conclusion in mathematics, betwixt which and the premises it is indeed absolutely requisite there be an apparent, necessary connexion: But it is far other-
145 wise in the sudden judgments men make of distance. We are not to think that brutes and children, or even grown reasonable men, whenever they perceive an object to approach, or depart from them, do it by virtue of geometry and demonstration.

demonstration: deduction

150 25 That one idea may suggest another to the mind it will suffice that they have been observed to go together, without any demonstration of the necessity of their coexistence, or

These *innumerable instances* might include such things as the wonderful smell at low tide, heartburn after a rich meal, and joint pain before a storm.

without so much as knowing what it is that makes them so to coexist. Of this there are innumerable instances of which no one can be ignorant.

26 Thus, greater confusion having been con-   155
stantly attended with nearer distance, no sooner is the former idea perceived, but it suggests the latter to our thoughts. And if it had been the ordinary course of Nature that the farther off an object were placed, the more confused it should appear, it is certain the very same perception that now makes us think an object approaches would then have made us to imagine it went   160
farther off. That perception, abstracting from custom and experience, being equally fitted to produce the Idea of great distance, or small distance, or no distance at all.

27 *Thirdly,* An object being placed at the distance above specified, and brought nearer to the eye, we may nevertheless prevent, at least for some time, the appearances growing more confused, by straining the eye. In which case that sensation supplies the place of confused   165
vision in aiding the mind to judge of the distance of the object; it being esteemed so much the nearer by how much the effort or straining of the eye in order to distinct vision is greater.

distinct vision: to focus the image

28 I have here set down those sensations or ideas that seem to be the constant and gen-   170
eral occasions of introducing into the mind the different ideas of near distance. It is true in most cases that divers other circumstances contribute to frame our idea of distance, to wit, the particular number, size, kind, etc., of the things seen. Concerning which, as well as all other the forementioned occasions which suggest distance, I shall only observe they have none of them, in their own nature, any relation or connexion with it: Nor is it possible they should ever signify   175
the various degrees thereof, otherwise than as by experience they have been found to be connected with them.

. . .

41 From what hath been premised it is a manifest consequence that a man born blind, being made to see, would at first have no idea of distance by sight; the sun and stars, the remotest objects as well as the nearer, would all seem to be in his eye, or rather in his mind. The   180
objects intromitted by sight would seem to him (as in truth they are) no other than a new set of thoughts or sensations, each whereof is as near to him as the perceptions of pain or pleasure, or the most inward passions of his soul. For our judging objects perceived by sight to be at any distance, or without the mind, is (*vid.* sect. 28) intirely the effect of experience, which one in those circumstances could not yet have attained to.   185

42 It is indeed otherwise upon the common supposition that men judge of distance by the angle of the optic axes, just as one in the dark, or a blind-man by the angle comprehended by two sticks, one whereof he held in each hand. For if this were true, it would follow that one blind from his birth being made to see, should stand in need of no new experience in order to

190 perceive distance by sight. But that this is false has, I think, been sufficiently demonstrated.

43 And perhaps upon a strict inquiry we shall not find that even those who from their birth have grown up in a continued habit of seeing are
195 irrecoverably prejudiced on the other side, to wit, in thinking what they see to be at a distance from them. For at this time it seems agreed on all hands, by those who have had any thoughts of that matter, that colours, which are the proper and imme-
200 diate object of sight, are not without the mind. But then it will be said, by sight we have also the ideas of extension, and figure, and motion; all which may well be thought without, and at some distance from the mind, though colour should not. In
205 answer to this I appeal to any man's experience, whether the visible extension of any object doth not appear as near to him as the colour of that object; nay, whether they do not both seem to be in the very same place. Is not the extension we see coloured, and is it possible for us, so much as in thought, to separate and abstract colour from extension? Now, where the extension is there surely is the figure, and there the motion
210 too. I speak of those which are perceived by sight.

44 But for a fuller explication of this point, and to shew that the immediate objects of sight are not so much as the ideas or resemblances of things placed at a distance, it is requisite that we look nearer into the matter and carefully observe what is meant in common discourse, when one says that which he sees is at a distance from him. Suppose, for example, that look-
215 ing at the moon I should say it were fifty or sixty semidiameters of the earth distant from me. Let us see what moon this is spoken of: It is plain it cannot be the visible moon, or anything like the visible moon, or that which I see, which is only a round, luminous plain of about thirty visible points in diameter. For in case I am carried from
220 the place where I stand directly towards the moon, it is manifest the object varies, still as I go on; and by the time that I am advanced fifty or sixty semidiameters of the earth, I shall be so far from being near a small, round, luminous flat that I shall per-
225 ceive nothing like it; this object having long since disappeared, and if I would recover it, it must be by going back to the earth from whence I set out. Again, suppose I perceive by sight the faint and obscure idea of something which I doubt whether it be a man, or a tree, or a tower, but judge it to be at the distance of about a mile. It is plain I cannot mean that what I see is a mile off, or that it is the image or likeness of anything
230 which is a mile off, since that every step I take towards it the appearance alters, and from being

sufficiently demonstrated: It is not apparent what demonstrations Berkeley has in mind. As of 1709 there were no known cases of vision restored to people born blind. The first such case, published in 1728 by the surgeon William Cheselden, seemed to support Berkeley's view, as have many—but not all—subsequent cases. See Degenaar (1996); Gregory and Wallace (1963); Senden (1932).

not without the mind: not outside the mind

thirty visible points: Berkeley is referring to the proportion of the visual field covered by the full moon as viewed from earth. As you get closer to the moon it covers a larger proportion of your visual field and you begin to see details of the surface.

obscure, small, and faint, grows clear, large, and vigorous. And when I come to the mile's end, that which I saw first is quite lost, neither do I find any thing in the likeness of it.

45 In these and the like instances the truth of the matter stands thus: Having of a long time experienced certain ideas, perceivable by touch, as distance, tangible figure, and solidity, to have been connected with certain ideas of sight, I do upon perceiving these ideas of sight forth- 235 with conclude what tangible ideas are, by the wonted ordinary course of Nature like to follow. Looking at an object I perceive a certain visible figure and colour, with some degree of faint- ness and other circumstances, which from what I have formerly observed, determine me to think that if I advance forward so many paces or miles, I shall be affected with such and such ideas of touch: So that in truth and strictness of speech I neither see distance it self, nor any- 240 thing that I take to be at a distance. I say, neither distance nor things placed at a distance are themselves, or their ideas, truly perceived by sight. This I am persuaded of, as to what concerns my self: and I believe whoever will look narrowly into his own thoughts and examine what he means by saying he sees this or that thing at a distance, will agree with me that what he sees only suggests to his understanding that after having passed a certain distance, to be measured 245 by the motion of his body, which is perceivable by touch, he shall come to perceive such and such tangible ideas which have been usually connected with such and such visible ideas. But that one might be deceived by these suggestions of sense, and that there is no necessary con- nexion between visible and tangible ideas suggested by them, we need go no farther than the next looking-glass or picture to be convinced. Note that when I speak of tangible ideas, I take 250 the word idea for any the immediate object of sense or understanding, in which large signifi- cation it is commonly used by the moderns.

46 From what we have shewn it is a manifest consequence that the ideas of space, outness, and things placed at a distance are not, strictly speaking, the object of sight; they are not oth- erwise perceived by the eye than by the ear. 255 Sitting in my study I hear a coach drive along the street; I look through the casement and see it; I walk out and enter into it; thus, common speech would incline one to think I heard, saw, and touched the same thing, to wit, the coach. It is nevertheless certain, the ideas intromitted 260 by each sense are widely different and distinct from each other; but having been observed con- stantly to go together, they are spoken of as one and the same thing. By the variation of the noise I perceive the different distances of the coach, and know that it approaches before I look out. Thus by the ear I perceive distance, just after the same manner as I do by the eye.

> *outness:* the property of existing outside the mind

47 I do not nevertheless say I hear distance in like manner as I say that I see it, the ideas per- 265 ceived by hearing not being so apt to be confounded with the ideas of touch as those of sight are. So likewise a man is easily convinced that bodies and external things are not properly the object of hearing; but only sounds, by the mediation whereof the idea of this or that body or distance is suggested to his thoughts. But then one is with more difficulty brought to discern the difference there is betwixt the ideas of sight and touch: Though it be certain a man no more 270 sees and feels the same thing than he hears and feels the same thing.

48 One reason of which seems to be this. It is thought a great absurdity to imagine that one and the same thing should have any more than one extension and one figure. But the extension and figure of a body, being let into the mind two ways, and that indifferently either by sight

275 or touch, it seems to follow that we see the same extension and the same figure which we feel.

49 But if we take a close and accurate view of things, it must be acknowledged that we never see and feel one and the same object. That which is seen is one thing, and that which is felt is another. If the visible figure and extension be not the same with the tangible figure and extension, we are not to infer that one and the same thing has divers extensions. The true con-

280 sequence is that the objects of sight and touch are two distinct things. It may perhaps require some thought rightly to conceive this distinction. And the difficulty seems not a little increased, because the combination of visible ideas hath constantly the same name as the combination of tangible ideas wherewith it is connected: Which doth of necessity arise from the use and end of language.

285 50 In order therefore to treat accurately and unconfusedly of vision, we must bear in mind that there are two sorts of objects apprehended by the eye, the one primarily and immediately, the other secondarily and by intervention of the former. Those of the first sort neither are, nor appear to be, without the mind, or at any distance

290 off; they may indeed grow greater or smaller, more confused, or more clear, or more faint, but they do not, cannot approach or recede from us. Whenever we say an object is at a distance, whenever we say it draws near, or goes farther *off,* we

295 must always mean it of the latter sort, which properly belong to the touch, and are not so truly perceived as suggested by the eye in like manner as thoughts by the ear.

> Berkeley is not talking about primary and secondary qualities of objects (see 2.2); rather, he is making something like the distinction Reid (see 2.2) makes between sensations and perceptions.

51 No sooner do we hear the words of a familiar language pronounced in our ears, but the ideas corresponding thereto present themselves to our minds: in the very same instant the sound and the meaning enter the understanding:

300 So closely are they united that it is not in our power to keep out the one, except we exclude the other also. We even act in all respects as if we heard the very thoughts themselves. So likewise the secondary objects, or those which are only suggested

305 by sight, do often more strongly affect us, and are more regarded than the proper objects of that sense; along with which they enter into the mind, and with which they have a far more strict connexion, than ideas have with words. Hence it is we find it so difficult to discriminate between the

310 immediate and mediate objects of sight, and are so prone to attribute to the former what belongs only to the latter. They are, as it were, most closely twisted, blended, and incorporated together. And the prejudice is confirmed and riveted in our thoughts by a long tract of time, by

> Berkeley made much of the parallels, as he saw them, between language and perception; see §147 on p. 110. He discusses his language theory of perception at greater length in the fourth dialogue of *Alciphron* (Berkeley, 1732/1950); see also Turbayne (Berkeley, 1963).

the use of language, and want of reflexion. However, I believe any one that shall attentively consider what we have already said, and shall say, upon this subject before we have done (especially if he pursue it in his own thoughts) may be able to deliver himself from that prejudice! Sure I am it is worth some attention, to whoever would understand the true nature of vision. 315

. . .

121 We have shewn the way wherein the mind by mediation of visible ideas doth perceive or apprehend the distance, magnitude, and situation of tangible objects. We come now to inquire more particularly concerning the difference between the ideas of sight and touch, which are called by the same names, and see whether there be any idea common to both 320 senses. From what we have at large set forth and demonstrated in the foregoing parts of this treatise, it is plain there is no one selfsame numerical extension perceived both by sight and touch; but 325 that the particular figures and extensions perceived by sight, however they may be called by the same names and reputed the same things with those perceived by touch, are nevertheless different, and have an existence distinct and sep- 330 arate from them: So that the question is not now concerning the same numerical ideas, but whether there be any one and the same sort or species of ideas equally perceivable to both senses; or, in other words, whether extension, 335 figure, and motion perceived by sight are not specifically distinct from extension, figure, and motion perceived by touch.

> *situation*: location

> *selfsame numerical extension:* When we say that two things are the *same,* it is usually clear from the context that they are *indistinguishable* but *numerically different,* that is, there are two of them. Here Berkeley has a different meaning of *same* in mind: there is no *one* extension perceived both by sight and touch. Rather, there is an extension perceived by sight and another extension perceived by touch.

. . .

> *trine:* threefold

126 Some, perhaps, may think pure space, *vacuum,* or trine dimension to be equally the object of sight and touch: But though we have a 340 very great propension to think the ideas of outness and space to be the immediate object of sight, yet, if I mistake not, in the foregoing parts of this essay that hath been clearly demonstrated to be a mere delusion, arising from the quick and sudden suggestion of fancy, which so closely connects the idea of distance with those of sight, that we are apt to think it is it self a proper and immediate object of that sense till 345 reason corrects the mistake.

> *no abstract ideas of figure:* Berkeley makes this case in §122–§125, which we have omitted.

127 It having been shewn that there are no abstract ideas of figure, and that it is impossible for us by any precision of thought to frame an idea of extension separate from all other visible and 350

tangible qualities which shall be common both to sight and touch: The question now remaining is, whether the particular extensions, figures, and motions perceived by sight be of the same kind with the particular extensions, figures, and motions perceived by touch? In answer to which I shall venture to lay down the following proposition: *The extension, figures, and motions perceived*

355   *by sight are specifically distinct from the ideas of touch called by the same names, nor is there any such thing as one idea or kind of idea common to both senses.* This proposition may without much difficulty be collected from what hath been said in several places of this essay. But because it seems so remote from, and contrary to, the received notions and settled opinion of mankind, I shall attempt to demonstrate it more particularly and at large by the following arguments.

360   128 When upon perception of an idea I range it under this or that sort, it is because it is perceived after the same manner, or because it has a likeness or conformity with, or affects me in the same way as, the ideas of the sort I rank it under. In short, it must not be intirely new, but have something in it old and already perceived by me. It must, I say, have so much at least in common with the ideas I have before known and named as to make me give it the same name

365   with them. But it has been, if I mistake not, clearly made out that a man born blind would not at first reception of his sight think the things he saw were of the same nature with the objects of touch, or had anything in common with them; but that they were a new set of ideas, perceived in a new manner, and intirely different from all he had ever perceived before: So that he would not call them by the same name, nor repute them to be of the same sort with any thing

370   he had hitherto known.

      129 *Secondly,* light and colours are allowed by all to constitute a sort or species intirely different from the ideas of touch: Nor will any man, I presume, say they can make themselves perceived by that sense: But there is no other immediate object of sight besides light and colours. It is therefore a direct consequence that there is no idea common to both senses.

375   130 It is a prevailing opinion, even amongst those who have thought and writ most accurately concerning our ideas and the ways whereby they enter into the understanding, that something more is perceived by sight than barely light and colours with their variations. Mr. Locke termeth sight, 'The most comprehensive of all our senses, conveying to our minds the ideas of light and colours, which are peculiar only to that sense; and also the far different

380   ideas of space, figure, and motion.' *Essay on Humane Understand. B.* ii. C. 9. S. 9. Space or distance, we have shewn, is not otherwise the object of sight than of hearing. *vid.* sect. 46. And as for figure and extension, I leave it to anyone that shall calmly attend to his own clear and distinct ideas to decide whether he has any idea intromitted immediately and properly by sight save only light and colours: Or whether it be possible for him to frame in his mind a distinct

385   abstract idea of visible extension or figure exclusive of all colour: and on the other hand, whether he can conceive colour without visible extension? For my own part, I must confess I am not able to attain so great a nicety of abstraction: in a strict sense, I see nothing but light and colours, with their several shades and variations. He who beside these doth also perceive by sight ideas far different and distinct from them hath that faculty in a degree more perfect

390   and comprehensive than I can pretend to. It must be owned that by the mediation of light and colours other far different ideas are suggested to my mind: but so they are by hearing, which

beside sounds which are peculiar to that sense, doth by their mediation suggest not only space, figure, and motion, but also all other ideas whatsoever that can be signified by words.

131 *Thirdly,* it is, I think, an axiom universally received that quantities of the same kind may be added together and make one intire sum. Mathematicians add lines together: but they do not add a line to a solid, or conceive it as making one sum with a surface: These three kinds of quantity being thought incapable of any such mutual addition, and consequently of being compared together in the several ways of proportion, are by them esteemed intirely disparate and heterogeneous. Now let any one try in his thoughts to add a visible line or surface to a tangible line or surface, so as to conceive them making one continued sum or whole. He that can do this may think them homogeneous: but he that cannot, must by the foregoing axiom think them heterogeneous: A blue and a red line I can conceive added together into one sum and making one continued line: but to make in my thoughts one continued line of a visible and tangible line added together is, I find, a task far more difficult, and even insurmountable: and I leave it to the reflexion and experience of every particular person to determine for himself.

132 A farther confirmation of our tenet may be drawn from the solution of Mr. Molyneux's problem, published by Mr. Locke in his *Essay:* Which I shall set down as it there lies, together with Mr. Locke's opinion of it, '"Suppose a man born blind, and now adult, and taught by his touch to distinguish between a cube and a sphere of the same metal, and nighly of the same bigness, so as to tell, when he felt one and

> William Molyneux (1656–1698) had posed this question in a letter to Locke in 1693.

t'other, which is the cube and which the sphere. Suppose then the cube and sphere placed on a table, and the blind man to be made to see: *Quaere,* Whether by his sight, before he touched them, he could now distinguish and tell which is the globe, which the cube?" To which the acute and judicious proposer answers: "Not. For though he has obtained the experience of how a globe, how a cube, affects his touch, yet he has not yet attained the experience that what affects his touch so or so must affect his sight so or so: Or that a protuberant angle in the cube that pressed his hand unequally shall appear to his eye as it doth in the cube." I agree with this thinking gentleman, whom I am proud to call my friend, in his answer to this his problem; and am of opinion that the blind man at first sight would not be able with certainty to say which was the globe which the cube, whilst he only saw them' *(Essay on Humane Understanding,* B. ii. C. 9. S. 8).

> Locke's answer to Molyneux's question is consistent with his "blank slate" theory; see 4.2.

133 Now, if a square surface perceived by touch be of the same sort with a square surface perceived by sight, it is certain the blind man here mentioned might know a square surface as soon as he saw it: It is no more but introducing into his mind by a new inlet an idea he has been already well acquainted with. Since, therefore, he is supposed to have known by his touch that a cube is a body terminated by square surfaces, and that a sphere is not terminated by square

395

400

405

410

415

420

425

430

surfaces: upon the supposition that a visible and tangible square differ only *in numero* it follows that he might know, by the unerring mark of the square surfaces, which was the cube, and which
435   not, while he only saw them. We must therefore allow either that visible extension and figures are specifically distinct from tangible extension and figures, or else that the solution of this problem given by those two thoughtful and ingenious men
440   is wrong.

> *in numero:* in number (rather than in kind). The two symbols below
>
> $ \$ \$
>
> are different in number only. That is, the one on the left is not the same one as the one on the right, but it is the same sign. Whereas these
>
> $ \&   \$
>
> are different in kind.

134 Much more might be laid together in proof of the proposition I have advanced: but what has been said is, if I mistake not, sufficient to convince any one that shall yield a reasonable attention: And as for those that will not be at the pains of a little thought, no multiplication of words will ever suffice to make them under-
445   stand the truth, or rightly conceive my meaning.

135 I cannot let go the above-mentioned problem without some reflexion on it. It hath been made evident that a man blind from his birth would not, at first sight, denominate any thing he saw by the names he had been used to appropriate to ideas of touch. . . . Cube, sphere, table are words he has known applied to things perceivable by touch, but to things perfectly
450   intangible he never knew them applied. Those words in their wonted application always marked out to his mind bodies or solid things which were perceived by the resistance they gave: But there is no solidity, no resistance or protrusion, perceived by sight. In short, the ideas of sight are all new perceptions, to which there be no names annexed in his mind: he cannot therefore understand what is said to him concerning them: And to ask of the two bodies he saw
455   placed on the table which was the sphere, which the cube? were to him a question downright bantering and unintelligible; nothing he sees being able to suggest to his thoughts the idea of body, distance, or in general of any thing he had already known.

136 It is a mistake to think the same thing affects both sight and touch. If the same angle or square which is the object of touch be also the object of vision, what should hinder the blind
460   man at first sight from knowing it? For though the manner wherein it affects the sight be different from that wherein it affected his touch, yet, there being beside this manner or circumstance, which is new and unknown, the angle or figure, which is old and known, he cannot choose but discern it.

. . .

138 I shall . . . proceed to consider what may be alledged, with greatest appearance of rea-
465   son, against the proposition we have shewn to be true: For where there is so much prejudice to be encountered, a bare and naked demonstration of the truth will scarce suffice. We must also satisfy the scruples that men may raise in favour of their preconceived notions, shew

whence the mistake arises, how it came to spread, and carefully disclose and root out those false persuasions that an early prejudice might have implanted in the mind.

139 *First,* therefore, it will be demanded how visible extension and figures come to be called by the same name with tangible extension and figures, if they are not of the same kind with them? It must be something more than humour or accident that could occasion a custom so constant and universal as this, which has obtained in all ages and nations of the world, and amongst all ranks of men, the learned as well as the illiterate. 470

140 To which I answer, we can no more argue a visible and tangible square to be of the same species from their being called by the same name than we can that a tangible square and the monosyllable consisting of six letters whereby it is marked are of the same species because they are both called by the same name. It is customary to call written words and the things they signify by the same name: For words not being regarded in their own nature, or otherwise than as they are marks of things, it had been superfluous, and beside the design of language, to have given them names distinct from those of the things marked by them. The same reason holds here also. Visible figures are the marks of tangible figures, and from sect. 59 it is plain that in themselves they are little regarded, or upon any other score than for their connexion with tangible figures, which by nature they are ordained to signify. And because this language of nature doth not vary in different ages or nations, hence it is that in all times and places visible figures are called by the same names as the respective tangible figures suggested by them, and not because they are alike or of the same sort with them. 475, 480, 485

We have not included section 59.

141 But, say you, surely a tangible square is liker to a visible square than to a visible circle: It has four angles and as many sides: so also has the visible square: but the visible circle has no such thing, being bounded by one uniform curve without right lines or angles, which makes it unfit to represent the tangible square but very fit to represent the tangible circle. Whence it clearly follows that visible figures are patterns of, or of the same species with, the respective tangible figures represented by them: that they are like unto them, and of their own nature fitted to represent them, as being of the same sort: and that they are in no respect arbitrary signs, as words. 490, 495

142 I answer, it must be acknowledged the visible square is fitter than the visible circle to represent the tangible square, but then it is not because it is liker, or more of a species with it, but because the visible square contains in it several distinct parts, whereby to mark the several distinct corresponding parts of a tangible square, whereas the visible circle doth not. The square perceived by touch hath four distinct, equal sides, so also hath it four distinct equal angles. It is therefore necessary that the visible figure which shall be most proper to mark it contain four distinct equal parts corresponding to the four sides of the tangible square, as likewise four other distinct and equal parts whereby to denote the four equal angles of the tangible square. And accordingly we see the visible figures contain in them distinct visible parts, answering to the distinct tangible parts of the figures signified or suggested by them. 500, 505

143 But it will not hence follow that any visible figure is like unto, or of the same species with, its corresponding tangible figure, unless it be also shewn that not only the number but also the kind of the parts be the same in both. To illustrate this, I observe that visible figures represent tangible figures much after the same manner that written words do sounds. Now, in this respect words are not arbitrary, it not being indifferent what written word stands for any sound: But it is requisite that each word contain in it so many distinct characters as there are variations in the sound it stands for. Thus the single letter *a* is proper to mark one simple uniform sound; and the word *adultery* is accommodated to represent the sound annexed to it, in the formation whereof there being eight different collisions or modifications of the air by the organs of speech, each of which produces a difference of sound, it was fit the word representing it should consist of as many distinct characters, thereby to mark each particular difference or part of the whole sound: And yet no body, I presume, will say the single letter *a*, or the word *adultery*, are like unto, or of the same species with, the respective sounds by them represented. It is indeed arbitrary that, in general, letters of any language represent sounds at all: but when that is once agreed, it is not arbitrary what combination of letters shall represent this or that particular sound. I leave this with the reader to pursue, and apply it in his own thoughts.

144 It must be confessed that we are not so apt to confound other signs with the things signified, or to think them of the same species, as we are visible and tangible ideas. But a little consideration will shew us how this may be without our supposing them of a like nature. These signs are constant and universal, their connexion with tangible ideas has been learnt at our first entrance into the world; and ever since, almost every moment of our lives, it has been occurring to our thoughts, and fastening and striking deeper on our minds. When we observe that signs are variable, and of human institution; when we remember there was a time they were not connected in our minds with those things they now so readily suggest; but that their signification was learned by the slow steps of experience: This preserves us from confounding them. But when we find the same signs suggest the same things all over the world; when we know they are not of human institution, and cannot remember that we ever learned their signification, but think that at first sight they would have suggested to us the same things they do now: All this persuades us they are of the same species as the things respectively represented by them, and that it is by a natural resemblance they suggest them to our minds.

145 Add to this that whenever we make a nice survey of any object, successively directing the optic axis to each point thereof, there are certain lines and figures described by the motion of the head or eye, which being in truth perceived by feeling, do nevertheless so mix themselves, as it were, with the ideas of sight, that we can scarce think but they appertain to that sense. Again, the ideas of sight enter into the mind several at once, more distinct and unmingled than is usual in the other senses beside the touch. Sounds, for example, perceived at the same instant, are apt to coalesce, if I may so say, into one sound: But we can perceive at the same time great variety of visible objects, very separate and distinct from each other. Now tangible extension being made up of several distinct coexistent parts, we may hence gather another reason that may dispose us to imagine a likeness or analogy between the immediate objects of sight and touch. But nothing, certainly, doth more contribute to blend and confound

them together than the strict and close connexion they have with each other. We cannot open our eyes but the ideas of distance, bodies, and tangible figures are suggested by them. So swift and sudden and unperceived is the transition from visible to tangible ideas that we can scarce forbear thinking them equally the immediate object of vision.   550

146 The prejudice which is grounded on these, and whatever other causes may be assigned thereof, sticks so fast that it is impossible without obstinate striving and labour of the mind to get intirely clear of it. But then the reluctancy we find in rejecting any opinion can be no argument of its truth to whoever considers what has been already shewn with regard to the prejudices we entertain concerning the distance, magnitude, and situation of objects; prejudices so familiar to our minds, so confirmed and inveterate, as they will hardly give way to the clearest demonstration.   555

147 Upon the whole, I think we may fairly conclude that the proper objects of vision constitute an universal language of the Author of nature, whereby we are instructed how to regulate our actions in order to attain those things that are necessary to the preservation and well-being of our bodies, as also to avoid whatever may be hurtful and destructive of them. It is by their information that we are principally guided in all the transactions and concerns of life. And the manner wherein they signify and mark unto us the objects which are at a distance is the same with that of languages and signs of human appointment, which do not suggest the things signified by any likeness or identity of nature, but only by an habitual connexion that experience has made us to observe between them.   560   565

148 Suppose one who had always continued blind be told by his guide that after he has advanced so many steps he shall come to the brink of a precipice, or be stopt by a wall; must not this to him seem very admirable and surprizing? He cannot conceive how it is possible for mortals to frame such predictions as these, which to him would seem as strange and unaccountable as prophesy doth to others. Even they who are blessed with the visive faculty may (though familiarity make it less observed) find therein sufficient cause of admiration. The wonderful art and contrivance wherewith it is adjusted to those ends and purposes for which it was apparently designed, the vast extent, number, and variety of objects that are at once with so much ease and quickness and pleasure suggested by it: All these afford subject for much and pleasing speculation, and may, if any thing, give us some glimmering, analogous praenotion of things which are placed beyond the certain discovery and comprehension of our present state.   570   575

. . .

For Discussion

1. What are the three different coaches that Berkeley hears, sees, and rides in? What does his distinction tell us about the relation between an object and our perception of it?

2. Is Berkeley's distinction between mediate and immediate objects of sight the same as Wundt's?

3. If you say, "I see a tree," Berkeley claims you are mistaken.

   a. What is the mistake?
   b. What do you see?

FIGURE 1   (Eds.) An illustration of Berkeley's §4. Angle a (left panel) is smaller than angle b (right panel); therefore the point of concurrence (intersection) of the optic axes is more distant from viewer A than from viewer B; therefore the viewed object (triangle) appears closer to B than to A.

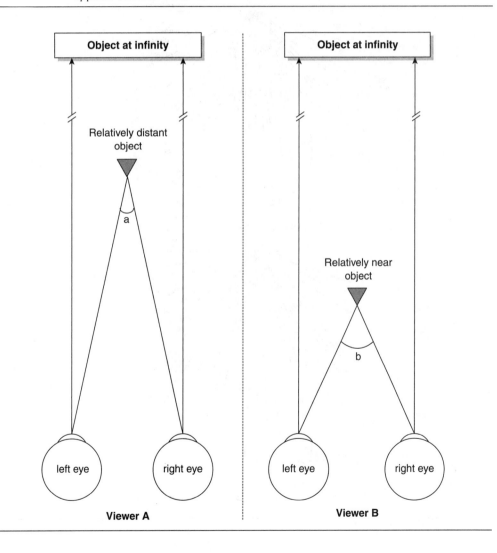

FIGURE 2   (Eds.) An illustration of Berkeley's §6. It is supposed, says Berkeley, that the greater divergence of the visual rays when the viewed object (triangle) is near (top panel) is sensed by the viewer and interpreted as a perception of the object as relatively near. The lesser divergence (greater parallelism) of the rays when the object is distant, on the other hand, is interpreted as a perception of the object as relatively far away.

Berkeley rejects this hypothesis on the grounds that the visual rays themselves are not perceived; only their end points are, and these tell us nothing about the divergence of the rays.

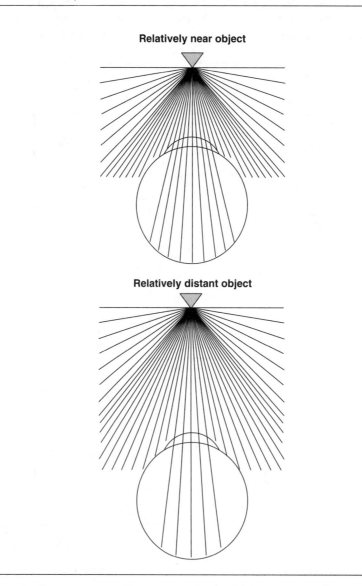

Relatively near object

Relatively distant object

Thomas Reid (1710–1796)
Essays on the Intellectual Powers of Man (1785)

Essay II: Of the Powers We Have by Means of Our External Senses

P*hilosophy* and *common sense* don't often appear in the same sentence. Philosophers point out that common sense is hard to define and may not exist. Conversely, people to whom common sense is obvious often find philosophy nonsensical. Thomas Reid was sympathetic to both sides, and—for reasons that are evident in the present reading—his way of thinking became known as *common sense philosophy.*

Reid was born near Aberdeen, Scotland. Both his parents came from families prominent in intellectual and clerical circles, and Reid was educated accordingly. After finishing his studies at Marischal College, he served briefly as the college librarian and in 1737 became minister in the village of New Machar. His parishioners were pleased with him, but Reid's interests lay elsewhere. In 1752 he returned to Aberdeen as professor of philosophy at King's College. Here he taught mathematics, physics, and logic, in addition to philosophy, and in 1764 he published his *Inquiry Into the Human Mind.* Shortly thereafter, Reid succeeded Adam Smith as the professor of moral philosophy at the University of Glasgow. Here he taught only philosophy but even so had insufficient time for his own work. In 1780 Reid retired in order to devote more time to writing and produced the *Essays on the Intellectual Powers of Man,* from which the present reading is taken, in 1785, and the *Essays on the Active Powers of the Human Mind* in 1788.

Source: Reid, T. (1969). *Essays on the Intellectual Powers of Man*. Cambridge, MA: MIT Press. Reprinted from Vols. 2 and 3 of *The Works of Thomas Reid*, published in 1814–1815 by Samuel Etheridge, Jr., Charlestown, MA.

Reid's ideas remained very influential in the half century after his death, but in more recent times he has become rather inconspicuous. This is unfortunate, for he has something to say and says it well. From a psychological perspective, Reid's most important contribution is his clear distinction between *sensation* and *perception,* words that have often been, and continue to be, used interchangeably. Reid argues that these words ought to be used to refer to two different aspects of the process by which the mind becomes aware of the world.

CHAPTER V. OF PERCEPTION

In speaking of the impressions made on our organs in perception, we build upon facts borrowed from anatomy and physiology, for which we have the testimony of our senses. But being now to speak of perception itself, which is solely an act of the mind, we must appeal to another authority. The operations of our minds are known not by sense, but by consciousness, the authority of which is as certain and as irresistible as that of sense.

In order, however, to our having a distinct notion of any of the operations of our own minds, it is not enough that we be conscious of them, for all men have this consciousness: it is further necessary that we attend to them while they are exerted, and reflect upon them with care, while they are recent and fresh in our memory. It is necessary that, by employing ourselves frequently in this way, we get the habit of this attention and reflection; and therefore, for the proof of facts which I shall have occasion to mention upon this subject, I can only appeal to the reader's own thoughts, whether such facts are not agreeable to what he is conscious of in his own mind.

If, therefore, we attend to that act of our mind which we call the perception of an external object of sense, we shall find in it these three things. *First,* Some conception or notion of the object perceived. *Secondly,* A strong and irresistible conviction and belief of its present existence. And, *thirdly,* That this conviction and belief are immediate, and not the effect of reasoning.

1st, It is impossible to perceive an object without having some notion or conception of that which we perceive. We may indeed conceive an object which we do not perceive; but when we perceive the object, we must have some conception of it at the same time; and we have commonly a more clear and steady notion of the object while we perceive it, than we have from memory or imagination when it is not perceived. Yet, even in perception, the notion which our senses give of the object may be more or less clear, more or less distinct, in all possible degrees.

Thus we see more distinctly an object at a small than at a great distance. An object at a great distance is seen more distinctly in a clear than in a foggy day. An object seen indistinctly with the naked eye, on account of its smallness, may be seen distinctly with a microscope. The objects in this room will be seen by a person in the room less and less distinctly as the light of the day fails; they pass through all the various degrees of distinctness according to the degrees of the light, and at last, in total darkness, they are not seen at all. What has been said of the objects of sight is so easily applied to the objects of the other senses, that the application may be left to the reader.

In a matter so obvious to every person capable of reflection, it is necessary only further to observe, that the notion which we get of an object, merely by our external sense, ought not to be confounded with that more scientific notion which a man, come to the years of understanding, may have of the same object, by attending to its various attributes, or to its various parts, and their relation to each other, and to the whole. Thus the notion which a child has of a jack for roasting

jack: a device for turning the spit in a roasting oven. On the other side of the English Channel Reid might have called it a *rotisserie.*

meat, will be acknowledged to be very different from that of a man who understands its construction, and perceives the relation of the parts to one another, and to the whole. The child sees the jack and every part of it as well as the man. The child, therefore, has all the notion of it which sight gives; whatever there is more in the notion which the man forms of it, must be derived from other powers of the mind, which may afterward be explained. This observation is made here only, that we may not confound the operations of different powers of the mind, which, by being always conjoined after we grow up to understanding, are apt to pass for one and the same.

2dly, In perception we not only have a notion more or less distinct of the object perceived, but also an irresistible conviction and belief of its existence. This is always the case when we are certain that we perceive it. There may be a perception so faint and indistinct, as to leave us in doubt whether we perceive the object or not. Thus, when a star begins to twinkle as the light of the sun withdraws, one may, for a short time, think he sees it, without being certain, until the perception acquires some strength and steadiness. When a ship just begins to appear in the utmost verge of the horizon, we may at first be dubious whether we perceive it or not: but when the perception is in any degree clear and steady, there remains no doubt of its reality; and when the reality of the perception is ascertained, the existence of the object perceived can no longer be doubted.

By the laws of all nations, in the most solemn judicial trials wherein men's fortunes and lives are at stake, the sentence passes according to the testimony of eye or ear witnesses of good credit. An upright judge will give a fair hearing to every objection that can be made to the integrity of a witness, and allow it to be possible that he may be corrupted; but no judge will ever suppose, that witnesses may be imposed upon by trusting to their eyes and ears: and if a skeptical counsel should plead against the testimony of the witnesses, that they had no other evidence for what they declared, but the testimony of their eyes and ears, and that we ought not to put so much faith in our senses, as to deprive men of life or fortune upon their testimony; surely no upright judge would admit a plea of this kind. I believe no counsel, however skeptical, ever dared to offer such an argument; and if it was offered, it would be rejected with disdain.

> *imposed upon:* deceived

> *a plea of this kind:* It doesn't weaken Reid's argument, but in fact such pleas are no longer unheard of. Our senses may not deceive us, but our perceptions—on which testimony is based—are prone to error.

Can any stronger proof be given, that it is the universal judgment of mankind that the evidence of sense is a kind of evidence which we may securely rest upon in the most momentous concerns of mankind; that it is a kind of evidence against which we ought not to admit any reasoning; and therefore, that to reason either for or against it, is an insult to common sense?

The whole conduct of mankind, in the daily occurrences of life, as well as the solemn procedure of judicatories in the trial of causes, civil and criminal, demonstrates this. I know only of two exceptions that may be offered against this being the universal belief of mankind.

The first exception is that of some lunatics, who have been persuaded of things that seem to contradict the clear testimony of their senses. It is said there have been lunatics and hypochondriacal persons, who seriously believed themselves to be made of glass; and, in consequence of this, lived in continual terror of having their brittle frame shivered into pieces.

85   All I have to say to this is, that our minds, in our present state, are, as well as our bodies, liable to strong disorders; and as we do not judge of the natural constitution of the body, from the disorders or diseases to which it is subject from accidents, so neither ought we to judge of the natural powers of the mind from its disorders, but from its sound state. It is natural to man, and common to the species, to have two hands, and two feet; yet I have seen a man, and a very

90   ingenious one, who was born without either hands or feet. It is natural to man to have faculties superior to those of brutes; yet we see some individuals, whose faculties are not equal to those of many brutes; and the wisest man may, by various accidents, be reduced to this state. General rules that regard those whose intellects are sound, are not overthrown by instances of men whose intellects are hurt by any constitutional or accidental disorder.

95   The other exception that may be made to the principle we have laid down, is that of some philosophers who have maintained, that the testimony of sense is fallacious, and therefore ought never to be trusted. Perhaps it might be a sufficient answer to this to say, that there is nothing so absurd which some philosophers have not maintained. It is one thing to profess a doctrine of this kind, another seriously to believe it, and to be governed by it in the conduct of

100   life. It is evident, that a man who did not believe his senses, could not keep out of harm's way an hour of his life; yet, in all the history of philosophy, we never read of any skeptic that ever stepped into fire or water because he did not believe his senses, or that showed, in the conduct of life, less trust in his senses than other men have. This gives us just ground to apprehend, that philosophy was never able to conquer that natural belief which men have in their senses; and

105   that all their subtle reasonings against this belief were never able to persuade themselves.

It appears, therefore, that the clear and distinct testimony of our senses carries irresistible conviction along with it, to every man in his right judgment.

I observed, 3dly, That this conviction is not only irresistible but it is immediate; that is, it is not by a train of reasoning and argumentation that we come to be convinced of the existence

110   of what we perceive; we ask no argument for the existence of the object, but that we perceive it; perception commands our belief upon its own authority, and disdains to rest its authority upon any reasoning whatsoever.

The conviction of a truth may be irresistible, and yet not immediate. Thus, my conviction that the three angles of every plain triangle, are equal to two right angles, is irresistible, but it is not

115   immediate: I am convinced of it by demonstrative reasoning. There are other truths in mathematics of which we have not only an irresistible, but an immediate conviction. Such are the axioms. Our belief of the axioms in mathematics is not grounded upon argument. Arguments are

120   grounded upon them, but their evidence is discerned immediately by the human understanding.

> *Axioms* are propositions that are self-evidently true, such as that two things that are both equal to a third thing are equal to each other.

It is, no doubt, one thing to have an immediate conviction of a self evident axiom; it is another thing to have an immediate conviction of the existence of what we see: but the conviction is equally immediate and equally irresistible in both cases. No man thinks of seeking a reason to believe what he sees; and, before we are capable of reasoning, we put no less confi- 125 dence in our senses than after. The rudest savage is as fully convinced of what he sees and hears, and feels, as the most expert logician. The constitution of our understanding determines us to hold the truth of a mathematical axiom as a first principle, from which other truths may be deduced, but it is deduced from none; and the constitution of our power of perception determines us to hold the existence of what we distinctly perceive as a first principle, from 130 which other truths may be deduced, but it is deduced from none. What has been said of the irresistible and immediate belief of the existence of objects distinctly perceived, I mean only to affirm with regard to persons so far advanced in understanding, as to distinguish objects of mere imagination from things which have a real existence. Every man knows that he may have a notion of Don Quixote, or of Garagantua, without any belief that such persons ever existed; 135 and that of Julius Cesar and of Oliver Cromwell, he has not only a notion, but a belief that they did really exist. But whether children, from the time that they begin to use their senses, make a distinction between things which are only conceived or imagined, and things which really exist, may be doubted. Until we are able to make this distinction, we cannot properly be said to believe or to disbelieve the existence of any thing. The belief of the existence of any thing 140 seems to suppose a notion of existence; a notion too abstract, perhaps, to enter into the mind of an infant. I speak of the power of perception in those that are adult, and of a sound mind, who believe that there are some things which do really exist; and that there are many things conceived by themselves, and by others, which have no existence. That such persons do invariably ascribe existence to every thing which they distinctly perceive, without seeking reasons 145 or arguments for doing so, is perfectly evident from the whole tenor of human life.

The account I have given of our perception of external objects, is intended as a faithful delineation of what every man, come to years of understanding, and capable of giving attention to what passes in his own mind, may feel in himself. In what manner the notion of external objects, and the immediate belief of their existence, is produced by means of our senses, I am not able to 150 show, and I do not pretend to show. If the power of perceiving external objects in certain circumstances, be a part of the original constitution of the human mind, all attempts to account for it will be vain. No other account can be given of the constitution of things, but the will of Him that made them. As we can give no reason why matter is extended and inert, why the mind thinks, and is conscious of its thoughts, but the will of Him who made both; so I suspect we can give no other 155 reason why, in certain circumstances, we perceive external objects, and in others, do not.

The Supreme Being intended, that we should have such knowledge of the material objects that surround us, as is necessary in order to our supplying the wants of nature, and avoiding the dangers to which we are constantly exposed; and he has admirably fitted our powers of perception to this purpose. [If] the intelligence we have of external objects were to be got by 160 reasoning only, the greatest part of men would be destitute of it; for the greatest part of men hardly ever learn to reason; and in infancy and childhood no man can reason. Therefore, as this intelligence of the objects that surround us, and from which we may receive so much benefit

or harm, is equally necessary to children and to men, to the ignorant and to the learned, God
165 in his wisdom conveys it to us in a way that puts all upon a level. The information of the senses
is as perfect, and gives as full conviction to the most ignorant, as to the most learned.

CHAPTER XVI. OF SENSATION

Having finished what I intend, with regard to that act of mind which we call the perception of
an external object, I proceed to consider another, which, by our constitution, is conjoined with
perception, and not with perception only, but with many other acts of our minds; and that is
170 sensation. To prevent repetition, I must refer the reader to the explication of this word given
in Essay I. chap. 1.

The passage to which Reid refers is this:

Sensation is a name given by philosophers to an act of mind, which may be distinguished from
all others by this, that it hath no object distinct from the act itself. Pain of every kind is an uneasy
sensation. When I am pained, I cannot say that the pain I feel is one thing, and that my feeling it
is another thing. They are one and the same thing, and cannot be disjoined, even in imagination.
Pain, when it is not felt, has no existence. It can be neither greater nor less in degree or duration,
nor any thing else in kind, than it is felt to be. It cannot exist by itself, nor in any subject, but in a
sentient being. No quality of an inanimate insentient being can have the least resemblance to it.

. . .

I shall add an observation concerning the word *feeling*. This word has two meanings. First,
it signifies the perceptions we have of external objects, by the sense of touch. When we
speak of feeling a body to be hard or soft, rough or smooth, hot or cold, to feel these things,
is to perceive them by touch. They are external things, and that act of the mind by which we
feel them, is easily distinguished from the objects felt: secondly, the word *feeling* is used to
signify the same thing as *sensation,* which we have just now explained; and, in this sense, it
has no object; the feeling and the thing felt are one and the same.

Perhaps betwixt feeling, taken in this last sense, and sensation, there may be this small difference, that sensation is most commonly used to signify those feelings which we have by our
external senses and bodily appetites, and all our bodily pains and pleasures. But there are *feelings* of a nobler nature accompanying our affections, our moral judgments, and our determinations in matters of taste, to which the word *sensation* is less properly applied. (pp. 27–29)

Almost all our perceptions have corresponding sensations which constantly accompany
them, and, on that account, are very apt to be confounded with them. Neither ought we to
expect, that the sensation, and its corresponding perception, should be distinguished in com-
175 mon language, because the purposes of common life do not require it. Language is made to

serve the purposes of ordinary conversation; and we have no reason to expect that it should make distinctions that are not of common use. Hence it happens, that a quality perceived, and the sensation corresponding to that perception, often go under the same name.

This makes the names of most of our sensations ambiguous, and this ambiguity has very much perplexed philosophers. It will be necessary to give some instances, to illustrate the distinction between our sensations and the objects of perception. 180

When I smell a rose, there is in this operation both sensation and perception. The agreeable odour I feel, considered by itself, without relation to any external object, is merely a sensation. It affects the mind in a certain way; and this affection of the mind may be conceived, without a thought of the rose, or any other object. This sensation can be nothing else than it is felt to 185 be. Its very essence consists in being felt; and when it is not felt, it is not. There is no difference between the sensation and the feeling of it; they are one and the same thing. It is for this reason, that we before observed, that, in sensation, there is no object distinct from that act of the mind by which it is felt; and this holds true with regard to all sensations.

Let us next attend to the perception which we have in smelling a rose. Perception has always 190 an external object; and the object of my perception, in this case, is that quality in the rose which I discern by the sense of smell. Observing that the agreeable sensation is raised when the rose is near, and ceases when it is removed, I am led, by my nature, to conclude some quality to be in the rose, which is the cause of this sensation. This quality in the rose is the object perceived; and that act of my mind, by which I have the conviction and belief of this quality, is what in this 195 case I call perception.

But it is here to be observed, that the sensation I feel, and the quality in the rose which I perceive, are both called by the same name. The smell of a rose is the name given to both: so that this name has two meanings; and the distinguishing its different meanings removes all perplexity, and enables us to give clear and distinct answers to questions, about which philoso- 200 phers have held much dispute.

Thus, if it is asked, whether the smell be in the rose, or in the mind that feels it? The answer is obvious: that there are two different things signified by the smell of a rose; one of which is in the mind, and can be in nothing but in a sentient being; the other is truly and properly in the rose. The sensation which I feel is in my mind. The mind is the sentient being; and as the rose 205 is insentient, there can be no sensation, nor any thing resembling sensation in it. But this sensation in my mind is occasioned by a certain quality in the rose, which is called by the same name with the sensation, not on account of any similitude, but because of their constant concomitancy.

All the names we have for smells, tastes, sounds, and for the various degrees of heat and 210 cold, have a like ambiguity; and what has been said of the smell of a rose may be applied to them. They signify both a sensation, and a quality perceived by means of that sensation. The first is the sign, the last the thing signified. As both are conjoined by nature, and as the purposes of common life do not require them to be disjoined in our thoughts, they are both expressed by the same name: and this ambiguity is to be found in all languages, because the reason of it 215 extends to all.

The same ambiguity is found in the names of such diseases as are indicated by a particular painful sensation; such as the toothache, the headache. The toothache signifies a painful sensation, which can only be in a sentient being; but it signifies also a disorder in the body,
220 which has no similitude to a sensation, but is naturally connected with it.

Pressing my hand with force against the table, I feel pain, and I feel the table to be hard. The pain is a sensation of the mind, and there is nothing that resembles it in the table. The hardness is in the table, nor is there any thing resembling it in the mind. Feeling is applied to both; but in a different sense; being a word common to the act of sensation, and to that of perceiv-
225 ing by the sense of touch.

I touch the table gently with my hand, and I feel it to be smooth, hard, and cold. These are qualities of the table perceived by touch; but I perceive them by means of a sensation which indicates them. This sensation not being painful, I commonly give no attention to it. It carries my thought immediately to the thing signified by it, and is itself forgotten, as if it had never
230 been. But by repeating it, and turning my attention to it, and abstracting my thought from the thing signified by it, I find it to be merely a sensation, and that it has no similitude to the hardness, smoothness, or coldness of the table which are signified by it.

It is indeed difficult, at first, to disjoin things in our attention which have always been conjoined, and to make that an object of reflection which never was so before; but some pains
235 and practice will overcome this difficulty in those who have got the habit of reflecting on the operations of their own minds.

Although the present subject leads us only to consider the sensations which we have by means of our external senses, yet it will serve to illustrate what has been said, and I apprehend is of importance in itself to observe, that many operations of mind, to which we give one name,
240 and which we always consider as one thing, are complex in their nature, and made up of several more simple ingredients, and of these ingredients sensation very often makes one. Of this we shall give some instances.

The appetite of hunger includes an uneasy sensation, and desire of food. Sensation and desire are different acts of mind. The last, from its nature, must have an object; the first has no
245 object. These two ingredients may always be separated in thought; perhaps they sometimes are, in reality; but hunger includes both.

Benevolence toward our fellow creatures includes an agreeable feeling; but it includes also a desire of the happiness of others. The ancients commonly called it desire: many moderns choose rather to call it a feeling. Both are right; and they only err who exclude either of the
250 ingredients. Whether these two ingredients are necessarily connected, is perhaps difficult for us to determine, there being many necessary connections which we do not perceive to be necessary; but we can disjoin them in thought. They are different acts of the mind.

An uneasy feeling, and a desire, are in like manner the ingredients of malevolent affections; such as malice, envy, revenge. The passion of fear includes an uneasy sensation or feeling, and
255 an opinion of danger; and hope is made up of the contrary ingredients. When we hear of a heroic action, the sentiment which it raises in our mind is made up of various ingredients. There is in it an agreeable feeling, a benevolent affection to the person, and a judgment or opinion of his merit.

If we thus analyze the various operations of our minds, we shall find, that many of them which we consider as perfectly simple, because we have been accustomed to call them by one name, are compounded of more simple ingredients; and that sensation or feeling, which is only a more refined kind of sensation, makes one ingredient, not only in the perception of external objects, but in most operations of the mind. 260

A small degree of reflection may satisfy us, that the number and variety of our sensations and feelings is prodigious: for, to omit all those which accompany our appetites, passions, and affections, our moral sentiments, and sentiments of taste, even our external senses furnish a 265 great variety of sensations differing in kind, and almost in every kind an endless variety of degrees. Every variety we discern, with regard to taste, smell, sound, colour, heat and cold, and in the tangible qualities of bodies, is indicated by a sensation corresponding to it.

The most general and the most important division of our sensations and feelings, is into the agreeable, the disagreeable, and the indifferent. Every thing we call pleasure, happiness, or 270 enjoyment, on the one hand, and on the other, every thing we call misery, pain, or uneasiness, is sensation or feeling: for no man can for the present be more happy, or more miserable than he feels himself to be. He cannot be deceived with regard to the enjoyment or suffering of the present moment.

But I apprehend, that besides the sensations that are either agreeable or disagreeable, there 275 is still a greater number that are indifferent. To these we give so little attention that they have no name, and are immediately forgotten, as if they had never been; and it requires attention to the operations of our minds to be convinced of their existence.

For this end we may observe, that to a good ear every human voice is distinguishable from all others. Some voices are pleasant, some disagreeable; but the far greater part can 280 neither be said to be one or the other. The same thing may be said of other sounds, and no less of tastes, smells, and colours and if we consider that our senses are in continual exercise while we are awake, that some sensation attends every object they present to us, and that familiar objects seldom raise any emotion pleasant or painful, we shall see reason, besides the agreeable and disagreeable, to admit a third class of sensations, that may be 285 called indifferent.

The sensations that are indifferent, are far from being useless. They serve as signs to distinguish things that differ; and the information we have concerning things external, comes by their means. Thus, if a man had no ear to receive pleasure from the harmony or melody of sounds, he would still find the sense of hearing of great utility. Though sounds gave him nei- 290 ther pleasure nor pain of themselves, they would give him much useful information and the like may be said of the sensations we have by all the other senses.

As to the sensations and feelings that are agreeable or disagreeable, they differ much, not only in degree, but in kind and in dignity. Some belong to the animal part of our nature, and are common to us with the brutes: others belong to the rational and moral part. The 295 first are more properly called *sensations*, the last *feelings*. The French word *sentiment* is common to both.

300 The intention of nature in them is for the most part obvious, and well deserving our notice. It has been beautifully illustrated by a very elegant French writer, in his Théorie des sentimens agréables.

> The elegant French writer is Louis-Jean Lévesque de Pouilly (1691–1750). His book was published in 1747 and was translated in 1749 as *The Theory of Agreeable Sensations*.

305 The Author of nature, in the distribution of agreeable and painful feelings, has wisely and benevolently consulted the good of the human species, and has even shown us, by the same means, what tenor of conduct we ought to hold. For, *first,* The painful sensations of the animal kind are admonitions to avoid what would hurt us; and the agreeable sensations of this kind, invite us to those actions that are necessary to the preservation of the individual, or of the kind. 2dly, By the same means nature invites us to moderate bodily exercise, and admonishes us to avoid idleness and inactivity on the one hand, and

310 excessive labour and fatigue on the other. 3dly, The moderate exercise of all our rational powers gives pleasure. 4thly, Every species of beauty is beheld with pleasure, and every species of deformity with disgust; and we shall find all that we call beautiful, to be something estimable or useful in itself, or a sign of something that is estimable or useful. 5thly, The benevolent affections are all accompanied with an agreeable feeling, the malevolent with the contrary. And,

315 6thly, The highest, the noblest, and most durable pleasure, is that of doing well, and acting the part that becomes us; and the most bitter and painful sentiment, the anguish and remorse of a guilty conscience. These observations, with regard to the economy of nature in the distribution of our painful and agreeable sensations and feelings, are illustrated by the author last mentioned, so elegantly and judiciously, that I shall not attempt to say any thing upon them

320 after him.

I shall conclude this chapter by observing, that as the confounding our sensations with that perception of external objects, which is constantly conjoined with them, has been the occasion of most of the errors and false theories of philosophers with regard to the senses; so the distinguishing these operations seems to me to be the key that leads to a right understanding of both.

325 Sensation, taken by itself, implies neither the conception nor belief of any external object. It supposes a sentient being, and a certain manner in which that being is affected; but it supposes no more. Perception implies an immediate conviction and belief of something external; something different both from the mind that perceives, and from the act of perception. Things so different in their nature ought to be distinguished; but by our constitution they are always

330 united. Every different perception is conjoined with a sensation that is proper to it. The one is the sign, the other the thing signified. They coalesce in our imagination. They are signified by one name, and are considered as one simple operation. The purposes of life do not require them to be distinguished.

It is the philosopher alone who has occasion to distinguish them, when he would analyze

335 the operation compounded of them. But he has no suspicion that there is any composition in it; and to discover this requires a degree of reflection which has been too little practised even by philosophers.

species: This word is, among other things, a metaphysical term denoting emanations (from objects) that make contact with the sense organs, thus causing awareness of the objects.

Reid explains and discusses primary and secondary qualities in Chapter XVII, next page.

In the old philosophy, sensation and perception were perfectly confounded. The sensible species coming from the object, and impressed 340 upon the mind, was the whole; and you might call it sensation or perception as you pleased.

Des Cartes and Locke, attending more to the operations of their own minds, say, that the sensations by which we have notice of secondary quali- 345 ties, have no resemblance to any thing that pertains to body; but they did not see that this might with equal justice be applied to the primary qualities. Mr. Locke maintains, that the sensations we have from primary qualities are resemblances of those qualities. This shows how grossly the most inge- 350 nious men may err with regard to the operations of their minds. It must indeed be acknowledged, that it is much easier to have a distinct notion of the sensations that belong to secondary, than of those that belong to the primary qualities. The reason of this will appear in the next chapter.

But had Mr. Locke attended with sufficient accuracy to the sensations which he was every day and every hour receiving from primary qualities, he would have seen, that they can as little 355 resemble any quality of an inanimated being, as pain can resemble a cube or a circle.

What had escaped this ingenious philosopher was clearly discerned by bishop Berkeley. He had a just notion of sensations, and saw that it was impossible that any thing in an insentient being could resemble them; a thing so evident in itself, that it seems wonderful that it should have been so long unknown. 360

But let us attend to the consequence of this discovery. Philosophers, as well as the vulgar, had been accustomed to comprehend both sensation and perception under one name, and to consider them as one uncompounded opera-tion. Philosophers, even more than the vulgar, gave the name of sensation to the whole opera- 365 tion of the senses; and all the notions we have of material things were called ideas of sensation. This led bishop Berkeley to take one ingredient of a complex operation for the whole; and having clearly discovered the nature of sensation, taking 370 it for granted, that all that the senses present to the mind is sensation, which can have no resemblance to any thing material, he concluded that there is no material world.

vulgar: The Latin *vulgus* meant *the common people,* and Reid uses it in this sense, with no pejorative connotation, to refer to people who use language in an everyday, commonsensical way.

If the senses furnished us with no materials of thought but sensations, his conclusion must be just; for no sensation can give us the conception of material things, far less any argument to prove their existence. But if it is true that by our senses we have not only a variety of sensa- 375 tions, but likewise a conception, and an immediate natural conviction of external objects, he reasons from a false supposition, and his arguments fall to the ground.

CHAPTER XVII. OF THE OBJECTS OF PERCEPTION; AND FIRST, OF PRIMARY AND SECONDARY QUALITIES

The objects of perception are the various qualities of bodies. Intending to treat of these *only* in general, and chiefly with a view to explain the notions which our senses give us of them,

380 I begin with the distinction between primary and secondary qualities. These were distinguished very early. The Peripatetic system confounded them, and left no difference. The distinction was again revived by Des Cartes and Locke, and a sec-

385 ond time abolished by Berkeley and Hume. If the real foundation of this distinction can be pointed out, it will enable us to account for the various revolutions in the sentiments of philosophers concerning it.

> *peripatetic:* From the Greek *peripatein,* to walk around. According to tradition, Aristotle and his students liked to walk around while philosophizing, so Aristotle is sometimes referred to as *the peripatetic* and his philosophy as the *Peripatetic school* or *system.*

390 Every one knows that extension, divisibility, figure, motion, solidity, hardness, softness, and fluidity, were by Mr. Locke called *primary qualities of body;* and that sound, colour, taste, smell,

> See Locke (1690), Bk. 2, Ch. 8, §9, 10.

and heat or cold, were called *secondary qualities.* Is there a just foundation for this distinc-

395 tion? Is there any thing common to the primary which belongs not to the secondary? And what is it?

I answer, that there appears to me to be a real foundation for the distinction; and it is this: that our senses give us a direct and a distinct notion of the primary qualities, and inform us what they are in themselves: but of the secondary qualities, our senses give us only a relative and

400 obscure notion. They inform us only, that they are qualities that affect us in a certain manner, that is, produce in us a certain sensation; but as to what they are in themselves, our senses leave us in the dark.

Every man capable of reflection may easily satisfy himself, that he has a perfectly clear and distinct notion of extension, divisibility, figure, and motion. The solidity of a body means no

405 more, but that it excludes other bodies from occupying the same place at the same time. Hardness, softness, and fluidity, are different degrees of cohesion in the parts of a body. It is fluid, when it has no sensible cohesion; soft when the cohesion is weak; and hard when it is strong. Of the cause of this cohesion we are ignorant, but the thing itself we understand perfectly, being immediately informed of it by the sense of touch. It is evident, therefore, that of

410 the primary qualities we have a clear and distinct notion; we know what they are, though we may be ignorant of their causes.

I observed further, that the notion we have of primary qualities is direct, and not relative only. A relative notion of a thing, is, strictly speaking, no notion of the thing at all, but only of some relation which it bears to something else.

Thus gravity sometimes signifies the tendency of bodies toward the earth; sometimes it signifies the cause of that tendency. When it means the first, I have a direct and distinct notion of gravity: I see it, and feel it, and know perfectly what it is; but this tendency must have a cause: we give the same name to the cause; and that cause has been an object of thought and of speculation. Now what notion have we of this cause when we think and reason about it? It is evident, we think of it as an unknown cause, of a known effect. This is a relative notion, and it must be obscure, because it gives us no conception of what the thing is, but of what relation it bears to something else. Every relation which a thing unknown bears to something that *is* known, may give a relative notion of it; and there are many objects of thought, and of discourse, of which our faculties can give no better than a relative notion.

Having premised these things to explain what is meant by a relative notion, it is evident, that our notion of primary qualities is not of this kind; we know what they are, and not barely what relation they bear to something else.

It is otherwise with secondary qualities. If you ask me, what is that quality or modification in a rose which I call its smell, I am at a loss to answer directly. Upon reflection I find, that I have a distinct notion of the sensation which it produces in my mind. But there can be nothing like to this sensation in the rose, because it is insentient. The quality in the rose is something which occasions the sensation in me; but what that something is, I know not. My senses give me no information upon this point. The only notion therefore my senses give is this, that smell in the rose is an unknown quality or modification, which is the cause or occasion of a sensation which I know well. The relation which this unknown quality bears to the sensation with which nature has connected it, is all I learn from the sense of smelling: but this is evidently a relative notion. The same reasoning will apply to every secondary quality.

Thus I think it appears, that there is a real foundation for the distinction of primary from secondary qualities; and that they are distinguished by this, that of the primary we have by our senses a direct and distinct notion; but of the secondary only a relative notion, which must, because it is only relative, be obscure; they are conceived only as the unknown causes or occasions of certain sensations with which we are well acquainted.

The account I have given of this distinction is founded upon no hypothesis. Whether our notions of primary qualities are direct and distinct, those of the secondary relative and obscure, is a matter of fact, of which every man may have certain knowledge by attentive reflection upon them. To this reflection I appeal, as the proper test of what has been advanced, and proceed to make some reflections on this subject.

1st, The primary qualities are neither sensations, nor are they resemblances of sensations. This appears to me self-evident. I have a clear and distinct notion of each of the primary qualities. I have a clear and distinct notion of sensation. I can compare the one with the other; and when I do so, I am not able to discern a resembling feature. Sensation is the act, or the feeling, I dispute not which, of a sentient being. Figure, divisibility, solidity, are neither acts nor feelings. Sensation supposes a sentient being as its subject;

415

420

425

430

435

440

445

450

455

Clear and distinct ideas were very important in Descartes' thought; see *Meditation IV.*

for a sensation that is not felt by some sentient being, is an absurdity. Figure and divisibility suppose a subject that is figured and divisible, but not a subject that is sentient.

2dly, We have no reason to think, that the sensations by which we have notice of secondary qualities resemble any quality of body. The absurdity of this notion has been clearly shown by Des Cartes, Locke, and many modern philosophers. It was a tenet of the ancient philosophy, and is still by many imputed to the vulgar, but only as a vulgar error. It is too evident to need proof, that the vibrations of a sounding body do not resemble the sensation of sound, nor the effluvia of an odorous body the sensation of smell.

> *tenet of the ancient philosophy:* Aristotle taught that like can be perceived only by like; whatever is in the perceiver, there must be some of the same in the object.

3dly, The distinctness of our notions of primary qualities prevents all questions and disputes about their nature. There are no different opinions about the nature of extension, figure, or motion, or the nature of any primary quality. Their nature is manifest to our senses, and cannot be unknown to any man, or mistaken by him, though their causes may admit of dispute.

The primary qualities are the object of the mathematical sciences, and the distinctness of our notions of them enables us to reason demonstratively about them to a great extent. Their various modifications are precisely defined in the imagination, and thereby capable of being compared, and their relations determined with precision and certainty.

It is not so with secondary qualities. Their nature not being manifest to the sense, may be a subject of dispute. Our feeling informs us that the fire is hot; but it does not inform us what that heat of the fire is. But does it not appear a contradiction, to say we know that the fire is hot, but we know not what that heat is? I answer, there is the same appearance of contradiction in many things, that must be granted. We know that wine has an inebriating quality; but we know not what that quality is. It is true, indeed, that if we had not some notion of what is meant by the heat of fire, and by an inebriating quality, we could affirm nothing of either with understanding. We have a notion of both; but it is only a relative notion. We know that they are the causes of certain known effects.

4thly, The nature of secondary qualities is a proper subject of philosophical disquisition; and in this, philosophy has made some progress. It has been discovered, that the sensation of smell is occasioned by the effluvia of bodies; that of sound by their vibration. The disposition of bodies to reflect a particular kind of light occasions the sensation of colour. Very curious discoveries have been made of the nature of heat, and an ample field of discovery in these subjects remains.

> By philosophy, Reid means natural philosophy, which we now call natural sciences.

5thly, We may see why the sensations belonging to secondary qualities are an object of our attention, while those which belong to the primary are not.

The first are not only signs of the object perceived, but they bear a capital part in the notion we form of it. We conceive it only as that which occasions such a sensation, and therefore cannot reflect upon it without thinking of the sensation which it occasions. We have no other mark whereby to distinguish it. The thought of a secondary quality, therefore, always carries us back to the sensation which it produces. We give the same name to both, and are apt to confound them together.   500

But having a clear and distinct conception of primary qualities, we have no need when we think of them to recall their sensations. When a primary quality is perceived, the sensation immediately leads our thought to the quality signified by it, and is itself forgotten. We have no occasion afterward to reflect upon it; and so we come to be as little acquainted with it, as if we had never felt it. This is the case with the sensations of all primary qualities, when they are not   505
so painful or pleasant as to draw our attention.

When a man moves his hand rudely against a pointed hard body, he feels pain, and may easily be persuaded that this pain is a sensation, and that there is nothing resembling it in the hard body; at the same time he perceives the body to be hard and pointed, and he knows that these qualities belong to the body only. In this case, it is easy to distinguish what he feels from   510
what he perceives.

Let him again touch the pointed body gently, so as to give him no pain; and now you can hardly persuade him that he feels any thing but the figure and hardness of the body; so difficult it is to attend to the sensations belonging to primary qualities, when they are neither pleasant nor painful. They carry the thought to the external object, and immediately disappear and are forgotten.   515
Nature intended them only as signs; and when they have served that purpose they vanish.

We are now to consider the opinions both of the vulgar, and of philosophers upon this subject. As to the former, it is not to be expected that they should make distinctions which have no connection with the common affairs of life; they do not therefore distinguish the primary from the secondary qualities, but speak of both as being equally qualities of the external object.   520
Of the primary qualities they have a distinct notion, as they are immediately and distinctly per-ceived by the senses; of the secondary, their notions, as I apprehend, are confused and indis-tinct, rather than erroneous. A secondary quality is the unknown cause or occasion of a well known effect; and the same name is common to the cause and the effect. Now, to distinguish clearly the different ingredients of a complex notion, and, at the same time, the different mean-   525
ings of an ambiguous word, is the work of a philosopher; and is not to be expected of the vulgar, when their occasions do not require it.

I grant, therefore, that the notion which the vulgar have of secondary qualities, is indistinct and inaccurate. But there seems to be a contradiction between the vulgar and the philosopher upon this subject, and each charges the other with a gross absurdity. The vulgar say, that fire   530
is hot, and snow cold, and sugar sweet; and that to deny this is a gross absurdity, and contra-dicts the testimony of our senses. The philosopher says, that heat, and cold, and sweetness, are nothing but sensations in our minds; and it is absurd to conceive, that these sensations are in the fire, or in the snow, or in the sugar.

I believe this contradiction between the vulgar and the philosopher is more apparent than real;   535
and that it is owing to an abuse of language on the part of the philosopher, and to indistinct notions on the part of the vulgar. The philosopher says, there is no heat in the fire, meaning, that the fire has not the sensation of heat. His meaning is just; and the vulgar will agree with him, as

soon as they understand his meaning; but his language is improper; for there is really a quality
in the fire, of which the proper name is heat; and the name of heat is given to this quality, both
by philosophers and by the vulgar, much more frequently than to the sensation of heat. This
speech of the philosopher, therefore, is meant by him in one sense; it is taken by the vulgar in
another sense. In the sense in which they take it, it is indeed absurd, and so they hold it to be. In
the sense in which he means it, it is true; and the vulgar, as soon as they are made to understand
that sense, will acknowledge it to be true. They know as well as the philosopher, that the fire does
not feel heat; and this is all that he means by saying there is no heat in the fire.

In the opinions of philosophers about primary and secondary qualities, there have been, as was
before observed, several revolutions. They were distinguished long before the days of Aristotle,
by the sect called Atomists; among whom Democritus made a capital figure. In those times, the
name of *quality* was applied only to those we call secondary qualities; the primary being considered as essential to matter, were not called qualities. That the atoms, which they held to be the
first principles of things, were extended, solid, figured, and moveable, there was no doubt; but
the question was, whether they had smell, taste and colour? or, as it was commonly expressed,
whether they had qualities? The Atomists maintained, that they had not; that the qualities were
not in bodies, but were something resulting from the operation of bodies upon our senses.

> Democritus put it this way:
>
> > Sweet exists by convention, bitter by convention, colour by convention; atoms and void
> > alone exist in reality.... We know nothing accurately in reality, but only as it changes
> > according to the bodily condition, and the constitution of those things that flow upon the
> > body and impinge upon it. (Freeman 1957, fragment 9)

It would seem, that when men began to speculate upon this subject, the primary qualities
appeared so clear and manifest, that they could entertain no doubt of their existence wherever
matter existed; but the secondary so obscure, that they were at a loss where to place them. They
used this comparison; as fire, which is neither in the flint nor in the steel, is produced by their col-
lision, so those qualities, though not in bodies, are produced by their impulse upon our senses.

This doctrine was opposed by Aristotle. He believed taste and colour to be substantial forms
of bodies, and that their species, as well as those of figure and motion, are received by the senses.

> In regard to all sense generally we must understand that sense is that which is receptive of sensible
> forms apart from their matter, as wax receives the imprint of the signet ring apart from the iron or
> gold of which it is made: it takes the imprint which is of gold or bronze, but not qua gold or bronze.
> And similarly sense as relative to each sensible is acted upon by that which possesses color, flavor,
> or sound, not in so far as each of those sensibles is called a particular thing, but in so far as it

(Continued)

(Continued)

possesses a particular quality and in respect of its character or form.... It might be asked whether what is unable to smell would be in any way acted upon by an odor, or that which is incapable of seeing by a color, and so for the other sensibles. But, if the object of smell is odor, the effect it produces, if it produces an effect at all, is smelling. Therefore none of the things that are unable to smell can be acted upon by odor, and the same is true of the other senses.... Is it not... the case that not all body can be affected by smell and sound, and that the bodies which are so affected are indeterminate and shifting; for example, air? For odor in the air implies that the air has been acted upon in some way. What then is smelling besides a sort of suffering or being acted upon? Or shall we say that the act of smelling implies sense-perception, whereas the air, after it has been acted upon, so far from perceiving, at once becomes itself perceptible to sense? (Aristotle, 4th cent. BCE/1907, II/12)

In believing, that what we commonly call *taste* and *colour* is something really inherent in body, and does not depend upon its being tasted and seen, he followed nature. But, in believing that our sensations of taste and colour are the forms or species of those qualities received 565 by the senses, he followed his own theory, which was an absurd fiction. Des Cartes not only showed the absurdity of sensible species received by the senses, but gave a more just and more intelligible account of secondary qualities than had been given before. Mr. Locke followed him, and bestowed much pains upon this subject. He was the first, I think, that gave them the name of secondary qualities, which has been very generally adopted. He distinguished the sensation 570 from the quality in the body, which is the cause or occasion of that sensation, and showed that there neither is nor can be any similitude between them.

As Descartes (1644/1985, §198) put it:

[W]e are not entitled to say that anything reaches the brain except for the local motion of the nerves themselves. And we see that this local motion produces not only sensations of pain and pleasure but also those of light and sound. If someone is struck in the eye, so that the vibration of the blow reaches the retina, this will cause him to see many sparks of flashing light, yet the light is not outside his eye. ... [W]e know that the nature of our soul is such that different local motions are quite sufficient to produce all the sensations in the soul. What is more, we actually experience the various sensations as they are produced in the soul, and we do not find that anything reaches the brain from the external sense organs except for motions of this kind. In view of all this we have every reason to conclude that the properties in external objects to which we apply the terms light, colour, smell, taste, sound, heat and cold—as well as the other tactile qualities and even what are called 'substantial forms'—are, so far as we can see, simply various dispositions in those objects which make them able to set up various kinds of motions in our nerves which are required to produce all the various sensations in our soul.

Reid might also have mentioned Galileo(1623/1957, p. 274), who put it this way:

> Now I say that whenever I conceive any material or corporeal substance, I immediately feel the
> need to think of it as bounded, and as having this or that shape; as being large or small in relation
> to other things, and in some specific place at any given time; as being in motion or at rest; as
> touching or not touching some other body; and as being one in number, or few, or many. From
> these conditions I cannot separate such a substance by any stretch of my imagination. But that
> it must be white or red, bitter or sweet, noisy or silent, and of sweet or foul odor, my mind does
> not feel compelled to bring in as necessary accompaniments. Without the senses as our guides,
> reason or imagination unaided would probably never arrive at qualities *like* these. Hence I think
> that tastes, odors, colors, and so on are no more than mere names so far as the object in which
> we place them is concerned, and that they reside only in the consciousness. Hence if the living
> creature were removed, all these qualities would be wiped away and annihilated. But since we
> have imposed upon them special names, distinct from those of the other and real qualities
> mentioned previously, we wish to believe that they really exist as actually different from those.

575

580

585

590

By this account, the senses are acquitted of putting any fallacy upon us; the sensation is real,
and no fallacy; the quality in the body, which is the cause or occasion of this sensation, is likewise real, though the nature of it is not manifest to our senses. If we impose upon ourselves,
by confounding the sensation with the quality that occasions it, this is owing to rash judgment,
or weak understanding, but not to any false testimony of our senses.

. . .

Bishop Berkeley, having adopted the sentiments common to philosophers, concerning the
ideas we have by our senses, to wit, that they are all sensations, saw more clearly the necessary
consequence of this doctrine; which is, that there
is no material world; no qualities primary or secondary; and, consequently, no foundation for any
distinction between them. He exposed the absurdity of a resemblance between our sensations and
any quality, primary or secondary, of a substance
that is supposed to be insentient. Indeed, if it is
granted that the senses have no other office but to
furnish us with sensations, it will be found impossible to make any distinction between primary
and secondary qualities, or even to maintain the existence of a material world.

> Some of these arguments appear in
> Berkeley's *New Theory of Vision* (1709/1948),
> but his more extreme views were
> developed in the *Principles of Human
> Knowledge* (1710/1949b).

From the account I have given of the various revolutions in the opinions of philosophers
about primary and secondary qualities, I think it appears, that all the darkness and intricacy that
thinking men have found in this subject, and the errors they have fallen into, have been owing
to the difficulty of distinguishing clearly sensation from perception; what we feel from what we
perceive.

The external senses have a double province; to make us feel, and to make us perceive. They furnish us with a variety of sensations, some pleasant, others painful, and others indifferent; at the same time they give us a conception, and an invincible belief of the existence of external objects. This conception of external objects is the work of nature. The belief of their existence, which our senses give, is the work of nature; so likewise is the sensation that accompanies it. This conception and belief which nature produces by means of the senses, we call *perception*. The feeling which goes along with the perception, we call *sensation*. The perception and its corresponding sensation are produced at the same time. In our experience we never find them disjoined. Hence we are led to consider them as one thing, to give them one name, and to confound their different attributes. It becomes very difficult to separate them in thought, to attend to each by itself, and to attribute nothing to it which belongs to the other.

. . .

CHAPTER XVIII. OF OTHER OBJECTS OF PERCEPTION

. . .

That we perceive certain disorders in our own bodies by means of uneasy sensations, which nature has conjoined with them, will not be disputed. Of this kind are toothache, headache, gout, and every distemper and hurt which we feel. The notions which our sense gives of these, have a strong analogy to our notions of secondary qualities. Both are similarly compounded, and may be similarly resolved, and they give light to each other.

In the toothache, for instance, there is, first, a painful feeling; and, secondly, a conception and belief of some disorder in the tooth, which is believed to be the cause of the uneasy feeling. The first of these is a sensation, the second is perception; for it includes a conception and belief of an external object. But these two things, though of different natures, are so constantly conjoined in our experience, and in our imagination, that we consider them as one. We give the same name to both; for the toothache is the proper name of the pain we feel; and it is the proper name of the disorder in the tooth which causes that pain. If it should be made a question, whether the toothache be in the mind that feels it, or in the tooth that is affected? much might be said on both sides, while it is not observed that the word has two meanings. But a little reflection satisfies us, that the pain is in the mind, and the disorder in the tooth. If some philosopher should pretend to have made a discovery, that the toothache, the gout, the headache, are only sensations in the mind, and that it is a vulgar error to conceive that they are distempers of the body, he might defend his system in the same manner as those, who affirm that there is no sound nor colour nor taste in bodies, defend that paradox. But both these systems, like most paradoxes, will be found to be only an abuse of words.

> *no sound nor colour*: The paradox is resolved by re-wording this claim: There is no sound-as-sensation nor color-as-sensation in bodies.

595

600

605

610

615

620

625

630 We say that we *feel* the toothache, not that we perceive it. On the other hand, we say that we *perceive* the colour of a body, not that we feel it. Can any reason be given for this difference of phraseology? In answer to this question, I apprehend, that both when we feel the toothache, and when we see a coloured body, there is sensation and perception conjoined. But, in the toothache, the sensation being very painful, engrosses the attention; and therefore we speak of it, as if it were felt only, and not perceived: whereas, in seeing a coloured body, the sensa-

635 tion is indifferent, and draws no attention. The quality in the body, which we call its colour, is the only object of attention; and therefore we speak of it, as if it were perceived, and not felt. Though all philosophers agree that in seeing colour there is sensation, it is not easy to persuade the vulgar, that, in seeing a coloured body, when the light is not too strong, nor the eye inflamed, they have any sensation or feeling at all.

640 There are some sensations, which, though they are very often felt, are never attended to, nor reflected upon. We have no conception of them; and therefore, in language, there is neither any name for them, nor any form of speech that supposes their existence. Such are the sensations of colour and of all primary qualities; and therefore those qualities are said to be perceived, but not to be felt. Taste and smell, and heat and cold, have sensations that are often agreeable or

645 disagreeable, in such a degree as to draw our attention; and they are sometimes said to be felt, and sometimes to be perceived. When disorders of the body occasion very acute pain, the uneasy sensation engrosses the attention, and they are said to be felt, not to be perceived.

There is another question relating to phraseology, which this subject suggests. A man says, he feels pain in such a particular part of his body; in his toe, for instance. Now, reason assures

650 us, that pain being a sensation, can only be in the sentient being, as its subject, that is, in the mind. And though philosophers have disputed much about the place of the mind, yet none of them ever placed it in the toe. What shall we say then in

655 this case? Do our senses really deceive us, and make us believe a thing which our reason deter-

the place of the mind: The leading candidates were the heart, liver, and brain; by Reid's time most had accepted the brain as being—somehow—the seat of the mind.

mines to be impossible? I answer, 1st, that when a man says, he has pain in his toe, he is perfectly understood, both by himself, and those who hear him. This is all that he intends. He really feels what he and all men call a pain in the toe; and there is no deception in the matter. Whether

660 therefore there be any impropriety in the phrase or not, is of no consequence in common life. It answers all the ends of speech, both to the speaker and the hearers.

In all languages, there are phrases which have a distinct meaning; while, at the same time, there may be something in the structure of them that disagrees with the analogy of grammar, or with the principles of philosophy. And the reason is, because language is not made either

665 by grammarians or philosophers. Thus we speak of feeling pain, as if pain was something distinct from the feeling of it. We speak of a pain coming and going, and removing from one place to another.

removing: moving

Such phrases are meant by those who use them in a sense that is neither obscure nor false. But the philosopher puts them into his alembic, reduces them to their first principles, draws out of them a sense that was never meant, and so imagines that he has discovered an error of the vulgar.

> alembic: (from Arabic, "still") laboratory apparatus used for distillation

I observe, 2dly, that when we consider the sensation of pain by itself, without any respect to its cause, we cannot say with propriety, that the toe is either the place, or the subject of it. But it ought to be remembered, that when we speak of pain in the toe, the sensation is combined in our thought, with the cause of it, which really is in the toe. The cause and the effect are combined in one complex notion, and the same name serves for both. It is the business of the philosopher to analyze this complex notion, and to give different names to its different ingredients. He gives the name of *pain* to the sensation only, and the name of *disorder* to the unknown cause of it. Then it is evident that the disorder only is in the toe, and that it would be an error to think that the pain is in it. But we ought not to ascribe this error to the vulgar, who never made the distinction, and who under the name of pain comprehend both the sensation and its cause.

Cases sometimes happen, which give occasion even to the vulgar to distinguish the painful sensation from the disorder which is the cause of it. A man who has had his leg cut off, many years after feels pain in a toe of that leg. The toe has now no existence; and he perceives easily, that the toe can neither be the place, nor the subject of the pain which he feels; yet it is the same feeling he used to have from a hurt in the toe; and if he did not know that his leg was cut off, it would give him the same immediate conviction of some hurt or disorder in the toe.

The same phenomenon may lead the philosopher in all cases, to distinguish sensation from perception. We say, that the man had a deceitful feeling, when he felt a pain in his toe after the leg was cut off; and we have a true meaning in saying so. But, if we will speak accurately, our sensations cannot be deceitful; they must be what we feel them to be, and can be nothing else. Where then lies the deceit? I answer, it lies not in the sensation, which is real, but in the seeming perception he had of a disorder in his toe. This perception, which nature had conjoined with the sensation, was in this instance fallacious.

The same reasoning may be applied to every phenomenon that can, with propriety, be called a deception of sense. As when one, who has the jaundice, sees a body yellow, which is really white; or when a man sees an object double, because his eyes are not both directed to it; in these, and other like cases, the sensations we have are real, and the deception is only in the perception which nature has annexed to them.

Nature has connected our perception of external objects with certain sensations. If the sensation is produced, the corresponding perception follows even when there is no object, and in that case is apt to deceive us. In like manner, nature has connected our sensations with certain impressions that are made upon the nerve and brain: and, when the impression is made, from whatever cause, the corresponding sensation and perception immediately follows. Thus, in the man who feels pain in his toe after the leg is cut off, the nerve that went to the toe, part

710 of which was cut off with the leg, had the same impression made upon the remaining part, which, in the natural state of his body, was caused by a hurt in the toe: and immediately this impression is followed by the sensation and perception which nature connected with it.

In like manner, if the same impressions, which are made at present upon my optic nerves by the objects before me, could be made in the dark, I apprehend that I should have the same sensations, and see the same objects which I now see. The impressions and sensations would 715 in such a case be real, and the perception only fallacious.

...

FOR DISCUSSION

1. In the context of Reid's discussion, what point of view or set of facts does "common sense" refer to?
2. What is an example of a perception without a corresponding sensation?
3. How would Reid explain a phrase such as "The stone feels cold?"
4. What is the role of learning in perception, according to Reid?
5. What is a "relative notion"? What are some examples other than those given by Reid?

Hermann von Helmholtz
(1821–1894)
Treatise on Physiological Optics (1867)

§26. Concerning the Perceptions in General

Few people master a science, and fewer master several sciences. Fewer still make lasting and vitally important contributions to each of them. Physiologists, mathematicians, psychologists, and physicists are all proud to call Helmholtz one of their own.

Helmholtz was born in Potsdam, where his father taught philology and philosophy at the gymnasium. As a student (at the same gymnasium) Helmholtz was most interested in physics, but to attend the university, he was obliged to switch to medicine in order to qualify for a government scholarship. Helmholtz enrolled at the Royal Friedrich-Wilhelm Institute of Medicine and Surgery in Berlin, but he spent as much time as he could reading mathematics and philosophy. When he graduated, in 1843, Helmholtz owed the next 10 years of his life to the Prussian government (a condition of the scholarship he had received), and was assigned as army doctor to a regiment at Potsdam.

Helmholtz continued to devote his spare time to his real interests, which appear to have been nearly everything other than medicine. His work in physiology and in physics led to his 1847 paper *Über die Erhaltung der Kraft* (On the Conservation of Energy), which other scientists immediately saw to be very important. Helmholtz was released from the rest of his indenture and was given the chair in physiology at the University of Königsberg.

Source: Helmholtz's Treatise on Physiological Optics, vol. 3, ch. 26. Translated from the Third German Edition by James P. C. Southall. Published by the Optical Society of America in 1925; reprinted in 1962 by Dover Publications.

The principle of conservation of energy, one of the foundations of modern physics, says that in a physical system energy can be transformed—from heat to motion, for example, or vice versa—but cannot be gained or lost. Helmholtz saw that living organisms can be seen as physical systems and further saw that this perspective has implications for understanding the nervous system. Previous generations of physiologists, including Helmholtz's teacher Johannes Müller, believed that the nerves worked by a principle called *vitalism,* that a nerve impulse represented the instantaneous passage along the nerve of some mysterious vital force. Helmholtz demonstrated that this view of nerve action could not be right. With a frog's leg in contact with a timing device, Helmholtz could electrically stimulate the leg's motor nerve; the leg would then twitch, thus stopping the timer. By stimulating the nerve at two different distances from the muscle and noting the difference in response time, Helmholtz was able to measure the speed of the nerve impulse (Helmholtz, 1850). This measurement showed that the impulse is not instantaneous, which in turn showed that the vitalist position was untenable, and cleared the way for a new physical concept of the nerve impulse.

In 1851 Helmholtz invented the ophthalmoscope, the device that is used to this day to examine the inside of the eye. The list goes on, but these examples suffice to show Helmholtz as a first-class thinker, a creative experimenter, and a gifted inventor.

Helmholtz's importance for psychology comes not only from his physiological achievements, but also from his work on the senses, which produced the massive *On the Sensations of Tone as a Physiological Basis for a Theory of Music* (1863) and the more massive *Treatise on Physiological Optics* (1867), from which the present reading is taken. Helmholtz matters not because he knew everything there was to know or because he wrote massive books, but because he was among the first to recognize that much of the perceptual process is unconscious and, more important, to see the significance of this fact.

In the first volume of the *Optics,* Helmholtz explains the anatomy of the eye and its optical characteristics. In the second, he deals with visual sensations, sensitivity, and color vision. Chapter 26 comes at the beginning of the third volume, which is devoted to visual perception. At the end of the chapter, Helmholtz adds a brief historical review of the problems he has discussed. We have moved it to the beginning, as it makes a good introduction to Helmholtz's arguments and helps to put his own contributions in their proper context.

T he earlier history of the theory of the sense-perceptions is practically the same as the history of philosophy, as given at the end of §17. The investigations of the physiologists of the seventeenth and eighteenth centuries generally did not go beyond the image on the retina, for they supposed that when it was formed, everything was settled. Hence they were little troubled by the questions as to why we see objects erect and why we see them single, in spite of two   5
inverted retinal images. Among philosophers Descartes (1637/1954, 1644/1985) was the first to take any deep interest in visual perceptions as related to the knowledge of his time. He considered the qualities of sensation as being essentially subjective, but he regarded the ideas of the quantitative relations of size, form, motion, position, duration, number of objects, etc., as something that could be correctly perceived objectively. However, in order to explain the cor-   10
rectness of these ideas, he assumes, as the idealistic philosophers did who came after him, a system of *innate ideas* which are in harmony with the things. This theory was subsequently developed in its most logical and purest form by Leibniz (1704/1951b).

Berkeley (1709/1948) made a profound study of the influence of memory on the visual perceptions and their concomitant inductive conclusions. He says concerning them that they take   15
place so quickly that we are not aware of them unless we are deliberately on the watch for them. It is true this empirical basis led him to assert that not only the qualities of sensation but the perceptions also were mainly merely internal processes having no correspondence with anything outside. What led him into making this false conclusion was the error contained in the proposition that the cause (the object perceived) must be of the same kind as its effect (the   20
idea), that is, must be a mental entity also, and not a real object.

In his theory of the human understanding, Locke (1690) denied the existence of innate ideas and attempted to establish an empirical basis for all understanding; but this attempt ended in Hume's (1748/1999) denying all possibility of objective knowledge.

The most essential step for putting the problem in its true light was taken by Kant   25
(1787/1934) in his *Critique of Pure Reason,* in which he derived all real content of knowledge from experience. But he made a distinction between this and whatever in the form of our apperceptions and ideas was conditioned by the peculiar ability of our mind. Pure thinking *a priori* can yield only formally correct propositions, which, while they may certainly appear to be absolutely binding as necessary laws of thought and imagination, are, however, of no real sig-   30
nificance for actuality; and hence they can never enable us to form any conclusion about facts of possible experience.

According to this view perception is recognized as an effect produced on our sensitive faculty by the object perceived; this effect, in its minuter determinations, being just as dependent on what causes the effect as on the nature of that on which the effect is produced. This point   35
of view was applied to the empirical relations especially by Johannes Müller in his theory of the Specific Energy of the Senses (Minkowski, 1911, pp. 129–152).

The subsequent idealistic systems of philosophy associated with the names of J. G. Fichte, Schelling and Hegel all emphasized the theory that idea is essentially dependent on the nature of the mind; thus neglecting the influence which the thing causing the effect has on the effect.   40
Consequently, their views have had slight influence on the theory of the sense-perceptions.

Kant had briefly represented space and time as given forms of all apperception, without going farther and investigating how much might be derived from experience in the more minute formation of individual apperceptions of space and time. This investigation was out-
45 side of his special work. Thus, for example, he regarded the geometrical axioms as being propo-sitions in space-apperception which were given to start with;—a view which is not at all settled yet. His lead was followed by Müller (1826) and the group of physiologists who tried to develop the *intuition theory* of space-apperception. Müller himself assumed that the retina might "sense" itself in its space-extension by virtue of an innate ability for it, and that the sen-
50 sations of the two retinas are fused together in this case. The one who has recently tried to carry out this view in its most logical form and to adapt it to newer discoveries is E. Hering (1861–64).

Prior to Müller, Steinbuch (1811) had tried to explain individual apperceptions of space by means of the movements of the eye and of the body. Among the philosophers, Herbart (1816, 1825), Lotze (1852, 1856), Waitz (1849) and Cornelius (1861, 1864) attacked the same problem.
55 From the empirical side, it was Wheatstone especially who, by inventing the stereoscope, gave a powerful incentive to the investigation of the influence of experience on our visual apper-ceptions. In addition to minor contributions which I myself have made to the solution of this problem in various works, attempts to give an *empirical* view may be found in the writings of Nagel (1861), Wundt (1862) and Classen (1862). In the succeeding chapters, more will be said
60 with reference to these investigations and the points of controversy.

[Chapter 26 begins here. —Eds.]

The sensations aroused by light in the nervous mechanism of vision enable us to form con-ceptions as to the existence, form and position of external objects. These ideas are called *visual perceptions.* In this third subdivision of Physiological Optics we must try to analyze the scientific
65 results which we have obtained concerning the conditions which give rise to visual perceptions.

. . .

The general rule determining the ideas of vision that are formed whenever an impression is made on the eye, with or without the aid of optical instruments, is that *such objects are always imagined as being present in the field of vision as would have to be there in order to produce the same impression on the nervous mechanism, the eyes being used under ordinary normal conditions.*
70 To employ an illustration which has been mentioned before, suppose that the eyeball is mechanically stimulated at the outer corner of the eye. Then we imagine that we see an appear-ance of light in front of us somewhere in the direction of the bridge of the nose. Under ordi-nary conditions of vision, when our eyes are stimulated by light coming from outside, if the region of the retina in the outer corner of the eye is to be stimulated, the light actually has to
75 enter the eye from the direction of the bridge of the nose. Thus, in accordance with the above rule, in a case of this kind we substitute a luminous object at the place mentioned in the field of view, although as a matter of fact the mechanical stimulus does not act on the eye from in front of the field of view nor from the nasal side of the eye, but, on the contrary, is exerted on the outer surface of the eyeball and more from behind. The general validity of the above rule
80 will be shown by many other instances that will appear in the following pages.

In the statement of this rule mention is made of the ordinary conditions of vision, when the visual organ is stimulated by light from outside; this outside light, coming from the opaque objects in its path that were the last to be encountered, and having reached the eye along rectilinear paths through an uninterrupted layer of air. This is what is meant here by the normal use of the organ of vision and the justification for using this term is that this mode of stimulation occurs in such an enormous majority of cases that all other instances where the paths of the rays of light are altered by reflections or refractions, or in which the stimulations are not produced by external light, may be regarded as rare exceptions. This is because the retina in the fundus of the firm eyeball is almost completely protected from the actions of all other stimuli and is not easily accessible to anything but external light.

85

90

fundus: the deepest or lowest part (from Latin fundus, bottom, as in fundamental); here, the back, inner lining of the eye

. . .

Thus it happens, that when the modes of stimulation of the organs of sense are unusual, incorrect ideas of objects are apt to be formed; which used to be described, therefore, as *illusions of the senses.* Obviously, in these cases there is nothing wrong with the activity of the organ of sense and its corresponding nervous mechanism which produces the illusion. Both of them have to act according to the laws that govern their activity once for all. It is rather simply an illusion in the judgment of the material presented to the senses, resulting in a false idea of it.

95

100

The psychic activities that lead us to infer that there in front of us at a certain place there is a certain object of a certain character, are generally not conscious activities, but unconscious ones. In their result they are equivalent to a *conclusion,* to the extent that the observed action on our senses enables us to form an idea as to the possible cause of this action; although, as a matter of fact, it is invariably simply the nervous stimulations that are perceived directly, that is, the actions, but never the external objects themselves. . . .

105

These unconscious conclusions derived from sensation are equivalent in their consequences to the so-called *conclusions from analogy.* Inasmuch as in an overwhelming majority of cases, whenever the parts of the retina in the outer corner of the eye are stimulated, it has been found to be due to external light coming into the eye from the direction of the bridge of the nose, the inference we make is that it is so in every new case whenever this part of the retina is stimulated; just as we assert that every single individual now living will die, because all previous experience has shown that all men who were formerly alive have died. But, moreover, just because they are not free acts of conscious thought, these unconscious conclusions from analogy are irresistible, and the effect of them cannot be overcome by a better understanding of the real relations. It may be ever so clear how we get an idea of a luminous phenomenon in the field of vision when pressure is exerted on the eye; and yet we cannot get rid of the conviction that this appearance of light is actually there at the given place in the visual field; and we cannot seem to comprehend that there is a luminous phenomenon at the place where the retina is stimulated. It is the same way in case of all the images that we see in optical instruments.

110

115

120

On the other hand, there are numerous illustrations of fixed and inevitable associations of ideas due to frequent repetition, even when they have no natural connection, but are dependent merely on some conventional arrangement, as, for example, the connection between the written letters of a word and its sound and meaning. Still to many physiologists and psychologists the connection between the sensation and the conception of the object usually appears to be so rigid and obligatory that they are not much disposed to admit that, to a considerable extent at least, it depends on acquired experience, that is, on psychic activity. On the contrary, they have endeavoured to find some mechanical mode of origin for this connection through the agency of imaginary organic structures. With regard to this question, all those experiences are of much significance which show how the judgment of the senses may be modified by experience and by training derived under various circumstances, and may be adapted to the new conditions. Thus, persons may learn in some measure to utilize details of the sensation which otherwise would escape notice and not contribute to obtaining any idea of the object. On the other hand, too, this new habit may acquire such a hold that when the individual in question is back again in the old original normal state, he may be liable to illusions of the senses.

Facts like these show the widespread influence that experience, training and habit have on our perceptions. But how far their influence really does extend, it would perhaps be impossible to say precisely at present. Little enough is definitely known about infants and very young animals, and the interpretation of such observations as have been made on them is extremely doubtful. Besides, no one can say that infants are entirely without experience and practice in tactile sensations and bodily movements. Accordingly, the rule given above has been stated in a form which does not anticipate the decision of this question. It merely expresses what the result is. And so it can be accepted even by those who have entirely different opinions as to the way ideas originate concerning objects in the external world.

Another general characteristic property of our sense-perceptions is, that we are not in the habit of observing our sensations accurately, except as they are useful in enabling us to recognize external objects. On the contrary, we are wont to disregard all those parts of the sensations that are of no importance so far as external objects are concerned. ... A common experience, illustrative of this sort of thing, is for a person who has some ocular trouble that impairs his vision to become suddenly aware of the so-called mouches volantes in his visual field, although the causes of this phenomenon have been there in the vitreous humor all his life. Yet now he will be firmly persuaded that these corpuscles have developed as the result of his ocular ailment, although the truth simply is

mouches volantes: (French, "flying flies") Commonly known as *floaters,* these are small blobs, specks, or threads in the visual image caused by debris "floating" in the eye's vitreous body. Because the debris moves with the eye, it is not possible to look directly at it, but because it drifts (slowly) through the vitreous, the retina does not cancel out its image. Most people have some floaters. The easiest way to see them is to lie on your back, so they will float toward the fovea, and look at a bright uniform background, such as a blue sky or a white ceiling.

that, owing to his ailment, the patient has been paying more attention to visual phenomena. No doubt, also, there are cases where one eye has gradually become blind, and yet the patient has continued to go about for an indefinite time without noticing it, until he happened one day to close the good eye without closing the other, and so noticed the blindness of that eye.[1]   165

double images: Hold up an index finger at arm's length, directly in front of you, and the other index finger halfway between your nose and your first finger. With both eyes open, focus on the nail of the far finger. You will see two images of the near finger. Now focus on the nail of the near finger. You will see two images of the far finger.

When a person's attention is directed for the first time to the double images in binocular vision, he is usually greatly astonished to think that he had never noticed them before, especially when he reflects that the only objects he has ever seen single were those few that happened at the moment to be about as far from his eyes as the point of fixation. The great majority of objects, comprising all those that were farther or nearer than this point, were all seen double.   170   175

Accordingly, the first thing we have to learn is to pay heed to our individual sensations. Ordinarily we do so merely in case of those sensations that enable us to find out about the world around us. In the ordinary affairs of life the sensations have no other importance for us. Subjective sensations are of interest chiefly for scientific investigations only. If they happen to be noticed in the ordinary activity of the senses, they merely distract the attention. Thus while we may attain an extraordinary degree of delicacy and precision in objective observation, we not only fail to do so in subjective observations, but indeed we acquire the faculty in large measure of overlooking them and of forming our opinions of objects independently of them, even when they are so pronounced that they might easily be noticed.   180   185

The most universal sign by which subjective visual phenomena can be identified appears to be by the way they accompany the movement of the eye over the field of view. Thus, the after-images, the *mouches volantes,* the blind spot, and the "luminous dust" of the dark field all participate in the motions of the eye, and coincide successively with the various stationary objects in the visual field. On the other hand, if the same phenomena recur again invariably at the same places in the visual field, they may be regarded as being objective and as being connected with external bodies. This is the case with contrast phenomena produced by after-images.   190

An *after-image* is what you see, for example, after looking at a light bulb. No matter where you look, the "image" of the bulb remains in the same part of your visual field.

The *blind spot* is a region of the retina where the axons of the ganglion cells converge and exit the eyeball. There are no receptors here.

---

[1] Nearly everybody has a dominant eye, which governs the other eye; and in which the vision is superior to that in the other eye. But not many persons are aware of the fact. (J.P.C.S.)

Luminous dust is Helmholtz's description of visual experience in the complete absence of light:

> [T]he field of vision of a healthy human being is never entirely free from appearances of this kind which have been called the *chaotic light* or *luminous dust of the dark visual field*. It plays such an important part in many phenomena, like after-images, for example, that we shall call it the *self-light* or *intrinsic light* of the retina. When the eyes are closed, and the dark field is attentively examined, often at first after-images of external objects that were previously visible will still be perceived. . . . This effect is soon superseded by an irregular feebly illuminated field with numerous fluctuating spots of light, often similar in appearance to the small branches of the blood-vessels or to scattered stems of moss and leaves. . . . A quite common appearance seems to be what Goethe describes as floating cloud-ribbons. . . . The background of the visual field, on which these phenomena are projected is never entirely black; and alternate fluctuations of bright and dark are visible there, frequently occurring in rhythm with the movements of respiration. . . . Moreover, with every movement of the eyes or eyelids, and with every change of accommodation, there are accompanying variations of this "luminous dust." (1867/1962, Vol. 2, pp. 12–13)

A simple after-image contrast phenomenon can be induced as follows: Find a smooth, flat, well-illuminated surface that is all one color. Stare at the center of the surface for 30–60 seconds, and then put a small scrap of white or gray paper on the surface. You will see a negative after-image on the paper: If the surface is red, the paper will look green, and vice versa; if the surface is blue, the paper will look yellow, and vice versa. Helmholtz's point here is that this after-image (the contrast phenomenon), unlike the light-bulb after-image, is located wherever you put the white paper, not wherever you look.

195   The same difficulty that we have in observing subjective sensations, that is, sensations aroused by internal causes, occurs also in trying to analyze the compound sensations, invariably excited in the same connection by any simple object, and to resolve them into their separate components. In such cases experience shows us how to recognize a compound aggregate of sensations as being the sign of a simple object. Accustomed to consider the sensation-complex

200   as a connected whole, generally we are not able to perceive the separate parts of it without external help and support. Many illustrations of this kind will be seen in the following pages. For instance the perception of the apparent direction of an object from the eye depends on the combination of those sensations by which we estimate the adjustment of the eye, and on being able to distinguish those parts of the retina where light falls from those parts where it does not

205   fall. The perception of the solid form of an object of three dimensions is the result of the combination of two different perspective views in the two eyes. The gloss of a surface, which is apparently a simple effect, is due to differences of colouring or brightness in the images of it in the two eyes. These facts were ascertained by theory and may be verified by suitable experiments. But usually it is very difficult, if not impossible, to discover them by direct observation and analysis of the sensations alone. Even with sensations that are much more involved and always associ-

210   ated with frequently recurring complex objects, the oftener the same combination recurs, and

the more used we have become to regarding the sensation as the normal sign of the real nature of the object, the more difficult it will be to analyze the sensation by observation alone. By way of illustration, it is a familiar experience that the colours of a landscape come out much more brilliantly and definitely by looking at them with the head on one side or upside down than they do when the head is in the ordinary upright position. In the usual mode of observation all we try to do is to judge correctly the objects as such. We know that at a certain distance green surfaces appear a little different in hue. We get in the habit of overlooking this difference, and learn to identify the altered green of distant meadows and trees with the corresponding colour of nearer objects. In the case of very distant objects like distant ranges of mountains, little of the colour of the body is left to be seen, because it is mainly shrouded in the colour of the illuminated air. This vague blue-grey colour, bordered above by the clear blue of the sky or the red-yellow of the sunset glow, and below by the vivid green of meadows and forests, is very subject to variations by contrast. To us it is the vague and variable colour of distance. The difference in it may, perhaps, be more noticeable sometimes and with some illuminations than at other times. But we do not determine its true nature, because it is not ascribed to any definite object. We are simply aware of its variable nature. But the instant we take an unusual position, and look at the landscape with the head under one arm, let us say, or between the legs, it all appears like a flat picture; partly on account of the strange position of the image in the eye, and partly because, as we shall see presently, the binocular judgment of distance becomes less accurate. It may even happen that with the head upside down the clouds have the correct perspective, whereas the objects on the earth appear like a painting on a vertical surface, as the clouds in the sky usually do. At the same time the colours lose their associations also with near or far objects, and confront us now purely in their own peculiar differences (Rood, 1861). Then we have no difficulty in recognizing that the vague blue-grey of the far distance may indeed be a fairly saturated violet, and that the green of the vegetation blends imperceptibly through blue-green and blue into this violet, etc. This whole difference seems to me to be due to the fact that the colours have ceased to be distinctive signs of objects for us, and are considered merely as being different sensations. Consequently, we take in better their peculiar distinctions without being distracted by other considerations.

215
220
225
230
235
240
245

> *saturated:* A color with no white mixed in is said to be saturated; as more white is added the color becomes less saturated. For example, in bright sunshine a flower garden produces fairly saturated greens, blues, yellows, and reds; in fog, or at a great distance (or both), the same garden yields relatively unsaturated greens, blues, yellows, and reds.

The connection between the sensations and external objects may interfere very much with the perception of their simplest relations. A good illustration of this is the difficulty about perceiving the double images of binocular vision when they can be regarded as being images of one and the same external object.

In the same way we may have similar experiences with other kinds of sensations. The sensation of the *timbre* of a sound, as I have shown elsewhere (Helmholtz, 1863), consists of a series of sensations of its partial tones (fundamental and harmonics); but it is exceedingly difficult to

250

analyze the compound sensation of the sound into these elementary components. The tactile sensation of wetness is composed of that of coldness and that of smoothness of surface. Consequently, on inadvertently touching a cold piece of smooth metal, we often get the impression of having touched something wet. Many other illustrations of this sort might be adduced. They all indicate that we are exceedingly well trained in finding out by our sensations the objective nature of the objects around us, but that we are completely unskilled in observing the sensations *per se;* and that the practice of associating them with things outside of us actually prevents us from being distinctly conscious of the pure sensations.

Consequently, it may often be rather hard to say how much of our apperceptions *(Anschauungen)* as derived by the sense of sight is due directly to sensation, and how much of them, on the other hand, is due to experience and training. The main point of controversy between various investigators in this territory is connected also with this difficulty. Some are disposed to concede to the influence of experience as much scope as possible, and to derive from it especially all notion of space. This view may be called the *empirical theory (empiristische Theorie).* Others, of course, are obliged to admit the influence of experience in the case of certain classes of perceptions; still with respect to certain elementary apperceptions that occur uniformly in the case of all observers, they believe it is necessary to assume a system of innate apperceptions that are not based on experience, especially with respect to space-relations. In contradistinction to the former view, this may perhaps be called the *intuition theory (nativistische Theorie)* of the sense-perceptions.

In my opinion the following fundamental principles should be kept in mind in this discussion.

Let us restrict the word *idea (Vorstellung)* to mean the image of visual objects as retained in the memory, without being accompanied by any present sense-impressions; and use the term *apperception (Anschauung)* to mean a perception *(Wahrnehmung)* when it is accompanied by the sense-impressions in question. The term *immediate perception (Perzeption)* may then be employed to denote an apperception of this nature in which there is no element whatever that is not the result of direct sensations, that is, an apperception such as might be derived without any recollection of previous experience. Obviously, therefore, one and the same apperception may be accompanied by the corresponding sensations in very different measure. Thus idea and immediate perception may be combined in the apperception in the most different proportions.[2]

A person in a familiar room which is brightly lighted by the sun gets an apperception that is abundantly accompanied by very vivid sensations. In the same room in the evening twilight he will not be able to recognize any objects except the brighter ones, especially the windows. But whatever he does actually recognize will be so intermingled with his recollections of the furniture that he can still move about in the room with safety and locate articles he is trying to

---

[2] It is very difficult to find the precise English equivalents for these metaphysical terms, which will prove satisfactory to everybody. And it may not be quite possible to restrict the English word "idea," for example, to the definition here given. It is doubtful whether the author himself is scrupulously careful throughout the remainder of this work to distinguish these shades of meaning always exactly. (J.P.C.S.)

find, even when they are only dimly visible. These images would be utterly insufficient to enable him to recognize the objects without some previous acquaintance with them. Finally, 290 he may be in the same room in complete darkness, and still be able to find his way about in it without making mistakes, by virtue of the visual impressions formerly obtained. Thus, by continually reducing the material that appeals to the senses, the perceptual-image (*Anschauungsbild*) can ultimately be traced back to the pure memory-image (*Vorstellungsbild*) and may gradually pass into it. In proportion as there is less and less material appeal to the 295 senses, a person's movements will, of course, become more and more uncertain, and his apperception less and less accurate. Still there will be no peculiar abrupt transition, but sensation and memory will continually supplement each other, only in varying degrees.

But even when we look around a room of this sort flooded with sunshine, a little reflection shows us that under these conditions too a large part of our perceptual-image may be due to 300 factors of memory and experience. The fact that we are accustomed to the perspective distortions of pictures of parallelepipeds and to the form of the shadows they cast has much to do with the estimation of the shape and dimensions of 305 the room, as will be seen hereafter. Looking at the room with one eye shut, we think we see it just as distinctly and definitely as with both eyes. And yet we should get exactly the same view in case every point in the room were shifted arbitrarily to 310 a different distance from the eye, provided they all remained on the same lines of sight.

> A *parallelepiped* is a solid figure with six faces; each face is a parallelogram and opposite faces are parallel to one another. The most common parallelepipeds, which are probably what Helmholtz has in mind, are those with right angles: books, bricks, boxes, boards, and the like.

Thus in a case like this we are really considering an extremely multiplex phenomenon of sense; but still we ascribe a perfectly definite explanation to it, and it is by no means easy to realize that the monocular image of such a familiar object necessarily means a much more meagre perception than would be obtained with both 315 eyes. Thus too it is often hard to tell whether or not untrained observers inspecting stereoscopic views really notice the peculiar illusion produced by the instrument.

> A *stereoscopic view* is one in which the two eyes are shown slightly different views of the same scene, as in a Viewmaster or a 3-D movie or a magic eye picture. The *peculiar illusion* Helmholtz refers to is simply the perception of depth produced by a stereoscopic view.

We see, therefore, how in a case of this kind 320 reminiscences of previous experiences act in conjunction with present sensations to produce a perceptual image (*Anschauungsbild*) which imposes itself on our faculty of perception with overwhelming power, without our being conscious of how much of it is due to memory and 325 how much to present perception.

Still more remarkable is the influence of the comprehension of the sensations in certain cases, especially with dim illumination, in which a visual impression may be misunderstood at first, by not knowing how to attribute the correct depth-dimensions; as when a distant light, for example,

330   is taken for a near one, or *vice versa.* Suddenly it dawns on us what it is, and immediately, under the influence of the correct comprehension, the correct perceptual image also is developed in its full intensity. Then we are unable to revert to the previous imperfect apperception.

This is very common especially with complicated stereoscopic drawings of forms of crystals and other objects which come out in perfect clearness of perception the moment we once suc-
335   ceed in getting the correct impression.

Similar experiences have happened to everybody, proving that the elements in the sense-perceptions that are derived from experience are just as powerful as those that are derived from present sensations. All observers who have thoroughly investigated the theory of the sense-perceptions, even those who were disposed to allow experience as little scope as pos-
340   sible, have always admitted this.

Hence, at all events it must be conceded that, even in what appears to the adult as being direct apperception of the senses, possibly a number of single factors may be involved which are really the product of experience; although at the time it is difficult to draw the line between them.

Now in my opinion we are justified by our previous experiences in stating that no indu-
345   bitable present sensation can be abolished and overcome by an act of the intellect; and no matter how clearly we recognize that it has been produced in some anomalous way, still the illusion does not disappear by comprehending the process. The attention may be diverted from sensations, particularly if they are feeble and habitual; but in noting those relations in the external world, that are associated with these sensations, we are obliged to observe the
350   sensations themselves. Thus we may be unmindful of the temperature-sensation of our skin when it is not very keen, or of the contact-sensations produced by our clothing, as long as we are occupied with entirely different matters. But just as soon as we stop to think whether it is warm or cold, we are not in the position to convert the feeling of warmth into that of coldness; maybe because we know that it is due to strenuous exertion and not to the tem-
355   perature of the surrounding air. In the same way the apparition of light when pressure is exerted on the eyeball cannot be made to vanish simply by comprehending better the nature of the process, supposing the attention is directed to the field of vision and not, say, to the ear or the skin.

On the other hand, it may also be that we are
360   not in the position to isolate an impression of sensation, because it involves the composite sense-symbol of an external object. However, in this case the correct comprehension of the object shows that the sensation in question has been perceived
365   and used by the consciousness.

My conclusion is, that nothing in our sense-perceptions can be recognized as sensation which can be overcome in the perceptual image and converted into its opposite by factors that are
370   demonstrably due to experience.

> *composite sense-symbol:* The complete set of sensory events occasioned by a given object. For example, we may not be able to separate the red-sensation of an apple from its weight-sensation in our hand, but, says Helmholtz, the fact that we correctly perceive the thing as an apple (rather than, say, a painted lead model of an apple) means that the sensations nevertheless occurred and were available to the process responsible for our perception of an apple.

Whatever, therefore, can be overcome by factors of experience, we must consider as being itself the product of experience and training. By observing this rule, we shall find that it is merely the qualities of the sensation that are to be considered as real, pure sensation; the great majority of space-apperceptions, however, being the product of experience and training.

Still it does not follow that apperceptions, which persist in spite of our better conscious   375
insight and continue as illusions, might not be due to experience and training. Our knowledge of the changes of colour produced in distant objects by the haziness of the atmosphere, of perspective distortions, and of shadow is undoubtedly a matter of experience. And yet in a good landscape picture we shall get the perfect visual impression of the distance and the solid form of the buildings in it, in spite of knowing that it is all depicted on canvas.   380

. . . In this matter we must remember, as was intimated above, that the sensations are interpreted just as they arise when they are stimulated in the normal way, and when the organ of sense is used normally.

We are not simply passive to the impressions that are urged on us, but we *observe,* that is, we adjust our organs in those conditions that enable them to distinguish the impressions most   385
accurately. Thus, in considering an involved object, we accommodate both eyes as well as we can, and turn them so as to focus steadily the precise point on which our attention is fixed, that is, so as to get an image of it in the fovea of each eye; and then we let our eyes traverse all the noteworthy points of the object one after another. If we are interested in the general shape of the object and are trying to get as good an idea as we can of its relative dimensions, we assume   390
a position such that, without having to turn the head, we can survey the whole surface, enabling us at the same time to view as symmetrically as possible those dimensions we wish to compare. Thus, in looking at an object, as, for example, a building with prominent horizontal and vertical lines, we like to stand opposite to it with the centres of rotation of the two eyes in a horizontal line. This position of the eyes can be controlled at any moment by separating   395
the double images; which in the case mentioned here are in the same horizontal plane.

Unquestionably, our reason for choosing this definite mode of seeing is because in this way we can observe and compare most accurately; and, consequently, in this so-called *normal* use of the eyes we learn best how to compare our sensations with the reality. And so we obtain also the most correct and most accurate perceptions by this method.   400

But if, from necessity or on purpose, we employ a different mode of looking at objects, that is, if we view them merely indirectly or without focusing both eyes on them, or without surveying them all over, or if we hold the head in some unusual position, then we shall not be able to have as accurate apperceptions as when the eyes are used in the normal fashion. Nor are we so well trained in interpreting what we see under such circumstances as in the other case.   405
Hence there is more scope for interpretation, although, as a rule, we are not clearly aware of this uncertainty in the explanation of our sense-perceptions. When we see an object in front of us, we are obliged to assign it to some definite place in space. We cannot think of it as having some dubious intermediate position between two different places in space. Without any recollections coming to our aid, we are wont to interpret the phenomenon as it would have to   410
be interpreted if we had received the same impression in the normal and most accurate mode

of observation. Thus certain illusions enter into the perception, unless we concentrate our eyes on the objects under observation, or when the objects are in the peripheral part of the visual field, or if the head is held to one side, or if we do not focus the object with both eyes at once.

. . .

415   Thus far the sensations have been described as being simply *symbols* for the relations in the external world. They have been denied every kind of similarity or equivalence to the things they denote. Here we touch on the much disputed point as to how far our ideas agree in the main with their objects; that is, whether they are true or false, as one might say. Some have asserted that there is such an agreement, and others have denied it. In favour of it, a *pre-established har-*
420   *mony* between nature and mind was assumed. Or it was maintained that there was an *identity* of nature and mind, by regarding nature as the product of the activity of a general mind; the human mind being supposed to be an emanation from it. The *intuition theory* of space-apperceptions is connected with these views to the extent that, by some innate mechanism and a certain pre-established harmony, it admits of the origin of perceptual images that are supposed
425   to correspond with reality, although in a rather imperfect fashion.

Or else the agreement between ideas and their objects was denied, the ideas being explained therefore as illusions. Consequently, it was necessary to deny also the possibility of all knowledge of any objects whatsoever. This was the attitude of certain so-called "sensational" philosophers in England in the eighteenth century. However, it is not my purpose
430   here to undertake an analysis of the opinions of the various philosophical schools on this question. That would be much too extensive a task in this place. I shall confine myself therefore merely to inquiring what I think should be the attitude of an investigator toward these controversies.

Our apperceptions and ideas are *effects* wrought on our nervous system and our con-
435   sciousness by the objects that are thus apprehended and conceived. Each effect, as to its nature, quite necessarily depends both on the nature of what causes the effect and on that of the person on whom the effect is produced. To expect to obtain an idea which would reproduce the nature of the thing conceived, that is, which would be true in an absolute sense, would mean to expect an effect which would be perfectly independent of the nature of the
440   thing on which the effect was produced; which would be an obvious absurdity. Our human ideas, therefore, and all ideas of any conceivable intelligent creature, must be images of objects whose mode is essentially co-dependent on the nature of the consciousness which has the idea, and is conditioned also by its idiosyncrasies.

In my opinion, therefore, there can be no possible sense in speaking of any other truth of
445   our ideas except of a *practical* truth. Our ideas of things *cannot* be anything but symbols, natural signs for things which we learn how to use in order to regulate our movements and actions. Having learned correctly how to read those symbols, we are enabled by their help to adjust our actions so as to bring about the desired result; that is, so that the expected new sensations will arise. Not only is there *in reality* no other comparison at all between ideas and things—all the
450   schools are agreed about this—but any other mode of comparison is entirely *unthinkable* and has no sense whatever. This latter consideration is the conclusive thing, and must be grasped

in order to escape from the labyrinth of conflicting opinions. To ask whether the idea I have of a table, its form, strength, colour, weight, etc., is true *per se,* apart from any practical use I can make of this idea, and whether it corresponds with the real thing, or is false and due to an illusion, has just as much sense as to ask whether a certain musical note is red, yellow, or blue. Idea   455
and the thing conceived evidently belong to two entirely different worlds, which no more admit of being compared with each other than colours and musical tones or than the letters of a book and the sound of the word they denote.

Were there any sort of similarity of correspondence between the idea in the head of a person *A* and the thing to which the idea belongs, another intelligent person *B,* conceiving both the   460
thing itself and *A's* idea of it, according to the same laws, might be able to find some similarity between them or at least to suppose so; because the same sort of thing represented (conceived) in the same way would have to give the same kinds of images (ideas). Now I ask, what similarity can be imagined between the process in the brain that is concomitant with the idea of a table and the table itself? Is the form of the table to be supposed to be outlined by elec-   465
tric currents? And when the person with the idea has the idea that he is walking around the table, must the person then be outlined by electric currents? Perspective projections of the external world in the hemispheres of the brain (as they are supposed to be) are evidently not sufficient for representing the idea of a bodily object. And granted that a keen imagination is not frightened away by these and similar hypotheses, such an electrical reproduction of the   470
table in the brain would be simply another bodily object to be perceived, but no idea of the table. However, it is not simply persons with materialistic opinions who try to refute the proposed statement, but also persons with idealistic views. And for the latter I should think the argument would be still more forcible. What possible similarity can there be between the idea, some modification of the incorporeal mind that has no extension in space, and the body of the   475
table that occupies space? As far as I am aware, the idealistic philosophers have never once investigated even a single hypothesis or imagination in order to show this connection. And by the very nature of this view it is something that cannot be investigated at all.

In the next place as to the *properties* of objects in the external world, a little reflection reveals that all properties attributable to them may be said to be simply *effects* exerted by them either   480
on our senses or on other natural objects. Colour, sound, taste, smell, temperature, smoothness, and firmness are properties of the first sort, and denote effects on our organs of sense. Smoothness and firmness denote the degree of resistance either to the gliding contact or pressure of the hand. But other natural bodies may be employed instead of the hand. And the same thing is true in testing other mechanical properties such as elasticity and weight. Chemical   485
properties are described by certain reactions, that is, by effects exerted by one natural body on others. It is the same way with any other physical property of a body, optical, electrical, or magnetic. In every case we have to do with the mutual relations between various bodies and with the effects depending on the forces that different bodies exert on each other. For all natural forces are such as are exerted by one body on others. When we try to think of mere matter with-   490
out force, it is void of properties likewise, except as to its different distribution in space and as to its motion. All properties of bodies in nature are manifested therefore simply by being so

situated as to interact with other bodies of nature or with our organs of sense. But as such interaction may occur at any time, particularly too as it may be produced by us voluntarily at any
495   moment, and as then we see invariably the peculiar sort of interaction occurring, we attribute
to the objects a permanent capacity for such effects which is always ready to become effective.
This permanent capacity is a so-called characteristic *property*.

The result is that in point of fact the characteristic *properties* of natural objects, in spite of this
name, do not denote something that is peculiar to the individual object by itself, but invariably
500   imply some relation to a second object (including our organs of sense). The kind of effect must,
of course, depend always on the peculiarities both of the body producing it and of the body
on which it is produced. As to this there is never any doubt even for an instant, provided we
have in mind those properties of bodies that are manifested when two bodies belonging to the
external world react on each other, as in the case of chemical reactions. But in the case of prop-
505   erties depending on the mutual relations between things and our organs of sense, people have
always been disposed to forget that here too we are concerned with the reaction toward a special reagent, namely, our own nervous system; and that colour, smell, and taste, and feeling of
warmth or cold are also effects quite essentially
depending on the nature of the organ that is
510   affected. Doubtless, the reactions of natural
objects to our senses are those that are most frequently and most generally perceived. For both
our welfare and convenience they are of the most
powerful importance. The reagent by which we
515   have to test them is something we are endowed with by nature, but that does not make any
difference in the connection.

> The properties of objects that Helmholtz
> discusses here are those that some earlier
> writers had called *secondary properties*. (See,
> e.g., 2.2.)

Hence there is no sense in asking whether vermilion as we see it, is really red, or whether this is
simply an illusion of the senses. The sensation of red is the normal reaction of normally formed eyes
to light reflected from vermilion. A person who is red-blind will see vermilion as black or as a dark
520   grey-yellow. This too is the correct reaction for an
eye formed in the special way his is. All he has to
know is that his eye is simply formed differently
from that of other persons. In itself the one sensation
is not more correct and not more false than the
525   other, although those who call this substance red
are in the large majority. In general, the red colour of
vermilion exists merely in so far as there are eyes
which are constructed like those of most people.
Persons who are red-blind have just as much right to
530   consider that a characteristic property of vermilion is

> We use *vermilion* primarily to refer to a
> certain brilliant shade of orange-red (also
> called *China red*), but the word also
> designates the pigment originally used to
> create this color. The pigment is made by
> crushing *cinnabar*, a naturally occurring
> form of mercury sulfide mined by the
> Romans as a source of mercury.

that of being black. As a matter of fact, we should not speak of the light reflected from vermilion
as being red, because it is not red except for certain types of eyes. When we speak of the properties of bodies with reference to other bodies in the external world, we do not neglect to name also

the body with respect to which the property exists. Thus we say that lead is soluble in nitric acid, but not in sulphuric acid. Were we to say simply that lead is soluble, we should notice at once that the statement is incomplete, and the question would have to be asked immediately, Soluble in what? But when we say that vermilion is red, it is implicitly understood that it is red for our eyes and for other people's eyes supposed to be made like ours. We think this does not need to be mentioned, and so we neglect to do so, and can be misled into thinking that red is a property belonging to vermilion or to the light reflected from it, entirely independently of our organs of sense. The statement that the waves of light reflected from vermilion have a certain length is something different. That is true entirely without reference to the special nature of our eye. Then we are thinking simply of relations that exist between the substance and the various systems of waves in the aether.

> *aether* (or *ether*): Many earlier physical theories postulated an ether, a distinct form of matter responsible for carrying such things as electrical and magnetic forces, and thus the electromagnetic waves (which we experience as light) that Helmholtz refers to. In the 20th century physicists have generally found ethers to be superfluous concepts. Ether is an example of what Wundt (1.3) calls a *supplementary concept*.

The only respect in which there can be a real agreement between our perceptions and the reality is the time-sequence of the events with their various peculiarities. Simultaneity, sequence, the regular recurrence of simultaneity or sequence, may occur likewise in the sensations as well as in the events. The external events, like their perceptions, proceed in time; and so the temporal relations of the latter may be the faithful reproduction of the temporal relations of the former. The sensation of thunder in the ear succeeds the sensation of lightning in the eye, just in the same way as the sound vibrations in the air due to the electrical discharge reach the place where the observer is later than the vibrations of the luminiferous aether. Yet here it certainly should be noted that the time-sequence of the sensations is not quite a faithful reproduction of the time-sequence of the external events, inasmuch as the transmission from the organs of sense to the brain takes time, and in fact a different time for different organs. Moreover, in case of the eye and the ear, the time has to be added that it takes light and sound to reach the organ. Thus at present we see the fixed stars as they were various long periods of years ago.

As to the representation of space-relations, there certainly is something of this sort in the peripheral nerve terminals in the eye and to a certain extent in the tactile skin, but still only in a limited way; for the eye gives only perspective surface-images, and the hand reproduces the objective area on the surface of a body by shaping itself to it as congruently as possible. A direct image of a portion of space of three dimensions is not afforded either by the eye or by the hand. It is only by comparing the images in the two eyes, or by moving the body with respect to the hand, that the idea of solid bodies is obtained. Now since the brain itself has three dimensions, of course, there is still another conceivable possibility, and that is to fancy by what mechanism in the brain itself images of three dimensions can arise from external objects in space. But I cannot see any necessity for such an assumption nor even any probability for it. The idea of a body in space, of a table, for instance, involves a quantity of separate observations. It comprises the whole series of images which this table would present to me in looking at it from different sides and at different distances; besides the whole series of tactile impressions that would be obtained by touching the surface at various places in succession. Such an idea of a single individual body is, therefore, in fact a *conception (Begriff)* which grasps, and includes an infinite number of single, successive apperceptions, that can all be deduced from it; just as the species "table" includes all individual tables and expresses their common peculiarities. The idea of a single individual table which I carry in my mind is correct and exact, provided I can deduce from it correctly the precise sensations I shall have when my eye and my hand are brought into this or that definite relation with respect to the table. Any other sort of similarity between such an idea and the body about which the idea exists, I do not know how to conceive. One is the mental symbol of the other. The kind of symbol was not chosen by me arbitrarily, but was forced on me by the nature of my organ of sense and of my mind. This is what distinguishes this sign-language of our ideas from the arbitrary phonetic signs and alphabetical characters that we use in speaking and writing. A writing is correct when he who knows how to read it forms correct ideas by it. And so the idea of a thing is correct for him who knows how to determine correctly from it in advance what sense-impressions he will get from the thing when he places himself in definite external relations to it. Incidentally, it does not matter at all what sort of mental symbols we employ, provided they constitute a sufficiently varied and ordered system. Nor does it matter either how the words of a language sound, provided there are enough of them, with sufficient means of denoting their grammatical relations to one another.

On this view of the matter, we must be on our guard against saying that all our ideas of things are consequently *false,* because they are not *equal* to the things themselves, and that hence we are not able to know anything as to the *true nature* of things. That they cannot be equal to things, is in the nature of knowledge. Ideas are merely pictures of things. Every image is the image of a thing merely for him who knows how to read it, and who is enabled by the aid of the image to form an idea of the thing. Every image is similar to its object in one respect, and dissimilar in all others, whether it be a painting, a statue, the musical or dramatic representation of a mental mood, etc. Thus the ideas of the external world are images of the regular sequence of natural events, and if they are formed correctly according to the laws of our thinking, and we are able by our actions to translate them back into reality again, the ideas we have are also the *only true* ones for our mental capacity. All others would be false.

In my opinion, it is a mistake, therefore, to try to find pre-established harmony between the laws of thought and those of nature, an identity between nature and mind, or whatever we may call it. A system of signs may be more or less perfect and convenient. Accordingly, it will be more or less easy to employ, more exact in denoting or more inexact, just as is the case with different languages. But otherwise each system can be adapted to the case more or less well. If there were not a number of similar natural objects in the world, our faculty of forming shades of conception would indeed not be of any use to us. Were there no solid bodies, our geometrical faculties would necessarily remain undeveloped and unused, just as the physical eye would not be of any service to us in a world where there was no light. If in this sense anybody wishes to speak of an adaptation of our laws of mind to the laws of nature, there is no objection to it. Evidently, however, such adaptation does not have to be either perfect or exact. The eye is an extremely useful organ practically, although it cannot see distinctly at all distances, or perceive all sorts of aether vibrations, or concentrate exactly in one point all the rays that issue from a point. Our intellectual faculties are connected with the activities of a material organ, namely the brain, just 620 as the faculty of vision is connected with the eye. Human intelligence is wonderfully effective in the world, and brings it under a strict law of causation. Whether it necessarily must be able to control whatever is in the world or can happen—I can see no guarantee for that.

We must speak now of the manner in which our ideas and perceptions are formed by inductive conclusions. The best analysis of the nature of 625 our conclusions I find in J. S. Mill's *Logic*. As long as the premise of the conclusion is not an injunction imposed by outside authority for our conduct and belief, but a statement related to reality, which can therefore be only the result of experience, the 630

> The reference is to Mill's *A System of Logic Ratiocinative and Inductive,* first published in 1843.

conclusion, as a matter of fact, does not tell us anything new or something that we did not know already before we made the statement. Thus, for example:

Major: All men are mortal.

Minor: Caius is a man.

Conclusion: Caius is mortal. 635

The major premise, that all men are mortal, which is a statement of experience, we should scarcely venture to assert without knowing beforehand whether the conclusion is correct, namely, that Caius, who is a man, either is dead or will die. Thus we must be sure of the conclusion before we can state the major premise by which we intend to prove it. That seems to be proceeding in a circle. The real relation evidently is, that, in common with other folks, we 640 have observed heretofore without exception that no person has ever survived beyond a certain age. Observers have learned by experience that Lucius, Flavius and other individuals of their acquaintance, no matter what their names are, have all died; and they have embraced this experience in the general statement, that *all* men die. Inasmuch as this final result occurred regularly 645 in all the instances they observed, they have felt justified in explaining this general law as being valid also for all those cases which might come up

> Helmholtz is describing the process of *inductive reasoning* or *induction.*

for observation hereafter. Thus we preserve in our memory the store of experiences heretofore accumulated on this subject by ourselves and others in the form of the general statement 650 which constitutes the major premise of the above conclusion.

However, the conviction that Caius would die might obviously have been reached directly also without formulating the general statement in our consciousness, by having compared his case with all those which we knew previously. Indeed, this is the more usual and original method of reasoning by induction. Conclusions of this sort are reached without conscious reflection, 655 because in our memory the same sort of thing in cases previously observed unites and reinforces

them; as is shown especially in those cases of inductive reasoning where we cannot succeed in deducing from previous experiences a rule with precisely defined limits to its validity and without any exceptions. This is the case in all complicated processes. For instance, from analogy with
660   previous similar cases, we can sometimes predict with tolerable certainty what one of our acquaintances will do, if under certain circumstances he decides to go into business; because we know his character and that he is, let us say, ambitious or timid. We may not be able to say exactly how we have estimated the extent of his ambition or timidity, or why this ambition or timidity of his will be enough to decide that his business will turn out as we expect.
665   In the case of conclusions properly so-called, which are reached consciously, supposing they are not based on injunctions but on facts of experience, what we do, therefore, is really nothing more than deliberately and carefully to retrace those steps in the inductive generalizations of our experiences which were previously traversed more rapidly and without conscious reflection, either by ourselves or by other observers in whom we have confidence. But although
670   nothing essentially new is added to our previous knowledge by formulating a general principle from our previous experiences, still it is useful in many respects. A definitely stated general principle is much easier to preserve in the memory and to be imparted to others than to have to do this same thing with every individual case as it arises. In formulating it we are led to test accurately every new case that occurs, with reference to the correctness of the generalization.
675   In this way every exception will be impressed on us twice as forcibly. The limits of its validity will be recalled much sooner when we have the principle before us in its general form, instead of having to go over each separate case. By this sort of conscious formulation of inductive reasoning, there is much gain in the convenience and certainty of the process; but nothing essentially new is added that did not exist already in the conclusions which were reached by
680   analogy without reflection. It is by means of these latter that we judge the character of a person from his countenance and movements, or predict what he will do in a given situation from a knowledge of his character.

Now we have exactly the same case in our sense-perceptions. When those nervous mechanisms whose terminals lie on the right-hand portions of the retinas of the two eyes have been
685   stimulated, our usual experience, repeated a million times all through life, has been that a luminous object was over there in front of us on our left. We had to lift the hand toward the left to hide the light or to grasp the luminous object; or we had to move toward the left to get closer to it. Thus while in these cases no particular conscious conclusion may be present, yet the essential and original office of such a conclusion has been performed, and the result of it has
690   been attained; simply, of course, by the unconscious processes of association of ideas going on in the dark background of our memory. Thus too its results are urged on our consciousness, so to speak, as if an external power had constrained us, over which our will has no control.

These inductive conclusions leading to the formation of our sense-perceptions certainly do lack the purifying and scrutinizing work of conscious thinking. Nevertheless, in my opinion, by
695   their peculiar nature they may be classed as *conclusions,* inductive conclusions unconsciously formed.

There is one circumstance quite characteristic of these conclusions which operates against their being admitted in the realm of conscious thinking and against their being formulated in the normal form of logical conclusions. This is that we are not able to specify more closely what has taken place in us when we have experienced a sensation in a definite nerve fibre, and how it differs from corresponding sensations in other nerve fibres. Thus, suppose we have had a sensation of light in certain fibres of the nervous mechanism of vision. All we know is that we have had a sensation of a peculiar sort which is different from all other sensations, and also from all other visual sensations, and that whenever it occurred, we invariably noticed a luminous object on the left. Naturally, without ever having studied physiology, this is all we can say about the sensation, and even for our own imagination we cannot localize or grasp the sensation except by specifying it in terms of the conditions of its occurrence. I have to say, "I see something bright there on my left." That is the only way I can describe the sensation. After we have pursued scientific studies, we begin to learn that we have nerves, that these nerves have been stimulated, and that their terminals in fact lie on the right-hand side of the retina. Then for the first time we are in a position to define this mode of sensation independently of the mode in which it is ordinarily produced.

> *except in terms of the bodies:* The only words we have for describing smells are the names of things (smoke, lilacs, boiled cabbage) we have learned to associate with specific sensations, which themselves remain indescribable.

It is the same way with most sensations. The sensations of taste and smell usually cannot be described even as to their quality except in terms of the bodies responsible for them; although we do have a few rather vague and more general expressions like "sweet," "sour," "bitter" and "sharp."

These judgments, in which our sensations in our ordinary state of consciousness are connected with the existence of an external cause, can never once be elevated to the plane of conscious judgments. The inference that there is a luminous object on my left, because the nerve terminals on the right-hand side of my retina are in a state of stimulation, can only be expressed by one who knows nothing about the inner structure of the eye by saying, "There is something bright over there on my left, because I see it there." And accordingly from the standpoint of everyday experience, the only way of expressing the experience I have when the nerve terminals on the right-hand side of my eyeball are stimulated by exerting pressure there, is by saying, "When I press my eye on the right-hand side, I see a bright glow on the left."

There is no other way of describing the sensation and of identifying it with other previous sensations except by designating the place where the corresponding external object appears to be. Hence, therefore, these cases of experience have the peculiarity that the connection between the sensation and an external object can never be expressed without anticipating it already in the designation of the sensation, and without presupposing the very thing we are trying to describe.

...

Finally, the tests we employ by voluntary movements of the body are of the greatest importance in strengthening our conviction of the correctness of the perceptions of our senses. And thus, as contrasted with purely passive observations, the same sort of firmer

740 conviction arises as is derived by the process of experiment in scientific investigations. The peculiar ultimate basis, which gives convincing power to all our conscious inductions, is the law of causation. If two natural phenomena have frequently been observed to occur together, such as thunder and lightning, they seem to be regularly connected together, and we infer that there must be a common basis for both of them. And if this causal connection has invariably acted heretofore, so that thunder and lightning accompany each other, then in the future too like

745 causes must produce like effects, and the result must be the same in the future. However, so long as we are limited to mere observations of such phenomena as occur by themselves without our help, and without our being able to make experiments so as to vary the complexity of causes, it is difficult to be sure that we have really ascertained all the factors that may have some influence on the result. There must be an enormous variety of cases where the law is obeyed,

750 and the law must define the result with great precision, if we are to be satisfied with a case of mere observation. This is the case with the motions of the planetary system. Of course, we cannot experiment with the planets, but the theory of universal gravitation as propounded by Newton gives such a complete and exact expla-

755 nation of the comparatively complicated apparent motions of the heavenly bodies, that we no longer hesitate about considering it as being sufficiently proved. And yet there are Reich's experiments on the gravitational attraction of lead balls, Foucault's

760 experiment on the deviation of the plane of vibration of a pendulum in consequence of the earth's rotation, and the experimental determinations of the velocity of light in traversing terrestrial distances as made by Foucault and Fizeau, that are of

765 the utmost value in strengthening our conviction experimentally also.

Ferdinand Reich (1799–1882), the discoverer of the element indium, was one of many 19th century scientists who replicated Henry Cavendish's 1797 measurement of the earth's gravitational constant. Jean Foucault (1819–1868), the inventor of the gyroscope, showed that the path of a freely swinging pendulum changes as the earth rotates. Armand Fizeau (1819–1896) devised an ingenious method for measuring the speed of light in 1849. Foucault later improved the method and obtained a more accurate value.

. . .

The same great importance which experiment has for the certainty of our scientific convic- tions, it has also for the unconscious inductions of the perceptions of our senses. It is only by voluntarily bringing our organs of sense in various relations to the objects that we learn to be

770 sure as to our judgments of the causes of our sensations. This kind of experimentation begins in earliest youth and continues all through life without interruption.

If the objects had simply been passed in review before our eyes by some foreign force with- out our being able to do anything about them, probably we should never have found our way about amid such an optical phantasmagoria; any more than mankind could interpret the

775 apparent motions of the planets in the firmament before the laws of perspective vision could be applied to them. But when we notice that we can get various images of a table in front of us simply by changing our position; and that we can sometimes have one view and sometimes another, just as we like at any time, by a suitable change of position; and that the table may

vanish from sight, and then be there again at any moment we like, simply by turning the eyes toward it; we get the conviction based on experiment, that our movements are responsible for the different views of the table, and that whether we see it just at this moment or do not see it, still we can see it whenever we like. Thus by our movements we find out that it is the stationary form of the table in space which is the cause of the changing image in our eyes. We explain the table as having existence independent of our observation, because at *any moment we like,* simply by assuming the proper position with respect to it, we can observe it.

780

785

The essential thing in this process is just this principle of experimentation. Spontaneously and by our own power, we vary some of the conditions under which the object has been perceived. We know that the changes thus produced in the way that objects look depend solely on the movements we have executed. Thus we obtain a different series of apperceptions of the same object, by which we can be convinced with experimental certainty that they are simply apperceptions, and that it is the common cause of them all. In fact we see children also experimenting with objects in this way. They turn them constantly round and round, and touch them with the hands and the mouth, doing the same things over and over again day after day with the same objects, until their forms are impressed on them; in other words, until they get the various visual and tactile impressions made by observing and feeling the same object on various sides.

790

795

In this sort of experimentation with objects some of the changes in the sense-impressions are found to be due to our own will; whereas others, that is, all that depend on the nature of the object directly before us, are urged upon us by a necessity which we cannot alter as we like, and which we feel most when it arouses disagreeable sensations or pain. Thus we come to recognize something independent of our will and imagination, that is, an external cause of our sensations. This is shown by its persisting independently of our instantaneous perception; because at any moment we like, by suitable manipulations and movements, we can cause to recur each one of the series of sensations that can be produced in us by this external cause. Thus this latter is recognized as an object existing independently of our perception.

800

805

The idea and the cause here combine, and it is a question whether we have a right to assume this cause in the original perception of the senses. Here again the difficulty is that we are not able to describe the processes except in the language of metaphysics, whereas the reflection of the consciousness in itself is not yet distinctly contained in the original form of the conscious perception.

Natural consciousness, which is entirely absorbed in the interest of observing the external world, and has little inducement to direct its attention to the Ego that appears always the same amid the multicoloured variations of outside objects, is not in the habit of noticing that the *properties* of the objects that are seen and touched are their effects, partly on other natural bodies, but mainly on our senses. Now as our nervous system and our sensation-faculty, as being the constant reagent on which the effect is exerted, is thus left out of account entirely, and as the difference of the effect is regarded as being simply a difference in the object from which it proceeds, the effect can no longer be recognized as an effect (for every effect must be the effect on something else), and so comes to be considered objectively as being a property of the body and merely as belonging to it. And then as soon as we recall that we perceive these properties,

810

815

820   our impression, consequently, seems to us to be a pure image of the external state of affairs reflecting only that external condition and depending solely on it.

But if we ponder over the basis of this process, it is obvious that we can never emerge from the world of our sensations to the apperception of an external world, except by inferring from the changing sensation that external objects are the causes of this change. Once the idea of
825   external objects has been formed, we may not be concerned any more as to how we got this idea, especially because the inference appears to be so self-evident that we are not conscious of its being a new result.

Accordingly, the law of causation, by virtue of which we infer the cause from the effect, has to be considered also as being a law of our thinking which is prior to all experience. Generally, we
830   can get no experience from natural objects unless the law of causation is already active in us. Therefore, it cannot be deduced first from experiences which we have had with natural objects.

. . .

The law of sufficient basis amounts simply to the requirement of wishing to understand everything. The process of our comprehension with respect to natural phenomena is that we try to find *generic notions* and *laws of nature.* Laws of nature are merely generic notions for the
835   changes in nature. But since we have to assume the laws of nature as being valid and as acting independently of our observation and thinking, whereas as generic notions they would concern at first only the method of our thinking, we call them *causes* and *forces.* Hence, when we cannot trace natural phenomena to a law, and therefore cannot make the law objectively responsible as being the cause of the phenomena, the very possibility of comprehending such
840   phenomena ceases.

However, we must try to comprehend them. There is no other method of bringing them under the control of the intellect. And so in investigating them we must proceed on the supposition that they are comprehensible. Accordingly, the law of sufficient reason is really nothing more than the *urge* of our intellect to bring all our perceptions under its own control. It is
845   not a law of nature. Our intellect is the faculty of forming general conceptions. It has nothing to do with our sense-perceptions and experiences, unless it is able to form general conceptions or laws. These laws are then objectified and designated as causes. But if it is found that the natural phenomena are to be subsumed under a definite causal connection, this is certainly an objectively valid fact, and corresponds to special objective relations between natural phe-
850   nomena, which we express in our thinking as being their causal connection, simply because we do not know how else to express it.

Just as it is the characteristic function of the eye to have light-sensations, so that we can *see* the world only as a *luminous phenomenon,* so likewise it is the characteristic function of the intellect to form general conceptions, that is, to search for causes; and hence it can *conceive*
855   *(begreifen)* of the world only as being *causal* connection. We have other organs besides the eye for comprehending the external world, and thus we can feel or smell many things that we cannot see. Besides our intellect there is no other equally systematized faculty, at any rate for comprehending the external world. Thus if we are unable to *conceive* a thing, we cannot imagine it as existing.

FOR DISCUSSION

1. Helmholtz says, "it is invariably simply the nervous stimulations that are perceived directly, that is, the actions, but never the external objects themselves." How does Reid express the same idea?

2. What are some consequences of Helmholtz's claim that the conclusions, or inferences, that constitute our perceptions are unconscious?

3. What does Helmholtz mean by "real agreement between our perceptions and the reality" (p. 152, lines 546)? What are the various ways in which perceptions can be similar to and different from external objects and events?

4. What similarities does Helmholtz see between the process of perception and the process of science?

J. J. Gibson (1904–1979)
The Perception of the Visual World (1950)

Chapter 5: A Psychophysical Theory of Perception

In 1892 William James wrote

Mental facts cannot properly be studied apart from the physical environment of which they take cognizance. The great fault of the older rational psychology was to set up the soul as an absolute spiritual being with certain faculties of its own by which the several activities of remembering, imagining, reasoning, willing, etc. were explained, almost without reference to the peculiarities of the world with which these activities deal. But the richer insight of modern days perceives that our inner faculties are *adapted* in advance to the features of the world in which we dwell. . . . Mind and world in short have evolved together, and in consequence are something of a mutual fit. (1892, pp. 3–4; emphasis in original)

It is hard to imagine a better introduction to the book that J. J. Gibson wrote half a century later.

James Jerome Gibson is the un-Helmholtz. Gibson's agenda is not so much to overthrow Helmholtz as to show that his approach to vision—static, laboratory-based, centered on the retina—does not explain much of vision as we experience it, moving around in the world. Gibson's approach to vision is everything that Helmholtz's is not—dynamic, naturalistic, and centered on the stimulus. The crucial fact for Helmholtz is that a single three-dimensional world is projected onto two two-dimensional surfaces, and he wants to know how we turn those two images into a single perception of the world. By contrast, the crucial fact for Gibson is that we effortlessly "pick up" information from the world, and he wants to identify the properties of that world that make this possible.

Source: Gibson, J. J. (1950). *The perception of the visual world*. Boston: Houghton Mifflin. Reprinted with permission.

At the beginning of World War II, the theoretical problem of space perception became a practical problem almost overnight. The skills of aviation began to be of vital interest to millions of individuals. The abstract question of how one can see a third dimension based only on a pair of retinal images extended in two dimensions became very concrete and important to the man who was required to get about in the third dimension. If the visual world of the airplane pilot   5
were not in fairly close correspondence with the material world on which he had to land his airplane such as a carrier-deck, the practical consequences could be disastrous. The theories of space perception, therefore, became of more than academic interest in the rapidly developing field of aviation psychology.

But the fact was that all the evidence from the laboratories and all the theories of ingenious   10
men had little practical application to the problem of flying. The theory of the binocular and the monocular cues for depth, perfected eighty years before by Helmholtz, could explain how a pilot might see one point as nearer than another point. But the pilot was not looking at points of   15
color in a visual field; he was typically looking at the ground, the horizon, the landing field, the direction of his glide, not to mention several instruments, and visualizing a space of air and terrain in which he himself was moving—very fast and possibly in a cold sweat.   20

> *binocular and monocular cues:* Gibson lists and explains these under the heading "The Cues for Distance as Stimulation Gradients," p. 174.

ABSTRACT SPACE AND THE WORLD OF THE FLIER

> A *stereoscope* is a device that presents each of the two eyes with a slightly different view of the same scene, as in a Viewmaster or a 3-D movie, or a magic eye picture. Gibson's *figures of the stereoscope* is the perception of depth created by a stereoscopic view.

> The *artificial horizon,* an instrument now found in all airplanes, was perfected in 1929 by the American inventor Elmer Sperry (1860–1930).

The space in which the pilot flies is not the abstract space of theories, nor the lines and figures of the stereoscope, nor the space of the usual laboratory apparatus for studying depth perception. It does not consist of objects at varying empty distances. It   25
consists chiefly of one basic object, a continuous surface of fundamental importance—the ground. A pilot who cannot see the ground or sea is apt to lose touch with reality in his flying. A visual field of blue sky, or fog, or total darkness yields an inde-   30
terminate space which is the nearest thing to no space at all. Only a substitute for the ground and its horizon in the form of instruments will permit him to maintain the level flight of the airplane under such conditions and to proceed from one place to   35
another. The spatial situation which needs to be analysed, therefore, must involve the ground and everything that it implies. Instead of calling it a space it would be better to call it a world.

The conception of an empty space of three dimensions was a conception of philosophers and physicists. It was appropriate for the analysis of the abstract world of events defined by
40 Newton. It was and still is of enormous value for analysis in the physical sciences. But the fact that it simplifies such problems does not make it the best starting point for the problem of visual perception. Space, time, points, and instants are useful terms, but not the terms with which to start the analysis of how we see, for no one has ever seen them.[1]

The world with a ground under it—the visual world of surfaces and edges—is not only the
45 kind of world in which the pilot flies; it is the prototype of the world in which we all live. In it, one can stand and move about. It conditions and provides support for motor activity. A ground is necessary for bodily equilibrium and posture, for kinesthesis and locomotion, and indirectly for all behavior which depends on these adjustments.

An out-of-doors world is one in which the lower portion of the visual field (corresponding
50 to the upper portion of each retinal image) is invariably filled by a projection of the terrain. The upper portion of the visual field is usually filled with a projection of the sky. Between the upper and lower portions is the skyline, high or low as the observer looks down or up, but always cutting the normal visual field in a horizontal section. This is the kind of world in which our primitive ancestors lived. It was also the environment in which took place the evolution of visual
55 perception in their ancestors. During the millions of years in which some unknown animal species evolved into our human species, land and sky were the constant visual stimuli to which the eyes and brain responded. In the typical indoors world of civilized man, a ceiling and walls take the place of the horizon and sky, but the floor is still an equivalent to the ground. This basic surface is the background for the objects to which we normally give attention and, as we
60 learned in Chapter 3, its horizontal axis is implicit in every visual field whatever the posture of the body may be. It is little noticed, but on the average and over the ages it must have determined the fundamental pattern of retinal images for all or most terrestrial animals.[2]

The classical theories of space perception conceived the third dimension to be a line extending outward from the eye. Space was therefore empty between the eye and the object
65 fixated. The perceived distance of this object seemed to be what needed explanation, and the

---

[1] The theories of space-perception which flourished in the 19th century were all theories of abstract, empty space. The experiments concerned lines and points in an indeterminate visual field, as seen in a stereoscope or a depth-perception apparatus. The theories and the experiments alike may be characterized as *geometrical*. They were great intellectual achievements (the theories of the "horopter" are an example), but they will not be considered at present. The theory of disparate retinal images as it applies to surfaces rather than abstract points will be restated in the next chapter, and the conception of geometrical space will be treated in Chapter 10. [The horopter (Gr., "boundary of seeing") is the set of points in the visual field, at a given fixation distance, that fall on corresponding retinal points. Each point on the horopter falls on locations in the left and right retinas that correspond to one another and therefore produce single (fused) vision of that point. (Eds.)]

[2] So universally is the ground taken to be the background of objects that the mere location of one patch of color *above* another in the visual field tends to make it appear more distant. Height in the visual field can be a genuine clue to distance only if upright posture, a level ground, and a tendency for objects to be *on* the ground are assumed. This point will come up in later chapters.

explanation was sought in the consequences of the possession of two eyes. It would have been better to seek an explanation of the sensory continuum of distance as such which, once visible, determines how distant all the objects within it are. But this explanation was impossible so long as the continuum of distance was conceived as the third dimension. The solution of the difficulty is to recognize that the continuum of distance depends on a determinate surface   70
which extends away from the observer in the third dimension. Such a surface is projected as an image which is spread out on the retina, not confined to a point.

Figure 1 illustrates the two formulations of the problem. The points A, B, C, and D are not discriminable on the retina. Distance along this line may be a fact of geometry but it is not one of vision. The points W, X, Y, and Z at corresponding distances *are* discriminable on the retina.   75
They represent the image of an extended surface, the points being, for example, highlights on the surface. It may be noted that the retinal spots become progressively closer together as the distance increases. What kind of a theory, we may now ask, is implied by this latter formulation of the problem? How is a surface seen?

STIMULUS CORRELATES

The first place to look for an explanation is obviously the retinal image. If, contrary to past teach-   80
ing, there are exact concomitant variations in the image for the important features of the visual world a psychophysical theory will be possible. The image, according to the evidence in Chapter 4, is a good correlate (but not a copy) of the physical environment. It may also prove to be a good correlate of perception, despite an entrenched opinion to the contrary. The reti-   85
nal image, it is true, is not much to look at when one compares it with the elaborate reality of the visual world, but the fact is that it is not something to be looked at; it is a stimulus. The question is not how much it resembles the visual world but whether it contains enough variations to account for all the features of the visual world.

If we can analyse the retinal image for its stimulus variations, we shall open up the possibility of experimental control of these variations. Given a means of producing them, an experimenter,   90
and an observer, it can be determined whether the variations are or are not in psycho-physical correspondence with the observer's perceptions. This is the method by which the sensory capacities, so called, of men and animals have been determined. The test is simple: does a specific variation in the observer's experience (or behavior) correspond to a variation of the physical stimulus? Although this experiment has seldom been applied to what are tradition-   95
ally called perceptions, it can and should be performed (Gibson, 1948).[3]

It is, of course, a departure from tradition to conceive that a surface, or an outline, or the depth of a surface should have a specific stimulus. The stimulus for vision, we are accustomed

---

[3] Students of psychology will recall, in this connection, that the Gestalt theory denied any one-to-one correspondence between the stimulation of receptors and the experience which resulted. The assumption of such a fixed correspondence was called the "constancy hypothesis." It seemed to be untenable since everyday visual experience was so demonstrably unlike its retinal image. The aim of this chapter is to reassert the constancy hypothesis on the basis of a broader conception of stimulation.

FIGURE 1   Two Formulations of the Problem of Distance Perception

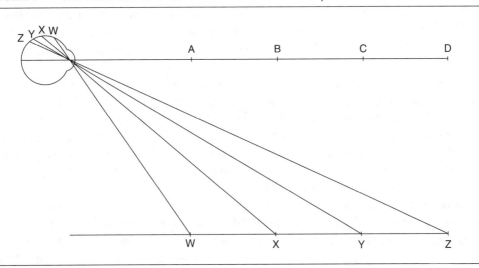

to think, is simply light energy. But such a definition reflects the preoccupation of nearly a hundred years of research on color vision and light-dark discrimination, the outcome of which still
leaves us ignorant of the vision employed in everyday living. The higher animals do not simply
react to the direction of light as a plant does; they have a specialized neural surface, the retina,
on which their environment is projected by
means of focused light. As a result they can react
indirectly to the environment itself, and the point
would be missed by insisting that they are actually reacting only to light. In what respects is this
projected light a stimulus?

> *focused light:* an image, as distinct from
> mere light stimulation

THE HYPOTHESIS OF ORDINAL STIMULATION

Before attempting to answer this question it would be useful to agree on just what the term "stimulus" is to mean, for it is a much misused word. Let us assume that a stimulus is a type of variable
physical energy falling within certain ranges of variation (the limits being called absolute thresh-
olds) which excites a receptor or a set of receptors differentially. If it does not release physiological activity in a receptor-mechanism it is not a stimulus. As the energy varies successively, the
excitation varies concomitantly in some specific way. This is a strict definition of a stimulus. For
our present purposes, as applied to the retina, we wish to extend the term to mean also a simultaneous variation over the set of receptors, or a differential excitation of different receptors, and

> Note that Gibson is talking about order or succession in space, not in time.

the order of such a variation. For the extended meaning the term ordinal stimulation will be used. "Ordinal" simply refers to order or succession. This is what has usually, but inaccurately, been called pattern stimulation. 120

In this book, the term "stimulus" will always refer to the light energy on the retina, never to the object from which light is reflected. The term "stimulus-object" will never be used, since it can serve as a cloak for ignorance. The distinction of Heider (1927) and Koffka (1935) between the "distant" stimulus (the object) and the "proximal" stimulus (the image) is illuminating just because it implies, and just so long as it implies, that the latter stimulates the organism. The term "stimulus situation" likewise will never be used since the situation does not exist in the retina any more than the object does, and the question is how both are seen. 125

How can we specify the order of visual stimulation? The retinal image as a physical event may be treated as an infinite series of geometrical points or as a finite number of minute areas of arbitrary size. The latter is the more useful assumption for our purpose. In either case the 130

> *geometrical points:* as in the Cartesian plane, where every point is a unique location on the (X,Y) coordinates

image can vary in two fundamental ways: first in the character or "color" of the focused light at a given spot, and second in the distribution of these spots, or their geometrical relations to one another. This second variable is the one that makes all the difficulty. It is not easy to deal with the complexities of distribution or arrangement in a mathematically precise way. Nevertheless this variable is the one on which everyday perception depends. Let us assume, as a start, that organisms can react specifically to the order of the light-spots as well as to the character of the light in each spot. 135

140

> *minute areas:* A familiar example would be the pixels (*picture elements*) of computer monitors and video displays.

How an organism can do so, we do not know—that is another question. But if it can react differently to a spot-sequence such as "black-gray-white" from the way it does to the sequence "white-gray-black," then the order is the effective fact and it would be legitimate to invent for it the term ordinal stimulation.[4] 145

---

[4] As will appear in a later chapter, there is evidence that organisms can react specifically to a *successive* order of stimulation of the same spot as well as to an *adjacent* order of stimulation of different spots. Both kinds of order are present in retinal stimulation. The *successive* order "black-gray-white" yields a lightening effect and the reverse a darkening effect; the *adjacent* order yields a patterning effect. A co-variance of successive and adjacent order seems to be the essential condition for visual motion. For the present we are concerned only with adjacent order.

The term *order* is often used by philosophers and artists in a very inclusive sense. It may mean form, pattern, arrangement, position, direction, and even magnitude or distance. The term is here used, however, in an exact and literal sense to refer to that characteristic which numbers have of making a sequence which is not the same in one direction as in the other.

The spots or elements of the image, in this analysis, are to be understood as arbitrary units of area. Like the points of geometry and optics they have only a logical existence. They are
150 necessary to a mathematical treatment of retinal stimulation, but they are not to be considered the elements of visual experience, or the sensory units of perception. They are analytical fictions, and they do not add up to a visual field any more than the geometrical points employed in the operations of a surveyor add up to the surface of the earth which he surveys. It should be emphasized that the fundamental variations in light energy and in order or arrangement
155 which constitute the retinal image are both abstractions.

The prevailing assumption about pattern vision has always been that the ocular mechanism enables the organism to respond to a specific set of *ray-directions* (Troland, 1930, Vol. 2, p. 85). Each hypothetical light ray was supposed to be an individual stimulus. It has been argued, however, that light rays are analytic
160 fictions. Furthermore, the homogeneous total field experiment demonstrates that when every ray has the same wave length and intensity there is no perception, and this experiment implies that the organism *cannot* respond to ray-direc-
165 tions as such. What the retina does respond to is a differential intensity in adjacent order over the retina. The necessary condition for pattern vision is an *inhomogeneity* of the set of hypothetical rays, not the rays themselves. The ray-direction
170 theory of the stimulus, the point-theory of objective space, and the local-sign theory of subjective space all collapse together if this implication is correct and require a thorough reformulation.

> The *homogeneous total field*, or *Ganzfeld*, is what is perceived when the entire retina is uniformly stimulated. The field is featureless and of indeterminate depth. Regardless of the color of the light used, the field soon becomes gray. Splitting a ping-pong ball and wearing the two halves as monocles can provide a rough idea of the experience.

Considering the retinal image as an array of small adjacent areas of different radiant energy, let us try to state the kinds of order into which the elements might fall. For the sake of simplicity
175 we may consider a hypothetical case in which there are only two levels of light intensity in the image and no differences of wavelength. An element may be relatively "light" or "dark," but nothing more. If the former it may be indicated by the letter *l* and if the latter by *d*. The simplest of all orders would then be *llllllll* or *dddddddd*. All the elements of the order are the same. This is what Koffka has called homogeneous retinal
180 stimulation (1935, p. 110). In a two dimensional array it is the stimulus correlate of visual fields like the sky, absolute darkness, or the "film-colors." The experience is one of pure areal color, seen at an indeterminate distance.

> A *film color* is what is perceived in a colored Ganzfeld before it turns gray.

185 A second type of order would be one containing a single step or jump, such as *llllddddd* or *ddddllllll*. This order may occur along one or both dimensions of an array of elements and, when it does, what we call lines or discontinuous areas will appear in the visual field. Presumably this

The *margins or outlines* correspond to the transitions from *l* to *d* and vice versa. Such discontinuities, or edges, are very important in more recent theories of vision; see Marr, 2.5.

type of order is a stimulus correlate for the margins or outlines which are the necessary conditions for seeing figures and shapes.[5]

190

```
lllldddd ddddllll  11111111 dddddddd
lllldddd ddddllll  11111111 dddddddd
lllldddd ddddllll  dddddddd 11111111
lllldddd ddddllll  dddddddd 11111111
```

A third type of order would be one similar to *llddllddl*, which contains a cyclical or alter-   195
nating change. It is a reasonable hypothesis that when such an order is found in both dimensions of an array of elements there will occur the visual quality of texture, and that this is the stimulus correlate of a visual surface. The varieties of texture in experience are innumerable, of course, but the varieties of a cyclical order of elements could be equally enormous in number. With only the two elements *l* and *d*, there are many repetitive sequences   200
possible; when all the levels of intensity and wave length are taken into account the variety of cycles become incalculable. The assumption is that the microstructure or texture of a visual surface is the phenomenal correlate of some repetitive type of retinal stimulation. If physical surfaces have regular structures peculiar to them, as wood, cloth, or earth have, the regularity will be projected in a focused image, and this repetitive character of the stim-   205
ulation, in turn, may well be the basis for the perception of a surface.[6]

The three kinds of order just defined are hypothetical stimuli for pure visual extent, for outlines, and for surfaces in the abstract. But we need to account for surfaces as they are seen in three dimensions, and for the background surface best exemplified by the terrain. For that it is necessary to consider a serial or progressive order of elements in the retinal image, or gra-   210
dients as forms of stimulation.

---

[5] It must be remembered that we are describing what first happens on the retina, not what might happen at later stages in the physiological process of seeing. The occurrence of a margin or outline in perception is determined primarily by the step from light to dark but also of course by the subsequent events in the optic nervous system. The latter may be guessed at from such phenomena as brightness contrast at a border and the inhibition of one border in perception by an adjacent border or a succeeding one, all of which suggest some kind of a process of "contour-building." The significant experiments on this problem are described by Bartley (1941) in his chapter on visual contour. The stages intermediate between a true contour and a shadow penumbra have been studied by MacLeod (1947) together with the accompanying effects (contrast or constancy) on the areas separated by the contour or penumbra. Here also there is presumably some kind of interaction between adjacent areas.

[6] A striking illustration of this point has been suggested by Dr. Leonard Carmichael. Many of the great classical painters, especially those Dutch painters who worked with magnifying glasses and the finest of brushes, could simulate velvet, satin, the texture of flower-petals, and even the peculiar sheen of a drop of water on the flower by the precise arrangement of spots of pigment. The microstructure of the paint was quite different from the microstructure of the real fabric, the real petal, or the real water-drop. What the painter could reproduce was the *microstructure of the light reflected from these surfaces*. Qualities of lustre, softness, hardness, wetness, and the like are very clear in these paintings. The analysis of visual texture will be carried further in the next chapter.

RETINAL GRADIENTS AS VARIABLES OF STIMULATION—TEXTURE

Consider for a moment the physical environment from which light is reflected and which is projected on the retina. The problem of distance perception has been reduced to the question of how we can see surfaces parallel to the line of sight (Figure 1). These will be called longitudinal surfaces to distinguish them from frontal surfaces, which are perpendicular to the line of sight. The former are best exemplified by the ground; the latter are characteristic of objects. The surfaces of the physical environment and its parts are either longitudinal, frontal, or somewhere between these two extremes.

In Figure 2 the material surface *AB* is a longitudinal surface, and the surface *BC* is a frontal surface. In the retinal image *ab*, there exists a gradient of texture from coarse to fine, whereas in the retinal image *bc* no such gradient occurs, and the texture is uniform throughout. The diagram may be conceived either as a cross-sectional view from the side (*AB* is a floor or the ground), or from above (*AB* is a wall to the right of the observer). The slant of a surface is something that we can see, and the surfaces of the visual world are in fairly good agreement with the surfaces of the physical environment with respect to slant. Moreover, as everybody knows, a photograph or a painting can serve as a good substitute for a physical environment in yielding a picture-world with surfaces which seem to slant or confront us just about as they did in the original. The picture surface is flat, but we have all learned to neglect that impression and to see an array of longitudinal, transverse and slanting surfaces which make up the "space" of the picture.

> Notice that the points at which the rays intersect *AB* and *BC* are evenly spaced, dividing the two equal distances (*AB* and *BC*) into four equal intervals. Because *BC* is perpendicular to the line of sight, the points on the retina (on *bc*) corresponding to the equally spaced points on *BC* are likewise equally spaced. Because *AB*, however, is not perpendicular to the line of sight, the points on the retina (on *ab*) corresponding to the equally spaced points on *AB* are *not* equally spaced. Rather, there is a *gradient*: Moving from *a* to *b*, equal distances on the perceived surface are represented by progressively smaller distances on the retina.

The retinal stimulus-variable which makes possible the perception of a longitudinal surface must be a continuous change of some sort in the image of that surface. To the distance of the physical surface at successive points there must correspond a variation in the image at the projected points. Then, as the image differs progressively from point to point, the perceived surface can differ correspondingly in its distance or depth. There must, in other words, be a stimulation gradient.

We can now define a fourth type of order among the elements of a retinal image. It would be a serial change in the length of the cycles of a repetitive order. An example might be *ddddlllldddlllddllddlldl*. If a repetitive order is the stimulus for visual texture, this would constitute a gradient of the density of texture.

FIGURE 2   The Optical Projection of a Longitudinal and a Frontal Surface

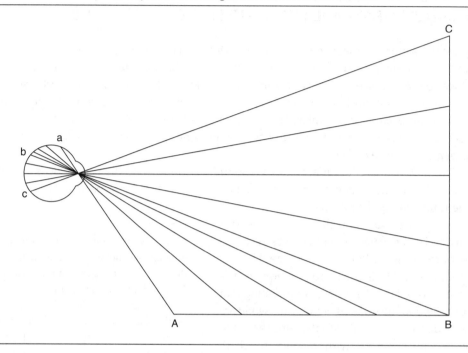

We know from ordinary experience that the texture of different surfaces may vary from coarse to fine. The various grades of sandpaper used by carpenters differ in just this respect. Figure 3 shows the same texture in various grades of density. When the image of a single surface varies progressively in this way, it may be that the gradient of density is an adequate stimulus for the impression of continuous distance.   250

In order to verify this hypothesis a program of experiments would be necessary, and a beginning on such a program will be described in subsequent chapters. The hypothesis can be illustrated in a preliminary way by examining pictures with respect to the impression of depth and distance which they yield. Figure 4 shows two examples of textured surfaces found in a natural environment in which a gradient from coarse to fine runs from the bottom to the top of the picture. Although the elements of the texture in the two cases are of different shape and mean size, the gradients in both pictures are similar. In both pictures there appears a continuous increase in the visible distance of the surface. The impression of a ground extending away from the observer is fairly compelling. In Figure 5, many different gradients of texture-density are combined to yield a complex scene. Half a dozen different kinds of texture are visible in the photograph.   255   260

These photographs represent surfaces which are familiar in everyday vision. Although the gradient of texture is the only noticeable variation to be discovered in them, they are interpreted by most observers from cues present in the picture and are given a meaning. The meanings   265

FIGURE 3   Grades of Texture

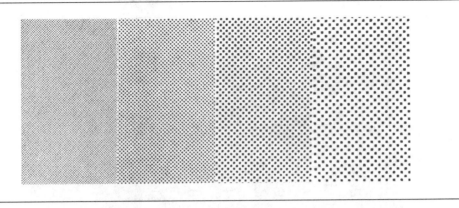

FIGURE 4   Gradients of Natural Texture and the Resulting Impression of Continuous Distance

usually assigned to the upper pictures are a ploughed field and a field of growing alfalfa, which are correct. It is possible to suppose that the interpretation is the cause of the depth-impression. Such would be the explanation given by an empirical theory of space-perception. Figure 6, however, was constructed artificially out of line-segments, with a gradient of lines and gaps

270

FIGURE 5 Texture-Perspective and the Impression of Receding Surfaces (Courtesy of Professor R. B. MacLeod)

decreasing toward the top of the picture. The impression of a surface extended in distance is clear in this picture as well as in the others. This result suggests that the gradation of texture elements, not the familiarity of elements, is the principal cause of a depth-impression. The last picture may also be interpreted as a level terrain extending off to the horizon, but there are no actual cues for such a meaning, and we may conclude that the impression of distance is an immediate process, while the interpretation follows upon it. "Immediate process" does not imply an innate intuition of distance; it only implies that the impression of distance may have a definable stimulus just as the so-called "sensations" have.

275

The line segments of Figure 6 were not drawn so as to fall one above the other in straight lines converging to the horizon, but were instead offset. Aligning them would have induced the familiar appearance of linear perspective. The gradient of texture is not the same thing as ordinary perspective, although the two are united by underlying principles as will be shown. The projected size of things in the environment does decrease as their distance increases from the observer and as their size approaches zero or "vanishes" at the horizon. In this respect the texture of a longitudinal surface and the perspective of objects are alike. But the former leads us to a general phenomenon, of which the latter is only a special case. The artificial texture of Figure 6 might have been drawn with the line segments at the bottom of the picture twice as

280

285

FIGURE 6   A Gradient of Artificial Texture and the Impression of Continuous Distance

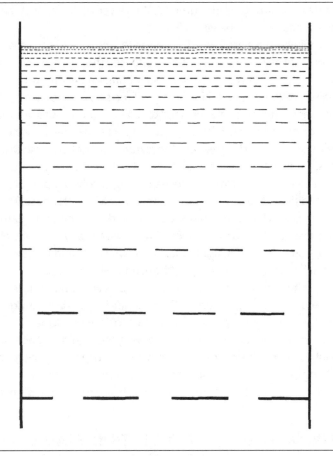

long as they are and the line segments above also twice as long all the way up to the level
290   where they diminish to zero. In other words the horizontal dimensions, but not the vertical
ones, could have been proportionally increased. The resulting impression of distance on a surface, however, would have remained as strong as before. The only change would have been a
faster rate of decrease of the line segments from the bottom to the top of the picture, or a larger
angle of convergence of the theoretical lines connecting their ends (linear perspective). So long
295   as the elements approach a vanishing level at the top of such a picture, the impression of a sort
of disembodied terrain is the result. An increase in the gross size of the lines suggests an
impression either of larger texture elements or of viewing the terrain from a lower position,
down near the ground. In perceiving distance on a real terrain, similarly, the gross size of the
texture elements on the retina will vary depending on whether they are predominantly sand,

grass, bushes, or trees, and also on whether the observer is flying an airplane, perched on a tele- 300
phone pole, standing, or sitting on the ground. Whatever their size may be, however, they
diminish to zero in a gradient up the visual field.

The hypothesis implies that a gradient of texture in the visual field corresponds to distance in
the material environment on the one hand, and to distance in the visual world on the other. If true,
this principle should apply not only to distance-perception on the ground, in aerial and out-of- 305
doors space, but also to distance-perception in the civilized spaces of rooms and other man-made
surfaces. In order to apply the principle, we need to remember the types of surfaces already distinguished: longitudinal, frontal, and slanting, with respect to the line of sight. Gradients of texture on man-made surfaces may decrease, but the texture does not diminish to a zero limit as that
of the terrain does. On such bounded surfaces, the rate of the gradient is a function of the slant 310
of the surface. A gradient of texture may decrease rapidly, slowly, or not at all, and these are the
three respective conditions for a longitudinal, a slanting, or a frontal surface. The texture of a surface faced directly does not change from coarse to fine, and correspondingly an unchanging texture gives the impression of a frontal surface. When there is any gradient of texture, it may
decrease upwards, from left to right, right to left, or downwards, and these are the four respec- 315
tive conditions for a floor, a left-hand wall, a right-hand wall, and a ceiling. These rules are illustrated in Figure 7, where an artificial gradient has been constructed in each of these four
directions. It can be compared with the similar figure beside it which lacks any gradient and where
the surface, insofar as a surface is represented, appears to lie in the plane of the picture.

If the slant of any plane surface, such as a floor or wall, has a unique gradient of texture, then 320
the changing slant of a curved surface or one with edges, such as an object possesses, should
have a unique change of the gradient of texture. It therefore seems possible that a change of
gradient may be a stimulus for the impression of depth and relief in an object.

THE CUES FOR DISTANCE AS STIMULATION GRADIENTS

The historical origins of the traditional cues for distance have already been discussed in
Chapter 2. The accepted list of these criteria or signs usually includes the following: 325

1. Linear perspective.

2. The apparent size of objects whose real size is known.

3. The relative apparent motion of objects as the observer moves his head. This is often
called motion parallax.

4. The covering of a far object by a near one, or the superposition of one contour on 330
another produced when one object "eclipses" another.

5. The change in color of distant objects, to which is sometimes appended the loss of
sharp outline and detail. This is called aerial perspective.

6. The degree of upward angular location of the object in the visual field, the ground
and skyline being necessarily implied as the background. 335

FIGURE 7   A Gradient of Density in Four Different Directions, as Compared with an Even Density

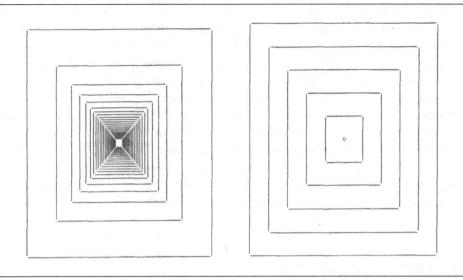

7. The relative brightness of the object. This has been conceived by some writers to be an inverse indicator of its distance; optically, however, this is based on a misconception. It is sometimes mistakenly assumed that the more distant an object is in the ordinary environment the lower will be the intensity of its retinal image, but this

340   principle applies only to point-sources, not to reflecting surfaces.

8. The relation of the lighted to the shadowed areas of an object, or shading. This is an indicator or sign, not of distance but of the depth or relief of a single object.

The "secondary" signs listed above have traditionally been considered less important than the "primary" signs of distance and depth listed below:

345   9. The disparity of the binocular images of the object as a cue to its depth, and the relative disparities (crossed and uncrossed) of different objects as cues to their relative depth.

10. The degree of convergence of the eyes on a fixated object, the convergence being inversely related to its distance.

11. The degree of accommodation of the lens for a fixated object necessary to maximize

350   the definition of the image.

Since we have now reformulated the problem of distance and suggested a theory of texture gradients, these factors in depth perception must be re-examined. For when they are considered as variables of perception rather than as facts of knowledge—once we understand that they apply to an array of objects in the visual field rather than to a single object—they may all

355   prove to be gradients of stimulation, or related to such gradients.

Linear perspective, for example, might be a special result of the decrease in size of figures in the visual field from the lower margin to the horizon.[7] Motion parallax, as seen from a train window, might be a special result of the gradients of deformation which fill the visual field when the observer moves. Superposition of one shape on another is best understood by analyzing the outline between them, and this outline may prove to involve a step separating two continuous gradients. Aerial perspective is, for the most part, a simple gradient of hue in the visual field, a gradient running toward the violet end of the spectrum. The shading on a curved surface is obviously a gradient, as every artist knows. It would be surprising but significant if retinal disparity, like the other signs of depth, could be defined as a gradient of stimulation—not of the single retina, it is true, but a gradient of the theoretically combined images of the two retinas. A visual field obtained with both eyes open, as we shall see, always contains a gradient of "double images." Finally, the cue of upward height in the visual field becomes intelligible in the light of a "ground-theory" instead of an "air-theory" of visual space, inasmuch as the ground embodies and is a precondition for the gradients mentioned.

360

365

. . .

THE CONCEPT OF GRADIENT

The word gradient means nothing more complex than an increase or decrease of something along a given axis or dimension. As such it is related to the plots or curves of analytical geometry. The gradient of a railroad or highway, for example, is its change of altitude with distance. This change may be positive or negative or zero (the last being a level gradient), and it may also be rapid or slow, corresponding to a steep or a moderate gradient. The gradient may itself change, as the slope of a road does in hilly country. When the change is very abrupt—if the slope of a road should end at a cliff—it is properly thought of not as a gradient but as a step or discontinuity. These concepts appear to be admirably adapted for describing the retinal image, since both gradients and steps of stimulation can be found within it.[8]

370

375

. . .

---

[7] Linear perspective is also a geometrical technique for drawing the edges of straight-sided objects, but the two meanings should not be confused.

[8] In Bartley's work on vision (1941), he has used the term gradient to refer to a change in the luminous intensity of stimulation at a border within the retinal image. He is thinking of a microscopic shadow-edge as it falls on the mosaic of retinal cells which can be considered a gradient since the change must be distributed over the width of a number of cells. This is what was called a *step* above. It might be termed a *microgradient* as distinguished from a *macrogradient*. Visual contours, visual acuity, and the elements of visual texture all seem to involve *microgradients* of luminous intensity. The cues for the depth or slant of a surface, on the other hand, seem to involve macrogradients over a considerable dimension of the retina. A gradient of the density of texture would be one case. A gradient of shading in the hollows of a surface or the shading toward the unlighted side of a curved object would be another. The penumbra of a shadow is such a gradient according to MacLeod (1947), and he has demonstrated with "artificial penumbrae" the different effects of a steep gradient as compared with a gentle gradient.

THE CONCEPT OF PSYCHOPHYSICAL CORRESPONDENCE

380

385

The correspondence of the variables of perception to the variables of stimulation is exemplified in Figure 8. Four pairs of such variables are given. The lower line of each pair represents a variable of experience. Each line is to be regarded as continuous. Points on the upper line represent possibilities or instances of stimulation, and points on the lower line represent descriptions or judgments of the ensuing sensory impression, but these "points" are not isolable. They cannot be thought of as stimuli and sensations respectively; the points are simply numbers in a serial order. The variable of physics and the variable of experience in each case are in a one-to-one correspondence. In terms of the geometrical model, for every point on the upper line there is one and only one point on the lower line. The lines (or numbers) need not be conceived as scales possessing units of length. For present purposes they are continuous series merely. An introduction to the problem of scaling the variables of physics and of experience—the

FIGURE 8 Examples of Psychophysical Correspondence

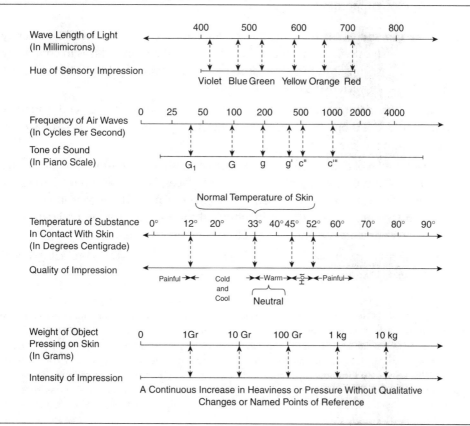

"dimensions of consciousness"—is to be found in Stevens (1946), and the background of this   390
problem is given by Boring (1933).[9]

A few pairs of corresponding points are indicated by dotted lines. It is noteworthy that, for
some variables like temperature and others like weight, the correspondence of sensory qualities to their physical variables may be shifted by adaptation. For example, after holding the
hand in warm water, a stimulus which formerly felt warm now feels neutral and a stimulus   395
which formerly felt neutral now feels cold. The correspondence has been displaced, but it is still
a specific and regular correspondence (Gibson, 1937). It is reasonable to suppose that the spatial qualities of the world, as well as the "sensory" qualities illustrated above, may undergo a
shift in their correspondence to stimulation without a destruction of the correspondence.
Something of this sort probably occurs in the process of getting adapted to eyeglasses.   400

SUMMARY

A theory of visual space perception has now been outlined. Its strength or weakness can be
estimated better if its postulates are made clear. It may be useful, therefore, to summarize the
theory in a series of propositions.

1. It was assumed that the fundamental condition for seeing a visual world is an array of
    physical surfaces reflecting light and projected on the retina. This is in contrast with   405
    the usual assumption that the problem of perception should start from the
    geometrical characteristics of abstract "space."

2. In any environment, these surfaces are of two extreme types, frontal and longitudinal.
    A frontal surface is one transverse to the line of sight, and a longitudinal surface is one
    parallel with the line of sight.   410

3. The perception of depth, distance, or the so-called third dimension, is reducible to the
    problem of the perception of longitudinal surfaces. When no surface is present in
    perception because of homogeneous retinal stimulation, distance is indeterminate.
    Although the ground is the main longitudinal surface, the walls and ceilings of man-
    made environments constitute three other geometrical types.   415

4. The general condition for the perception of a surface is the type of ordinal stimulation
    which yields texture.

---

[9] Boring has also discussed the seeming paradox (exemplified by auditory "volume") that there may exist more dimensions of sensory experience than there are simple dimensions of the physical stimulus (Boring, 1935). The difficulty is
resolved if one defines the dimensions of the stimulus as those variables of stimulation, *however mathematically complex*, with which the variations in discriminative response prove to be correlated as the outcome of a psychophysical
experiment. [The "volume" knob on your radio should be labelled "intensity," for that is what it controls—i.e. the sound
pressure level produced by the radio. This single physical stimulus dimension—intensity—is experienced most
directly as loudness, but the sound has a second perceptual dimension, namely the volume of space that the sound
seems to fill. (Eds.)]

5. The general condition for the perception of an edge, and hence for the perception of a *bounded* surface in the visual field, is the type of ordinal stimulation consisting of an abrupt transition. The simplest and best understood kind of retinal transition is one of brightness.

6. The perception of an object in depth is reducible to the problem of the changing slant of a curved surface or the differing slants of a bent surface. In either case the problem is similar to that of how we see a longitudinal surface.

7. The general condition for the perception of a longitudinal or slanted surface is a kind of ordinal stimulation called a gradient. The gradient of texture has been described, and it has been suggested that gradients dependent on outlines, a gradient of retinal disparity, a gradient of shading, a deformation gradient when the observer moves, and possibly others, all have the function of stimulus-correlates for the impression of distance on a surface.

CONCLUSION

The correspondence of the visual *field* to the total retinal image is an anatomical point-for-point correspondence which is not hard to understand. The correspondence of the visual *world* to the total retinal image is an ordinal correspondence which is more difficult to analyse and specify. But the latter correspondence *is no less literal and exact,* we may believe, than the former, and it is clear that the way to determine it is to find the obscure variations of the projected image which yield coordinate variations in perception.

FOR DISCUSSION

1. About what do Helmholtz and Gibson agree and disagree?

2. What is the significance of Gibson's identification of the stimulus as the light on the retina rather than as the object(s) in the outside world from which that light is reflected?

3. What does Gibson seem to say about Reid's distinction between sensation and perception?

4. What is the difference between the visual *field* and the visual *world*?

David Marr (1945–1980)

Visual Information Processing: The Structure and Creation of Visual Representations (1980)

When the first computers appeared, in the mid-twentieth century, the idea of artificial intelligence (AI) was not far behind. It seemed obvious, to many computer scientists, psychologists, mathematicians, science-fiction writers, and others, that it was only a matter of time before computers would be powerful enough to run programs that would exhibit intelligent behavior. They were certainly right about the powerful part.

As for the intelligent part, the results have been mixed. No doubt some people have been disappointed, or even embarrassed, by AI's failure to live up to its expectations, but from a psychological perspective the entire experience has taught us important things about the mind. Consider the 1968 sci-fi classic, *2001: A Space Odyssey*.

One of the main characters is a HAL 9000, a computer that flew the spaceship in the movie. This entailed navigating and controlling all the ship's engines, rockets, cryogenic hibernation pods, you name it. HAL was able to do all this by receiving inputs from various sensors, by running programs that evaluated the sensory input and made decisions, and by sending its decisions to control various parts of the ship. HAL and the crew communicated with one another in ordinary spoken English. In 1968, all of what HAL could do was fantasy. Since then, many of HAL's functions have become reality. Computers now play chess, checkers, and other games very well. They fly airplanes, work on assembly lines, and control nuclear reactors.

But some of HAL's abilities have turned out to be far more difficult to program into a computer than anyone understood in 1968. We have learned that the things that computers are good at have one thing in common: They are tasks that can be carried out by following rules

Source: Marr, D. (1980). Visual information processing: The structure and creation of visual representations. *Philosophical Transactions of the Royal Society, London, B, 290*, 199–218. Reprinted with permission of the Royal Society of London.

that we (humans) can articulate. Rule-based systems can control machinery, play games, diagnose illnesses, manage inventory, and many other things, often better than humans can. Rule-based approaches to machine vision and speech recognition, on the other hand, have failed quite convincingly. It seems that whatever it is that people do that enables them to use language or to see the world and move around in it cannot be captured in rules that a computer can follow.

One of the people most responsible for discerning the significance of this failure for theories of vision is David Marr. Marr was born in Essex, England. At Trinity College, Cambridge, he earned a BS and an MS in mathematics and then went on to a doctorate in theoretical neuroscience. His dissertation, published as three papers (Marr, 1969, 1970, 1971), articulated a new theory of brain function and established Marr as one of those extraordinary people who can look at what everyone else is looking at and see something completely different. After the three brain papers, Marr became interested in vision. He left England in 1973 for a post in MIT's Artificial Intelligence Laboratory, where, in collaboration with Tomaso Poggio and others, he more or less invented the field of computational neuroscience, in which mathematical models are used to describe functions of the brain.

In 1977 Marr joined MIT's department of psychology. In the following year he was diagnosed with acute leukemia. In his last months, Marr worked furiously to complete *Vision: A Computational Investigation Into the Human Representation and Processing of Visual Information*. The book, published posthumously in 1982, had an enormous impact on both the study of human vision and the pursuit of machine vision. The present paper is essentially a synopsis of the book.

INTRODUCTION

Modern neurophysiology has learned much about the operation of the individual nerve cell, but disconcertingly little about the meaning of the circuits that they compose in the brain. The reason for this can be attributed, at least in part, to a failure to recognize what it means to understand a complex information-processing system; for a complex system cannot be understood as a simple extrapolation from the properties of its elementary components. One does not formulate, for example, a description of thermodynamical effects by using a large set of equations one for each of the particles involved. One describes such effects at their own level, that of an enormous collection of particles, and tries to show that in principle, the microscopic and macroscopic descriptions are consistent with one another.

 5

The core of the problem is that a system as complex as a nervous system or a developing embryo must be analysed and understood at several different levels. Indeed, in a system that solves an information-processing problem, we may distinguish four important levels of description (Marr & Poggio 1977; Marr 1977a). At the lowest level, there is basic component and circuit analysis: how do transistors (or neurons) or diodes (or synapses) work? The second level is the study of particular mechanisms: adders, multipliers and memories, these being assemblies made from basic components. The third level is that of the algorithm, the scheme for a computation; and the top level contains the *theory* of the computation. A theory of addition, for example, would encompass the meaning of that operation, quite independent of the representation of the numbers to be added, i.e., whether they are, say, arabic or roman. But it would also include the realization that the first of these representations is the more suitable of the two. An algorithm, on the other hand, is a particular method by which to add numbers. It therefore applies to a particular representation, since plainly an algorithm that adds arabic numerals would be useless for roman. At still a further level down, one comes upon a mechanism for addition—say a pocket calculator—which simply implements a particular algorithm. . . .

 10

 15

 20

 25

Now each of the four levels of description will have its place in the eventual understanding of perceptual information processing, and of course there are logical and causal relations among them. But the important point is that the four levels of description are only loosely related. Too often in attempts to relate psychophysical problems to physiology there is confusion about the level at which a problem arises; is it related, for instance, mainly to the physical mechanisms of vision (like the after-images such as the one seen after staring at a light bulb) or mainly to the computational theory of vision (like the ambiguity of the Necker cube)? More disturbingly, although the top level is the most

 30

 35

psychophysical . . . physiology: Psychophysics is the study of the quantitative relation between stimulus and percept, without regard to physiology, which is concerned with the biological structure and function of the sensory system.

neglected, it is also the most important. This is because the nature of computations that underlie perception depend more upon the computational *problems* that have to be solved than

40   upon the particular hardware in which their solutions are implemented. To phrase the matter another way, an algorithm is likely to be understood more readily by understanding the nature of the problem that it deals with than by examining the mechanism (and the hardware) by which it is embodied. There is, after all, an analogue to all of this in physics, where a thermodynamical approach represented, at least historically, the first stage in the study of matter:
45   it succeeded in producing a theory of gross properties such as temperature. A description in terms of mechanisms or elementary components—in this case atoms and molecules— appeared some decades afterwards.

Our main point, therefore, is that the topmost of our four levels, that at which the necessary structure of computation is defined, is a crucial but neglected one. Its study is separate from
50   the study of particular algorithms, mechanisms or hardware, and the techniques needed to pursue it are new. In the rest of this article, I summarize some examples of vision theories at the uppermost level.

CONVENTIONAL APPROACHES

Omitted here is Marr's description of some of the background to his work: (1) Wertheimer's (1938) work on apparent motion, and his observation that we see the motion of the whole (e.g., of a flock of geese) rather than of the individual constituents of the whole (this goose, that goose, . . .); (2) the single-cell recording work of Kuffler (1953) and of Hubel & Wiesel (1962, 1968); (3) Julesz's (1971) invention of the random-dot stereogram, showing that stereopsis alone can provide a perception of depth; and (4) Shepard & Metzler's (1971) mental rotation studies, which stimulated speculation about the nature of mental representations of visually perceived objects.

. . .

Interesting and important though these findings are, one must sometimes be allowed the luxury of pausing to reflect upon the overall trends that they represent, in order to take stock
55   of the kind of knowledge that is accessible through these techniques. For we repeat: perhaps the most striking feature of neurophysiology and psychophysics at present is that they *describe* the behaviour of cells or of subjects, but do not *explain* it. What are the visual areas of the cerebral cortex actually doing? What are the problems in doing it that need explaining, and at what level of description should such explanations be sought?

A COMPUTATIONAL APPROACH TO VISION

60   In trying to come to grips with these problems, our group at the M.I.T. Artificial Intelligence Laboratory has adopted a point of view that regards visual perception as a problem primarily

grey-level intensity array: Imagine an image projected on a big sheet of graph paper. For each square, measure the intensity of the light falling on that square, and fill the square with a shade of gray (the higher the intensity, the lighter the shade, the lower, the darker). The finished product is a representation of the image as a gray-level intensity array. (The number of different shades of gray—which include black and white—is typically some power of two, but the specific number does not matter for Marr's present purposes.)

in information processing. The problem begins with a large, grey-level intensity array, which suffices to approximate an image such as the world might cast upon the retinas of the eyes, and it culminates in a *description* that depends on that array, and on the purpose that the viewer brings to it. Our particular concern in this article will be with the derivation of a description well suited for the recognition of three-dimensional shapes.

The Primal Sketch

It is a commonplace that a scene and a drawing of the scene appear very similar, despite the completely different grey-level images to which they give rise. This suggests that the artist's symbols correspond in some way to natural symbols that are computed out of the image during the normal course of its interpretation. Our theory therefore asserts that the first operation on an image is to transform it into a primitive but rich description of the way its intensities change over the visual field, as opposed to a description of its particular intensity values in and of themselves. This yields a description of markedly reduced size that still captures the important aspects required

values: intensity and color

for image analysis. We call it a *primal sketch* (Marr 1976). Consider, for example, an intensity array of 1000 by 1000, or 10^6 points in all. Even if the possible intensity at any one point were merely black or white—two different brightnesses—the number of all possible arrays would still be 2^{10^6}. In a real image, however, there tend to be continuities of intensity—areas where brightness varies uniformly—and this tends to eliminate possibilities in which the black and white oscillate wildly. It also tends to simplify the array. Typically, therefore, a primal sketch need not include a set of values for every point in an image. As stored in a computer, it will instead con-

Marr's point is that many of the 2^{10^6} possible intensity arrays would rarely or never occur naturally.

stitute an array with numbers representing the directions, magnitudes, and spatial extents of intensity changes assigned to certain specific points in an image, points that tend to be places of locally high or low intensity. The positions of these points, particularly their arrangement among their immediate neighbours—that is to say, the local geometry of the image—must also be made explicit in the primal sketch, as it would otherwise be lost. (It was implicit, of course, in the 1000 by 1000 array, but we are no longer retaining data for each of those 10^6 places.) One way to do this is to specify 'virtual lines'—directions and distances—between neighbouring points of interest in the sketch.

FIGURE 1   The image (*a*), which is 320 × 320 pixels, has been convolved with $\nabla^2 G$, a centre-surround operator with central excitatory region of width $2\sigma = 6$, 12, and 24 pixels. These filters span approximately the range of filters that operate in the human fovea. The zero-crossings of the filtered images are shown in (*b*), (*c*) and (*d*). These are the precursors of the raw primal sketch. (From Marr & Hildreth, 1980. Reprinted with permission.)

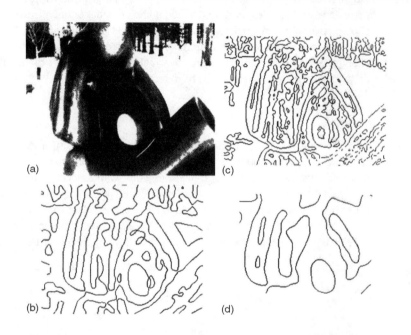

100   The process of computing the primal sketch involves several steps. The first is the derivation of the *raw primal sketch* (see Marr & Hildreth 1980), which involves detecting and representing the intensity changes in the image. First, the image is filtered through a set of medium band-pass second differential operators $\nabla^2 G$, (where ∇^2 is the Laplacian and G is a Gaussian distribution), and the zero-crossings in the filtered images are found (see figure 1). This representation

105   of the intensity changes is probably complete (Marr, Poggio, & Ullman 1979). Although in general there is no reason why the zero-crossings found by the different channels should be related, in practice they will be. The reason is that most intensity changes in an image arise from physical phenomena that are spatially localized. This constraint allowed Marr & Hildreth to formulate the *spatial coincidence assumption* which states: If a zero-crossing is present in a set of

110   independent $\nabla^2 G$ channels over a contiguous range of sizes, and it has the same position and orientation in each channel, then the set of such zero-crossings may be taken to indicate the presence of an intensity change in the image that is due to a single physical phenomenon (a change in reflectance, illumination, depth or surface orientation).

We have retained the preceding paragraph to call attention to the fact that in Marr's model low-level vision is understood as digital image processing. That is, the image is represented as an array of intensity values; to say that the image is "filtered through a set of medium bandpass second differential operators," or "independent $\nabla^2 G$ channels," is to say that the visual system subjects the array to computations that look for change in the rate of (spatial) change of intensity. Such places are called "zero-crossings" and tend to correspond to edges and other discontinuities in the visual scene. The "size" of a Laplacian-of-Gaussian (or "Marr edge detector") channel refers to the size of the region of the visual array that it uses in its computations. If the region is large, the channel will filter out small changes, and therefore detect only relatively salient discontinuities; the smaller the region, the less filtering and the more "edges" will be detected.

FIGURE 2   The primal sketch makes explicit information held in an intensity array (*a*). There are two kinds of information: one (*b*) concerns changes in intensity, represented by orientated edge, bar, and blob primitives, together with associated parameters that measure the contrast and spatial extent of the intensity change; and the other (*c*) is the local geometry of significant places in the image. Such places are marked by place-tokens, which can be defined in a variety of ways, and the geometric relations between them are represented by virtual lines (Marr, 1976, figures 7 and 12a, Reprinted with permission).

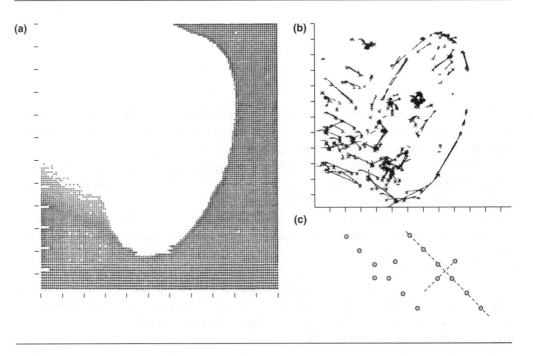

This assumption allows one to combine the zero-crossings from different channels into edge-segment descriptors, bars and blobs (see figure 2b), which constitute the raw primal sketch. To obtain the full primal sketch, these primitive elements are grouped, perhaps hierarchically, into units called place-tokens, which associate properties like length, width, brightness and so forth with positions in the image (Marr 1976). Virtual lines may then be used to represent the local geometry of these place-tokens (see figure 2c and Stevens 1978).

Recently, Marr & Ullman (1981) have extended the work of Marr & Hildreth to include the detection and use of directional selectivity. They have proposed specific roles for the X and Y channels found originally by Enroth-Cugell & Robson (1966), and in an explicit model for one class of cortical simple cell, they showed how to combine X and Y information to form a directionally selective unit.

Modules of Early Visual Processing

The primal sketch of an image is typically a large and unwieldy collection of data, even despite its simplification relative to a grey-level array; for this is the unavoidable consequence of the irregularity and complexity of natural images. The next computational problem is thus its decoding. Now the traditional approach to machine vision assumes that the essence of such a decoding is a process called *segmentation,* whose purpose is to divide a primal sketch, or more generally an image, into regions that are meaningful, perhaps as physical objects. Tenenbaum & Barrow (1976), for example, applied knowledge about several different types of scene to the segmentation of images of landscapes, an office, a room, and a compressor. Freuder (1975) used a similar approach to identify a hammer in a simple scene. Upon finding a blob, his computer program would tentatively label it as the head of a hammer, and begin a search for confirmation in the form of an appended shaft. If this approach were correct, it would mean that a central problem for vision is arranging for the right piece of specialized knowledge to be made available at the appropriate time in the segmentation of an image. Freuder's work, for example, was almost entirely devoted to the design of a system that made this possible. But despite considerable efforts over a long period, the theory and practice of segmentation remain rather primitive, and here again we believe that the main reason lies in the failure to formulate precisely the goals of this stage of the processing—a failure, in other words, to work at the topmost level of visual theory. What, for example, is an object? Is a head an object? Is it still an object if it is attached to a body? What about a man on horseback?

What, indeed, is an object? The answer seems perfectly obvious until we try to articulate it. One of the most challenging ways to articulate a concept is to explain it to a computer. It's true that we see objects all around us, but approaching the study of visual perception from this perspective has been unsuccessful because there are no objects in the raw data of vision. Rather, there are intensities and hues, which the eye and brain apparently organize into edges and surfaces and depth, some of which in turn are organized into objects. To put it another way, *object* is meaningful only in the context of conscious experience. For describing the stimulus, the visual array, or the intermediate stages of vision, *object* is meaningless.

> *descending influence:* often referred to as top-down or knowledge-driven processes (as distinct from bottom-up or data-driven processes)

Marr (1978) argued that the early stages of visual information processing ought instead to squeeze the last possible ounce of information   150
from an image before taking recourse to the descending influence of "high-level" knowledge about objects in the world. Let us turn, then, to a brief examination of the physics of the situation. As noted earlier, the visual process begins with arrays of intensities projected upon the retinas of the eyes. The principal factors that determine   155
these intensities are (1) the illuminant, (2) the surface reflectance properties of the objects viewed, (3) the shapes of the visible surfaces of these objects, and (4) the vantage point of the viewer.

> *the illuminant:* the intensity and other characteristics of the light falling on the visual scene

Thus if the analysis of the input intensity arrays is to   160
operate autonomously, at least in its early stages, it can only be expected to extract information about these four factors. In short, early visual processing must be limited to the recovery of localized physical properties of the visible *surfaces* of a viewed object, particularly local surface dispositions (orientation and depth) and surface material properties (colour, texture, shininess, and so on). More abstract matters such as a description   165
of overall three-dimensional shape must come after this more basic analysis is complete.

An example of early processing is stereopsis. Imagine that images of a scene are available from two nearby points at the same horizontal level—the analogue of the images that play upon the   170
retinas of your left and right eyes. The images are somewhat different, of course, in consequence of the slight difference in vantage point. Imagine further that a particular location on a surface in the scene is chosen from one image; that the corre-   175
sponding location is identified in the other image;

> *stereopsis* means "seeing with two eyes." Because the two eyes see things from different positions, images on the left and right retinas are slightly different. (This is called *retinal disparity*.) But our visual perception is (usually) unitary, which means that the visual system somehow fuses the two images.

and that the relative positions of the two versions of that location are measured. This information will suffice for the calculation of depth—the distance of that location from the viewer. Notice that methods based on grey-level correlation between the pair of images fail to be suitable because a mere grey-level measurement does not reliably define a point on a physical surface. To put the matter plainly, numerous points in a surface might fortuitously be the same shade of grey, and differences in the vantage points of the observer's eyes could change the shade as well. The matching must evidently be based instead on objective markings that lie upon the surface, and so one had to use changes in reflectance. One way of doing this is to obtain a primitive description of the intensity changes that exist in each image (such as a primal sketch), and then to match these descriptions. After all, the line segments, edge segments, blobs, and edge termination points included in such a description correspond quite closely to boundaries and reflectance changes on physical surfaces. The stereo problem—the determination of depth given a stereo pair of images—may thus be reduced to that of matching two primitive descriptions, one from each eye; and to help in this task there are physical constraints that translate into two rules for how the left and right descriptions are combined.

Uniqueness

Each item from each image may be assigned at most one disparity value, that is to say, a unique position relative to its counterpart in the stereo pair. This condition rests on the premise that the items to be matched have a physical existence, and can be in only one place at a time.

Continuity

Disparity varies smoothly almost everywhere. This condition is a consequence of the cohesiveness of matter, and it states that only a relatively small fraction of the area of an image is composed of discontinuities in depth.

. . .

A second example of early visual processing concerns the derivation of structure from motion. It has long been known that as an object moves relative to the viewer, the way its appearance changes provides information that we can use to determine its shape (Wallach & O'Connell 1953). The motion analogue of a random-dot stereogram is illustrated in figure 3, and as expected, humans can easily perceive shape from a succession of frames, each of which on its own is merely a set of random-dots. In various papers and a forthcoming book on the subject, Ullman (1979*a, b*) decomposed the problem into two parts: matching the elements that occur in consecutive images, and deriving shape information from measurements of their changes in position. Ullman then showed that these problems can be solved mathematically. His basic idea is that, in general, nothing can be inferred about the shape of an object given only a set of sequential views of it; some extra assumptions have to be made. Accordingly, he formulates an assumption of rigidity, which states that if a set of moving points has a *unique* interpretation as a rigid body in motion, that interpretation is correct. (The assumption is based

FIGURE 3 The motion analogue of the random-dot stereogram. Two transparent, concentric cylinders are rotated in opposite directions. Each has dots scattered on its surface. A cine camera photographs the scene from the side, and each frame contains only a pattern of random dots. When a human watches the film, however, he immediately perceives the two counter-rotating cylinders. (From Ullman, 1979b. Reprinted with permission.)

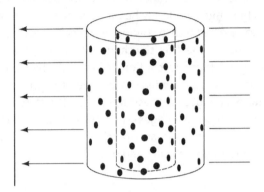

on a theorem, which he proves, stating that three distinct views of four non-coplanar points on a rigid body are sufficient to determine uniquely their three-dimensional arrangement in space.) From this he derives a method for computing structure from motion. The method gives results that are quantitatively superior to the ability of humans to determine shape from   215
motion, and which fail in qualitatively similar circumstances. Ullman has also devised a set of simple algorithms by which the method may be implemented.

The 2½-D Sketch

Both of the techniques of image analysis discussed in the preceding paragraphs provide information about the relative distances to various places in an image. In stereopsis, it is the matching of points in a stereo pair that leads to such information. In structure from motion, it   220
is the matching of points in successive images. More generally, however, we know that vision provides several sources of information about shapes in the visual world. The most direct, perhaps, are the aforementioned stereo and motion, but texture gradients in a single image are nearly as effective. Furthermore, the theatrical techniques of facial make-up reveal the sensitivity of perceived shapes to shading (see Horn 1975), and colour sometimes suggests the man-   225
ner in which a surface reflects light. It often happens that different parts of a scene are open to inspection by different techniques. Yet different as the techniques are, they all have two important characteristics in common: they rely on information from the image rather than *a priori* knowledge about the shapes of the viewed objects, and the information that they specify concerns the depth or surface orientation at arbitrary points in an image, rather than the   230
depth or orientation associated with particular objects (see table 1).

TABLE 1   The form in which various early visual processes deliver information about the changes in a scene

information source	natural parameter
stereo	disparity, hence especially δr and Δr
motion	r, hence $\delta r, \Delta r$
shading	s
texture gradients	s
perspective cues	s
occlusion	Δr
contour	s

Key:

r is depth
δr is small, local change in depth
Δr is large changes in depth

s is local surface orientation

> By *change*, Marr also means *difference*.

To make the most efficient use of different and often complementary channels of information deriving from stereopsis, from motion, from contours, from texture, from colour, from
shading, they need to be combined in some way. The computational question that now arises
235   is thus how best to do this, and the natural answer is to seek some representation of the visual
scene that makes explicit just the information that these processes can deliver. We seek, in
other words, a representation of surfaces in an image that makes explicit their shapes and orientations, much as the arabic representation of a number makes explicit its composition by
powers of ten. It might be contrasted with the representation of a surface as a mathematical
240   expression, in which the orientation is only implicit, and not at all apparent. We call such a representation the 2½-D sketch (Marr & Nishihara 1978; Marr 1978), and in the particular candidate
for it shown in figure 4, surface orientation is represented by covering an image with needles.
The length of each needle defines the dip of the surface at that point, so that zero length corresponds to a surface that is perpendicular to the vector from the viewer to the point, and
245   increasing lengths denote surfaces that dip increasingly away from the viewer. The orientation
of each needle defines the local direction of dip.

Our argument is that the 2½-D sketch is useful because it makes explicit information about
the image in a form that is closely matched to what image analysis can deliver. To put it another
way, we can formulate the goals of this stage of visual processing as being primarily the con-
250   struction of this representation, discovering, for example, what are the surface orientations in
a scene, which of the contours in the primal sketch correspond to surface discontinuities and

FIGURE 4   Illustration of the 2½-dimensional sketch. In (a), the perspective views of small squares placed at various orientations to the viewer are shown. The dots with arrows show a way of representing the orientations of such surfaces symbolically. In (b), this representation is used to show the surface orientations of two cylindrical surfaces in front of a background orthogonal to the viewer. The full 2½-dimensional sketch would include rough distances to the surfaces as well as their orientations, contours where surface orientation changes sharply, and contours where depth is discontinuous (subjective contours). A considerable amount of computation is required to maintain these quantities in states that are consistent with one another and with the structure of the outside world (see Marr 1978, §3). (From Marr & Nishihara, 1978, figure 2. Reprinted with permission.)

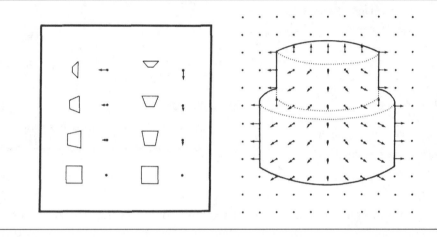

should therefore be represented in the 2½-D sketch, and which contours are missing in the primal sketch and need to be inserted into the 2½-D sketch to bring it into a state that is consistent with the nature of three-dimensional space. This formulation avoids the difficulties associated with the terms 'region' and 'object'—the difficulties inherent in the image segmentation approach; for the grey level intensity array, the primal sketch, the various modules of early visual processing, and finally the 2½-D sketch itself deal only with discovering the properties of *surfaces* in an image. One is pleased about that, for we know of ourselves as perceivers that surface orientation can be associated with unfamiliar shapes, so its representation probably precedes the decomposition of the scene into objects. One is thus free to ask precise questions about the computational structure of the 2½-D sketch and of processes to create and maintain it. We are currently much occupied with these matters.   255

260

LATER PROCESSING PROBLEMS

The final components of our visual processing theory concern the application of visually derived surface information for the representation of three-dimensional shapes in a way that is suitable specifically for recognition (Marr & Nishihara 1978). By this we mean the ability to recognize a shape   265 as being the same as a shape seen earlier, and this in essence depends on being able to describe shapes consistently each time they are seen, whatever the circumstances of their positions relative to the viewer. The problem with local surface representations such as the 2½-D sketch is that the description depends as much on the viewpoint of the observer as it does on the structure of the shape. In order to factor out a description of a shape that depends on its structure alone, the representation must be based on readily identifiable geometric features of the overall shape, and the dispositions of these features must de specified relative to the shape in itself. In brief, the coordinate system must be 'object-centred,' not 'viewer-centred.' One aspect of this deals with the nature of the representation scheme that is to be used, and another with how to obtain it from the 2½-D sketch. We begin by discussing the first, and will then move on to the second.

FIGURE 5   The portrayal of animals by a small number of pipe-cleaners serves to show that the representation of a three-dimensional shape need not make explicit its surface to describe it so well that it can easily be recognized. The success of the representation is due, one suspects, in large measure to the correspondence between the pipe-cleaners and the axes of the volumes that they stand for. (From Marr & Nishihara, 1978, figure 1. Reprinted with permission.)

The 3-D model representation

The most basic geometric properties of the volume occupied by a shape are (1) its average location (or centre of mass), (2) its overall size, as exemplified, for example, by its mean diameter or volume, and (3) its principal axis of elongation or symmetry, if one exists. A description based on these qualities would certainly be inadequate for an application such as shape recognition; after all, one can tell little about the three-dimensional structure of a shape given only its position, size and orientation. But if a shape itself has a natural decomposition into components that can be so described, this volumetric scheme is an effective means for describing the relative spatial arrangement of those components. The illustration of figure 5 shows a familiar version of this type of description, the stick figure (see Blum 1973). The recognizability of the animal shapes depicted in the illustration is surprising considering the simplicity of representation used to describe them. The reason that such a description works so well lies, we think, in (1) the volumetric (as opposed to surface-based) definition of the primitive elements—the sticks—used by the representation, (2) the relatively small number of elements used, and (3) the relation of elements to each other rather than to the viewer. In short, this type of shape representation is volumetric, modular, and can be based on object-centred coordinates. Figure 6 illustrates the scheme of representation that was developed from these ideas. Here the description of a shape is composed of a hierarchy of stick-figure specifications that we call 3-D models. In the simplest, a single axis element is used to specify the location, size and orientation of the entire shape; the human body displayed in the illustration will serve as an instance. This element is also used to define a coordinate system that will specify the dispositions of subsidiary axes, each of these specifying in turn a coordinate system for 3-D models of 'arm,' 'hand,' and so on. This hierarchical structure makes it possible to treat any component of a shape as a shape in itself. It also provides flexibility in the detail of a description.

Shapes admitting 3-D model descriptions

If the scheme for a given shape is to be uniquely defined and stable over unimportant variations such as viewpoint—if, in a word it is to be canonical—its definition must take advantage of any salient geometrical characteristics that the shape possesses inherently. If a shape has natural axes, then those should be used. The coordinate system for a sausage should take advantage of its major axis, and for a face, of its axis of symmetry.

> *canonical:* invariant, lawlike; for example, a canonical scheme for elbow macaroni is that it is curved, cylindrical, and hollow, even though some or all of these properties are not apparent from some viewpoints or when illuminated in certain ways.

FIGURE 6   The arrangement of 3-D models into the representation of a human shape. First the overall form—the 'body'—is given an axis. This yields an object-centred coordinate system which can then be used to specify the arrangement of the 'arms', 'legs', 'torso' and 'head'. The position of each of these is specified by an axis of its own, which in turn serves to define a coordinate system for specifying the arrangement of further subsidiary parts. This gives us a hierarchy of 3-D models, shown here extending downwards as far as the ringers. The shapes in the figure are drawn as if they were cylindrical, but that is purely for illustrative convenience. (From Marr & Nishihara, 1978, figure 3. Reprinted with permission.)

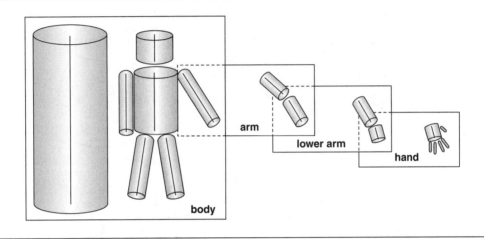

Highly symmetrical objects, like a sphere, a square, or a circular disk, will inevitably lead to ambiguities in the choice of coordinate systems. For a shape as regular as a sphere this poses no great problem, because its description in all reasonable systems is the same. One can even allow other factors, like the direction of motion or spin, to influence the choice of coordinate frame. For other shapes, the existence of more than one possible choice probably means that one has to represent the object in several ways, but this is acceptable provided that their number is small. For example, there are four possible axes on which one might wish to base the coordinate system for representing a door, namely the midlines along its length, its width, and its thickness, and also the axis of its hinges. (This last would be especially useful to represent how the door opens.) For a typewriter, there are two reasonable choices, an axis parallel to its width, because that is usually its largest dimension, and the axis about which a typewriter is roughly symmetrical.

In general, if an axis can be distinguished in a shape, it can be used as the basis for a local coordinate system. One approach to the problem of defining object-centred coordinates is therefore to examine the class of shapes having an axis as an integral part of their structure. Consider, accordingly, the class of so-called *generalized cones,* each of these being the surface swept out by moving a cross section of constant shape but smoothly varying size along an axis, as shown in figure 7. Binford (1971) has drawn attention to this class of constructions,

FIGURE 7   The definition of a generalized cone. It is the surface created by moving a cross-section along a given smooth axis. The cross section may vary smoothly in size, but its shape remains constant. Several examples are shown here. In each, the cross section is shown at several positions along the trajectory that spins out the construction.

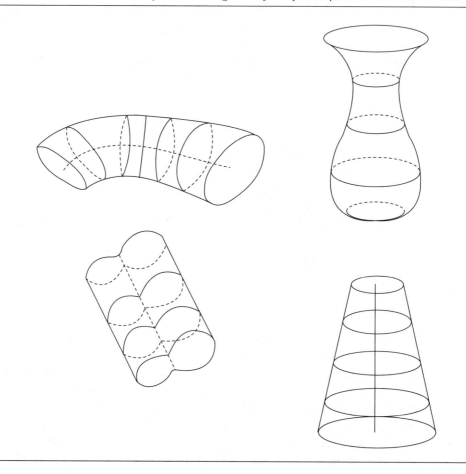

suggesting that it might provide a convenient way of describing three-dimensional surfaces   330
for the purposes of computer vision (see also Agin 1972; Nevatia 1974). We regard it as an
important class not because the shapes themselves are easily describable, but because the
presence of an axis allows one to define a canonical local coordinate system. Fortunately, many
objects, especially those whose shape was achieved by growth, are described quite naturally
in terms of one or more generalized cones. The animal shapes of figure 7 provide some   335
examples; the individual sticks are simply the axes of generalized cones that approximate the
shapes of parts of these creatures. Many artefacts can also be described in this way—say a car
(a small box sitting atop a longer one) or a building (a box with a vertical axis.)

It is important to remember, however, that there exist surfaces that cannot conveniently be approximated by generalized cones, for example a cake that has been transected at some arbitrary plane, or the surface formed by a crumpled newspaper. Cases like the cake could be dealt with by introducing a suitable surface primitive for describing the plane of the cut, in much the same way as an axis in the 3-D model representation is a primitive that describes a volumetric element. But the crumpled newspaper poses apparently intractable problems.

Finding the natural coordinate system

Even if a shape possesses a canonical coordinate frame, one still is faced with the problem of finding it from an image. Our own interest in this problem grew from the question of how to interpret the *outlines* of objects as seen in a two-dimensional image (Marr 1977*b*), and our

FIGURE 8   'Rites of Spring' by Pablo Picasso. We immediately interpret such silhouettes in terms of particular three-dimensional surfaces—this despite the paucity of information in the image itself. In order to do this, we plainly must invoke certain *a priori* assumptions and constraints about the nature of the shapes.

starting point was the observation that when one looks at the silhouettes in Picasso's 'Rites of Spring' (reproduced here in figure 8), one perceives them in terms of very particular three-dimensional shapes, some familiar, some less so. This is quite remarkable, because the silhouettes could in theory have been generated by an infinite variety of three-dimensional shapes which, from other viewpoints, would have no descernible similarities to the shapes we perceive. One can perhaps attribute part of the phenomenon to a familiarity with the depicted shapes, but not all of it, because one can use the medium of a silhouette to convey a new shape, and because even with considerable effort it is difficult to imagine the more bizarre three-dimensional surfaces that could have given rise to the same silhouettes. The paradox, then, is that the bounding contours in Picasso's 'Rites' apparently tell us more than they should about the shape of the figures. For example, neighbouring points on such a contour could in general arise from widely separated points on the original surface, but our perceptual interpretation usually ignores this possibility.

350

355

360

The first observation to be made is that the contours that bound these silhouettes are contours of surface discontinuity, which are precisely the contours with which the 2½-D sketch is concerned. Secondly, because we can interpret the silhouettes as three-dimensional shapes, then implicit in the way we interpret them must lie some *a priori* assumptions that allow us to infer a shape from an outline. If a surface violates these assumptions, our analysis will be wrong, in the sense that the shape that we assign to the contours will differ from the shape that actually caused them. An everyday example is the shadowgraph, where the appropriate arrangement of one's hands can, to the surprise and delight of a child, produce the shadow of a duck or a rabbit.

365

370

> *surface discontinuity:* The contour, or outline, is the boundary between parts of the object's surface visible to the viewer and parts that are hidden from the viewer.

What assumptions is it reasonable to suppose that we make? To explain them, we need to define the four constructions that appear in figure 9. These are (1) a three-dimensional surface Σ, (2) its image or silhouette S_v as seen from a viewpoint V, (3) the bounding contour C_v of S_v, and (4) the set of points on the surface that project onto the contour C_v. We shall call this last the *contour generator* of C_v and we shall denote it by Γ_v

375

380

> *contour generator:* Look at an object. Now imagine a plane, perpendicular to the line of sight, passing through the object so that all the object's forward-facing surface points are in front of the plane, and all rearward-facing surface points are behind the plane. The set of points that lie in the plane and on the surface of the objects are the contour generator.

Observe that the contour C_v, like the contours in the work of Picasso, imparts very little information about the three-dimensional surface that caused it. Indeed, the only obvious feature available in the contour is the distinction between convex and concave places—that is to say, the presence of inflexion points. In order that these inflections be

385

> An *inflection point* is a point where something changes direction.

FIGURE 9   Four structures of importance in studying the a *priori* conditions mentioned in figure 8. *(a)* A three-dimensional surface Σ; *(b)* its silhouette, S_y, as seen from viewpoint V; *(c)* the contour C_y of S_y; *(d)* the set of points Γ_y on E that project onto the contour. Finally, *(e)* illustrates schematically the meaning of the phrase 'all distant viewing directions that lie in a plane'.

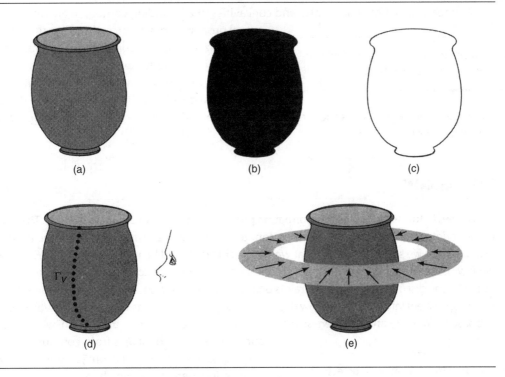

(a)   (b)   (c)

(d)   (e)

'reliable,' one needs to make some assumptions about the way in which the contour was generated, and we choose the following restrictions (Marr 1977*b*).

(1) Each point on the contour generator Γ_y projects to a different point on the contour C_y.

(2) Nearby points on the contour C_y arise from nearby points on the contour generator Γ_y.

(3) The contour generator Γ_y lies wholly in a single plane.

The first and second restrictions say that each point on the contour of the image comes from one point on the surface (which is an assumption that facilitates the analysis but is not of fundamental importance), and that where the surface looks continuous in the image, it really is continuous in three dimensions. The third restriction is simply the demand that the difference between convex and concave contour segments reflects properties of the surface, rather than of the imaging process.

It turns out to be a theorem that if the surface is smooth (for our purposes, if it is twice 400
differentiable with continuous second derivative) and if restrictions 1–3 hold for all distant
viewing positions in any one plane (as illustrated in figure 11), then the viewed surface is a generalized cone with straight axis. (The converse is also true: if the surface is a generalized cone
with straight axis, then conditions 1–3 will be found to be true.)

This means that if the convexities and concavities of a bounding contour in an image are 405
actual properties of a surface, then that surface is
a generalized cone or is composed of several such

> *actual properties:* as opposed to a function of vantage point, as in a shadowgraph

cones. In brief, the theorem says that a natural
link exists between generalized cones and the
imaging process itself. The combination of these 410
two must mean, we think, that generalized cones will play an intimate role in the development
of vision theory.

DISCUSSION

I have tried in this survey of visual information processing to make two principal points. The first
is methodological: namely, that it is important to be very clear about the nature of the understanding that we seek. The results that we try to achieve should be precise ones, at the level of 415
what we call a computational theory. The critical act in formulating computational theories turns
out to be the discovery of valid constraints on the way the world is structured—constraints that
provide sufficient information to allow the processing to succeed. Consider stereopsis, which presupposes continuity and uniqueness in the world, or structure from visual motion, which presupposes rigidity, or shape from contour, which 420
presupposes the three restrictions just discussed, or

> *spatial coincidence:* An edge is "detected," or inferred, where several edge candidates (zero crossings), picked out by different sizes of spatial filter, coincide.

even edge detection, which presupposes the
assumption of spatial coincidence. The discovery of
constraints that are valid and universal leads to
results about vision that have the same quality of 425
permanence as results in other branches of science.

The second point is that the critical issues for vision seem to me to revolve around the nature
of the representations and the nature of the processes that create, maintain and eventually
interpret them. I have suggested an overall framework for visual information processing (summarized in table 2) that includes three categories of representation upon which the process- 430
ing is to operate. The first encompasses representations of intensity variations and their local
geometry in the input to the visual system. One among these, the primal sketch, is expressly
intended to be an efficient description of these variations which captures just that information
required by the image analysis to follow. The second category encompasses the representations of visible surfaces—the descriptions, in other words, of the physical properties of the sur- 435
faces that caused the images in the first place. The nature of these representations, the

2½-dimensional sketch in particular, is determined primarily by what information can be extracted by modules of image analysis such as stereopsis and structure from motion. Like the primal sketch of the previous category, the 2½-dimensional sketch is intended to be a final or
440 output representation: this is where the separate contributions from the various image-analysis modules can be combined into a unified description. The third category encompasses all representations that are subsequently constructed from information contained in the 2½-D sketch. The designs of these tertiary representations are determined largely by the use to which they are to be put, as for the 3-D model representation, to be used for shape recognition. If one
445 had wanted instead, for example, to represent a shape simply for later *reproduction,* say by the milling of a block of metal, then the 2½-D sketch would itself have been sufficient, as the milling process depends explicitly on information about local depth and orientation, such as that sketch can provide.

TABLE 2   A framework for the derivation of shape information from images

image(s)	
↓	
primal sketch(es)	Describes the intensity changes present in an image, labels distinguished locations like termination points, and makes explicit local two-dimensional geometrical relations
↓	
2½-D sketch	Represents contours of surface discontinuity, and depth and orientation of visible surface elements, in a coordinate frame that is centred on the viewer
↓	
3-D model representation	Shape description that includes volumetric shape primitives of a variety of sizes, whose positions are defined by using an object-centred coordinate system. This representation imposes considerable modular organization on its descriptions

Finally, a remark of a rather different nature. As
450 we have seen, some aspects of human early visual processing, like stereopsis, have apparently been understood well enough to implement them in machines (Marr & Poggio, 1979; Grimson & Marr, 1979). The computational power required by
455 these early processes is prohibitive, and until recently the prospects for real-time implementation of human-like early vision were remote. It now appears, however, that the emerging VLSI and CCD technologies will be able to supply the
460 necessary processing power. This could make the next two decades very interesting.

VLSI, or Very-Large-Scale Integration, was, in the 1980s, the state of the art in the fabrication of integrated circuits ("chips"). It allowed many tens of thousands of transistors to be created on a single chip, which was roughly a tenfold increase over LSI, the previous standard.

A *CCD,* or charge-coupled device, is an optical sensor that produces a pixelated image (such as the gray-level intensity array that Marr uses at the beginning of the paper). Today CCDs are the guts of such things as scanners and digital cameras.

FOR DISCUSSION

1. What does Marr's gray-level array correspond to in Gibson's description of vision?

2. Why does segmentation seem—intuitively at least—to be the right way to decode the primal sketch? What, in Marr's view, is wrong with it?

3. In the context of Marr's theory, what is an object?

4. What does the 2½-D sketch add to the primal sketch? What salient feature of the world, as we perceive it, is still missing from the 2½-D sketch?

5. What is the fundamental difference between the way the visual world is represented in the 2½-D sketch and the way it is represented in the 3-D model?

Part III

Opening the Black Box

A spacecraft from an advanced civilization in a distant galaxy lands in Central Park. The crew are the toast of the town, even though no one can figure out how to communicate with them. They seem to be visiting, systematically, every pizzeria in New York, which takes some time. Meanwhile, their ship is turned over to NASA. After a while, the NASA folks learn how to fly the thing. They discover how to use its navigational instruments and determine that it is fueled by sunlight. Even after they have taken it completely apart and put it back together, however, they have no idea *how* it works—they don't know *how* it turns sunlight into propulsion, *how* the knobs and levers make it go this way or that way, *how* the navigation system gets the ship from here to there and back again. In short, they have what scientists and engineers sometimes call a *black box:*

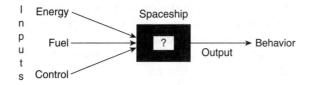

Everything NASA knows about the ship is in the form *if (input) then (output);* for example:

> If we push the green button, then the door will open.

> If the red light is on and we push the green button, then the door will not open.

Psychology begins in the same way:

> If I look someone in the eye when we are introduced, and repeat the person's name, I am more likely to be able to remember it.

> When I turn out the light, I can see almost nothing, but after a while I can see much more.

Every time the dog hears the can opener, she goes to the kitchen.

When I am with other people, I eat more than when I am alone.

and so on

We know thousands of such things about ourselves and others, but we often want to do more than simply identify an if-then relation. After all, there must be something going on inside the black box, some causal connection between the input and the output, between the *if* and the *then*. If my *mind* is the part of me that remembers and forgets, then there's something about the way my mind works that is responsible for the fact that if I look someone in the eye and repeat their name I am more likely to remember it.

Something is happening in there, but we cannot study that process directly. Therefore we develop a theory of the box—of what's in it, of how it works—to account for our observations of the relation between the box's inputs and its outputs, and then we try to test our theory.

Most psychological research necessarily begins with description, that is, with the box closed. Sooner or later, though, it is only natural to want to know not only what happens, but how and why it happens. At that point the box must be opened. When talking about black boxes in the context of psychology, there may be a temptation to take the metaphor too literally and to suppose that the skull is the box, which we literally open so as to peer at the brain. Not necessarily. We can learn about what's going on inside in other ways.

The readings in this section describe some of the tools that have been developed as ways of describing and understanding what goes on in the box. The most obvious such tool, of course, is to *introspect,* to look (*spect*) inside (*intro*) our own minds. As Titchener describes it, introspection was conceived as a way to build a systematic account of the kinds of things that are in the mind and how they are organized. Despite its obviousness, however, introspection was not the first black-box tool to be developed. Fechner (see Additional Readings) developed his psychophysics, a way of quantifying the relation between stimuli and sensations, and Donders developed his reaction-time logic for making inferences about psychological processes, before introspection was widely adopted.

Introspection was rejected by many people for many reasons. For Freud, introspection was inadequate because the things he was looking for—memories and motives—were not visible to the introspecting eye. Freud's black-box tool, psychoanalysis, was an elaborate way of interpreting—not merely observing—behavior to uncover the mind's hidden content. For Skinner, on the other hand, the problem with introspection was not that it could not see far enough, but that it was looking in the wrong direction. Behaviorism's solution to the problem of opening the black box was very clear: Don't. It is unnecessary to open the black box, Skinner argues, because everything we suppose we will find inside it can be explained in terms of behavior and its consequences.

In the second half of the 20th century, the development of the computer offered a metaphor for thinking about how the mind works, and it provided a way to test those ideas. Simon and Kotovsky showed how a psychological theory framed in terms of information processing can be tested by turning the theory into a program and running it on a computer. The 20th century also saw the appearance of brain imaging, a powerful set of black-box tools that offer views of the living brain. As Posner, Petersen, Fox, and Raichle explain, it has become possible to measure and record, in various ways, the intensity and location of brain activity corresponding to mental events (sensations, thoughts, memories, etc.) and to the presentation of specific stimuli. These imaging tools are gradually drawing a map of the brain's functions.

ADDITIONAL READINGS

Pierre Flourens   *Investigations of the properties and functions of the nervous system in vertebrate animals* (1824)

> Flourens pioneered the ablation method for investigating the localization of function in the brain.

Paul Broca   *Remarks on the seat of the faculty of articulate language, followed by an observation of aphemia* (1861)

> Broca was one of the first to see that naturally occurring brain damage provides important clues to the localization of function in the human brain.

Hermann Ebbinghaus   *Memory* (1885)

> In his famous memory experiments, Ebbinghaus upset the conventional wisdom that mental processes (e.g., memory) were unobservable and therefore outside the realm of science. Inspired by Fechner, Ebbinghaus studied memory indirectly, by measuring behavior that is (presumably) a function of hidden mental processes.

Allen Newell & Herbert Simon   *GPS, a program that simulates human thought* (1961)

> GPS, or General Problem Solver, is one of the landmarks of the early and ambitious period of artificial intelligence. Newell and Simon argue that GPS solves logic problems in approximately the same way as human subjects, evidence that human thought is a matter of information processing.

James McClelland, David Rumelhart, & Geoffrey Hinton   *The appeal of PDP* (1986)

> Twenty-five years after GPS, the limitations of the information-processing model of human thought were becoming clear. A new generation of psychologists and computer scientists were attracted to a different model, known as parallel distributed processing (PDP), or connectionism. This paper is a nontechnical introduction to PDP and a discussion of its advantages over the information-processing point of view.

Allan Collins & M. Ross Quillian   *Retrieval time from semantic memory* (1969)

> A classic experiment in which the reaction time methods developed by Donders and Cattell are used to test a model of how knowledge (semantic memory) is organized in the human mind.

Wilder Penfield   *The mystery of the mind* (1975)

> Penfield, a neurosurgeon, found that direct electrical stimulation of the human cortex yielded reports of various sensory and cognitive experiences.

F. C. Donders (1818–1889)
On the Speed of Mental Processes (1868–1869)

In 1850 Helmholtz measured the speed of nerve impulses, demonstrating conclusively that nerves did not, as some had thought, simply conduct electric current. Whatever they did conduct moved much more slowly, and knowing this was an important clue to the nature of the nerve impulse.

About 15 years later, Donders measured the speed of the work that nerve impulses do. He is sometimes said to have measured the "speed of thought," but this is misleading. Rather, Donders measured the time required to make a response in a simple cognitive task. By itself, this measurement is of no particular interest, but Donders saw that comparing such measurements for two slightly different tasks could reveal something about the mental processes involved in those tasks. Both Helmholtz's measurement (described by Donders, below) and Donders's were the fruit of considerable technical ingenuity and skill, and both are milestones in the history of psychology.

Franciscus Cornelius Donders was born in Tilburg, in the Netherlands, and studied medicine in Utrecht. In 1848 he became professor of physiology at the University of Utrecht, and 10 years later he established the Netherlands' first ophthalmology clinic. The clinic quickly became internationally important, not only as a hospital but as a center of research and teaching. (Another ophthalmologist at Donders's clinic was Herman Snellen, immortalized on the walls of doctors' offices in the *Snellen Chart* for measuring visual acuity.)

Donders's research led him to an understanding of ocular problems such as farsightedness and astigmatism, and he became the world's expert on visual defects of accommodation and refraction. His massive treatise *On the anomalies of refraction and accommodation of the eye*, published in 1864, helped to establish the medical field of ophthalmology.

Source: Donders, F. C. (1969). On the speed of mental processes (W. G. Koster, Trans.). *Acta Psychologica, 30,* 412–431. Reprinted with permission. [We have converted Donders's fractional time intervals to decimal numbers.]

A few years later, Donders published the results of his studies of the speed of mental processes, and the importance of his work was immediately apparent. His techniques were adopted and developed by others, particularly in Wilhelm Wundt's laboratory at Leipzig, where the American psychologist James McKeen Cattell, then a graduate student, conducted many reaction-time studies (Cattell, 1886a, 1886b, 1887). Since then, reaction time, or "mental chronometry," as it is sometimes called, has been used in countless studies. (Examples are Collins & Quillian, 1969, and Sternberg, 1966.) It remains one of the experimental psychologist's most versatile tools (for a review, see Luce, 1986).

While philosophy is occupied in the abstract with the contemplation of mental phenomena, physiology, having at its disposal the results of philosophy, has to investigate the relation between those phenomena and the action of the brain. In the domain of morphology that relation immediately leaps to the eye. Considering the known facts of comparative anatomy and anthropology, any doubt concerning the existence of such a relation is untenable. But physiology cannot be content with that general result. Along with disorders observed in the case of pathological changes, physiology tries to locate the various mental faculties as much as possible by experimentation, and especially to trace the nature of the action accompanying the mental phenomena. It therefore relates the study on chemical composition and the metabolism of its components with the investigation of the fine structure of the brain. It finds that with the loss of blood or suppressed action of the heart, consciousness is lost, it learns from this that the regular supply of blood is a necessary condition for mental processes, and concludes that metabolism is at the root of brain life. Further, it establishes that, as in all other organs, the blood undergoes a change as a consequence of the nourishment of the brain, and discovers in comparing the incoming and outflowing blood that oxygen has been consumed, that carbonic acid has been formed and that heat has been generated. It knows that the heat may have originated from other forms of energy, for instance from electromotive action that it may postulate in the brain, after proving its existence in morphologically and chemically related nerves. It further aims at tracing, by means of continuing research, all phases of the chemical process in the living brain, and to follow closely the series of transformations, beginning with chemical energy and ending up with heat. And convinced that the phenomena can be reduced to laws only by measuring and evaluating, it will not rest before it has established, not only the nature of such conversions, but also their quantity and that of the converted substances, and has thus found the equivalent of the different forms of energy.

But will it ever be possible for the function of the mind to be included in the chain of transforming forces? As far as we can see now there is no prospect of this whatever. The essence of all forms of work and energy we know and measure, is motion or the condition of motion, and nobody can imagine how from motion, in whatever way combined, consciousness or any other sort of mental function may be born. In form and nature mental function has a character completely of its own, as we perceive it in the first place in ourselves. Nowhere does it show a transition or an affinity to other natural phenomena, and the law of conservation of energy, valid for all known natural forces and forming the guiding principle in every investigation, is absolutely powerless to bring the mental phenomena under its control. For, apart from their specific nature, which makes their creation from chemical bonds as inconceivable as their transformation into thermal movement or electrical movement, they can neither be

> *morphology:* the study of the form and structure of organisms

> *conservation of energy:* Helmholtz (1847) established that in a physical system energy can be transformed (for example, from heat to motion or vice versa) but cannot be gained or lost.

5

10

15

20

25

30

35

40

measured nor evaluated, and we know no unit by which to express sensation, reason and will in figures.

The question physiology has to pose itself is simply this: What happens in the brain during
45 the processes of sensation, reason and will? It is readily understood that this formulation does not and indeed must not, prejudge anything. But we must also admit that the complete answering of this question, i.e. a complete knowledge of the functioning of the brain, with which each mental process is connected, does not carry us a step further in the understanding of *the nature* of their relation. An explanation of mental phenomena, in the sense in which
50 we consider phenomena explained, would be attainable only if they could be reduced to a universal law, such as the one on the conservation of energy, and, as we have seen, this possibility seems a priori ruled out.

But will all quantitative treatment of mental processes be out of the question then? By no means! An important factor seemed to be susceptible to measurement: I refer to the time
55 required for simple mental processes. For answering the question whether we are entitled to apply the generally proved relation to special cases—in other words, whether we may assume that there is an absolute correspondence between diverse
60 functions in the brain and the diversity in each particular sensation, each private mental picture, each expression of the will—it seems that the determination of that duration of time is not without importance. . . .

> *generally proved relation:* that is, the relation between brain function and mental process referred to in the previous paragraph

Barely 25 years ago, the time in which excited nerves carried their commands to the brain and the brain activated the muscles, was supposed to be 'infinitely short.' Johannes Müller, to
65 whom the first place among the physiologists of his time is due, not only pronounced the conduction velocity in the nerves unknown, but he even went so far as to predict that the means of determining this velocity would no doubt always be denied us. And yet a short time later, in 1845, Du Bois-Reymond sketched in general terms a scheme for such a determination, and as early as 1850 Helmholtz carried out the measurements.

70 The method was simple. Helmholtz excited the motor nerves at two points, the one close to the nerve-muscle junction, the other at a greater distance. In both cases he determined the time that elapsed before the muscle contracted. The differences in times indicated the conduction time of the
75 nerve between the two excited points, and from this the conduction velocity could be obtained. It appeared to be no greater than 100 feet per second.[1] This is a speed surpassed by birds in their flight, approached by race-horses, and attained by our hand when arm motions are quickest.

> This is a crude estimate. The speed of the nerve impulse varies considerably from one kind of nerve fiber to another. What matters here is not how fast the impulse travels but that its speed is finite.

80 This result was obtained with frogs. . . . [R]ecently the conduction velocity of a motor-nerve has been measured successfully in man in as easy and conclusive a way as in the frog, and

---

[1] About 30 metres per second (translator's note).

Here is Helmholtz's setup:

Think of the myographion as a stopwatch that is started when an electrical stimulus is delivered, and stopped when the thumb moves. The muscle that moves the thumb is stimulated at location A and then at B. Subtracting time A from time B gives the time taken by a nerve impulse to travel from location B to A.

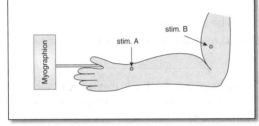

belied: contradicted

consequently with complete exclusion of the mental process of the brain. It is Helmholtz again who indicated the right course. He excited the nerves of the muscles of the ball of the thumb in succession at the wrist and above the fold of the elbow, whilst elbow, forearm and hand were fixed immovably in a plasterjacket: in both cases the muscles referred to contracted and the moments of contraction could be recorded via a lever on the 'myographion.' The result obtained was very satisfactory. As a matter of fact, with a very small deviation a conduction velocity was found of 33 metres per second, which is only a little more than found in the case of frog nerves.

. . .

Thus the conduction velocity in the nerves is known and the prediction of Johannes Müller has been brilliantly belied. It is worth noting that the theory created the courage to venture upon the solution of the problems referred to as insoluble. In fact, the theoretical notion that propagation cannot be considered as a progressive force or movement, but rather as a chemical and associated electromotive process, renovating itself at each point, prompted the surmise that conduction in nerves could not be so extraordinarily rapid, and that the shortness of the nerves could not be an absolute obstacle to empirical determination.

Would thought also not have the infinite speed usually associated with it, and would it not be possible to determine the time required for shaping a concept or expressing one's will? For years this question has intrigued me.

We have described above the method used in the study of the propagation velocity in sensory nerves. In these experiments the time that elapses between the stimulus and the response includes a particular mental process. The same is true of those experiments in which the stimulus acted on one of the other sense-organs. On this subject the first comparative research was done by Hirsch, the well-known astronomer of Neufchatel. The time elapsing between stimulus and response he called *physiological time,* and with unchanged response, for instance a movement of the hand, he found that this time was shortest after stimulating the skin (close to the brain of course), longer after stimulation of the ear, and still longer after stimulation of the eye. In general this result was confirmed by later experiments. From the combined experiments, including those of myself and my students, I calculated the physiological time for the three sense-organs mentioned, *viz.* touch, hearing and vision, as being approx. 0.143, 0.167, and 0.200 sec respectively.

85

90

95

100

105

110

115

120

But what proportion of this forms part of the mental process proper? On this point we are completely in the dark. In that short lapse of time much has to be done. When we follow the process from the moment of the stimulus up to that of the response, we can distinguish:

(1) the action on the sensory elements in the sense-organs;

125

(2) the communication with the peripheral ganglion cells and the increase required for a discharge ('Schwelle' of Fechner);

Schwelle: (German, "threshold") In psychophysics this refers to the minimum energy or, as in the present context, change in energy that the subject can detect.

(3) the conduction in the sensory nerves up to the ganglion cells of the medulla;

130

(4) the increase in activity in these ganglion cells;

(5) the conduction to the nerve cells of the organ of conception;

(6) the increase in activity of these nerve cells;

(7) the increase in activity of the nerve cells of the organ of will;

(8) the conduction to the nerve cells governing movement;

135

(9) the increase in activity in these cells;

(10) the conduction in the motor-nerves to the muscle;

(11) the latency in the action of the muscle;

(12) the increase in activity up to the moment of overcoming the resistance of the response.

The whole process can be completed in 0.143 of a second; even 0.111 has been found as a

140   minimum. The times required for the separate stages of the process cannot be determined. Only the conduction velocity in the nerves can approximately be taken into account, and this then leads to the result that the mental process of conception and expression of the will lasts less than $1/10$ of a second, but it does not allow us to claim that it takes any time at all. The truth is that these experiments teach us only about the limits of the maximum, while as to the min-

145   imum they give no decisive answer at all.

The idea occurred to me to interpose into the process of the physiological time some new components of mental action. If I investigated how much this would lengthen the physiological time, this would, I judged, reveal the time required for the interposed term.

. . .

150   In the first series of experiments identical electrodes were placed on both feet. The arrangement was such that by tilting a Pohl seesaw[2] an

The Pohl seesaw is simply the means by which the experimenter determines to which foot the impulse is delivered.

---

[2] The Pohl seesaw is described by De Jaager (Inaug. Diss. De Jaager l.c.[loc. cit.] p. 16, 17 and plate I). It appears to be a sort of two-way switch (translator's note). (De Jaager, 1865/1970).

electric impulse could be delivered to either the right or the left foot. The experiments were now executed in two ways: (a) in the first it was known to which foot the impulse was to be offered and the response was to be made by the hand on the same side; (b) in the second it was not known to which foot the impulse was to be offered but the response had also to be made by the hand on the stimulated side. In the latter case more time was required than in the first, and the difference represented the time required for deciding which side had been stimulated and for establishing the action of the will on the right or left side. For the rest the whole process was identical in both cases. It appeared that the mental action interposed in this manner required 0.067 of a second, as calculated from the average values. Previously it was found that response with the left hand lasted 0.009 second longer than with the right hand, which difference was taken into account.

This was the first determination of the duration of a well-defined neural process. It concerned the decision in a choice and an action of the will in response to that decision.

The same experiment was made with stimuli acting on the sense-organ of vision. Here the physiological time was ascertained with a simple response to light and with a differential response to a red and to a white light.[3] In the latter experiments the response to red light had to be given with the right hand, to white light with the left. In this case the decision in the choice and the related response appeared to require more time than in the previous experiments: averaged over 5 subjects it was 0.154 sec; the lowest average was 0.122 in the case of Mr. Place; the highest, 0.184, fell to my debit, since my age was twice that of other observers. Later on we will return to the cause of the difference between stimulation of the skin and of the eye.

In these experiments the signal was given with one of the hands. Later I carried out another series of experiments in which the stimuli were special letter-symbols, either uncovered or suddenly illuminated by an induction spark, and the response consisted in pronouncing the sound. In this case the interposed mental process requires 0.166 as calculated from the averages and 0.124 as calculated from the minima. This method lent itself further to experiments in which one vowel-symbol had to be recognised not out of two but out of five and to be pronounced as a sound. In this way we made no fewer than 5 series of observations on different days and it appeared that, with the wider choice out of five, some more time is indeed required than with the choice out of two, *viz.* 0.170 as calculated from the averages and 0.163 as calculated from the minima.

> The *induction spark*—produced in the same way as the ignition spark in a gasoline engine—was Donders's way of brightly and briefly illuminating a visual stimulus. The precise control of brief stimulus presentation remains an important technical challenge in experimental psychology, though the spark has been replaced by the photostrobe (the technology behind a camera's flash) and, more recently, by the computer monitor.

Finally, the same experiments were carried out with stimulation of the ear. In this case the stimulus consisted in the sound of a vowel and the response was the repetition of the same

155

160

165

170

175

180

185

190

---

[3] See De Jaager [1865/1970], p. 21–32: the method was not exact enough to trust the difference between the minima.

vowel. Two subjects A and B are seated before the mouth of the phonautograph. Whilst the cylinder is turned, A utters a vowel and B has to repeat it as quickly as possible. The beginning of the vibration caused by the two sounds is to be seen on the line P (figure 1) at *a* and *b,* and the time lapse between the two can be deduced from the vibrations S of a tuning-fork recorded simultaneously. The experiments were carried out in two ways, (a) while the subject knew what vowel-sound was to be presented and had only to repeat the same sound as soon as possible, (b) while the subject did not know what vowel was to be presented, and thus had to form a clear idea of the

> The *phonautograph,* patented in 1857 by Édouard-Léon Scott, a French printer, was the first device capable of recording sound. The record was a line scratched on a soot-covered drum by a needle connected to a diaphragm that vibrated in response to sound spoken or played into a horn. Scott's machine was intended for the study of sound, and could only record; reproduction came 21 years later with Edison's phonograph, based on the same basic idea as the phonautograph.

vowel-sound in order to repeat it. In my first experiments with De Jaager I responded in 0.180 second on the average, in the case of a known sound *ki*[4] and in 0.268 second in the case of an unknown sound, the result being a difference of 0.088 second; with longer times—especially at the beginning—De Jaager obtained an identical difference of 0.088 second. Later on, in seven series in which I myself had to respond to the sound, I found 0.201 second on the average for a known sound and 0.284 second for an unknown one, hence a difference of 0.083 second; as calculated from the minima this difference was reduced to 0.067 second. In four other series, in which I had to repeat either the previously known stimulus or one out of *only two* unknown stimuli, the repetition of the known sound required a little less time (0.184 second) and the increment for the unknown sound was only 0.056 second as calculated from the averages or 0.0615 second as calculated from the minima.

FIGURE 1   The phonautograph record referred to in the text. The upper trace is the regular vibration of a tuning fork of known frequency, in this case 261 cps. On the lower trace, the vibrations beginning at *a* are the record of the stimulus (the vowel spoken by A), and the vibrations beginning at *b* are the record of the response (the same vowel spoken by B). There are 33 fork cycles between *a* and *b,* which means the response began 33/261, or 0.126 sec after the stimulus began.

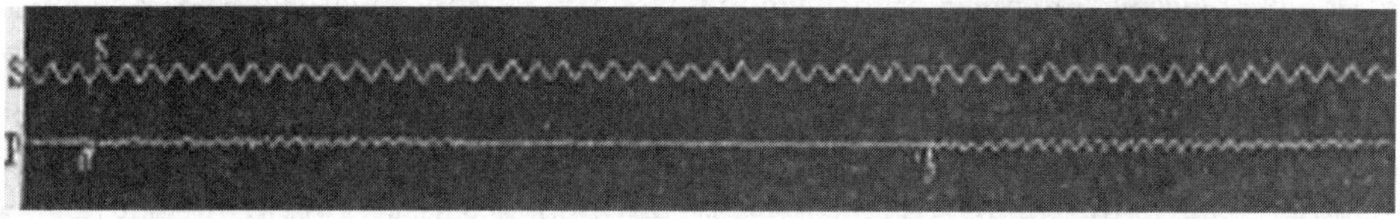

---

[4] Pronounced key (translator's note).

Summing up the results obtained, it appears that the time required for a decision and the appropriate response is:

		second
(1)	stimulation of the *skin;* choice, calculated from the averages	0.066
(2)	stimulation of the *eye;*	
	(a) two colours, choice, five subjects, calculated from the averages	0.184, 0.122, 0.159, 0.134, 0.172
	(b) two vowel-symbols, choice, calculated from the averages	0.166
	calculated from the minima	0.124
	(c) five vowel-symbols, calculated from the averages	0.170
	calculated from the minima	0.163
(3)	stimulation of the *ear;*	
	(a) two vowel-sounds, calculated from the averages	0.056
	calculated from the minima	0.0615
	(b) five vowel-sounds, with myself, initially, calculated from the averages later, calculated from the averages	0.088 0.083
	calculated from the minima	0.067
The same with four other subjects		
calculated from the averages		0.088
calculated from the averages		0.069
calculated from the averages		0.087
calculated from the averages		0.088

Some of the differences immediately attract attention. First of all: why does the choice require less time in the case of differences in sound (0.056 second) than in that of differences in colour (0.122 second)? The answer is that the response given to the sound is the simple imitation which has become natural by training, more so than the conventional response with the right or the left hand in the case of differences in colour. Consequently, prolonged training will result in a higher speed of response in the case of colour experiments. With the imitation of vowel-sounds, on the other hand, the maximum speed appeared to have been effectively reached, and thus the values obtained here tell us immediately the minimum time required for decision in a simple choice, including the corresponding expression of the will, *viz.* 0.056 second. However, with stimulation of the skin in which the response was likewise conventional (movement also of right or left hand) the same interposed process required only 0.066 second, thus little more than with the trained response to vowel-sounds. This result is not surprising either. We made the subjects respond with the right hand to the stimulus on the right side, and with the left hand to the stimulus on the left side. The tendency to respond in this way is already present as a consequence of habit or training: for, when movement of the right hand was required with stimulation of the left side or the other way round, then the time lapse was longer and errors common. I would make a final remark. The recognition of vowel-symbols and the

235 response to them require about double the time needed for recognising vowel-sounds and making the appropriate response, and we have certainly as much training in seeing and pronouncing vowel-symbols as in hearing and repeating them. I was very struck by this result. The reason may lie in the different stages of the complex process. I believe, however, it must be looked for in the purely mental process. I calculated from joint observations with different subjects that the response to light usually requires somewhat more time than the response to

240 sound. Combining the results, obtained with myself as a subject, of 8 series of experiments with responses to light and 12 series with responses to sound, I find that they are equal, *viz.* for the former 0.1953 second, for the latter 0.1952 second.

Of course, such a complete resemblance is accidental, the more so as in some experiments

245 single vowels were used, in others vowels with plosives, the corresponding physiological times differing a little. Yet this shows that the physio- logical times for sound and light do not notice-

> A *plosive* is a speech sound—such as *p, t, d*—made by stopping the flow of air and then releasing it in a burst.

ably diverge in my case. I also believe I may assume that the distinguishing of two colours

250 takes place as quickly as distinguishing two sounds, and that with enough training the time required to make a response to the distinction of the former sort might be reduced to that required by the latter. The reason for the difference is to be found, I suppose, in the form of the symbol, which is not so quickly distinguished by the mind as is the sound. To account for this difference we have to analyse somewhat more closely the impression of

255 the sound and of the form of the symbol. On the retina that impression is very complex. A number of sensory elements, each transmitting to the brain the excitation it received together with its own local sign, are suddenly excited, and from this our conception of the form is con-

260 structed. The elements excited are quite differ- ent when the symbol is large from when it is small, and yet an *a* remains an *a,* an *i* an *i.* A small deviation of the axis of vision also makes the whole picture of the letter-symbol fall on differ-

265 ent elements of the retina. Thus the process of conceiving of the form is necessarily very com- plex, and it is not surprising that it takes more time than that of an impression of light in gen-

> *Local sign* is a term used by Lotze (1856/1885), referring to a postulated sensory quality unique to each visual or tactile receptor. Thus, when a retinal cell is active, it provides the visual system information about the intensity of the light falling on it, and, according to Lotze, it also tells the visual system where it is—its location.

eral, or even a colour that acts on certain sensory elements or only represents a particular

270 type of energy. For such a process, prolonged by the time required for differential expres- sion of the will, 0.16 second is comparatively not much. And now, how is the concept of a sound formed? For many sounds the process may be as complex as for instantaneously illuminated small forms. After all, normal sounds are composed of a number of individual vibrations that also bring into action different nerve fibres and each pitch has its own

system of nerve fibres that receives the impression,: the only thing that makes the process   275
appear more simple is the relation between the individual tones which, at each pitch, are
again mainly what are called the harmonics. But, although the process is made up in that
way for sound in general, this does not apply to vowels. Whatever the pitch of the voice
with which it is produced, for each vowel the tuning of the oral cavity is absolute, as I
demonstrated already ten years ago, and in this connection any vowel has its absolute, vir-   280
tually invariable harmonics. Thus, with the sound of the same vowel at any pitch some of
the same tones are produced, and each time some of the same nerve fibres are excited,
which, when a vowel-sound may be expected, characterise it immediately. That is why the
conception of vowel-timbre does not suggest such a complex process as is considered necessary for the conception of a vowel-symbol.   285

After measuring the combined time lapse in which the discrimination between two or
more impressions as well as the corresponding expression of the will is possible, the question arose whether the times required for the two stages of this process could not be established separately.

It seemed to me one would approach this problem by making it a necessary condition that   290
a response should be made only to one stimulus, ignoring all others.

Thus, vowel-sounds were established as stimuli without further indication, but only one, for
instance *i*, had to be responded to with *i*, the others were not to be responded to at all. The
subject strains his ears for the recognition of *i* and keeps the position of the parts of the mouth
and the mechanism ready so that, upon recognising the *i*, he has only to breathe out to pro-   295
duce the corresponding sound, just as in the case where a subject knowing that an *i* was to be
heard had to respond with *i*. In this sort of experiment no choice is now required for the
response: only the distinction, the recognition of *i*, is interposed in the normal process. And,
indeed, it was found that less time was required than for responding to each vowel sound with
the identical sound. Of the many experiments carried out by myself in this way, I will only insert   300
the results of three series, carried out on the same evening and in such a sequence that as far
as fatigue played a role, it was distributed uniformly over the three experimental procedures:

(a) responding to a known sound;
(b) responding to an unknown sound;
(c) responding to one of the unknown sounds.   305

With each of these ways the average duration and the minimum were recorded:

For
(a) the average duration 201, the minimum 170.5 thousandths of a second
(b) the average duration 284, the minimum 237.5
(c) the average duration 237, the minimum 212.6   310

the following values are now found:

from the averages	from the minima	averaged
b–a = 83	67	75
c–a = 36	42	39

315   In these experiments, then, the time required for the conception of a certain sound (longer duration with method c than with method a) was only a little more than half of that required for that same conception combined with the corresponding expression of the will. The development of a conception takes 0.039 seconds for myself, i.e. nearly .04 of a second, and a little less, just over .036 of a second, is required for expression of the will. In the foregoing we have

320   reported experiments with other persons who needed less time for the combined process. In these experiments, too, the time for both stages is probably to be divided into about equal parts. From the determination they made with the c-method this fact cannot, however, be deduced satisfactorily. It has appeared to me that to many people the c-method offers certain difficulties. They give the response, when they ought to have remained silent. And if this happens

325   only once, the whole series must be rejected: for, how can we be certain that when they had to make the response and did make it, they had properly waited until they were sure to have dis-

> Marks on the cylinder recorded the occurrence of stimuli and of responses; unused revolutions corresponded to the passage of time during which nothing happened.

330   criminated? In addition, since the very vowel-sound to which a response has to be made is presented only now and then the method is invariably accompanied by the drawback that most revolutions of the cylinder remain unused. For that reason I attach much value to the results of the three series mentioned above and obtained with myself as a subject, utilising the

335   three methods described for each series, in which the experiments turned out to be faultless.
     Meanwhile one could still doubt whether with the procedure used it is really the time required for a certain conceptual process that is being measured. Is it not rather the difference of time which we find between the determination of the nature of the vowel-sound and the simple hearing of it? Our answer to this is in the negative. Anyone who has carried out the

340   experiments knows that where the object is only to give a response in general, the response is made to anything that happens. Although one is waiting under tension for a visual stimulus, one will also respond involuntarily to a sound, and vice versa; and likewise to a shock, an electrical impulse, in a word to any strong impression. One does not wait till one hears, but only till one perceives, and with the method used one thus finds the time that elapses between the first

345   moment of perception and the complete conception of the nature of the sound, i.e. the time required for the development of a certain conception.
     I carried out these same experiments, using the c-method, when the stimulus was *seeing* a vowel-symbol. The time required for recognition was then rather short, scarcely longer than

with vowel-sounds. This result is certainly remarkable when one considers that the discrimination of vowel-symbols, as appeared to us in the experiments with the a- and b-methods,   350
requires much more time than the discrimination of vowel-sounds. Yet I believe that it can be
explained. In the experiments with the b-method one could not conceive beforehand what
impression one was to receive: one even had to refrain from doing so in order to be able to
respond with equal speed to any vowel-symbol that might be presented. A relatively long interval was now required for discrimination. On the other hand, in the experiments with the   355
c-method of which we are speaking here, all vowel-symbols could, indeed, also be presented,
but one had to respond to only one of them; with the others one had to keep silent, and thus
one could and even had to have a conception of that one symbol in order to give immediately
on establishing the equivalence of impression and conception, the response prepared in the
mechanism. In experiments on stereoscopic vision published elsewhere the great influence of   360
a predetermined conception on the recognition of forms became very clear to me.

   With other stimuli, too, such as electrical impulses on the skin, experiments may be made
using the c-method, but here only in relation with a presented choice. Nor is one limited to the
choice of a sound as a response. For on hearing all the sounds or only a predetermined vowel-
sound one can make a movement with the hand, and the difference again indicates the time   365
required for a certain conception; but comparison with the differential response to each of the
sounds is then excluded, and the experiments would not have served their purpose if I had not
had the idea of recording the sound as a response.

FOR DISCUSSION

1. What is the significance, for Donders, of Helmholtz's measurement of the speed of the
   nerve impulse?

2. What does Donders mean by "conception and expression of the will" (p. 211, line 142)
   and "action of the will" (p. 212, line 159)?

3. What is a possible consequence of Donders's decision to throw out trials in which the
   subject made a mistake (p. 217, line 325) and then repeat the trial?

4. What are some other possible applications of Donders's methods?

3.2

E. B. Titchener (1867–1927)
An Outline of Psychology (1896)

Chapter 1. The Meaning and Problem of Psychology

Chapter 2. Sensation as a Conscious Element— The Method of Investigating Sensation

Chapter 3. The Quality of Sensation

Chapter 5. Affection as a Conscious Element— The Methods of Investigating Affection

Titchener's student, E. G. Boring (1886–1968) summarized his teacher this way: "Titchener was an Englishman who represented the German psychological tradition in America" (Boring, 1950, p. 410). As an undergraduate at Oxford, Titchener studied philosophy. The British philosophical tradition of empiricism and associationism (see, e.g., readings by Locke [4.2], Berkeley [2.1], Reid [2.2]) was deeply psychological, but in the late 19th century psychology as an experimental science had not yet taken root in England. Thus, to pursue his interest in scientific psychology Titchener was obliged, like many of his American contemporaries, to go to Germany, and specifically to Leipzig, where in 1879 Wundt (see 1.3) had established the first psychological laboratory.

Titchener went to Leipzig in 1890 and completed his doctorate 2 years later. He had hoped to return to England, but Oxford was still not interested in experimental psychology. Instead he went to Cornell, where he replaced his friend Frank Angell, who himself had left Wundt

Source: Titchener, E. B. (1896). *An outline of psychology.* New York: Macmillan.

only a year earlier and had set up a laboratory at Cornell. Titchener spent the rest of his life at Cornell. In those 35 years he worked out a rigorously empirical and, by most standards, rather narrowly defined vision of the content and method of psychology. Titchener saw psychology as the scientific study of the mind—the normal, adult, human mind—by means of introspection. Titchener's narrow and rigid conception of psychology, and perhaps certain aspects of his personality, effectively isolated him from most of American psychology and psychologists. Toward the end of Titchener's career the behaviorist movement—the antithesis of Titchener's interests and methods—began to gather steam, and when he died his system went with him.

While still an undergraduate, Titchener had translated the third edition (1887) of Wundt's *Grundzüge der physiologischen Psychologie* ("Fundamentals of Physiological Psychology"; by "physiological" Wundt meant, roughly, "experimental"). He also translated Wundt's fourth (1893) and fifth (1902–1903) editions. This last is the only one of the three translations that Titchener published, and it remains the only version of Wundt's *Grundzüge* in English. To help meet the need for experimental psychology in English, Titchener also wrote his own books, beginning with *An Outline of Psychology* (1896), modeled on a book by Külpe (*Grundriss der Psychologie,* 1893; translated by Titchener in 1895). In keeping with Titchener's conception of psychology, his own book is mainly concerned with the structure and contents of consciousness: sensation, perception, attention, feeling, association, memory, reasoning, and purposeful action. Not surprisingly, given his time in Leipzig, there is also a chapter on reaction time studies.

Titchener left no intellectual heirs, and history has not been kind to his reputation. His books are out of print, and when he is mentioned today it is often with a derisive snort. Titchener is mostly remembered for his insistence on introspection as *the* method of experimental psychology. Subsequent generations of psychologists have had nothing but scorn for introspection and, therefore, for Titchener. Nonetheless, introspection was widely used in prebehaviorist times and is an important idea in the history of psychology. In the following selections from the *Outline,* Titchener explains what introspection is and what we can learn from it.

CHAPTER 1: THE MEANING AND PROBLEM OF PSYCHOLOGY

§ 3. Mental Process, Consciousness and Mind.—Psychology is sometimes defined, technically as well as popularly, as the 'science of mind.' The psychologist can accept this definition . . . if 'mind' is understood to mean simply the sum total of mental processes experienced by the individual during his lifetime. Ideas, feelings, impulses, etc., are mental processes; the whole
5   number of ideas, feelings, impulses, etc., experienced by me during my life constitutes my 'mind.'

   . . .

   It is clear that mind lasts longer than any single mental process; it is a sum or series of mental processes. It must be noted further that the processes which make up mind do not occur one by one; our mental experience, even in moments of extreme preoccupation or concentration,
10   is complex. As you read this page, your mind is composed of a large number of processes: the sense of the printed page; satisfaction or dissatisfaction with that sense; pressures from your clothing, chair, etc.; internal sensations and feelings which make up your bodily comfort or discomfort, which inform you of the position of your limbs, etc.; probably a medley of sounds from neighbouring rooms or from the street, and so on. Just as life consists of a sum of simultaneous
15   processes,—secretion and excretion, decomposition and recomposition,—so mind is a stream of processes, more or less numerous, which run their course in time together.

   My 'consciousness' is the sum of mental processes which make up my experience *now;* it is the mind of any given 'present' time. We might, perhaps, consider it as a cross-section of mind. This section may be either artificial or natural. We may deliberately cut across mind, in order to
20   investigate it for psychological purposes. We have then interfered with the natural succession of our mental processes. On the other hand, mind falls of itself into a series of consciousnesses, each separate consciousness being dominated by some particular group of processes. . . .

§ 4. The Problem of Psychology.—The aim of the psychologist is threefold. He seeks (1) to analyse concrete (actual) mental experience into its simplest components, (2) to discover how
25   these elements combine, what are the laws which govern their combination, and (3) to bring them into connection with their physiological (bodily) conditions.

   (1) We saw above that all science begins with analysis. The original material of science is complex; science itself introduces order into chaos by reducing the complex to its elements, by tracing the proportion of identical elements in different complexes, and by determining
30   (where that is possible) the relations of the elements to one another. Psychology is no exception to the rule. Our concrete mental experience, the experience of 'real life,' is always complex. However small a fragment we may seize upon,—a single wish, a single idea, a single resolution,—we find invariably that close inspection of it will reveal its complexity, will show that it is composed of a number of more rudimentary processes. The first object of the psychologist,
35   therefore, is to ascertain the *nature and number of the mental elements*. He takes up mental experience, bit by bit, dividing and subdividing, until the division can go no further. When that point is reached, he has found a conscious element.

The mental or conscious elements are those mental processes which cannot be further analyzed, which are absolutely simple in nature, and which consequently cannot be reduced, even
in part, to other processes.   40

. . .

(2) Analysis needs to be tested in two ways. We must always ask, with regard to it: Has it
gone as far as it can go? and: Has it taken account of all the elements which are contained in
the experience? To answer the first question, the analysis must be repeated: analysis is its own
test. When one psychologist says that a process is elemental, other psychologists repeat his
analysis for themselves, trying to carry it further than he could do. If they stop short where he   45
did, he was right; if they find his 'simple' process to be complex, he was wrong. As regards the
second question, on the other hand, the test of analysis is *synthesis*. When we have analysed a
complex into the elements *a, b, c,* we test our analysis by trying to put it together again, to get
it back from *a, b* and *c.* If the complex can be thus restored, the analysis is correct; but if the combination of *a, b* and *c* does not give us back the original complex, the analyst has failed to dis-   50
cover some one or more of its ingredients. Hence the psychologist, when he has analysed
consciousness, must put together the results of his analysis, must synthetise, and compare his
reconstruction of mental experience with the experience as originally given. If the two tally, his
work on that mental experience is done, and he can pass on to another; if not, he must repeat
his analysis, watching constantly for the factors which he had previously missed.   55

If the conscious elements were 'things,' the task of reconstruction of an experience would
not be difficult. We should put the simple bits of mind together, as the bits of wood are put
together in a child's puzzle-map or kindergarten cube. But the conscious elements are
'processes': they do not fit together, side to side and angle to angle; they flow together, mix
together, overlapping, reinforcing, modifying or arresting one another, in obedience to cer-   60
tain psychological laws. The psychologist must, therefore, in the second place, seek to ascertain the *laws which govern the connection of the mental elements*. Knowledge of these laws
renders the synthesis of elements into a concrete experience possible, and is of assistance also
in subsequent analysis.

. . .

(3) Every mental process is connected with a bodily process; we do not know anything of   65
mind apart from body. Mind and body, that is, always go together in our experience. And ordinary observation will convince us that body influences mind in various ways. Consciousness
when the eyes are closed is different from con-
sciousness when the eyes are open; if the bodily
state varies, the mental state varies also; the drop-   70
ping of the eyelids prevents the ether waves from
gaining access to the sensitive parts of the eyes,
and with this physical fact go the mental facts of
the sensation of darkness, the 'feeling' of bodily
unsteadiness and uncertainty, etc. The mind of a   75

ether waves: light waves. Until about the
end of the 19th century it was generally
assumed that light travels through a specific
medium, a quasi-substance that fills the
void of space and the void between air
molecules.

man who has been blind from his birth is essentially different from the mind of one endowed with normal vision. Where the latter sees, the former hears and touches: I *see* my path, but the blind man *hears* and *'feels'* his way. Even the highest and most abstract processes of thought give evidence of the close connection of mind with body. We cannot think, unless we have ideas in which to think; and ideas are built up from impressions received through bodily sense-organs. . . . .

> *We cannot think:* Here Titchener echoes Locke's theory of the origin of ideas; see 4.2.

CHAPTER 2: SENSATION AS A CONSCIOUS ELEMENT. THE METHOD OF INVESTIGATING SENSATION

§ 7. The Definition of Sensation.—Ideas are always complex, made up of separate parts. Our way of using a single word to express them—though there are good reasons for it—is likely to mislead us upon this matter: it tempts us to think that they are simple and uniform in their nature. Hence it requires some effort and trouble to analyse an idea, even if (as is often the case) it owes its existence to the combined action of several sense-organs. But every idea can be resolved into elements, *i.e.*, elemental *processes;* and these elements are termed *sensations.*

. . .

We may compare the sensation, the element of the idea, to the elements treated of in chemical science. The idea is a compound; it consists of a number of elemental processes, travelling side by side in consciousness: it therefore resembles the compound bodies analysed in the chemical laboratory. But the sensation resists analysis, just as do the chemical elements oxygen and hydrogen. It stands to the idea as oxygen and hydrogen stand to water. Whatever test we put it to,—however persistent our attempt at analysis and however refined our method of investigation,—we end where we began: the sensation remains precisely what it was before we attacked it. 'Cold,' 'blue,' 'salt,' cannot be divided up into any simpler modes of experience.

. . .

§ 8. The Attributes of Sensation.—Although the sensation is an element of mind, that is, a process which cannot be split up into simpler processes, yet it has various aspects or attributes—presents different sides, so to speak—each of which may be separately examined by the psychologist. Some sensations have four such aspects; every sensation has at least three. The four are quality, intensity, extent and duration. The process is *itself,* and not some other process (quality); it is stronger or weaker than other sensations (intensity); it spreads over a certain portion of space, greater or less (extent); and it lasts a certain, longer or shorter period of time (duration).

> Today *quality* usually refers to *how good* something is, but its older sense has to do with *what* something is, for example, green, b-flat, cheesy.

. . .

If any one of them disappears, the whole sensation disappears with it. A tone which is of no duration, which does not last for any time at all, is not a tone; and a point of light which has no extent cannot give rise to a sensation of sight,—it is just nothing. . . . 110

. . .

§ 9. The Method of Investigating Sensation.—Every science has its own special material to deal with, and consequently its own special methods of working upon that material for the discovery of facts and laws. Physics and chemistry follow 'physical' and 'chemical' methods: and no progress can be made by the student in either science until he has learned the right *way* to 115 work, *i.e.*, has grasped the significance of method. The special method employed by psychology is that of introspection or self-observation. We 'look into' the mind, each for himself; or we observe ourselves,—in order to find out what processes are going on at the time, and how they are influencing one another.

This 'looking into' one's mind or observation of one's own mental processes must not be 120 understood literally, however, as if consciousness were one thing, existing of itself, and the 'I,' the observer, could stand apart and watch it from the outside. The 'I,' the watching, and the conscious phenomenon observed, are all alike conscious processes; so that when 'I observe myself,' all that happens is that a new set of processes is introduced into the consciousness of the moment.

But this introduction of new processes must, it would seem, bring about a change in the particular experience which one sets out to observe. And it is imperative to keep that experience 125 unchanged: a method of observation which involved an alteration of the facts to be observed would not be worth much. Direct introspection—observation of a process which is still running its course—is, as a matter of fact, entirely worthless; it defeats its own object.

. . .

Psychological introspection, however, does not consist in the effort to follow up a process during its course. The rule for introspection, in the sphere of sensation, is as follows: *Be as attentive as* 130 *possible to the object or process which gives rise to the sensation, and, when the object is removed or the process completed, recall the sensation by an act of memory as vividly and completely as you can.*

The object or process which gives rise to a sensation is termed the *stimulus* to that sensation. If we attend to the stimulus, the sensation becomes clearer, and has a more enduring 135 place in consciousness than it would have gained in its own right. Hence we can best observe those sensations to whose stimuli we have been especially attentive. We avoid any interference with the workings of consciousness by postponing our observation of the process which we wish to examine until after it has run its full course, and the stimulus which occasioned it has ceased to affect us. We then call it back, look at it from all points of view, and dissect it. 140 Introspective examination must be a *post mortem* examination.

. . .

But this introspection, it may well be said, cannot furnish very reliable results. The individual can apply the method to one consciousness only—his own; and we all know how easy it is for a single observer to make mistakes, and how necessary to have more witnesses

145 than one, if a fact is to be securely established. There is no guarantee that other individuals would come to the same conclusion, from an examination of their consciousnesses; and no means of comparing the conclusions reached by different individuals under similar circumstances.

The first objection is unanswerable. But although we can never apply the introspective
150 method to any consciousness except our own, we can arrange matters so that other individuals may be brought forward as witnesses to the facts which we ourselves have observed. This end is attained by the employment of the method under experimental conditions.

An experiment is a trial, test, or observation, carefully made under certain special conditions: the object of the conditions being (1) to render it possible for any one who will to *repeat* the
155 test, in the exact manner in which it was first performed, and (2) to help the observer to rule out disturbing influences during his observation, and so to get at the desired result in a *pure* form. If we say precisely how we have worked, other investigators can go through the same processes, and judge whether our conclusion is right or wrong; and if we do the work in a fitting place, with fitting instruments, without hurry or interruption, guarding against any influ-
160 ence which is foreign to the matter in hand, and which might conceivably alter our observation, we may be sure of obtaining 'pure' results, results which follow directly from the conditions laid down by us, and are not due to the operation of any unforeseen or unregulated causes. Experiment thus secures accuracy of observation, and the connection of every result with its own conditions; while it enables observers in all parts of the world to work together upon one
165 and the same psychological problem.

. . .

The rule of experimental introspection, in the sphere of sensation, runs as follows: Have yourself placed under such conditions that there is as little likelihood as possible of external interference with the test to be made. Attend to the stimulus, and, when it is removed, recall the sensation by an act of memory. Give a verbal account of the processes constituting your
170 consciousness of the stimulus. The account must be written down by the assistant, who has arranged for you the conditions under which the test is to be made. His description of the conditions, and your description of the experience, furnish data from which other psychologists can work.

In whichever form it is employed, the introspective method demands the exercise of *mem-*
175 *ory*. Care must therefore be taken to work with memory at its best: the interval of time which elapses between experience and the account of experience must not be so short that memory has not time to recover the experience, or so long that the experience has become faded and blurred. In its experimental form, introspection demands further an exact use of *language*. The terms chosen to describe the experience must be
180 definite, sharp, and concrete. The conscious process is like a fresco, painted in great sweeps of colour and with all sorts of intermediary and mediating lights and shades: words are little blocks of stone, to be used in the composition of a mosaic.

> Titchener's fresco/mosaic metaphor exactly describes the fundamental challenge of digital photography.

If we are required to represent the fresco by a mosaic, we must see to it that our blocks be of 185
small size and of every obtainable tint and hue. Otherwise, our representation will not come
very near to the original.

. . .

§ 10. General Rules for the Introspection of Sensation.—The 'experimental conditions'
which are necessary to render the results of introspection scientifically valuable will, of course,
differ in the case of different sensations. The rules which apply in the sense of sight do not hold, 190
without modification, in that of hearing. But there are certain conditions which must always be
regarded, in whatever department of sensation we are working: or, to put the matter from the
other side, there are certain errors to which we are always liable, and which we must constantly
guard against.

(1) When we introspect, we must be absolutely *impartial* and unprejudiced. We must not 195
let ourselves be biassed by any preconceived idea. . . .

(2) When we introspect, we must have our *attention* under control. The attention must
not be permitted either to flag or to wander.

(3) When we introspect, body and mind must be *fresh.*

(4) When we introspect, our *general disposition,* physical and mental, should be 200
favourable. We must feel well, feel comfortable, feel good-tempered, and feel
interested in the subject.

These are the most important of the general rules to be followed in introspection. Can we
ever be quite sure that we have followed them?

Even when we think that all possible precautions have been taken, it must often be the 205
case that certain of the required conditions are left unfulfilled . . . . Now there is a method,
employed both in science and in practical life, which helps us to set up a working standard,
a norm with which all individual results may be compared, under the most various and fluctuating circumstances: the method of averages. We make a large number of observations,
and take their average. This mean result will not represent the observer at his very best, but 210
will indicate the normal or average performance which may be expected of him when the
conditions under which he observes are as favourable as human nature can make and keep
them. . . .

The 'facts' of the psychology of sensation are, then, average results obtained from
observers trained in introspection under experimental conditions of both a general and a 215
special character. The former we have learned to know as impartiality, attention, freshness,
and favourable disposition. The latter we shall discuss (under the heading of *Method)* in following chapters.

§ 11. The Classification of Sensations.—Every sensation comes to us from a definite bodily
organ. We may therefore divide sensations into groups or classes, according to the various 220

sense-organs which the body possesses, and speak of eye sensations, ear sensations, nose sensations, skin sensations, muscle sensations, joint sensations, etc.

This list, if completed, would be perfectly accurate. But it is convenient to make some further divisions and subdivisions, which are justified by differences in the nature of the stimuli necessary to arouse sensations of certain kinds. Classification by *stimulus,* in addition to the classification by sense-organs, is useful in two ways.

Sensations in general fall into two principal groups, according as their stimulus is external (originating outside the body) or internal (originating within the body). Light, the stimulus to vision, is an external stimulus; muscular contraction, the stimulus to muscular sensation, is an internal stimulus. We therefore distinguish between *sensations of the special senses,* which are stimulated from without, and *organic sensations,* the stimulus to which consists in a certain state, or change of state, of the internal bodily organ from which they come. There is one, and only one, sensation quality which is common to every department of sense, whether external or internal: the quality of pain. We shall therefore speak of pain as a *common sensation.*

The nature of the stimulus may differ within the same sense. Light is the stimulus to sensations from the eye. But the physicist recognises two kinds of light,—white or mixed light, and pure or coloured light (light of one wave-length or of one vibration-rate); and we have two corresponding groups of sensations,—sensations of brightness (black, grey, white), and sensations of colour. Sound is the stimulus of hearing: but sound may be produced both by a single shock or concussion of the air and by an air-wave; and we have two corresponding types of auditory sensation,—the simple noise (shock), and the simple tone (wave).

Our list will, then, take final shape as follows . . . .

I. Sensations of the Special Senses (external stimulus).

    1. Visual sensations.

        a. Sensations of brightness (stimulus: mixed light).
        b. Sensations of colour (stimulus: homogeneous or pure light).

    2. Auditory sensations.

        a. Sensations of noise (stimulus: sound concussion or shock).
        b. Sensations of tone (stimulus: sound-wave).

    3. Olfactory sensations (stimulus: odorous particles carried by a draught of air).

    4. Gustatory sensations (stimulus: the chemical constitution of certain substances, which enables them to excite the organs of taste).

    5. Cutaneous sensations.

        a. Sensations of pressure (stimulus: mechanical affection of the skin).
        b. Sensations of temperature (stimulus: thermal affection of the skin).

II. Organic Sensations (internal stimulus).

    6. Muscular sensations (stimulus: contraction of muscle).

    7. Tendinous sensations (stimulus: pull or, strain upon tendon).

    8. Articular sensations (stimulus: rubbing or jamming together of surfaces of joint).   260

    9. Sensations from the alimentary canal.

        a. From the pharynx (stimulus: dryness of mucous membrane).
        b. From the oesophagus (stimulus: antiperistaltic reflex).
        c. From the stomach (stimulus: dryness of gastric mucous membrane).

  10. Circulatory sensations (stimulus: change in circulation).   265

  11. Respiratory sensations (stimulus: change in breathing).

  12. Sexual sensations (stimulus: change in blood-supply, or in secretory activity, of the sex organs).

  13. Sensation of the 'static sense' (stimulus: change in the distribution of pressure from the water of the semicircular canals of the internal ear).   270

III. Common Sensation (external or internal stimulus).

> In chapter 3 Titchener follows the above list, discussing each type of sensation in turn and describing the methods by which the number of different sensory qualities of that type is determined. We have included illustrative examples from each of Titchener's categories (special, organic, common) of sensation.

CHAPTER 3: THE QUALITY OF SENSATION

I. Sensations of Special Sense

§ 12. The Quality of Visual Sensations.—The stimulus to vision is light. Physical theory regards light as a wave movement in the ether with which space is filled. Light is either mixed or pure (homogeneous): mixed, if it consists of waves of every possible length, travelling together; and pure (homogeneous), if its waves are all of the same length. Mixed light always   275 excites the sensation of brightness; a single pure light, the sensation of some colour.

    (1) *Sensations of Brightness.*—We have only five names, in ordinary conversation, to indicate different kinds or qualities of brightness: black, white, grey, dark grey and light grey. When put

280 to a rigid test, however, the eye is found to be capable of distinguishing 700 brightness qualities, varying from the deepest black to the most brilliant white.

The *method* by which we determine the number of brightness qualities is as follows. Four
circular pieces (discs) of cardboard are prepared, two of dead black and two of white. A cut is
made in each, from outer edge to centre, so that a black and a white can be fitted together,
and a white sector, of any desired width, laid over the black surface. The backs of the discs are
285 divided up into degrees and fractions of degrees, in order that the amount of white which
replaces the original black in a particular experiment may be accurately measured.

For purposes of experiment, the discs are mounted in pairs—a white behind a black—
upon 'colour wheels,' which allow of their rapid rotation. When the discs are combined in this
way, presenting a black and white surface, and are rapidly rotated, they give rise to a sensa-
290 tion of grey. The object of the first experiment is to discover, by the comparison of an all-
black disc with a surface in which there is a slight trace of white, what mixture of black and
white is just different in sensation from dead black; the object of the second, to discover what
amount of white must be added to black to make a grey just different in sensation from the
grey of the first mixture; and so on. Each of these 'just different' brightness sensations is a
295 conscious element.

. . .

(2) *Sensations of Colour.*—The colours of the solar spectrum, which may be taken as standard or normal colours, are named: red, orange, yellow, green, blue, indigo-blue and violet.
. . . But here again, the eye, when placed under experimental conditions, is found to distinguish
far better than language does: we can discriminate, if the purples are included in the sum,
300 about 150 spectral colour qualities . . . . Every 'just different' colour is a conscious element.

Colour sensations, of a quite simple nature, but different from the colours of the spectral
series, are produced by the mixture of mixed with
pure light. Thus pink results from the mixing of red
and white; brown from that of black and yellow;
mauve from that of purple and white. Each of the
305 150 spectral colours may be combined in this way
with each of the 700 brightness qualities. But the
more white or black we mix with a colour, the

> A pure spectral color is said to be *saturated;*
> as more achromatic ("white") light is mixed
> with it, it becomes more *desaturated.*

harder does it become to distinguish that colour from other colours. Hence, instead of having
310 150x700 colour sensations of this mixed origin, we have only about 150 x 200, or 30,000.

. . .

We possess, therefore, about 700 +150 + 30,000 qualities of visual sensation: we have to
search in the structure and function of the eye for the conditions of some 30,850 conscious
elements. For the qualities are all equally elemental as sensations, however different the
physical processes (stimuli) with which they are connected.

. . .

FIGURE 1   Two Discs, Cut for Mounting upon the Colour Wheel. The figure shows the way in which they are fitted together for rotation

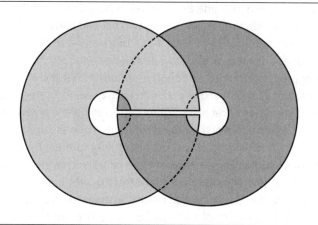

II. Organic Sensations

§17. The Quality of Muscular, Tendinous and Articular Sensations.—

. . .

In the sphere of organic sensation . . . it is very difficult to detach any single sensation from those which ordinarily accompany it. The simple qualities are here so closely woven together that the psychologist does not even know what to look for, when he begins his analysis. And the sense-organs within the body are not separated as are those upon its surface: muscle and tendon, *e.g.*, pass directly into each other. Nevertheless, careful experiments made during the last few years upon the normal individual, and careful observations of pathological cases (anaesthesia or insensitiveness of particular internal organs), have thrown some light upon the nature of the elementary processes included under the general title of organic sensations.

. . .

(2) *Tendinous Sensation.*—Like the muscles to which they are attached, the tendons are supplied with sensory nerves. The nerve-endings in tendon, however, are different in form from those in muscle or skin. The specific quality of tendinous sensation is not the quality of pressure, but that of tension or strain.

Method.—Lay your arm and hand, palm upwards, upon a table. Place a small ball, or other round object, in the palm, and close the fingers lightly round it. Note carefully the sensations which you are receiving from hand and arm. Now grasp the ball as tightly with the fingers as you can. You obtain, almost immediately, a new sensation, that of strain. This sensation quality is different from any skin sensation (pressure, heat, cold) and from the muscular sensation observed in the preceding experiment.

315

320

325

330

The new quality might, however, proceed from the joints, since in curling your fingers over
the ball you have altered the mutual pressure of various articular surfaces. You may easily
assure yourself that it does not. Let your arm hang down loosely by your side. Attach a fairly
heavy weight by a string to the forefinger. The weight pulls the surfaces of the elbow and other
joints apart; so that there is no pressure or friction of one surface against another. But you soon
get the sensation of strain throughout the arm.

If the sensation of strain is different from any sensation obtainable from skin or muscle, and
is independent of stimulation of the joints, it must come from the tendons.

. . .

III. Common Sensation

§ 21. Pain.—Excessive stimulation of any sense-organ, or direct injury to any sensory nerve,
occasions the common sensation of pain. A concrete pain, such as is excited by a dazzling light
or a cut of the finger, contains three distinct factors: a sensation of special sense or organic sensation, the common sensation of pain, and a severe unpleasantness. In extreme pain, the first
of these factors is far outweighed by the other two. But we always know that it is the finger
which is cut, a tooth that is aching, the alimentary canal which is giving us colic pains, etc.; and
this knowledge of locality comes from a sensation of special sense or specific organic quality.

. . .

Method.—It is difficult to assure oneself of the qualitative similarity of pains set up in different
sense departments, because the presence of pain is extremely unfavourable to introspection.
But the following method may be successfully employed. Press a blunt rod down upon your
chest, until the pressure becomes painful, and let an assistant, when you give the word, sound
a painfully shrill tone upon a piston whistle. After a few trials you will be able to introspect well
enough to convince yourself that the two pains have the same quality.

§ 22. The Total Number of Elementary Sensations.—Putting together the results of the foregoing Sections, we obtain the following list of sensation qualities:

Eye	30,850	Alimentary canal	3?
Ear (audition)	11,550	Blood-vessels	?
Nose	?	Lungs	1?
Tongue	4	Sex organs	1
Skin	3	Ear (static sense)	1
(Muscle	1)	All organs (pain)	1
Tendon	1		
(Joint	1)	More than	42,415

Each one of these forty thousand qualities is a *conscious element,* distinct from all the rest, and
altogether simple and unanalysable. Each one may be blended or connected with others in various ways, to form *perceptions* and *ideas.* A large part of psychology is taken up with the determination of the laws and conditions which govern the formation of these sensation complexes.

The above list represents the full resources of the normal mind. It must not be supposed, however, that every normal individual has had experience of all the qualities enumerated. It is safe to say that no one, not even the most experienced psychologist, has seen all the possible visual qualities, heard all the possible tones, smelled all the possible scents, etc. The list is a summary of the results obtained by many observers in the course of minute investigations of our capacity of discrimination in the various fields of sense.   365

. . . [W]hen all allowances are made, the average number of conscious elements must run into the tens of thousands. And the permutations and combinations even of 10,000 elements would give a very large stock of ideas.

CHAPTER 5: AFFECTION AS A CONSCIOUS ELEMENT. THE METHODS OF INVESTIGATING AFFECTION

§ 31. The Definition of Affection.—We can quite well conceive of *a* mind which should be entirely made up of sensation processes and the processes arising from the interconnection and intermixture of sensations (perceptions and ideas). Certain mythologies represent the divine mind to be of this type: it is omniscient (*i.e.,* the ideas of which it consists form the total sum of all possible ideas), but it is also indifferent (unfeeling) and contemplative (inactive). Mind as we observe it, however, is of a very different nature. The living organism is exposed through its sense-organs to all manner of stimuli, and its mental processes are in large measure the sensation   370

Certain mythologies: Plato and Aristotle, and other Greeks, seemed to conceive of god in this way.

     375

processes directly aroused by these stimuli. But the organism is not indifferent. It not only senses: it *feels*. It not only receives impressions and has sensations: it receives impressions in a certain *way*.   380

When we have spoken in previous Sections of the effect of stimulation upon a bodily organ, we have thought of the body as entirely passive. We have pictured the stimulus as forcing its way through the organ, and setting up some change in it and in the brain, just as we might have pictured the photographer's acid eating away the surface of the sensitive plate. . . .   385

It will be readily understood that we cannot classify affections as we classified sensations; that there are no different orders or groups of affections as there are of sensations. There are many sense-organs, and each organ furnishes one or two groups or classes of sensations: but there is only one affective organ,—the whole body. It will be seen, further, that there cannot be so many qualities of affection as there are, *e.g.,* of sight or hearing. We have a large number of sensations of colour, because ether-waves of different lengths set up different chemical processes within the retina; we have a large number of sensations of tone, because air-waves of different lengths throw different fibres of the basilar membrane into vibration. But there are only two bodily processes to give rise to affective processes: the building-up process (anabolism) and the breaking-down process (catabolism). We should expect, then, to find no   390

     395

more than two qualities of affection. And introspection tells us that the expectation is correct. The anabolic bodily processes correspond to the conscious quality of *pleasantness,* catabolic processes to that of *unpleasantness.* These are the only qualities of affection.

400   In our definition of sensation, we took account of its simplicity as a conscious process, and of its bodily conditions. Of the simplicity of affection—pleasantness and unpleasantness— there can be no doubt: neither of its two qualities can be analysed into more simple and ele- mentary components. It is, as we have seen, unlike sensation in that it is not connected with a bodily process in a definite bodily organ. The organism, as a whole, receives the impressions

405 made upon it in a certain way: an affection is the conscious process arising from its 'way of receiving' a particular impression.

§ 32. Affection and Sensation.—The processes of pleasantness and unpleasantness seem, at least in many cases, to bear a strong resemblance to certain concrete experiences which we have analysed, provisionally, as complexes of sensations. Thus pleasantness may suggest

410 health, drowsiness, bodily comfort; and unpleasantness pain, discomfort, overtiredness, etc. . . . Beyond this there is no resemblance: a sensation process is radically different from a pleasantness or unpleasantness. The following considerations will be enough to make the fact clear.

    (1) The first great difference between sensations on the one hand and pleasantness and

415 unpleasantness on the other is that the former are looked upon as more or less common property,—as inherent, so to speak, in the objects which give rise to them, and therefore as pos- sible parts of every one's experience,—while the latter are our own peculiar property. Blue seems to belong to the sky; but the pleasantness of the blue is in me. . . .

    The same difference is observed even when we compare the affective processes with those

420 sensations which are occasioned from within, by a change in the state of a bodily organ. The unpleasantness of a toothache is far more personal to me than the pain of it. The pain is 'in the tooth'; the unpleasantness is as wide as consciousness. . . .

    We may put this first difference between sensation and affection briefly as follows: Sensations are objective and local, affections are subjective and coextensive with

425 consciousness.

    It is an obvious corollary to this statement that two affections cannot run their course as conscious processes at the same time. Nothing can be at once pleasant and unpleasant.

    'Why, then,' it may be asked, 'do we hear of "mixed feelings"? Why does Shakespeare make Juliet say: "Parting is such sweet sorrow"—*i.e.,* a

430 pleasant unpleasantness? Or how can Tennyson's Geraint look at the dinnerless mowers with "humorous ruth"—*i.e.,* again, with a pleasant unpleasant feeling?' The answer is that the ner- vous system may very well be exposed, at different

435 quarters, to stimuli some of which are catabolic

> *Ruth* can mean pity or compassion, or it can mean anguish over one's misdeeds.
>
> *Humorous ruth* is from Tennyson's *Geraint and Enid* (1859), part of his Arthurian epic *Idylls of the King.*

and some anabolic; some of which, that is, if felt by themselves, would be felt pleasantly, and some of which, if felt alone, would be felt unpleasantly. And the attention may oscillate, as it were, between the one group and the other; so that pleasantness and unpleasantness succeed each another in consciousness with great rapidity. The boy leaves home for school with 'mixed feelings'; he is sorry to go (unpleasantness), but his new watch partly reconciles him to   440
his fate (pleasantness). Nevertheless, at any given moment he is either glad or sorry; watch-consciousness and parting-consciousness succeed each other rapidly, but never overlap; there is no moment of combined joy and sorrow.

(2) If we are exposed for a long time together to the same stimulus (and if the sensation which the stimulus arouses is not of a kind to pass over into pain), we cease to be affected by   445
it at all. The cookery of a foreign country is, when we first make acquaintance with it, distinctly pleasant or unpleasant; but in either case quickly becomes indifferent. Dwellers in the country do not find the pleasure in country scents and odours that the townsman does; they have 'grown used' to their surroundings. . . .

Habituation to an experience, then, weakens or destroys the pleasantness or unpleasantness   450
which originally attached to it. There is no similar weakening or destruction of sensations. . . .

(3) The more closely we attend to a sensation, the clearer does it become, and the longer and more accurately do we remember it. We cannot attend to an affection at all. If we attempt to do so, the pleasantness or unpleasantness at once eludes us and disappears, and we find ourselves attending to some obtrusive sensation or idea which we had no desire to observe. If we wish to   455
get pleasure from a beautiful picture, we must attend to the picture: if, with our eyes on it, we try to attend to our feelings, the pleasantness of the experience is gone.

. . .

We see, then, that there are strong reasons for regarding affection as different from sensation. It must be carefully noted that the statements just given of these reasons do not tell us *how* 'red,' a sensation, differs from 'pleasant,' an affection, in mental experience. They are suf-   460
ficient indication that a real difference exists; but the difference itself cannot be described,—it must be experienced.

§ 33. The Methods of Investigating Affection.—There are two chief difficulties in the way of affective investigation. We cannot attend to a pleasantness or unpleasantness; and we can describe our affective experience only in a roundabout way. Hence if we were confined   465
exclusively to the employment of psychological method,—the method of experimental introspection,—we should find it very hard to give an adequate account of affective experience. Fortunately, we can supplement this direct method by an indirect, physiological method, which allows us to infer the presence and intensity of affective processes from their bodily consequences.

. . .

(1) *Psychological Method.*—A series is formed of stimuli which belong to the same sense   470
department (coloured papers, woollen fabrics, etc.). Each in turn is presented to the observer,

who gives it his complete attention, and when it has produced its full effect for sensation, asks himself whether it is pleasant or unpleasant, and whether it is more or less pleasant or unpleasant than preceding impressions. The rule of experimental introspection in the sphere of affection will accordingly run as follows: *Have yourself placed under such conditions that there is as little likelihood as possible of external interference with the test to be made. Attend to each stimulus as it is presented, and, when it is removed, form an idea of the pleasantness or unpleasantness which you felt during its observation. Put this idea into words, stating whether it is an idea of pleasurable affection, unpleasurable affection or indifference, and (2) in the two former cases, whether it is an idea of much or little, more or less, pleasantness or unpleasantness.* The assistant's account of the conditions, and your own verbal translation *(i.e.,* translation into ideas) of your affective experience furnish data from which other psychologists can work.

. . .

(2) *Physiological Method.*—Affection appears when there is a general alteration of the nervous system, including its highest co-ordinating organ, by way of anabolism or catabolism: in the one case we have pleasantness, in the other unpleasantness. Such an alteration will, of course, show itself in certain bodily effects. Seeing these effects, and knowing that the cause of them—the nervous change—is the bodily condition of affection, we are able to turn them to account for psychological purposes.

The principal bodily effects are four in number. We find that pleasantness is attended (1) by increase of bodily volume, due to the expansion of arteries running just beneath the skin; (2) by deepened breathing; (3) by heightened pulse; and (4) by increase of muscular power. Unpleasantness is accompanied by the reverse phenomena of lessened volume, light breathing, weak pulse, and diminished muscular power. There are special physiological instruments by which each of these manifestations can be measured. . . .

FOR DISCUSSION

1. Does everything in psychology fall unambiguously into Titchener's categories of thing and process?

2. Why is the nature of the mind not, in Titchener's view, a psychological question? What kind of question is it if it's not psychological?

3. What assumptions are involved in Titchener's expectation that two observers will make similar introspections under the same conditions?

4. Titchener likens consciousness to a fresco, and the words the introspector uses to describe it to mosaic stones. Choose an example of a conscious process; let this be the fresco. What mosaic stones are available to describe it?

5. What, in Titchener's view (or in yours) do we learn from enumerating all the elementary sensations?

6. Instead of ROYGBIV, suppose English possessed only two color words. What would be the consequences for Titchener's approach to the study of color sensations?

7. What do we stand to learn from Titchener's methods of studying the affections?

8. Does Titchener consider psychology to be a branch of philosophy, a natural science, or both?

9. What are the elements of vision according to Titchener? Compare his analysis to Marr's (2.5).

10. What place, if any, does introspection as Titchener describes it have in a richer and more sophisticated experimental psychology?

11. Why can't we introspect about pleasantness and unpleasantness?

Sigmund Freud (1856–1939)
The Psychopathology of Everyday Life (1901)

from *Chapter 2. The Forgetting of Foreign Words*

Freud is so strongly identified with his famous creation—psychoanalysis—that we need to remind ourselves occasionally that things might have been very different. Freud's medical training—in neurology—came at the end of a century that had witnessed, among other things, extraordinary advances in our understanding of the brain and of the rest of the nervous system. As a young neurologist, Freud was a philosophic and scientific descendant of the great 19th century German physiologists, and he began his career as a research scientist, investigating such things as the gonads of eels. By all accounts Freud's work was excellent, and he would have been happy to stay with it. But the glass ceiling of Viennese anti-Semitism seemed to rule out that option, and in 1882 Freud, who desperately wanted to get married, reluctantly gave up research and went into practice. This led to his encounter with hysteria and his famous collaboration with Josef Breuer, the first step on the path to psychoanalysis.

Freud was, among other things, ambitious. In early letters to friends and colleagues his desire to leave his mark on the world is palpable. A century later, the mark is unmistakable. People still read Freud. Many Freudian concepts are part of everyday discourse, and *Freudian* itself is an everyday adjective. On the other hand, scientific psychology has largely abandoned Freud. But regardless of what anyone thinks about the value of Freud's theory as a way of understanding minds and behavior and about the value of his methods for treating people with various symptoms, Freud's place in the history of ideas is secure. Here it does not matter whether we think he was right or wrong, but only that his ideas left their mark on the intellectual landscape.

Source: Freud, S. (1965). *The psychopathology of everyday life* (Alan Tyson, Trans.). New York: Norton. Copyright 1965, 1960 by James Strachery. Translation copyright Alan Tyson. Reprinted with permission of W.W. Norton & Company, Inc. and Sigmund Freud Copyrights/Paterson Marsh, Ltd.

Freud's immense influence arguably revolves around his basic claim that most of our behavior is a product of an unconscious but very active part of the mind. This unconscious is full of unacceptable urges, intolerable memories, conflicts, defense mechanisms, and so forth. Part of Freud's lasting significance in the history of ideas is that psychoanalysis was conceived as a means of opening the black box of the unconscious. As a psychologist, Freud wanted to know about the unconscious in general. What structures, forces, processes are found in every mind's unconscious part? As a psychiatrist, Freud wanted to know about a given patient's unconscious. What is in there that might account, in psychoanalytic theory, for that patient's symptoms? Freud believed that his method was at once a way to probe a given patient's unconscious and a way to investigate the unconscious generally.

An important premise of Freud's system is that psychopathology—a word that for Freud covered a much broader territory than its current meaning of *mental illness*—is not limited to neurotics, but manifests itself in seemingly innocent and meaningless everyday occurrences such as slips of the tongue, errors in reading and writing, and forgetting. In the present case, a young man quotes a line from Virgil's *Aeneid* but leaves out a word. In an analytic *tour de force,* Freud leads him through a series of associations that illuminate the unconscious motive for forgetting that word.

The current vocabulary of our own language, when it is confined to the range of normal usage, seems to be protected against being forgotten. With the vocabulary of a foreign language it is notoriously otherwise. The disposition to forget it extends to all parts of speech, and an early stage in functional disturbance is revealed by the fluctuations in the control we have over our stock of foreign words—according to the general condition of our health and to the degree of our tiredness. I shall give [an] analysis, . . . which . . . concerns the forgetting of a non-substantival word in a Latin quotation. Perhaps I may be allowed to present a full and clear account of this small incident.

Last summer—it was once again on a holiday trip—I renewed my acquaintance with a certain young man of academic background. I soon found that he was familiar with some of my psychological publications. We had fallen into conversation—how I have now forgotten—about the social status of the race to which we both belonged; and ambitious feelings prompted him to give vent to a regret that his generation was doomed (as he expressed it) to atrophy, and could not develop its talents or satisfy its needs.

He ended a speech of impassioned fervour with the well-known line of Virgil's in which the unhappy Dido commits to posterity her vengeance on Aeneas: '*Exoriare . . . .*' Or rather, he *wanted* to end it in this way, for he could not get hold of the quotation and tried to conceal an obvious gap in what he remembered by changing the order of the words: '*Exoriar(e) ex nostris ossibus ultor.*' At last he said irritably: 'Please don't look so scornful: you seem as if you were gloating over my embarrassment. Why not help me? There's something missing in the line; how does the whole thing really go?'

'I'll help you with pleasure,' I replied, and gave the quotation in its correct form: '*Exoriar(e) ALIQUIS nostris ex ossibus ultor.*'

protected: We are often temporarily unable to produce a word. Freud is presumably saying that we do not permanently lose the vocabulary of our native language.

functional disturbance: Freud is suggesting that an early symptom of unconscious conflict is the forgetting of foreign words.

non-substantival word: roughly, something other than a noun or verb; the word in question (see below) is an indefinite pronoun.

familiar: By this time Freud had published *The Interpretation of Dreams* (1900) and, with Breuer, *Studies on Hysteria* (1895).

the race: The young man is, like Freud, a Jew.

atrophy: to wither, waste. At the turn of the century the position of Jews in Austria was already precarious, and many social and professional opportunities were closed to them, as Freud knew only too well.

commits to posterity: passes along to future generations. In Roman mythology Dido, queen of Carthage, has fallen in love with the Trojan refugee Aeneas. When, at Jupiter's command, Aeneas leaves for Italy (where his descendants will found Rome), Dido throws herself on a pyre, but not before giving vent to her queenly anger in a speech that includes the line: *Exoriare aliquis nostris ex ossibus ultor,* "Let someone rise up from my bones as an avenger" (Virgil, *Aeneid,* IV/625).

'How stupid to forget a word like that! By the way, you claim that one never forgets a thing without some reason. I should be very curious to learn how I came to forget the indefinite pronoun *'aliquis'* in this case.'

I took up this challenge most readily, for I was hoping for a contribution to my collection. So I said: 'That should not take us long. I must only ask you to tell me, *candidly* and *uncritically*, whatever comes into your mind if you direct your attention to the forgotten word without any definite aim.'[1]

'Good. There springs to my mind, then, the ridiculous notion of dividing up the word like this: *a* and *liquis.'*

45

50

> *reliquien*: relics, such as bits of bone or hair, alleged to be the remains of saints

'What does that mean?' 'I don't know.' 'And what occurs to you next?' 'What comes next is *Reliquien, liquefying, fluidity, fluid.* Have you discovered anything so far?'

'No. Not by any means yet. But go on.'

55

> *accusation:* For many centuries Jews have been periodically accused of using Christian blood in their rituals.

'I am thinking,' he went on with a scornful laugh, 'of *Simon of Trent,* whose relics I saw two years ago in a church at Trent. I am thinking of the accusation of ritual blood-sacrifice which is being brought against the Jews again just now, and of Kleinpaul's book in which he regards all these supposed victims as incarnations, one might say new editions, of the Saviour.'

60

> Rudolf Kleinpaul (1845–1918), a contemporary art historian. The book in question is Kleinpaul (1892).

'The notion is not entirely unrelated to the subject we were discussing before the Latin word slipped your memory.'

65

> *the subject:* anti-semitism

'True. My next thoughts are about an article that I read lately in an Italian newspaper. Its title, I think, was "What St. Augustine says about Women." What do you make of that?'

70

'I am waiting.'

'And now comes something that is quite clearly unconnected with our subject.'

'Please refrain from any criticism and—'

'Yes, I understand. I am thinking of a fine old gentleman I met on my travels last week. He was a real original, with all the appearance of a huge bird of prey. His name was Benedict, if it's of interest to you.'

75

> The name *Benedict* means blessed, as in *benediction.*

> Freud is referring to his method of free association, which he used in his practice as a way into a patient's unconscious. Ideational elements are thoughts, memories, motives, and other unconscious lumber.

---

[1] This is the general method of introducing concealed ideational elements to consciousness. Cf. my *Interpretation of Dreams* (1900), Chapter II.

'Anyhow, here are a row of saints and Fathers of the Church: St. Simon, St. Augustine, St. Benedict. There was, I think, a Church Father called Origen. Moreover, three of these names are
80   also first names, like Paul in Kleinpaul.'

'Now it's St. Januarius and the miracle of his blood that comes into my mind—my thoughts seem to me to be running on mechanically.'

> *St. Januarius*, or San Gennaro, is the patron saint of Naples.

'Just a moment: St. Januarius and St. Augustine
85   both have to do with the calendar. But won't you remind me about the miracle of his blood?'

> It is unlikely that Freud needs to be reminded.

'Surely you must have heard of that? They keep the blood of St. Januarius in a vial inside a church at Naples, and on a particular holy day it miracu-
90   lously liquefies. The people attach great impor-tance to this miracle and get very excited if it's delayed, as happened once at a time when the French were occupying the town. So the general in command—or have I got it wrong? was it
95   Garibaldi?—took the reverend gentleman aside and gave him to understand, with an unmistak-able gesture towards the soldiers posted outside, that he hoped the miracle would take place very soon. And in fact it did take place . . . '

> St. Januarius's blood in a vial is an example of a relic.

> The miracle can be duplicated in various ways, for example, with a mixture of olive oil, beeswax, and iron oxide (rust); see Nickell and Fischer (1992).

> *the reverend gentleman*: the priest

100   'Well, go on. Why do you pause?'

'Well, something has come into my mind . . . but it's too intimate to pass on . . . Besides, I don't see any connection, or any necessity for saying it.'

'You can leave the connection to me. Of course I
105   can't force you to talk about something that you find

> The ellipses (. . .) here are Freud's, and represent pauses in the conversation.

distasteful; but then you mustn't insist on learning from me how you came to forget your *aliquis*.'

'Really? Is that what you think? Well then, I've suddenly thought of a lady from whom I might easily hear a piece of news that would be very awkward for both of us.'

'That her periods have stopped?'
110   'How could you guess that?'

'That's not difficult any longer; you've prepared the way sufficiently. Think of the calendar saints, the blood that starts to flow on a particular day, the disturbance when the event fails to take place, the open threats that the miracle must be vouchsafed, or else . . . In fact you've made use of the miracle of St. Januarius to manufacture
115   a brilliant allusion to women's periods.'

'Without being aware of it. And you really mean to say that it was this anxious expectation that made me unable to produce an unimportant word like *aliquis*?'

> Lack of awareness is central to Freud's ideas. The anxiety about a possible pregnancy causes the recall failure via a complex set of associations that the subject is unaware of.

sacrificed as a child: Freud sees St. Simon representing a possible solution to the object of the young man's anxiety: abortion.

'It seems to me undeniable. You need only recall   120
the division you made into a-liquis, and your associations: relics, liquefying, fluid. St. Simon was sacrificed
as a child—shall I go on and show how he comes in?
You were led on to him by the subject of relics.'

'No, I'd much rather you didn't. I hope you don't take these thoughts of mine too seriously,   125
if indeed I really had them. In return I will confess to you that the lady is Italian and that I went
to Naples with her. But mayn't all this just be a matter of chance?'

'I must leave it to your own judgement to decide whether you can explain all these connections by the assumption that they are matters of chance. I can however tell you that every case
like this that you care to analyse will lead you to "matters of chance" that are just as striking.'[2]   130

I have several reasons for valuing this brief analysis; and my thanks are due to my former
travelling-companion who presented me with it. In the first place, this is because I was in this
instance allowed to draw on a source that is ordi-
narily denied to me. For the examples collected
here of disturbances of a psychical function in daily   135
life I have to fall back mainly on self-observation. I
am anxious to steer clear of the much richer material provided by my neurotic patients, since it might
otherwise be objected that the phenomena in

This case substantiates Freud's view that there is psychopathology in everyday life, in mentally healthy people as well as in neurotics, and that no behavior is random.

question are merely consequences and manifestations of neurosis. My purpose is therefore par-   140
ticularly well served when a person other than myself, not suffering from nervous illness, offers
himself as the object of such an investigation.

. . .

disturbance in reproduction: any misremembering of verbal material; here, the omission of *aliquis*

The disturbance in reproduction occurred in
this instance from the very nature of the topic hit
upon in the quotation, since opposition uncon-   145
sciously arose to the wishful idea expressed in it.
The circumstances must be construed as follows.
The speaker had been deploring the fact that the

Eugen Bleuler (1857–1939) was a Swiss psychiatrist, best known for his extensive studies of schizophrenia, a word he coined.

This footnote was added in 1924, by which time Freud had become quite famous and his ideas had aroused some opposition.

[2] This short analysis has received much attention in the literature of the subject and has provoked lively discussion. Basing
himself directly on it, Bleuler (1919) has attempted to determine mathematically the credibility of psycho-analytic interpretations, and has come to the conclusion that it has a higher
probability value than thousands of medical 'truths' which
have gone unchallenged, and that it owes its exceptional position only to the fact that we are not yet accustomed to take
psychological probabilities into consideration in science.

present generation of his people was deprived of
150 its full rights; a new generation, he prophesied
like Dido, would inflict vengeance on the oppres-
sors. He had in this way expressed his wish for
descendants. At this moment a contrary thought
intruded. 'Have you really so keen a wish for
155 descendants? That is not so. How embarrassed
you would be if you were to get news just now
that you were to expect descendants from the
quarter you know of. No: no descendants—however much we need them for vengeance.' This
160 contradiction then asserts itself by . . . setting up
an external association between one of its
ideational elements and an element in the wish

> *wishful idea:* the young man's wish, like that expressed by Dido, that his descendants will avenge him

> *This contradiction:* between the young man's abstract wish for descendants who will avenge his generation of Jews on their gentile oppressors and his personal wish to avoid the complications of marriage and fatherhood

that has been repudiated; this time, indeed, it does so in a most arbitrary fashion by making use
of a roundabout associative path which has every appearance of artificiality.

. . .

For Discussion

1. Freud's interpretation of the young man's slip seems to him "undeniable." Why? What
   alternative explanations are there?

2. Compare Freud's method of free association with Titchener's introspection. What
   would Titchener have to say about Freud's method?

Herbert A. Simon (1916–2001)
Kenneth Kotovsky (b. 1939)
Human Acquisition of Concepts for Sequential Patterns (1963)

A t the age of 19, Herbert Simon did a study, in his native Milwaukee, of the city government's decision-making process, and it is fair to say that decision making remained Simon's primary interest for the rest of his life—indeed, he later told his student and collaborator Edward Feigenbaum, "I am a monomaniac. What I am a monomaniac about is decisionmaking" (Feigenbaum, 2001). Simon cared nothing for academic labels or disciplinary boundaries; he followed his interest in decision making across many fields. His BA and PhD, both from the University of Chicago, were in political science. Simon spent most of his graduate years at the University of California, Berkeley, directing a group studying municipal administration. He returned to Chicago in 1942 to take a faculty position in political science at the Illinois Institute of Technology and became involved with some of the leading economists of the day at the Cowles Commission for Research in Economics, located at the time at the University of Chicago. In 1949 Simon left Chicago to join the Carnegie Institute's new Graduate School of Industrial Administration. He stayed at Carnegie for the rest of his career. In addition to industrial administration, Simon was university professor of computer science and psychology, and he was a member of the Departments of Philosophy and of Social and Decision Sciences. In 1975 Simon and his long-time collaborator Allen Newell received the Association for Computing Machinery's Turing Award. Simon was also recognized by the American Psychological Association, the International Joint Conference on Artificial Intelligence (which Simon would have preferred to call "complex information processing"), and the Institute for Operations Research and the Management Sciences, and he won the 1978 Nobel Prize in economics.

Source: Simon, H. A., & Kotovsky, K. (1963). Human acquisition of concepts for sequential patterns. *Psychological Review, 70,* 534–546. Reprinted with permission.

Kenneth Kotovsky is professor of psychology at Carnegie-Mellon University. This article was his first of many collaborations with Simon in the area of problem solving. More than 4 decades later, Kotovsky continues to pursue this fascinating aspect of human cognition.

Simon and Kotovsky's paper is included here as a choice specimen of the information-processing approach to psychology. This approach represents a significant departure from other psychological paradigms in at least two important ways. First, information processing is deliberately and necessarily quantitative; that is, it asserts that a theory of a given psychological process must be reasonable and explicit about the amount of information that is being stored and manipulated. Second, information processing took psychological theory well beyond the narrow stimulus-response boundaries of the dominant behaviorist paradigm.

In most research on the acquisition of concepts, a *concept* is taken to mean a subclass of some class of objects, or, alternatively, a procedure for identifying a particular object as belonging to, or not belonging to such a subclass. The usual behavioral evidence that a subject has attained a concept is that he is able to sort objects that embody the concept from objects that do not. For example, we would say that a subject had attained the concept "red" if, on instructions to sort a pile of variously colored objects, he placed all the red objects in one pile and all the others in another.

There is no necessary relation between the ability to identify objects exemplifying a concept and the ability to produce examples of the concept. A familiar example of the lack of relation between these two abilities is the discrepancy between an individual's reading vocabulary and his speaking vocabulary (his ability to understand and his ability to produce words in a language). In experiments on memorization, the same discrepancy is familiar as the difference between ability to recognize and ability to recall.

There are some kinds of concepts, however, where we commonly measure attainment by ability to *produce* an object satisfying the concept rather than mere ability to *identify* an object as belonging to the concept. Prominent among these are concepts in the form of *serial patterns.* For example, the sequence abababa embodies the concept of "simple alternation of the characters a and b." We might test the subject's attainment of the concept by presenting him with a sequence of characters and asking him to decide whether it embodies the concept or not. More often, however (e.g., in the Thurstone Letter Series Completion Test), we ask him to demonstrate his attainment of the concept by presenting him with a sequence that embodies it, and requiring him to extrapolate the sequence. Thus, we would say that he had attained the concept, or recognized the pattern, embodied in the sequence given above if he were able to write down ba as the next two characters in the sequence.[1]

In this paper we propose to explain in what form a human subject remembers or "stores" a serial pattern; how he produces the serial pattern from the remembered concept or rule; and how he acquires the concept or rule by induction from an example. The theory takes the form of a computer program that simulates the processes of sequence production and rule acquisition, and that creates in the computer memory symbolic structures to represent the stored concept.[2]

> *induct,* or induce, means to formulate a general rule from one or (usually) more particulars. For example, if we notice that the plants we neglect to water tend to wither, me might induce the rule *plants need water.*

---

[1] Notice that neither in concept identification nor concept production is it essential that the concept be referred to by a name, or even have a name. We shall not consider in this paper the relation between concept naming, on the one hand, and concept identification or production, on the other.

[2] On the methodological issues involved in the use of computer programs to express and test psychological theories see Newell and Simon (1962). Laughery and Gregg (1962) and Feldman, Tonge, and Kanter (1961) have incorporated similar mechanisms for detecting and generating serial patterns in tasks somewhat different from the one considered in this paper.

Three kinds of evidence will be offered in support of the theory. First, an "existence" proof is provided—it is shown that the kinds of symbolic representations and information processes postulated in the theory are sufficient to permit a mechanism endowed with them to induct, produce, and extrapolate patterns. Second, the theory is shown to be parsimonious in a certain sense—the processes and forms of representation postulated in it are basically the same as those that have previously been used to explain certain forms of problem solving, and rote learning behavior. A mechanism possessing the basic capabilities for performing these other tasks has also the capabilities for performing tasks of the kind we are considering here. Third, the predictions of the theory show good qualitative agreement with the gross behavior of human subjects in the same tasks, in particular, predicting the relative difficulty of different tasks.

> For more on the description of serial patterns, see, for example, Kotovsky and Simon (1973), Restle (1970), Simon and Greeno (1974), and Simon and Sumner (1968).

> In scientific contexts, *parsimonious* (cheap, miserly) is used to describe a theory that postulates few or no new causal mechanisms. A parsimonious theory is not necessarily a simple theory.

The theory casts considerable light on the psychological processes involved in series completion tasks. It indicates that task difficulty is closely related to immediate memory requirements. It suggests what kinds of errors may be expected from human subjects in series completion tasks. It provides a clear-cut and operational referent for the notion of "meaningful" as distinct from rote organization of material in memory.

CHARACTERIZATION OF SEQUENTIAL PATTERNS

In Table 1 are shown 25 Thurstone letter series completion problems. The first 10 problems, designated by the letters A through J, were used as training problems with our human subjects, the last 15 designated by the numbers 1 through 15, as test problems. The test problems vary widely in difficulty, the number of subjects in a group of 67 who solved each problem ranging from 27 to 65.

In explaining human behavior in this problem solving task we seek, first, to form a plausible hypothesis about "what is learned": about the way in which a subject stores such patterns in memory in order to remember them, reproduce them, and extrapolate them. The first part of our theory, based on a simple "language" for characterizing serial patterns, postulates that such patterns are represented in memory by symbolic structures built from the vocabulary of such a language.

It is obvious that if a subject is able to extrapolate a sequence, he holds in memory something different from the bare sequence with which he was presented. The sequence, taken by itself, provides no basis for its own extrapolation. Indeed, from a strict mathematical standpoint, there is no uniquely defined correct answer to a serial pattern extrapolation task. Consider, for example, the sequence 1, 2, 3, 4, ... What is its continuation? One answer might be 5 but another, equally valid, would be 1 (i.e., 1, 2, 3, 4, 1, 2, 3, 4, 1 . . .). Still another would be 2 (i.e., 1, 2, 3, 4, 2, 4, 6, 8, 3, 6, 9, 12, . . .).

What is common to all these alternative solutions is that each is produced by a rule that is capable of continuing the sequence indefinitely. It is pragmatically true, although not logically necessary, that for the items commonly used on serial pattern tests it is easy to get consensus about the correct continuation. Presumably, the reason for this is that one sequence is suffi-   75
ciently "simpler" or "more obvious" than others, that almost all persons who find an answer find that one first. But it must be emphasized that this is a psychological, not a logical, matter.

It is also not logically necessary that a given continuation be associated uniquely with a particular rule. There may be several different ways of obtaining the same continuation, or of representing a particular rule. Indeed we shall encounter some examples of such multiple pos-   80
sibilities as we go along.

We must begin, then, by saying something about what the subjects bring to the task—for what they bring will certainly affect their criteria of simplicity, the kinds of patterns they will discover, and how difficult it will be for them to discover them. We assume the subjects have in memory the English alphabet, and the alphabet backwards. (There are some alternatives to the latter assump-   85
tion, but we make it, at present, for simplicity.) We assume the subjects have the concept of "same" or "equal"—e.g., c is the same as c. We assume they have the concept of "next" on a list—e.g., d is next to c on the alphabet, and f to g on the backward alphabet. We assume they are able to pro-duce a cyclical pattern—e.g., to cycle on the list a, b in order to produce abababababa. . . . Finally, we assume that they are able to keep track of a small number of symbols in immediate memory—   90
for present purposes, we need to assume only the capacity to keep track of two symbols simulta-neously. We may call these the first and second symbols in immediate memory, respectively.

Now, using a simple language capable of handling only the concepts that have just been described, representations can be constructed for all of the serial patterns in Table 1, and many others. It will be easiest to show how this is done by considering four examples of gradually   95
increasing complexity.

Pattern 3: atbataatbat . This sequence can be described most simply if we mark it off in peri-ods of three-letter lengths: atb ata atb at__. Having done this, we observe that the first posi-tion in each period is occupied by an a, the second position, by a t. We refer to these patterns as *simple cycles* of a's and t's, respectively. The third position in the period is occupied by the   100
cycle ba ba. . . . We refer to a pattern of this kind as a "cycle on the list b,a," Hence, we can describe the entire Pattern 3 by the notation :

3. [a, t, (b,a)]

Pattern 2: aaabbbcccdd Again, this sequence can be marked off in periods of three letters; but in this case, there are simple relations among the letters *within* each period (they are, in fact,   105
identical). One way in which we can describe Pattern 2 is by the notation :

M here stands for (immediate) memory.	[MI=Alpha]
	2. [MI, MI, MI, N(M1)]

TABLE 1 Letter Series Completion Problems

Training problems

Your task is to write the correct letter in the blank.

Read the row of letters below.

   A. abababab__

The next letter in this series would be a.

Write the letter a in the blank.

Now read the next row of letters and decide what the next letter should be.

Write that letter in the blank.

   B. cadaeafa__

You should have written the letter g. Now read the series of letters below and fill in each blank with a letter.

   C. aabbccdd__
   D. abxcdxefxghx__
   E. axbyaxbyaxb__

You will now be told what your answers should have been.

Now work the following problems for practice. Write the correct letter in each blank.

   F. rsrtrurvr__
   G. abcdabceabcfabc__
   H. mnlnknjn__
   I. mnomoompom__
   J. cegedeheeeiefe__

You will now be told the correct answers.

Test problems

1. cdcdcd__	9. urtustuttu__
2. aaabbbcccdd__	10. abyabxabwab__
3. atbataatbat—	11. rscdstdetuef__
4. abmcdmefmghm__	12. npaoqapraqsa__
5. defgefghfghi__	13. wxaxybyzczadab__
6. qxapxbqxa__	14. jkqrklrslmst__
7. aduacuaeuabuafua__	15. pbnonmnmlmlk__
8. mabmbcmcdm__	

The notation is interpreted as follows: we set a variable, Ml, equal to the first letter, a, of the alphabet. Each period is executed by producing Ml three times, and then replacing Ml by the *next* (N) letter of the alphabet. An alternative representation of this pattern is shown as Example 2b in Table 2. We shall refer to it later. 110

Pattern 13: wxaxybyzczadab_. This sequence is more complicated than the previous two, but can again be analyzed in terms of a period of three symbols; with internal relations among the first two symbols of each period. One description of this pattern is: 115

[Ml=Alph;w:M2=Alph;a]

13. [Ml, N(M1), Ml, M2, N(M2)]

Here are two variables, Ml and M2, corresponding to alphabetic sequences; but the Ml sequence begins with w, while the M2 sequence begins with a. Notice that when we come to the end of the list for such a sequence, we begin again at the beginning—z is followed by a. 120 Thus, these alphabetic sequences are identical with what we have called cycles on a list; in this case, the list is the alphabet, (a . . . z).

Pattern 15: pononmnmlmlk_. Our final example, also based on a period of three, can be represented in the same notation as the others, with the addition of one new operator:

[M2 = Ml = Balph;p] 125

15. [M2, N(M2), M2, N(M2), N(M1), E(M2,M1)]

There are two variables, Ml and M2, which follow the sequence of the alphabet backwards (Balph), starting with the letter p. The variable M2 is produced, then the next letter of the sequence, then the next; then the next in sequence to Ml is found, and M2 is set equal (E) to the new Ml.

Table 2 gives pattern descriptions for the entire set of 15 test problems in the notation we 130 have just introduced. We remark again that the descriptions are not necessarily unique—in many, if not all, cases, it is fairly easy to find alternative descriptions of the patterns. Those provided appear intuitively to be the simplest among the alternatives we have found. In the case of Patterns 1, 2, and 6, we give two alternatives.

The pattern descriptions contain all the information contained in the sequences from which 135 they were derived. They can be used to reconstruct the sequences. More than that, they can be used to extrapolate the sequences indefinitely—hence they can be used to perform the task with which the subjects were confronted in the Letter Series Completion Test. Thus, we may assert that anyone who has learned the pattern description has learned the concept embodied in the corresponding sequence. Our central hypothesis about human concept attainment in 140 situations involving serial patterns is the converse of this assertation, namely: *subjects attain a serial pattern concept by generating and fixating a pattern description of that concept.*

GENERATING SEQUENCES

We have now achieved our first objective: to formulate a simple, parsimonious language of pattern description, based on plausible hypotheses about what subjects bring to the serial pattern

TABLE 2   Pattern Descriptions of the Test Problems

Example	Initialization	Sequence iteration
1a.	M1 = (c, d,); c	M1, N(M1)
1b.	—	c, d
2a.	M1 = Alph; a	M1, M1, M1, N(M1)
2b.	M1 = Alph; a	M1(3), N(M1)
3.	M1 = (b, a); b	a, t, M1, N(M1)
4.	M1 = Alph; a	M1, N(M1), M1, N(M1), m
5.	M1 = M2 = Alph; d	M1, N(M1), M1, N(M1), M1, N(M1), M1, N(M2), E(M1, M2)
6a.	M1 = (q, p); q: M2 = (a, b); a	M1, N(M1), x, M2, N(M2)
6b.	—	q, x, a, p, x, b
7.	M1 = Alph; d; M2 = Balph; c	a, M1, N(M1), u, a, M2, N(M2), u
8.	M1 = Alph; a	m, M1, N(M1), M1
9.	M1 = Alph; r	u, M1, N(M1), t
10.	M1 = Balph; y	a, b, M1, N(M1)
11.	M1 = Alph; r: M2 = Alph; c	M1, N(M1), M1, M2, N(M2), M2
12.	M1 = Alph; n: M2 = Alph; p	M1, N(M1), M2, N(M2), a
13.	M1 = Alph; w: M2 = Alph; a	M1, N(M1), M1, M2, N(M2)
14.	M1 = Alph; j: M2 = Alph; q	M1, N(M1), M1, M2, N(M2), M2
15.	M1 = M2 = Balph; p	M1, N(M1), M1, N(M1), M1, N(M2), E(M1, M2)

Note:—Alph = alphabet; Balph = alphabet backwards.

task. Our next tasks are *(a)* to propose a mechanism that would enable a subject, holding such a pattern description in memory, to produce and extrapolate a sequence; and *(b)* to propose a mechanism that would enable a subject to induct such pattern descriptions from segments of letter sequences. We consider first the possible structure of a sequence generator.

Information processing theories already exist that seek to explain how humans perform certain other tasks, including problem solving—the General Problem Solver (GPS)—and rote memory—the Elementary Perceiver and Memorizer (EPAM). In constructing our present theory, we wish to avoid creating elaborate mechanisms ad hoc, and seek, instead, to build the hypothesized system from the same elementary mechanisms that have been used in GPS and EPAM.

See Newell and Simon (1961) for a description of GPS, and Feigenbaum (1961) for a description of EPAM.

Our language of pattern description makes this easy to do, since the processes required to produce sequences fitting the list descriptions can be formulated naturally and simply in the list processing language that has been used in constructing these earlier theories.

A list processing language, as its name implies, is a system of processes for acting upon symbolic information represented in the form of lists and list structures (lists of lists). Among the fundamental processes in such a language are the process of writing or producing a symbol, the process of copying a symbol (i.e., writing a symbol that is the same as the given symbol), and the process of finding the symbol that is next to a given symbol on a list. In addition, there are processes for inserting symbols in lists, deleting symbols from lists, and otherwise modifying lists and list structures.[3]

We can see rather immediately that processes of these kinds will enable the subject, having stored the pattern description, to produce and extrapolate the sequence. By way of example, let us consider in detail Pattern 9 in Table 2. To produce the sequence described by the pattern, we simply interpret the pattern description, symbol by symbol, as follows:

Hold the letter "r" on the list named "Alphabet" in immediate memory.

Produce the letter "u."

Produce the letter that is in immediate memory (initially, this will be "r").

Put the next letter on the list in immediate memory (on the first round, this will move the pointer to "s").

Produce the letter "t."

Return to Step 2, and repeat the sequence as often as desired.

Any mechanism that follows the program outlined in Steps 1 through 6 will produce the sequence: urtust-uttuut.... Thus, all that is required to construct such a mechanism, is to give it the capacity to interpret the symbols in the pattern description, and to execute the actions they signify—actions like "hold in immediate memory," "produce," "find next on a list," "repeat."

The second part of our theory, then, is a program, written in IPL-V—that is capable of generating sequences from pattern descriptions by executing the elementary list processes called for by the descriptions. As we have seen, the program is extremely simple. We postulate: *normal adult beings have stored in memory a program capable of interpreting and executing descriptions of serial patterns. In its essential structure, the program is like the one we have just described.*

Our main evidence for these assertions is that the program we have written, containing the mechanisms and processes we have described, is in fact capable of generating and extrapolating letter series from stored descriptions. We are not aware that any alternative mechanism has been hypothesized capable of doing this. Further, the basic processes incorporated in the

---

[3] We cannot enter here into a full discussion of the reasons for supposing that human thinking processes are fundamentally list processes. For a general nontechnical introduction to this point of view see Miller, Galanter, and Pribram (1960). The particular list processing language that has been used to define GPS, EPAM, and the theory set forth in this paper is IPL-V (Information Processing Language V). The language is described in Newell (1961)....

190   program are processes that have already been shown to be efficacious in simulating human problem solving and memorizing behavior.

PATTERN GENERATOR

We come, finally, to the question of how subjects induct a pattern description from the pattern segment that is presented to them. Our answer to this question again takes the form of a pro-gram that is capable of doing just this, in cases where the pattern is not too complex. We shall
195   describe the program, and then consider the reasons for supposing it bears a close family resemblance to the programs used by human subjects.

The inputs to the pattern generator are the letter sequences presented to the subject. The out-puts of the generator are the corresponding pattern descriptions. By considering what is involved in translating a sequence (Table 1) into its pattern description (Table 2), we can achieve some
200   understanding of what is involved in the generator. Basically a description characterizes a sequence in terms of some initial conditions—for example, the symbol to be stored at the outset in imme-diate memory—and some relations among symbols—for example, that one symbol follows another in the alphabet. The main task, then, of the pattern generator is to detect these initial con-ditions and relations in the given sequence, and to arrange them in the corresponding pattern.

205   There is gross behavioral evidence that the subjects accomplish these tasks by first discov-ering a periodicity in the sequence. Sequence 1, for example, has a period of two, for every other symbol is a c. Similarly, Sequence 2 has a period of three, for it consists of segments of three equal symbols each. The pattern generator seeks periodicity in the sequence by looking for a relation that repeats at regular intervals. Thus, it discovers that the *same* symbol occurs
210   in every second position in Sequence 1, and that the *next* symbol occurs at every fourth posi-tion starting with the first in Sequence 5. If this kind of periodicity is not found, the pattern gen-erator looks for a relation that is *interrupted* at regular intervals—Sequence 2 provides an example, where the relation of "same" is interrupted at every third position. Thus, to discover periodicity in the sequence, the pattern generator needs merely the capacity to detect relations
215   like "same" and "next" with familiar alphabets.

Once a basic periodicity has been discovered, the details of the pattern are supplied in almost the same way—by detecting and recording the relations—of equal and next—that hold between successive symbols within a period or between symbols in corresponding positions of successive periods. The pattern of Sequence 9, for example, records that a period of three
220   was discovered; that the first position in the period is always occupied by the same symbol—u, and the third position always by t. In the second position, however, each successive period has the symbol next in the alphabet to the second symbol in the previous period.

A number of different variants of the pattern generator have been written, all of them, however, based on these same simple relation recognizing processes. The several variants show different
225   degrees of success in describing the 15 test sequences. A particular pattern generator may fail to describe a given pattern for either one of several reasons. It may be unfamiliar with an alphabet used in constructing the pattern. It may not have a sufficiently wide repertoire of relations it can

test. It may have inadequate means for organizing and recording as a coherent pattern description the relations it discovers. All of these reasons for failure can be identified in our experiments.

We would expect that among our human subjects, also, different levels of performance on the Letter Series Tests might be associated with the same kinds of limitations. We shall raise this point again when we look at some of the data on human performance and its comparison with the computer simulation. 230

Some information on the performance of four variants of the program—A, B, C, and D—is provided in Table 3. The program became progressively more powerful, Variant A solving 3 of the 15 problems; Variant B, 6; Variant C, 7; and Variant D, 13. Except for Problem 3, all problems solved by a less powerful variant were solved by the more powerful variants. There is no *logical* necessity for this ordering relation to hold, but as an empirical matter it would be rather difficult to construct a 235

TABLE 3 Problems Failed by Group of 12 Subjects, and by Variants of the Computer Program

Problem number	Subjects [a]												Program variants			
	1	2	3	4	5	6	7	8	9	10	11	12	A	B	C	D
1																
2													X			
3				X		X								X	X	X
4													X			
5		X	X	X	X		X	X	X	X	X	X	X	X	X	X
6				X			X			X	X					
7						X	X	X	X	X	X	X	X	X	X	X
8										X	X	X	X			
9			X			X		X	X	X	X	X	X			
10										X	X		X	X	X	
11					X	X	X	X	X	X	X	X	X	X	X	
12					X	X	X	X	X		X	X	X	X	X	
13				X	X	X	X			X				X	X	X
14			X				X	X	X	X	X	X	X	X	X	X
15				X		X	X	X	X		X	X	X	X	X	X
Total correct	15	14	12	10	10	9	8	8	7	6	6	6	3	6	7	13

Note:—X = problem missed.

a. In order of performance.

240 variant that would succeed on the "hard" problems and fail on the "easy" ones. Thus, the programs reveal a "natural" metric of difficulty—a point we shall discuss further in the next section.

The pattern generator—we shall not attempt to distinguish among the several variants—constitutes the third part of our theory of human serial pattern learning. We postulate: *normal adult human beings have stored in memory a program, essentially like the pattern generator just described, capable of detecting relations and recording a pattern description for a simple sequence.*

EXAMINATION OF SOME EMPIRICAL DATA

245 Thus far we have been concerned primarily with describing a set of programs capable of doing what human subjects demonstrably can to discover, remember, and produce simple serial patterns. We have been able to find some quite simple mechanisms, incorporating elementary symbol manipulating and list manipulating processes, that have this capacity. The next stage in inquiry is to see what light these mechanisms—hypothesized as an explanation of human

250 performance in these tasks—can cast on the behavior of subjects in the laboratory; and conversely, to seek more positive tests of the validity of the explanation.

The data we shall discuss here were obtained by giving the Letter Series Completion Test to two sets of subjects. Since our main interest was in analyzing differences in difficulty among problems rather than differences in ability among subjects, no special care was taken to

255 obtain samples representative of any particular population. The first group, 12 subjects, ranged from college graduates to housewives. The second group, 67 subjects, comprised an entire class of high school seniors. Problems 1–15 of Table 1 were administered to the 12 subjects individually and to the 67 subjects as a group.

The three columns of Table 4 show for each problem: (1) the number of subjects in the first

260 group who solved it, (2) the number of subjects in the second group who solved it, and (3) whether it was solved (S), or left unsolved (U) by Variant C of the computer program.[4] The problems of less than median difficulty, as defined by the numbers of subjects solving them, are shown in boldface type in Columns 1 and 2.

The three columns of Table 5 show: (1) the average time per problem for those subjects in

265 the group of 12 who obtained the problem solution, (2) the average time spent by all subjects in the first group on each problem, and (3) the time spent per problem by Variant D of the program (which solved 13 of the 15 problems). The times that were below median in Columns 1 and 2 are shown in boldface type.

Considering both tables together, we have four measures of problem difficulty for the

270 human subjects—two measures of numbers of subjects who solved the problems, and two measures of problem solving time. Not surprisingly, there is a high level of agreement among

---

[4] Variant C was used for this comparison because it solved about half (7 out of 15) of the problems, thus permitting them to be divided evenly into "easy" and "hard."

TABLE 4   Problem Difficulty: Comparison of Human Subjects with Variant C of Program

| Problem number | Number of subjects obtaining correct solution | | Program[a] |
	Group of 12	Group of 67	
1	**12**	**65**	**S**
2	**12**	**61**	**S**
3	**10**	**60**	U
4	**12**	**57**	**S**
5	2	45	U
6	**8**	**48**	**S**
7	5	27	U
8	**9**	**49**	**S**
9	5	43	**S**
10	**9**	**51**	**S**
11	4	39	U
12	5	42	U
13	7	43	U
14	6	**48**	U
15	5	34	U

Note:—Problems shown in boldface were below median in difficulty for subjects in question.

a. S = solved, U = failed.

the four measures as to which problems were easy, and which hard. On all four measures, Problems 1, 2, 3, 4, 8, and 10 ranked below the medians in difficulty, as did Problem 6 on two measures (number solving) and Problem 9 on two measures (problem solving time). Problems 14 and 11 were each below median on one measure, while Problems 5, 7, 12, 13, and 15 were above the median in difficulty on all four measures. For purposes of gross comparison, we will call the eight problems in the first two groups the easy ones, and the seven problems in the last two groups the hard ones.

To see whether there is anything in our theory that would account for these differences in difficulty, we examine the pattern descriptions in Table 2. By common sense inspection of the pattern descriptions, it is clear that the easier problems have simpler descriptions—we could have made an almost perfect prediction of which problems would be above median in difficulty simply by counting the number of symbols in their pattern descriptions. (There is some ambiguity for Problem 6, which is neither as difficult as Description 6a would suggest, nor as simple as Description 6b would imply.)

TABLE 5   Comparison of 12 Subjects with Variant D of Program: Time per Problem

| Problem number | Seconds per subject | | Seconds |
	Subjects who solved	All subjects	Program D
1	**6.0**	**6.0**	**9**
2	**3.8**	**3.8**	28
3	**24.7**	**23.0**	18[a]
4	**16.8**	**16.8**	**23**
5	27.5	40.6	35
6	37.0	31.4	**19**
7	37.8	49.2	19[a]
8	**24.9**	**24.9**	**23**
9	**18.8**	**28.7**	**17**
10	**20.9**	**20.7**	**18**
11	**21.5**	37.3	35
12	49.8	49.0	**24**
13	61.7	65.5	29
14	41.2	47.8	36
15	48.0	56.8	30

Note:—Times below median shown in boldface.

a. Program D failed to solve problem.

But the lengths of the descriptions do not tell the whole story. If we now examine the patterns more closely we see that *all* of the patterns for the hard problems, and *none* of the patterns for the easy ones (except 6a) call for two positions in immediate memory. To extrapolate these more difficult sequences, the subject has to keep his place in two separate lists, but only in one at most, for the easier sequences. Moreover, to build up the patterns for the former sequences, the subject had to detect and keep track of relations on two distinct lists, as against one for the latter sequences.

An alternative hypothesis would be that the length of period was the source of difficulty. It is true that all the patterns with a period of four or more symbols (Patterns 5, 7, 11, and 14) are among the hard ones; but Patterns 12, 13, and 15, which have periods of three, are hard; while Patterns 3, 4, 8, and 10, which also have periods of three, are easy. Although the evidence is far from conclusive, number of positions in immediate memory appears to be more closely related to difficulty than length of period.

We cannot undertake here a detailed analysis of the errors made by our subjects, but we can make one observation that helps explain why Problem 9 appeared rather more difficult (in terms of failure to solve, not solution time) than its pattern description would have predicted. The main process, we have hypothesized, for solving these problems is to detect relations between adjoining symbols, or symbols in corresponding positions of successive periods. But towards the end of the sequence in Problem 9—the symbols tuttu—there are a number of spurious relations of "equals" and "next" that are not part of the pattern. Discovery of these relations, and failure to check them through the earlier part of the sequence, would lead to wrong answers. For example, the partial sequence given above could reasonably be extrapolated by annexing the symbol t.

COMPARISONS WITH PROGRAM PERFORMANCE

We have seen that one part of our theory—the pattern descriptions—allows us to make predictions about the relative difficulty of serial pattern problems for human subjects. It may be objected that the test is subjective, since we cannot know that the patterns used by the subjects are the same as those we have written down. The objection would be more convincing if it could be shown that the patterns could be described in a manner quite different from the one we have proposed. But there is additional evidence we can bring to bear on the question, derived from the programs used to generate the patterns—the third part of our theory.

Of the several variants of the pattern generating program we have studied, Variant C will be considered here, because it solved 7 of the 15 problems, hence found about half of them "easy" and half "hard." From Table 4 it can be seen that the program solved none of the problems we have previously labeled hard, and all but one (Problem 3) of the problems previously labeled easy. Hence the pattern generator also provides excellent predictions of the relative difficulty of the problems for human subjects.

A closer investigation of the program's failure with the hard problems showed that the difficulties arose specifically in keeping track of the lists associated with distinct positions in immediate memory. The program was incapable of organizing the parts of the pattern into an overall structure when two immediate memory positions were involved. We take this as additional evidence for the plausibility of our hypothesis that this was the locus, also, of the difficulties the less successful human subjects encountered. A more powerful version of the program, Variant D, overcame most of these difficulties, and failed only on Problems 3 and 7. A still more powerful version has solved all but Problem 7.

A few more words are in order about Problems 3 and 6. Problem 6 was solved by Variant C relatively rapidly, but the pattern discovered was 6b rather than 6a. With respect to Problem 3, we must simply say that the program of Variant C was different from that of most of the human subjects. (It might be mentioned, however, that the fourth and sixth ranking in the group of 12 adult subjects also missed this problem.) The occurrence of a following b in Sequence 3 led the program to attempt to use the relation of "next on the backward alphabet" instead of describing the pattern in terms of the circular list (a, b). It did not do enough checking to discover and correct its error. The majority of the human subjects either did not make that error, or were able to correct it.

In the third column of Table 5 we have recorded the times spent by Variant D on each of the 15 problems. There is a modest positive correlation between the times taken by the program and the subjects (Column 1), but the agreement cannot be claimed to be close. Analysis suggests that the time required by the program depended much more on *length of period* than

> *positive correlation:* This means that, on the whole, the more time the program took, the more time the subjects took. It does not mean that the program and the subjects took the same amount of time.

did the time required by the human subjects. If we consider only the nine patterns of Period 3, the correlation of times is very much improved. Since the theory does not postulate that the relative times required for the several elementary processes will be the same for the computer as for human subjects, there is no real justification for comparing human with computer times between tasks that have quite different "mixes" of the elementary processes.

Among the patterns of Period 3, Pattern 2 took the human subjects a very short time, but the program a rather long time. We would conjecture that in this case, the program was slow because it lacked a concept that most of the subjects had—the concept of repeating a symbol a fixed number of times (see Tables 1 and 2). Thus, while the program discovered Pattern 2a, we believe that most subjects represented the pattern in a manner more nearly resembling 2b.

We have mentioned these details because they illustrate how a theory of the sort we have proposed permits one to examine the microstructure of the data, and to develop quite specific hypotheses about the processes that human subjects use in performing these tasks. Of course, to test these hypotheses we shall require additional observations, particularly observations like those we have reported on problem solving tasks, which record not simply the success or failure of the subject, but as much detail as can be detected of behavior during the problem solving process. The possibility of confronting the theory with such detail greatly facilitates its testing and improvement.

CONCLUSION

In this paper we have set forth a theory, comprising a language for pattern description and a program, to explain the processes used by human subjects in performing the Thurstone Letter Series Completion task. We have devised measures of problem difficulty based on the pattern descriptions and upon the ability of variants of the program to solve particular problems. These measures of problem difficulty correlate well with measures derived from the behavior of the human subjects. By analysis of the pattern descriptions and programs, we have been able to form, and partially test, some hypotheses as to the main sources of problem difficulty. By detailed comparison with the human behavior, we have formed some conjectures about the detail of processes that can be subjected to additional tests in the further development of the theory.

We conclude on the basis of the evidence presented here that the theory provides a tenable explanation for the main pattern forming and pattern extrapolating processes involved in the performance of the letter series completion task. Different variants of the theory can be used to account for individual differences among human subjects in performing this task.

375

FOR DISCUSSION

1. What are some examples of serial pattern learning in everyday life?

2. The authors suggest that the human mind is likely to find the simplest pattern in a given sequence. Is this a reasonable assumption? What, in this context, constitutes simplicity?

3. What are some aspects or examples of human pattern learning that this approach might not capture?

4. In what way does Simon and Kotovsky's research (and other work like it) open the black box?

B. F. Skinner (1904–1990)
About Behaviorism (1974)

Chapter 4. Operant Behavior

No one is indifferent to B. F. Skinner. For some, he had all the answers; for others, he wasn't even asking the right questions. For better or for worse, his agenda and his methods strongly shaped American psychology and provided an explanation of behavior and mental life that the public could understand, misunderstand, embrace, despise, and oversimplify.

Burrhus Frederic Skinner grew up in Susquehanna, Pennsylvania. As an undergraduate, at Hamilton College, he majored in English literature and hoped to become a writer. He soon decided, however, that he had nothing to say. While casting about for another path he read Watson and Pavlov, who convinced him that behaviorist psychology was the way to go. In 1928 he enrolled as a graduate student at Harvard. It was in his graduate and postdoctoral years at Harvard that he laid the theoretical and methodological foundations for his lifelong study of operant conditioning. In 1936 Skinner took a teaching position at the University of Minnesota, and in 1945 he became chair of psychology at Indiana University. In 1948 he returned, permanently, to Harvard.

Skinner was a prolific writer, publishing more than 20 books and nearly 200 papers in the period 1930–1990. Most of them are technical, but Skinner, like Freud, devoted considerable energy to making his system accessible to the general reading public. Probably the most important efforts in that direction are Skinner's (1948) novel *Walden Two,* which depicts a utopian society run by operant methods, and the manifesto *Beyond Freedom and Dignity* (1971), in which Skinner applies behavioral methods to such conventional concepts as free will.

There are recent biographies by Bjork (1993) and Wiener (1996). Skinner wrote a short autobiography (in Boring & Lindzey, 1967) and a longer one in three installments (Skinner, 1976, 1979, 1983). An accessible, brief introduction to Skinner's ideas is Nye's (1992) *Legacy of B. F. Skinner.*

It is not clear whether Skinner believed that there was nothing in the black box or simply that it could not be opened, but in either case he may seem an odd choice for this section. We have included Skinner here not because he has anything to say about how to study the mind (other than "Don't!"), but because he provides a clear and detailed view of an alternative to studying the mind. In the present reading Skinner argues that our everyday, commonsense explanations of behavior as caused by mental states—feelings, ideas, purposes, and the like— are misguided, and he offers a guide to translating such explanations into another language, one in which the units of explanation are not mental states but behavior and consequences.

The process of operant conditioning described in the preceding chapter is simple enough. When a bit of behavior has the kind of consequence called reinforcing, it is more likely to occur again.

> Note that a thing or event is classified as a reinforcer (or punisher) not because of what it *is* (e.g., food, shock) but because of what it *does* to behavior.

5 A positive reinforcer strengthens any behavior that produces it: a glass of water is positively reinforcing when we are thirsty, and if we then draw and drink a glass of water, we are more likely to do so again on similar occasions. A negative reinforcer strengthens any behavior that reduces or terminates it: when we take off a shoe that is pinching, the reduction in pressure is

10 negatively reinforcing, and we are more likely to do so again when a shoe pinches.

The process supplements natural selection. Important consequences of behavior which could not play a role in evolution because they were not

15 sufficiently stable features of the environment are made effective through operant conditioning during the lifetime of the individual, whose power in dealing with his world is thus vastly increased.

> For example, your ability to mobilize your body when threatened is a product of natural selection (of genes) over the lifetime of your species. Your habit of avoiding restrooms in bus stations is a product of natural selection (of behaviors) over your lifetime—or of your mother's advice.

THE FEELINGS OF REINFORCERS

The fact that operant conditioning, like all physio-

20 logical processes, is a product of natural selection throws light on the question of what kinds of consequences are reinforcing and why. It is commonly said that a thing is reinforcing because it feels, looks, sounds, smells, or tastes good, but from the

25 point of view of evolutionary theory a susceptibility to reinforcement is due to its survival value and not to any associated feelings.

> *product of natural selection:* Skinner is arguing that the *capacity* for operant conditioning is built in, acquired (by the species) through selection on a Darwinian scale—over many generations—but that *specific behaviors* are acquired (by the individual) through selection on a Skinnerian scale—within one lifetime.

The point may be made for the reinforcers which play a part in the conditioning of reflexes.

30 Salivation is elicited by certain chemical stimuli on the tongue (as other secretions are elicited by other stimuli in later stages of digestion) because the effect has contributed to the survival of the species. A person may report that a substance

35 tastes good, but it does not elicit salivation because it tastes good. Similarly, we pull our hand

> The *conditioning of reflexes* that Skinner refers to here is *classical* or *Pavlovian* conditioning. A reflex is a built-in (i.e., unlearned) neural mechanism. It is said to be *conditioned* when the stimulus that naturally elicits the reflexive response (e.g., a puff of air on the cornea) has been repeatedly paired with an otherwise neutral stimulus (e.g., a green light). Thus the eyeblink reflex has been conditioned to the green light.

> *collateral product:* a side effect

> *susceptibility:* that is, to being reinforced by salt and sugar

away from a hot object, but not because the object *feels* painful. The behavior occurs because appropriate mechanisms have been selected in the course of evolution. The feelings are merely collateral products of the conditions responsible for the behavior.

The same may be said of operant reinforcers. Salt and sugar are critical requirements, and individuals who were especially likely to be reinforced by them have more effectively learned and remembered where and how to get them and have therefore been more likely to survive and transmit this susceptibility to the species. It has often been pointed out that competition for a mate tends to select the more skillful and powerful members of a species, but it also selects those more susceptible to sexual reinforcement. As a result, the human species, like other species, is powerfully reinforced by sugar, salt, and sexual contact. This is very different from saying that these things reinforce *because* they taste or feel good.

Feelings have dominated the discussion of rewards and punishments for centuries. One reason is that the conditions we report when we say that a taste, odor, sound, picture, or piece of

> *contingencies:* relations between behaviors and consequences, either quantitative (e.g., every 7th response is reinforced) or logical (e.g., if a response occurs while the green light is on, it is reinforced).

music is delicious, pleasant, or beautiful are part of the immediate situation, whereas the effect they may have in changing our behavior is much less salient—and much less likely to be "seen," because the verbal environment cannot establish good contingencies. According to the philosophy of hedonism, people act to achieve pleasure and escape from or avoid pain, and the effects referred to in Edward L. Thorndike's famous Law of Effect were feelings: "satisfying" or "annoying." The verb "to like" is a synonym of "to be pleased with"; we say "If you like" and "If you please" more or less interchangeably.

40

45

50

55

60

65

Edward L. Thorndike (1874–1949) was one of the first to conceive of learning in strictly objective terms, independent of any consideration of an animal's (unobservable) representation of what it knows. The law of effect that Skinner refers to came from Thorndike's famous "puzzle box" studies:

Of several responses made to the same situation, those which are accompanied or closely followed by satisfaction to the animal will, other things being equal, be more firmly connected with the situation, so that, when it recurs, they will be more likely to recur; those which are accompanied or closely followed by discomfort to the animal will, other things being equal, have their connections with that situation weakened, so that, when it recurs, they will be less likely to occur. The greater the satisfaction or discomfort, the greater the strengthening or weakening of the bond. (Thorndike, 1911, p. 244)

The law of effect and Pavlov's conditioned reflex became two of the cornerstones of American behaviorism.

Some of these terms refer to other effects of reinforcers—satisfying, for example, is related to satiation—but most refer to the bodily states generated by reinforcers. It is sometimes possible to discover what reinforces a person simply by asking him what he likes or how he feels about things. What we learn is similar to what we learn by testing the effect of a reinforcer: he

70 is talking about what has reinforced him in the past or what he sees himself "going for." But this does not mean that his feelings are causally effective; his answer reports a collateral effect.

The expressions "I like Brahms," "I love Brahms,"
75 "I enjoy Brahms," and "Brahms pleases me" may easily be taken to refer to feelings, but they can be regarded as statements that the music of Brahms is reinforcing. A person of whom the expressions are true will listen to the radio when it plays
80 Brahms rather than turn it off, buy and play records of Brahms, and go to concerts where Brahms is played. The expressions have antonyms ("I dislike Brahms," "I hate Brahms," "I detest Brahms," and "Brahms bores me"), and a person
85 for whom Brahms is thus aversive will act to avoid or escape from hearing him. These expressions do not refer to instances of reinforcement but rather to a general susceptibility or the lack of it.

. . .

> Skinner's use of quotation marks is potentially confusing. Sometimes, as in the Brahms example, they simply indicate made-up specimens of verbal behavior. More often they identify a word, phrase, or sentence as foreign to Skinner's point of view. (Longer passages may be direct quotations, but most seem to be a sentence or two that Skinner created to express an opposing view.)

> *general susceptibility:* the capacity (or lack thereof) to be reinforced, for example, by the experience of listening to Brahms, as distinct from a history of instances in which one was (or failed to be) so reinforced

WANTS, NEEDS, DESIRES AND WISHES

Some mentalistic terms refer to conditions which affect both the susceptibility to reinforce-
90 ment and the strength of already reinforced behavior. We use "want" to describe a shortage: a hungry man wants food in the same sense that food is wanting. "Needs" originally meant violent force, restraint, or compulsion, and we still make a distinction between wanting to act (because of positively reinforcing consequences) and needing to act (because not acting will

have aversive consequences), but for most purposes the terms are interchangeable. We say that a car needs gasoline and, much less idiomatically, that gasoline is wanting, but to say that 95 a person "wants to get out" suggests aversive control. The significant fact is that a person who needs or wants food is particularly likely to be reinforced by food and that he is particularly likely to engage in any behavior which has previously 100 been reinforced with food. A person under aversive control is particularly likely to be reinforced if he escapes and to engage in any behavior which has led to escape.

> *aversive control:* negative reinforcement, as defined in Skinner's first paragraph

. . .

An event is not reinforcing *because* it reduces a need. Food is reinforcing even when it does not satiate, and deprivation can be changed in ways which are not reinforcing. The relation 105 between a state of deprivation and the strength of appropriate behavior is presumably due to survival value. If behavior leading to ingestion were strong at all times, a person would grossly overeat and use his energies inefficiently. 110

> *deprivation . . . reinforcing:* A state of deprivation (e.g., of food) can be reduced in a way (e.g., by a feeding tube) that does not reinforce any behavior.

It is a mistake to say that food is reinforcing *because* we feel hungry or *because* we feel the need for food, or that we are more likely to engage in food-reinforced behavior because we feel hungry. It is the *condition* felt as hunger which would have 115 been selected in the evolution of the species as most immediately involved in operant reinforcement.

> *the condition felt as hunger:* the aversive state (which in mentalese we call *hunger* but which in Skinner's conception is a strictly physiological condition) whereby our body signals its need for food, from which we can escape by eating (thus providing the body what it needs). Skinner's point is that the capacity for this physiological condition has been selected in the evolution of the species. This capacity allows each individual to learn (i.e., to be reinforced for) behaviors that lead to food.

The states associated with wanting and needing are more likely to be felt if no relevant behavior is at the moment possible. The lover writes "I want you" 120 or "I need you" when nothing else can be done, and if he is doing anything else, aside from writing, it must be a matter of existing in the state which he describes with these expressions. If behavior then becomes possible, it is easy to say that it was caused by the want or need rather than by the depri- 125 vation or aversive stimulation responsible for both the behavior and the state felt.

Desiring, longing, hoping, and yearning are more closely related to a current absence of appropriate behavior because they terminate when action begins. "I miss you" could almost be thought of as a metaphor based on target practice, equivalent to "My behavior with respect to you as a person cannot reach its mark" or "I look for you and fail to find you." The lover in the arms 130 of his beloved is not instantly free of wanting and needing her, but he is no longer missing her or longing or yearning for her. Wishing is perhaps most exclusively a reference to a heightened state of deprivation or aversive stimulation when no behavior is possible. A person may wish that he could act ("I wish I could go") or he may wish for the consequences ("I wish I were there").

135   The effects of operant reinforcement are often represented as inner states or possessions. When we reinforce a person we are said to give him a motive or incentive, but we infer the motive or the incentive from the behavior. We call a person highly motivated when all we know is that he behaves energetically.

        Depriving a person of something he needs or wants is not a forceful act, and the effect builds
140   up slowly, but states of deprivation are given a more dramatic role when they are called drives or urges. Freud saw men mercilessly "driven by powerful biological forces dwelling in the depths of the mind or personality." We are said to be at the mercy of sex, hunger, and hatred, even though they are said to supply the psychic energy needed for action. Freud's libido has been defined as "emotional or psychic energy derived from primitive biological urges." These
145   metaphors are based on aversive control. The coachman does *drive* his horses by whipping them until they move forward, and, in the case of hunger at least, strong internal stimulation may have a similar function, but deprivation as such is not a driving force.

        . . .

IDEA AND WILL

The consequences which shape and maintain the behavior called an operant are not present in the
150   setting in which a response occurs; they have become part of the history of the organism. The current setting may affect the probability of a response, as we shall see in the next chapter, but it is not the only thing that does so. To alter a
155   probability is not to *elicit* a response, as in a reflex.

        A person may feel or otherwise observe some of the conditions associated with the probability that he will behave in a given way. For example, he may say that he "feels like going," that he
160   "wants to go," that he "should like to go," or that he "wishes to go." The same terms are used to identify reinforcers—as in saying, "I feel like a drink," "I want a drink," "I should like a drink," or "I wish I had a drink." It is possible that the report "I
165   feel like going" is close to "I feel now as I have felt in the past when I have gone"; and "I want to go" may be a report of deprivation or a shortage. "I wish" is, as we have seen, probably closer to a report of a sheer probability of action. Whether or not a person feels or otherwise observes the likelihood of a response, the simple fact is that at some point a response occurs.

170   To distinguish an operant from an elicited reflex, we say that the operant response is "emitted." (It might be better to say simply that it appears, since emission may imply that behavior

> *to alter . . . not to elicit:* There is a fundamental distinction between *operant* behavior, in which a certain action—an operant—is freely emitted, and *respondent* behavior, in which a specific action—a response—is automatically elicited by a specific stimulus. Skinner blurs the distinction by using *response* instead of *behavior* to refer to an (emitted, not elicited) operant.

> Notice that, contrary to some caricatures of Skinner's views, he does not deny the existence of mental states, but only their causal efficacy. In terms of the mind/body problem (see Part I) he is an epiphenomenalist.

exists inside the organism and then comes out. But the word need not mean ejection; light is not in the hot filament before it is emitted.) The principal feature is that there seems to be no necessary prior causal event. We recognize this when we say that "it occurred to him to go" as if to say that "the act of going occurred to him." "Idea" is used to represent behavior in this sense (we say   175
"the idea occurred to him"), but in expressions like "to get an idea," or "to borrow an idea" the word suggests an independent entity. Nevertheless, when we say, "I have an idea; let's try the rear door; it may be unlocked," what is "had" is the behavior of trying the rear door. When a person successfully imitates a dancing teacher, he may be said to "get the idea," although what he gets is   180
nothing more than behavior similar to that of the teacher. Nor need we refer to more than behavior when we say that a person who laughs at a joke

> *what is "had":* What if the behavior is prevented—did I then never have the idea?

has "got the point," or that a person who responds appropriately to a passage in a book has "got its meaning."   185

The apparent lack of an immediate cause in operant behavior has led to the invention of an initiating event. Behavior is said to be put into play when a person wills to act. The term has a confusing history. The simple future, as in "He will go," takes on an additional meaning when we say, "He *will* go in spite of the danger." Willing is close to choosing, particularly when the choice   190

> *unheralded:* outwardly uncaused

is between acting or not acting; to will or to choose is evidently as unheralded as to act. By attributing otherwise unexplained behavior to an

> *raison d'être:* (French, "reason for existing") purpose

act of will or choice, one seems to resolve puzzlement. That is perhaps the principal *raison d'etre* of   195
the concept; behavior is satisfactorily accounted for as long as we have no reason to explain the act
of will. But the conditions which determine the form of probability of an operant are in a person's history. Since they are not conspicuously represented in the current setting, they are easily overlooked. It is then easy to believe that the will is free and that the person is free to   200
choose. The issue is determinism. The spontaneous generation of behavior has reached the same stage as the spontaneous generation of maggots and micro-organisms in Pasteur's day.

> Skinner's rejection of uncaused events is by no means unique or original. His determinist view of human behavior and his denial of free will, however, in combination with his stated view that the purpose of psychology is the prediction and control of behavior, made him a popular target for critics on the political left, many of whom saw in Skinner's writings a prescription for a totalitarian state (see, for example, Chomsky, 1971, and Szasz, 1974). There is no evidence that Skinner himself had any such political leanings, but there are legitimate moral, political, and philosophical questions about any science that deals with the control of behavior. Not all criticism of Skinner's ideas is ideological; see, for example, Chomsky (1959), Dennett (1978), and Rozycki (1995).

"Freedom" usually means the absence of restraint or coercion, but more comprehensively it means a lack of any prior determination: "All things that come to be, except acts of will, have causes." . . .

The conspicuousness of the causes is at issue when reflex behavior is called involuntary—one is not free to sneeze or not to sneeze; the initiating cause is the pepper. Operant behavior is called voluntary, but it is not really uncaused; the cause is simply harder to spot. The critical condition for the apparent exercise of free will is positive reinforcement, as the result of which a person feels free and calls himself free and says he does as he *likes* or what he *wants* or is *pleased* to do.

. . .

PURPOSE AND INTENTION

Possibly no charge is more often leveled against behaviorism or a science of behavior than that it cannot deal with purpose or intention. A stimulus-response formula has no answer, but operant behavior is the very field of purpose and intention. By its nature it is directed toward the future: a person acts *in order that* something will happen, and the order is temporal. "Purpose" was once commonly used as a verb, as we now use "propose." "I propose to go" is similar to "I intend to go." If instead we speak of our purpose or intention in going, it is easy to suppose that the nouns refer to things.

A good deal of misunderstanding has arisen from the fact that early representations of purpose were spatial. The racer's purpose is to reach the goal, and we play parcheesi with the purpose of bringing our pieces home. In the mazes in which purposive behavior was once studied, organisms moved toward the place where reinforcement was to occur. To use goal for purpose ("What is his goal in life?") is to identify it with a terminus. But it is meaningless, for example, to say that the goal—let alone the purpose—of life is death, even though the ultimate termination is death. One does not live in order to die or with the purpose of dying, whether we are speaking in terms of natural selection or operant conditioning.

> *refer to things:* rather than to actions. Skinner is saying that our mistake is in putting purpose in the organism rather than in the organism's behavior.

Goals and purposes are confused in speaking of purpose in a homing device. A missile reaches its target when its course is appropriately controlled, in part by information coming from the target during its flight. Such a device is sometimes said to "have purpose built into it," but the feedback used in guidance (the heart of cybernetics) is not reinforcement, and the missile has no purpose in the present sense. . . .

> During World War II, Skinner developed a missile guidance system that used three pigeons (in the nosecone) pecking at images of the target. It worked, but the army lost interest and did not use it. See *Pigeons in a Pelican* (in Skinner, 1959); also Glines (2005). The nosecone is on display at the Smithsonian's National Museum of American History.
>
> For a different and important perspective on feedback in purposive behavior, see Miller, Galanter, and Pribram (1960).

Not all consequences are reinforcing, and much of the effect of those which are depends upon the contingencies. Psychoanalysts have often said that the gambler's true purpose is to punish himself by losing. It is almost always the case that the gambler eventually loses, and the behavior therefore has that consequence, but it is not therefore reinforcing. Gambling can be demonstrated in many other species and is explained by a special schedule of reinforcement to be noted in a moment. The ultimate loss (the "negative utility") does not offset the effect of the schedule.

> Skinner does not accept the punishment explanation because, by definition, behavior that is punished extinguishes, but gambling is notoriously resistant to repeated and consistent negative consequences.

> We can find no report of naturally occurring behavior, in nonhuman species, that constitutes gambling. It is more likely that Skinner is referring to the fact that a schedule of reinforcement (see below) can be devised such that an organism—be it a rat pressing a lever for food or a human pulling a lever for silver dollars—will work harder and harder for less and less reward. Skinner's point is that the "gambling" organism's behavior is under the control of the contingencies and immune to any consideration of long-term (future) consequences (e.g., exhaustion, starvation, bankruptcy).

. . .

Seeking or looking for something seems to have a particularly strong orientation toward the future. We learn to look for an object when we acquire behavior which commonly has the consequence of discovering it. Thus, to look for a match is to look in a manner previously reinforced by finding matches. To seek help is to act in ways which have in the past led to help. If past consequences have not been very explicit, we are likely to look in vague and unproductive ways. People can usually say what they are looking for and why they are looking in a given place, but like other species they also may not be able to do so.

Many features of the debate about purpose in human behavior are reminiscent of the debate about purpose in evolution. As the *Columbia Encyclopedia* puts it:

A still prevalent misunderstanding of evolution is the belief that an animal or plant changes in order to better adapt to its environment; e.g., that it develops an eye for the purpose of seeing. Since mutation is a random process and since most mutations are harmful rather than neutral or beneficial to the organism, it is evident that the occurrence of a variation is itself a matter of chance, and that one cannot speak of a will or purpose on the part of the individual to develop a new structure or trait that might prove helpful.

FEELINGS ASSOCIATED WITH SCHEDULES OF REINFORCEMENT

260   The probability that a person will respond in a given way because of a history of operant reinforcement changes as the contingencies change. Associated bodily conditions can be felt or observed introspectively, and they are often cited as the causes of the states or changes in probability.

When a given act is almost always reinforced, a person is said to have a feeling of confidence. A tennis player reports that he practices a particular shot "until he feels confident"; the basic
265   fact is that he practices until a certain proportion of his shots are good. . . .

When reinforcement is no longer forthcoming, behavior undergoes "extinction" and appears rarely, if at all. A person is then said to suffer a loss of confidence, certainty, or sense of power. Instead,

> *extinction:* disappearance of the behavior

270   his feelings range from a lack of interest through disappointment, discouragement, and a sense of impotence to a possibly deep depression, and these feelings are then said—erroneously—to explain the absence of the behavior. For example, a person is said to be unable to go to work because he is discouraged or depressed, although his not going, together with what he feels, is due to a lack of reinforcement either in his work or in some other part of his life.

> Skinner has just described what happens when most or all responses are reinforced (continuous reinforcement) and what happens when no responses are reinforced (extinction), and below he talks about what happens when some responses are reinforced and others are not (intermittent reinforcement). Skinner devoted an enormous amount of time to studies of how the acquisition, maintenance, and extinction of a behavior are affected by the *schedule of reinforcement,* or contingencies (Skinner & Ferster, 1957). The simplest schedules (other than continuous reinforcement and extinction) are classified as either *fixed* or *variable* and as either *interval* or *ratio.* In a fixed-interval schedule, the first response made after a specified period of time (the interval) since the last reinforced response is reinforced, and the cycle begins again. In a fixed-ratio schedule, every *n*th response is reinforced. In a variable-interval schedule, the duration of the interval varies, in some specified way, about a specified mean. In a variable-ratio schedule, *n* varies, in some specified way, about a specified mean.

. . .

275   Most reinforcements occur intermittently, and the schedules on which they are programmed generate conditions which are described with a wide range of terms. The so-called ratio schedules supply many good examples. When the ratio of responses to reinforcements is favorable, the behavior is commonly attributed to (1) diligence, industry, or ambition, (2) determination, stubbornness, staying power, or perseverance (continuing to respond over long
280   periods of time without results), (3) excitement or enthusiasm, or (4) dedication or compulsion.

The ratio of responses to reinforcements may be "stretched" until it becomes quite unfavorable. This has happened in many incentive systems, such as the piece-rate pay of home industries in the nineteenth century. The schedule generates a dangerously high level of activity, and those interested in the welfare of workers usually oppose it. It is not unknown, however, in daily life. A writer who makes his living by writing one article or story after another is on a kind of fixed-ratio schedule, and he is often aware of one result: the completion of one article is often followed by a period resembling extinction during which he is unable to start a new one. The condition is sometimes called "abulia," defined as a lack of will power, or a neurotic inability to act, and this is often cited as the source of the trouble, in spite of the fact that the schedule produces a similar effect in a wide range of species.

> *piece-rate pay:* An arrangement in which a worker is paid a fixed amount for completing a fixed number of pieces (e.g., shirt collars).

Variable-ratio schedules, in which reinforcement occurs after a given average number of responses but in which the next response to be reinforced cannot be predicted, are particularly interesting. A favorable history in which the average is slowly enlarged is said to generate will power, together with large amounts of psychic energy, or libido. . . .

All gambling systems are based on variable-ratio schedules of reinforcement, although their effects are usually attributed to feelings. It is frequently said, for example, that people gamble because of the excitement, but the excitement is clearly a collateral product. It is also sometimes said that people gamble "to satisfy their sense of mastery, to dominate, to win"—in spite of the fact that gamblers almost always eventually lose. The inconsistency is explained by calling the gambler who ruins himself and his family "compulsive" or "pathological," his "irrational" behavior thus being attributed to an illness. His behavior is "abnormal" in the sense that not everyone responds with similar dedication to the prevailing contingencies, but the fact is simply that not everyone has been exposed to a program through which a highly unfavorable ratio is made effective. The same variable-ratio schedule affects those who explore, prospect, invent, conduct scientific research, and compose works of art, music, or literature, and in these fields a high level of activity is usually attributed to dedication rather than compulsion or irrationality.

> *made effective:* This is done by starting with a favorable ratio ("beginner's luck") and gradually stretching it.

It is characteristic of intermittent reinforcement that behavior may be sustained over long periods of time with very little return. This has been explained by saying, "Human beings are creatures of hope and not genetically designed to resign themselves," but there is nothing essentially human about the effects, and it is not hope or resignation but the contingencies which are the conspicuous and accessible cause.

AVERSIVE STIMULI AND PUNISHMENT

320   Aversive stimuli, which generate a host of bodily conditions felt or introspectively observed, are the stimuli which function as reinforcers when they are reduced or terminated. They have different effects when related to behavior in other ways. In respondent conditioning, if a previously neutral stimulus, such as a bell, is frequently followed after an interval by a noxious stimulus, such as an electric shock, the bell comes to elicit reac-
325   tions, primarily in the autonomic nervous system, which are felt as anxiety. The bell has become a conditioned aversive stimulus, which may then have the effect of changing the probability of any positively reinforced behavior in
330   progress. Thus, a person engaged in a lively conversation may begin to speak less energetically or more erratically or may stop speaking altogether at the approach of someone who has treated him aversively. On the other hand, his negatively reinforced behavior may be strengthened, and he may act more compulsively or aggressively or move to
335   escape. His behavior does not change because he feels anxious; it changes because of the aversive contingencies; which generate the condition felt as anxiety. The change in feeling and the change in behavior have a common cause.

> *conditioned aversive stimulus:* The *un*conditioned aversive stimulus is the shock.

Punishment is easily confused with negative reinforcement, sometimes called "aversive control." The same stimuli are used, and negative reinforcement might be defined as the pun-
340   ishment of not behaving, but punishment is designed to remove behavior from a repertoire, whereas negative reinforcement generates behavior.

Punishing contingencies are just the reverse of reinforcing. When a person spanks a child or threatens to spank him because he has misbehaved, he is *presenting* a negative reinforcer rather than removing one, and when a govern-
345   ment fines an offender or puts him in prison, it is removing a positive reinforcer (or a situation in which behavior has occasionally been positively reinforced) rather than presenting a negative one. If the effect were simply the reverse of the
350   effect of reinforcement, a great deal of behavior

> *presenting a negative reinforcer:* It might make more sense to call it an aversive stimulus, but Skinner means the spanking, actual or threatened.

could be easily explained; but when behavior is punished, various stimuli generated by the behavior or the occasion are conditioned in the respondent pattern, and the punished behavior is then displaced by incompatible behavior conditioned as escape or avoidance. A punished person remains "inclined" to behave in a punishable way, but he avoids pun-
355   ishment by doing something else instead, possibly nothing more than stubbornly doing nothing.

In the above paragraph, Skinner seems to contradict himself, saying first that punishment is the reverse of reinforcement and a few sentences later saying that it is not. Elsewhere, Skinner holds that reinforcement (favorable consequences) directly strengthens behavior but that punishment is not simply the other side of the coin. In Skinner's view, punishment does not directly weaken behavior. Instead, punishment relies on negative reinforcement of escape from or avoidance of a classically conditioned aversive emotional response. Finally, it is only fair to point out that Skinner consistently maintained that punishment is not very effective.

What a person feels when he is in a situation in which he has been punished or when he has engaged in previously punished behavior depends upon the type of punishment, and this often depends in turn upon the punishing agent or institution. If he has been punished by his peers, he is said to feel shame; if he has been punished by a religious agency,   360
he is said to feel a sense of sin; and if he has been punished by a governmental agency, he is said to feel guilt. If he acts to avoid further punishment, he may moderate the condition felt as shame, sin, or guilt but he does not act because of his feelings or because his feelings are then changed; he acts because of the punishing contingencies to which he has been exposed.   365

The condition felt as shame, guilt, or a sense of sin is not due simply to an earlier occurrence of an aversive stimulus. A thunderstorm may set up conditions felt as anxiety and during a storm positively reinforced behavior may be weakened, and negatively reinforced (such as flight or concealment) strengthened, but this condition is not felt as guilt. The point has been made by saying that "a person cannot feel guilty if he has no object-directed impulses to   370
feel guilty about." More exactly, he feels guilty only when he behaves, or tends to behave, in a punishable way.

. . .

THE MIND IN OPERANT BEHAVIOR

In most of this chapter I have been concerned with feelings or states of mind which may be interpreted as collateral products of the contingencies which generate behavior. It remains for us to consider other mentalistic processes which are said to be needed if operant condition-   375
ing is to take place. The mind is not merely a spectator; it is said to play an active role in the determination of behavior.

Many English idioms containing the word "mind" suggest a probability of action, as in "I have a mind to go." Mind is often represented as an agent, scarcely to be distinguished from the person who has the mind. "It crossed my *mind* that I should go" is scarcely more than "It   380
occurred to *me* that I should go." When responses of glands or smooth muscle (under control

of the autonomic nervous system) are brought under operant control by making reinforcement contingent upon them, the result is said to demonstrate the control of "mind over matter"; but what it demonstrates is that a person may respond with his glands or his smooth muscles under operant contingencies. A mechanical arm designed to be operated by muscles normally operating some other part of the body is said to be "thought-operated" or "operated by the mind," although it is operated by the person who originally moved some other part of his body. When people shoot other people, it is said that "minds kill, not guns," and that "a man's mind was the instrument directly responsible for the assassination of John F. Kennedy and Martin Luther King" but people are shot by people, not by minds.

> *by people:* that is, by behaving organisms

The view that mental activity is essential to operant behavior is an example of the view that feelings or introspectively observed states are causally effective. When a person replies to the question "Will you go tomorrow?" by saying, "I don't know, I never know how I will feel," the assumption is that what is in doubt is the feeling rather than the behavior—that the person will go if he feels like going rather than that he will feel like going if he goes. Neither statement is, of course, an explanation.

There is an interesting parallel between Skinner's explanation here and the famous James-Lange theory of emotion:

> Our natural way of thinking about these coarser emotions is that the mental perception of some fact excites the mental affection called the emotion, and that this latter state of mind gives rise to the bodily expression. My theory, on the contrary, is that *the bodily changes follow directly the perception of the exciting fact, and that our feeling of the same changes as they occur is the emotion.* Common-sense says, we lose our fortune, are sorry and weep; we meet a bear, are frightened and run; we are insulted by a rival, are angry and strike. The hypothesis here to be defended says that this order of sequence is incorrect, that the one mental state is not immediately induced by the other, that the bodily manifestations must first be interposed between, and the more rational statement is that we feel sorry because we cry, angry because we strike, afraid because we tremble, and not that we cry, strike, or tremble because we are sorry, angry, or fearful, as the case may be. Without the bodily states following on the perception, the latter would be purely cognitive in form, pale, colorless, destitute of emotional warmth. We might then see the bear and judge it best to run, receive the insult and deem it right to strike, but we should not actually *feel* afraid or angry. (James, 1892, pp. 375–376)

(Continued)

(Continued)

Both Skinner and James suggest that our belief that our mental state is the cause of our behavior is an illusion. There are important differences, too. James is talking about those mental states we call emotions; Skinner is talking about all mental states. More fundamentally, Skinner argues that our feelings are "collateral effects" of the causes of our behavior, whereas for James the feeling and the behavior do not have the same cause.

There are other words referring to mental activities said to be more specifically required by behavior. People must "judge" what will or will not occur if they do or do not act in certain ways. The dog in the Pavlovian experiment salivates in anticipation of food or because it "expects" food. In operant experiments a rat presses a lever because it "anticipates" that food will be delivered or expects food to be delivered when it does so. "In social learning theory the potential of the occurrence of a behavior is considered to be a function of the expectancy that the behavior will lead to a particular reinforcement or reinforcements and the value of these reinforcements in a given situation." We should have to translate these statements in some such way as this: "The probability of behavior depends upon the kind of frequency of reinforcement in similar situations in the past." A person may well feel conditions associated with "judging," "anticipating," and "expecting," but he does not need to do so.

Operant behavior is also said to require the "association" of ideas. The fact that a baby learns to avoid a hot stove is said to imply that "the baby has the ability to associate his act with getting burned." But, as in a conditioned reflex, touching and burning are associated in the contingencies. Reinforcement is also said to "supply information": "With other than very young children we can never say that the major effect of reinforcement is other than a source of information used by the child to confirm or change his expectations and to develop new and tentative solutions." Increasing the probability that people will respond in certain ways is sometimes said to be a matter of "raising consciousness." How fast a rat will run in a maze is said to depend upon whether it "knows that food is any longer available in the end box." I shall return to knowledge, information, and consciousness in later chapters.

> *associated in the contingencies:* Skinner rejects Locke's "association of ideas," (see 4.2) because ideas (and therefore associations between them) are unobservable, and replaces it with an association of observable things—in this case touching (the behavior, not the idea) and burning (the consequence, not the idea).

Another supposed mental process said to be needed in operant conditioning is understanding. People must "understand the regularities upon which they can count." Their action must be "grounded on the understanding of how things behave." Another state said to be needed is belief. People must believe that what they are doing has some chance of obtaining

400

405

410

415

420

425

430   what they want or avoiding something to which they are averse. But the chances are in the con-
      tingencies. The relation of beliefs to other conditions, such as wants and needs, can be easily
      stated, to say that "desires enter into the causation of beliefs" is simply to say that the proba-
      bility of behavior with which a belief is associated depends not only upon reinforcement but
      upon a state of deprivation or aversive stimulation.

435   It is sometimes said, that operant conditioning is simply one aspect of the pursuit of hap-
      piness, and the expression will help to summarize several points in this chapter. Happiness is
      a feeling, a by-product of operant reinforcement.
      The things which make us happy are the things

      a by-product of operant reinforcement: as
      opposed to a *goal,* if we may use such a
      word

      which reinforce us, but it is the things, not the feel-
440   ings, which must be identified and used in pre-
      diction, control, and interpretation. Pursuit
      suggests purpose: we act to achieve happiness.
      But pursuit, like search, is simply behavior which has been reinforced by achieving something.
      Behavior becomes pursuit only after reinforcement. It has been said that the pursuit of happi-
445   ness cannot be an explanation of behavior because "nothing proves that men in modern
      societies are happier than men in archaic societies," but operant reinforcement is effective quite
      apart from any ultimate gain, as the negative utility of gambling abundantly demonstrates.

FOR DISCUSSION

1. Could Skinner's explanation of the reinforcing properties of sugar, salt, and sex also explain the reinforcing properties of alcohol, nicotine, and caffeine?

2. What are some examples of "collateral products" (lines 41 and 374) other than verbal statements?

3. Why does Skinner argue that we like something because it is reinforcing rather than the other way around?

4. How would you rewrite Thorndike's Law of Effect in light of Skinner's discussion of the feelings of reinforcers?

5. What is Skinner's explanation of how someone becomes a compulsive gambler?

6. Why is the feedback used in guiding a missile (or cruise control, thermostat, etc.) not reinforcement?

7. How would the idea of culture be worked into Skinner's way of explaining behavior?

8. Translate the following mentalese sentences into Skinnerese:
   a. I love you.
   b. I have no idea what's wrong with this car.
   c. I hope your mother enjoyed the show.
   d. I wish I were an Oscar Mayer wiener.
   e. OK, OK, I get the point: you want me to take out the trash.

9. Skinner says (p. 268, line 182) "Nor need we refer to more than behavior when we says that . . . a person who responds appropriately to a passage in a book has 'got its meaning'"

   a. What is an appropriate response to a passage in a book?
   b. If an appropriate response does not occur, can we infer that the person doesn't understand the passage?

10. What does the sentence *I need a cup of coffee* mean in mentalese? In Skinnerese? Does Skinner deny that we have a conscious experience to which we give the name "need"?

11. How might Skinner explain the establishment of superstitious behaviors and why they are so hard to extinguish?

Michael I. Posner (b. 1936)
Steven E. Petersen (b. 1952)
Peter T. Fox (b. 1951)
Marcus E. Raichle (b. 1937)
Localization of Cognitive Operations in the Human Brain (1988)

In the early nineteenth century the Viennese physician and anatomist Franz Joseph Gall (1758–1828) and his student Johann Gaspar Spurzheim (1776–1832) developed *phrenology,* a theory about the relation between psychological characteristics and the brain. The theory identifies a set of faculties, or mental functions:

1. impulse to reproduce
2. parental love
3. friendly attachment, fidelity
4. valor, self-defense
5. murder, carnivorousness

6. sense of cunning
7. larceny, sense of property
8. pride, arrogance, love of authority
9. ambition and vanity
10. circumspection

Source: Posner, M. I., Petersen, S. E., Fox, P. T., & Raichle, M. E. (1988). Localization of cognitive operations in the human brain. *Science, 240,* 1627–1631. Reprinted with permission from AAAS.

11. memory for things and facts

12. sense of locality

13. memory for people

14. verbal memory and comprehension

15. faculty of language

16. sense (aesthetic) of color

17. sense for sounds, musical talent

18. sense of quantity, time

19. mechanical skill

20. comparative perspicuity

21. metaphysical perspicuity

22. wit, causality, sense of inference

23. poetic talent

24. good nature, compassion, moral sense

25. mimicry

26. sense of God and religion

27. perseverance, firmness

As a statement of basic cognitive abilities and of the ways in which people differ from one another, this list is not unreasonable. But phrenology was not just a vague theory of individual differences. Gall claimed that the brain consists of a number of "organs," each of which is responsible for a different faculty. Thus phrenology was a theory of what is often referred to as *localization of function;* that is, a theory of where in the brain different psychological functions are carried out.

If we believe there is a relation between the development of particular mental organs and their size, then the shape of the skull should tell us something about the relative development of the organs. Thus phrenology seemed to offer a way (feeling the bumps on the skull) to assess a wide range of personal characteristics long before the advent of psychological testing. This "applied" side of phrenology became wildly popular, especially in England and America, in the mid-19th century, but it eventually came to be seen as a carnival sideshow rather than a science, and Gall earned a reputation as a quack. No one now takes phrenology seriously, but Gall's claim that different mental functions take place in different places in the brain—the idea of localization—has motivated a substantial amount of brain research for nearly 2 centuries.

Since Gall, a number of strategies for gathering evidence about localization have emerged. Pierre Flourens (1794–1867) established the first experimental approach, in which he first observed an animal's behavior, then destroyed some part of the animal's brain, and then observed its behavior again. Any behavior that is missing after the surgery, Flourens reasoned, must be caused or controlled by the part of the brain that is now missing. By systematically destroying different parts of the brain in different animals, Flourens established the first empirical, though very broad, localization of brain functions. The cerebral hemispheres were apparently responsible for perception, memory, judgment, and volition; the cerebellum coordinated motor functions; and the medulla controlled vital functions.

Another strategy amounts to Flourens's method in reverse. Doctors had long been familiar with many cases of sudden and strange changes in a patient's behavior, such as the loss of speech (expressive aphasia) or the inability to recognize familiar objects (visual agnosia). If these changes were caused by damage to the brain, it ought to be possible to identify the site of the damage in a postmortem examination. In this way Paul Pierre Broca (1824–1880) found, in 1861, a region of the left frontal lobe to be responsible for aspects of both speaking and writing (but not language comprehension), and in 1874 Karl Wernicke (1848–1905) identified a location in the left temporal lobe as the culprit in a certain kind of receptive aphasia (inability to understand speech).

Around the same time, surgical techniques and understanding of electricity had reached a point that allowed the direct electrical stimulation of the brain. In 1870 Gustav Fritsch (1837–1927) and Eduard Hitzig (1838–1907) discovered the motor cortex using this method in a dog. By 1876 David Ferrier (1843–1924) had produced a fairly detailed map of this region in a monkey. Shortly thereafter he located vision in the occipital region.

Richard Caton (1842–1926) found that instead of electrically stimulating the brain, he could measure the brain's own electrical activity. Connecting a sensitive galvanometer directly to the surface of the cortex in various animals, Caton found that he could measure a voltage—indicating electrical activity—and that this voltage changed when the animal made a certain movement or was subjected to a certain stimulus. Others soon found that, in the absence of movement or stimulus, there is a regular cyclic variation, a "brain wave." In 1929 Hans Berger (1873–1941) announced that he had succeeded in measuring brain electrical activity through the scalp, a technique known as *electroencephalography* ("electric head writing"), or EEG.

Techniques and instruments for measuring electrical activity, either through the skull, from the surface of the brain, or from within the brain, have continued to develop, but in the last few decades technologies have emerged that offer something new: images of the living brain. Positron emission tomography (PET) and functional magnetic resonance imaging (fMRI) both take advantage, in different ways, of an idea that has been around for quite a while.

F. C. Donders (1868/1969) (see 3.1) pointed out that blood flowing out of the brain contains less oxygen than blood flowing in. Angelo Mosso (1846–1910) supplied a second key, described here by James:

> The brain itself is an excessively vascular organ, a sponge full of blood, in fact; and another of Mosso's inventions showed that when less blood went to the arms, more went to the head. The subject to be observed lay on a delicately balanced table which could tip downward either at the head or at the foot if the weight of either end were increased. The moment emotional or intellectual activity began in the subject, down went the balance at the head-end, in consequence of the redistribution of blood in his system. But the best proof of the immediate afflux of blood to the brain during mental activity is due to Mosso's observations on three persons whose brain had been laid bare by lesion of the skull. By means of apparatus described in his book [Mosso, 1881], this physiologist was enabled to let the brain pulse record itself directly by a tracing. The intra-cranial blood-pressure rose immediately whenever the subject was spoken to, or when he began to think actively, as in solving a problem in mental arithmetic. Mosso [1881] gives in his work a large number of reproductions of tracings which show the instantaneity of the change of blood-supply, whenever the mental activity was quickened by any cause whatever, intellectual or emotional. . . . The fluctuations of the blood-supply to the brain were independent of respiratory changes, and followed the quickening of mental activity almost immediately. We must suppose a very delicate adjustment whereby the

circulation follows the needs of the cerebral activity. Blood very likely may rush to each region of the cortex according as it is most active, but of this we know nothing. (James, 1890, pp. 98–99)

Just as activity in a given part of the brain produces electrical signals, it is accompanied by increased blood flow and increased oxygen metabolism in that region. PET and fMRI have finally given brain researchers tools to see the activity of the brain as reflected in its circulation and metabolism. For more on the history of the study of the brain see Brazier (1961), Finger (1994), and Raichle (1998).

The present reading explains how these tools are used to study the localization of function. The authors have all been active in developing the methods they describe. Michael Posner, a psychologist, has been one of the most prominent cognition researchers for nearly half a century. He is now professor emeritus at the University of Oregon and adjunct professor at the Weill Medical College in New York (Sackler Institute). Steven Petersen is a biologist at Washington University Medical School, where he is a professor in the Departments of Neurology and Radiology, an associate professor in the Departments of Anatomy and Neurobiology, Neurosurgery, and Psychology, and chief of the Neuropsychology Division. Peter Fox, a neurologist, is director of the Research Imaging Center at the University of Texas Health Science Center. Marcus Raichle is professor of Radiology, Neurology, Neurobiology, Biomedical Engineering and Psychology at Washington University School of Medicine and codirector of the Division of Radiological Sciences at the Mallinckrodt Institute of Radiology.

Among other things, their paper shows that the study of localization—whether by means of PET scans or bumps on the skull—demands a theory of function. One cannot speak of *where* in the brain something happens without a notion of what the various *somethings*—mental functions—are.

The question of localization of cognition in the human brain is an old and difficult one (Churchland, 1986). However, current analyses of the operations involved in cognition (Anderson, 1980) and new techniques for the imaging of brain function during cognitive tasks (Raichle, 1983) have combined to provide support for a new hypothesis. The hypothesis is that

5   elementary operations forming the basis of cognitive analyses of human tasks are strictly local-ized. Many such local operations are involved in any cognitive task. A set of distributed brain areas must be orchestrated in the performance of even simple cognitive tasks. The task itself is not performed by any single area of the brain, but the operations that underlie the perfor-mance are strictly localized. This idea fits generally with many network theories in neuroscience

10   and cognition. However, most neuroscience network theories of higher processes (Mesulam, 1981; Goldman-Rakic, 1988) provide little information on the specific computations performed at the nodes of the network, and most cognitive network models provide little or no informa-tion on the anatomy involved (McClelland & Rumelhart, 1986). Our approach relates specific mental operations as developed from cognitive models to neural anatomical areas.

15   The study of reading and listening has been one of the most active areas in cognitive science for the study of internal codes involved in information processing (Posner, 1986). In this arti-cle we review results of studies on cognitive tasks that suggest several separate codes for pro-cessing individual words. These codes can be accessed from input or from attention. We also review studies of alert monkeys and brain-lesioned patients that provide evidence on the local-

20   ization of an attention system for visual spatial information. This system is apparently unnec-essary for processing single, foveally centered words. Next, we introduce data from positron emission tomography (PET) concerning the neural systems underlying the coding of individual visual

25   (printed) words. These studies support the find-ings in cognition and also give new evidence for an anterior attention system involved in language processing. Finally, we survey other areas of cognition for which recent findings support the

30   localization of component mental operations.

> *codes:* In this context *code* refers to the activity in the nervous system, or part of it, corresponding to a subjective state or to a hypothesized cognitive process. The authors' goal is not to "break" the codes but to enumerate and identify them.

INTERNAL CODES

The most advanced efforts to develop cognitive models of information processing have been in the area of the coding of individual words through reading and listening (Posner, 1986; Marshall & Newcombe, 1973; LaBerge & Samuels, 1974; Carr & Pollatsek, 1985; Coltheart,

35   1985). These efforts have distinguished between a number of internal codes related to the visual, phonological, articulatory, and semantic analysis of a word. Operations at all these levels appear to be involved in understanding a word.

The findings discussed here are based on the reaction time logic devised by Donders; see 3.1.

This view began with efforts to develop detailed measurements of the time it takes to execute operations on codes thought to be involved in reading. Figure 1 shows the amount of time needed to determine if two simultaneously shown visual letters or words belong to the same category (Posner, Lewis, & Conrad, 1972). The reaction time to match pairs of items that are physically identical (for example, AA) is faster than reaction time for matches of the same letters or words in the opposite case (Aa), which are in turn faster than matches that have only a common category (Ae). These studies have been interpreted as involving a mental operation of matching based on different codes. In the case of visual identity the code is thought to be the visual form, whereas in cross-case matching it is thought to be the letter or word name. The idea that a word consists of separable physical, phonological, and semantic codes and that operations may be performed on them separately has been basic to many theories of reading and listening (Marshall & Newcombe, 1973; LaBerge & Samuels, 1974; Carr & Pollatsek, 1985; Coltheart, 1985). Thus the operation of rotating a letter to the upright position is thought to be performed on the visual code (Cooper, 1976), whereas matching to determine if two words rhyme is said to be performed on a phonological representation of the words (Kleiman, 1975). These theories suggest that mental operations take place on the basis of codes related to separate neural systems.

visual identity: same-case pairs

elementary: an operation that cannot be further divided into constituent operations

It is not easy to determine if any operation is elementary or whether it is based on only a single code. Even a simple task such as matching identical items can involve parallel operations on both physical and name codes. Indeed, there has been controversy over the theoretical implications of these matching experiments (Boles & Eveland, 1983; Proctor, 1981). Some results have suggested that both within- and cross-case matches are performed on physical (visual) codes, whereas others have suggested that they are both performed on name codes (Boles & Eveland, 1983; Proctor, 1981). A basic question is to determine whether operations performed on different codes involve different brain areas. This question cannot be resolved by performance studies, since they provide only indirect evidence about localization of the operations performed on different codes.

It has been widely accepted that there can be multiple routes by which codes interact. For example, a visual word may be sounded out to produce a phonological code and then the phonology is used to develop a meaning (Posner, 1986; Marshall & Newcombe, 1973; LaBerge & Samuels, 1974; Carr & Pollatsek, 1985; Coltheart, 1985). Alternately, the visual code may have direct access to a semantic interpretation without any need for developing a phonological code (Posner, 1986; Marshall & Newcombe, 1973; LaBerge & Samuels, 1974; Carr & Pollatsek, 1985;

interpretation: here, code

40

45

50

55

60

65

70

75

FIGURE 1   Results of reaction time studies in which subjects were asked to classify whether pairs of letters were either both vowels or both consonants (A) or whether pairs of words were both animals or both plants (B). Reaction times are in milliseconds. Each study involved 10 to 12 normal subjects. Standard deviations are typically 20 % of the mean value. Data argue in favor of these matches being made on different internal codes (Posner, 1986; Marshall & Newcombe, 1973; LaBerge & Samuels, 1974; Carr & Pollatsek, 1985; Coltheart, 1985). Abbreviations: PI, physical identity; NI, name identity; and RI, rule identity. [Graph redrawn and revised by editors from Posner, Lewis & Conrad (1972) with permission of MIT Press.]

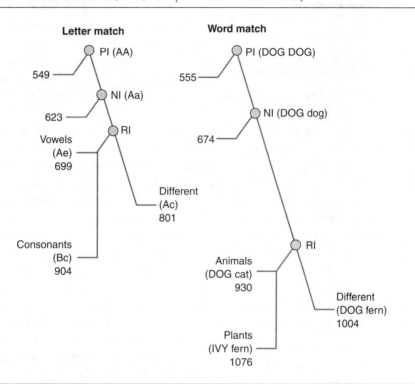

Coltheart, 1985). These routes are thought to be somewhat separate because patients with one form of reading difficulty have great trouble in sounding out nonsense material (for example, the nonword "caik"), indicating they may have a poor ability to use phonics, but they have no problems with familiar words even when the words have irregular pronunciation (for example, pint). Other patients have no trouble with reading non-words but have difficulty with highly familiar irregular words. Although there is also reason to doubt that these routes are entirely separate, it is often thought that the visual to semantic route is dominant in skilled readers (Marshall & Newcombe, 1973; LaBerge & Samuels, 1974; Carr & Pollatsek, 1985; Coltheart, 1985).

VISUAL SPATIAL ATTENTION

Another distinction in cognitive psychology is between automatic activation of these codes and controlled processing by means of attention (Posner, 1986; Marshall & Newcombe, 1973; LaBerge & Samuels, 1974; Carr & Pollatsek, 1985; Coltheart, 1985). Evidence indicates that a word may activate its internal visual, phonological, and even semantic codes without the person having to pay attention to the word. The evidence for activation of the internally stored visual code of a word is particularly good. Normal subjects show evidence that the stimulus duration necessary for perceiving individual letters within words is shorter than for perceiving the same letter when it is presented in isolation (Reicher, 1969; McClelland & Rumelhart, 1981). This idea suggests that feedback from the stored visual word assists in obtaining information about the individual letters (Reicher, 1969; McClelland & Rumelhart, 1981).

> This paradoxical result is known as the *word superiority effect.*

What is known about the localization of attention? Cognitive, brain lesion, and animal studies have identified a posterior neural system involved in visual spatial attention. Patients with lesions of many areas of the brain show neglect of stimuli from the side of space opposite the lesion (DeRenzi, 1982). These findings have led to network views of the neural system underlying visual spatial attention (Mesulam, 1981; Goldman-Rakic, 1988). However, studies performed with single-cell recording from alert monkeys have been more specific in showing three brain areas in which individual cells show selective enhancement due to the requirement that the monkey attend to a visual location (Mountcastle, 1978; Wurtz, Goldberg, & Robinson, 1980; Petersen, Robinson, & Keys, 1985). These areas are the posterior parietal lobe of the cerebral cortex, a portion of the thalamus (part of the pulvinar), and areas of the midbrain related to eye movements—all areas in which clinical studies of lesioned patients find neglect of the environment opposite the lesion.

Recent studies of normal (control) and patient populations have used cues to direct attention covertly to areas of the visual field without eye movements (Posner, Walker, Friedrich, & Rafal, 1984). Attention is measured by changes in the efficiency of processing targets at the cued location in comparison with other uncued locations in the visual field. These studies have found systematic deficits in shifting of covert visual attention in patients with injury of the same three brain areas suggested by the monkey studies. When the efficiency of processing is measured precisely by a reaction time test, the nature of the deficits in the three areas differs. Patients with lesions in the parietal lobe show very long reaction times to targets on the side opposite the lesion only when their attention has first been drawn to a different location in the direction of the lesion (Posner, Walker, Friedrich, & Rafal, 1984). This increase in reaction time for uncued but not [for] cued contralesional targets is consistent with a specific deficit in the patient's ability to disengage attention from a cued location when the target is in

> *direct attention . . . without eye movements:*
> Normally what we are looking at is what we are (visually) paying attention to, and vice versa. Here, however, the subject's job (see Figure 2) was to look at (fixate) one location while attending to a different location.

90

95

100

105

110

115

120

125

the contralesional direction. In contrast, damage to the midbrain not only greatly lengthens overall reaction time but increases the time needed to establish an advantage in reaction time at the
cued location in comparison to the uncued location (Posner, Cohen, & Rafal, 1982; Posner, Rafal,
Choate, & Vaughan, 1985). This finding is consistent with the idea that the lesion causes a slow-
130 ing of attention movements. Damage to the thalamus (Rafal & Posner, 1987) produces a pattern
of slowed reaction to both cued and uncued targets on the side opposite the lesion. This pattern
suggests difficulty in being able to use attention to speed processing of targets irrespective of the
time allowed to do so (engage deficit). A similar deficit has been found in monkeys performing
this task when chemical injections disrupt the performance of the lateral pulvinar (Petersen,
135 Robinson, & Keys, 1985). Thus the simple act of shifting attention to the cued location appears to
involve a number of distinct computations (Fig. 2) that must be orchestrated to allow the cognitive performance to occur. We now have an idea of the anatomy of several of these computations.

Damage to the visual spatial attention system also produces deficits in recognition of
visual stimuli. Patients with lesions of the right parietal lobe frequently neglect (fail to report)
140 the first few letters of a nonword. However, when shown an actual word that occupied the
same visual angle, they report it correctly (Sieroff, Pollatsek, & Posner, 1988; Sieroff & Posner,
1988). Cognitive studies have often shown a superiority of words over nonwords (Reicher, 1969;
McClelland & Rumelhart, 1981). Our results fit with the idea that words do not require scanning
by a covert visual spatial attention system.

ATTENTION FOR ACTION

145 In cognitive studies it is often suggested that attention to stimuli occurs only after they have
been processed to a very high degree (Allport, 1980; Duncan, 1980). In this view, attention is
designed mainly to limit the conflicting actions taken toward stimuli. This form of attention is
often called "attention for action." Our studies of patients with parietal lesions suggest that the
posterior visual-spatial attention system is connected to a more general attention system that
150 is also involved in the processing of language stimuli (Posner, Inhoff, Friedrich, & Cohen, 1987).
When normal subjects and patients had to pay close attention to auditory, or spoken, words, the
ability of a visual cue to draw their visual spatial attention was retarded. Cognitive studies have
been unclear on whether access to meaning requires attention. Although semantic information
may be activated without attention being drawn to the specific lexical unit (Marcel, 1983), atten-
155 tion strongly interacts with semantic activation (Henik, Friedrich, & Kellogg, 1983; Hoffman &
Macmillan, 1985). Considerable evidence shows that attention to semantic information limits the
range of concepts activated. When a person attends to one meaning of a word, activation of
alternative meanings of the same item tends to be suppressed (Neely, 1977).

PET IMAGING OF WORDS

How do the operations suggested by cognitive theories of lexical access relate to brain sys-
160 tems? Recently, in a study with normal persons, we used PET to observe brain processes that

FIGURE 2 The flow chart (bottom) shows that experimental setup. The subject fixates the center box (+). Then a light appears in either the right-hand (R) box (as shown here) or in the left-hand (L) box. The light, or cue, serves to draw the subject's visual attention, covertly and without eye movements, to either L or R. Then a target appears, either in L or R, and the time between the onset of the cue and the subject's response is measured. Each trial corresponds to a cell of the table below:

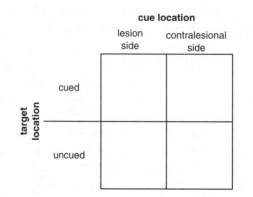

The authors use patters of reaction times in the four cells to infer deficits in the disengage state (parietal), the move state (midbrain), and the engage stage (thalamus). [Eds.]

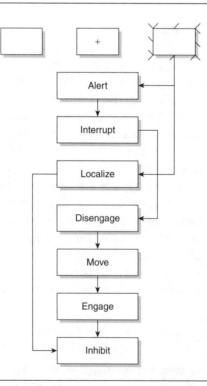

Source: Flowchart reprinted from (Posner, Inhoff, Friedrich, and Cohen, 1987) with permission of the Psychonomic Society.

are active during single word reading (Petersen, Fox, Posner, Mintun, & Raichle, 1988). This method allows examination of averaged changes in cerebral blood flow in localized brain areas during 40 seconds of cognitive activity (Fox, Mintun, Reiman, & Raichle, 1988). During this period we presented words at a rate of one per second. Previous PET studies have suggested

TABLE 1   Conditions for PET Subtractive Studies of Words

Control state	*Stimulus state*	*Computations*
Fixation	Passive words	Passive word processing, attention
Repeat words	Generate word use	Semantic association, attention
Passive words	Monitor category	Semantic association, attention (many targets)*

*The extent of attentional activation increases with the number of targets.

165 that a difference of a few millimeters in the location of activations will be sufficient to separate them (Fox, Mintun, Raichle, Miezin, Allman, & Van Essen, 1986).

To isolate component mental operations we used a set of conditions shown in Table 1. By subtracting the control state from the stimulus state, we attempted to isolate areas of activation related to those mental operations present in the stimulus state but not in the control state. For example, 170 subtraction of looking at the fixation point, without any stimuli, from the presentation of passive visual words allowed us to examine the brain areas automatically activated by the word stimuli.[1]

Visual word forms. We examined changes in cerebral blood flow during passive looking at foveally presented nouns. This task produced five areas of significantly greater activation than found in the fixation condition. They all lie within the occipital lobe: two along the calcarine fis- 175 sure in left and right primary visual cortex and three in left and right lateral regions (Fig. 3). As one moves to more complex naming and semantic activation tasks, no new posterior areas are active. Thus the entire visually specific coding takes place within the occipital lobe. Activated areas are found as far anterior as the occipital temporal boundary. Are these activations specific to visual words? The presentation of auditory words does not produce any activation in this area. 180 Visual stimuli known to activate striate cortex (for example, checkerboards or dot patterns) do not activate the prestriate areas used in word reading (Fox et al., 1986; Fox, Miezin, Allman, Van Essen, & Raichle, 1987). All other cortical areas active during word reading are anterior. Thus it seems reasonable to conclude that visual word forms are developed in the occipital lobe.

It might seem that occipital areas are too early in the system to support the development 185 of visual word forms. However, the early development of the visual word form is supported by our evidence that patients with right parietal lesions do not neglect the left side of foveally

---

[1] The use of subtraction to infer mental processes was used by F. C. Donders in 1868 for reaction time data. [See 3.1.] The method has been disputed because it is possible that subjects use different strategies as the task is made more complex. By using PET, we can study this issue. For example, when subtracting the fixation control from the generate condition, one should obtain only those active areas found in passive (minus fixation) plus repeat (minus passive) plus generate (minus repeat). Our preliminary analyses of these conditions generally support the method.

centered words even though they do neglect the initial letters of nonword strings (Sieroff, Pollatsek, & Posner, 1988; Sieroff & Posner, 1988). The presence of pure alexia from lesions of the occipital temporal boundary (Damasio & Damasio, 1983) also supports the development of the visual word form in the occipital area.

> *alexia:* the inability to read words (printed or written)

190

Precise computational models of how visual word forms are developed (McClelland & Rumelhart, 1986; Reicher, 1969; McClelland & Rumelhart, 1981) involve parallel computations from feature, letter, and word levels and precise feedback among these levels. The prestriate visual system would provide an attractive anatomy for models relying on such abundant feedback. However, presently we can only tentatively identify the general occipital areas that underlie the visual processing of words.

195

Semantic operations. We used two tasks to study semantic operations. One task required the subject to generate and say aloud a use for each of 40 concrete nouns (for example, a subject may say "pound" when presented with the noun "hammer"). We subtracted the activations from repeating the nouns to eliminate strictly sensory and motor activations. Only two general areas of the cortex were found to be active (Fig. 3, square symbols). A second semantic task required subjects to note the presence of dangerous animals in a list of 40 visually presented words. We subtracted passive presentation of the word list to eliminate sensory processing. No motor output was required and subjects were asked to estimate only the frequency of targets after the list was presented. The same two areas of cortex were activated (Fig. 3, circles).

200

205

One of the areas activated in both semantic tasks was in the anterior left frontal lobe. . . . This area is strictly left lateralized and appears to be specific to semantic language tasks. Moreover, lesions of this area produce deficits in word fluency tests (Benton, 1968). Thus we have concluded that this general area is related to the semantic network supporting the type of word associations involved in the generate and monitoring tasks.

210

Phonological coding. When words are presented in auditory form, the primary auditory cortex and an area of the left temporoparietal cortex that has been related to language tasks are activated (Geschwind, 1965). This temporoparietal left-lateralized area seemed to be a good candidate for phonological processing. It was surprising from some perspectives that no visual word reading task activated this area. However, all of our visual tasks involved single common nouns read by highly skilled readers. According to cognitive theories of reading (Marshall & Newcombe, 1973; LaBerge & Samuels, 1974; Carr & Pollatsek, 1985; Coltheart, 1985), these tasks should involve the visual to semantic route. One way of requiring a phonological activation would be to force subjects to tell whether two simultaneous words (for example, pint-tint or row-though) rhymed. This method has been used in cognitive studies to activate phonological codes (Kleiman, 1975). Recent data from our laboratory (Petersen, Fox, Posner, & Raichle, unpublished data) show that this task does produce activation near the supramarginal gyrus. We also assume that word reading that involves difficult words or requires storage in short-term memory or is performed by unskilled readers would also activate phonological operations.

215

220

225

FIGURE 3   Areas activated in visual word reading on the lateral aspect of the cortex (a) and on the medial aspect (b). Triangles refer to the passive visual task minus fixation (a, left hemisphere; a, right hemisphere). Only occipital areas are active. Squares refer to generate minus repeat task. Circles refer to monitor minus passive words task. Solid circles and squares in (a) denote left hemisphere activation; however, in (b), on the midline it is not possible to determine if activation is left or right. The lateral area is thought to involve a semantic network while the midline areas appear to involve attention (Petersen, Fox, Posner, Mintun, & Raichle, 1988. Reprinted with permission.).

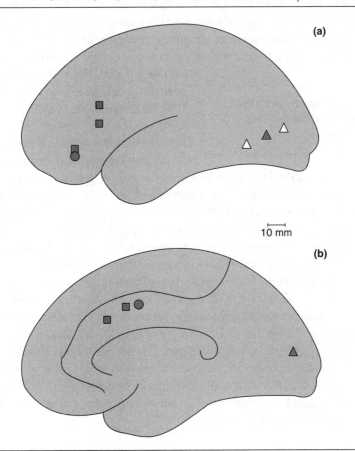

Anterior attention. There is no evidence of activation of any parts of the posterior visual spatial attention system (for example, parietal lobe) in any of our PET language studies. However, it is possible to show that simple tasks that require close monitoring of visual input or that use visual imagery (Petersen, Fox, Miezin, & Raichle, 1988) do activate this parietal system. We conclude, in agreement with the results of our lesion work (Sieroff, Pollatsek, & Posner, 1988; Sieroff & Posner, 1988), that visual word reading is automatic in that it does not require activation of the visual spatial attention system.

In recent cognitive theories the term attention for action is used to summarize the idea that attention seems to be involved in selecting those operations that will gain control of output systems (Allport, 1980). This kind of attention system does not appear to be related to any particular sensory or cognitive content and is distinct from the more strictly visual functions assigned to the visual spatial attention system. Although attention for action seems to imply motor acts, internal selections involved in detecting or noting an event may be sufficient to involve attention in this sense (Fox, Mintun, Reiman, & Raichle, 1988). Whenever subjects are active in this way, we see an increase in blood flow in areas of the medial frontal lobe (Fig. 3B, square symbols). When motor output is involved (for example, naming words), these areas tend to be more superior and posterior (supplementary motor area); but when motor activity is subtracted away or when none is required, they appear to be more anterior and inferior (anterior cingulate gyrus). The anterior cingulate has long been thought to be related to attention (Mesulam, 1981; Goldman-Rakic, 1988) in the sense of generating actions, since lesions of this area produce akinetic mutism (Damasio & Van Hoesen, 1983).

> *akinetic mutism:* a condition in which the patient is apparently alert but does not speak or move voluntarily

We tested the identification of the anterior cingulate with attention and the left lateral frontal area with a word association network. This was done by applying a cognitive theory that attention would not be much involved in the semantic decision of whether a word belonged to a category (for example, dangerous animal) but would be involved in noting the targets even though no specific action was required. The special involvement of attention with target detection has been widely argued by cognitive studies (Duncan, 1980). These studies have suggested that monitoring produces relatively little evidence of heavy attentional involvement, but when a target is actually detected there is evidence of strong interference so that the likelihood of detecting a simultaneous target is reduced. Thus we varied the number of dangerous animals in our list from one (few targets) to 25 (many targets). We found that blood flow in the anterior cingulate showed much greater change with many targets than with few targets. The left frontal area showed little change in blood flow between these conditions. Additional work with other low-target vigilance tasks not involving semantics also failed to activate the anterior cingulate area.[2] Thus the identification of the anterior cingulate with some part of an anterior attention system that selects for action receives some support from these results.

CONCLUSIONS

The PET data provide strong support for localization of operations performed on visual, phonological, and semantic codes. The ability to localize these operations in studies of average blood

---

[2] The studies of the visual monitoring task were conducted by S. E. Petersen, P. T. Fox, M. I. Posner, and M. E. Raichle. Unpublished studies on vigilance were conducted by J. Pardo, P. T. Fox, M. I. Posner, and M. E. Raichle, using somatosensory and visual tasks.

flow suggests considerable homogeneity in the neural systems involved, at least among the right-handed subjects with good reading skills who were used in our study.

270   The PET data on lexical access complement the lesion data cited here in showing that mental operations of the type that form the basis of cognitive analysis are localized in the human brain. This form of localization of function differs from the idea that cognitive tasks are performed by a particular brain area. Visual imagery, word reading, and even shifting visual attention from one location to another are not performed by any single brain area. Each of them involves a large number of component computations that must be orchestrated to perform the

275   cognitive task.

        Our data suggest that operations involved both in activation of internal codes and in selective attention obey the general rule of localization of component operations. However, selective attention appears to use neural systems separate from those involved in passively collecting information about a stimulus. In the posterior part of the brain, the ventral occipital lobe appears to

280   develop the visual word form. If active selection or visual search is required, this is done by a spatial system that is deficient in patients with lesions of the parietal lobe (Friedrich, Walker, & Posner, 1985; Riddoch & Humphreys, 1987). Similarly, in the anterior brain the lateral left frontal lobe is involved in the semantic network for coding word associations. Local areas within the anterior cingulate become increasingly involved when the output of the computations within the semantic

285   network is to be selected as a relevant target. Thus the anterior cingulate is involved in the computations in selecting language or other forms of information for action. This separation of anterior and posterior attention systems helps clarify how atten-

290   tion can be involved both in early visual processing and in the selection of information for output.

> *early visual processing:* the preconscious, preperceptual work of parsing the visual scene into objects, movement, depth; see Marr (2.5)

        Several other research areas also support our general hypothesis. In the study of visual imagery, models distinguish between a set of operations involved in the generation of an image and those involved in scanning the image once

295   it is generated (Kosslyn, 1980). Mechanisms involved in image scanning share components with those in visual spatial attention. Patients with lesions of the right parietal lobe have deficits both in scanning the left side of an image (Bisiach & Luzzatti, 1978) and in responding to visual input to their left (Bisiach & Luzzatti, 1978). Although the right hemisphere plays an important role in visual scanning, it apparently is deficient in operations needed to generate an image.

300   Studies of patients whose cerebral hemispheres have been split during surgery show that the isolated left hemisphere can generate complex visual images whereas the isolated right hemisphere cannot (Kosslyn, Holtzman, Farah, & Gazzaniga, 1985).

        Patients with lesions of the lateral cerebellum have a deficit in timing motor output and in their threshold for recognition of small temporal differences in sensory input (Ivry, Keele, &

305   Diener, 1988). These results indicate that this area of the cerebellum performs a critical computation for timing both motor and sensory tasks. Similarly, studies of memory have indicated that the hippocampus performs a computation needed for storage in a manner that will allow

conscious retrieval of the item once it has left current attention. The same item can be used as part of a skill even though damage to the hippocampus makes it unavailable to conscious recollection (Squire, 1986).

The joint anatomical and cognitive approach discussed in this article should open the way to a more detailed understanding of the deficits found in the many disorders involving cognitive or attentional operations in which the anatomy is poorly understood. For example, we have attempted to apply the new knowledge of the anatomy of selective attention to study deficits in patients with schizophrenia (Posner, Early, & Reiman, 1988).

310

315

FOR DISCUSSION

1. The authors assert that "PET data provide strong support for localization of operations performed on visual, phonological, and semantic codes"(p. 292, line 265). What is the nature of that support?

2. Do the authors either assume or conclude that the modularity they find is innate?

Part IV

Nativism and Empiricism

aka
Heredity and Environment

If you want to say something disparaging about someone's intelligence, you might say that he couldn't think his way out of a paper bag. This is insulting because it denies someone a basic human ability. Not only can we all think our way out of paper bags, we can avoid obstacles, navigate forest trails and city streets, tie knots, solve Rubik's cube, and much more.

Where do these basic abilities—call them aspects of spatial reasoning—come from? Why do we all have them? There are several possibilities. First, our spatial reasoning abilities could be partly or entirely learned—they could be something that each of us, individually and independently, learns to do. Second, they could be partly or entirely innate—something specified in our genes. Or, of course, they could be partly learned and partly innate.

The question *Where does our spatial reasoning come from?* can be replaced by any number of analogous questions about the mind's abilities: Where does our ability to use language come from? Where does our ability to count come from? Where does our ability to see the world in three dimensions come from? And so on. For all such cases our goal is to determine to what extent the ability is learned and to what extent it is innate.

Note that *our* in the above questions refers to *all of us,* the whole species. About any mental ability, habit, or characteristic that is found in all (or virtually all) humans, we can ask three questions:

1. Where does it come from?

2. Why does one human have more of it than another?

3. Why does one group of humans have more of it than another group?

Questions 2 and 3 are often conspicuous and contentious, but question 1 is older and more basic. Question 1 is the subject of the readings in this section. The view that a universal ability is due mostly (or entirely) to heredity ("nature") is known as *nativism,* and the view that it is mostly (or entirely) acquired from the environment and experience ("nurture") is called *empiricism.*

Hereditary can refer to either characteristics that we all share or to individual characteristics. For example, consider your eyes. Some aspects of your eyes—that you have two of them, that they are sensitive to certain wavelengths of light, and so on—are built into you *as a human*. Other aspects—that they are brown or blue, that the upper lid is or isn't folded—are built into you *as an individual*. Having eyes comes with membership in our species; having green eyes or folded lids comes with membership in your family. Heredity is just as important an idea in the context of the things that make us all humans as it is in the context of the things that make us different from one another.

There are traits—such as those just mentioned—and disorders that we inherit directly and unambiguously from our parents, but there are skills, interests, and idiosyncrasies that we clearly do not inherit—at least not genetically—from anybody, such as a habit of interrupting people, say, or an interest in stamp collecting, though we may inherit a predisposition to such interests. In between lies a vast range of physical, behavioral, and psychological traits—such things as alcoholism, aggression, schizophrenia, gender orientation, cognitive abilities, and so on—whose sources are not so clear. Things that we inherit genetically are *heritable;* they are part of our *heredity.* Things we do not inherit genetically are *learned;* they are *acquired from our environment.*

Heredity and environment are rather lopsided alternatives. Heredity is a clearly defined mechanism, and the environment is everything else: culture, family, race, class, language, neonatal environment, geography, climate, politics, war and peace, religion, education, and so on. To make things more difficult, many environmental factors run in families: Children tend to speak their parents' language, practice their parents' religion, occupy their parents' social class, and so on. Consequently some of our "learned" characteristics may be hard to distinguish from inherited ones. Your parents' role in determining, for example, the language you speak is probably just as big as their role in determining what you look like; so, we can't distinguish environment from heredity on the basis of the degree of resemblance between parents and children. Instead, we need to ask whether, for a given set of parents (or, more precisely, for a given embryo), the offspring's characteristic might have been something other than what it is. With respect to what you look like, the answer is clearly no: you would look pretty much as you do whether or not you were raised by your biological parents. But the language you speak, of course, could easily have been something else.

The readings in this section deal with untangling the roles of heredity and environment in some of the human qualities that we all appear to possess. Descartes and Locke are concerned with the question of the origin of ideas, an ancient and difficult problem. There are certain ideas—such as those represented by the words *number, solidity, not, more, existence,* and so on—that seem to be universal. Are these somehow built into the mind? Or does every individual mind acquire each of those ideas for itself, just as any mind must acquire other ideas—goulash, big bang, bebop—that are not shared by all humans?

Helmholtz, like Berkeley (2.1), is concerned with a subset of the question of innate ideas, namely those having to do with perception. Among other things, our perceptual systems make it possible for us to get around in a three-dimensional world. We can do this by seeing what's around us, by feeling it, and by hearing it, but regardless of which sense we use, we must have ideas of *space* and *distance,* for without these our sensations—visual, tactile, or auditory—would have no value as navigation aids. The question, then, is whether these ideas are innate or learned.

Darwin, Freud, Watson, and the Brelands are concerned—in very different ways—with broad ranges of behavior, both ordinary and not so ordinary. How much behavior can be explained as resulting from various built-in dispositions, urges, drives? How much cannot? Is it possible that little is built in, that all behavior is somehow learned? (See also Skinner, 3.5.)

Among the mind's many furnishings, the ability to speak and understand a language is one of the richest. Everyone learns a language, very quickly, and at a time when cognitive abilities are not well developed. How does this happen? Do we learn our language from scratch, or, as Chomsky argues, do we have some help in the form of innate ideas about the structure of language?

ADDITIONAL READINGS

Plato   *Meno* and *Phaedo* (4th century BCE)

These dialogues both contain discussions of Plato's doctrine of reminiscence, the idea that knowledge—at least of certain things—is innate in us, having been acquired by the soul in an earlier life.

Gottfried Wilhelm Leibniz   *New essays on the human understanding* (1704)

A point-by-point critique of Locke's *Essay on Human Understanding*. Leibniz accepts Locke's "blank slate" but points out that it cannot be entirely blank: the mind must at least be equipped with what it needs to acquire ideas from sensory experience. Leibniz's argument is further developed by Hume and Kant.

David Hume   *Enquiry concerning human understanding* (1748)

Hume argues that some of our fundamental ideas—time, cause and effect, and the self—are not acquired from the world of sensory experience but rather are the necessary consequence of unavoidable habits of thought.

Etienne Bonnot de Condillac   *Treatise on the sensations* (1754)

In a fascinating thought experiment, Condillac starts with a statue of a man and gives it a sense of smell. Solely from its olfactory sensations, the statue conceives such ideas as number and time. As Condillac adds senses, the statue acquires more and more ideas, demonstrating the plausibility of what Locke had simply asserted, that is that all ideas come through the senses.

Immanuel Kant   *Critique of pure reason* (1781, rev. 1787)

The Critique is as challenging to the reader as it is important to philosophy. Going beyond Leibniz and Hume, Kant claims that the nature of thought is determined by what he calls the "pure categories of the understanding," a set of built-in (and universal) cognitive dispositions.

Francis Galton   *Hereditary genius,* ch. 3: "Classification of men according to their natural gifts" (1869)

Galton suggests some ways to measure and assess human intelligence and presents data that support his notion that intellectual ability is largely hereditary. Along the way, he makes a major contribution to the fledgling field of statistics.

Carl Jung   *The concept of the collective unconscious* (1936)

In addition to the personal unconscious, Jung believes there is a collective unconscious, whose contents are inherited. These consist of instincts and memories shared by all humans, and are made manifest in myth, religion, and other cultural artifacts.

Jean Piaget   *The construction of reality in the child* (1937)

Piaget describes the child's gradual cognitive and perceptual differentiation between self, world, and others.

Nikolaas Tinbergen   *The study of instinct,* ch. 2 (1951)

Tinbergen was a pioneer of the field of ethology, the study of behavior in its natural setting. One of ethology's main concerns is to clarify the concept of instinct and to determine its contribution to the behavior of a given species.

Eleanor J. Gibson & Richard Walk   *The visual cliff* (1960)

Is depth perception innate? Gibson and Walk devised an ingenious technique for studying this question in the laboratory. Their results were not entirely unambiguous, but the experiment remains a landmark in the field.

David Hubel & Torsten Wiesel   *Receptive fields of single neurones in the cat's striate cortex* (1959)

Hubel & Wiesel identified neurons in the visual cortex that respond selectively to certain low-level features of the stimulus, such as edges with specific orientations. They have reviewed their work in, for example, Hubel (1982), Hubel and Wiesel (1979).

Jerome Lettvin, Humberto Maturana, Warren McCulloch, & Walter Pitts   *What the frog's eye tells the frog's brain* (1959)

This paper did much to establish that the visual system is more active and more complex than had been thought, by showing that a considerable amount of image processing takes place in the frog's retina.

Jerome Kagan, J. Steven Reznick, & Nancy Snidman   *Biological bases of childhood shyness* (1988)

Kagan et al. describe a longitudinal study that followed extremely inhibited and uninhibited children from age 2 to age 7½. The temperamental differences between the two groups remained and these differences correlated with physiological reaction measures.

Diane Halpern   *Sex differences in intelligence* (1997)

A wonderfully evenhanded review of the research literature on sex differences in cognitive functioning, complete with a discussion of the implications of these differences for education.

Steven Pinker   *How the mind works* (1997)

A thorough look at cognition from an evolutionary point of view.

Steven Pinker   *The blank slate: The modern denial of human nature* (2002)

>   Pinker views Locke and his descendants as denying that there is such a thing as "human nature," that is, a common set of built-in capabilities and dispositions, and sets out to refute them.

Arthur Jensen   *How much can we boost IQ and scholastic achievement?* (1969)

>   The IQ in question is that of blacks, and Jensen's answer is: not much. This paper ignited a furious controversy, some of it scientific, over the heritability of IQ and the link between race and IQ.

Richard Lewontin   *Race and intelligence* (1970)

>   A reply to Jensen; Lewontin is strongly critical, on methodological grounds, of Jensen's conclusions.

Stephen Jay Gould   *The mismeasure of man* (1996)

>   A history of efforts to measure human intelligence and of the misuses of some of the results.

René Descartes (1596–1650)
Notes Directed Against a Certain Programme (1648)

Henri de Roy (1598–1679)—known academically by his Latin name, Henricus Regius—professor of medicine at the University of Utrecht, had been an enthusiastic disciple of Descartes, but relations deteriorated when, in 1646, Regius published his *Principles of Physics*. Regius not only appropriated some of Descartes' ideas—ideas which Descartes had not yet published—but also distorted them. Descartes was not pleased and publicly repudiated Regius, who in turn published a statement ("programme") sharply critical of Descartes' philosophy in 1647.

Neither Regius nor Descartes was identified by name, but there was no mystery about the identity of the author or of the target. Descartes' purpose in the *Notes Directed Against a Certain Programme* was to provide a point-by-point rebuttal of Regius's arguments, but in the process he also provides a lucid and concise statement of some of his most important ideas. In particular, the *Notes* contain a useful explanation of Descartes' views on innate ideas.

Source: Descartes, R. (1911). *The philosophical works of Descartes.* (E. S. Haldane & G. R. T. Ross, Eds. & Trans.). London: Cambridge University Press. Reprinted with permission.

. . .

In article twelve he appears to dissent from me only in words, for when he says that *the mind has no need of innate ideas, or notions, or axioms,* and at the same time allows it the faculty of thinking (to be considered natural or innate), he makes an affirmation in effect identical with mine, but denies it in words. For I never wrote or concluded that the mind required innate ideas which were in some sort different from its faculty of thinking; but when I observed the existence in me of certain thoughts which proceeded, not from extraneous objects nor from the determination of my will, but solely from the faculty of thinking which is within me, then, that I might distinguish the ideas or notions (which are the forms of these thoughts) from other thoughts *adventitious* or *factitious*, I termed the former 'innate.' In the same sense we say that in some families generosity is innate, in others certain diseases like gout or gravel, not that on this account the babes of these families suffer from these diseases in their mother's womb, but because they are born with a certain disposition or propensity for contracting them.

> *adventitious:* from extraneous objects
> *factitious:* from the determination of his will

The conclusion which he deduces in *article* XIII from the preceding article is indeed wonderful. '*For this reason*' he says (i.e. because the mind has no need of innate ideas, but the faculty of thinking of itself is sufficient), '*all common notions, engraven on the mind, owe their origin to the observation of things or to tradition*'—as though the faculty of thinking could of itself execute nothing, nor perceive nor think anything save what it received from observation or tradition, that is, from the senses. So far is this from being true, that, on the contrary, any man who rightly observes the limitations of the senses, and what precisely it is that can penetrate through this medium to our faculty of thinking must needs admit that no ideas of things, in the shape in which we envisage them by thought, are presented to us by the senses. So much so that in our ideas there is nothing which was not innate in the mind, or faculty of thinking, except only these circumstances which point to experience—the fact, for instance, that we judge that this or that idea, which we now have present to our thought, is to be referred to a certain extraneous thing, not that these extraneous things transmitted the ideas themselves to our minds through the organs of sense, but because they transmitted something which gave the mind occasion to form these ideas, by means of an innate faculty, at this time rather than at another. For nothing reaches our mind from external objects through the organs of sense beyond certain corporeal movements, as our author himself affirms, in article XIX, taking the doctrine from my Principles; but even these movements, and the figures which arise from them, are not conceived by us in the shape they assume in

> *corporeal movements:* physical activity of the sense organs and nervous system

the organs of sense, as I have explained at great length in my Dioptrics. Hence it follows that the ideas of the movements and figures are themselves innate in us. So much the more must the ideas of pain, colour, sound and the like be innate, that our mind may, on occasion of certain corporeal movements, envisage these ideas, for they have no likeness to the corporeal movements. Could anything be imagined more preposterous than that all common

Dioptrics: optics. Descartes' first publication (1637), characteristically anonymous, was titled *Discourse on the Method of rightly conducting one's reason and seeking the truth in the sciences, and in addition the Optics, the Meteorology and the Geometry, which are essays in this Method.* (Subsequent generations have reduced this to *Discourse and Essays*.) In the first part of the Optics Descartes offers a fascinating argument to show that sensations are not copies but rather signs of things in the outside world. Later writers, particularly Berkeley (see 2.1) and Helmholtz (2.3) reached a similar conclusion in different ways.

notions which are inherent in our mind should arise from these movements, and should be incapable of existing without them? I should like our friend to instruct me as to what corporeal move- 45 ment it is which can form in our mind any common notion, e.g. the notion that 'things which are equal to the same thing are equal to one another' or any other he pleases; for all these movements are particular, but notions are universal having no 50 affinity with movements and no relation to them.

He goes on to affirm, *in article* XIV, that even the idea of God which is in us is the outcome, not of our faculty of thinking, as being native to it, but of *Divine Revelation or tradition, or observation*. The 55 error of this assertion we shall the more readily realise if we reflect that anything can be said to be the outcome of another, either because this other is its proximate and primary cause, without which it could not exist, or only because it is a remote and accidental cause, which, certainly, gives the primary cause occasion to produce its effect at one time rather than at another. Thus 60 all workmen are the primary and proximate causes of their works, but those who give them orders, or promise them reward, that they may perform these works, are accidental and remote causes, because, probably, they would not have performed the tasks unbidden. There is no doubt that tradition or observation is a remote cause, inviting us to bethink ourselves of the idea which we may have of God, and to present it vividly to our thought. But no one can 65 maintain that this is the proximate and efficient cause, except the man who thinks that we can apprehend nothing regarding God save this name *'God,'* and the corporeal figure which painters exhibit to us as a representation of God. For observation, if it takes place through the medium of sight, can of its own proper power present nothing to the mind beyond pictures, and pictures consisting only of a permutation of corporeal movements, as *our author* himself 70 instructs us. If it takes place through the medium of hearing, it presents nothing beyond words and voices; if through the other senses, it has nothing in it which can have reference to God. And surely it is manifest to every man that sight, of itself and by its proper function, presents nothing beyond pictures, and hearing nothing beyond voices or sounds, so that all these things that we think of, beyond these voices or pictures, as being symbolised by them, are presented 75 to us by means of ideas which come from no other source than our faculty of thinking, and are accordingly together with that faculty innate in us, that is, always existing in us potentially; for existence in any faculty is not actual but merely potential existence, since the very word 'faculty' designates nothing more or less than a potentiality. But that with regard to God we can comprehend nothing beyond a name or a bodily effigy, no one can affirm, save a man who 80 openly professes himself an atheist, and moreover destitute of all intellect.

. . .

... By innate ideas I never understood anything other than that which he himself, on page 6 of his second pamphlet, affirms in so many words to be true, viz. that *'there is innate in us by nature a potentiality whereby we know God'*; but that these ideas are *actual,* or that they are some kind of species different from the faculty of thought I never wrote nor concluded. On the contrary, I, more than any other man, am utterly averse to that empty stock of scholastic entities—so much so, that I cannot refrain from laughter when I see that mighty heap which our hero—a very inoffensive fellow no doubt—has laboriously brought together to prove that *infants have no notion of God so long as they are in their mother's womb*—as though in this fashion he was bringing a magnificent charge against me.

> *scholastic entities:* a reference to the Platonic notion that ideas, or forms, are real things that exist independently of being thought. According to this doctrine there is an idea of every thing that can be thought or thought about—momentum, book, gorilla, justice, kryptonite, and so on. These ideas are real, they exist—not as physical books and gorillas, but as ideas.

For Discussion

1. What does Descartes mean by ideas that proceed from extraneous objects? What might be some examples?

2. What does Descartes mean by ideas that proceed from the determination of his will? What might be some examples?

3. What does Descartes mean by ideas that proceed solely from his faculty of thinking? What might be some examples?

4. What can the power of thinking achieve on its own?

John Locke (1632–1704)
An Essay Concerning Human Understanding (1690)

Book 1, Chapter 1. Introduction

Book 2, Chapter 1. Of Ideas in General and Their Original

    Chapter 2. Of Simple Ideas

    Chapter 3. Of Ideas of One Sense

    Chapter 4. Of Solidity

    Chapter 5. Of Simple Ideas of Divers Senses

    Chapter 6. Of Simple Ideas of Reflection

    *Chapter 7. Of Simple Ideas of Both
            Sensation and Reflection*

Aside from having large ships named after them, England's Queen Elizabeth I (1533–1603) and Elizabeth II (b. 1926) have little in common. The first made war and peace, sent explorers all over the globe, and turned England into a major European power; the second is a ceremonial head of state with very little power. The most important part of this transformation of the monarchy took

---

Source: Locke, J. (n.d.). *An essay concerning human understanding*. New York: Dutton.

place in the 17th century. When, in 1625, Charles I inherited the throne from his father, James I, he also inherited James's difficult relations with Parliament, and proceeded to make them worse. Some of the conflict had to do with religion, but the nub of the issue was power. Charles believed he ruled by divine right, but Parliament, and much of England, was outgrowing this ancient idea. Civil war broke out in 1642 and continued off and on until 1649, when Charles I was found guilty of treason and beheaded. Parliament established the Commonwealth and governed England without a monarch until 1653, when Oliver Cromwell took power and ruled as a military dictator. After Cromwell's death in 1658 the Commonwealth returned briefly, and in 1660 Charles II, who had fled to France when his father was executed, was restored to the throne. Charles was succeeded in 1685 by his brother, James II. A Catholic, James faced opposition across the political spectrum, and in 1688 his opponents took the extraordinary step of inviting the Dutch prince William of Orange (James's nephew, but a Protestant) and his wife Mary (James's daughter, but a Protestant) to England to oust James. William arrived with an army, James fled to France, and Parliament invited William and Mary to rule jointly. Forty years after the execution of Charles I, it was clear that Parliament, not God, was to be the source of the monarch's right to rule.

Woven among these upheavals is the life of John Locke. His family were Puritans, gentry (i.e., people who owned land but were not nobles) in the south of England. Locke was educated at Christ Church, Oxford, studying classics and philosophy and, later, medicine. His life took a decisive turn in 1666, when he became the friend, confidant, and physician of Anthony Ashley Cooper (1621–1683), who was later made Earl of Shaftesbury, a shrewd, intelligent, and generally progressive politician. His association with Shaftesbury provided Locke with the leisure, security, and intellectual stimulation that allowed him to develop as a philosopher. It was during his time as a member of Shaftesbury's household that Locke began writing what would later become the present *Essay.*

Shaftesbury, alternately in and out of favor with the powers that be, was twice imprisoned in the Tower of London and died in self-exile in Holland. Locke, too, sometimes thought it healthier to live abroad. From 1675 to 1679 he lived in France, and from 1683 to 1689 in Holland; both periods were very stimulating and productive. On his second return to England Locke published two books that he had been working on for years. Both books were widely read, and their influence on the development of 18th century thought is impossible to overstate.

Given the political turmoil he lived through, Locke's interest in the philosophical foundations of government is not surprising. In the *Two Treatises of Government,* which he published anonymously (not an uncommon practice in his day), Locke argued against the divine right of kings and eloquently advocated a civil society based on religious tolerance, liberty, and education. Locke's political and social thought deeply influenced succeeding generations of thinkers in France, England, and the American colonies, and it is fair to say that the U.S. constitution owes a good deal to him.

Locke's other great work is the *Essay Concerning Human Understanding.* If Locke were writing the book today, he would call it something like *Principles of Psychology,* but in 1690 *psychology* had not yet made its way into English. For Locke and his contemporaries, *the understanding* is what we would usually call *the mind.* But call it what you will, 17th century psychology was quite a different animal from its modern descendant. In the *Essay* you will find no discussion of personality, motives, group dynamics, and the like. Locke was concerned with the question *What sorts of things make up the contents of the mind? How do they get there? What sorts of things does the mind do with them?*

Depending on one's point of view, the most celebrated or the most notorious idea in the *Essay* is the doctrine that has come to be known as the *blank slate*. The blank slate has become many things to many people, but what it was to Locke sometimes gets lost in their enthusiasm or scorn. As Locke explains, the blank slate is a theory of the origin of ideas. Both words can be misconstrued, but Locke has in mind the origin *within the individual* of ideas representing classes of objects, actions, and mental events. How is it, for example, that the concept of "book"—not the perception or memory of some particular book—is part of your mental vocabulary? Locke answers that it is through experience, and no one would disagree. If we replace "book" with other concepts—"alternative," "negation," or "god," say—Locke's answer does not change. Some will agree with him (see, e.g., 4.4), but some will disagree, arguing that some concepts could not be learned from the environment and therefore must somehow be innate (see, e.g., 4.1 and 4.8; also Pinker, 2002).

BOOK I

Chapter 1. Introduction

1. *An inquiry into the understanding, pleasant and useful.*—Since it is the understanding that sets man above the rest of sensible beings, and gives him all the advantage and dominion which he has over them, it is certainly a subject, even for its

5 nobleness, worth, our labour to inquire, into. The understanding, like the eye, whilst it makes us see and perceive all other things takes no notice of itself; and it requires art and pains to set it at a distance, and make it its own object. But whatever be

10 the difficulties that lie in the way of this inquiry, whatever it be that keeps us so much in the dark to ourselves, sure I am that all the light we can let in upon our own minds, all the acquaintance we can make with our own understandings, will not only be very pleasant, but bring us great advantage in directing our thoughts in the search of other things.

> *Sensible beings* are not those who behave sensibly but those who are sentient, that is, have sensations.

> *art and pains:* skill and effort

. . .

15 3. *Method.*—It is therefore worthwhile to search out the bounds between opinion and knowledge, and examine by what measures, in things whereof we have no certain knowledge, we ought to regulate our assent, and moderate our persuasions. In order whereunto, I shall pursue this following method:—

First. I shall inquire into the original of those ideas,

20 notions, or whatever else you please to call them, which a man observes, and is conscious to himself he has in his mind, and the ways whereby the understanding comes to be furnished with them.

> *original:* origin, source

Secondly. I shall endeavour to show what knowledge the understanding hath by those

25 ideas, and the certainty, evidence, and extent of it.

Thirdly. I shall make some inquiry into the nature and grounds of faith or opinion; whereby I mean, that assent which we give to any proposition as true, of whose truth yet we have no certain knowledge: and here we shall have occasion to examine the reasons and degrees of assent.

4. *Useful to know the extent of our comprehension.*—If by this inquiry into the nature of the

30 understanding, I can discover the powers thereof, how far they reach, to what things they are in any degree proportionate, and where they fail us, I suppose it may be of use to prevail with the busy mind of man to be more cautious in meddling with things exceeding its comprehension, to stop when it is at the utmost extent of its tether, and to sit down in a quiet ignorance of those things which, upon examination, are found to be beyond the reach of our

35 capacities. We should not then, perhaps, be so forward, out of an affectation of an universal

knowledge, to raise questions, and perplex ourselves and others with disputes, about things to which our understandings are not suited, and of which we cannot frame in our minds any clear or distinct perceptions, or whereof (as it has, perhaps, too often happened) we have not any notions at all. If we can find out how far the understanding can extend its view, how far it has faculties to attain certainty, and in what cases it can only judge and guess, we may learn   40
to content ourselves with what is attainable by us in this state.

  . . .

8. *What "idea" stands for.*—Thus much I thought necessary to say concerning the occasion of this inquiry into human understanding. But, before I proceed on to what I have thought on this subject, I must here, in the entrance, beg pardon of my reader for the frequent use of the word "idea" which he will find in the following treatise. It being that term which, I think, serves best   45
to stand for whatsoever is the object of the understanding when a man thinks, I have used it to express whatever is meant by phantasm, notion, species, or whatever it is which the mind can be employed about in thinking; and I could not avoid frequently using it.

  I presume it will be easily granted me, that there are such *ideas* in men's minds. Every one is conscious of them in himself; and men's words and actions will satisfy him that they are in   50
others.

  Our first inquiry, then, shall be, how they come into the mind.

> Locke's first inquiry is actually not about how ideas come into the mind. Rather, he devotes the next three chapters to refuting various versions of the claim that there are innate ideas in the mind. Most of these versions are straw men, and the arguments are of little philosophical or psychological interest. We proceed, then, to Book 2, where Locke sets out his views about the origin of ideas.

BOOK 2

Chapter 1. Of Ideas in General, and Their Original

1. *Idea is the object of thinking.*—Every man being conscious to himself, that he thinks, and that which his mind is applied about, whilst thinking, being the ideas that are there, it is past doubt that men have in their mind several ideas, such as are those expressed by the words, "white-   55
ness, hardness, sweetness, thinking, motion, man, elephant, army, drunkenness," and others. It is in the first place then to be inquired, How he comes by them? I know it is a received doctrine, that men have native ideas and original characters stamped upon their minds in their very first being. This opinion I have at large examined already; and, I suppose, what I have said in the foregoing book will be much more easily admitted, when I have shown whence the under-   60
standing may get all the ideas it has, and by what ways and degrees they may come into the mind; for which I shall appeal to every one's own observation and experience.

2. *All ideas come from sensation or reflection.*—Let us then suppose the mind to be, as we say, white paper, void of all characters, without any ideas; how comes it to be furnished? Whence comes it by that vast store, which the busy and boundless fancy, of man has painted on it with an almost endless variety? Whence has it all the materials of reason and knowledge? To this I answer, in one word, From experience: in that all our knowledge is founded, and from that it ultimately derives itself. Our observation, employed either about external sensible objects, or about the internal operations of our minds, perceived and reflected on by ourselves, is that which supplies our understandings with all the materials of thinking. These two are the fountains of knowledge, from whence all the ideas we have, or can naturally have, do spring.

Locke's *white paper* is not a new image; Aristotle used it to describe the relation of the mind and its thoughts:

The question might arise: assuming that the mind is something simple and impassive and, in the words of Anaxagoras, has nothing in common with anything else, how will it think, if to think is to be acted upon? For it is in so far as two things have something in common that the one of them is supposed to act and the other to be acted upon. Again, can mind itself be its own object? For then either its other objects will have mind in them, if it is not through something else, but in itself, that mind is capable of being thought, and if to be so capable is everywhere specifically one and the same; or else the mind will have some ingredient in its composition which makes it, like the rest, an object of thought. Or shall we recall our old distinction between two meanings of the phrase "to be acted upon in virtue of a common element," and say that the mind is in a manner potentially all objects of thought, but is actually none of them until it thinks: potentially in the same sense as in a tablet which has nothing actually written upon it the writing exists potentially? This is exactly the case with the mind. Moreover, the mind itself is included among the objects which can be thought. For where the objects are immaterial that which thinks and that which is thought are identical. Speculative knowledge and its object are identical. (We must, however, inquire why we do not think always.) On the other hand, in things containing matter each of the objects of thought is present potentially. Consequently material objects will not have mind in them, for the mind is the power of becoming such objects without their matter; whereas the mind will have the attribute of being its own object. (1907, III, 4)

Aristotle's phrase was *pinakis agraphos,* "tablet without writing." When Aristotle was translated into Latin, this became *tabula rasa,* which in English becomes the (in)famous *blank slate.* It is important to note that some modern writers have extended the meaning of *blank slate* to refer not only to the mind's repertory of ideas at birth, but also to character and ability.

3. *The object of sensation one source of ideas.*—First. Our senses, conversant about particular sensible objects, do convey into the mind several distinct perceptions of things, according to those various ways wherein those objects do affect them; and thus we come by those ideas we

have of yellow, white, heat, cold, soft, hard, bitter, sweet, and all those which we call sensible   75
qualities; which when I say the senses convey into the mind, I mean, they from external
objects convey into the mind what produces there those perceptions. This great source of most
of the ideas we have, depending wholly upon our senses, and derived by them to the understanding, I call "sensation."

4. *The operations of our minds the other source of them.*—Secondly. The other fountain, from   80
which experience furnisheth the understanding with ideas, is the perception of the operations
of our own minds within us, as it is employed about the ideas it has got; which operations, when
the soul comes to reflect on and consider, do furnish the understanding with another set of ideas
which could not be had from things without; and such are perception, thinking, doubting,
believing, reasoning, knowing, willing, and all the different actings of our own minds; which we,   85
being conscious of, and observing in ourselves, do from these receive into our understanding
as distinct ideas, as we do from bodies affecting our senses. This source of ideas every man has
wholly in himself; and though it be not sense as having nothing to do with external objects, yet
it is very like it, and might properly enough, be called "internal sense." But as I call the other "sensation," so I call this "reflection," the ideas it affords being such only as the mind gets by reflect-   90
ing on its own operations within itself. By reflection, then, in the following part of this discourse,
I would be understood to mean that notice which the mind takes of its own operations, and the
manner of them, by reason whereof there come to be ideas of these operations in the understanding. These two, I say, viz., external material things as the objects of sensation, and the operations of our own minds within as the objects of reflection, are, to me, the only originals from   95
whence all our ideas take their beginnings. The term "operations" here, I use in a large sense, as
comprehending not barely the actions of the mind about its ideas, but, some sort of passions
arising sometimes from them, such as is the satisfaction or uneasiness arising from any thought.

5. *All our ideas are of the one or the other of these.*—The understanding seems to me not to have
the least glimmering of any ideas which it doth not receive from one of these two. External objects   100
furnish the mind with the ideas of sensible qualities, which are all those different perceptions they
produce in us; and the mind furnishes the understanding with ideas of its own operations.

These, when we have taken a full survey of them, and their several modes, combinations,
and relations, we shall find to contain all our whole stock of ideas; and that we have nothing
in our minds which did not come in one of these two ways. Let any one examine his own   105
thoughts, and thoroughly search into his understanding, and then let him tell me, whether all
the original ideas he has there, are any other than of the objects of his senses, or of the operations of his mind considered as objects of his reflection; and how great a mass of knowledge
soever he imagines to be lodged there, he will, upon taking a strict view, see that he has not
any idea in his mind but what one of these two   110
hath imprinted, though perhaps with infinite variety compounded and enlarged by the understanding, as we shall see hereafter.

---

how great . . . soever: however great

6. Observable in children,—He that attentively considers the state of a child at his first coming
into the world, will have little reason to think him stored with plenty of ideas that are to be the
matter of his future knowledge. It is by degrees he comes to be furnished with them; and
though the ideas of obvious and familiar qualities imprint themselves before the memory
begins to keep a register of tune and order, yet it is often so late before some unusual qualities come in the way, that there are few men that cannot recollect the beginning of their
acquaintance with them; and, if it were worth
while, no doubt a child might be so ordered as to
have but a very few even of the ordinary ideas till
he were grown up to a man. But all that are born

ordered: raised, brought up

into the world being surrounded with bodies that perpetually and diversely affect them, variety of ideas whether care be taken about it, or no, are imprinted on the minds of children. Light
and colours are busy at hand everywhere when the eye is but open; sounds and some tangible qualities fail not to solicit their proper senses, and force an entrance to the mind; but yet I
think it will be granted easily, that if a child were kept in a place where he never saw any other
but black and white till he were a man, he would have no more ideas of scarlet or green, than
he that from his childhood never tasted an oyster or a pineapple has of those particular relishes.

7. Men are differently furnished with these according to the different objects they converse with.—
Men then come to be furnished with fewer or more simple ideas from without, according as the
objects they converse with afford greater or less variety; and from the operations of their minds
within, according as they more or less reflect on them. For, though he that contemplates the
operations of his mind cannot but have plain and clear ideas of them; yet, unless he turn his
thoughts that way, and considers them attentively, he will no more have clear and distinct ideas
of all the operations of his mind, and all that may be observed therein, than he will have all the
particular ideas, of any landscape, or of the parts and motions of a clock, who will not turn his
eyes to it, and with attention heed all the parts of it. The picture or clock may be so placed that
they may come in his way every day; but yet he will have but a confused idea, of all the parts they
are made of, till he applies himself with attention to consider them each in particular.

8. Ideas of reflection later, because they need attention.—And hence we see the reason why it is pretty
late before most children get ideas of the operations of their own minds; and some have not any
very clear or perfect ideas of the greatest part of them all their lives:—because, though they pass
there continually, yet like floating visions, they make not deep impressions enough to leave in the
mind clear, distinct, lasting ideas, till the understanding turns inwards upon itself, reflects on its own
operations, and makes them the object of its own
contemplation. Children, when they come first into
it, are surrounded with a world of new things, which,
by a constant solicitation of their senses, draw the

solicitation: stimulation

mind constantly to them, forward to take notice of new, and apt to be delighted with the variety
of changing objects. Thus the first years are usually employed and diverted in looking abroad.

Men's business in them is to acquaint themselves with what is to be found without; and so, growing up in a constant attention to outward sensations, seldom make any considerable reflection on what passes within them till they come to be of riper years; and some scarce ever at all.   155

   . . .

22. Follow a child from its birth, and observe the alterations that time makes, and you shall find, as the mind by the senses comes more and more to be furnished with ideas, it comes to be more and more awake, thinks more the more it has matter to think on. After some time it begins to know the objects, which, being most familiar with it, have made lasting impressions. Thus it comes by degrees to know the persons it daily converses with, and distinguish them from strangers; which   160 are instances and effects of its coming to retain and distinguish the ideas the senses convey to it: and so we may observe how the mind, by degrees, improves in these, and advances to the exercise of those other faculties of enlarging, compounding, and abstracting its ideas, and of reasoning about them, and reflecting upon all these; of which I shall have occasion to speak more hereafter.

23. If it shall be demanded, then, when a man begins to have any ideas? I think, the true answer   165 is, When he first has any sensation. For since there appear not to be any ideas in the mind before the senses have conveyed any in, I conceive that ideas in the understanding are coeval with sensation; which is such an impression or motion made in some part of the body as produces some perception in the understanding. It is about these   170 impressions made on our senses by outward objects, that the mind seems first to employ itself in such operations as we call "perception, remembering, consideration, reasoning."

> *coeval:* simultaneous

24. *The original of all our knowledge.*—In time the mind comes to reflect on its own operations about the ideas got by sensation, and thereby stores itself with a new set of ideas, which I call   175 "ideas of reflection." These are the impressions that are made on our senses by outward objects, that are extrinsical to the mind; and its own operations, proceeding from powers intrinsical and proper to itself, which, when reflected on by itself,   180 become also objects of its contemplation, are, as I have said, the original of all knowledge. Thus the first capacity of human intellect is, that the mind is fitted to receive the impressions made on it, either through the senses by outward objects, or by its own operations when it reflects on them. This is the first step a man makes towards the discovery of anything, and the groundwork whereon to build all those notions which ever he shall have naturally in this world. All   185 those sublime thoughts which tower above the clouds, and reach as high as heaven itself, take their rise and footing here: in all that great extent wherein the mind wanders in those remote speculations it may seem to be elevated with, it stirs not one jot beyond those ideas which sense or reflection have offered for its contemplation.

> *impressions:* physical effects of external stimuli; sensations

190   **25.** *In the reception of simple ideas, the understanding is for the most part passive.*—In this part the understanding is merely passive; and whether or no it will have these beginnings and, as it were, materials of knowledge, is not in its own power. For the objects of our senses do many of them obtrude their particular ideas upon our minds, whether we will or no; and the operations of our minds will not let us be without at least some obscure notions of them. No man can

195   be wholly ignorant of what he does when he thinks. These simple ideas, when offered to the mind, the understanding can no more refuse to have, nor alter when they are imprinted, nor blot them out and make new ones itself, than a mirror can refuse, alter or obliterate the images or ideas, which the objects set before it do therein produce. As the bodies that surround us do diversely affect our organs, the mind is forced to receive the impressions, and cannot avoid the

200   perception of those ideas that are annexed to them.

Chapter 2. Of Simple Ideas

1. *Uncompounded appearances.*—The better to understand the nature, manner, and extent of our knowledge, one thing is carefully to be observed concerning the ideas we have; and that is, that some of them are simple, and some complex.

    Though the qualities that affect our senses are, in the things themselves, so united and
205   blended that there is no separation, no distance between them; yet it is plain the ideas they produce in the mind enter by the senses simple and unmixed. For though the sight and touch often take in from the same object at the same time different ideas—as a man sees at once
210   motion and colour, the hand feels softness and warmth in the same piece of wax—yet the simple ideas thus united in the same subject are as per-

> *united and blended:* The qualities of an object—for example, the redness, smoothness, and softness of a ripe tomato—are not separate in the object.

fectly distinct as those that come in by different senses; the coldness and hardness which a man feels in a piece of ice being as distinct ideas in the mind as the smell and whiteness of a lily, or
215   as the taste of sugar and smell of a rose: and there is nothing can be plainer to a man than the clear and distinct perception he has of those simple ideas; which, being each in itself uncompounded, contains in it nothing but one uniform appearance or conception in the mind, and is not distinguishable into different ideas.

2. *The mind can neither make nor destroy them.*—These simple ideas, the materials of all our
220   knowledge, are suggested and furnished to the mind only by those two ways above mentioned, viz., sensation and reflection. When the understanding is once stored with these simple ideas, it has the power to repeat, compare, and unite them, even to an almost infinite variety, and so can make at pleasure new complex ideas. But it is not in the power of the most exalted wit or enlarged understanding, by any quickness or variety of thoughts, to invent or
225   frame one new simple idea in the mind, not taken in by the ways before mentioned; nor can

much-what: very nearly

any force of the understanding destroy those that are there: the dominion of man in this little world of his own understanding, being much-what the same as it is in the great world of visible things, wherein his power, however managed by art and skill, reaches no farther than to compound 230 and divide the materials that are made to his hand but can do nothing towards the making the least particle of new matter, or destroying one atom of what is already in being. The same inability will everyone find in himself, who shall go about to fashion, in his understanding any simple idea not received in by his senses from external objects, or by reflection, from the operations of his own mind about them. I would have anyone try to fancy any taste which had never 235 affected his palate, or frame the idea of a scent he had never smelt; and when he can do this, I will also conclude, that a blind man hath *ideas* of colours, and a deaf man true, distinct notions of sounds.

. . .

Chapter 3. Of the Ideas of One Sense

1. *Division of simple ideas.*—The better to conceive the ideas we receive from sensation, it may not be amiss for us to consider them in reference to the different ways whereby they make their 240 approaches to our minds, and make themselves perceivable by us.

First, then, there are some which come into our minds by one sense only.

Secondly. There are others that convey themselves into the mind by more senses than one.

Thirdly. Others that are had from reflection only.

Fourthly. There are some that . . . are suggested to the mind, by all the ways of sensation 245 and reflection.

We shall consider them apart under these several heads.

1.   There are some ideas which have admittance only through one sense, which is peculiarly adapted to receive them. Thus light and colours, as white, red, yellow, blue, with their several degrees or shades and mixtures, as green, scarlet, purple, sea green, and the rest, come in only 250 by the eyes; all kinds of noises, sounds, and tones, only by the ears; the several tastes and smells, by the nose and palate. And if these organs, or the nerves which are the conduits to convey them from without to their audience in the brain, the mind's presence-room, (as I may so call it) are, any of them, so disordered as not to perform their functions, they have no postern to be 255 admitted by, no other way to bring themselves into view, and be received by the understanding.

postern: a rear gate; in this context, a back door, an alternate means of access

260   The most considerable of those belonging to the touch are heat, and cold, and solidity; all the rest—consisting almost wholly in the sensible configuration, as smooth and rough; or else more or less firm adhesion of the parts, as hard and soft, tough and brittle—are obvious enough.

...

Chapter 4. Of Solidity

1. *We receive this idea from touch.*—The idea of solidity we receive by our touch; and it arises from the resistance which we find in body to the entrance of any other body into the place it possesses, till it has left it. There is no idea which we receive more constantly from sensation
265   than solidity. Whether we move or rest, in what posture soever we are, we always feel something under us that supports us, and hinders our farther sinking downwards; and the bodies which we daily handle make us perceive that whilst they remain between them, they do, by an insurmountable force, hinder the approach of the parts of our hands that press them. That which thus hinders the approach of two bodies, when they are moving one towards another,
270   I call "solidity." I will not dispute whether this acceptation of the word "solid" be nearer to its original signification than that which mathematicians use it in; it suffices that, I think, the common notion of "solidity," will allow, if not justify this use of it; but if anyone think it better to call it "impenetrability," he has my consent. Only I have thought the term "solidity" the more proper to
275   express this idea, not only because of its vulgar use in that sense, but also because it carries something more of positive in it than "impenetrability,"

> *vulgar:* common, everyday

which is negative, and is perhaps, more a consequence of solidity than solidity itself. This, of all other, seems the idea most intimately connected with and essential to body, so as nowhere else
280   to be found or imagined but only in matter; and though our senses take no notice of it but in masses of matter, of a bulk sufficient to cause a sensation in us; yet the mind, having once got this idea from such grosser sensible bodies, traces it farther and considers it, as well as figure, in the minutest particle of matter that can exist, and
285   finds it inseparably inherent in body, wherever or however modified.

> *figure:* shape, form (but not any specific shape)

...

6. *What it is.*—If anyone asks me, what this solidity is, I send him to his senses to inform him: let him put a flint or a foot-ball between his hands, and then
290   endeavour to join them, and he will know. If he thinks this not a sufficient explanation of solidity,

> *flint:* a stone; *foot-ball:* a rugby or soccer ball

what it is, and wherein it consists, I promise to tell him what it is, and wherein it consists, when he tells me what thinking is, or wherein it consists; or explains to me what extension or motion is, which perhaps seems much easier. The simple ideas we have are such as experience teaches them us; but if, beyond that, we endeavour by words to make them clearer in the mind, we shall succeed no better than if we went about to clear up the darkness of a blind man's mind by talking, and to discourse into him the ideas of light and colour. The reason of this I shall show in another place. 295

Chapter 5. Of Simple Ideas of Divers Senses

extension: the property of taking up space (but not any specific space)

The ideas we get by more than one sense are of space or extension, figure, rest and motion: for 300
these make perceivable impressions both on the eyes and touch; and we can receive and convey into our minds the ideas of our extension, figure, motion, and rest of bodies, both by seeing and feeling. But having occasion to speak more at large of these in another place, I here only enumerate them. 305

Chapter 6. Of Simple Ideas of Reflection

Simple ideas of reflection are the operations of the mind about its other ideas.—The mind, receiving the ideas mentioned in the foregoing chapters from without, when it turns its view inward upon itself, and observes its own actions about those ideas it has, takes from thence other ideas, which are as capable to be the objects of its contemplation as any of those it received from foreign things. 310
The idea of perception, and idea of willing, we have from reflection.—The two great and principal actions of the mind, which are most frequently considered, and which are so frequent that everyone that pleases may take notice of them in himself, are these two: perception or thinking, and volition or willing. The power of thinking is called "the understanding," and the power of volition is called "the will;" and these two powers or abilities in the mind are denominated "faculties." 315
ulties." Of some of the modes of these simple ideas of reflection, such as are remembrance, discerning, reasoning, judging, knowledge, faith, &c., I shall have occasion to speak hereafter.

Chapter 7. Of Simple Ideas of Both Sensation and Reflection

1. *Pleasure and pain.*—There be other simple ideas which convey themselves into the mind by all the ways of sensation and reflection; viz., pleasure or delight, and its opposite, pain or uneasiness; power, existence, unity. 320

affection: stimulation; that which affects our senses

2. Delight or uneasiness, one or other of them, join themselves to almost all our ideas both of sensation and reflection; and there is scarce any affection of our senses from without, any retired

325   thought of our mind within, which is not able to produce in us pleasure or pain. By "pleasure" and "pain," I would be understood to signify whatsoever delights or molests us; whether it arises from the thoughts of our minds, or anything operating on our bodies. For whether we call it "satisfaction, delight, pleasure, happiness," &c., on the one side; or "uneasiness, trouble, pain, torment, anguish, misery," &c., on the other; they are still but different degrees of the same

330   thing, and belong to the ideas of pleasure and pain, delight or uneasiness; which are the names I shall most commonly use for those two sorts of ideas.

3. The infinitely wise Author of our being—having given us the power over several parts of our bodies, to move or keep them at rest as we think

335   fit, and also by the motion of them to move our-

> *Author of our being:* God

selves and other contiguous bodies, in which consist all the actions of body; having also given a power to our minds, in several instances, to choose amongst its ideas which it will think on, and to pursue the inquiry of this or that subject with consideration and attention—to excite us to these actions of thinking and motion that we are capable of, has been

340   pleased to join to several thoughts and several sensations a perception of *delight.* If this were wholly separated from all our outward sensations and inward thoughts, we should have no reason to prefer one thought or action to another, negligence to attention, or motion to rest: and so we should neither stir our bodies, nor employ our minds; but let our thoughts (if I may so call it) run adrift, without any direction or design; and suffer the ideas of our minds, like

345   unregarded shadows, to make their appearances there as it happened, without attending to them: in which state man, however furnished with the faculties of understanding and will, would be a very idle, unactive creature, and pass his time only in a lazy, lethargic dream. It has therefore pleased our wise Creator to annex to several objects, and to the ideas which we receive from them, as also to several of our thoughts, a concomitant pleasure, and that

350   in several objects to several degrees, that those faculties which be had endowed us with might not remain wholly idle and unemployed by us.

4. *Pain* has the same efficacy and use to set us on work that pleasure has, we being as ready to employ our faculties to avoid that, as to pursue this: only this is worth our consideration—that pain is often produced by the same objects and ideas that produce pleasure in us. This their

355   near conjunction, which makes us often feel pain in the sensations where we expected pleasure, gives us new occasion of admiring the wisdom and goodness of our Maker, who, designing the preservation of our being, has annexed pain to the application of many things to our bodies, to warn us of the harm that they will do, and as advices to withdraw from them. But He, not designing our preservation barely, but the preservation of every part and organ in its per-

360   fection, hath in many cases annexed pain to those very ideas which delight us. Thus heat, that is very agreeable to us in one degree, by a little greater increase of it proves no ordinary torment; and the most pleasant of all sensible objects, light itself, if there be too much of it, if increased beyond a due proportion to our eyes, causes a very painful sensation: which is wisely

and favourably so ordered by nature, that when any object does by the vehemency of its oper-   365
ation disorder the instruments of sensation, whose structures cannot but be very nice and delicate, we might by the pain be warned to withdraw before the organ be quite put out of order,
and so be unfitted for its proper functions for the future. The consideration of those objects that
produce it may well persuade us, that this is the end or use of pain; for though great light be
insufferable to our eyes, yet the highest degree of darkness does not at all disease them,
because the causing no disorderly motion in it leaves that curious organ unharmed in its nat-   370
ural state. But yet excess of cold as well as heat pains us because it is equally destructive to that
temper which is necessary to the preservation of life, and the exercise of the several functions
of the body, and which consists in a moderate degree of warmth, or, if you please, a motion of
the insensible parts of our bodies confined within certain bounds.

    . . .

7. *Existence and unity.*—Existence and unity are two other ideas that are suggested to the   375
understanding by every object without, and every idea within. When ideas are in our minds,
we consider them as being actually there, as well as we consider things to be actually without
us: which is, that they exist, or have existence: and whatever we can consider as one thing,
whether a real being or idea, suggests to the understanding the idea of unity.

8. *Power.*—Power also is another of those simple ideas which we receive from sensation and   380
reflection. For, observing in ourselves that we can at pleasure move several parts of our bodies which were at rest, the effects also that natural bodies are able to produce in one another
occurring every moment to our senses, we both these ways get the idea of power.

9. *Succession.*—Besides these there is another idea, which though suggested by our senses yet
is more constantly offered us by what passes in our own minds; and that is the idea of succes-   385
sion. For if we look immediately into ourselves, and reflect on what is observable there, we shall
find our ideas always, whilst we are awake or have any thought, passing in train, one going and
another coming without intermission.

10. *Simple ideas the materials of all our knowledge.*—These, if they are not all, are at least (as I
think) the most considerable of those simple ideas which the mind has, and out of which is   390
made all its other knowledge: all of which it receives only by the two forementioned ways of
sensation and reflection.

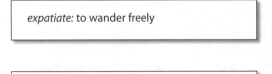

expatiate: to wander freely

inane: empty space; void

Nor let anyone think these too narrow bounds
for the capacious mind of man to expatiate in,
which takes its flight farther than the stars, and   395
cannot be confined by the limits of the world; that
extends its thoughts often even beyond the
utmost expansion of matter, and makes excur-
sions into that incomprehensible inane. I grant all
this; but desire anyone to assign any simple idea   400

which is not received from one of those inlets before mentioned, or any complex idea not made out of those simple ones. Nor will it be so strange to think these few simple ideas sufficient to employ the quickest thought or largest capacity, and to furnish the materials of all that various knowledge and more various fancies and opinions of all mankind, if we consider how many

405 words may be made out of the various composition of twenty-four letters; or if, going one step farther, we will but reflect on the variety of combinations may be made with, barely one of the above-mentioned ideas, viz., number, whose

410 stock is inexhaustible and truly infinite; and what a large and immense field doth extension alone afford the mathematicians?

> *24 letters:* In Locke's day *J* and *U* were still relative newcomers to the alphabet used for writing English. At first they were equivalent to *I* and *V*, respectively, and were not always counted as members of the alphabet. In any case Locke himself used 26 letters.

FOR DISCUSSION

1. How many elephants must we experience in order to have the *idea* of elephant? Through which sense must this experience take place?

2. What, if anything, guarantees that two people will have the same *elephant* idea?

3. Where do ideas such as *vertebrate, fireproof, invisible,* and *congruent* come from?

4. What, in Locke's conception, is *thinking?* What does the understanding (mind) do with its ideas once it has them?

Charles Darwin (1809–1882)
The Origin of Species
(1859)

Chapter 8. Instinct

In 1825 it was generally expected that sons would follow in their fathers' footsteps, so it was no surprise to anyone that Robert Darwin, a prosperous country doctor, packed his sons Erasmus and Charles off to Edinburgh, then the Athens of the medical world. But Charles found medicine alternately boring and revolting, and he was soon sent to Cambridge, where he would become an Anglican clergyman. Darwin did not distinguish himself in formal academic pursuits, but he learned a great deal in the woods and fields around Cambridge, doing what he always liked best—observing nature and collecting specimens. He also got to know a number of people with similar interests, people who would be useful to him throughout his career.

When Darwin graduated in 1831, he was prepared to find a parish somewhere and settle down as a country parson and gentleman naturalist. Instead, one of his Cambridge professors, John Stevens Henslow, a botanist, recommended him for the post of naturalist on HMS *Beagle,* a ship that was to spend two years surveying and mapping the eastern and western coasts of South America. By the time the *Beagle* returned, five years later, Darwin had amassed a huge and important collection of specimens from unknown parts of the world. This collection alone would have earned Darwin a distinguished position in the community of English and European naturalist-scientists, but an even more important cargo was in Darwin's head.

On the voyage Darwin read a great deal, including the *Principles of Geology* (1830) by Charles Lyell (1797–1875), who argued, controversially, that the present form of the earth's surface was not the result of periodic cataclysms (such as Noah's flood), as the going theory had it, but was

---

Source: Darwin, C. (1936). *The origin of species* (6th ed.). New York: Modern Library. [First edition published 1859; sixth edition published 1872.]

instead the product of slow, continuous processes—such as erosion, glaciation, and lava flows—operating over a very long time. Theologically, Lyell's theory was dynamite, and Darwin was not looking for trouble. Nevertheless, five years of sailing around the world showed him so many examples of exactly what Lyell was talking about that he could no longer doubt it. Moreover, the animals he saw raised interesting questions. Why were there so many species? Why were they distributed in a given way? Why were some species so similar to one another? Darwin began to wonder if there could be slow, continuous processes in biology, like those Lyell had described in geology.

Many people today identify Darwin as the author of the theory of evolution, but this does not do Darwin justice. The idea of evolution—the idea that species change, die out, and come into being—had been in the air for a couple of generations. Indeed, Darwin's own grandfather, Erasmus Darwin (1731–1802) had been an evolutionist. Evolution is a question of fact: Do species change? Do they come and go? Even before Darwin's *Beagle* specimens, evidence had been accumulating, in the form of fossils of extinct species, that the answer was yes. Darwin contributed substantially to the evidence for the fact of evolution, but his real achievement was to find an explanation of evolution. Thus, we should identify Darwin as the author of the theory of evolution by natural selection, for that was his explanation:

> can we doubt (remembering that many more individuals are born than can possibly survive) that individuals having any advantage, however slight, over others, would have the best chance of surviving and of procreating their kind? On the other hand, we may feel sure that any variation in the least degree injurious would be rigidly destroyed. This preservation of favourable individual differences and variations, and the destruction of those which are injurious, I have called Natural Selection, or the Survival of the Fittest. Variations neither useful nor injurious would not be affected by natural selection, and would be left either a fluctuating element, as perhaps we see in certain polymorphic species, or would ultimately become fixed, owing to the nature of the organism and the nature of the conditions. (1936, pp. 63–64)

Darwin was not the first to explain how evolution might happen. The French naturalist Jean Baptiste Lamarck (1744–1829) had proposed that species change, and become better adapted to their environments, through the inheritance of acquired characteristics. There is no genetic mechanism that allows an acquired characteristic (e.g., exceptional strength) to be passed on to the next generation, but Lamarck did not know that, and neither did Darwin, who did not absolutely rule out Lamarck's mechanism of change.

Neither was Darwin the only one to explain evolution by natural selection. After the *Beagle,* Darwin began thinking and writing about natural selection, among many other things. By 1858 he had done quite a lot of thinking, and he had told some of his friends of his big idea, but he had not published anything about it. That year he received a letter from Alfred Russel Wallace (1823–1913). Like Darwin, Wallace was an English naturalist and a talented collector with a particular interest in beetles. Wallace had spent many years in the Amazon region (seeking, among other things, the origin of species), and he was now in Malaysia, suffering from malaria. In a sudden insight he had realized that the origin of species might be explained through natural selection, and he was writing to Darwin, as a distinguished naturalist, to see what he thought of the idea.

With Wallace in Malaysia, it would not have been difficult for Darwin, in England, to lose Wallace's letter, quickly publish his theory, and thereby establish himself as the discoverer of natural selection. But Darwin did roughly the opposite. He consulted his friends, who quickly arranged for a paper by Darwin and another by Wallace to be read before the Linnaean Society, thus establishing the two men as equal and independent discoverers. (Oddly, the members of the Linnaean Society did not grasp the significance of what they had heard.) In 1859 Darwin finally published a much briefer (502 pages) account of his theory than he had planned. Unlike the Linnaean Society, the reading public immediately grasped the significance of the book, *The Origin of Species by Means of Natural Selection or the Preservation of Favored Races in the Struggle for Life*. Thus it was Darwin's name, not Wallace's, that became firmly and permanently attached to the idea.

Darwin's natural selection, like Lyell's geological processes, is a simple idea that applies to everything and takes a long time. For Lyell, everything means the whole surface of the earth; for Darwin it means every characteristic of an organism that it can pass on to its descendants. Among the many such characteristics are some aspects of behavior. Darwin saw that if a behavior (a) varied and (b) was hereditary, it must be subject to natural selection.

Many instincts are so wonderful that their development will probably appear to the reader a difficulty sufficient to overthrow my whole theory. I may here premise that I have nothing to do with the origin of the mental powers, any more than I have with that of life itself. We are concerned only with the diversities of instinct and of the other mental faculties in animals of the same class.

> Here and throughout the reading it is important to understand *wonderful* in its older sense of *amazing* rather than in its present sense of *very good*.

I will not attempt any definition of instinct. It would be easy to show that several distinct mental actions are commonly embraced by this term; but every one understands what is meant, when it is said that instinct impels the cuckoo to migrate and to lay her eggs in other birds' nests. An action, which we ourselves require experience to enable us to perform, when performed by an animal, more especially by a very young one, without experience, and when performed by many individuals in the same way, without their knowing for what purpose it is performed, is usually said to be instinctive. But I could show that none of these characters are universal. A little dose of judgment or reason, as Pierre Huber expresses it, often comes into play, even with animals low in the scale of nature.

> Jean Pierre Huber (1777–1840), Swiss entomologist

Frederick Cuvier and several of the older metaphysicians have compared instinct with habit. This comparison gives, I think, an accurate notion of the frame of mind under which an instinctive action is performed, but not necessarily of its origin. How unconsciously many habitual actions are performed, indeed not rarely in direct opposition

> Cuvier (Fr., 1769–1832) was a pioneer in paleontology and comparative anatomy.

to our conscious will! yet they may be modified by the will or reason. Habits easily become associated with other habits, with certain periods of time, and states of the body. When once acquired, they often remain constant throughout life. Several other points of resemblance between instincts and habits could be pointed out. As in repeating a well-known song, so in instincts, one action follows another by a sort of rhythm; if a person be interrupted in a song, or in repeating anything by rote, he is generally forced to go back to recover the habitual train of thought; so P. Huber found it was with a caterpillar, which makes a very complicated hammock; for if he took a caterpillar which had completed its hammock up to, say, the sixth stage of construction, and put it into a hammock completed up only to the third stage, the caterpillar simply re-performed the fourth, fifth, and sixth stages of construction. If, however, a caterpillar were taken out of a hammock made up, for instance, to the third stage, and were put into one finished up to the sixth stage, so that much of its work was already done for it, far from deriving any benefit from this, it was much embarrassed, and in order to complete its hammock, seemed forced to start from the third stage, where it had left off, and thus tried to complete the already finished work.

The inheritance of a habitual action would be an example of Lamarck's evolution through inheritance of acquired characteristics. Modern evolutionary biology does not consider this a possibility.

If we suppose any habitual action to become inherited—and it can be shown that this does sometimes happen—then the resemblance between what originally was a habit and an instinct becomes so close as not to be distinguished. If Mozart, instead of playing the pianoforte at three years old with wonderfully little practice, had played a tune with no practice at all, he might truly be said to have done so instinctively. But it would be a serious error to suppose that the greater number of instincts have been acquired by habit in one generation, and then transmitted by inheritance to succeeding generations. It can be clearly shown that the most wonderful instincts with which we are acquainted, namely, those of the hive-bee and of many ants, could not possibly have been acquired by habit.

It will be universally admitted that instincts are as important as corporeal structures for the welfare of each species, under its present conditions of life. Under changed conditions of life, it is at least possible that slight modifications of instinct might be profitable to a species; and if it can be shown that instincts do vary ever so little, then I can see no difficulty in natural selection preserving and continually accumulating variations of instinct to any extent that was profitable. It is thus, as I believe, that all the most complex and wonderful instincts have originated. As modifications of corporeal structure arise from, and are increased by, use or habit, and are diminished or lost by disuse, so I do not doubt it has been with instincts. But I believe that the effects of habit are in many cases of subordinate importance to the effects of the natural selection of what may be called spontaneous variations of instincts;—that is of variations produced by the same unknown causes which produce slight deviations of bodily structure.

unknown causes: In 1859 neither Darwin nor anyone else had any idea of what we now know as *genes.*

No complex instinct can possibly be produced through natural selection, except by the slow and gradual accumulation of numerous slight, yet profitable, variations. Hence, as in the case of corporeal structures, we ought to find in nature, not the actual transitional gradations by which each complex instinct has been acquired—for these could be found only in the lineal ancestors of each species—but we ought to find in the collateral lines of descent some evidence of such gradations; or we ought at least to be able to show that gradations of some kind are possible; and this we certainly can do. I have been surprised to find, making allowance for the instincts of animals having been but little observed except in Europe and North America, and for no instinct being known amongst extinct species, how very generally gradations, leading to the most complex instincts, can be discovered. Changes of instinct may sometimes be facilitated by the same species having different instincts at different periods of life, or at different seasons of the year, or when placed under different circumstances, &c.; in which case either the one or the other instinct might be preserved by natural selection. And such instances of diversity of instinct in the same species can be shown to occur in nature.

Again, as in the case of corporeal structure, and conformably to my theory, the instinct of each species is good for itself, but has never, as far as we can judge, been produced for the exclusive good of others. One of the strongest instances of an animal apparently performing an action for the sole good of another, with which I am acquainted, is that of aphides voluntarily yielding, as was first observed by Huber, their sweet excretion to ants: that they do so voluntarily, the following facts show. I removed all the ants from a group of about a dozen aphides on a dockplant, and prevented their attendance during several hours. After this interval, I felt sure that the aphides would want to excrete. I watched them for some time through a lens, but not one excreted; I then tickled and stroked them with a hair in the same manner, as well as I could, as the ants do with their antennæ; but not one excreted.

> *aphides:* aphids, tiny insects that feed, usually in large colonies, on the juices of various plants, such as roses, often causing substantial damage. To humans aphids are pests, but for many species of ants (and other insects) they are a source of *honeydew,* sweet, concentrated, partially digested plant sap excreted in large amounts. Aphids often form symbiotic relations with ants, who guard the aphids and their eggs in return for honeydew.

Afterwards I allowed an ant to visit them, and it immediately seemed, by its eager way of running about, to be well aware what a rich flock it had discovered; it then began to play with its antennas on the abdomen first of one aphis and then of another; and each, as soon as it felt the antennæ, immediately lifted up its abdomen and excreted a limpid drop of sweet juice, which was eagerly devoured by the ant. Even the quite young aphides behaved in this manner, showing that the action was instinctive, and not the result of experience. It is certain, from the observations of Huber, that the aphides show no dislike to the ants: if the latter be not present they are at last compelled to eject their excretion. But as the excretion is extremely viscid, it is no doubt a convenience to the aphides to have it removed; therefore probably they do not excrete solely for the good of the ants. Although there is no evidence that any animal performs an action for the exclusive good of another species, yet each tries to take advantage of the instincts of others, as each takes advantage of the weaker bodily structure of other species. So again certain instincts cannot be considered as absolutely perfect; but as details on this and other such points are not indispensable, they may be here passed over.

As some degree of variation in instincts under a state of nature, and the inheritance of such variations, are indispensable for the action of natural selection, as many instances as possible ought to be given; but want of space prevents me. I can only assert that instincts certainly do vary—for instance, the migratory instinct, both in extent and direction, and in its total loss. So it is with the nests of birds, which vary partly in dependence on the situations chosen, and on the nature and temperature of the country inhabited, but often from causes wholly unknown to us: Audubon has given several remarkable cases of differences in the nests of the same species in the northern and southern

> John James Audubon (1785–1851) was a French-Haitian-American ornithologist, famous for his stunning paintings of birds, published as *The Birds of America* between 1827 and 1838.

vermilion: powdered cinnabar (an ore of mercury), used as a brilliant red pigment

probably Thomas Andrew Knight (1759–1838), English botanist

Propolis is resin collected by bees from tree buds and used as a glue in their hives.

A *decorticated* tree is one that has had its bark (cortex) removed.

desert islands: deserted islands

wildness: fearfulness

United States. Why, it has been asked, if instinct be variable, has it not granted to the bee "the ability to use some other material when wax was deficient"? But what other natural material could bees use? They will work, as I have seen, with wax hardened with vermilion or softened with lard. Andrew Knight observed that his bees, instead of laboriously collecting propolis, used a cement of wax and turpentine, with which he had covered decorticated trees. It has lately been shown that bees, instead of searching for pollen, will gladly use a very different substance, namely oatmeal. Fear of any particular enemy is certainly an instinctive quality, as may be seen in nestling birds, though it is strengthened by experience, and by the sight of fear of the same enemy in other animals. The fear of man is slowly acquired, as I have elsewhere shown, by the various animals which inhabit desert islands; and we see an instance of this even in England, in the greater wildness of all our large birds in comparison with our small birds; for the large birds have been most persecuted by man. We may safely attribute the greater wildness of our large birds to this cause; for in uninhabited islands large birds are not more fearful than small; and the magpie, so wary in England, is tame in Norway, as is the hooded crow in Egypt.

That the mental qualities of animals of the same kind, born in a state of nature, vary much, could be shown by many facts. Several cases could also be adduced of occasional and strange habits in wild animals, which, if advantageous to the species, might have given rise, through natural selection, to new instincts. But I am well aware that these general statements, without the facts in detail, will produce but a feeble effect on the reader's mind. I can only repeat my assurance, that I do not speak without good evidence.

INHERITED CHANGES OF HABIT OR INSTINCT IN DOMESTICATED ANIMALS

The possibility, or even probability, of inherited variations of instinct in a state of nature will be strengthened by briefly considering a few cases under domestication. We shall thus be enabled to see the part which habit and the selection of so-called spontaneous variations have played in

modifying the mental qualities of our domestic animals. It is notorious how much domestic animals vary in their mental qualities. With cats, for instance, one naturally takes to catching rats, and
another mice, and these tendencies are known to be inherited. One cat, according to Mr. St. John,
always brought home game-birds, another hares or rabbits, and another hunted on marshy
ground and almost nightly caught woodcocks or snipes. A number of curious and authentic
instances could be given of various shades of disposition and of taste, and likewise of the odd-
est tricks, associated with certain frames of mind or periods of time, being inherited. But let us look
to the familiar case of the breeds of the dogs: it cannot be doubted that young pointers (I have
myself seen a striking instance) will sometimes point and even back other dogs the very first time
that they are taken out; retrieving is certainly in some degree inherited by retrievers ; and a tendency to run round, instead of at, a flock of sheep, by shepherd dogs. I cannot see that these
actions, performed without experience by the young, and in nearly the same manner by each
individual, performed with eager delight by each breed, and without the end being known—for
the young pointer can no more know that he points to aid his master, than the white butterfly
knows why she lays her eggs on the leaf of the cabbage—I cannot see that these actions differ
essentially from true instincts. If we were to behold one kind of wolf, when young and without
any training, as soon as it scented its prey, stand motionless like a statue, and then slowly crawl
forward with a peculiar gait; and another kind of wolf rushing round, instead of at, a herd of deer,
and driving them to a distant point, we should assuredly call these actions instinctive. Domestic
instincts, as they may be called, are certainly far less
fixed than natural instincts; but they have been
acted on by far less rigorous selection, and have
been transmitted for an incomparably shorter
period, under less fixed conditions, of life.

less rigorous selection: Darwin is referring to selection that takes place in the course of domestic breeding.

How strongly these domestic instincts, habits,
and dispositions are inherited, and how curiously they become mingled, is well shown when
different breeds of dogs are crossed. Thus it is known that a cross with a bull-dog has affected
for many generations the courage and obstinacy of greyhounds; and a cross with a greyhound
has given to a whole family of shepherd-dogs a tendency to hunt hares. These domestic
instincts, when thus tested by crossing, resemble natural instincts, which in a like manner
become curiously blended together, and for a long period exhibit traces of the instincts of
either parent: for example, Le Roy describes a dog, whose great-grandfather was a wolf, and
this dog showed a trace of its wild parentage only in one way, by not coming in a straight line
to his master, when called.

Domestic instincts are sometimes spoken of as actions which have become inherited solely
from long-continued and compulsory habit; but this is not true. No one would ever have
thought of teaching, or probably could have
taught, the tumbler-pigeon to tumble,—an action
which, as I have witnessed, is performed by young
birds, that have never seen a pigeon tumble. We
may believe that some one pigeon showed a

Tumblers are domestic pigeons with a habit of turning somersaults in flight.

slight tendency to this strange habit, and that the long-continued selection of the best indi- 200
viduals in successive generations made tumblers what they now are; and near Glasgow there
are house-tumblers, as I hear from Mr. Brent, which cannot fly eighteen inches high without
going head over heels. It may be doubted whether any one would have thought of training a
dog to point, had not some one dog naturally shown a tendency in this line; and this is known
occasionally to happen, as I once saw, in a pure terrier: the act of pointing is probably, as many 205
have thought, only the exaggerated pause of an animal preparing to spring on its prey. When
the first tendency to point was once displayed, methodical selection and the inherited effects
of compulsory training in each successive generation would soon complete the work; and
unconscious selection is still in progress, as each man tries to procure, without intending to
improve the breed, dogs which stand and hunt best. . . . 210

Natural instincts are lost under domestication: a remarkable instance of this is seen in those
breeds of fowls which very rarely or never become "broody," that is, never wish to sit on their
eggs. Familiarity alone prevents our seeing how largely and how permanently the minds of our
domestic animals have been modified. It is scarcely possible to doubt that the love of man has
become instinctive in the dog. All wolves, foxes, jackals, and species of the cat genus, when kept 215
tame, are most eager to attack poultry, sheep, and pigs; and this tendency has been found
incurable in dogs which have been brought home as puppies from countries such as Tierra del
Fuego and Australia, where the savages do not keep these domestic animals. How rarely, on
the other hand, do our civilised dogs, even when quite young, require to be taught not to attack
poultry, sheep, and pigs! No doubt they occasionally do make an attack, and are then beaten; 220
and if not cured, they are destroyed; so that habit and some degree of selection have probably concurred in civilising by inheritance our dogs. . . .

Hence, we may conclude, that under domestication instincts have been acquired, and natural instincts have been lost, partly by habit, and partly by man selecting and accumulating,
during successive generations, peculiar mental habits and actions, which at first appeared from 225
what we must in our ignorance call an accident. In some cases compulsory habit alone has
sufficed to produce inherited mental changes; in other cases, compulsory habit has done nothing, and all has been the result of selection, pursued both methodically and unconsciously: but
in most cases habit and selection have probably concurred.

Special Instincts

We shall, perhaps, best understand how instincts in a state of nature have become modified by 230
selection by considering a few cases. I will select only three,—namely, the instinct which leads the
cuckoo to lay her eggs in other birds' nests; the slave-making instinct of certain ants; and the cell-making power of the hive-bee. These two latter instincts have generally and justly been ranked by naturalists 235
as the most wonderful of all known instincts.

> We have included Darwin's discussion of cuckoos and ants, but not his fascinating (but lengthy) discussion of bees.

Instincts of the Cuckoo.—It is supposed by some naturalists that the more immediate cause of the instinct of the cuckoo is, that she lays her eggs, not

240   daily, but at intervals of two or three days; so that, if she were to make her own nest and sit on her own eggs, those first laid would have to be left for some time unincubated, or there would be eggs and young birds of different ages in the same nest.

> Unless he specifies otherwise, when Darwin says *cuckoo* he means the (parasitic) European cuckoo. In what follows, much of Darwin's argument hinges on differences among the European, American, and Australian cuckoos, and so it is necessary to keep track of which bird he is talking about.

245   If this were the case, the process of laying and hatching might be inconveniently long, more especially as she migrates at a very early period; and the first hatched young would probably have to be fed by the male alone. But the American cuckoo is in this predicament; for she makes her own nest, and has eggs and young successively hatched, all at the same time. It has been both asserted and denied that the American cuckoo

250   occasionally lays her eggs in other birds' nests; but I have lately heard from Dr. Merrell, of Iowa, that he once found in Illinois a young cuckoo together with a young jay in the nest of a Blue jay (Garrulus cristatus); and as both were nearly full feathered, there could be no mistake in their identification. I could also give several instances of various birds which have been known occasionally to lay their eggs in other birds' nests. Now let us suppose that the ancient progenitor

255   of our European cuckoo had the habits of the American cuckoo, and that she occasionally laid an egg in another birds' nest. If the old bird profited by this occasional habit through being enabled to migrate earlier or through any other cause; or if the young were made more vigorous by advantage being taken of the mistaken instinct of another species than when reared by their own mother, encumbered as she could hardly fail to be by having eggs and young of dif-

260   ferent ages at the same time; then the old birds or the fostered young would gain an advantage. And analogy would lead us to believe, that the young thus reared would be apt to follow by inheritance the occasional and aberrant habit of their mother, and in their turn would be apt to lay their eggs in other birds' nests, and thus be more successful in rearing their young. By a continued process of this nature, I believe that the strange instinct of our cuckoo has been gen-

265   erated. It has, also, recently been ascertained on sufficient evidence, by Adolf Muller, that the cuckoo occasionally lays her eggs on the bare ground, sits on them, and feeds her young. This rare event is probably a case of reversion to the long-lost, aboriginal instinct of nidification.

> *nidification:* nest building

270   It has been objected that I have not noticed other related instincts and adaptations of structure in the cuckoo, which are spoken of as necessarily co-ordinated. But in all cases, speculation on an instinct known to us only in a single species, is useless, for we have hitherto had no facts to guide us. Until recently the instincts of the European and of the non-parasitic American cuckoo alone were known; now, owing to Mr. Ramsay's observations, we

275   have learnt something about three Australian species, which lay their eggs in other birds' nests. The chief points to be referred to are three: first, that the common cuckoo, with rare

exceptions, lays only one egg in a nest, so that the large and voracious young bird receives ample food. Secondly, that the eggs are remarkably small, not exceeding those of the sky-lark,—a bird about one-fourth as large as the cuckoo. That the small size of the egg is a real case of adaptation we may infer from the fact of the non-parasitic American cuckoo laying full-sized eggs. Thirdly, that the young cuckoo, soon after birth, has the instinct, the strength, and a properly shaped back for ejecting its foster-brothers, which then perish from cold and hunger. This has been boldly called a beneficent arrangement, in order that the young cuckoo may get sufficient food, and that its foster-brothers may perish before they had acquired much feeling!

Turning now to the Australian species; though these birds generally lay only one egg in a nest, it is not rare to find two and even three eggs in the same nest. In the Bronze cuckoo the eggs vary greatly in size, from eight to ten times in length. Now if it had been of an advantage to this species to have laid eggs even smaller than those now laid, so as to have deceived certain foster-parents, or, as is more probable, to have been hatched within a shorter period (for it is asserted that there is a relation between the size of eggs and the period of their incubation), then there is no difficulty in believing that a race or species might have been formed which would have laid smaller and smaller eggs; for these would have been more safely hatched and reared. Mr. Ramsay remarks that two of the Australian cuckoos, when they lay their eggs in an open nest, manifest a decided preference for nests containing eggs similar in colour to their own. The European species apparently manifests some tendency towards a similar instinct, but not rarely departs from it, as is shown by her laying her dull and pale-coloured eggs in the nest of the Hedge-warbler with bright greenish-blue eggs. Had our cuckoo invariably displayed the above instinct, it would assuredly have been added to those which it is assumed must all have been acquired together. The eggs of the Australian Bronze cuckoo vary, according to Mr. Ramsay, to an extraordinary degree in colour; so that in this respect, as well as in size, natural selection might have secured and fixed any advantageous variation.

In the case of the European cuckoo, the offspring of the foster-parents are commonly ejected from the nest within three days after the cuckoo is hatched; and as the latter at this age is in a most helpless condition, Mr. Gould was formerly inclined to believe that the act of ejection was performed by the foster-parents themselves. But he has now received a trustworthy account of a young cuckoo which was actually seen, whilst still blind and not able even to hold up its own head, in the act of ejecting its foster-brothers. One of these was replaced in the nest by the observer, and was again thrown out. With respect to the means by which this strange and odious instinct was acquired, if it were of great importance for the young cuckoo, as is probably the case, to receive as much food as possible soon after birth, I can see no special difficulty in its having gradually acquired, during successive generations, the blind desire, the strength, and structure necessary for the work of ejection; for those young cuckoos which had such habits and structure best developed would be the most securely reared. The first step towards the acquisition of the proper instinct might

John Gould (1804–1881), English ornithologist

280

285

290

295

300

305

310

315

have been more unintentional restlessness on the part of the young bird, when somewhat advanced in age and strength; the habit having been afterwards improved, and transmitted to an earlier age. I can see no more difficulty in this, than in the unhatched young of other birds acquiring the instinct to break through their own shells;—or than in young snakes acquiring in their upper jaws, as Owen has remarked, a transitory sharp tooth for cutting through the tough egg-shell. For if each part is liable to individual varia-tions at all ages, and the variations tend to be inherited at a corresponding or earlier age,—propositions which cannot be disputed,—then the instincts and structure of the young could be slowly modified as surely as those of the adult; and both cases must stand or fall together with the whole theory of natural selection.

> Richard Owen (1804–1892), English anatomist and paleontologist who coined the word *dinosaur* in 1841

...

Slave-making instinct.—This remarkable instinct was first discovered in the Formica (Polyerges) rufescens by Pierre Huber, a better observer even than his celebrated father. This ant is absolutely dependent on its slaves; without their aid, the species would certainly become extinct in a single year. The males and fertile female do no work of any kind, and the workers or sterile females, though most energetic and courageous in capturing slaves, do no other work. They are inca-pable of making their own nests, or of feeding their own larvæ. When the old nest is found incon-venient, and they have to migrate, it is the slaves which determine the migration, and actually carry their masters in their jaws. So utterly helpless are the masters, that when Huber shut up thirty of them without a slave, but with plenty of the food which they like best, and with their own larvæ and pupæ to stimulate them to work, they did nothing; they could not even feed them-selves, and many perished of hunger. Huber then introduced a single slave (F. fusca), and she instantly set to work, fed and saved the survivors; made some cells and tended the larvæ, and put all to rights. What can be more extraordinary than these well-ascertained facts? If we had not known of any other slave-making ant, it would have been hopeless to speculate how so wonderful an instinct could have been perfected.

Another species, Formica sanguinea, was likewise first discovered by P. Huber to be a slave-making ant. This species is found in the southern parts of England, and its habits have been attended to by Mr. F. Smith, of the British Museum, to whom I am much indebted for information on

> *Formica* is the Latin for *ant.*

> *celebrated father:* François Huber (1750–1830), Swiss entomologist

> Ant species discussed in this section:
> *F. rufescens* (master), *F. fusca* (slave; small, black), *F. sanguinea* (master; large, red), *F. flava* (small, yellow)

> Frederick Smith (1805–1879), English entomologist

this and other subjects. Although fully trusting to the statements of Huber and Mr. Smith, I tried to approach the subject in a sceptical frame of mind, as any one may well be excused for doubting the existence of so extraordinary an instinct as that of making slaves. Hence, I will give the observations which I made in some little detail. I opened fourteen nests of F. sanguinea, and found a few slaves in all. Males and fertile females of the slave species (F. fusca) are found only in their own proper communities, and have never been observed in the nests of F. sanguinea. The slaves are black and not above half the size of their red masters, so that the contrast in their appearance is great. When the nest is slightly disturbed, the slaves occasionally come out, and like their masters are much agitated and defend the nest: when the nest is much disturbed, and the larvæ and pupæ are exposed, the slaves work energetically together with their masters in carrying them away to a place of safety. Hence, it is clear, that the slaves feel quite at home. During the months of June and July, on three successive years, I watched for many hours several nests in Surrey and Sussex, and never saw a slave either leave or enter a nest. As, during these months, the slaves are very few in number, I thought that they might behave differently when more numerous; but Mr. Smith informs me that he has watched the nests at various hours during May, June, and August, both in Surrey and Hampshire, and has never seen the slaves, though present in large numbers in August, either leave or enter the nest. Hence he considers them as strictly household slaves. The masters, on the other hand, may be constantly seen bringing in materials for the nest, and food of all kinds. During the year 1860, however, in the month of July, I came across a community with an unusually large stock of slaves, and I observed a few slaves mingled with their masters leaving the nest, and marching along the same road to a tall Scotch-fir-tree, twenty-five yards distant, which they ascended together, probably in search of aphides or cocci. According to Huber, who had ample opportunities for observation, the slaves in Switzerland habitually work with their masters in making the nest, and they alone open and close the doors in the morning and evening; and, as Huber expressly states, their

Cocci, or coccids, also known as *scale insects*, are very small insects that cover themselves in waxy secretions.

principal office is to search for aphides. This difference in the usual habits of the masters and slaves in the two countries, probably depends merely on the slaves being captured in greater numbers in Switzerland than in England.

One day I fortunately witnessed a migration of F. sanguinea from one nest to another, and it was a most interesting spectacle to behold the masters carefully carrying their slaves in their jaws instead of being carried by them, as in the case of F. rufescens. Another day my attention was struck by about a score of the slave-makers haunting the same spot, and evidently not in search of food; they approached and were vigorously repulsed by an independent community of the slave-species (F. fusca), sometimes as many as three of these ants clinging to the legs of the slave-making F. sanguinea. The latter ruthlessly killed their small opponents, and carried their dead bodies as food to their nest, twenty-nine yards distant, but they were prevented from getting any pupæ to rear as slaves. I then dug up a small parcel of the pupæ of F. fusca from another nest, and put them down on a bare spot near the place of combat; they were eagerly seized and carried off by the tyrants, who perhaps fancied that, after all, they had been victorious in their late combat.

400   At the same time I laid on the same place a small parcel of the pupæ of another species, F. flava, with a few of these little yellow ants still clinging to the fragments of their nest. This species is sometimes, though rarely, made into slaves, as has been described by Mr. Smith. Although so small a species, it is very courageous, and I have seen it ferociously attack other ants. In one instance I found to my surprise an independent community of F. flava under a stone beneath a
405   nest of the slave-making F. sanguinea; and when I had accidentally disturbed both nests, the little ants attacked their big neighbours with surprising courage. Now I was curious to ascertain whether F. sanguinea could distinguish the pupæ of F. fusca, which they habitually make into slaves, from those of the little and furious F. flava, which they rarely capture, and it was evident that they did at once distinguish them; for we have seen that they eagerly and instantly seized
410   the pupæ of F. fusca, whereas they were much terrified when they came across the pupæ, or even the earth from the nest, of F. flava, and quickly ran away; but in about a quarter of an hour, shortly after all the little yellow ants had crawled away, they took heart and carried off the pupæ.

One evening I visited another community of F. sanguinea, and found a number of these ants returning home and entering their nests, carrying the dead bodies of F. fusca (showing that it
415   was not a migration) and numerous pupæ. I traced a long file of ants burthened with booty, for about forty yards back, to a very thick clump of heath, whence I saw the last individual of F. sanguinea emerge, carrying a pupa; but I was not able to find the desolated nest in the thick heath. The nest, however, must have been close at hand, for two or three individuals of F. fusca were rushing about in the greatest agitation, and one was perched motionless with its own pupa in
420   its mouth on the top of a spray of heath, an image of despair over its ravaged home.

Such are the facts, though they did not need confirmation by me, in regard to the wonderful instinct of making slaves. Let it be observed what a contrast the instinctive habits of F. sanguinea present with those of the continental F. rufescens. The latter does not build its own nest, does not determine its own migrations, does not collect food for itself or its young, and can-
425   not even feed itself: it is absolutely dependent on its numerous slaves. Formica sanguinea, on the other hand, possesses much fewer slaves, and in the early part of the summer extremely few: the masters determine when and where a new nest shall be formed, and when they migrate, the masters carry the slaves. Both in Switzerland and England the slaves seem to have the exclusive care of the larvæ, and the masters alone go on slave-making expeditions. In
430   Switzerland the slaves and masters work together, making and bringing materials for the nest; both, but chiefly the slaves, tend, and milk, as it may be called their aphides; and thus both collect food for the community. In England the masters alone usually leave the nest to collect building materials and food for themselves, their slaves and larvæ. So that the masters in this country receive much less service from their slaves than they do in Switzerland.

435   By what steps the instinct of F. sanguinea originated I will not pretend to conjecture. But as ants which are not slave-makers will, as I have seen, carry off the pupæ of other species, if scattered near their nests, it is possible that such pups originally stored as food might become developed; and the foreign ants thus unintentionally reared would then follow their proper

instincts, and do what work they could. If their presence proved useful to the species which had seized them—if it were more advantageous to this species to capture workers than to procreate them—the habit of collecting pupæ, originally for food, might by natural selection be strengthened and rendered permanent for the very different purpose of raising slaves. When the instinct was once acquired, if carried out to a much less extent even than in our British *F. sanguinea*, which, as we have seen, is less aided by its slaves than the same species in Switzerland, natural selection might increase and modify the instinct—always supposing each modification to be of use to the species—until an ant was formed as abjectly dependent on its slaves as is the *Formica rufescens*.

440

445

. . .

Objections to the Theory of Natural Selection as Applied to Instincts

It has been objected to the foregoing view of the origin of instincts that "the variations of structure and of instinct must have been simultaneous and accurately adjusted to each other, as a modification in the one without an immediate corresponding change in the other would have been fatal." The force of this objection rests entirely on the assumption that the changes in the instincts and structure are abrupt. To take as an illustration the case of the larger titmouse (Parus major) alluded to in a previous chapter; this bird often holds the seeds of the yew between its feet on a branch, and hammers with its beak till it gets at the kernel. Now what special difficulty would there be in natural selection preserving all the slight individual variations in the shape of the beak, which were better and better adapted to break open the seeds, until a beak was formed, as well constructed for this purpose as that of the nuthatch, at the same time that habit, or compulsion, or spontaneous variations of taste, led the bird to become more and more of a seed-eater? In this case the beak is supposed to be slowly modified by natural selection, subsequently to, but in accordance with, slowly changing habits or taste; but let the feet of the titmouse vary and grow larger from correlation with the beak, or from any other unknown cause, and it is not improbable that such larger feet would lead the bird to climb more and more until it acquired the remarkable climbing instinct and power of the nuthatch. In this case a gradual change of structure is supposed to lead to changed instinctive habits. To take one more case: few instincts are more remarkable than that which leads the swift of the Eastern Islands to make its nest wholly of inspissated saliva. Some birds build their nests of mud, believed to be moistened with saliva, and one of the swifts of North America makes its nest (as I have seen) of sticks agglutinated with saliva, and even with flakes of this substance. Is it then very improbable that the natural selection of individual swifts, which secreted more and more saliva, should at last produce a species with instincts leading it to neglect other materials, and to make its nest exclusively

450

455

460

465

470

inspissated: thickened, condensed

475 of inspissated saliva? And so in other cases. It must, however, be admitted that in many instances we cannot conjecture whether it was instinct or structure which first varied.

. . .

Summary

I have endeavoured in this chapter briefly to show that the mental qualities of our domestic animals vary, and that the variations are inherited. Still more briefly I have attempted to show that instincts vary slightly in a state of nature. No one will dispute that instincts are of the highest importance to each animal. Therefore there is no real difficulty, under changing conditions

480 of life, in natural selection accumulating to any extent slight modifications of instinct which are in any way useful. In many cases habit or use and disuse have probably come into play. I do not pretend that the facts given in this chapter strengthen in any great degree my theory; but none of the cases of difficulty, to the best of my judgment, annihilate it. On the other hand, the fact that instincts are not always absolutely perfect and are liable to mistakes:—that no instinct can

485 be shown to have been produced for the good of other animals, though animals take advantage of the instincts of others;—that the canon in natural history, of "Natura non facit saltum," is applicable to instincts as well as to corporeal structure, and is plainly explicable on the foregoing views,

490 but is otherwise inexplicable,—all tend to corroborate the theory of natural selection.

> *Natura non facit saltum* (L.): Nature does not make leaps.

This theory is also strengthened by some few other facts in regard to instincts; as by that common case of closely allied, but distinct species, when inhabiting distant parts of the world and living under considerably different conditions of life, yet often retaining nearly the same

495 instincts. For instance, we can understand, on the principle of inheritance, how it is that the thrush of tropical South America lines its nest with mud, in the same peculiar manner as does our British thrush; how it is that the Horn-bills of Africa and India have the same extraordinary instinct of plastering up and imprisoning the females in a hole in a tree, with only a small hole left in the plaster through which the males feed them and their young when hatched; how it

500 is that the male wrens (Troglodytes) of North America build "cock-nests," to roost in, like the males of our Kitty-wrens,—a habit wholly unlike that of any other known bird. Finally, it may not be a logical deduction, but to my imagination it is far more satisfactory to look at such instincts as

505 the young cuckoo ejecting its foster-brothers,— ants making slaves,—the larvæ of ichneumonidæ

> A troglodyte is a cave dweller, and *Troglodytes* is a genus of wrens who typically nest in cavities.

feeding within the live bodies of caterpillars,—not as specially endowed or created instincts, but as small consequences of one general law leading to the advancement of all organic beings,—namely, multiply, vary, let the strongest live and the weakest die.

FOR DISCUSSION

1. Why is it important for Darwin to show that instincts vary within species and between species?

2. How does Darwin explain the loss of instinct under domestication?

3. How does the loss of instinct under domestication support Darwin's overall claim about instincts?

4. What is Darwin's distinction between habit and instinct, and what is its significance?

5. What happens when a characteristic that is selected for becomes maladaptive? How does natural selection work under those circumstances? (See Darwin's discussion (lines 330–351) of F. rufescens's dependence on its slaves.)

Hermann von Helmholtz
(1821–1894)
The Facts of Perception (1878)

When in 1690 Locke famously compared the mind at birth to a blank slate (see 4.2), he was joining an argument already long in progress. His claim that "there appear not to be any ideas in the mind, before the senses have conveyed any in" had been around for a long time in a Latin phrase of unknown origin: *Nihil est in intellectu quod non prius fuerit in sensu.* (There is nothing in the mind that was not first in the senses.) Leibniz (1704/1951, p. 409) quoted this phrase to characterize Locke's argument, but added *excipe: nisi ipse intellectus* (except the mind).[1]

Later in the eighteenth century, Kant expanded, to put it mildly, on Leibniz's insight. Kant argued that certain basic mental categories are necessary to any perception and therefore cannot be learned. Kant begins his *Critique of Pure Reason* (1787/1934) with these observations:

> That all our knowledge begins with experience there can be no doubt. For how is it possible that the faculty of cognition should be awakened into exercise otherwise than by means of objects which affect our senses, and partly of themselves produce representations, partly rouse our powers of understanding into activity, to compare, to connect, or to separate these, and so to convert the raw material of our sensuous impressions into a knowledge of objects, which is called experience? In respect of time, therefore, no knowledge of ours is antecedent to experience, but begins with it.
>
> But, though all our knowledge begins with experience, it by no means follows that

---

Source: Helmholtz, H. von. (1971). *Selected writings of Hermann von Helmholtz* (R. Kahl, Ed.). Middletown, CT: Wesleyan University Press. Reprinted with permission. [The text was an address given on the anniversary of the founding of the University of Berlin in 1878.]

[1] See Leibniz's *New Essays concerning Human Understanding* (1704/1951), a point-by-point examination of Locke's Essay. On the origin of *Nihil . . .* , see Cranefield (1970).

all arises out of experience. For, on the contrary, it is quite possible that our empirical knowledge is a compound of that which we receive through impressions, and that which the faculty of cognition supplies from itself (sensuous impressions giving merely the occasion), an addition which we cannot distinguish from the original element given by sense, till long practice has made us attentive to, and skilful in separating it. It is, therefore, a question which requires close investigation, and not to be answered at first sight, whether there exists a knowledge altogether independent of experience, and even of all sensuous impressions? Knowledge of this kind is called *a priori,* in contradistinction to empirical knowledge, which has its sources *a posteriori,* that is, in experience. (p. 25)

In the present reading Helmholtz critically discusses Kant's position from a physiological and psychological point of view. He finds that some of Kant's claims make sense in that light, but others do not. Helmholtz's claims for empiricism—for the doctrine of *Nihil . . .*—are as adamant as Locke's, but they are more sophisticated. Where Locke's argument was based on reason, Helmholtz's is based on the more detailed and nuanced understanding of sensation and perception that emerged in the nineteenth century—an understanding to which Helmholtz himself contributed enormously (see 2.3).

[For biographical information, see 2.3.]

. . .

Shortly before the beginning of the present century, Kant expounded a theory of that which, in cognition, is prior or antecedent to all experience; that is, he developed a theory of what he called the *transcendental* forms of intuition and thought. These are forms into which the content of our sensory experience must necessarily be fitted if it is to be transformed into ideas.

5   As to the qualities of sensations themselves, Locke had earlier pointed out the role which our bodily and mental structure or organization plays in determining the way things appear to us. Along this latter line, investigations of the physiology of

10   the senses, in particular those which Johannes

> *transcendental:* In Kant's use, this refers to necessary, or *a priori,* foundations of (empirical) knowledge.

Müller carried out and formulated in the law of the specific energies of the senses, have brought (one can almost say, to a completely unanticipated degree) the fullest confirmation. Further, these investigations have established the nature of—and in a very decisive manner have clarified the significance of—the antecedently given subjective forms of intuition. This

15   subject has already been discussed rather frequently, so I can begin with it at once today.

> Müller (1801–1858) was one of the leading physiologists of his time. His law of specific nerve energies is found in the fifth book of his monumental *Elements of Physiology* (1842):
>
>> Sensation consists in the sensorium receiving through the medium of the nerves, and as the result of the action of an external cause, a knowledge of certain qualities or conditions, not of external bodies, but of the nerves of sense themselves; and these qualities of the nerves of sense are in all different, the nerve of each sense having its own peculiar quality or energy. (p. 1065) . . . The nerve of each sense seems to be capable of one determinate kind of sensation only, and not of those proper to the other organs of sense; hence one nerve of sense cannot take the place and perform the function of the nerve of another sense. (p. 1069) . . . It is not known whether the essential cause of the peculiar "energy" of each nerve of sense is seated in the nerve itself, or in the parts of the brain and spinal cord with which it is connected; but it is certain that the central portions of the nerves included in the encephalon are susceptible of their peculiar sensations, independently of the more peripheral portion of the nervous cords which form the means of communication with the external organs of sense. (p. 1072)

Among the various kinds of sensations, two quite different distinctions must be noted. The most fundamental is that among sensations which belong to different senses, such as the differences among blue, warm, sweet, and high-pitched. In an earlier work I referred to these as differences in the *modality* of the sensations. They are so fundamental as to exclude any pos-

20   sible transition from one to another and any relationship of greater or less similarity. For example, one cannot ask whether sweet is more like red or more like blue.

Johann Gottlieb Fichte (1762–1814) rejected the view that there is an external world that exists independently of human will and values. In his idealism the ultimate reality is ego, which Fichte conceived as what we do (rather than what we are).

The second distinction, which is less fundamental, is that among the various sensations of the same sense. I have referred to these as differences in *quality*. Fichte thought of all the qualities of a single sense as constituting a *circle of quality;* what I have called differences of modality, he designated differences between circles of quality. Transitions and comparisons are possible only within each circle; we can cross over from blue through violet and carmine to scarlet, for example, and we can say that yellow is more like orange than like blue.

Physiological studies now teach that the more fundamental differences are completely independent of the kind of external agent by which the sensations are excited. They are determined solely and exclusively by the nerves of sense which receive the excitations. Excitations of the optic nerves produce only sensations of light, whether the nerves are excited by objective light (that is, by the vibrations in the ether), by electric currents conducted through the eye, by a blow on the eyeball, or by a strain in the nerve trunk during the eyes' rapid movements in vision. The sensations which result from the latter processes are so similar to those caused by objective light that for a long time men believed it was possible to produce light in the eye itself. It was Johannes Müller who showed that internal production of light does not take place and that the sensation of light exists only when the optic nerve is excited.

Every sensory nerve, then, when excited by even the most varied stimuli, produces a sensation only within its own specific circle of quality. The same external stimulus, therefore, if it strikes different nerves, produces diverse sensations, which are always within the circles of quality of the nerves excited. The same vibrations of the ether which the eye experiences as light, the skin feels as heat. The same vibrations of the air which the skin feels as a flutter, the ear hears as sound.

. . .

It is apparent that all these differences among the effects of light and sound are determined by the way in which the nerves of sense react. Our sensations are simply effects which are produced in our organs by objective causes; precisely how these effects manifest themselves depends principally and in essence upon the type of apparatus that reacts to the objective causes. What information, then, can the qualities of such sensations give us about the characteristics of the external causes and influences which produce them? Only this: our sensations are signs,

apparatus: sense organ

not images, of such characteristics. One expects an image to be similar in some respect to the object of which it is an image; in a statue one expects similarity of form, in a drawing similarity of perspective, in a painting similarity of color. A sign, however, need not be similar in any way to that of which it is a sign. The sole relationship between them is that the same object, appearing under the same conditions, must evoke the same sign; thus different signs always signify different causes or influences.

To popular opinion, which accepts on faith and trust the complete veridicality of the images which our senses apparently furnish of external objects, this relationship may seem very insignificant. In truth it is not, for with it something of the greatest importance can be accom-
65 plished: we can discover the lawful regularities in the processes of the external world. All natural laws assert that from initial conditions which are the same in some specific way, there always follow consequences which are the same in some other specific way. If the same kinds of things in the world of experience are indicated by the same signs, then the lawful succession of equal effects from equal causes will be related to a similar regular succession in the
70 realm of our sensations. If, for example, some kind of berry in ripening forms a red pigment and sugar at the same time, we shall always find a red color and a sweet taste together in our sensations of berries of this kind.

Thus, even if in their qualities our sensations are only signs whose specific nature depends completely upon our makeup or organization, they are not to be discarded as empty appear-
75 ances. They are still signs of something—something existing or something taking place—and given them we can determine the laws of these objects or these events. And that is something of the greatest importance!

Thus, our physiological makeup incorporates a pure form of intuition, insofar as the qualities of
80 sensation are concerned. Kant, however, went further. He claimed that, not only the qualities of sense experience, but also space and time are determined by the nature of our faculty of intuition, since we cannot perceive anything in the

> *pure form of intuition:* Helmholtz refers to the fact that activity of a given sensory nerve will always be experienced within the same sensory modality; see note (p. 339) about Müller.

85 external world which does not occur at some time and in some place and since temporal location is also a characteristic of all subjective experience. Kant therefore called time the a priori and necessary transcendental form of the inner, and space the corresponding form of the outer, intuition. Further, Kant considered that spatial characteristics belong no more to the world of
90 reality (the *dinge an sich*) than the colors we see belong to external objects. On the contrary, according to him, space is carried to objects by our eyes.

> *dinge an sich:* "things in themselves," things as they are, as opposed to things as they are perceived

Even in this claim scientific opinion can go along with Kant up to a certain point. Let us consider whether any sensible marks are present
95 in ordinary, immediate experience to which all perception of objects in space can be related. Indeed, we find such marks in connection with the fact that our body's movement sets us in varying spatial relations to the objects we perceive, so that the impressions which these objects make upon us change as we move. The impulse to move, which we initiate through the innervation of our motor nerves, is immediately perceptible. We *feel* that we are doing some-
100 thing when we initiate such an impulse. We do not know directly, of course, all that occurs; it is only through the science of physiology that we learn how we set the motor nerves in an excited condition, how these excitations are conducted to the muscles, and how the muscles

in turn contract and move the limbs. We are aware, however, without any scientific study, of the perceptible effects which follow each of the various innervations we initiate.

The fact that we become aware of these effects through frequently repeated trials and   105
observations can be demonstrated in many, many ways. Even as adults we can still learn the innervations necessary to pronounce the words of a foreign language, or in singing to produce some special kind of voice formation. We can learn the innervations necessary to move our ears, to turn our eyes inward or outward, to focus them upward or downward, and so on. The only difficulty in learning to do these things is that we must try to do them by using innervations   110
which are unknown, innervations which have not been necessary in movement previously executed. We know these innervations in no form and by no definable characteristics other than the fact that they produce the observable effects intended. This alone distinguishes the various innervations from one another.

If we initiate an impulse to move—if we shift our gaze, say, or move our hands, or walk back   115
and forth—the sensations belonging to some circles of quality (namely, those sensations due to objects in space) may be altered. Other psychical states and conditions that we are aware of in ourselves, however, such as recollections, intentions, desires, and moods, remain unchanged. In this way a thoroughgoing distinction may be established in our immediate experience between the former and the latter. If we use the term *spatial* to designate those   120
relations which we can alter directly by our volition but whose nature may still remain conceptually unknown to us, an awareness of mental states or conditions does not enter into spatial relations at all.

All sensations of external senses, however, must be preceded by some kind of innervation, that is, they must be spatially determined. Thus space, charged with the qualities of our sen-   125
sations of movement, will appear to us as that through which we move or that about which we gaze. In this sense spatial intuition is a subjective form of intuition, just as the qualities of sensation (red, sweet, cold) are. Naturally, this does not mean that the determination of the position of a specific object is only an illusion, any more than the qualities of sensation are.

From this point of view, space is the necessary form of outer intuition, since we consider only   130
what we perceive as spatially determined to constitute the external world. Those things which are not perceived in any spatial relation we think of as belonging to the world of inner intuition, the world of self-consciousness.

Space is an a priori form of intuition, necessarily prior to all experience, insofar as the perception of it is related to the possibility of motor volitions, the mental and physical capacity for   135
which must be provided by our physiological make-up before we can have intuitions of space.

signs or marks: bodily movements

There can be no doubt about the relationship between the sensible signs or marks mentioned above and the changes in our perception of objects in space which result from our movements.   140
. . . We still must consider the question, however, whether it is *only* from this source that all the specific characteristics of our intuition of space originate. To this end we must reflect further upon some of the conclusions concerning perception at which we have just arrived.

145 Let us try to set ourselves back to the state or condition of a man without any experience at all. In order to begin without any intuition of space, we must assume that such an individual no longer recognizes the effects of his own innervations, except to the extent that he has now learned how,
150 by means of his memory of a first innervation or by the execution of a second one contrary to the first, to return to the state out of which he originally moved. Since this mutual self-annulment of different innervations is completely independent of
155 what is actually perceived, the individual can discover how to initiate innervations without any prior knowledge of the external world.

Let us assume that the man at first finds himself to be just one object in a region of stationary
160 objects. As long as he initiates no motor impulses, his sensations will remain unchanged. However, if he makes some movement (if he moves his eyes or his hands, for example, or moves forward), his sensations will change. And if he returns (in mem-
165 ory or by another movement) to his initial state, all his sensations will again be the same as they were earlier.

If we call the entire group of sensation aggregates which can potentially be brought to con-
170 sciousness during a certain period of time by a specific, limited group of volitions the temporary *presentabilia*—in contrast to the *present,* that is, the sensation aggregate within this group which is the object of immediate awareness—then our
175 hypothetical individual is limited at any one time to a specific circle of *presentabilia,* out of which, however, he can make any aggregate present at any given moment by executing the proper movement. Every individual member of this group of
180 *presentabilia,* therefore, appears to him to exist at every moment of the period of time, regardless of his immediate present, for he has been able to observe any of them at any moment he wished to do so. This conclusion—that he could have

---

Helmholtz's approach here is similar to that of Condillac (1754/1930), who brought a statue to life and gave it one sense at a time. He then describes the growth of the statue's ideas of the world (time, space, and so on) as it acquires each sense. The point of Condillac's statue, like that of Helmholtz's present argument, is that all the mind's ideas—here, the concept of space—can be acquired through experience, and do not need to be built in.

What Helmholtz has just said is that the first thing we learn is that for a given movement (e.g., turn head left 30 degrees), we can make another movement (turn head right 30 degrees) that undoes the first movement. When we make the first movement, what we see—it doesn't matter what it is—is different from what we saw initially, and when we make the second movement, our perception is back to where we started out.

---

sensation aggregates: A sensation aggregate is the complete set of sensations that is experienced at a given moment. The *presentabilia,* or *presentables,* then, are the aggregates that, in a given stimulus context, are available to the observer, who may switch between sensation aggregates by means of certain voluntary motions. As a simple example, stare straight ahead, and close your left eye. The visual sensation you have now is one of the sensation aggregates that is available to you in this stimulus context. Without shifting your gaze, open your left eye and close your right. Now you have another sensation aggregate. These two aggregates are the presentabilia corresponding to "a specific, limited group of volitions," namely opening one eye and closing the other.

Later research has supported Helmholtz's implicit notion that voluntary motion is an essential ingredient in the development of spatial perception; see Held and Hein (1963); Walk, Shepherd, and Miller (1988).

observed them at any other moment of the period — if he had wished—should be regarded as a kind of inductive inference, since from any moment a successful inference can easily be made to any other moment of the given period of time.

In this way the idea of the simultaneous and continuous existence of a group of different but adjacent objects may be attained. *Adjacent* is a term with spatial connotations, but it is legitimate to use it here, since we have used *spatial* to define those relations which can be changed by volition. Moreover, we need not restrict the term *adjacent* so that it refers only to material objects. For example, it can legitimately be said that "to the right it is bright, to the left dark," and "forward there is opposition, behind there is nothing," in the case where "right" and "left" are only names for specific movements of the eyes and "forward" and "behind" for specific movements of the hands.

circles of presentabilia: Helmholtz is defining an object as the set of sensation aggregates that it permits, thus obviating the need for an (innate) concept of object.

At other times the circles of *presentabilia* related to this same group of volitions are different. In this way circles of *presentabilia*, along with their individual members, come to be something given to us, that is, they come to be *objects*. Those changes which we are able to bring about or put an end to by familiar acts of volition come to be separated from those which do not result from and cannot be set aside by such acts. This last statement is negative: in Fichte's quite appropriate terminology, the Non-Ego forces the recognition that it is distinct from the Ego.

When we inquire into the empirical conditions under which our intuition of space is formed, we must concentrate in particular upon the sense of touch, for the blind can form complete intuitions of space without the aid of vision. Even if space turns out to be less rich in objects for them than for people with vision, it seems highly improbable that the foundation of the intuition of space is completely different for the two classes of people. If, in the dark or with our eyes closed, we try to perceive only by touch, we are definitely able to feel the shapes of the objects lying around us, and we can determine them with accuracy and certainty. Moreover, we are able to do this with just one finger or even with a pencil held in the hand the way a surgeon holds a probe. Ordinarily, of course, if we want to find our way about in the dark we touch large objects with five or ten fingertips simultaneously. In this way we get from five to ten times as much information in a given period of time as we do with one finger. We also use the fingers to measure the sizes of objects, just as we measure with the tips of an open pair of compasses.

Berkeley (2.1) has a similar concern with the relation between vision and touch. Assuming that the objects of our perceptions are our sensations, what can it mean that we give the same name (e.g., *doorknob*) to a visual sensation and to a tactile sensation? How do we establish that there is in fact some external body that is the cause of both sensations?

230

It should be emphasized that with the sense of touch, the fact that we have an extended skin surface with many sensitive points on it is of secondary importance. What we are able to find out, for example, about the impression on a medal by the sensations in the skin when our hand is stationary is very slight and crude in comparison with what we can discover even

235

with the tip of a pencil when we move our hand. With the sense of sight, perception is more complicated due to the fact that besides the most sensitive spot on the retina, the *fovea centralis,* or pit, which in vision rushes as it were about the

240

visual field, there are also a great many other sensitive points acting at the same time and in a much richer way than is the case with the sense of touch.

> Another example of Helmholtz's point is the fact that a blind person reads Braille not by pressing her palm on the page but by moving her fingertips along each line of type.

> *rushes . . . about the visual field:* By running our fingers over an object we can pick up a good deal of information about it; likewise, by moving our eyes we are able to "point" the fovea—the retinal region of highest acuity—at important or interesting features in different parts of the visual field.

. . .

It is thus that our knowledge of the spatial arrangement of objects is attained. Judgments

245

concerning their size result from observations of the congruence of our hand with parts or points of an object's surface, or from the congruence of the retina with parts or points of the retinal image.

A strange consequence—a characteristic of the ideas in the minds of individuals with at least some experience—follows from the fact that the perceived spatial ordering of things originates

250

in the sequences in which the qualities of sensations are presented by our moving sense organs: the objects in the space around us appear to possess the qualities of our sensations. They appear to be red or green, cold or warm, to have an odor or a taste, and so on. Yet these qualities of sensations belong only to our nervous system and do not extend at all into the space around us. Even when we know this, however, the illusion does not cease, for *it is the*

255

primary and fundamental truth. The illusion is quite simply the sensations which are given to us in spatial order to begin with.

You can see how the most fundamental properties of our spatial intuition can be obtained in this way. Commonly, however, an intuition is taken to be something which is simply given, something which occurs without reflection or effort, something which

260

above all cannot be reduced to other mental processes. This popular interpretation, at least insofar as the intuition of space is concerned, is due in part to certain theorists in physiological optics and in part to a strict adherence to the philosophy of Kant. As is well known, Kant taught, not only that the general form of the intuition of space is given transcendentally, but also that this form possesses, originally and prior to all pos-

265

sible experience, certain more specific characteristics which are commonly given expression in the axioms of geometry. These axioms may be reduced to the following propositions:

1. Between two points there is only one possible shortest line. We call such a line *straight*.

2. A plane is determined by three points. A plane is a surface which contains completely any straight line between any two of its points.

3. Through any point there is only one possible line parallel to a given straight line. Two straight lines are parallel if they lie in the same plane and do not intersect upon any finite extension.

Kant used the alleged fact that these propositions of geometry appear to us necessarily true, along with the fact that we cannot imagine or represent to ourselves any irregularities in spatial relations, as direct proof that the axioms must be given prior to all experience. It follows that the conception of space contained in them or implied by them must also constitute a transcendental form of intuition independent of all experience.

. . .

The memory traces of previous experience play an . . . extensive and influential role in our visual observations. An observer who is not completely inexperienced receives without moving his eyes (this condition can be realized experimentally by using the momentary illumination of an electric discharge or by carefully and deliberately staring) images of the objects in front of him which are quite rich in content. We can easily confirm with our own eyes, however, that these images are much richer and especially much more precise if the gaze is allowed to move about the field of vision, in this way making use of the kind of spatial observations which I have previously described as the most fundamental. Indeed, we are so used to letting our eyes wander over the objects we are looking at that considerable practice is required before we succeed in making them—for purposes of research in physiological optics—fix on a point without wandering.

In my work on physiological optics I have tried to explain how our knowledge of the field open to vision is gained from visual images experienced as we move our eyes, given that there are some perceptible differences of location on the retina among otherwise qualitatively similar sensations. Following Lotze's terminology, these spatially different retinal sensations were called *local signs*. It is not necessary to know prior to visual experience that these signs are local signs, that is, that they are related to various objective differences in place. The fact that people blind from birth who afterward gain their sight by an operation cannot, before they have touched them, distinguish between such simple

> *Local sign* refers to a postulated sensory quality unique to each visual or tactile receptor. Thus when a retinal cell is active it provides the visual system with information about the intensity of the light falling on it, and, according to Rudolf Hermann Lotze (1817–1881), it also tells the visual system where it is—its local sign.

forms as a circle and a square by the use of their eyes has been confirmed even more fully by recent studies.

Investigations in physiology show that with the eyes alone we can achieve rather precise and reliable comparisons of various lines and angles in the field of vision, provided that through the eyes' normal movements the images of these figures can be formed quickly one after another on the retina. We can even estimate the actual size and distance of objects which are not too far away from us with considerable accuracy by means of changing perspectives in our visual field, although making such judgments in the three dimensions of space is much more complicated than it is in the case of a plane image. As is well known, one of the greatest difficulties in drawing is being able to free oneself from the influence which the idea of the true size of a perceived object involuntarily has upon us. These are all facts which we would expect if we obtain our knowledge of local signs through experience. We can learn the changing sensory signs of something which remains objectively constant much more easily and reliably than we can the signs of something which changes with every movement of the body, as perspective images do.

To a great many physiologists, however, whose point of view we shall call nativistic, in contrast to the empirical position which I have sought to defend, the idea that knowledge of the field of vision is acquired is unacceptable. It is unacceptable to them because they have not made clear to themselves what even the example of learning a language shows so clearly, namely, how much can be explained in terms of the accumulation of memory impressions. Because of this lack of appreciation of the power of memory, a number of different attempts have been made to account for at least part of visual perception through innate mechanisms by means of which specific sensory impressions supposedly induce specific innate spatial ideas. In an earlier work I tried to show that all hypotheses of this kind which had been formulated were insufficient, since cases were always being discovered in which our visual perceptions are more precisely in agreement with reality than

> Helmholtz is probably referring to volume 3 of his *Optics* (1867/1962).

is stated in these hypotheses. With each of them we are forced to the additional assumption that ultimately experience acquired during movement may very well prevail over the hypothetical inborn intuition and thus accomplish in opposition to it what, according to the empirical hypothesis, it would have accomplished without such a hindrance.

Thus nativistic hypotheses concerning knowledge of the field of vision explain nothing. In the first place, they only acknowledge the existence of the facts to be explained, while refusing to refer these facts to well-confirmed mental processes which even they must rely on in certain cases. In the second place, the assumption common to all nativistic theories—that ready-made ideas of objects can be produced by means of organic mechanisms—appears much more rash and questionable than the assumption of the empirical theory that the noncognitive materials of experience exist as a result of external influences and that all ideas are formed out of these materials according to the laws of thought.

In the third place, the nativistic assumptions are unnecessary. The single objection that can be raised against the empirical theory concerns the sureness of the movements of many newborn or newly hatched animals. The smaller the mental endowment of these animals, the sooner they learn how to do all that they are capable of doing. The narrower the path on which their thoughts must travel, the easier they find their way. The newborn human child, on the other hand, is at first awkward in vision; it requires several days to learn to judge by its visual images the direction in which to turn its head in order to reach its mother's breast.

The behavior of young animals is, in general, quite independent of individual experience. Whatever these instincts are which guide them—whether they are the direct hereditary transmission of their parents' ideas, whether they have to do only with pleasure and pain, or whether they are motor impulses related to certain aggregates of experience—we do not know. In the case of human beings the last phenomenon is becoming increasingly well understood. Careful and critically employed investigations are most urgently needed on this whole subject.

Such investigations have been carried out by, for example, Gibson and Walk (1960).

Arrangements such as those which the nativistic hypotheses assume can at best have only a certain pedagogical value; that is, they may facilitate the initial understanding of uniform, lawful relations. And the empirical position is, to be sure, in agreement with the nativistic on a number of points—for example, that local signs of adjacent places on the retina are more similar than those farther apart and that the corresponding points on the two retinas are more similar than those that do not correspond. For our present purposes, however, it is sufficient to know that complete spatial intuition can be achieved by the blind and that for people with vision, even if the nativistic hypotheses should prove partially correct, the final and most exact determinations of spatial relations are obtained through observations made while moving in various ways.

I should like, now, to return to the discussion of the most fundamental facts of perception. As we have seen, we not only have changing sense impressions which come to us without our doing anything; we also perceive while we are being active or moving about. In this way we acquire knowledge of the uniform relations between our innervations and the various aggregates of impressions included in the circles of *presentabilia*. Each movement we make by which we alter the appearance of objects should be thought of as an experiment designed to test whether we have understood correctly the invariant relations of the phenomena before us, that is, their existence in definite spatial relations.

The persuasive force of these experiments is much greater than the conviction we feel when observations are carried out without any action on our part, for with these experiments the chains of causes run through our consciousness. One factor in these causes is our volitions, which are known to us by an inner intuition; we know, moreover, from what motives they arise. In these volitions originates the chain of physical causes which results in the final effect of the experiment, so we are dealing with a process passing from a known beginning to a known result. The two essential conditions necessary for the highest degree of conviction are (1) that our volitions not be determined by the physical causes which simultaneously determine the physical processes and (2) that our volitions not influence psychically the resulting perceptions.

. . .

What we unquestionably can find as a fact, without any hypothetical element whatsoever, is the lawful regularity of phenomena. From the very first, in the case where we perceive stationary objects distributed before us in space, this perception involves the recognition of a uniform or lawlike connection between our movements and the sensations which result from them.

390 Thus even the most elementary ideas contain a mental element and occur in accordance with the laws of thought. Everything that is added in intuition to the raw materials of sensation may be considered mental, provided of course that we accept the

395 extended meaning of *mental* discussed earlier.

> *extended meaning:* Helmholtz is referring to the *unconscious inference* by which perception is generated.

If "to conceive" means "to form concepts," and if it is true that in a concept we gather together a class of objects which possess some common characteristic, then it follows by analogy that the concept of some phenomenon which changes in time must encompass that which remains the same during that period of time. As

400 Schiller said, the wise man

> Seeks for the familiar law amidst the awesome multiplicity of accidental occurrences,
>
> Seeks for the eternal Pole Star amidst the constant flight of appearances.[2]

That which, independently of any and everything else, remains the same during all temporal changes, we call a *substance;* the invariant relation between variable but related quantities

405 we call a *law.* We perceive only the latter directly. Knowledge of substances can be attained only through extensive investigation, and as further investigation is always possible, such knowledge remains open to question. At an earlier time both light and heat were thought to be substances; later it turned out that both were only transitory forms of motion. We must therefore always be prepared for some new analysis of what are now known as the chemical elements.

410 The first product of the rational conception of phenomena is its lawfulness or regularity. If we have fully investigated some regularity, have established its conditions completely and with certainty and, at the same time, with complete generality, so that for all possible subsequent cases the effect is unequivocally determined—and if we have therefore arrived at the conviction that the law is true and will continue to hold true at all times and in all cases—then we rec-

415 ognize it as something existing independently of our ideas, and we label it a *cause,* or that which underlies or lies behind the changes taking place. (Note that the meaning I give to the word *cause* and its application are both exactly specified, although in ordinary language the word is also variously used to mean antecedent or motive.)

Insofar as we recognize a law as a power analogous to our will, that is, as something giving

420 rise to our perceptions as well as determining the course of natural processes, we call it a *force.* The idea of a force acting in opposition to us arises directly out of the nature of our simplest perceptions and the way in which they occur. From the beginning of our lives, the changes which we cause ourselves by the acts of our will are distinguished from those which are neither made nor can be set aside by our will. Pain, in particular, gives us the most compelling

---

[2] Friedrich von Schiller, *Der Spaziergang* ("The Walk").

awareness of the power or force of reality. The emphasis falls here on the observable fact that   425
the perceived circle of *presentabilia* is not created by a conscious act of our mind or will. Fichte's
Non-Ego is an apt and precise expression for this. In dreaming, too, that which a person
believes he sees and feels does not appear to be called forth by his will or by the known relations of his ideas, for these also may often be unconscious. They constitute a Non-Ego for the
dreamer too. It is the same for the idealists who see the Non-Ego as the world of ideas of the   430
World Spirit.

We have in the German language a most appropriate word for that which stands behind the
changes of phenomena and acts, namely, "the real" *(das Wirkliche)*. This word implies only action;
it lacks the collateral meaning of existing as substance, which the concept of "the actual" *(das
Reelle)* or "the essential" *(das Sachliche)* includes. In the concept of "the objective" *(das Objective)*,   435
on the other hand, the notion of the complete form of objects is introduced, something that
does not correspond to anything in our most basic perceptions. In the case of the logically consistent dreamer, it should be noted, we must use the words "effective" and "real" *(wirksam* and
wirklich) to characterize those psychical conditions or motives whose sensations correspond
uniformly to, and which are experienced as the momentary states of, his dreamed world.   440

In general, it is clear that a distinction between thought and reality is possible only when we
know how to make the distinction between that which the ego can and that which it cannot
change. This, however, is possible only when we know the uniform consequences which
volitions have in time. From this fact it can be seen that conformity to law is the essential condition which something must satisfy in order to be considered real.   445

I need not go into the fact that it is a *contradictio in abjecto* to try to present the actual
(das Reelle) or Kant's *ding an sich* in positive state-
ments without comprehending it within our
forms of representation. This fact has been
pointed out often enough already. What we can   450
attain, however, is knowledge of the lawful order in the realm of reality, since this can actually be presented in the sign system of our sense impressions.

contradictio in abjecto: an absurdity

All things transitory

But as symbols are sent.[3]

I take it to be a propitious sign that we find Goethe with us here, as well as further along on   455
this same path. Whenever we are dealing with a question requiring a broad outlook, we can
trust completely his clear, impartial view as to where the truth lies. He demanded of science
that it be only an artistic arrangement of facts and that it form no abstract concepts concerning them, for he considered abstract concepts to be empty names which only hide the facts.
In somewhat the same sense, Gustav Kirchhoff has recently stated that the task of the most   460

---

[3] *Faust,* Part II. Translated by Bayard Taylor.

abstract of the natural sciences, mechanics, is to describe completely and in the simplest possible way the kinds of motion appearing in nature.

As to the question whether abstract concepts hide the facts or not, this indeed happens if we remain in the realm of abstract concepts and do not examine their factual content, that is, if we do not try to make clear what new and observable invariant relations follow from them. A correctly formulated hypothesis, as we observed a moment ago, has its empirical content expressed in the form of a general law of nature. The hypothesis itself is an attempt to rise to more general and more comprehensive uniformities or regularities. Anything new, however, that an hypothesis asserts about facts must be established or confirmed by observation and experiment. Hypotheses which do not have such factual reference or which do not lead to trustworthy, unequivocal statements concerning the facts falling under them should be considered only worthless phrases.

Every reduction of some phenomenon to underlying substances and forces indicates that something unchangeable and final has been found. We are never justified, of course, in making an unconditional assertion of such a reduction. Such a claim is not permissible because of the incompleteness of our knowledge and because of the nature of the inductive inferences upon which our perception of reality depends.

Every inductive inference is based upon the belief that some given relation, previously observed to be regular or uniform, will continue to hold in all cases which may be observed. In effect, every inductive inference is based upon a belief in the lawful regularity of everything that happens. This uniformity or lawful regularity, however, is also the condition of conceptual understanding. Thus belief in uniformity or lawful regularity is at the same time belief in the possibility of understanding natural phenomena conceptually. If we assume that this comprehension or understanding of natural phenomena can be achieved—that is, if we believe that we shall be able to discern something fundamental and unchanging which is the cause of the changes we observe—then we accept a regulative principle in our thinking. It is called the law of causality, and it expresses our belief in the complete comprehensibility of the world.

Conceptual understanding, in the sense in which I have just described it, is the method by which the world is submitted to our thoughts, facts are ordered, and the future predicted. It is our right and duty to extend the application of this method to all occurrences, and significant results have already been achieved in this way. We have no justification other than its results, however, for the application of the law of causality. We might have lived in a world in which every atom was different from every other one and where nothing was stable. In such a world there would be no regularity whatsoever, and our conscious activities would cease.

The law of causality is in reality a transcendental law, a law which is given a priori. It is impossible to prove it by experience, for, as we have seen, even the most elementary levels of experience are impossible without inductive inferences, that is, without the law of causality. And even if the most complete experience should teach us that everything previously observed has occurred uniformly—a point concerning which we are not yet certain—we could conclude only by inductive inferences, that is, by presupposing the law of causality, that the law of causality will also be valid in the future. We can do no more than accept the proverb, "Have faith and keep on!"

The earth's inadequacies

Will then prove fruitful.[4]

That is the answer we must give to the question: what is true in our ideas? In giving this answer we find ourselves at the foundation of Kant's system and in agreement with what has always seemed to me the most fundamental advance in his philosophy.   505

I have frequently noted in my previous works the agreement between the more recent physiology of the senses and Kant's teachings. I have not meant, of course, that I would swear *in verba magistri* to all his more minor points. I believe that the most fundamental advance of recent times   510
must be judged to be the analysis of the concept of intuition into the elementary processes of thought. Kant failed to carry out this analysis or resolution; this is one reason why he considered the axioms of geometry to be transcendental propositions. It has   515
been the physiological investigations of sense perception which have led us to recognize the most basic or elementary kinds of judgment, to inferences which are not expressible in words. These judgments or inferences will, of course, remain   520
unknown and inaccessible to philosophers as long as they inquire only into knowledge expressed in language.

> The Roman poet Horace (1st century BCE) wrote *Nullius addictus iurare in verba magistri* ("I am not bound to believe in the word of any master") (Epistles, book I, epistle 1, line 14). A condensed version, *Nullius in verba,* is the motto of the Royal Society, and Helmholtz expresses the same independent empirical spirit by saying that he will not "swear to the word of the master."

. . .

FOR DISCUSSION

1. Is the specific quality of a sensation (e.g., blue, warm, sweet) built into the mind, determined by the stimulus, or learned?

2. Why and how does Helmholtz reject Kant's claim that space and time are innate ideas?

3. Give an example of the "lawlike connection between our movements and the sensations which result from them" (p. 349, line 390).

4. What are examples of things the ego can and cannot change?

5. How is Helmholtz's empiricism different from Locke's (4.2)?

6. What do you think Chomsky would say about Helmholtz's notion that we do not need to build in things like object constancy because we can learn from experience?

---

[4] Faust, Part II.

Sigmund Freud (1856–1939)
Instincts and Their Vicissitudes (1915)

Like any physician, Freud made his living treating patients. To do this he had to regard a given patient as an individual, and to focus on the ways—neurotic symptoms, compulsions, obsessions, phobias, and the like—in which this patient differed from other people. Then he needed to determine the specific and unique features of the patient's life experience that might explain the symptoms; only then could Freud relieve the symptoms.

Seeing patients fed his family, but in his heart Freud thought of himself as a scientist, and in that capacity his goal was not simply to describe individual differences (which in the psychiatric context tend to be pathological symptoms), but to discover universal features of the mind. Familiar examples of these features are the tripartite self (id/ego/superego), the stages of psychosexual development (oral/anal/phallic/genital), and ego defense mechanisms (regression, displacement, sublimation, and so forth).

These two faces of Freud's work were not, however, independent of one another. On the contrary: neither could have existed without the other. Treating patients supplied Freud with vital raw material for his theoretical work (see, for example, *Studies on Hysteria* [Breuer & Freud, 1895]), and his theories of the mind provided a context in which to understand a given patient's pathology.

Instinct is a problematic word. There is disagreement among psychologists, ethologists, and social scientists over what instincts are and whether any exist in humans. Among those who accept instincts, there is further disagreement about how many instincts we have and what they are. We will attempt to sidestep this issue by noting that the German *Trieb,* which has been translated here as *instinct,* means something closer to its English cognate *drive.* (German also

Source: Freud, S. (1957). *Standard Edition of the Complete Psychological Works of Sigmund Freud* (J. Strachey, Ed., v. 14). London: Hogarth Press. Reprinted with permission of Sigmund Freud Copyrights, The Institute of Psycho-Analysis, Hogarth Press, Random House, Ltd., and Perseus Books Group. [Bracketed material in the text and in the footnotes is by Freud's translator(s) and editor(s).]

has the word *instinkt,* which Freud uses elsewhere.) Which word we use matters less than that we try to understand what Freud means by a *Trieb.*

In the present reading Freud does two things, corresponding to his two interdependent roles as scientist and healer. On the one hand, he describes the human instincts, and on the other, he describes the ways these instincts can vary and express themselves in different ways.

. . .

A conventional basic concept . . . which is indispensable to us in psychology, is that of an 'instinct.' Let us try to give a content to it by approaching it from different angles.

First, from the angle of *physiology*. This has given us the concept of a 'stimulus' and the pattern of the reflex arc, according to which a stimulus applied to living tissue (nervous substance) *from* the outside is discharged by action *to* the outside. This action is expedient in so far as it withdraws the stimulated substance from the influence of the stimulus, removes it out of its range of operation.

> *Stimulus,* as Freud uses the word here, has a narrower meaning than it does in the context of sensation and perception. Freud is speaking of stimuli as substances and events that the organism must do something about ("discharge").

What is the relation of 'instinct' to 'stimulus'? There is nothing to prevent our subsuming the concept of 'instinct' under that of 'stimulus' and saying that an instinct is a stimulus applied to the mind. But we are immediately set on our guard against *equating* instinct and mental stimulus. There are obviously other stimuli to the mind besides those of an instinctual kind, stimuli which behave far more like physiological ones. For example, when a strong light falls on the eye, it is not an instinctual stimulus; it *is* one, however, when a dryness of the mucous membrane of the pharynx or an irritation of the mucous membrane of the stomach makes itself felt.[1]

We have now obtained the material necessary for distinguishing between instinctual stimuli and other (physiological) stimuli that operate on the mind. In the first place, an instinctual stimulus does not arise from the external world but from within the organism itself. For this reason it operates differently upon the mind and different actions are necessary in order to remove it. Further, all that is essential in a stimulus is covered if we assume that it operates with a single impact, so that it can be disposed of by a single expedient action. A typical instance of this is motor flight from the source of stimulation. These impacts may, of course, be repeated and summated, but that makes no difference to our notion of the process and to the conditions for the removal of the stimulus. An instinct, on the other hand, never operates as a force giving a *momentary* impact but always as a *constant* one. Moreover, since it impinges not from without but from within the organism, no flight can avail against it. A better term for an instinctual stimulus is a 'need.' What does away with a need is 'satisfaction.' This can be attained only by an appropriate ('adequate') alteration of the internal source of stimulation.

Let us imagine ourselves in the situation of an almost entirely helpless living organism, as yet unorientated in the world, which is receiving stimuli in its nervous substance. This organism will very soon be in a position to make a first distinction and a first orientation. On the one hand, it will be aware of stimuli which can be avoided by muscular action (flight); these it ascribes to an external world. On the other hand, it will also be aware of stimuli against which such action is of no avail and whose character of constant pressure persists in spite of it; these stimuli are the signs of an internal world, the evidence of instinctual needs. The perceptual

---

[1] Assuming, of course, that these internal processes are the organic basis of the respective needs of thirst and hunger.

substance of the living organism will thus have found in the efficacy of its muscular activity a basis for distinguishing between an 'outside' and an 'inside.' 40

We thus arrive at the essential nature of instincts in the first place by considering their main characteristics—their origin in sources of stimulation within the organism and their appearance as a constant force—and from this we deduce one of their further features, namely, that no actions of flight avail against them. In the course of this discussion, however, we cannot fail to be struck by something that obliges us to make a further admission. In order to guide us in deal- 45 ing with the field of psychological phenomena, we do not merely apply certain conventions to our empirical material as basic *concepts,* we also make use of a number of complicated *postulates.* We have already alluded to the most important of these, and all we need now do is to state it expressly. This postulate is of a biological nature, and makes use of the concept of 'purpose' (or perhaps of expediency) and runs as follows: the nervous system is an apparatus which 50 has the function of getting rid of the stimuli that reach it, or of reducing them to the lowest possible level; or which, if it were feasible, would maintain itself in an altogether unstimulated condition. Let us for the present not take exception to the indefiniteness of this idea and let us assign to the nervous system the task—speaking in general terms—of *mastering stimuli.* We then see how greatly the simple pattern of the physiological reflex is complicated by the intro- 55 duction of instincts. External stimuli impose only the single task of withdrawing from them; this is accomplished by muscular movements, one of which eventually achieves that aim and there-after, being the expedient movement, becomes a hereditary disposition. Instinctual stimuli, which originate from within the organism, cannot be 60 dealt with by this mechanism. Thus they make far higher demands on the nervous system and cause it to undertake involved and interconnected activities by which the external world is so changed as to afford satisfaction to the internal source of stim- 65 ulation. Above all, they oblige the nervous system to renounce its ideal intention of keeping off stim-

> *becomes hereditary:* Movements that are more effective with respect to the organism's goal of "mastering stimuli" enhance that organism's reproductive fitness and are therefore more likely to be preserved—in the species—than less effective movements.

uli, for they maintain an incessant and unavoidable afflux of stimulation. We may therefore well conclude that instincts and not external stimuli are the true motive forces behind the advances that have led the nervous system, with its unlimited capacities, to its present high level of devel- 70 opment. There is naturally nothing to prevent our supposing that the instincts themselves are, at least in part, precipitates of the effects of external stimulation, which in the course of phylogenesis have brought about modifications in the living 75 substance.

> The *pleasure principle* might be thought of as the id's mission statement: to gratify needs immediately and to avoid pain. The idea was introduced in 1848 by Gustav Fechner (1801–1887), a physicist, mystic, and the founder of psychophysics, and taken up by Freud in his *Interpretation of Dreams* (1900).

When we further find that the activity of even the most highly developed mental apparatus is subject to the pleasure principle, i.e. is automatically regulated by feelings belonging to the 80 pleasure–unpleasure series, we can hardly reject the further hypothesis that these feelings reflect the manner in which the process of mastering stimuli takes place—certainly in the sense that unpleasurable feelings are connected with an increase and pleasurable feelings with a decrease of stimulus. We will, however, carefully preserve this assumption in its present highly indefinite form, until we succeed, if that is possible, in discovering what sort of relation exists between pleasure and unpleasure, on the one hand, and fluctuations in the amounts of stimulus affecting mental life, on the other. It is certain that many very various relations of this kind, and not very simple ones, are possible.[2]

If now we apply ourselves to considering mental life from a *biological* point of view, an 'instinct' appears to us as a concept on the frontier between the mental and the somatic, as the psychical representative of the stimuli originating from within the organism and reaching the mind, as a measure of the demand made upon the mind for work in consequence of its connection with the body.

We are now in a position to discuss certain terms which are used in reference to the concept of an instinct—for example, its 'pressure,' its 'aim,' its 'object' and its 'source.'

By the pressure [*Drang*] of an instinct we understand its motor factor, the amount of force or the measure of the demand for work which it represents. The characteristic of exercising pressure is common to all instincts; it is in fact their very essence. Every instinct is a piece of activity; if we speak loosely of passive instincts, we can only mean instincts whose *aim* is passive.

The aim [*Ziel*] of an instinct is in every instance satisfaction, which can only be obtained by removing the state of stimulation at the source of the instinct. But although the ultimate aim of each instinct remains unchangeable, there may yet be different paths leading to the same ultimate aim; so that an instinct may be found to have various nearer or intermediate aims,

---

[2] [It will be seen that two principles are here involved. One of these is the 'principle of constancy.' It is stated again in *Beyond the Pleasure Principle* (Freud, 1920, p. 9), as follows: 'The mental apparatus endeavours to keep the quantity of excitation present in it as low as possible or at least to keep it constant.' For this principle Freud, in the same work (ibid., p. 56), adopted the term 'Nirvana principle.' The second principle involved is the 'pleasure principle,' stated at the beginning of the paragraph to which this note is appended. It, too, is restated in *Beyond the Pleasure Principle* (ibid., p. 7): 'The course taken by mental events is automatically regulated by the pleasure principle. . . . [That course] takes a direction such that its final outcome coincides with . . . an avoidance of unpleasure or a production of pleasure.' Freud seems to have assumed to begin with that these two principles were closely correlated and even identical. Thus, in his 'Project for a scientific psychology' of 1895 (Freud, 1954, Part I, Section 8) he writes: 'Since we have certain knowledge of a trend in psychical life towards avoiding unpleasure, we are tempted to identify that trend with the primary trend towards inertia [i.e. towards avoiding excitation].' A similar view is taken in Chapter VII (E) of *The Interpretation of Dreams* (Freud, 1900, p. 598). In the passage in the text above, however, a doubt appears to be expressed as to the completeness of the correlation between the two principles. This doubt is carried farther in *Beyond the Pleasure Principle* (Freud, 1920, p. 8 & p. 63) and is discussed at some length in 'The Economic Problem of Masochism' (Freud, 1924). Freud there argues that the two principles cannot be identical, since there are unquestionably states of increasing tension which are pleasurable (e.g. sexual excitement), and he goes on to suggest (what had already been hinted at in the two passages in *Beyond the Pleasure Principle* just referred to) that the pleasurable or unpleasurable quality of a state may be related to a *temporal* characteristic (or rhythm) of the changes in the quantity of excitation present. He concludes that in any case the two principles must not be regarded as identical: the pleasure principle is a *modification* of the Nirvana principle. The Nirvana principle, he maintains, is to be attributed to the 'death instinct,' and its modification into the pleasure principle is due to the influence of the 'life instinct' or libido.]

which are combined or interchanged with one another. Experience permits us also to speak of instincts which are 'inhibited in their aim,' in the case of processes which are allowed to make 105 some advance towards instinctual satisfaction but are then inhibited or deflected. We may suppose that even processes of this kind involve a partial satisfaction.

The object [*Objekt*] of an instinct is the thing in regard to which or through which the instinct is able to achieve its aim. It is what is most variable about an instinct and is not originally connected with it, but becomes assigned to it only in consequence of being peculiarly fitted to 110 make satisfaction possible. The object is not necessarily something extraneous: it may equally well be a part of the subject's own body. It may be changed any number of times in the course of the vicissitudes which the instinct undergoes during its existence; and highly important parts are played by this displacement of instinct. It may happen that the same object serves for the satisfaction of several instincts simultaneously, a phenomenon which Adler [1908] has called 115 a 'confluence' of instincts [*Triebverschrankung*]. A particularly close attachment of the instinct to its object is distinguished by the term 'fixation.' This frequently occurs at very early periods of the development of an instinct and puts an end to its mobility through its intense opposition to detachment.

By the source [*Quelle*] of an instinct is meant the somatic process which occurs in an organ 120 or part of the body and whose stimulus is represented in mental life by an instinct. We do not know whether this process is invariably of a chemical nature or whether it may also correspond to the release of other, e.g. mechanical, forces. The study of the sources of instincts lies outside the scope of psychology. Although instincts are wholly determined by their origin in a somatic source, in mental life we know them only by their aims. An exact knowledge of the sources of 125 an instinct is not invariably necessary for purposes of psychological investigation; sometimes its source may be inferred from its aim.

Are we to suppose that the different instincts which originate in the body and operate on the mind are also distinguished by different *qualities,* and that that is why they behave in qualitatively different ways in mental life? This supposition does not seem to be justified; we are 130 much more likely to find the simpler assumption sufficient—that the instincts are all qualitatively alike and owe the effect they make only to the amount of excitation they carry, or perhaps, in addition, to certain functions of that quantity. What distinguishes from one another the mental effects produced by the various instincts may be traced to the difference in their sources. In any event, it is only in a later connection that we shall be able to make plain what 135 the problem of the quality of instincts signifies.[3]

What instincts should we suppose there are, and how many? There is obviously a wide opportunity here for arbitrary choice. No objection can be made to anyone's employing the concept of an instinct of play or of destruction or of gregariousness, when the subject-matter demands it and the limitations of psychological analysis allow of it. Nevertheless, we 140 should not neglect to ask ourselves whether instinctual motives like these, which are so highly specialized on the one hand, do not admit of further dissection in accordance with the

---

[3] [It is not clear what 'later connection' Freud had in mind.]

sources of the instinct, so that only primal instincts—those which cannot be further dissected—can lay claim to importance.

145   I have proposed that two groups of such primal instincts should be distinguished: the *ego,* or *self-preservative,* instincts and the *sexual* instincts. But this supposition has not the status of a necessary postulate, as has, for instance, our assumption about the biological purpose of the mental apparatus; it is merely a working hypothesis, to be retained only so long as it proves useful, and it will make little difference to the results of our work of description and classification

150 if it is replaced by another. The occasion for this hypothesis arose in the course of the evolution of psycho-analysis, which was first employed upon the psychoneuroses, or, more precisely, upon the group described as 'transference neuroses' (hysteria and obsessional neurosis); these showed that at the root of all such affections there is to be found a conflict between the claims of sexuality and those of the ego. . . . The contribution which biology has to make here

155 certainly does not run counter to the distinction between sexual and ego-instincts. Biology teaches that sexuality is not to be put on a par with other functions of the individual; for its purposes go beyond the individual and have as their content the production of new individuals— that is, the preservation of the species. It shows, further, that two views, seemingly equally well-founded, may be taken of the relation between the ego and sexuality. On the one view,

160 the individual is the principal thing, sexuality is one of its activities and sexual satisfaction one of its needs; while on the other view the individual is a temporary and transient appendage to the quasi-immortal germ-plasm,which is entrusted to him by the process of generation.

> *germ plasm:* the genetic material

   . . .

165   This much can be said by way of a general characterization of the sexual instincts. They are numerous, emanate from a great variety of organic sources, act in the first instance independently of one another and only achieve a more or less complete synthesis at a late stage. The aim which each of them strives for is the attainment of 'organ-pleasure';[4] only when synthesis is achieved do they enter the service of the reproductive function and thereupon

170 become generally recognizable as sexual instincts. At their first appearance they are attached to the instincts of self-preservation, from which they only gradually become separated; in their choice of object, too, they follow the paths that are indicated to them by the ego-instincts. A portion of them remains associated with the ego-instincts throughout life and fur-

175 nishes them with libidinal components, which in normal functioning easily escape notice and are revealed clearly only by the onset of illness. They

> *libidinal:* The libido is the energy associated with the sexual instincts.

are distinguished by possessing the capacity to act vicariously for one another to a wide extent and by being able to change their objects readily. In consequence of the latter

---

[4] ['Organ-pleasure' (i.e. pleasure attached to one particular bodily organ) seems to be used here for the first time by Freud.]

Sublimation (from Latin *sublimare,* to elevate) is a defense mechanism that allows an instinct that is denied direct gratification to be gratified indirectly through a more acceptable kind of behavior. Freud regarded much of artistic activity, for example, as sublimated expression of libido.

properties they are capable of functions which are far removed from their original purposive actions—capable, that is, of 'sublimation.'

Our inquiry into the various vicissitudes which instincts undergo in the process of development and in the course of life must be confined to the sexual instincts, which are the more familiar to us. Observation shows us that an instinct may undergo the following vicissitudes:—

Reversal into its opposite.

Turning round upon the subject's own self.

Repression.

Sublimation.

Since I do not intend to treat of sublimation here and since repression requires a special chapter to itself, it only remains for us to describe and discuss the two first points. Bearing in mind that there are motive forces which work against an instinct's being carried through in an unmodified form, we may also regard these vicissitudes as modes of *defence* against the instincts.

Reversal of an instinct into its opposite resolves on closer examination into two different processes: a change from activity to passivity, and a reversal of its content. The two processes, being different in their nature, must be treated separately.

Examples of the first process are met with in the two pairs of opposites: sadism–masochism and scopophilia–exhibitionism. The reversal affects only the *aims* of the instincts. The active aim (to torture, to look at) is replaced by the passive aim (to be tortured, to be looked at). Reversal of *content* is found in the single instance of the transformation of love into hate.

The turning round of an instinct upon the subject's own self is made plausible by the reflection that masochism is actually sadism turned round upon the subject's own ego, and that exhibitionism includes looking at his own body. Analytic observation, indeed, leaves us in no doubt that the masochist shares in the enjoyment of the assault upon himself, and that the exhibitionist shares in the enjoyment of [the sight of] his exposure. The essence of the process is thus the change of the *object,* while the aim remains unchanged. We cannot fail to notice, however, that in these examples the turning round upon the subject's self and the transformation from activity to passivity converge or coincide.

To elucidate the situation, a more thorough investigation is essential.

In the case of the pair of opposites sadism–masochism, the process may be represented as follows:

(a) Sadism consists in the exercise of violence or power upon some other person as object.

(b) This object is given up and replaced by the subject's self. With the turning round upon the self the change from an active to a passive instinctual aim is also effected.

(c) An extraneous person is once more sought as object; this person, in consequence of the alteration which has taken place in the instinctual aim, has to take over the role of the subject.[5]

220

Case *(c)* is what is commonly termed masochism. Here, too, satisfaction follows along the path of the original sadism, the passive ego placing itself back in phantasy in its first role, which has now in fact been taken over by the extraneous subject. Whether there is, besides this, a more direct masochistic satisfaction is highly doubtful. . . .

225   Our view of sadism is further prejudiced by the circumstance that this instinct, side by side with its general aim (or perhaps, rather, within it), seems to strive towards the accomplishment of a quite special aim—not only to humiliate and master, but, in addition, to inflict pains. Psychoanalysis would appear to show that the infliction of pain plays no part among the original purposive actions of the instinct. A sadistic child takes no account of whether or not he inflicts pains,

230   nor does he intend to do so. But when once the transformation into masochism has taken place, the pains are very well fitted to provide a passive masochistic aim; for we have every reason to believe that sensations of pain, like other unpleasurable sensations, trench upon sexual excitation and produce a pleasurable condition, for the sake

235   of which the subject will even willingly experience the unpleasure of pain. When once feeling pains has become a masochistic aim, the sadistic aim of

> *trench upon:* to verge, encroach. Baines's translation (Freud, 1915/1963) gives *extends into.*

causing pains can arise also, retrogressively; for while these pains are being inflicted on other people, they are enjoyed masochistically by the subject through his identification of himself with

240   the suffering object. In both cases, of course, it is not the pain itself which is enjoyed, but the accompanying sexual excitation—so that this can be done especially conveniently from the sadistic position. The enjoyment of pain would thus be an aim which was originally masochistic, but which can only become an instinctual aim in someone who was originally sadistic.

. . .

Rather different and simpler findings are afforded by the investigation of another pair of

245   opposites—the instincts whose respective aim is to look and to display oneself (scopophilia and exhibitionism, in the language of the perversions). Here again we may postulate the same stages as in the previous instance:—*(a)* Looking as an *activity* directed towards an extraneous object. *(b)* Giving up of the object and turning of the scopophilic instinct towards a part of the subject's own body; with this, transformation to passivity and setting up of a new aim—that

250   of being looked at. *(c)* Introduction of a new subject to whom one displays oneself in order to be looked at by him. Here, too, it can hardly be doubted that the active aim appears before the passive, that looking precedes being looked at. But there is an important divergence from what

---

[5] [Though the general sense of these passages is clear, there may be some confusion in the use of the word 'subject.' As a rule 'subject' and 'object' are used respectively for the person in whom an instinct (or other state of mind) originates, and the person or thing to which it is directed. Here, however, 'subject' seems to be used for the person who plays the active part in the relationship—the agent. The word is more obviously used in this sense in the parallel passage in lines 247–251 and elsewhere below.]

happens in the case of sadism, in that we can recognize in the case of the scopophilic instinct a yet earlier stage than that described as *(a)*. For the beginning of its activity the scopophilic instinct is auto-erotic: it has indeed an object, but that object is part of the subject's own body.   255
It is only later that the instinct is led, by a process of comparison, to exchange this object for an analogous part of someone else's body—stage *(a)*. This preliminary stage is interesting because it is the source of *both* the situations represented in the resulting pair of opposites, the one or the other according to which element in the original situation is changed. The follow-ing might serve as a diagrammatic picture of the scopophilic instinct:—   260

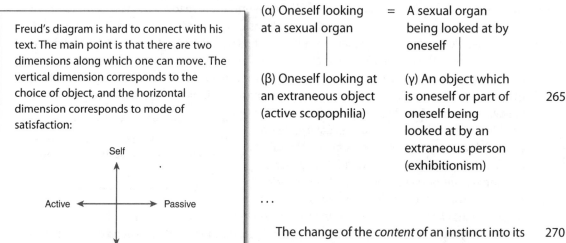

(α) Oneself looking   =   A sexual organ
at a sexual organ   being looked at by
                           oneself

Freud's diagram is hard to connect with his text. The main point is that there are two dimensions along which one can move. The vertical dimension corresponds to the choice of object, and the horizontal dimension corresponds to mode of satisfaction:

Self

Active ←——→ Passive

Other

(β) Oneself looking at   (γ) An object which
an extraneous object   is oneself or part of   265
(active scopophilia)   oneself being
                         looked at by an
                         extraneous person
                         (exhibitionism)

. . .

The change of the *content* of an instinct into its   270
opposite is observed in a single instance only—
the transformation of *love into hate*.[6] Since it is
particularly common to find both these directed
simultaneously towards the same object, their co-existence furnishes the most important example of ambivalence of feeling.   275

The case of love and hate acquires a special interest from the circumstance that it refuses to be fitted into our scheme of the instincts. It is impossible to doubt that there is the most intimate relation between these two opposite feelings and sexual life, but we are naturally unwilling to think of love as being some kind of special component instinct of sex-uality in the same way as the others we have been discussing. We should prefer to regard   280
loving as the expression of the *whole* sexual current of feeling; but this idea does not clear up our difficulties, and we cannot see what meaning to attach to an opposite content of this current.

---

[6] [In the German editions previous to 1924 this reads 'the transformation of *love and hate*.']

285 Loving admits not merely of one, but of three opposites. In addition to the antithesis 'loving–hating,' there is the other one of 'loving–being loved'; and, in addition to these, loving and hating taken together are the opposite of the condition of unconcern or indifference. The second of these three antitheses, loving–being loved, corresponds exactly to the transformation from activity to passivity and may be traced to an underlying situation in the same way as in the case of the scopophilic instinct. This situation
290 is that of *loving oneself,* which we regard as the characteristic feature of narcissism. Then, according as the object or the subject is replaced by an extraneous one, what results is the active aim of loving or the passive one of being loved—the latter remaining near to narcissism.

Perhaps we shall come to a better understanding of the several opposites of loving if we
295 reflect that our mental life as a whole is governed by *three polarities,* the antitheses

Subject (ego)–Object (external world),

Pleasure–Unpleasure, and

Active–Passive.

The antithesis ego–non-ego (external), i.e. subject–object, is, as we have already
300 said, thrust upon the individual organism at an early stage, by the experience that it can silence *external* stimuli by means of muscular action but is defenceless against *instinctual* stimuli. This antithesis remains, above all, sovereign in our intellectual activity and creates for research the basic situation which no efforts can alter. The polarity of pleasure–unpleasure is attached to a scale of feelings, whose paramount importance in
305 determining our actions (our will) has already been emphasized. The antithesis active–passive must not be confused with the antithesis ego-subject–external world-object. The relation of the ego to the external world is passive in so far as it receives stimuli from it and active when it reacts to these. It is forced by its instincts into a quite special degree of activity towards the external world, so that we might bring out the essential point if
310 we say that the ego-subject is passive in respect of external stimuli but active through its own instincts. The antithesis active–passive coalesces later with the antithesis masculine–feminine, which, until this has taken place, has no psychological meaning. The coupling of activity with masculinity and of passivity with femininity meets us, indeed, as a biological fact; but it is by no means so invariably complete and exclusive
315 as we are inclined to assume.

The three polarities of the mind are connected with one another in various highly significant ways. There is a primal psychical situation in which two of them coincide. Originally, at the very beginning of mental life, the ego is cathected with instincts and is to some extent capable of satisfying them on itself. We call this condition 'narcissism' and this way of obtaining satisfaction

cathected: invested with psychic energy

'auto-erotic.'[7] At this time the external world is not cathected with interest (in a general sense) and is indifferent for purposes of satisfaction. During this period, therefore, the ego-subject coincides with what is pleasurable and the external world with what is indifferent (or possibly unpleasurable, as being a source of stimulation). If for the moment we define loving as the relation of the ego to its sources of pleasure, the situation in which the ego loves itself only and is indifferent to the external world illustrates the first of the opposites which we found to 'loving.'[8]

In so far as the ego is auto-erotic, it has no need of the external world, but, in consequence of experiences undergone by the instincts of self-preservation, it acquires objects from that world, and, in spite of everything, it cannot avoid feeling internal instinctual stimuli for a time as unpleasurable. Under the dominance of the pleasure principle a further development now takes place in the ego. In so far as the objects which are presented to it are sources of pleasure, it takes them into itself, 'introjects' them (to use Ferenczi's [1909] term); and, on the other hand, it expels whatever within itself becomes a cause of unpleasure.

Thus the original 'reality-ego,' which distinguished internal and external by means of a sound objective criterion, changes into a purified 'pleasure-ego,' which places the characteristic of pleasure above all others. For the pleasure-ego the external world is divided into a part that is pleasurable, which it has incorporated into itself, and a remainder that is extraneous to it.

---

[7] Some of the sexual instincts are, as we know, capable of this auto-erotic satisfaction, and so are adapted to being the vehicle for the development under the dominance of the pleasure principle [from the original 'reality-ego' into the 'pleasure-ego'] which we are about to describe [in the next paragraphs of the text]. Those sexual instincts which from the outset require an object, and the needs of the ego-instincts, which are never capable of auto-erotic satisfaction, naturally disturb this state [of primal narcissism] and so pave the way for an advance from it. Indeed, the primal narcissistic state would not be able to follow the development [that is to be described] if it were not for the fact that every individual passes through a period during which he is helpless and has to be looked after and during which his pressing needs are satisfied by an external agency and are thus prevented from becoming greater.—[This very condensed footnote might have been easier to understand if it had been placed two or three paragraphs further on. It may perhaps be expanded as follows. In his paper '[Formulations on the] Two Principles of Mental Functioning' (1911/1958a) Freud had introduced the idea of the transformation of an early 'pleasure-ego' into a 'reality-ego.' In the passage which follows in the text above, he argues that there is in fact a still earlier *original* 'reality-ego.' This original 'reality-ego,' instead of proceeding directly into the *final* 'reality-ego,' is replaced, under the dominating influence of the pleasure principle, by a 'pleasure-ego.' The footnote enumerates those factors, on the one hand, which would favour this latter turn of events, and those factors, on the other hand, which would work against it. The existence of auto-erotic libidinal instincts would encourage the diversion to a 'pleasure-ego,' while the non-auto-erotic libidinal instincts and the self-preservative instincts would be likely instead to bring about a direct transition to the final adult 'reality-ego.' This latter result would, he remarks, in fact come about, if it were not that parental care of the helpless infant satisfies this second set of instincts, artificially prolongs the primary state of narcissism, and so helps to make the establishment of the 'pleasure-ego' possible.]

[8] [On p. 363 Freud enumerates the opposites of loving in the following order: (1) hating, (2) being loved and (3) indifference. In the present passage, and below on p. 365, he adopts a different order: (1) indifference, (2) hating and (3) being loved. It seems probable that in this second arrangement he gives indifference the first place as being the first to appear in the course of development.]

340   It has separated off a part of its own self, which it projects into the external world and feels as hostile. After this new arrangement, the two polarities coincide once more: the ego-subject coincides with pleasure, and the external world with unpleasure (with what was earlier indifference).

When, during the stage of primary narcissism, the object makes its appearance, the second opposite to loving, namely hating, also attains its development.

345   As we have seen, the object is brought to the ego from the external world in the first instance by the instincts of self-preservation; and it cannot be denied that hating, too, originally characterized the relation of the ego to the alien external world with the stimuli it introduces. Indifference falls into place as a special case of hate or dislike, after having first appeared as their forerunner. At the very beginning, it seems, the external world, objects, and what is hated are identical. If later on an object turns out to be a source of pleasure, it is loved, but it is also incor-

350   porated into the ego; so that for the purified pleasure-ego once again objects coincide with what is extraneous and hated.

Now, however, we may note that just as the pair of opposites love–indifference reflects the polarity ego–external world, so the second antithesis love–hate reproduces the polarity pleasure–unpleasure, which is linked to the first polarity. When the purely narcissistic stage has

355   given place to the object-stage, pleasure and unpleasure signify relations of the ego to the object. If the object becomes a source of pleasurable feelings, a motor urge is set up which seeks to bring the object closer to the ego and to incorporate it into the ego. We then speak of the 'attraction' exercised by the pleasure-giving object, and say that we 'love' that object. Conversely, if the object is a source of un-pleasurable feelings, there is an urge which endeav-

360   ours to increase the distance between the object and the ego and to repeat in relation to the object the original attempt at flight from the external world with its emission of stimuli. We feel the 'repulsion' of the object, and hate it; this hate can afterwards be intensified to the point of an aggressive inclination against the object—an intention to destroy it.

We might at a pinch say of an instinct that it 'loves' the objects towards which it strives for pur-

365   poses of satisfaction; but to say that an instinct 'hates' an object strikes us as odd. Thus we become aware that the attitudes of love and hate cannot be made use of for the relations *of instincts* to their objects, but are reserved for the relations of the *total ego* to objects. But if we consider linguistic usage, which is certainly not without significance, we shall see that there is a further limitation to the meaning of love and hate. We do not say of objects which serve the interests of

370   self-preservation that we *love* them; we emphasize the fact that we *need* them, and perhaps express an additional, different kind of relation to them by using words that denote a much reduced degree of love—such as, for example, 'being fond of,' 'liking' or 'finding agreeable.'

Thus the word 'to love' moves further and further into the sphere of the pure pleasure-relation of the ego to the object and finally becomes fixed to sexual objects in the narrower

375   sense and to those which satisfy the needs of sublimated sexual instincts. The distinction between the ego-instincts and the sexual instincts which we have imposed upon our psychology is thus seen to be in conformity with the spirit of our language. The fact that we are not in the habit of saying of a single sexual instinct that it loves its object, but regard the relation of the ego to its sexual object as the most appropriate case in which to employ the word

'love'—this fact teaches us that the word can only begin to be applied in this relation after there 380
has been a synthesis of all the component instincts of sexuality under the primacy of the genitals and in the service of the reproductive function.

It is noteworthy that in the use of the word 'hate' no such intimate connection with sexual
pleasure and the sexual function appears. The relation of *unpleasure* seems to be the sole decisive one. The ego hates, abhors and pursues with intent to destroy all objects which are a 385
source of unpleasurable feeling for it, without taking into account whether they mean a frustration of sexual satisfaction or of the satisfaction of self-preservative needs. Indeed, it may be
asserted that the true prototypes of the relation of hate are derived not from sexual life, but
from the ego's struggle to preserve and maintain itself.

So we see that love and hate, which present themselves to us as complete opposites in their 390
content, do not after all stand in any simple relation to each other. They did not arise from the
cleavage of any originally common entity, but sprang from different sources, and had each its
own development before the influence of the pleasure—unpleasure relation made them into
opposites.

It now remains for us to put together what we know of the genesis of love and hate. Love 395
is derived from the capacity of the ego to satisfy some of its instinctual impulses auto-erotically
by obtaining organ-pleasure. It is originally nar-
cissistic, then passes over on to objects, which
have been incorporated into the extended ego,
and expresses the motor efforts of the ego 400
towards these objects as sources of pleasure. It
becomes intimately linked with the activity of the
later sexual instincts and, when these have been
completely synthesized, coincides with the sexual
impulsion as a whole. Preliminary stages of love 405
emerge as provisional sexual aims while the sexual
instincts are passing through their complicated
development. As the first of these aims we recognize the phase of incorporating or devouring—a
type of love which is consistent with abolishing 410
the object's separate existence and which may
therefore be described as ambivalent. At the
higher stage of the pregenital sadistic-anal orga-

> Freud talked about the sexual instincts as
> having developmental stages. In the *oral*
> stage, satisfaction comes from taking things
> in through the mouth or biting things. In
> the *anal* stage, pleasure comes from
> holding onto or letting go of feces. In the
> *phallic* stage, sexual satisfaction is
> associated, for a boy, with the genitals, but
> there is no sexual activity because the
> object of such activity—the mother—would
> be inappropriate. For a girl this stage
> notoriously includes her discovery that she
> is without a penis. In the *genital* stage the
> sexual instinct matures and turns its
> attention to reproduction.

nization, the striving for the object appears in the form of an urge for mastery, to which injury
or annihilation of the object is a matter of indifference. Love in this form and at this preliminary 415
stage is hardly to be distinguished from hate in its attitude towards the object Not until the
genital organization is established does love become the opposite of hate.

Hate, as a relation to objects, is older than love. It derives from the narcissistic ego's primor-
dial repudiation of the external world with its outpouring of stimuli. As an expression of the reaction of unpleasure evoked by objects, it always remains in an intimate relation with the 420

self-preservative instincts; so that sexual and ego-instincts can readily develop an antithesis which repeats that of love and hate. When the ego-instincts dominate the sexual function, as is the case at the stage of the sadistic-anal organization, they impart the qualities of hate to the instinctual aim as well.

425 The history of the origins and relations of love makes us understand how it is that love so frequently manifests itself as 'ambivalent'—i.e. as accompanied by impulses of hate against the same object. The hate which is admixed with the love is in part derived from the preliminary stages of loving which have not been wholly surmounted; it is also in part based on reactions of repudiation by the ego-instincts, which, in view of the frequent conflicts between the inter-

430 ests of the ego and those of love, can find grounds in real and contemporary motives. In both cases, therefore, the admixed hate has as its source the self-preservative instincts. If a love-relation with a given object is broken off, hate not infrequently emerges in its place, so that we get the impression of a transformation of love into hate. This account of what happens leads on to the view that the hate, which has its real motives, is here reinforced by a regression of the love

435 to the sadistic preliminary stage; so that the hate acquires an erotic character and the continuity of a love-relation is ensured.

The third antithesis of loving, the transformation of loving into being loved, corresponds to the operation of the polarity of activity and passivity, and is to be judged in the same way as the cases of scopophilia and sadism.

440 We may sum up by saying that the essential feature in the vicissitudes undergone by instincts lies in *the subjection of the instinctual impulses to the influences of the three great polarities that dominate mental life*. Of these three polarities we might describe that of activity–passivity as the *biological,* that of ego–external world as the *real,* and finally that of pleasure–unpleasure as the *economic* polarity.

445 The instinctual vicissitude of *repression* will form the subject of an inquiry which follows.

That inquiry was the subject of *Repression* (1915), which Freud published shortly after the present paper. There Freud writes:

One of the vicissitudes an instinctual impulse may undergo is to meet with resistances the aim of which is to make the impulse inoperative. Under certain conditions . . . the impulse then passes into the state of *repression*. If it were a question of the operation of an external stimulus, obviously flight would be the appropriate remedy; with an instinct, flight is of no avail, for the ego cannot escape from itself. . . . [I]t is a condition of repression that the element of avoiding "pain" shall have acquired more strength than the pleasure of gratification. Psychoanalytic experience of the transference neuroses, moreover, forces us to the conclusion that repression is not a defence-mechanism present from the very beginning, and that it cannot occur until a sharp distinction has been established between what is conscious and what is unconscious: that *the essence of repression lies simply in the function of rejecting and keeping something out of consciousness.* (p. 104)

Freud later reformulated his instinct theory (in *An Outline of Psycho-Analysis* [1940], ch. 2), adding the notorious death instinct:

The forces which we assume to exist behind the tensions caused by the needs of the id are called *instincts*. They represent the somatic demands upon the mind. Though they are the ultimate cause of all activity, they are of a conservative nature; the state, whatever it may be, which an organism has reached gives rise to a tendency to re-establish that state so soon as it has been abandoned. It is thus possible to distinguish an indeterminate number of instincts, and in common practice this is in fact done. For us, however, the important question arises whether it may not be possible to trace all these numerous instincts back to a few basic ones. We have found that instincts can change their aim (by displacement) and also that they can replace one another—the energy of one instinct passing over to another. This latter process is still insufficiently understood. After long hesitancies and vacillations we have decided to assume the existence of only two basic instincts, *Eros* and *the destructive instinct*. (The contrast between the instincts of self-preservation and the preservation of the species, as well as the contrast between ego-love and object-love, fall within Eros.) The aim of the first of these basic instincts is to establish ever greater unities and to preserve them thus—in short, to bind together; the aim of the second is, on the contrary, to undo connections and so to destroy things. In the case of the destructive instinct we may suppose that its final aim is to lead what is living into an inorganic state. For this reason we also call it the *death instinct*. If we assume that living things came later than inanimate ones and arose from them, then the death instinct fits in with the formula we have proposed to the effect that instincts tend towards a return to an earlier state. In the case of Eros (or the love instinct) we cannot apply this formula. To do so would presuppose that living substance was once a unity which had later been torn apart and was now striving towards re-union.[9]

In biological functions the two basic instincts operate against each other or combine with each other. Thus, the act of eating is a destruction of the object with the final aim of incorporating it, and the sexual act is an act of aggression with the purpose of the most intimate union. This concurrent and mutually opposing action of the two basic instincts gives rise to the whole variegation of the phenomena of life. The analogy of our two basic instincts extends from the sphere of living things to the pair of opposing forces—attraction and repulsion—which rule in the inorganic world.[10]

Modifications in the proportions of the fusion between the instincts have the most tangible results. A surplus of sexual aggressiveness will turn a lover into a sex-murderer, while a sharp diminution in the aggressive factor will make him bashful or impotent.

---

[9] Creative writers have imagined something of the sort, but nothing like it is known to us from the actual history of living substance.

[10] This picture of the basic forces or instincts, which still arouses much opposition among analysts, was already familiar to the philosopher Empedocles of Acragas.

FOR DISCUSSION

1. What is Freud's definition of instinct? Is it a property of the mind or of the body? What is its purpose?

2. How, according to Freud, did we as a species acquire the instincts we have?

3. How and why does an instinct tend to produce behavior that is not easily recognized as an expression of that instinct?

4. In spite of obvious differences, it could be argued that there are some important similarities between the approaches Freud and Pavlov took to understanding complex human behavior. What are they?

John B. Watson (1878–1958)
What the Nursery Has to Say About Instincts (1926)

John Broadus Watson completed his PhD at the University of Chicago in 1903, and in 1907 he accepted a full professorship at Johns Hopkins University. About a year later, the department chair was arrested in a bordello and resigned. Watson took over as chair and also became editor of the prestigious *Psychological Review* (Fancher, 1996).

Watson's own early research had dealt with the study of animal behavior, and he was increasingly displeased about the fact that psychology was generally seen as the "study of the science of the phenomenon of consciousness" and that many psychologists felt that "behavior data . . . have no value *per se*" (Watson, 1913, p. 158). In 1913 Watson published "Psychology as the behaviorist views it" in *Psychological Review*. This paper, usually referred to as "The Behaviorist Manifesto," attempted to redefine psychology.

Although the impact of this manifesto was not immediate, over time it would have a profound effect on American psychology. In its first paragraph, Watson laid out what the new psychology would look like. It would seek, not to understand consciousness, but to predict and control behavior. It would be a "purely objective natural science" and would not use the introspective method. Finally, it would recognize "no dividing line between man and beast."

Watson wanted to make the study of animal behavior a legitimate part of psychology, and he also wanted the study of human experience to use behavioral techniques. He knew how to study other animals behaviorally, but he was unsure about how to approach the study of human behavior. He struggled for a few years to find the right method, and then he learned about the work Pavlov (see 5.2) and Bekhterev (1928/1932) had been doing on conditioning. Classical conditioning seemed to offer a way to think about the great variety of behaviors seen

Source: Bentley, M., Dunlap, K., Hunter, W. S., Koffka, K., Köhler, W., McDougall, W., Prince, M., Watson, J. B., Woodworth, R. S. (1926). *Psychologies of 1925: Powell lectures in psychological theory.* Worcester, MA: Clark University. Reprinted with permission. [The same article with only small modification appears in Watson, (1925), ch. 5 & 6.]

in humans. If a behavior occurs reflexively in response to a particular stimulus, and if that stimulus is temporally associated with another (neutral) stimulus, then the neutral stimulus can come to elicit the same behavior.

In 1920 Watson and a graduate student, Rosalie Rayner, did a now famous study (Watson & Rayner, 1920). Watson believed that there are just three innate emotional responses: *fear, rage,* and *love,* and that all emotional responses shown after infancy are acquired through a process of classical conditioning. Watson & Rayner conditioned Albert B. ("Little Albert"), an 11-month-old lad, to fear rats and other furry things by pairing the presence of the rat (a previously neutral or interesting stimulus for Albert B.) with a loud noise (a hammer striking a steel bar).

Watson and Rayner concluded that the study was successful; they had conditioned an emotional response. By pairing Albert B.'s innate (unconditioned) fear of sudden, loud noises, with the presence of the rat they had added a fear of rats to his repertoire, and this fear had generalized to similar stimuli (rabbit, dog, fur coat, etc.).[1]

Virtually all students of psychology have read about the Little Albert study. It appears in textbooks in introductory psychology, developmental psychology, learning theory, abnormal psychology, and other psychology subfields. Yet, as Harris (1979) points out its results are often distorted or misrepresented. Some of the errors are the result of authors relying too heavily on secondary sources, but some are due to the fact that Watson himself "altered or deleted" procedures or results in later descriptions of the study. There are also questions about the design of the experiment and the interpretation of the results. Harris reports, too, that subsequent researchers have not been able to replicate Watson and Rayner's results, and he concludes

> by itself the Albert study was not very convincing proof of the correctness of Watson's general view of personality and emotions. . . . It seems time, finally, to place the Watson and Rayner data in the category of "interesting but uninterpretable results." (p. 158)

The study with Albert B. was the last laboratory research Watson would do, for he was asked to leave Johns Hopkins in 1920 because he had been having an affair with Rayner. Watson went

---

[1] According to Rilling (2000), Watson's interest in Freud led him to study infancy and to center the Albert B. study on human emotions. The study supported Freud's idea that emotion could be transferred from one object to another, but it explained the transfer in terms of classical conditioning with no mention of the unconscious. The fact that Albert B. was thought to have shown stimulus generalization in the study is described by Watson and Rayner, not as generalization, but as transfer (a term similar to Freud's transference which in early psychoanalysis was what we would now call displacement).

Rilling points out that from 1910 to about 1920 Watson was interested in psychoanalysis and gave Freud substantial credit for a number of concepts and methods. In discussing methods appropriate to the study of emotions, for example, Watson (1919) includes free association, dream analysis, and slips of the tongue (pp. 208–209). In 1920, though, Watson began to attack Freud's ideas.

> The Freudians twenty years from now . . . when they come to analyze Albert's fear of a seal coat—assuming that he comes to analysis at that age—will probably . . . show that Albert at three years of age attempted to play with the pubic hair of the mother and was scolded violently for it. (Watson & Rayner, 1920, p. 14)

on to work for the J. Walter Thompson advertising agency, but he continued to write and speak about psychological issues for about a decade. Much of his writing after 1920 appeared in popular magazines and dealt with child rearing and the behaviorist position on a number of psychological issues. The article included here, however, is the text of a lecture he gave at Clark University in 1926 and is based on his discussion of instincts in *Behaviorism* (originally published in 1925 and revised in 1930). In it Watson assures us that instincts, capacities, talents, temperament, mental constitution, and personality characteristics are acquired, not innate. According to Watson, "man at birth is but an untrained ball of protoplasm and . . . the going concern he is to grow into is dependent almost wholly upon the kind of parents he has and the kind of environment he is to be nurtured in" (Watson, 1928a, p. 108). As a behaviorist, Watson says of an infant, "If he is healthy, if his reflexes are perfect . . . , if he has the use of fingers, toes, arms and eyes, I will shape him in any way I please" (Watson, 1928a, p. 108).

I. GENERAL CONSIDERATIONS

Introduction: In this brief course of lectures I wish to talk about how man is equipped to behave at birth—a subject that touches the very heart of human psychology.

When the array of facts about any subject is not very complete, it is only human nature to announce a thesis, that is, state what one is going to try to prove and then try to prove it by a
5   logical argument. I am in that position tonight. I have not the full set of facts about the so-called "instinctive" nature of man—I do not know who has; hence, please look upon these lectures both as logical presentations of what facts there are in the case and as a thesis which I am trying to defend. I shall present my thesis first.

The Thesis Presented

Man is an animal born with certain definite types of structure. Having that kind of structure,
10   he is forced to respond to stimuli at birth in certain ways (for example: breathing, heart beat, sneezing, and the like . . .). This repertoire of responses is in general the same for each of us. Yet there exists a certain amount of variation in each—the variation is probably merely proportional to the variation there is in structure (including in structure, of course, chemical constitution). . . . Let us call this group of reactions, man's *unlearned behavior.*
15   In this relatively simple list of human responses there is none corresponding to what is called an "instinct" by present-day psychologists and biologists. There are then for us no instincts—we no longer need the term in psychology. Everything we have been in the habit of calling an "instinct" today is a result largely of training—belonging to man's *learned behavior.*

> William McDougall was a contemporary of Watson's and a staunch advocate of the view that instincts are biological givens and very much a part of human nature. McDougall and Watson held a public debate on the issue of instincts in 1928. Their texts for the debate have been published, and the write-ups are a pleasure to read, primarily for the content of course, but the style, wit, and humor add a good deal (Watson & McDougall, 1928).

20   As a corollary from this, I wish to draw the conclusion that there is no such thing as an inheritance of *capacity, talent, temperament, mental constitution* and *characteristics.* These things again depend on training that goes on mainly in the cradle. The behaviorist would *not* say: "He inherits his father's capacity or talent for being a fine swordsman." He would say: "This child certainly has his father's slender build of body, the same type of eyes. His
25   build is wonderfully like his father's. He, too, has the build of a swordsman." And he

Like Freud, Watson believed that early experience influenced all of the experiences that followed and that a child was basically formed in the first years of life. "Slanting" or "shaping" were Watson's words to describe this powerful effect. As the twig is bent so grows the tree.

would go on to say: "–and his father is very fond of him. He put a tiny sword into his hand when he was a year of age, and in all their walks he talks sword play, attack and defense, the code of duelling and the like." A certain type of struc-   30
ture, plus early training—*slanting*—accounts for adult performance.

From research that has been done since 1926, one could argue with Watson's claim that none of the human qualities he lists—capacity, talent, temperament, mental constitution, or characteristics—has any hereditary basis. A number of researchers have looked at temperament, for example, and have reported evidence that it has a significant hereditary component (Chess & Thomas, 1996; Kagan, 1994, 1997, 2003; Kagan, Reznick, & Snidman, 1988; Kagan & Snidman, 2004; Scott, 1972; Scott & Fuller, 1965).

The Argument in Its Defence

Let me start by saying that man to the behaviorist is a *whole animal. When he reacts he reacts with each and every part of his body.* Sometimes he reacts more strongly with one group of muscles and glands than with another. We then say he is doing something. We have named many   35
of these acts—such as breathing, sleeping, crawling, walking, running, fighting, crying, etc. But please do not forget that each of these named acts involves the whole body.

We must begin, too, to think of man as a mammal—a primate—a two-legged animal with two arms and two delicate, mobile hands; as an animal that has a nine months embryonic life, a long helpless infancy, a slow developing childhood, eight years of adolescence and a total life   40
span of some three score years and ten.

We find this animal living in the tropics almost without shelter; going naked; living upon easily caught animals and upon fruit and herbs that require no cultivation. We find him in temperate regions, but dwelling here in well-built, steam-heated houses. We find the male always heavily clad even in summer, wearing a hat upon his head—the only naturally protected part   45
of his body. We find the female of this species dressed in the scantiest of clothes. We find the male working frantically (the female rarely) at almost every kind of vocation, from digging holes in the ground, damming up water like beavers, to building tall buildings of steel and concrete. Again we find man in arctic regions, clad in furs, eating fatty foods and living in houses built of snow and ice.   50

Everywhere we find man, we find him doing the strangest things, displaying the most divergent manners and customs. In Africa we find the blacks eating one another; in China we find men eating mainly rice and throwing it towards the mouth with dainty chopsticks. In other countries we find man using a metal knife and fork. So widely different is the adult behavior of the primitive

55 Australian bushmen from that of the dwellers in internal China, and both of these groups differ so widely in behavior from the cultivated Englishman, that the question is forced upon us—*Do all members of the genus homo, wherever they are found in biological history, start at birth with the same group of responses, and are these responses aroused by the same set of stimuli?* Put in another way, is the *unlearned,* birth equipment of man, which you have been in the habit of calling

60 *instincts,* the same wherever he is found, be it in Africa or in Boston, be it in the year six million B. C. or in 1925 A. D., whether born in the cotton fields of the South, in the Mayflower or beneath the silken purple quilts of European royalty?

> Although there is some disagreement about the exact timing of the evolution of humans, the genus *homo* is generally thought to have appeared only 1.5 to 2.5 million years ago, and the species *homo sapiens* ("modern man") is believed to have appeared no more than 200,000 years ago.
>
> Watson may have been a bit stereotypical in his descriptions of people in different climates and countries and continents—and, for that matter, of men and women in temperate climes. It is worth noting, however, that in terms of his views on racial, national, or ethnic differences, Watson frequently went out of his way to insist that there are no innate differences in any characteristics, other than peripheral ones, that are related to race, nationality, or ethnicity. He acknowledged that there are differences in achievements or accomplishments, but he argued that they are based on lack of opportunity and oppression. This view is consistent with his view that heredity plays no role in human behavior. Watson's views on gender differences are less clear.

The Genetic Psychologists' Answer

The genetic psychologist—the student best qualified to answer this question—hates to be

65 faced with it because his data are limited. But since he is forced to answer, he can give his honest conviction. His answer is, "Yes, within the limits of individual variation, man is born with the same general set of responses (let us wait before we

70 call them instincts, though) regardless of the station of his parents, regardless of the geological age in which he was born and regardless of the geographical zone in which he was born."

But you say, is there nothing in heredity—is

75 there nothing in eugenics—is there no advantage in being born an "F. F. V."—has there been no *progress* in human evolution? Let us examine a few of the questions you are now bursting to utter.

> Watson sometimes (as in this case) uses *genetic* to mean *developmental* and sometimes uses it in its more familiar current meaning of *innate*.

> *eugenics:* improvement in the quality of human beings through improvement in the gene pool. Over the years, the eugenics movement has been associated with selective breeding, the holocaust, laws prohibiting individuals with certain physical or mental conditions from marrying, the U.S. immigration acts of the 1920s, involuntary sterilization, "designer babies," and more. Eugenicists' goal is to encourage breeding among individuals with "good" genes and to discourage breeding among those with "bad" genes.

F. F. V.: First Families of Virginia. Families that can trace their ancestry to the English families who settled in Jamestown in 1607.

Certainly black parents will bear black children. . . . Certainly the yellow-skinned Chinese parents will bear yellow-skinned offspring. Certainly Caucasian parents will bear white children. But these differences are relatively slight. They are due among other things to differences in the amount and kind of pigments in the skin. I defy anyone to take these infants at birth, study their behavior, and mark off differences in behavior that will characterize white from black, and white or black from yellow. There will be differences in behavior but the burden of proof is upon the individual, be he biologist or eugenist, who claims that these racial differences are greater than the individual differences.

80

85

Although the title of this paper and Watson's introductory remarks suggest that he will be discussing instincts—common human qualities or innate behavioral tendencies—he actually devotes more attention to hereditary individual differences. But, the two are not completely different because there are individual differences in the strength of particular instincts. In any case, Watson felt that neither commonly shared instincts nor hereditary individual differences play a significant role in human behavior.

This lecture was originally delivered in 1925, soon after the Immigration Act of 1924 was passed to keep immigrants from eastern and southern Europe (the "unfit") out of the United States. Watson clearly did not agree with the scientific basis for this legislation.

In another article on instincts, Watson wrote:

the eugenist will ultimately tamper with the mating of men and women and is more dangerous than bolshevism. . . .

This belief in heredity of traits . . . has become a part of our mores. . . . It is a clever device (the Freudians would call it unconscious) for living forever. It is hard for most of us to believe when we are dead that we are dead all over, like Rover. (Watson, 1927, p. 229)

Again you say, "How about children born from parents who have large hands, with short stiff fingers, with extra fingers or toes? It can be shown that children from these parents inherit these peculiarities of structure." Our answer is: "Yes, thousands of variations are laid down in the germ plasm and will always appear (other factors being equal) in the offspring." Other inheritances are color of hair, color of eyes, texture of skin. . . . The biologist, knowing the makeup of the parents and grandparents, can predict many of even the finer structural characteristics of the offspring.

90

germ plasm: the genetic material, the carrier of heredity. We would now say DNA.

95

So let us hasten to admit—yes, there are heritable differences in form, in structure. Some people are born with long, slender fingers, with delicate throat structure; some are born tall, large, of prize-fighter build; others with delicate skin and eye coloring. These differences are

100

in the germ plasm and are handed down from parent to child. . . . But do not let these undoubted facts of inheritance lead you astray as they have some of the biologists. The mere presence of these structures tell us not one thing about function. This has been the source of a great deal of confusion in the subject we have under consideration tonight. Much of our structure laid down in heredity would never come to light, would never show in function, unless the organism were put in a certain environment, subjected to certain stimuli and forced to undergo training. Our hereditary structure lies ready to be shaped in a thousand different ways—the same structure mind you—depending on the way in which the child is brought up. To convince yourself, measure the right arm of the blacksmith, look at the pictures of strong men in our terrible magazines devoted to physical culture. Or turn to the poor bent back of the ancient bookkeeper. They are structurally shaped (within limits) by the kinds of lives they lead.

Are 'Mental' Traits Inherited?

But every one admits this about bone and tendons and muscles—"How about mental traits? Do you mean to say that great talent is not inherited? That criminal tendencies are not inherited? Surely we can prove that these things can be inherited." This was the older idea, the idea which grew up before we knew as much about what early shaping throughout infant life will do as we know now. The question is often put in specific form: "Look at the musicians who are the sons of musicians; look at Wesley Smith, the son of the great economist, John Smith—surely a chip off the old block if ever there was one." You already know the behaviorist's way of answering these questions. You know he recognizes no such thing as mental traits, dispositions or tendencies. Hence, to him, there is no sense to the question of the inheritance of talent as the question is ordinarily raised.

Wesley Smith early in life was thrown into an environment that fairly reeked with economic, political and social questions. His attachment for his father was strong. The path he took was a very natural one. He went into that life for the same reason that your son becomes a lawyer, a doctor or a politician. If the father is a shoemaker, a saloon keeper or a street cleaner, or engaged in any other non-socially recognized occupation, the son does not follow so easily in the father's footsteps, but that is another story. Why did Wesley Smith succeed in reaching eminence when so many sons who have famous fathers fail to attain equal eminence? Was it because this particular son inherited his father's talent? There may be a thousand reasons, not one of which lends any color to the view that Wesley Smith inherited the "talent" of his father. Suppose John Smith had had three sons who by hypothesis all had equal abilities and all began to work upon economics at the age of six months.[2] One was beloved by his father. He followed in his father's footsteps and, due to his father's tutorship, this son overtook and finally surpassed his father. Two years after the

| Watson's Smiths are presumably fictional. |

---

[2] And by this statement we do not mean that their genetic constitution is identical.

lounge lizard: According to the Online Etymology Dictionary (n.d.), the phrase was introduced in 1912 to describe men who flirted with women in tea rooms.

paresis: (general paresis) A disorder that includes intellectual impairment, personality change, inappropriate emotional reactions, hallucinations, and delusions. It is one of several possible late stages resulting from a syphilitic infection. If the syphilis is untreated, these symptoms can appear 10 to 15 years after the original infection.

The symptoms of general paresis look like a psychological disorder. When it was discovered that it is a late stage of syphilis, a disease with a physical cause, it gave much support to the idea that all psychological disorders have physical causes (the somatogenic approach to mental illness).

faculty psychology: An approach to the study of the mind that assumes that the mind has a fixed number of capacities or faculties such as will, intellect, reason, and memory. Its development is associated with Christian Wolff (1679–1754), a German philosopher. The most extreme version of the faculty approach was phrenology, a field developed by Franz Josef Gall (1758–1828) and based on the idea that different faculties are located in different parts of the brain, and that by feeling the bumps on a person's head you can determine which of their abilities and characteristics are most developed. Gall's ideas were totally discredited, but Reber and Reber (2001) suggest that some cognitive psychologists have revived the idea of mental faculties under the name of *modularity.*

birth of Wesley, the second son was born, but the father was taken up with the elder son. The second son was beloved by the mother who now got less of her husband's time, so she devoted her time to the second son. The second son could not follow so closely in the footsteps of his father; he was influenced naturally by what his mother was doing. 140 145

He early gave up his economic studies, entered society and ultimately became a "lounge lizard." The third son, born two years later, was unwanted. The father was taken up with the eldest son, the mother with the second son. The third son was also put to work upon economics, but receiving little parental care, he drifted daily towards the servants' quarters. An unscrupulous maid taught him to masturbate at three. At twelve the chauffeur made a homosexual out of him. Later, falling in with neighborhood thieves, he became a pickpocket, then a stool-pigeon and finally a drug fiend. He died in an insane asylum of paresis. There was nothing wrong with the heredity of any one of these sons. All by hypothesis had equal chances at birth. All could have been the fathers of fine, healthy sons if their respective wives had been of good stock (except possibly for the third son *after* he contracted syphilis). 150 155 160

You will probably say that I am flying in the face of the known facts of eugenics and experimental evolution—that the geneticists have proven that many of the behavior characteristics of the parents are handed down to the offspring—they will cite mathematical ability, musical ability, and many, many other types. My reply is that the geneticists are working under the banner of the old "faculty" psychology. One need not give very much weight to any of their present conclusions. Before the evening is over I hope to show you that there are no "faculties" and no stereotyped patterns of behavior which deserve the name either of "talent" or "instinct." 165 170 175

Differences in Structure and Differences in
Early Training Will Account for All Differences in Later Behavior

180 A while ago I said that, granting individual variation in structure, we could find no real proof that man's unlearned repertoire of acts has differed through the ages or that he has ever been either more or less capable of putting on complex training than in 1925. The fact that there are marked individual variations in structure among men has been known since biology began. But we have never sufficiently utilized it in analyzing man's behavior. Tonight I want to utilize still another fact only recently brought out by the behaviorists and other

185 students of animal psychology, namely, that *habit formation starts in all probability in embryonic life, and that even in the human young, environment shapes behavior so quickly that all of the older ideas about what types of behavior are inherited and what are learned break down.* Grant variations in structure at birth and rapid habit formation from birth, and you have a basis for explaining many of the so-called facts of inheritance of "mental" characteristics. Let

190 us take up these two points:

(1) Human Beings Differ in the Way They Are Put Together

Those of you who have physiological training have a good idea of the complexity of the material that goes into the human body. You realize the fact that there must be variation in the way these complicated tissues are put together. We have just brought out the fact that some

195 human beings are born with long fingers, some with short; some with long arm and leg bones, some with short; some with hard bones, and some with soft; some with over-developed glands; some with poorly functioning glands. Again you know that we can identify human beings by differences in their finger prints. No two human beings have ever had the same finger prints, yet you can mark off man's hand and foot prints from the tracks of all other animals.

200 No two human beings have bones exactly alike, yet any good comparative anatomist can pick out a human bone (and there are over 200 of them) from the bones of every other mammal. If so simple a thing as the markings on the fingers differ in every individual, you have absolute proof that general behavior will and must be different. They crawl differently, cry differently, differ in the frequency with which defaecation and urination occur, differ in early vocal efforts,

205 in requirements for food, in the speed and rapidity with which they use their hands—even identical twins show these differences—because they differ structurally and differ slightly in their chemical makeup. They differ likewise in the finer details of sense organ equipment, in the details of brain and cord structure, in the heart and circulatory mechanisms and in the length, breadth, thickness and flexibility of the striped muscular systems.

210 Yet with all of these structural differences "a man's a man for a' that"—all are made up of the same material and have the same general architectural plan regardless of habits.

(2) Differences in Early Training Make Men Still More Different

There are then admittedly these slight but significant differences in structure between one human being and every other human being. Differences in early training are even more

215 marked. I will not stop now to give much proof of this—the next two lectures will furnish it

abundantly. We now know that conditioned reflexes start in the human child at birth (and possibly before)—we know that there is no such thing as giving two children, even belonging to the same family, the same training. A doting young married couple have twins—a boy and a girl—they are dressed alike and fed alike. But the father pets and fondles the girl, surrounds her with love; the mother treats the boy in the same way, but the father wants the boy to fol- 220
low in his own footsteps. He is stern with him—he can't help shaping the boy his way. The mother wants the girl to be modest and maidenly. Soon they show great differences in behavior. They receive different training from infancy. The next children are born. Now the father is more taken up with affairs—he has to work harder. The mother is more taken up with social duties; servants are brought in. The younger children have brothers and sisters; they are 225
brought up in a wholly different world. . . .

The Conclusion We Draw

. . . [W]e have no real evidence of the inheritance of traits. I would feel perfectly confident in the ultimately favorable outcome of careful upbringing of a *healthy, well-formed baby* born of a long line of crooks, murderers, thieves and prostitutes. Who has any evidence to the contrary? Many, many thousands of children yearly, born from moral households and steadfast parents, 230
become wayward, steal or become prostitutes, through one mishap or another of nurture. Many more thousands of sons and daughters of the wicked grow up to be wicked because they couldn't grow up any other way in such surroundings. . . .

> *Give me a dozen* . . . : This sentence is often quoted, but the one that follows is typically omitted.

I should like to go one step further tonight and say, "Give me a dozen healthy infants, well- 235
formed, and my own specified world to bring them up in and I'll guarantee to take any one at random and train him to become any type of specialist I might select—a doctor, lawyer, artist, merchant-chief and, yes, even into beggar-man 240
and thief, regardless of his talents, penchants, tendencies, abilities, vocations and race of his ancestors." I am going beyond my facts and I admit it, but so have the advocates of the contrary and

> It's interesting that Watson seems to suggest here that infants come with "talents, penchants, tendencies, abilities."

they have been doing it for many thousands of years. Please note that when this experiment 245
is made I am to be allowed to specify the way they are to be brought up and the type of world they have to live in.

. . .

The behaviorist has an axe to grind, you say, by being so emphatic? Yes, he has—he would like to see the presuppositions and assumptions that are blocking us in our efforts to spend millions of dollars and years of patient research on infant psychology removed because then, and 250
only then, can we build up a real psychology of mankind.

Watson often imagined a society in which serious attention was given to child rearing:

> Will you believe the almost astounding truth that no well trained man or woman has ever watched the complete and daily development of a single child from its birth to its third year? Plants and animals we know about because we have studied them, but the human child until very recently has been a mystery.... How can we get facts on how to rear children unless we make the studies necessary to obtain them? (Watson, 1928b, p. 13)

Are There Any Instincts?

Let us, then, forever lay the ghost of inheritance of aptitudes, of "mental" characteristics, of special abilities (not based upon favorable structure such as throat formation in singing, hand in playing, structurally sound eyes, ears, etc.) and take up the more general question of what
255   the world has been in the habit of calling instincts.

It is not easy to answer this question. Up to the advent of the behaviorist, man was supposed to be a creature of many complicated instincts. A group of older writers, under the sway of the newly created theories of Darwin, vied with one another in finding new ... instincts in both man and animals. William James made a careful selection from
260   among these asserted instincts and gave man the following list: *Climbing, imitation, emulation and rivalry, pugnacity, anger, resentment, sympathy, hunting, fear, appropriation, acquisitiveness, kleptomania, constructiveness, play, curiosity, sociability, shyness,*

> Watson has left out *vocalization* and *secretiveness;* see James (1890, vol. 2, pp. 406–441).

265   *cleanliness, modesty, shame, love, jealousy, parental love.* James claims that no other mammal, not even the monkey, can lay claim to so large a list.

The behaviorist finds himself wholly unable to agree with James and the other psychologists who claim that man has unlearned activities of these complicated kinds. But you who are here tonight have been brought up on James or possibly even on a worse diet, and it will be hard to
270   dislodge his teaching. You say, "James says an instinct is 'a tendency to act in such a way as to bring about certain ends without having foresight of those ends.' Surely this formulation fits a lot of the early behavior of children and young animals." You think you understand it, anyway. At first it looks convincing. But when you test it out in terms of your own observations on young animals and children, you find that you have not a scientific definition but a metaphysical assumption. You
275   get lost in the sophistry of 'foresight' and 'end.'

I don't blame you for being confused. No subject in psychology today is more written about than the so-called instincts. In the past three years more than a hundred articles have been

> *sophistry:* logically invalid but often persuasive argument

written about instincts. The articles in general are of the armchair variety written by men who   280
have never watched the whole life history of animals and the early childhood of the human
young. Philosophy will never answer any questions about instincts. The questions asked are
factual ones—to be answered only by genetic observation. Let me hasten to add that the
behaviorist's knowledge of instinct also suffers from lack of observed facts but you cannot
accuse him of going beyond natural science in his inferences. Before attempting to answer the   285
question "What is an instinct?" let us take a little journey into mechanics. Possibly we may find
that we do not need the term after all.

A Lesson From the Boomerang

I have in my hand a hardwood stick. If I throw it forward and upward it goes a certain distance and drops to the ground. I retrieve the stick, put it in hot water, bend it at a certain angle,
throw it out again—it goes outward, revolving as it goes for a short distance, turns to the right   290
and then drops down. Again I retrieve the stick, reshape it slightly and make its edges convex.
I call it a boomerang. Again I throw it upward and outward. Again it goes forward revolving as
it goes. Suddenly it turns, comes back and gracefully and kindly falls at my feet. It is still a stick,
still made of the same material, but it has been shaped differently. *Has the boomerang an
instinct to return to the hand of the thrower?* No? Well, why does it return? Because it is made in   295
such a way that when it is thrown upward and outward with a given force it must return. . . . Let
me call attention to the fact here that all well made and well thrown boomerangs will return
to or near to the thrower's feet, but no two will follow exactly the same forward pathway or the
same return pathway, even if shot mechanically with the same application of force and at the
same elevation; yet they are all called boomerangs. This example may be a little unusual to you.   300
Let us take one a little easier. Most of us have rolled dice now and again. Take a die, load it in
a certain way, roll it, and the face bearing "six" will always come up when the die is thrown.
Why? The die must roll that way because of the way it was constructed. Again take a toy soldier. Mount it on a semi-circular loaded rubber base. No matter how you throw this soldier, he
will always bob upright, oscillate a bit, then come to a steady vertical position. *Has the rubber*   305
soldier an instinct to stand erect?

Notice that not until the boomerang, the toy soldier and the die are hurled into space do they
exhibit their peculiarities of motion. Change their form or their structure, or alter the material out
of which they are made (make them of iron instead of wood or rubber) and their characteristic
motion may markedly change. But man is made up of certain kinds of material—put together in   310
certain ways. If he is hurled into action (as a result of stimulation) may he not exhibit movement
(in advance of training) just as peculiar as (but no more mysterious than) that of the boomerang?[3]

---

[3] You will argue that in mechanics action and reaction are equal—that the boomerang is hit with a force equal to so many
ergs and that just that many ergs are used up in returning to the hand of the thrower (including the heat loss to the air)
but that when I touch a man with a hair and he jumps two feet high, the reaction is out of all proportion to the energy in
the stimulus. The reply is that in man the energy used in the reaction was stored. In dynamics you find the same thing when
a match touches off a powder blast or a breeze blows from a cliff a rocking boulder that destroys a house in the valley.

Concept of Instinct No Longer Needed in Psychology

This brings us to our central thought tonight. If the boomerang has no instinct (aptitude, capacity, tendency, trait, etc.) to return to the hand of the thrower; if we need no mysterious
315 way of accounting for the motion of the boomerang; if the laws of physics will account for its motions—cannot psychology see in this a much needed lesson in simplicity? Can it not dispense with instincts? Can we not say, "Man is built of certain materials put together in certain complex ways, and *as a corollary of the way he is put together and of the material out of which he is made—he must act [until learning has reshaped him] as he does act?"*
320 But you say: "That gives your whole argument away—you admit he does a lot of things at birth which he is forced to do by his structure—this is just what I mean by *instinct."* My answer is that we must now go to the facts. We can no longer postpone a visit to the nursery. I think you will find there, in the two or three years we shall study the infant and child, *little that will encourage you to keep sacred James' list of instincts.*

II. LABORATORY STUDIES ON THE GENESIS OF BEHAVIOR

325 During the past 25 years the students of animal behavior have been gathering a sound body of facts about the young of nearly every species of animal except that of man. We have lived with young monkeys, we have watched the growth of young rats, rabbits, guinea pigs, and birds of many species. We have watched them develop daily in our laboratories from the moment of birth to maturity. To check our laboratory results we have watched many of them
330 grow up in their own native habitat—in a natural environment.

These studies have enabled us to reach a fair understanding of both the *unlearned* and *learned* equipment of many species of animals. They have taught us that no one by watching the performance of the adult can determine what part of a complicated series of acts belongs in the *unlearned* category and what part belongs in the category of the *learned*. Best of all, they
335 have given us a method that we can apply to the study of the human young. Finally, animal studies have taught us that it is not safe to generalize from the data we gather on one species as to what will be true in another species. For example, the guinea pig is born with a heavy coat of fur and with a very complete set of motor responses. It becomes practically independent of the mother at three days of age. The white rat, on the other hand, is born in a very immature
340 state, has a long period of infancy; it becomes independent of the mother only at the end of thirty days. Such a wide divergence of birth equipment in two animal species so closely related (both rodents) proves how unsafe it is to generalize on the basis of infra-human animal studies as to what the unlearned equipment of man is.

Resistance to the Study of the Human Young

Until very recently we have had no reliable data on what happens during the first few years
345 of human infancy and childhood. Indeed there has been very great resistance to studying the

behavior of the human young. Society is in the habit of seeing them starve by hundreds, of seeing them grow up in dives and slums, without getting particularly wrought up about it. But let the hardy behaviorist attempt an experimental study of the infant or even begin systematic observation, and criticism begins at once. When experiments and observations are made in the maternity wards of hospitals there is naturally also considerable misunderstanding of the behaviorist's aims. The child is not sick, the behaviorist is not advancing clinical methods—therefore what good are such studies? Again, when the parents who have children under observation learn of it they become excited. They are ignorant of what you are doing and you have great difficulty in making them understand what you are doing. These difficulties at first confronted us in our work at the Johns Hopkins Hospital but, thanks to the broad-mindedness of Dr. J. Whitridge Williams, Dean of the Johns Hopkins Medical School, and of Dr. John Howland, physician-in-chief of the Harriet Lane Hospital, a satisfactory condition for study was finally arranged. It was arranged in such a way that psychological examination of the infants became a part of the regular routine of the care of all infants born in the hospital. I mention this because if any of you ever attempt to make such studies you will be confronted, until the work has become more generally accepted, with a similar set of difficulties.

> Watson and Rayner's study with Albert B. (see the Introduction) may indeed have generated some criticism.
>
> The fact that they conditioned fears in the infant would distress some. The fact that they did not undo the conditioning would dismay even more.

. . .

The Birth Equipment of the Human Young

Almost daily observation of several hundred infants from birth through the first thirty days of infancy and of a smaller number through the first years of childhood has given us the following set of (rough) facts on unlearned responses:[4]

Sneezing: This apparently can begin in a full-fledged way from birth. . . . habit factors apparently affect it very little indeed. . . .

Hiccoughing: This usually does not begin at birth but can be noticed in children from 7 days of age on with great ease. . . . So far as is known, this response is rarely conditioned under the ordinary conditions of life. . . .

Crying: The so-called birth cry takes place at the establishment of respiration. The lungs are not inflated until the stimulus of the air is present. As the air strikes the lungs and mucous membranes of the upper alimentary tract, the mechanism of breathing is gradually established. To establish breathing the infant has sometimes to be plunged into icy water. Coincident with the

---

[4] Mrs. Margaret Gray Blanton (1917), working in the psychological laboratory of the Johns Hopkins Hospital, has given us our best data upon this subject.

plunge into the icy water, the cry appears. It usually appears during the vigorous rubbing and slapping of the infant's back and buttocks—a method invariably employed to establish respiration. The birth cry itself differs markedly in different infants.

Hunger will bring out crying, noxious stimuli such as rough handling, circumcision or the lancing and care of boils will bring out cries even in extremely young infants. When the baby suspends itself with either hand crying is usually elicited.

Crying as such very shortly becomes conditioned. The child quickly learns that it can control the responses of nurse, parents and attendants by the cry, and uses it as a weapon ever thereafter. Crying in infants is not always accompanied by tears, although tears can sometimes be observed as soon as ten minutes after birth. Owing to the almost universal practice now of putting silver nitrate into the eyes shortly after birth, the normal appearance of tears is hard to determine. Tears have been observed usually, though, on a great many babies from the fourth day on. Tears, in all probability, are also conditioned very quickly, since they are a much more effective means of controlling the movements of nurses and parents than dry crying.

> *Silver nitrate* drops were routinely put in the newborn's eyes to prevent infection caused by vaginal bacteria encountered during delivery.

Numerous experiments have been carried out to see whether the crying of one infant in a nursery will serve as a stimulus to set off the rest of the children in the nursery. Our results are entirely negative. In order to more thoroughly control the conditions, we made phonographic records of a lusty crier. We would then reproduce this sound very close to the ear of, first, a sleeping infant, then a wakeful but quiet infant. The results again were wholly negative. Hunger contractions and noxious stimuli (also loud sounds) are unquestionably the unconditioned stimuli which call out crying.

. . . The cries of infants are so different that at night in a nursery it does not take very long to be able to name the child which is crying regardless of its location in the nursery.

. . .

Smiling: Smiling is due in all probability at first to the presence of kinaesthetic and tactual stimuli. It appears as early as the fourth day. It can most often be seen after a full feeding. Light touches on parts of the body, blowing upon the body, touching the sex organs and sensitive zones of the skin are the unconditioned stimuli that will produce smiling. Tickling under the chin and a gentle jogging and rocking of the infant will often bring out smiling.

Smiling is the response in which conditioning factors begin to appear as early as the thirtieth day. Mrs. Mary Cover Jones has made an extensive study of smiling. In a large group of children she found that conditioned smiling—that is, smiling when the experimenter smiles or says babyish words to the infant (both auditory and visual factors)—begins to appear at around the thirtieth day. In her total study of 185 cases, the latest age at which the conditioned smile first appeared was eighty days.

. . .

In addition to her research on smiling, Mary Cover Jones was "a pioneer of behavior therapy because of her work on the unconditioning of the fear reaction in infants" (Rutherford, 2000). In 1919 Jones, who was a friend of Rosalie Rayner, attended a series of lectures given by Watson (Jones, 1974). She learned about the Little Albert study on conditioned emotions (see the introduction to this reading) and was intrigued.

About 3 years after the conditioning of Little Albert, a case was presented to Jones that "seemed to be Albert grown a bit older" (Jones, 1924). Peter was almost 3 years old and was afraid of a white rat, a rabbit, a fur coat, a feather, and cotton wool. Peter showed the most fear in response to the rabbit, and so Jones tried to uncondition that fear. She used two methods to accomplish this—direct conditioning and social imitation. Direct conditioning involved associating the presence of the rabbit with the presence of food that Peter liked. In social imitation, Peter had the opportunity to see other children playing happily with the rabbit. Jones's techniques were successful. Peter became comfortable with the rabbit (and also with the rat, fur coat, etc.).

Jones notes that Watson served as an adviser for the work she reports in the above article.

Feeding Responses: Touching the face of a hungry baby at the corners of the mouth or on the cheek or on the chin will cause quick, jerky head movements which result in bringing the mouth near the source of stimulation. This has been observed many, many times from five hours of age onward. . . .   420

The whole group of feeding responses is most easy to condition. Conditioning can be most easily observed in a bottle fed baby. Even before reaching (occurring around the 120th day) the infant will get extremely active in its bodily "squirmings" the instant the bottle is shown. After reaching has developed, the mere sight of the bottle will carry out the lustiest kind of bodily movements. . . . So sensitive do infants become to the visual stimulus of the bottle that if it is   425
shown from 12 to 15 feet away, the response begins to appear. . . .

. . .

Blinking: Any newborn infant will close the lids when the eye (cornea) is touched or when a current of air strikes the eye. But no infant at birth will "blink" when a shadow rapidly crosses the eye as when a pencil or piece of paper is passed rapidly across the whole field of vision. The earliest reaction I have noted occurred on the 65th day. Mrs. Mary Cover Jones noted the reac-   430
tion in one infant at 40 days.

. . . Usually at 100 days the infant will blink whenever the stimulus is applied if at least one minute is allowed between stimulations. This reaction stays in the activity stream until death. We cannot prove it yet but this reaction looks to us very much like a conditioned visual eyelid response, as follows: 435

(U)S   (U)R

Contact with cornea   blink

but objects which touch the eye often cast a shadow, hence

440   (C)S   (U)R

Shadow   blink

> Blinking when the cornea is touched is a reflex. It is automatic, not conditioned or learned.
>
> Touching the cornea is the US (or UCS)— the unconditioned stimulus. Blinking is the UR (or UCR)—the unconditioned response.
>
> If there is a shadow just before cornea is touched, then the shadow (the CS, conditioned stimulus) itself will come to elicit blinking (the CR, conditioned response). This is a learned or conditioned response.
>
> This is the paradigm for classical (or Pavlovian) conditioning (see 5.2).

If this reasoning is correct, blinking at a shadow is not an *unlearned* response.

Handedness: We have already pointed out the
445   possibility of handedness being due to the long enforced intra-uterine position of the child (really a habit). . . .

At the age of approximately 120 days you can begin to get the baby to reach for a stick of gaudily striped peppermint candy. You must first pos-
450   itively condition him to the candy. This can be done long before the habit of reaching is established by visually stimulating the infant with the stick of candy and then putting the candy in the mouth or else putting it in the baby's hands. If the latter is done the baby puts the candy in its mouth. Usually by the 160th day the infant will reach readily for the candy as soon as it is exhibited. The infant is then ready to test for handedness.
455   In all, I have worked with about 20 babies during this interesting period. In making the test, the baby is held in the mother's lap so that both hands are equally free. The experimenter stands in front of the baby and extends the candy slowly towards the baby at the level of its eyes, using care to advance on a line between the two hands. When the candy gets just within reach (and usually not much before) the two hands get active, then one or the other or both
460   are lifted and advanced towards the candy. The hand touching it first is noted.

The results of all our tests of this nature, extending from the age of 150 days to one year, show no steady and uniform handedness. Some days the right is used more often, some days the left.

Baldwin (1903, pp. 69–76) had also done studies on handedness, with somewhat different results. His daughter served as the subject in a study that extended from her fourth to her tenth month. Baldwin looked at which hand she used to reach for objects at various locations and distances in front of her. The experiments were "planned with very great care" (p. 69). To be sure that her early experience had no effect on her handedness, his daughter was never carried (lest one hand be favored for holding on or reaching) and was not allowed to stand on her feet until the study was completed. No "preference for either hand was discernible" from her fifth to ninth month (right hand, 577 trials; left hand, 568 trials).

(Continued)

(Continued)

Baldwin also tested her handedness when the object was so far away that she had to strain to reach it. On these trials she used her right hand almost exclusively even when the object was on the left (right hand, 74 trials; left hand, 5 trials).

In an earlier report of this research, Baldwin (1894) suggested that handedness is related to the development of the two halves of the brain and that there is a strong inherited predisposition to favor one hand over the other for particular tasks.

The Conclusion We Draw

Our whole group of results on handedness leads us to believe that there is no fixed differentiation of response in either hand until social usage begins to establish handedness. Society soon thereafter steps in and says, "Thou shalt use thy right hand." Pressure promptly begins. "Shake hands with your right hand, Willy." We hold the infant so that it will wave "bye bye" with the right hand. *We force it to eat with the right hand. This in itself is a potent enough conditioning factor to account for handedness.* But you say, "Why is society right handed?" This probably goes back to primitive days. One old theory often advanced is probably the true one. The heart is on the left side. It was easy enough for our most primitive ancestors to *learn* that the men who carried their shields with the left hand and jabbed or hurled their spears with the right were the ones who most often came back bearing their shields rather than being borne upon them. If there is any truth in this it is easy enough to see why our primitive ancestors began to teach their young to be right handed.

...

If handedness is a habit socially instilled, should we or should we not change over the left handers—those hardy souls who have resisted social pressure? I am firmly convinced that if the job is done early enough and wisely enough, not the slightest harm results. I should want to do it before language develops very much. If I had the time I would attempt to prove tonight that from the beginning we begin *to verbalize our acts*—that is put acts into words and *vice versa*. Now changing over a left handed, talking child suddenly into a right handed child is likely to reduce the child to a 6 months infant. By interfering constantly with his acts you break down his manual habits, and at the same time *you may simultaneously interfere with speech* (since the word and the manual act are simultaneously conditioned). In other words, while he is relearning he will fumble not only with his hands but also with his speech. The child is reduced to sheer infancy again. The unorganized (emotional) visceral control of the body as a whole again become predominant. It takes wiser handling to change the child over at this age than the average parent or teacher is prepared to give.

The main problem is, I believe, settled: handedness is not an "instinct." It is possibly not even structurally determined. It is socially conditioned. But why we have 5% of out and out left

465

470

475

480

485

490 handers and from 10–15% who are mixtures—e.g. using right hand to throw a ball, write or eat, but the left hand to guide an axe or hoe, etc.—is not known.

. . .

> In addition to the learned and unlearned responses described above, Watson also discusses erection of penis; voiding of urine; defecation; eye movements; manual responses; turning the head; holding up head; crawling; hand movements; arm movements; leg and foot movements; trunk, leg, foot, and toe movements; standing and walking; vocal behavior; swimming; and grasping.

What Has Become of Instincts?

Are we not ready to admit that the whole concept of instinct is thus academic and meaningless? Even from the earliest moment we find habit factors present—present even in many acts so apparently simple that we used to call them physiological reflexes. Now turn to James'
495 list of instincts or turn to any other list of instincts. The infant is a graduate student in the subject of *learned responses* (he is multitudinously conditioned) by the time behavior such as James describes—imitation, rivalry, cleanliness and the other forms he lists—can be observed.

Actual observation thus makes it impossible for us any longer to entertain the concept of instinct. We have seen that every act has a genetic history. Is not the only correct scientific
500 procedure then to single out for study whatever act is in question and to watch and record its life history?

FOR DISCUSSION

1. Watson describes a number of structural and behavioral ways in which humans differ innately from one another. Are any of these differences things that we might think of as "capacity, talent, temperament, mental constitution, and characteristics"—all of which Watson argues are not innate?

2. Mary Cover Jones describes two techniques she found effective in extinguishing learned fears (see box on p. 386). What undesirable effects might each of these techniques have? Can you think of other possible techniques?

3. It has been said that Watson's behaviorism (and Skinner's radical behaviorism) could only have been developed in America. Do you agree?

4. How would Watson explain the instinctive drift reported by Breland and Breland [4.7]?

5. Could the definition of instinct that Watson ascribes to William James ("James says an instinct is 'a tendency to act in such a way as to bring about certain ends without having foresight of those ends.'") be applied to the behavior of the boomerang, the loaded die, and the weighted toy soldier (p. 382, lines 286–306)?

6. Why was it important to Watson to relate all human behavior to reflexes and not to instincts?

7. Fantz (1961, 1963) found that infants show an innate visual preference for human faces. What would Watson's response be to this finding?

Keller Breland (1915–1965)
Marian Breland (1920–2001)
The Misbehavior of Organisms (1961)

When the Japanese attacked Pearl Harbor in December 1941, B. F. Skinner (see 3.5) got serious about his idea of using pigeons to guide offensive missiles toward stationary targets. Skinner and Keller Breland, one of his graduate students at the University of Minnesota, began training pigeons and devising equipment that would make his idea a reality. They received some support from the National Defense Research Committee (NDRC) and $5,000 and some space in an old flour mill from General Mills. Skinner and Breland were later joined by Norman Guttman and two of Skinner's other students—William Estes and Marian Breland—who worked primarily on conditioning the pigeons. All the tests done on the project showed that trained pigeons were up to the task. Skinner's idea worked, and it worked very well, but the NDRC was never enthusiastic, and Skinner gave up Project Pigeon in 1944.[1]

The techniques that Skinner and his graduate students used to train the pigeons were based on principles of operant conditioning that Skinner had developed. Operant conditioning rests on the assumption that animals naturally behave, they act. If one of their behaviors (operants) is reinforced (something good happens after the behavior, or something bad goes away), the behavior is more likely to be repeated in the future. Reinforcement, then, can be used in animal training to increase the probability of a particular behavior being repeated, and the absence of reinforcement following a particular behavior can be used to decrease that probability. If, as usually happens, an animal does not happen to produce the particular behavior you want to see, you can use successive approximations to produce it, a process called "shaping." For example, if you want a pigeon to make a 360° turn, you could first give him a reinforcement (usually food) when he turns a little. After you have done this a few times, you could hold back

Source: Breland, K., & Breland, M. (1961). The misbehavior of organisms. *American Psychologist, 16,* 681–684.

[1] The material on Project Pigeon comes from Capshew (1997), Skinner (1958, 1960, 1979), and Glines (2005).

the reinforcement until he turns a little further, then a little further, and a little further until finally he receives reinforcement only when he turns all the way around. Before Project Pigeon, Skinner had already demonstrated the effectiveness of shaping and other operant conditioning techniques in training animals (rats or pigeons) to do quite complicated tasks.

After the Project Pigeon experience, Skinner began thinking about how operant conditioning could be used for behavioral engineering (Capshew, 1997). Two of his students—Keller and Marian Breland—also saw interesting possibilities based on their experience with Project Pigeon. They left academic life and ventured into another world, one that Skinner described as "the commercial production of behavior" (Skinner, 1958).

In 1943 the Brelands established Animal Behavior Enterprises (ABE) and trained animals to appear in commercials, at fairs, and in arcades (General Mills was their first client). They knew that working only with rats and pigeons would not draw crowds or advertising business, and so they began using operant conditioning techniques with a wide range of species. By 1950 the Brelands had made a success of ABE, and in order to expand their business, they moved from their farm in Minnesota to Hot Springs, Arkansas.

In 1954 they opened the IQ Zoo, a popular tourist attraction at which you could see all sorts of animals engaged in interesting and entertaining behaviors.[2] The Brelands continued their work for commercial clients (e.g., Sea World, Marineland, Quaker Oats, Mobil Oil, and Knott's Berry Farm) and accepted government contracts (e.g., the Navy Dolphin Project). After Keller Breland's death in 1965, Marian Breland continued the business. Bob Bailey, who had been working with the Brelands on the Navy Dolphin Project, became Marian's husband in 1976 and worked with her at ABE until it closed its doors in 1990.[3]

After 1990 Marian and Bob Bailey remained tireless proponents of their operant conditioning approach to animal training at workshops and training sessions across the country. The Brelands and the Baileys were committed to using humane methods of animal training. Like Skinner, they did not believe in the use of punishment. They developed effective and humane ways to train a variety of animal species, and they trained other people to use these techniques as well.

In the course of training animals Keller Breland had created the *bridging* technique, now widely used and usually called *clicker training*. A bridging signal is "one that bridges the time lag between the earning of the reward and the receiving of it" (Wolfert, 1957). The bridging signal (a click, a whistle, a bell) is a secondary reinforcer. Through a process of classical (or Pavlovian; see 5.2) conditioning, the animal is trained to associate the bridging signal (the conditioned stimulus, the CS) with a primary reinforcement (the unconditioned stimulus, the UCS—typically food). The bridging signal can then be used in training instead of food to shape an animal's behavior using operant conditioning techniques. Of course, the food should appear reasonably soon, especially in the early part of training, in order to maintain the relationship between the bridging signal and the food.

Despite its title—a play on Skinner's 1938 book, *The Behavior of Organisms*—the present reading was not intended to be an indictment of Skinnerian methods (Bailey & Bailey, 1993; Breland, 1961) but instead to point out a factor ("instinctive drift") that needs to be considered when training animals with operant techniques.

---

[2] The IQ Zoo changed hands, and names, several times in recent years. It isn't clear to us whether it still exists.

[3] The material on ABE and the IQ Zoo comes from Gillaspy and Bihm (2002), Bailey (2003), Wolfert (1957), and Cramer (2000).

There seems to be a continuing realization by psychologists that perhaps the white rat cannot reveal everything there is to know about behavior. Among the voices raised on this topic, Beach (1950) has emphasized the necessity of widening the range of species subjected to experimental techniques and conditions. However, psychologists as a whole do not seem to be heeding these admonitions, as Whalen (1961) has pointed out.

> Beach counted the number of psychological studies done with nonhuman animals and the number of different species used in these studies from 1911 to 1948. He found an increase in the number of studies but a decrease in the number of species studied after 1915. The white rat had come to represent all animals. Skinner (1938) argued that it is "reasonable" to study one representative species, but Beach asked in what ways the rat is representative. He described the advantages and disadvantages of this approach and concluded that the disadvantages far outweigh the advantages. He recommended a return to the study of comparative psychology.
>
> Whalen repeated Beach's study with data from 1956–1959 and concluded that nothing had changed, that "animal psychology will remain the science of rat learning."

Perhaps this reluctance is due in part to some dark precognition of what they might find in such investigations, for the ethologists Lorenz (1950, p. 233) and Tinbergen (1951, p. 6) have warned that if psychologists are to understand and predict the behavior of organisms, it is essential that they become thoroughly familiar with the instinctive behavior patterns of each new species they essay to study. Of course, the Watsonian (see 4.6) or neobehavioristically oriented experimenter is apt to consider "instinct" an ugly word. He tends to class it with Hebb's (1960) other "seditious notions" which were discarded in the behavioristic revolution, and he may have some premonition that he will encounter this bête noir in extending the range of species and situations studied.

> *ethology:* the study of animal behavior in natural settings

> *seditious:* inciting rebellion. Hebb was describing behaviorists' feelings about the word "instinct," not his own.
>
> *bête noir:* something one dislikes or avoids (Fr: "black beast")

We can assure him that his apprehensions are well grounded. In our attempt to extend a behavioristically oriented approach to the engineering control of animal behavior by operant conditioning techniques, we have fought a running battle with the seditious notion of instinct.[4] It might be of some interest to the psychologist to know how the battle is going and to learn something about the nature of the adversary he is likely to meet if and when he tackles new species in new learning situations.

---

[4] In view of the fact that instinctive behaviors may be common to many zoological species, we consider *species specific* to be a sanitized misnomer, and prefer the possibly septic adjective *instinctive.*

Our first report (Breland & Breland, 1951) in the *American Psychologist,* concerning our experiences in controlling animal behavior, was wholly affirmative and optimistic, saying in essence that the principles derived from the laboratory could be applied to the extensive control of behavior under nonlaboratory conditions throughout a considerable segment of the phylo-   30
genetic scale.

> In their 1951 article, the Brelands described the function of their business as the "mass production of conditioned operant behavior in animals" (p. 202), and they discussed their successful bringing together of modern behavioral science and professional animal training.
>
> They also give examples of some of their early successes: the hens who played piano, performed "tap dances" in costumes and shoes, "laid" any number of wooden eggs the audience called for; and a pig (Priscilla) who ate breakfast at a table, picked up dirty clothes and put them in a hamper, ran the vacuum around, and answered any yes-no question the audience asked.
>
> The Brelands go on to discuss the range of situations that call for animal training (e.g., "Seeing Eye" dogs) and the ease with which people can be trained to train animals using the techniques of operant conditioning.

When we began this work, it was our aim to see if the science would work beyond the laboratory, to determine if animal psychology could stand on its own feet as an engineering discipline. These aims have been realized. We have controlled a wide range of animal behavior and have made use of the great popular appeal of animals to make it an economically fea-   35
sible project. Conditioned behavior has been exhibited at various municipal zoos and museums of natural history and has been used for department store displays, for fair and trade convention exhibits, for entertainment at tourist attractions, on television shows, and in the production of television commercials. Thirty-eight species, totaling over 6,000 individual animals, have been conditioned, and we have dared to tackle such unlikely subjects as reindeer, cockatoos,   40
raccoons, porpoises, and whales.

Emboldened by this consistent reinforcement, we have ventured further and further from the security of the Skinner box. However, in this cavalier extrapolation, we have run afoul of a persistent pattern of discomforting failures. These failures, although disconcertingly frequent and seemingly diverse, fall into a very interesting pattern. They all represent breakdowns of   45
conditioned operant behavior. From a great number of such experiences, we have selected, more or less at random, the following examples.

The first instance of our discomfiture might be entitled, What Makes Sammy Dance? In the exhibit in which this occurred, the casual observer sees a grown bantam chicken emerge from a retaining compartment when the door automatically opens. The chicken walks over about   50
3 feet, pulls a rubber loop on a small box which starts a repeated auditory stimulus pattern (a four-note tune). The chicken then steps up onto an 18-inch slightly raised disc, thereby closing a timer switch, and scratches vigorously, round and round, over the disc for 15 seconds, at the rate of about two scratches per second until the automatic feeder fires in the retaining

55   compartment. The chicken goes into the compartment to eat, thereby automatically shutting the door. The popular interpretation of this behavior pattern is that the chicken has turned on the "juke box" and "dances."

The development of this behavioral exhibit was wholly unplanned. In the attempt to create quite another type of demonstration which required a chicken simply to stand on a platform
60   for 12–15 seconds, we found that over 50% developed a very strong and pronounced scratch pattern, which tended to increase in persistence as the time interval was lengthened. (Another 25% or so developed other behaviors—pecking at spots, etc.) However, we were able to change our plans so as to make use of the scratch pattern, and the result was the "dancing chicken" exhibit described above.

65   In this exhibit the only real contingency for reinforcement is that the chicken must depress the platform for 15 seconds. In the course of a performing day (about 3 hours for each chicken) a chicken may turn out over 10,000 unnecessary, virtually identical responses. Operant behaviorists would probably have little hesitancy in labeling this an example of Skinnerian "superstition" (Skinner, 1948) or "mediating" behavior, and we list it first to whet their explanatory
70   appetite.

> Skinner (1948) did a simple experiment to demonstrate the development of superstitious behavior in pigeons. A pigeon is placed in a cage. Every 15 seconds a food hopper swings into the cage, stays for 5 seconds, and then swings out. Skinner observed that many pigeons persist in whatever behavior they happened to be doing just before the hopper swung in. This was superstitious behavior and it was conditioned because of the temporal relationship between the behavior and the arrival of food—the behavior is performed and then the food appears. In the same way, any behavior may become conditioned (and therefore repeated) if it is followed by reinforcement, especially if the reinforcement consistently follows the behavior. The chicken's behavior can be seen as an example of the acquisition of a piece of superstitious behavior, particularly strong conditioning in this case because reinforcement regularly follows the behavior.

However, a second instance involving a raccoon does not fit so neatly into this paradigm. The response concerned the manipulation of money by the raccoon (who has "hands" rather similar to those of the primates). The contingency for reinforcement was picking up the coins and depositing them in a 5-inch metal box.
75   Raccoons condition readily, have good appetites, and this one was quite tame and an eager subject. We anticipated no trouble. Conditioning him to pick up the first coin was simple. We started out by reinforcing him for picking up a single coin. Then the metal container was introduced, with the requirement that he drop the coin into the container. Here we ran into the first bit of difficulty: he seemed to have a great deal of trouble letting go of the coin. He would rub it up against the inside of the container, pull it back out, and clutch it firmly for several seconds. However, he would finally
80   turn it loose and receive his food reinforcement. Then the final contingency: we put him on a ratio of 2, requiring that he pick up both coins and put them in the container.

Now the raccoon really had problems (and so did we). Not only could he not let go of the coins, but he spent seconds, even minutes, rubbing them together (in a most miserly fashion), and dipping them into the container. He carried on this behavior to such an extent that the practical application we had in mind—a display featuring a raccoon putting money in a piggy bank—simply was not feasible. The rubbing behavior became worse and worse as time went on, in spite of nonreinforcement.

85

gallinaceous birds: chickens and other ground-walking species

S_D: discriminative stimulus—a stimulus in the presence of which the animal is able to obtain reinforcements. It signals the potential availability of reinforcement.

For the third instance, we return, to the gallinaceous birds. The observer sees a hopper full of oval plastic capsules which contain small toys, charms, and the like. When the S_D (a light) is presented to the chicken, she pulls a rubber loop which releases one of these capsules onto a slide, about 16 inches long, inclined at about 30 degrees. The capsule rolls down the slide and comes to rest near the end. Here one or two sharp, straight pecks by the chicken will knock it forward off the slide and out to the observer, and the chicken is then reinforced by an automatic feeder. This is all very well—most chickens are able to master these contingencies in short order. The loop pulling presents no problems; she then has only to peck the capsule off the slide to get her reinforcement.

90

95

100

However, a good 20% of all chickens tried on this set of contingencies fail to make the grade. After they have pecked a few capsules off the slide, they begin to grab at the capsules and drag them backwards into the cage. Here they pound them up and down on the floor of the cage. Of course, this results in no reinforcement for the chicken, and yet some chickens will pull in over half of all the capsules presented to them.

105

Almost always this problem behavior does not appear until after the capsules begin to move down the slide. Conditioning is begun with stationary capsules placed by the experimenter. When the pecking behavior becomes strong enough, so that the chicken is knocking them off the slide and getting reinforced consistently, the loop pulling is conditioned to the light. The capsules then come rolling down the slide to the chicken. Here most chickens, who before did not have this tendency, will start grabbing and shaking.

110

The fourth incident also concerns a chicken. Here the observer sees a chicken in a cage about 4 feet long which is placed alongside a miniature baseball field. The reason for the cage is the interesting part. At one end of the cage is an automatic electric feed hopper. At the other is an opening through which the chicken can reach and pull a loop on a bat. If she pulls the loop hard enough the bat (solenoid operated) will swing, knocking a small baseball up the playing field. If it gets past the miniature toy players on the field and hits the back fence, the chicken is automatically reinforced with food at the other end of the cage. If it does not go far enough, or hits one of the players, she tries again. This results in behavior on an irregular ratio. When the feeder sounds, she then runs down the length of the cage and eats.

115

120

Our problems began when we tried to remove the cage for photography. Chickens that had been well conditioned in this behavior became wildly excited when the ball started to move. They would jump up on the playing field, chase the ball all over the field, even knock it off on the floor and chase it around, pecking it in every direction, although they had never had access to the ball before. This behavior was so persistent and so disruptive, in spite of the fact that it was never reinforced, that we had to reinstate the cage.

The last instance we shall relate in detail is one of the most annoying and baffling for a good behaviorist. Here a pig was conditioned to pick up large wooden coins and deposit them in a large "piggy bank." The coins were placed several feet from the bank and the pig required to carry them to the bank and deposit them, usually four or five coins for one reinforcement. (Of course, we started out with one coin, near the bank.)

Pigs condition very rapidly, they have no trouble taking ratios, they have ravenous appetites (naturally), and in many ways are among the most tractable animals we have worked with. However, this particular problem behavior developed in pig after pig, usually after a period of weeks or months, getting worse every day. At first the pig would eagerly pick up one dollar, carry it to the bank, run back, get another, carry it rapidly and neatly, and so on, until the ratio was complete. Thereafter, over a period of weeks the behavior would become slower and slower. He might run over eagerly for each dollar, but on the way back, instead of carrying the dollar and depositing it simply and cleanly, he would repeatedly drop it, root it, drop it again, root it along the way, pick it up, toss it up in the air, drop it, root it some more, and so on.

> *root:* dig with the snout or nose

We thought this behavior might simply be the dilly-dallying of an animal on a low drive. However, the behavior persisted and gained in strength in spite of a severely increased drive—he finally went through the ratios so slowly that he did not get enough to eat in the course of a day. Finally it would take the pig about 10 minutes to transport four coins a distance of about 6 feet. This problem behavior developed repeatedly in successive pigs.

There have also been other instances: hamsters that stopped working in a glass case after four or five reinforcements, porpoises and whales that swallow their manipulanda (balls and inner tubes), cats that will not leave the area of the feeder, rabbits that will not go to the feeder, the great difficulty in many species of conditioning vocalization with food reinforcement, problems in conditioning a kick in a cow, the failure to get appreciably increased effort out of the ungulates with increased drive, and so on. These we shall not dwell on in detail; nor shall we discuss how they might be overcome.

> *ungulates:* animals with hooves

These egregious failures came as a rather considerable shock to us, for there was nothing in our background in behaviorism to prepare us for such gross inabilities to predict and control the behavior of animals with which we had been working for years.

The examples listed we feel represent a clear and utter failure of conditioning theory. They are far from what one would normally expect on the basis of the theory alone. Furthermore, they are definite, observable; the diagnosis of theory failure does not depend on subtle statistical interpretations or on semantic legerdemain—the animal simply does not do what he has been conditioned to do.

> legerdemain: sleight-of-hand

It seems perfectly clear that, with the possible exception of the dancing chicken, which could conceivably, as we have said, be explained in terms of Skinner's superstition paradigm, the other instances do not fit the behavioristic way of thinking. Here we have animals, after having been conditioned to a specific learned response, gradually drifting into behaviors that are entirely different from those which were conditioned. Moreover, it can easily be seen that these particular behaviors to which the animals drift are clear-cut examples of instinctive behaviors having to do with the natural food getting behaviors of the particular species.

The dancing chicken is exhibiting the gallinaceous birds' scratch pattern that in nature often precedes ingestion. The chicken that hammers capsules is obviously exhibiting instinctive behavior having to do with breaking open of seed pods or the killing of insects, grubs, etc. The raccoon is demonstrating so-called "washing behavior." The rubbing and washing response may result, for example, in the removal of the exoskeleton of a crayfish. The pig is rooting or shaking—behaviors which are strongly built into this species and are connected with the food getting repertoire.

These patterns to which the animals drift require greater physical output and therefore are a violation of the so-called "law of least effort." And most damaging of all, they stretch out the time required for reinforcement when nothing in the experimental setup requires them to do so. They have only to do the little tidbit of behavior to which they were conditioned—for example, pick up the coin and put it in the container—to get reinforced immediately. Instead, they drag the process out for a matter of minutes when there is nothing in the contingency which forces them to do this. Moreover, increasing the drive merely intensifies this effect.

It seems obvious that these animals are trapped by strong instinctive behaviors; and clearly we have here a demonstration of the prepotency of such behavior patterns over those which have been conditioned.

We have termed this phenomenon "instinctive drift." The general principle seems to be that wherever an animal has strong instinctive behaviors in the area of the conditioned response, after continued running the organism will drift toward the instinctive behavior to the detriment of the conditioned behavior and even to the delay or preclusion of the reinforcement. In a very boiled-down, simplified form, it might be stated as "learned behavior drifts toward instinctive behavior."

> preclusion: prevention

All this, of course, is not to disparage the use of conditioning techniques, but is intended as a demonstration that there are definite weaknesses in the philosophy underlying these techniques. The pointing out of such weaknesses should make possible a worthwhile revision in behavior theory.

205 The notion of instinct has now become one of our basic concepts in an effort to make sense of the welter of observations which confront us. When behaviorism tossed out instinct, it is our feeling that some of its power of prediction and control were lost with it. From the foregoing examples, it appears that although it was easy to banish the Instinctivists from the science during the Behavioristic Revolution, it was not possible to banish instinct so easily.

210 And if, as Hebb suggests, it is advisable to reconsider those things that behaviorism explicitly threw out, perhaps it might likewise be advisable to examine what they tacitly brought in—the hidden assumptions which led most disastrously to these breakdowns in the theory.

Three of the most important of these tacit assumptions seem to us to be: that the animal comes to the laboratory as a virtual *tabula rasa,*
215 that species differences are insignificant, and that all responses are about equally conditionable to all stimuli.

It is obvious, we feel, from the foregoing account that these assumptions are no longer ten-
220 able. After 14 years of continuous conditioning and observation of thousands of animals, it is our reluctant conclusion that the behavior of any species cannot be adequately understood, predicted, or controlled without knowledge of its
225 instinctive patterns, evolutionary history, and ecological niche.

In spite of our early successes with the application of behavioristically oriented conditioning theory, we readily admit now that ethological
230 facts and attitudes in recent years have done more to advance our practical control of animal behavior than recent reports from American "learning labs."

Moreover, as we have recently discovered, if
235 one begins with evolution and instinct as the basic format for the science, a very illuminating viewpoint can be developed which leads naturally to a drastically revised and simplified conceptual framework of startling explanatory power (to be
240 reported elsewhere).

It is hoped that this playback on the theory will be behavioral technology's partial repayment to the academic science whose impeccable empiricism we have used so extensively.

> *tabula rasa:* blank slate. The phrase comes from Aristotle and Aquinas, but it is now most strongly associated with John Locke (see 4.2). His view was that it is only through experience that we acquire knowledge about the world. Nothing is given innately; the mind's ideas are acquired through experience.

> Garcia and Koelling (1966) did further work on these assumptions. They found that, among species that select their food by taste, if one feels ill after eating or drinking something with a particular taste, one will avoid that taste in the future. If, however, one is shocked after eating or drinking it, the conditioned avoidance will not occur. Some connections between a UCS and a CS are easier to make than others, and species differ from one another in the kinds of connections that are likely (e.g., species that rely on vision to select food do not show learned taste aversions but do show learned color aversions [Wilcoxon, Dragoin, & Kral, 1971]).

> *elsewhere:* Breland and Breland (1966)

FOR DISCUSSION

1. What is the biological advantage of the rapid development of learned taste aversions (note, p. 399)?

2. Why does "instinctive drift" not show up until the conditioned behavior has been in place for a while?

3. All Breland and Breland's examples involve eating behavior. Is "instinctive drift" likely to happen with other instinctive (biological) drives as well?

4. How is the "instinctive drift" described by Breland and Breland related to the caterpillar's hammock-building behaviors that Darwin describes (p. 323, lines 32–40)?

5. What would Watson (4.6) say about the Brelands' examples of "instinctive drift"?

Noam Chomsky (b. 1928)
Language and Mind (1968)

Linguistic contributions to the study of mind: future

At first glance it seems obvious that if there is anything in the mind that results from experience, it is our language. After all, no one can speak—or, as far as we can tell, understand speech—at birth, and clearly the language we speak is determined by the linguistic environment we are born into. Moreover, in the "wild child" cases that occasionally come to light, children deprived of exposure to language consistently fail to develop language. The first attempts to explain language acquisition were, not surprisingly, empiricist: whether we learn by imitation, by trial and error, or through instruction, our exposure to the target language is the source of all that we learn.

What could be wrong with this? As it turns out, plenty. Looking closely at what a child can do, linguistically, at different ages, Chomsky saw things that seem incompatible with the empiricist approach. If you have studied a foreign language, you know what an accomplishment it is to be able to speak like a 6-year-old. Yet the child accomplishes this quickly, with an incompletely developed brain and without formal instruction or apparent effort. Moreover, Chomsky pointed out that the child's linguistic environment—the specimens of language the child is exposed to—is *impoverished;* it does not contain enough or the right kinds of specimens to explain what the child is able to do. Chomsky gave this example in a 1996 BBC interview:[1]

QUESTION: What is it about the grammars of natural language that can't be inferred just from the input?

CHOMSKY: To infer anything from an input you have to have a specific method of deriving

Source: From *Language and mind, 3rd edition*, by Noam Chomsky. Reprinted by permission of Cambridge University Press. [The chapter was the third of three lectures given at the University of California, Berkeley, in 1967, and originally published in 1968 in the first edition of *Language and Mind*.]

[1] "Silent Children, New Language: Noam Chomsky Interviewed." Reprinted with permission of BBC.

information that leads you to that result. So we ask what aspect of grammar forces us to assume that there are highly specific ways of getting the result? Answer: every aspect. There are no generalised mechanisms known for looking at masses of data and yielding this specific analysis. They'll yield any analysis depending on how you tune them. When you begin to look at the actual properties of very simple expressions you can begin to determine the principles that are being used. So for example, take the sentence "John ate an apple." Let's say we've gotten to the point where the child understands that. We hear "John eats." Let's say the child understands that to mean John is eating something-or-other, not necessarily an apple. Well there's a kind of a principle. The principle says that if something is missing that belongs there, you understand it to mean something-or-other— okay, that's natural. Take it a step further. Take the sentence "John is too stubborn to talk to Bill." Okay, that means John is so stubborn that he won't talk to Bill. Drop out the last word Bill, just like we dropped out the last word apple, "John is too stubborn to talk to." Well, by the principle we just used it ought to mean John is so stubborn that he won't talk to someone-or-othser which is perfectly sensible but it doesn't mean that. It means that John is so stubborn that someone or other won't talk to him, John, so we invert the interpretation. We're dealing with tiny sentences, seven word sentences. Build this up a little bit it gets even more complex. "John is too clever for anyone to catch." Who's doing the catching? Well, you can figure it out.

On the basis of this and other sorts of evidence, Chomsky argues—to many, persuasively— that (1) the rules that the child is using could not have been derived exclusively from the speech specimens in the linguistic environment, and that therefore (2) some universal aspects of language—of all possible human languages—must be innate.

. . .

It is quite natural to expect that a concern for language will remain central to the study of human nature, as it has been in the past. Anyone concerned with the study of human nature and human capacities must somehow come to grips with the fact that all normal humans acquire language, whereas acquisition of even its barest rudiments is quite beyond the capacities of an otherwise intelligent ape—a fact that was emphasized, quite correctly, in Cartesian philosophy.[1] It is widely thought that the extensive modern studies of animal communication challenge this classical view; and it is almost universally taken for granted that there exists a problem of explaining the "evolution" of human language from systems of animal communication. However, a careful look at recent studies of animal communication seems to me to provide little support for these assumptions. Rather, these studies simply bring out even more clearly the extent to which human language appears to be a unique phenomenon, without significant analogue in the animal world. If this is so, it is quite senseless to raise the problem of explaining the evolution of human language from more primitive systems of communication that appear at lower levels of intellectual capacity. The issue is important, and I would like to dwell on it for a moment.

The assumption that human language evolved from more primitive systems is developed in an interesting way by Karl Popper [1966] in his recently published Arthur Compton Lecture, "Clouds and Clocks." He tries to show how problems of freedom of will and Cartesian dualism can be solved by the analysis of this "evolution." I am not concerned now

For example, Descartes writes,

> [I]t has never been observed that any brute animal has attained the perfection of using real speech, that is to say, of indicating by word or sign something relating to thought alone and not to natural impulse. Such speech is the only certain sign of thought hidden in a body. All human beings use it, however stupid and insane they may be, even though they may have no tongue and organs of voice; but no animals do. Consequently this can be taken as a real specific difference between humans and animals (Descartes, 1649/1991, p. 366).

The uniqueness of human language is for Descartes an important argument for the presence, in humans, of some "thinking substance."

---

[1] Modern attempts to train apes in behavior that the investigators regard as language-like confirm this incapacity, though it may be that the failures are to be attributed to the technique of operant conditioning and therefore show little about the animal's actual abilities. See, for example, Ferster [1964]. Ferster attempted to teach chimpanzees to match the binary numbers 001, . . ., 111 to sets of one to seven objects. He reports that hundreds of thousands of trials were required for 95 per cent accuracy to be achieved, even in this trivial task. Of course, even at this stage the apes had not learned the principle of binary arithmetic; they would not, for example, be able to match a four-digit binary number correctly, and, presumably, they would have done just as badly in the experiment had it involved an arbitrary association of the binary numbers to sets rather than the association determined by the principle of the binary notation. Ferster overlooks this crucial point and therefore concludes, mistakenly, that he has taught the rudiments of symbolic behavior. The confusion is compounded by his definition of language as "a set of symbolic stimuli that control behavior" and by his strange belief that the "effectiveness" of language arises from the fact that utterances "control almost identical performances in speaker and listener."

with the philosophical conclusions that he draws from this analysis, but with the basic assumption that there is an evolutionary development of language from simpler systems of the sort that one discovers in other organisms. Popper argues that the evolution of language passed through several stages, in particular a "lower stage" in which vocal gestures are used for expression of emotional state, for example, and a "higher stage" in which articulated sound is used for expression of thought—in Popper's terms, for description and critical argument. His discussion of stages of evolution of language suggests a kind of continuity, but in fact he establishes no relation between the lower and higher stages and does not suggest a mechanism whereby transition can take place from one stage to the next. In short, he gives no argument to show that the stages belong to a single evolutionary process. In fact, it is difficult to see what links these stages at all (except for the metaphorical use of the term "language"). There is no reason to suppose that the "gaps" are bridge-able. There is no more of a basis for assuming an evolutionary development of "higher" from "lower" stages, in this case, than there is for assuming an evolutionary development from breathing to walking; the stages have no significant analogy, it appears, and seem to involve entirely different processes and principles.

A more explicit discussion of the relation between human language and animal communication systems appears in a recent discussion by the comparative ethologist W. H. Thorpe (1967, pp. 2–10, and discussions on pp. 19, 84–85). He points out that mammals other than man appear to lack the human ability to imitate sounds, and that one might therefore have expected birds (many of which have this ability to a remarkable extent) to be "the group which ought to have been able to evolve language in the true sense, and not the mammals." Thorpe does not suggest that human language "evolved" in any strict sense from simpler systems, but he does argue that the characteristic properties of human language can be found in animal communication systems, although "we cannot at the moment say definitely that they are all present in one particular animal." The characteristics shared by human and animal language are the properties of being "purposive," "syntactic," and "propositional." Language is purposive "in that there is nearly always in human speech a definite intention of getting something over to somebody else, altering his behavior, his thoughts, or his general attitude toward a situation." Human language is "syntactic" in that an utterance is a performance with an internal organization, with structure and coherence. It is "propositional" in that it transmits information. In this sense, then, both human language and animal communication are purposive, syntactic, and propositional.

All this may be true, but it establishes very little, since when we move to the level of abstraction at which human language and animal communication fall together, almost all other behavior is included as well. Consider walking: Clearly, walking is purposive behavior, in the most general sense of "purposive." Walking is also "syntactic" in the sense just defined, as, in fact, Karl Lashley pointed out a long time ago in his important discussion of serial order in behavior (Lashley, 1951), to which I referred in the first lecture. Furthermore, it can certainly be informative; for example, I can signal my interest in reaching a certain goal by the speed or intensity with which I walk.

It is, incidentally, precisely in this manner that the examples of animal communication that
Thorpe presents are "propositional." He cites as an example the song of the European robin,
in which the rate of alternation of high and low pitch signals the intention of the bird to defend
its territory; the higher the rate of alternation, the greater the intention to defend the territory.
The example is interesting, but it seems to me to show very clearly the hopelessness of the
attempt to relate human language to animal communication. Every animal communication
system that is known (if we disregard some science fiction about dolphins) uses one of two
basic principles: Either it consists of a fixed, finite number of signals, each associated with a specific range of behavior or emotional state, as is illustrated in the extensive primate studies that
have been carried out by Japanese scientists for the past several years; or it makes use of a fixed,
finite number of linguistic dimensions, each of which is associated with a particular nonlinguistic dimension in such a way that selection of a point along the linguistic dimension determines and signals a certain point along the associated nonlinguistic dimension. The latter is the
principle realized in Thorpe's bird-song example. Rate of alternation of high and low pitch is a
linguistic dimension correlated with the non-linguistic dimension of intention to defend a territory. The bird signals its intention to defend a territory by selecting a correlated point along
the linguistic dimension of pitch alternation—I use the word "select" loosely, of course. The linguistic dimension is abstract, but the principle is clear. A communication system of the second
type has an indefinitely large range of potential signals, as does human language. The mechanism and principle, however, are entirely different from those employed by human language to express indefinitely many new thoughts, intentions, feelings, and so on. It is not
correct to speak of a "deficiency" of the animal system, in terms of range of potential signals;
rather the opposite, since the animal system admits in principle of continuous variation along
the linguistic dimension (insofar as it makes sense to speak of "continuity" in such a case),
whereas human language is discrete. Hence, the issue is not one of "more" or "less," but rather
of an entirely different principle of organization. When I make some arbitrary statement in a
human language—say, that "the rise of supranational corporations poses new dangers for
human freedom"—I am not selecting a point along some linguistic dimension that signals a
corresponding point along an associated nonlinguistic dimension, nor am I selecting a signal
from a finite behavioral repertoire, innate or learned.

Furthermore, it is wrong to think of human use of language as characteristically informative,
in fact or in intention. Human language can be used to inform or mislead, to clarify one's own
thoughts or to display one's cleverness, or simply for play. If I speak with no concern for modifying your behavior or thoughts, I am not using language any less than if I say exactly the same
things *with* such intention. If we hope to understand human language and the psychological
capacities on which it rests, we must first ask what it is, not how or for what purposes it is used.
When we ask what human language is, we find no striking similarity to animal communication
systems. There is nothing useful to be said about behavior or thought at the level of abstraction at which animal and human communication fall together. The examples of animal communication that have been examined to date do share many of the properties of human

gestural systems: When we talk to one another we move our hands, our bodies, our faces in ways that amplify, clarify, or contradict what we say. When we write, we cannot use these gestural systems, and must rely exclusively on words. Conversely, when speech is impossible or undesirable, we are limited to gestures. A fundamental difference between languages and gestural systems is that a language permits infinite combinations of words to express any imaginable meaning, whereas gestures are limited in the meanings they can convey.

gestural systems, and it might be reasonable to explore the possibility of direct connection in this case. But human language, it appears, is based on entirely different principles. This, I think, is an important point, often overlooked by those who approach human language as a natural, biological phenomenon; in particular, it seems rather pointless, for these reasons, to speculate about the evolution of human language from simpler systems—perhaps as absurd as it would be to speculate about the "evolution" of atoms from clouds of elementary particles.

As far as we know, possession of human language is associated with a specific type of mental organization, not simply a higher degree of intelligence. There seems to be no substance to the view that human language is simply a more complex instance of something to be found elsewhere in the animal world. This poses a problem for the biologist, since, if true, it is an example of true "emergence"—the appearance of a qualitatively different phenomenon at a specific stage of complexity of organization. Recognition of this fact, though formulated in entirely different terms, is what motivated much of the classical study of language by those whose primary concern was the nature of mind. And it seems to me that today there is no better or more promising way to explore the essential and distinctive properties of human intelligence than through the detailed investigation of the structure of this unique human possession. A reasonable guess, then, is that if empirically adequate generative grammars can be constructed and the universal principles that govern their structure and organization determined, then this will be an important contribution to human psychology, in ways to which I will turn directly, in detail.

The *generative grammar* of a language is the set of rules possessed and used by a speaker of that language to generate sentences that other speakers of that language will accept as well-formed, or "grammatical." The rules of generative grammar have nothing to do with the (prescriptive) rules we learned in school. No one taught us our generative grammar, and though we can use the generative rules we cannot easily articulate most of them.

As a simple example, consider the word *Humboldtian* that Chomsky uses in the next paragraph. You have probably not seen this word before, and it is quite possible that Chomsky had not seen it until he wrote it. Chomsky's ability to invent this word and your ability to understand it can be explained in the same way, by supposing that the generative grammar of English includes something like the following rule for forming an adjective from a noun:

If the noun ends in

a consonant	→	add -ian	(e.g., Humboldtian, Skinnerian, Jamesian)
a	→	add -n	(e.g., Georgian)
e, i, or y	→	add -an	(e.g., Lockean, Fermian, Chomskyan)
o or u	→	add -nic	(e.g., Platonic)

This is only a crude sketch; you will quickly think of plenty of exceptions (such as *Aristotelian*). But it is clear that this kind of rule accounts for the *generativity* of language, that is, our ability to construct and to understand words (and sentences) we have never encountered before.

For more detailed but very accessible discussions of generative grammar, see Pinker (1994, 1999).

In the course of these lectures I have mentioned some of the classical ideas regarding language structure and contemporary efforts to deepen and extend them. It seems clear that we must

140 regard linguistic competence—knowledge of a language—as an abstract system underlying behavior, a system constituted by rules that interact to determine the form and intrinsic meaning of a potentially infinite number of sentences. Such a system—a generative grammar—provides an explication of the Humboldtian idea of "form of language," which

145 in an obscure but suggestive remark in his great posthumous work, *Über die Verschiedenheit des Menschlichen Sprachbaues,* Humboldt [1836/1999] defines as "that constant and unvarying system of processes underlying the mental act of raising artic-

150 ulated structurally organized signals to an expression of thought." Such a grammar defines a language in the Humboldtian sense, namely as "a recursively generated system, where the laws of generation are fixed and invariant, but the scope and the specific manner in which they are applied remain entirely unspecified."

155 In each such grammar there are particular, idiosyncratic elements, selection of which determines one specific human language; and there are general universal elements, conditions on the form and organization of any human language, that

160 form the subject matter for the study of "universal grammar." Among the principles of universal grammar are those I discussed in the preceding

> *Linguistic competence* is more than our ability to speak a language; it is what we know that makes this possible.

> Wilhelm von Humboldt (1767–1835) was a Prussian statesman and linguistic scholar. The title translates as "On the variety of human grammars."

> *Universal grammar* is a postulated basic grammar shared by all natural languages, past, present, and future. It was defined in 1751 by James Harris as "that grammar which without regarding the several idioms of particular languages only respects those principles that are essential to them all" (Harris, 1751, p. 11). Compare this to Humboldt's definition of "form of language."

lecture—for example, the principles that distinguish deep and surface structure and that constrain the class of transformational operations that relate them. . . .

> The distinction between *surface structure*—the actual sequence of words in a sentence—and *deep structure*—the underlying structure of relations among the constituents of a sentence—is one of Chomsky's important insights. For example, the sentences *Edith played the part of Electra* and *The part of Electra was played by Edith* and *Did Edith play the part of Electra?* have different surface structures but are all generated from a single deep structure that represents the relation between Edith and the part of Electra. (The deep structure is not itself a sentence; it is often illustrated by a hierarchical tree diagram.) Conversely, the sentences *Our guests are ready to eat* and *Our peaches are ready to eat* have the same surface structure but different deep structures—the guests are ready to do something, the peaches to have something done to them. *Transformational operations* are the rules that determine the surface structures (sentences) that can be made from a given deep structure.

Chomsky's objection to the psychology of learning is that it has given the *how* priority over the *what*. This error is only compounded by methodological restrictions that, among other things, limit the *how*s that may be studied to those that manifest themselves directly in observable behavior.

The classic exposition of this critique is Chomsky's 1959 review of Skinner's *Verbal Behavior* (see footnote 7), a thorough and devastating examination of the intellectual and scientific foundations of behaviorism.

The theory of generative grammar, both particular and universal, points to a conceptual lacuna in psychological theory that I believe is worth mentioning. Psychology conceived as "behavioral science" has been concerned with behavior and acquisition or control of behavior. It has no concept corresponding to "competence," in the sense in which competence is characterized by a generative grammar. The theory of learning has limited itself to a narrow and surely inadequate concept of what is learned—namely a system of stimulus-response connections, a network of associations, a repertoire of behavioral items, a habit hierarchy, or a system of dispositions to respond in a particular way under specifiable stimulus conditions.[2] Insofar

165

170

175

---

[2] This limitation is revealed, for example, in such statements as this from W. M. Wiest (1967): "An empirical demonstration . . . that a child has learned the rules of grammar would be his exhibiting the verbal performance called 'uttering the rules of grammar.' That this performance is not usually acquired without special training is attested to by many grammar school teachers. One may even speak quite grammatically without having literally learned the rules of grammar." Wiest's inability to conceive of another sense in which the child may be said to have learned the rules of grammar testifies to the conceptual gap we are discussing. Since he refuses to consider the question of what is learned, and to clarify this notion before asking how it is learned, he can only conceive of "grammar" as the "behavioral regularities in the understanding and production of speech"—a characterization that is perfectly empty, as it stands, there being no "behavioral regularities" associated with (let alone "in") the understanding and production of speech. One cannot quarrel with the desire of some investigators to study "the acquisition and maintenance of actual occurrences of verbal behavior" (ibid.). It remains to be demonstrated that this study has something to do with the study of language. As of now, I see no indication that this claim can be substantiated.

180 as behavioral psychology has been applied to education or therapy, it has correspondingly limited itself to this concept of "what is learned." But a generative grammar cannot be characterized in these terms. What is necessary, in addition to the concept of behavior and learning, is a concept of what is learned—a notion of competence—that lies beyond the conceptual limits of behaviorist psychological theory. Like much of modern linguistics and modern phi-

185 losophy of language, behaviorist psychology has quite consciously accepted methodological restrictions that do not permit the study of systems of the necessary complexity and abstractness.[3] One important future contribution of the study of language to general psychology may be to focus attention on this conceptual gap and to demonstrate how it may be filled by the elaboration of a system of underlying competence in one domain of human intelligence.

190 There is an obvious sense in which any aspect of psychology is based ultimately on the observation of behavior. But it is not at all obvious that the study of learning should proceed directly to the investigation of factors that control behavior or of conditions under which a "behavioral repertoire" is established. It is first necessary to determine the significant characteristics of this behavioral repertoire, the principles on which it is organized. A meaningful study

195 of learning can proceed only after this preliminary task has been carried out and has led to a reasonably well-confirmed theory of underlying competence—in the case of language, to the formulation of the generative grammar that underlies the observed use of language. Such a study

200 will concern itself with the relation between the data available to the organism and the competence that it acquires; only to the extent that the abstraction to competence has been successful—in the case of language, to the extent that the postulated grammar is "descriptively adequate" in the sense described in Lecture 2—can

205 the investigation of learning hope to achieve meaningful results. If, in some domain, the organization of the behavioral repertoire is quite trivial and elementary, then there will be little harm in avoiding the intermediate stage of theory construction, in which we attempt to characterize accurately the competence that is acquired. But one cannot count on this being the case, and in the study of language it surely is not the case. With a richer and more adequate char-

210 acterization of "what is learned"—of the underlying competence that constitutes the "final state" of the organism being studied—it may be possible to approach the task of constructing a theory of learning that will be much less restricted in scope than modern behavioral psychology has proved to be. Surely it is pointless to accept methodological strictures that preclude such an approach to problems of learning.

. . .

215 Before turning to the general implications of the study of linguistic competence and, more specifically, to the conclusions of universal grammar, it is well to make sure of the status of these conclusions in the light of current knowledge of the possible diversity of language. In my first

> Before Chomsky, much research on language acquisition had focused on counting the number of words that children used or understood at different ages.

---

[3] See Chomsky (1969) for a discussion of the work of Quine and Wittgenstein from this point of view.

Whitney (1827–1894) was an American linguist and lexicographer. His claim is that so many languages are so different from one another that it is inconceivable that they are all built on the same grammar.

lecture, I quoted the remarks of William Dwight Whitney about what he referred to as "the infinite diversity of human speech," the boundless variety that, he maintained, undermines the claims of philosophical grammar to psychological relevance.

Philosophical grammarians had typically maintained that languages vary little in their deep structures, though there may be wide variability in surface manifestations. Thus there is, in this view, an underlying structure of grammatical relations and categories, and certain aspects of human thought and mentality are essentially invariant across languages, although languages may differ as to whether they express the grammatical relations formally by inflection or word order, for example. Furthermore, an investigation of their work indicates that the underlying recursive principles that generate deep structure were assumed to be restricted in certain ways—for example, by the condition that new structures are formed only by the insertion of new "propositional content," new structures that themselves correspond to actual simple sentences, in fixed positions in already formed structures. Similarly, the grammatical transformations that form surface structures through reordering, ellipsis, and other formal operations must themselves meet certain fixed general conditions, such as those discussed in the preceding lecture. In short, the theories of philosophical grammar, and the more recent elaborations of these theories, make the assumption that languages will differ very little, despite considerable diversity in superficial realization, when we discover their deeper structures and unearth their fundamental mechanisms and principles.

Inflections are word modifications such as endings that specify the word's function and its relation to other words. The most common inflections in English are the addition of -*s* to make a plural and of -*ed* to form the past tense. English relies primarily on word order to make clear the relations among words and is a relatively uninflected language. Other languages, such as Latin or Russian, rely much more on inflections.

It is interesting to observe that this assumption persisted even through the period of German romanticism, which was, of course, much preoccupied with the diversity of cultures and with the many rich possibilities for human intellectual development. Thus, Wilhelm von Humboldt, who is now best remembered for his ideas concerning the variety of languages and the association of diverse language structures with divergent "world-views," nevertheless held firmly that underlying any human language we will find a system that is universal, that simply expresses man's unique intellectual attributes. For this reason, it was possible for him to maintain the rationalist view that language is not really learned—certainly not taught—but rather develops "from within," in an essentially predetermined way, when the appropriate environmental conditions exist. One cannot really teach a first language, he argued, but can only "provide the thread along which it will develop of its own accord," by processes more like maturation than learning. This Platonistic element in Humboldt's thought is a pervasive one; for Humboldt, it was as natural to propose an essentially Platonistic theory of "learning" as it was for Rousseau to found his critique of repressive social institutions on a conception of human freedom that derives from strictly Cartesian assumptions regarding the limitations of mechanical explanation. And in general it seems appropriate to construe both the psychology and the linguistics of the romantic period as in large part a natural outgrowth of rationalist conceptions.[4]

The issue raised by Whitney against Humboldt and philosophical grammar in general is of great significance with respect to the implications of linguistics for general human psychology. Evidently, these implications can be truly far-reaching only if the rationalist view is essentially correct, in which case the structure of language can truly serve as a "mirror of mind," in both its particular and its universal aspects. It is widely believed that modern anthropology has established the falsity of the assumptions of the rationalist universal grammarians by demonstrating through empirical study that languages may, in fact, exhibit the widest diversity. Whitney's claims regarding the diversity of languages are reiterated throughout the modern period; Martin Joos, for example, is simply expressing the conventional wisdom when he takes the basic conclusion of modern anthropological linguistics to be that "languages can differ without limit as to either extent or direction" (Joos, 1966, p. 228).[5]

The belief that anthropological linguistics has demolished the assumptions of universal grammar seems to me to be quite false in two important respects. First, it misinterprets the

> The Platonistic element in Humboldt's thought is its nativism--the idea that language is in some sense built in. Plato's theory of learning, on the other hand, is unlike Humboldt's ideas about language acquisition. Plato held that knowledge of some things-- such as the truths of mathematics-is innate, but we are unaware of this knowledge until we "recollect" it through the process of rational inquiry. (See the dialogues *Meno* and *Phaedo* for examples.) In Plato's theory, learning does not happen automatically as part of normal development and therefore does not take place in everyone.

> Jean-Jacques Rousseau (1712–1778), a key figure in the French enlightenment, believed that man is by nature good but is debased by civil society and its institutions, such as government and private property.

> The debate between anthropological and Chomskyan linguistics continues. For a description of an Amazonian language that may violate Chomsky's universal grammar, see Everett (2005); for a less technical account, see Colapinto (2007).

---

[4] For some discussion of these matters, see Chomsky (1966).

[5] This is put forth as the "Boas Tradition." American linguistics, Joos maintains, "got its decisive direction when it was decided that an indigenous language could be described without any preexistent scheme of what a language must be" (Joos, 1966, p. 1). Of course this could not literally be true—the procedures of analysis themselves express a hypothesis concerning the possible diversity of language. But there is, nevertheless, much justice in Joos's characterization.

views of classical rationalist grammar, which held that languages are similar only at the deeper level, the level at which grammatical relations are expressed and at which the processes that provide for the creative aspect of language use are to be found. Second, this belief seriously misinterprets the findings of anthropological linguistics, which has, in fact, restricted itself   295
almost completely to fairly superficial aspects of language structure.

...

I think that if we contemplate the classical problem of psychology, that of accounting for human knowledge, we cannot avoid being struck by the enormous disparity between knowledge and experience—in the case of language, between the generative grammar that expresses   300
the linguistic competence of the native speaker and the meager and degenerate data on the basis of which he has constructed this grammar for himself. In principle the theory of learning should deal with this problem; but in fact it bypasses the prob-   305
lem, because of the conceptual gap that I mentioned earlier. The problem cannot even be formulated in any sensible way until we develop the concept of competence, alongside the concepts of learning and behavior, and apply this concept in some domain. The fact is that this con-   310
cept has so far been extensively developed and applied only in the study of human language. It is only in this domain that we have at least the first steps toward an account of competence, namely the fragmentary generative grammars that have been constructed for particular languages. As the study of language progresses, we can expect with some confidence that these grammars will be extended in scope and depth, although it will hardly come as a surprise if the   315
first proposals are found to be mistaken in fundamental ways.

> *meager and degenerate:* This is the central empirical component of Chomsky's argument that some aspect of language must be innate. His claim is that the amount and quality of language to which children are exposed is insufficient to explain language acquisition through a purely inductive process.

Insofar as we have a tentative first approximation to a generative grammar for some language, we can for the first time formulate in a useful way the problem of origin of knowledge. In other words, we can ask the question, What initial structure must be attributed to the mind that enables it to construct such a grammar from the data of sense? Some of the empirical con-   320
ditions that must be met by any such assumption about innate structure are moderately clear. Thus, it appears to be a species-specific capacity that is essentially independent of intelligence, and we can make a fairly good estimate of the amount of data that is necessary for the task to be successfully accomplished. We know that the grammars that are in fact constructed vary only slightly among speakers of the same language, despite wide variations not only in intelligence   325
but also in the conditions under which language is acquired. As participants in a certain culture, we are naturally aware of the great differences in ability to use language, in knowledge of vocabulary, and so on that result from differences in native ability and from differences in conditions of acquisition; we naturally pay much less attention to the similarities and to common knowledge, which we take for granted. But if we manage to establish the requisite psychic distance,   330
if we actually compare the generative grammars that must be postulated for different speakers

of the same language, we find that the similarities that we take for granted are quite marked and that the divergences are few and marginal. What is more, it seems that dialects that are superficially quite remote, even barely intelligible on first contact, share a vast central core of common rules and processes and differ very slightly in underlying structures, which seem to remain invariant through long historical eras. Furthermore, we discover a substantial system of principles that do not vary among languages that are, as far as we know, entirely unrelated.

The central problems in this domain are empirical ones that are, in principle at least, quite straightforward, difficult as they may be to solve in a satisfactory way. We must postulate an innate structure that is rich enough to account for the disparity between experience and knowledge, one that can account for the construction of the empirically justified generative grammars within the given limitations of time and access to data. At the same time, this postulated innate mental structure must not be so rich and restrictive as to exclude certain known languages. There is, in other words, an upper bound and a lower bound on the degree and exact character of the complexity that can be postulated as innate mental structure. The factual situation is obscure enough to leave room for much difference of opinion over the true nature of this innate mental structure that makes acquisition of language possible. However, there seems to me to be no doubt that this is an empirical issue, one that can be resolved by proceeding along the lines that I have just roughly outlined.

My own estimate of the situation is that the real problem for tomorrow is that of discovering an assumption regarding innate structure that is sufficiently rich, not that of finding one that is simple or elementary enough to be "plausible." There is, as far as I can see, no reasonable notion of "plausibility," no a priori insight into what innate structures are permissible, that can guide the search for a "sufficiently elementary assumption." It would be mere dogmatism to maintain without argument or evidence that the mind is simpler in its innate structure than other biological systems, just as it would be mere dogmatism to insist that the mind's organization must necessarily follow certain set principles, determined in advance of investigation and maintained in defiance of any empirical findings. I think that the study of problems of mind has been very definitely hampered by a kind of apriorism with which these problems are generally approached. In particular, the empiricist assumptions that have dominated the study of acquisition of knowledge for many years seem to me to have been adopted quite without warrant and to have no special status among the many possibilities that one might imagine as to how the mind functions.

. . .

Assuming the rough accuracy of conclusions that seem tenable today, it is reasonable to suppose that a generative grammar is a system of many hundreds of rules of several different types, organized in accordance with certain fixed principles of ordering and applicability and containing a certain fixed substructure which, along with the general principles of organization, is common to all languages. There is no a priori "naturalness" to such a system, any more than there is to the detailed structure of the visual cortex. No one who has given any serious thought to the problem of formalizing inductive procedures or "heuristic methods" is likely to set much store by the hope that such a system as a generative grammar can be constructed by methods of any generality.

Heuristic methods are based on "rules of thumb," that is, rules for making decisions or drawing inferences that usually work but are not guaranteed to work in every situation or to yield the optimal result in any situation.

Induction is reasoning from specific experiences or observations (usually many) to a general rule. For example, over and over a falling barometer is followed by bad weather, and eventually we may consolidate these experiences in the form of a rule: a falling barometer predicts a storm. The problem is that our experience is not limited to the barometer and the weather. How, then, did we come to associate these two phenomena—out of many—with one another?

The English philosopher Francis Bacon (1561–1626) advocated a purely inductive kind of science. Build no theories, make no hypotheses, but collect facts—any and all of them—and the laws of nature will emerge. It sounds good, but it doesn't work, because facts do not organize themselves. They can only be organized by an active intelligence with some expectation or preconception. This is how science works and, Chomsky argues, this is how the child learns language.

Empiricist theories of language acquisition posit what amounts to a Baconian child: a brain, devoid of any trace of language, confronted with a large and haphazard collection of facts—in this case specimens of linguistic behavior. Can this child inductively build a grammar? Chomsky says no, no more than a scientist with no notion of time and space can construct a theory of the universe exclusively by gazing up at the stars.

To my knowledge, the only substantive proposal to deal with the problem of acquisition of knowledge of language is the rationalist conception that I have outlined. To repeat: Suppose that we assign to the mind, as an innate property, the general theory of language that we have called "universal grammar." This theory encompasses the principles that I discussed in the preceding lec- 375
ture and many others of the same sort, and it specifies a certain subsystem of rules that provides a skeletal structure for any language and a variety of conditions, formal and substantive, that any further elaboration of the grammar must meet. The theory of universal grammar, then, provides a schema to which any particular grammar must conform. Suppose, furthermore, that we can make this schema sufficiently restrictive so that very few possible grammars conforming to the 380
schema will be consistent with the meager and degenerate data actually available to the language learner. His task, then, is to search among the possible grammars and select one that is not defi- nitely rejected by the data available to him. What faces the language learner, under these assump- tions, is not the impossible task of inventing a highly abstract and intricately structured theory on the basis of degenerate data, but rather the much more manageable task of determining whether 385
these data belong to one or another of a fairly restricted set of potential languages.

The tasks of the psychologist, then, divide into several subtasks. The first is to discover the innate schema that characterizes the class of potential languages—that defines the "essence" of human lan- guage. This subtask falls to that branch of human psychology known as linguistics; it is the problem of traditional universal grammar, of contemporary linguistic theory. The second subtask is 390
the detailed study of the actual character of the stimulation and the organism-environment interaction that sets the innate cognitive mechanism into operation. This is a study now being under- taken by a few psychologists, and it is particularly active right here in Berkeley. It has already led

to interesting and suggestive conclusions. One might hope that such study will reveal a succession of maturational stages leading finally to a full generative grammar.[6] A third task is that of
determining just what it means for a hypothesis about the generative grammar of a language to
be "consistent" with the data of sense. Notice that it is a great oversimplification to suppose that
a child must discover a generative grammar that accounts for all the linguistic data that has been
presented to him and that "projects" such data to an infinite range of potential sound-meaning
relations. In addition to achieving this, he must also differentiate the data of sense into those utterances that give direct evidence as to the character of the underlying grammar and those that
must be rejected by the hypothesis he selects as ill-formed, deviant, fragmentary, and so on.
Clearly, everyone succeeds in carrying out this task of differentiation—we all know, within tolerable limits of consistency, which sentences are well formed and literally interpretable, and which
must be interpreted as metaphorical, fragmentary, and deviant along many possible dimensions.
I doubt that it has been fully appreciated to what extent this complicates the problem of
accounting for language acquisition. Formally speaking, the learner must select a hypothesis
regarding the language to which he is exposed that rejects a good part of the data on which this
hypothesis must rest. Again, it is reasonable to suppose this is possible only if the range of tenable hypotheses is quite limited—if the innate schema of universal grammar *is* highly restrictive.
The third subtask, then, is to study what we might think of as the problem of "confirmation"—in
this context, the problem of what relation must hold between a potential grammar and a set of
data for this grammar to be confirmed as the actual theory of the language in question.

. . .

The way in which I have been describing acquisition of knowledge of language calls to mind
a very interesting and rather neglected lecture
given by Charles Sanders Peirce more than fifty
years ago, in which he developed some rather similar notions about acquisition of knowledge in general (Peirce, 1957). Peirce argued that the general
limits of human intelligence are much more narrow than might be suggested by romantic assumptions about the limitless perfectibility of man (or,
for that matter, than are suggested by his own
"pragmaticist" conceptions of the course of scientific progress in his better-known philosophical

> Peirce (1839–1914; pronounced *purse*) was a
> physicist and philosopher who made
> important contributions to modern formal
> logic. He founded the school of philosophy
> known as *pragmatism,* which he later renamed
> *pragmaticism* to distinguish his views from
> William James's version of pragmatism.

---

[6] It is not unlikely that detailed investigation of this sort will show that the conception of universal grammar as an innate
schematism is only valid as a first approximation; that, in fact, an innate schematism of a more general sort permits the
formulation of tentative "grammars" which themselves determine how later evidence is to be interpreted, leading to
the postulation of richer grammars, and so on. I have so far been discussing language acquisition on the obviously false
assumption that it is an instantaneous process. There are many interesting questions that arise when we consider how
the process extends in time. For some discussion relating to problems of phonology, see Chomsky (1970). Notice also
that it is unnecessary to suppose, even in the first approximation, that "very few possible grammars conforming to the
schema" will be available to the language learner. It is enough to suppose that the possible grammars consistent with
the data will be "scattered" in terms of an evaluation procedure.

studies). He held that innate limitations on admissible hypotheses are a precondition for successful theory construction, and that the "guessing instinct" that provides hypotheses makes use of inductive procedures only for "corrective action." Peirce maintained in this lecture that the history of early science shows that something approximating a correct theory was discovered with remarkable ease and rapidity, on the basis of highly inadequate data, as soon as certain problems were faced; he noted "how few were the guesses that men of surpassing genius had to make before they rightly guessed the laws of nature." And, he asked, "How was it that man was ever led to entertain that true theory? You cannot say that it happened by chance, because the chances are too overwhelmingly against the single true theory in the twenty or thirty thousand years during which man has been a thinking animal, ever having come into any man's head." A fortiori, the chances are even more overwhelmingly against the true theory of each language ever having come into the head of every four-year-old child. Continuing with Peirce: "Man's mind has a natural adaptation to imagining correct theories of some kinds. . . . If man had not the gift of a mind adapted to his requirements, he could not have acquired any knowledge." Correspondingly, in our present case, it seems that knowledge of a language—a grammar— can be acquired only by an organism that is "preset" with a severe restriction on the form of grammar. This innate restriction is a precondition, in the Kantian sense, for linguistic experience, and it appears to be the critical factor in determining the course and result of language learning. The child cannot know at birth which language he is to learn, but he must know that its grammar must be of a predetermined form that excludes many imaginable languages. Having selected a permissible hypothesis, he can use inductive evidence for corrective action, confirming or disconfirming his choice. Once the hypothesis is sufficiently well confirmed, the child knows the language defined by this hypothesis; consequently, his knowledge extends enormously beyond his experience and, in fact, leads him to characterize much of the data of experience as defective and deviant.

Peirce regarded inductive processes as rather marginal to the acquisition of knowledge; in his words, "Induction has no originality in it, but only tests a suggestion already made." To understand how knowledge is acquired, in the rationalist view that Peirce outlined, we must penetrate the mysteries of what he called "abduction," and we must discover that which "gives a rule to abduction and so puts a limit

430	
435	
440	
445	
450	
455	
460	
465	

a fortiori: all the more so

Peirce gave abduction a more general form:

We have a set of facts, F

We have an explanation, E, such that *If E then F.*

Therefore E is probably true.

Peirce saw such reasoning as the process by which scientific hypotheses are created.

What is going on in the mind of the language learner, according to Chomsky, is not the inductive reasoning assumed by the empiricists, but abductive reasoning as described by Peirce:

I have a set of language specimens (the facts);

I have a grammar that allows those specimens (the explanation);

Therefore the grammar is probably the right grammar.

upon admissible hypotheses." Peirce maintained that the search for principles of abduction leads us to the study of innate ideas, which provide the instinctive structure of human intelligence. But Peirce was no dualist in the Cartesian sense; he argued (not very persuasively, in my opinion) that there is a significant analogy between human intelligence, with its abductive restrictions, and animal instinct. Thus, he maintained that man discovered certain true theories only because his "instincts must have involved from the beginning certain tendencies to think truly" about certain specific matters; similarly, "You cannot seriously think that every little chicken that is hatched, has to rummage through all possible theories until it lights upon the good idea of picking up something and eating it. On the contrary, you think that the chicken has an innate idea of doing this; that is to say, that it can think of this, but has no faculty of thinking anything else. . . . But if you are going to think every poor chicken endowed with an innate tendency towards a positive truth, why should you think to man alone this gift is denied?"

No one took up Peirce's challenge to develop a theory of abduction, to determine those principles that limit the admissible hypotheses or present them in a certain order. Even today, this remains a task for the future. It is a task that need not be undertaken if empiricist psychological doctrine can be substantiated; therefore, it is of great importance to subject this doctrine to rational analysis, as has been done, in part, in the study of language. I would like to repeat that it was the great merit of structural linguistics, as of Hullian learning theory in its early stages and of several other modern developments, to have given precise form to certain empiricist assumptions.[7] Where this step has been taken, the inadequacy of the postulated mechanisms has been clearly demonstrated, and, in the case of language at least, we can even begin to see just why any methods of this sort must fail—for example, because they cannot, in principle, provide for the properties of deep structures and the abstract operations of formal grammar. Speculating about the future, I think it is not unlikely that the dogmatic character of the general empiricist framework

> *Structural* or *descriptive linguistics* grew out of the work of the Swiss linguist Ferdinand de Saussure (1857–1913), who taught that meaning resides in the relations among signs (sounds, words) rather than in a correspondence between words and things. The emphasis in structural linguistics has therefore been to describe a language as a system of signs. Chomsky's emphasis, by contrast, has been the transformational rules by which meanings give rise to utterances.

> Clark Hull (1884–1952) developed an associationist theory in which all learned behavior was seen as the result of making connections between stimuli and responses.

---

[7] In contrast, the account of language acquisition presented by B. F. Skinner (1957) seems to me either devoid of content or clearly wrong, depending on whether one interprets it metaphorically or literally (see Chomsky, 1959). It is quite appropriate when a theory is disproven in a strong form to replace it by a weaker variant. However, not infrequently this step leads to vacuity. The popularity of Skinner's concept of "reinforcement," after the virtual collapse of Hullian theory, seems to me a case in point. (Note that the Skinnerian concepts can be well defined and can lead to interesting results, in a particular experimental situation—what is at issue is the Skinnerian "extrapolation" to a wider class of cases.)

and its inadequacy to human and animal intelligence will gradually become more evident as specific realizations, such as taxonomic linguistics, behaviorist learning theory, and the perception models,[8] heuristic methods, and "general problem solvers" of the early enthusiasts of "artificial intelligence," are successively rejected on empirical grounds when they are made precise and on grounds of vacuity when they are left vague. And—assuming this projection to be accurate—it will then be possible to undertake a general study of the limits and capacities of human intelligence, to develop a Peircean logic of abduction.

Modern psychology is not devoid of such initiatives. The contemporary study of generative grammar and its universal substructure and governing principles is one such manifestation. Closely related is the study of the biological bases of human language, an investigation to which Eric Lenneberg has made substantial contributions (Lenneberg, 1967)....

Still more clearly to the point, I think, are the developments in comparative ethology over the past thirty years, and certain current work in experimental and physiological psychology. One can cite many examples: for example, in the latter category, the work of Bower suggesting an innate basis for the perceptual constancies; studies in the Wisconsin primate laboratory on complex innate releasing mechanisms in rhesus monkeys; the work of Hubel, Barlow, and others on highly specific analyzing mechanisms in the lower cortical centers of mammals; and a number of comparable studies of lower organisms (for example, the beautiful work of Lettvin and his associates on frog vision). There is now good evidence from such investigations that perception of line, angle, motion, and other complex properties of the physical world is based on innate organization of the neural system.

505

510

515

520

525

Perceptual constancy is the fact that the sensory input corresponding to an object can vary drastically, yet we do not perceive the object to change. If you close this book and hold it at arm's length with the cover facing you, its retinal image is a rectangle. Now turn the book a little bit. Its retinal image becomes a trapezoid, but you do not perceive a change in the book's shape. This applies similarly to size, color, brightness, motion, melody, and many other percepts.

An *innate releasing mechanism* is a hypothesized neural structure by means of which a specific stimulus (known as a *releaser* or *sign stimulus*) causes a specific and fixed response. A well-known example is Tinbergen's (1951) observation that a male stickleback (a small fish) will attack anything that is roughly its own size and has a red belly, whether it is another male stickleback or a stickleback-size piece of wood painted red on the bottom. This behavior is unlearned; the red "belly" *releases* the attack.

The *analyzing mechanisms* Chomsky refers to are cells in the visual system that respond to very specific features of sensory input, such as an edge with a certain orientation or motion in a certain direction. See, for example, Hubel and Wiesel (1979) or Lettvin, Maturana, McCulloch, and Pitts (1959).

---

[8] For a discussion of such systems and their limitations, see Minsky and Papert (1967).

In some cases at least, these built-in structures will degenerate unless appropriate stimulation takes place at an early stage in life, but although such experience is necessary to permit the innate mechanisms to function, there is no reason to believe that it has more than a

530 marginal effect on determining *how* they function to organize experience. Furthermore, there is nothing to suggest that what has so far been discovered is anywhere near the limit of complexity of innate structures. The basic techniques for exploring the neural mechanisms are only a few years old, and it is impossible to predict what order of specificity and complexity will be demonstrated when they come to be extensively applied. For the present, it

535 seems that most complex organisms have highly specific forms of sensory and perceptual organization that are associated with the *Umwelt* and the manner of life of the organism. There is little reason to doubt that what is true of lower organisms is true of humans as well. Particularly

> *Umwelt:* environment

540 in the case of language, it is natural to expect a close relation between innate properties of the mind and features of linguistic structure; for language, after all, has no existence apart from its mental representation. Whatever properties it has must be those that are given to it by the innate mental processes of the organism that has invented it and that invents it anew with each succeeding generation, along with whatever properties are associated with

545 the conditions of its use. Once again, it seems that language should be, for this reason, a most illuminating probe with which to explore the organization of mental processes.

Turning to comparative ethology, it is interesting to note that one of its earliest motivations was the hope that through the "investigation of the a priori, of the innate working hypotheses pre-

550 sent in subhuman organisms," it would be possible to shed light on the a priori forms of human thought. This formulation of intent is quoted from an early and little-known paper by Konrad Lorenz (1941). Lorenz goes on to express views very much

555 like those Peirce had expressed a generation earlier. He maintains:

> Lorenz (1903–1989) was a pioneer of the field of ethology, the study of animal behavior in natural settings, for which he shared (with ethologists Nikolaas Tinbergen and Karl von Frisch) the Nobel Prize for physiology or medicine in 1973.

One familiar with the innate modes of reaction of subhuman organisms can readily hypothesize that the a priori is due to hereditary differentiations of the central nervous system which have become characteristic of the species, producing hereditary

560 dispositions to think in certain forms.... Most certainly Hume was wrong when he wanted to derive all that is a priori from that which the senses supply to experience, just as wrong as Wundt or Helmholtz who simply explain it as an abstraction from preceding experience. Adaptation of the a priori to the real world has no more originated from "experience" than adaptation of the fin of the fish to the properties of water. Just as the

565 form of the fin is given a priori, prior to any individual negotiation of the young fish with the water, and just as it is this form that makes possible this negotiation, so it is also the

case with our forms of perception and categories in their relationship to our negotiation with the real external world through experience. In the case of animals, we find limitations specific to the forms of experience possible for them. We believe we can demonstrate the closest functional and probably genetic relationship between these animal a priori's and our human a priori. Contrary to Hume, we believe, just as did Kant, that a "pure" science of innate forms of human thought, independent of all experience, is possible.

Peirce, to my knowledge, is original and unique in stressing the problem of studying the rules that limit the class of possible theories. Of course, his concept of abduction, like Lorenz's biological a priori, has a strongly Kantian flavor, and all derive from the rationalist psychology that concerned itself with the forms, the limits, and the principles that provide "the sinews and connections" for human thought, that underlie "that infinite amount of knowledge of which we are not always conscious," of which Leibniz spoke. It is therefore quite natural that we should link these developments to the revival of philosophical grammar, which grew from the same soil as an attempt, quite fruitful and legitimate, to explore one basic facet of human intelligence.

. . . What seems to me important in ethology is its attempt to explore the innate properties that determine how knowledge is acquired and the character of this knowledge. Returning to this theme, we must consider a further question: How did the human mind come to acquire the innate structure that we are led to attribute to it? Not too surprisingly, Lorenz takes the position that this is simply a matter of natural selection. . . .

In fact, the processes by which the human mind achieved its present stage of complexity and its particular form of innate organization are a total mystery, as much so as the analogous questions about the physical or mental organization of any other complex organism. It is perfectly safe to attribute this development to "natural selection," so long as we realize that there is no substance to this assertion, that it amounts to nothing more than a belief that there is some naturalistic explanation for these phenomena. The problem of accounting for evolutionary development is, in some ways, rather like that of explaining successful abduction. The laws that determine possible successful mutation and the nature of complex organisms are as unknown as the laws that determine the choice of hypotheses.[9] With no knowledge of the laws that determine the organization and structure of complex biological systems, it is just as senseless to ask what the "probability" is for the human mind to have reached its present state as it is to inquire into the "probability" that a particular physical theory will be devised. And, as we have noted, it is idle to speculate about laws of learning until we have some indication of what kind of knowledge is attainable—in the case of language, some indication of the constraints on the set of potential grammars.

---

[9] It has been argued on statistical grounds—through comparison of the known rate of mutation with the astronomical number of imaginable modifications of chromosomes and their parts—that such laws must exist and must vastly restrict the realizable possibilities. See the papers by Eden (1967), Schutzenberger (1967), and Gavaudan (1967).

In studying the evolution of mind, we cannot guess to what extent there are physically possible alternatives to, say, transformational generative grammar, for an organism meeting certain other physical conditions characteristic of humans. Conceivably, there are none—or very few—in which case talk about evolution of the language capacity is beside the point. The vacuity of such speculation, however, has no bearing one way or another on those aspects of the problem of mind that can be sensibly pursued. It seems to me that these aspects are, for the moment, the problems illustrated in the case of language by the study of the nature, the use, and the acquisition of linguistic competence.

605

FOR DISCUSSION

1. How is (human) language different from the other forms of communication such as birdsongs and bird calls, sirens, traffic lights, referee signals, and so on?

2. What do all (human) languages have in common?

3. Chomsky is often understood to be saying that language is innate. In what ways does this characterization misrepresent his views?

4. What are some examples of the empirical problems facing the language learner?

5. Chomsky says "It seems that most complex organisms have highly specific forms of sensory and perceptual organization that are associated with the *Umwelt* and the manner of life of the organism." What are some examples of such associations?

6. Parents think they are teaching their children language when they point at things and name them. Chomsky disagrees. What, in his view, allows the child to learn a language?

7. At some age children begin using such words as gooses, mouses, goed, swimmed, and so forth. Does this fit with or conflict with Chomsky's theory of language acquisition? Explain.

Part V

Levels of Explanation

Imagine the following scene: Two psychologists are sitting by the side of a road, calmly eating their lunch. At a little distance, a chicken emerges from the shrubbery, walks across the road, and disappears from view on the other side. The psychologists, being in the business of studying behavior, begin to wonder about what they have just seen.

Psychologist A, who is a holist,[1] might ask himself *For what purpose did this particular being, which happens to be a chicken, cross the road?* or *How did this chicken anticipate that she would benefit from being on the other side of the road?* or *What aspect of the evolutionary history of Gallus domesticus is responsible for the tendency of chickens to behave in this way, and under what circumstances?*

Psychologist B, who is a reductionist,[2] might ask herself *What are the basic neural mechanisms in the chicken that initiated and coordinated the complex series of actions that resulted in the chicken being on the other side of the road?* or *How has this chicken's past behavior been shaped by environmental events such that she is now likely to cross the road?* or *What is the chain of learned associations between stimuli and responses that underlies this chicken's action?*

The two psychologists represent a continuum of explanations. At one end are explanations framed in terms of the largest possible unit, namely the chicken and her environment. At the other end are explanations framed in terms of the smallest possible units, such as molecules and cells or discrete stimuli and responses. In between might be explanations using intermediate units of analysis, such as different functional parts of the brain, the chicken's habits, or her personality.

---

[1] In the history and philosophy of science *holism* (or *emergentism*) is the doctrine that a system (such as a chicken) may have properties that do not derive from the system's parts but rather from the system as a whole, that is, from the specific way the parts work together. We use the term here to refer not to the doctrine but to a general characteristic of holistic explanations, namely that their unit of analysis is the system as a whole.

[2] Likewise, *reductionism* is the doctrine that to be meaningful an explanation must be expressed exclusively in terms of observable things and events. We use the term here to refer not to the doctrine but to a general characteristic of reductive explanations, namely that they tend to be fine-grained, to explain things in terms of the operation and interaction of relatively many and relatively small parts.

A great deal of the disagreement in psychology is between those who advance relatively holistic theories of the mind and behavior and those who propose relatively reductionist theories. It is crucial to understand that the argument is not about who is right; it is about what kind, that is, what level, of explanation is most appropriate and most useful in a given context.

Often it is quite obvious what level is appropriate, and there is no tension. For example, a holistic explanation of a car would be in terms of what the system does (it's a motorized vehicle that transports its driver and any passengers or cargo) and in terms of how its functioning is affected by internal and external variables (e.g., terrain, weather, load, tires). At this level, a theory of the car's operation would consist of such ideas as "motor," "transmission," "steering," and "brakes." It would explain an individual car's characteristics or malfunctioning in terms of these theoretical constructs, for example, "the car won't stop because there's something wrong with the brakes." A reductionist explanation, on the other hand, would seek to identify the fundamentals of the car, that is, the workings of all the discrete parts—cylinders, valves, bearings, sensors, and so on—and to describe them in terms of the basic electrical, mechanical, thermodynamic, and dynamic processes at work.

The difference between the two levels of explanation can be seen by taking them on the road. Approaching a stop sign, a driver needs to stop the car. The holistic driver thinks *I need to press on the brake pedal*. The reductionist driver thinks *I need to slow the rotation of the wheels; to do this I need to close the brake calipers on the brake discs attached to the wheels; to do this I need to make hydraulic fluid in the brake hoses move into the wheel cylinders; to do this I need to push the piston into the brake master cylinder; to do this I need to press my foot on the brake pedal*. Obviously, you want a holistic cab driver and a reductionist mechanic rather than the other way around.

There is often some justice in the criticism that the reductionist can't see the forest for the trees, and many social scientists are strongly antireductionist, pointing out, for example, that a group is not simply the sum of its members, just as the wall is not simply the sum of its bricks (and the brick is not simply the sum of its clay particles, and so on). Conversely, it is fair to say that many advances in science and technology depend on a reductionist approach. For example, many recent advances in medicine and agriculture were made possible by the achievements of molecular biology, a reductionist science. Likewise, the dramatic advances in our understanding of matter at the molecular, atomic, and subatomic level in the last two centuries have brought us radio, nuclear power and bombs, x-rays, crazy glue, carbon dating, gas chromatography, NutraSweet®, buckyballs, and a few other things.

As in the car example, the holist/reductionist question is often moot. No one would suggest, for example, trying to explain the movements of the continental plates by looking at the molecular structure of the rocks they are made of. Conversely, industrial chemists cannot formulate a new paint simply by specifying the properties they want their paint to have. But in psychology it is not always so clear whether we should be looking at the whole, the parts, or both, and a sensitivity to the issue is essential to understanding the history of psychology as well as its future.

Reductionism and holism are not a simple dichotomy; rather, they are two ends of a continuum. We can try to explain a given system in terms of its minutest parts or in terms of the system as a single whole, or at any level in between. The challenge is to choose the right level of explanation (or unit of analysis) for the question we're asking about the system.

The readings in this section occupy a range of positions on the reductionist–holist spectrum. Farthest toward the reductionist end is Kandel's work on the molecular biology of memory (described in Milner, Squire, & Kandel). Nearby is Pavlov and his conditioned reflex, a basic mechanism that seemed capable of explaining various seemingly complex behaviors. Closer to the middle but still on the reductionist side is Hebb. Tolman writes as a reductionist who is having doubts about the possibility and value of reductive explanations of certain kinds of behavior. At the holist end, Wertheimer argues that some aspects of perception cannot usefully be reduced and must be understood as wholes. Lewin makes a similar point about group behavior.

In addition to the readings in Part V, several others illustrate different levels of explanation:

1.8   John Searle   *Minds, brains, and science* (1984), ch. 1, 2

2.5   J. J. Gibson   *The perception of the visual world* (1950), ch. 5

2.6   David Marr   *Visual information processing: The structure and creation of visual representations* (1980)

3.5   B. F. Skinner   *About behaviorism* (1974), ch. 4

7.6   Samuel Guze   *Biological psychiatry: Is there any other kind?* (1989)

ADDITIONAL READINGS

Gustave Le Bon   *The crowd* (1895)

Le Bon came to believe that people in crowds often abandon their conscious personalities and individuality. The character of such crowds is not related to the character, motives, or morals of the individuals who make it up. Rather, a collective mind forms that leads people to respond to a variety of primitive unconscious forces.

Sigmund Freud   *Project for a scientific psychology* (1895)

Before fully developing psychoanalysis, Freud envisioned a reductionist and materialist psychology that would be able to explain all mental events in terms of neurological processes.

John Dewey   *The reflex arc concept in psychology* (1896)

The reflex arc is the neural pathway that leads from sensory receptor to the relevant muscle or gland. Dewey argues that rather than focusing on the structure of this pathway, we ought to consider the function of the reflex, the meaning of the connection between the stimulus event and the body's response to it.

Karl Lashley   *The problem of serial order in behavior* (1951)

This influential paper showed that rapid serially ordered behavior (e.g., typing, piano playing) cannot be explained in terms of stimulus-response chains; rather, the explanation must include some kind of central representation of the series.

Thomas Nagel   *What is it like to be a bat?* (1974)

This celebrated paper is not about what it is like to be a bat, because we cannot know that. This leads Nagel to a fundamental problem with reductionist (physicalist) approaches to the mind.

Valentino Braitenberg *Vehicles: Experiments in synthetic psychology* (1984)

This quirky and entertaining little book is an excellent demonstration of the relation between two levels of explanation.

Eric Kandel & Robert Hawkins   *The biological basis of learning and individuality* (1992)

An accessible review of the work by Kandel and his many collaborators on the cellular and molecular mechanisms that underlie simple learning phenomena.

Max Wertheimer (1880–1943)
Laws of Organization in Perceptual Forms (1923)

One of the most consistent themes in gestalt psychology is the idea that the mind does not piece the world together out of elementary units; rather, the mind grasps the world by its handles.

The philosopher Christian von Ehrenfels (1859–1932), who coined the term *Gestaltqualitäten* ("whole qualities" or "form qualities"), argued that perceptions consist of a number of elementary sensations plus a *Gestaltqualität*. Thus the whole (percept) is more than the sum of its parts (Ehrenfels, 1890). This idea strongly influenced Wertheimer, who encountered Ehrenfels as a student at Charles University, in Prague. In Frankfurt in 1910 Wertheimer began his studies of apparent motion (with Kurt Koffka [1886–1941] and Wolfgang Köhler [1887–1967] as his subjects and collaborators) that led to a 1912 paper that is often used to mark the beginning of the gestalt school of psychology. That paper described the conditions in which two stationary lights, blinking alternately, are seen as a single light moving back and forth, an effect known as the *phi phenomenon*. Wertheimer regarded the perceived motion as an example of a *Gestaltqualität* and argued that such phenomena show the inadequacy of a psychology in which the percept is completely determined by its constituent sensations. Wertheimer extended Ehrenfels's idea considerably, arguing that not only does the whole depend on the parts, but the parts depend on the whole; for Wertheimer, the whole is not only more than but *different from* the sum of its parts.

Wertheimer moved to the University of Berlin in 1922, returning to Frankfurt as chair of psychology in 1929. In 1933 Hitler came to power, and Wertheimer was quicker to grasp the full extent of the Nazi menace than many other Jews in German universities. He left for Prague, and

Source: From Ellis, W. D. (Ed. & Trans.). (1938). *A source book of gestalt psychology* (pp. 71–88). London: Routledge & Kegan Paul. Wertheimer's paper, here condensed and translated by Ellis, was originally published in 1923 as Untersuchungen zur Lehre von der Gestalt, part 2, in *Psychologische Forschung, 4,* 301–350.

then for New York, where he spent the rest of his life at the New School for Social Research (now New School University).

Wertheimer was not as prolific as he was influential. The 1912 paper on perceived motion and the 1923 paper on perceptual organization (the present reading) are the most important contributions to gestalt psychology published during Wertheimer's lifetime, but his book *Productive Thinking* (1945), published posthumously, extended the gestalt approach to the study of creative problem solving, which became part of the foundation of cognitive psychology. In the same vein are Karl Duncker's (1945) "On Problem Solving" and George Polya's (1945) *How to Solve It.*

For general expositions of gestalt psychology, see Köhler's (1929) *Gestalt Psychology* and Koffka's (1935) *Principles of Gestalt Psychology.* See also the interesting perspective on Wertheimer's intellectual legacy by his son, the psychologist Michael Wertheimer (1991).

The present reading describes the gestalt principles of perceptual organization, familiar to most introductory psychology students. The most important parts of this reading are the first sentence and the last footnote.

I stand at the window and see a house, trees, sky.

Theoretically I might say there were 327 brightnesses and nuances of colour. Do I *have* "327"? No. I have sky, house, and trees. It is impossible to achieve "327" as such. And yet even though such droll calculation were possible—and implied, say, for the house 120, the trees 90, the sky 117—I should at least have *this* arrangement and division of the total, and not, say, 127 and 100 and 100; or 150 and 177.

The concrete division which I *see* is not determined by some arbitrary mode of organization lying solely within my own pleasure; instead I see the arrangement and division which is given there before me. And what a remarkable process it is when some other mode of apprehension *does* succeed! I gaze for a long time from my window, adopt after some effort the most unreal attitude possible. And I *discover* that part of a window sash and part of a bare branch together compose an *N*. Or, I look at a picture. Two faces cheek to cheek. I see one (with its, if you will, "57" brightnesses) and the other ("49" brightnesses). I do not see an arrangement of 66 plus 40 nor of 6 plus 100. There *have* been theories which would require that I see "106." In reality I see two faces!

> *given there before me:* This way of thinking about perception was later articulated in much more detail by J. J. Gibson; see 2.4.

Or, I hear a melody (17 tones) with its accompaniment (32 tones). I hear the melody and accompaniment, not simply "49"—and certainly not 20 plus 29. And the same is true even in cases where there is no stimulus continuum. I hear the melody and its accompaniment even when they are played by an old-fashioned clock where each tone is separate from the others. Or, one sees a series of discontinuous dots upon a homogeneous ground not as a sum of dots, but as figures. Even though there may here be a greater latitude of possible arrangements, the dots usually combine in some "spontaneous," "natural" articulation—and any other arrangement, even if it can be achieved, is artificial and difficult to maintain.

> In his references to 57 brightnesses and 17 tones Wertheimer is ridiculing the reductionist perspective of E. B. Titchener (1867–1927), who saw psychology's task as identifying the sensory elements of consciousness. See Titchener's table of sensation qualities in 3.2, p. 231.

When we are presented with a number of stimuli we do not as a rule experience "a number" of individual things, this one and that and that. Instead larger wholes separated from and related to one another are given in experience; their arrangement and division are concrete and definite.

Do such arrangements and divisions follow definite principles? When the stimuli *abcde* appear together what are the principles according to which *abc/de* and not *ab/cde* is experienced? It is the purpose of this paper to examine this problem, and we shall therefore begin with cases of discontinuous stimulus constellations.

I. A row of dots is presented upon a homogeneous ground. The alternate intervals are 3 mm. and 12 mm.

FIGURE 1

Normally this row will be seen as *ab/cd,* not as *a/bc/de.* As a matter of fact it is for most people impossible to see the whole series simultaneously in the latter grouping.

We are interested here in what is actually *seen.* The following will make this clear. One sees a row of groups obliquely tilted from lower left to upper right *(ab/cd/ef).* The arrangement *a/bc/de* is extremely difficult to achieve. Even when it can be seen, such an arrangement is far less cer-   45
tain than the other and is quite likely to be upset by eye-movements or variations of attention.

FIGURE 2

This is even more clear in Fig. 3.

FIGURE 3

i.e. :—

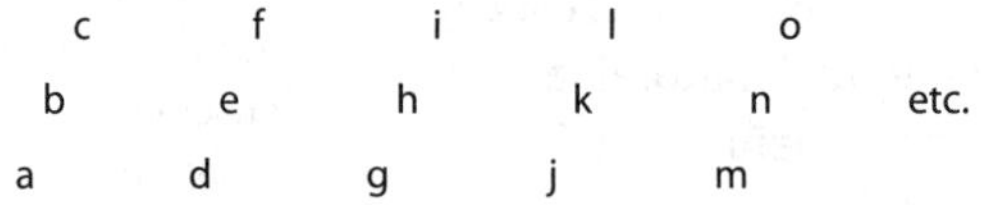

	c		f		i		l		o	
b		e		h		k		n		etc.
a		d		g		j		m		

Quite obviously the arrangement *abc/def/ghi* is greatly superior to *ceg/fhj/ikm.*
  . . .
Another example of seeing what the objective arrangement dictates is contained in Fig. 4 for vertical, and in Fig. 5 for horizontal groupings.   50

In all the foregoing cases we have used a relatively large number of dots for each figure. Using fewer we find that the arrangement is not so imperatively dictated as before, and reversing the more obvious grouping is comparatively easy. Examples: Figs. 6, 7.

It would be false to assume that Figs. 6 and 7 lend themselves more readily to reversal because fewer stimulus points (dots) are involved. Such incorrect reasoning would be based   55

FIGURE 4

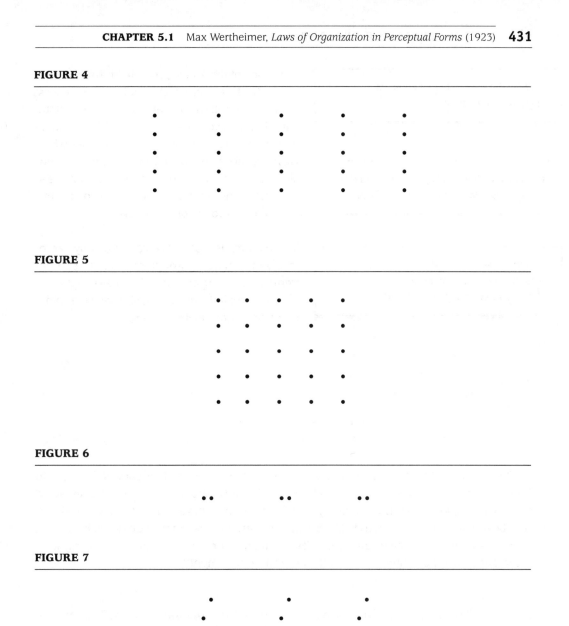

FIGURE 5

FIGURE 6

FIGURE 7

upon the proposition: "The more dots, the more difficult it will be to unite them into groups." Actually it is only the unnatural, artificial arrangement which is rendered more difficult by a larger number of points. The natural grouping (cf., e.g., Fig. 1, 2, etc.) is not at all impeded by increasing the number of dots. It never occurs, for example, that with a long row of such dots the process of "uniting" them into pairs is abandoned and individual points seen instead. It is not true that fewer stimulus points "obviously" yield simpler, surer, more elementary results.

60

interval: distance between adjacent elements (here, dots)

so on for the others: In Figure 2 this could be do-re, pause, do-re, pause, and so forth.

colour: These are the original figures; presumably Wertheimer means characteristics (shape, size, fill, etc.).

In each of the above cases that form of grouping is most natural which involves the smallest interval. They all show, that is to say, the predominant influence of what we may call *The Factor of Proximity*. Here is the first of the principles which we undertook to discover. That the principle holds also for auditory organization can readily be seen by substituting tap-tap, pause, tap-tap, pause, etc. for Fig. 1, and so on for the others. 65

70

II. Proximity is not, however, the only factor involved in natural groupings. This is apparent from the following examples. We shall maintain an identical proximity throughout but vary the colour of the dots themselves : 75

. . .

FIGURE 8

○ ○ ● ● ○ ○ ● ● ○ ○ ● ● ○ ○ ● ● ○ ○ ● ●

Thus we are led to the discovery of a second principle—viz. the tendency of like parts to band together—which we may call *The Factor of Similarity.* And again it should be remarked that this principle applies also to auditory experience. Maintaining a constant interval, the beats may be soft and loud (analogous to Fig. 8) thus: . .!!. .!! etc. Even when the attempt to hear some other arrangement succeeds, this cannot be maintained for long. The natural grouping soon 80 returns as an overpowering "upset" of the artificial arrangement.

. . .

III. What will happen when *two* such factors appear in the same constellation? They may be made to co-operate; or, they can be set in opposition—as, for example, when *one* operates to favour *ab/cd* while the *other* favours /*bc/de*. By appropriate variations, either factor may be weakened or strengthened. As an example, consider this arrangement: 85

FIGURE 9

.

● ○   ○ ●   ● ○   ○ ●

where both similarity and proximity are employed. An illustration of opposition in which similarity is victorious despite the preferential status given to proximity is this:

> *preferential status:* In Figure 10, each circle is closer to a dot than to another circle; each dot is closer to a circle than to another dot, yet we tend to group by similarity rather than proximity.

FIGURE 10

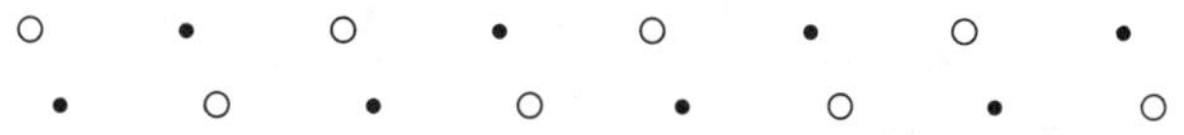

90   A less decided victory by similarity:

FIGURE 11

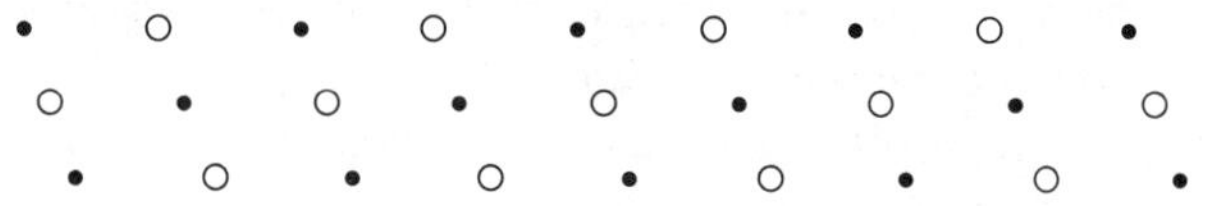

Functioning together towards the same end, similarity and proximity greatly strengthen the prominence here of verticality:

FIGURE 12

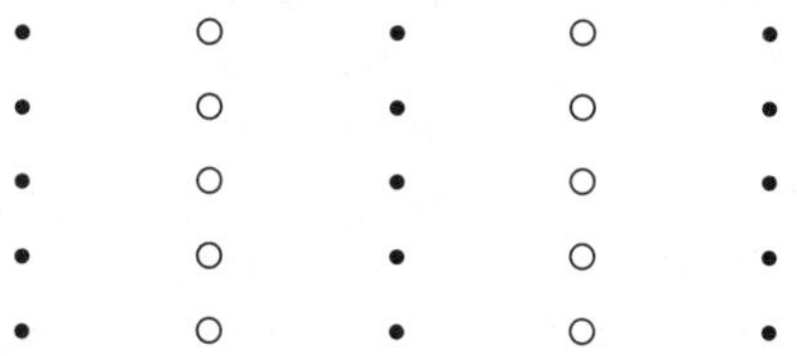

Where, in cases such as these, *proximity* is the predominant factor, a gradual increase of interval will eventually introduce a point at which *similarity* is predominant. In this way it is pos-
95   sible to test the strength of these Factors.

IV. A row of dots is presented:

FIGURE 13

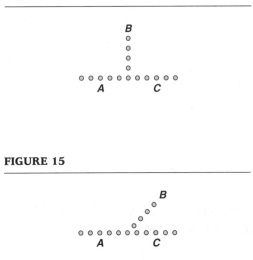

• • •	• • •	• • •	• • •
a b c	*d e f*	*g h i*	*j k l*

and then, without the subject's expecting it, but before his eyes, a sudden, slight shift upward is given, say, to *d, e, f* or to *d, e, f* and *j, k, 1* together. *This* shift is "pro-structural," since it involves an entire group of naturally related dots. A shift upward of, say, *c, d, e* or of *c, d, e* and *i, j, k* would be "contra-structural" because the common fate (i.e. the shift) to which these dots are subjected does *not* conform with their natural groupings.   100

> *natural groupings:* that is, natural according to the Factor of Proximity

Shifts of the latter kind are far less "smooth" than those of the former type. The former often call forth from the subject no more than bare recognition that a change has occurred; not so with   105
the latter type. Here it is as if some particular "opposition" to the change had been encountered. The result is confusing and discomforting. Sometimes a revolt against the originally dominant Factor of Proximity will occur and the shifted dots themselves thereupon constitute a new grouping whose common fate it has been to be shifted above the original row. The principle involved here may be designated *The Factor of Uniform Destiny* (or of "*Common Fate*").   110

. . .

VII. That spatial proximity will not alone account for organization can be shown by an example such as Fig. 14. Taken individually the points in *B* are in closer proximity to the individual points of *A* (or *C*) than the points of *A* and *C* are to each other. Nevertheless the perceived grouping is not   115
AB/C or *BC/A*, but, quite clearly "a horizontal line and a vertical line"—i.e. *AC/B*.

FIGURE 14

In Fig. 15 the spatial proximity of *B* and *C* is even greater, yet the result is still *AC/B*—i.e. horizontal-oblique. The same is true of the relationship *AB/C* in   120
Fig. 16. As Figs. 17–20 also show we are dealing now with a new principle which we may call *The Factor of Direction*. That direction may still be unequivocally given even when curved lines are used is of course obvious (cf. Figs. 21–24). The dom-   125
inance of this Factor in certain cases will be especially clear if one attempts to see Fig. 25 as *(abefil . . .)* *(cdghkm . . .)* instead of *(acegik . . .) (bdfhlm . . .).*

FIGURE 15

130 Suppose in Fig. 21 we had only the part designated as *A,* and suppose any two other lines were to be added. Which of the additional ones would join *A* as its continuation and which would appear as an appendage? As it is now drawn *AC* constitutes the continuity, *B* the

135 appendage. Figs. 26–31 represent a few such variations. Thus, for example, we see that *AC/B* is still the dominant organization even in Fig. 27 (where *C* is tangent to the circle implied by *A*). But in Fig. 28, when *B* is tangent to *A,* we still

140 have *AC/B.* Naturally, however, the length of *B* and *C* is an important consideration. . . . Certain arrangements are stronger than others, and seem to "triumph"; intermediate arrangements are less distinctive, more equivocal.

145 On the whole the reader should find no difficulty in *seeing* what is meant here. In designing a pattern, for example, one has a feeling how successive parts should follow one another; one knows what a "good" continuation is, how "inner

150 coherence" is to be achieved, etc.; one recognizes a resultant "good gestalt" simply by its own "inner necessity." A more detailed study at this juncture would require consideration of the

FIGURE 16

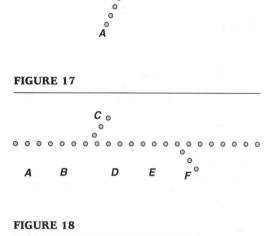

FIGURE 17

FIGURE 18

FIGURE 19

following: Additions to an incomplete object (e.g.
155 the segment of a curve) may proceed in a direction opposed to that of the original, or they may *carry on* the principle "logically demanded" by the original. It is in the latter case that "unity" will result. This does not mean, however, that "sim-
160 plicity" will result from an addition which is (piecewise considered) "simple." Indeed even a very "complicated" addition may promote unity of the resultant whole. "Simplicity" does not refer to the properties of individual parts; simplicity is a property of wholes. Finally, the addition must be viewed also in terms of such

FIGURE 20

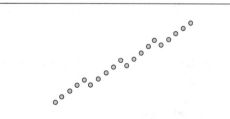

FIGURE 21

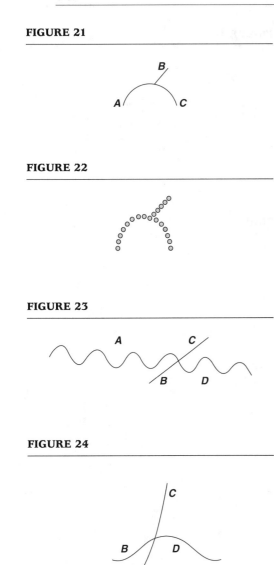

FIGURE 22

FIGURE 23

FIGURE 24

characteristic "whole properties" as closure, equi- 165
librium, and symmetry.[1]

From an inspection of Figs. 32–34 we are led to
the discovery of still another principle: *The Factor
of Closure.* If *A, B, C, D* are given and *AB/CD* consti- 170
tute two self-enclosed units, then *this* arrangement rather than *AC/BD* will be apprehended. It is
not true, however, that closure is necessarily the
dominant Factor in all cases which satisfy these
conditions. In Fig. 35, for example, it is not three 175
self-enclosed areas but rather *The Factor of the
"Good Curve"* which predominates.

. . .

VIII. Another Factor is that of past experience or
habit. Its principle is that if *AB* and *C* but not *BC*
have become habitual (or "associated") there is
then a tendency for *ABC* to appear as *AB/C*. Unlike 180
the other principles with which we have been
dealing, it is characteristic of this one that the *contents A, B, C* are assumed to be independent of the
constellation in which they appear. Their arrangement is on principle determined merely by extrin- 185
sic circumstances (e.g. drill).

There can be no doubt that some of our apprehensions are determined in this way.[2] Often arbitrary material can be arranged in arbitrary form
and, after a sufficient drill, made habitual. The dif- 190
ficulty is, however, that many people are inclined
to attribute to this principle the fundamental
structure of *all* apprehension. The situation in §VII,
they would say, simply involves the prominence of
habitual complexes. Straight lines, right angles, 195
the arcs of circles, squares—all are familiar from
everyday experience. And so it is also with the
intervals between parts (e.g. the spaces between
written words), and with uniformity of coloured surfaces. Experience supplies a constant drill
in such matters. 200

---

[1] Symmetry signifies far more than mere similarity of parts; it refers rather to the logical correctness of a part considered relative to the whole in which that part occurs.

[2] Example: 314 cm. is apprehended as *abc/de*, not as *ab/cde*—i.e. as 314 cm., not 31/4 cm. nor as 314c/m.

FIGURE 25

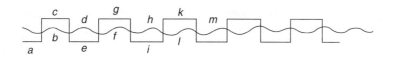

And yet, despite its plausibility, the doctrine of past experience brushes aside the real problems of apprehension much too easily. Its duty should be to demonstrate in each of the foregoing cases (1)

205 that the dominant apprehension was due to earlier experience (and to nothing else); (2) that non-dominant apprehensions in each instance had *not* been previously experienced; and, in general, (3) that in the *amassing* of experience none but adventitious factors

210 need ever be involved. It should be clear from our earlier discussions and examples that this programme could not succeed. A single example will suffice to show this. Right angles surround us from childhood (table, cupboard, window, corners of rooms, houses).

215 At first this seems quite self-evident. But does the child's environment consist of nothing but man-made objects? Are there not in nature (e.g. the branches of trees) fully as many obtuse and acute angles? But far more important than these is the following considera-

220 tion. Is it *true* that cupboards, tables, etc., actually present right angles to the child's eye? If we consider the literal reception of stimuli upon the retina, how often are *right angles* as such involved? Certainly less often than the *perception* of right angles. As a matter of fact

225 the conditions necessary for a literal "right angle" stimulation are realized but rarely in everyday life (viz. *only* when the table or other object appears in a frontal parallel plane). Hence the argument from experience is referring not to repetition of literal stimulus conditions,

230 but to repetition of phenomenal experience—and the problem therefore simply repeats itself.

Regardless of whether or not one believes that the relationships discussed in §VII depend upon past experience, the question remains in

235 either case: Do these relationships exhibit the

apprehension: perception

adventitious: chance

FIGURE 26

FIGURE 27

FIGURE 28

FIGURE 29

FIGURE 30

FIGURE 31

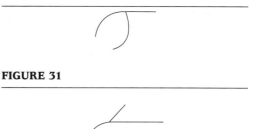

operations of intrinsic laws or not, and if so, which laws? Such a question requires experimental inquiry and cannot be answered by the mere expression "past experience." Let us take two arrangements which have been habitually experienced in the forms *abc* and *def* many thousands of times. I place them together and present *abcdef*. Is the result sure to be *abc/def*? Fig. 36, which is merely the combination of a W and an M, may be taken as an example. 240
One ordinarily sees not the familiar letters W and M, but a sinuation between two symmetrically curved uprights. If we designate parts of the W from left to right as *abc* and those of the M as *def*, the figure may be described as *ad/be/cf* (or as /*be*/ between /*ad*/ and /*cf*/; *not*, however, 245
as *abc/def*.

sinuation: a curlicue

FIGURE 32

FIGURE 33

FIGURE 34

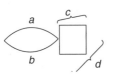

FIGURE 35

But the objection might be raised that while we are familiar enough with W and M, we are not accustomed to seeing them in *this* way (one above the other) and that this is why the other 250 arrangement is dominant. It would certainly be false, however, to consider this an "explanation." At best this mode of approach could show only why the arrangement W-M is *not* seen; the positive side would still be untouched. But apart from 255 this, the objection is rendered impotent when we arrange *abc* and *def* one above the other (Fig. 37) in a fashion quite as unusual as that given in Fig. 36. Nor is the argument admissible that the arrangements /*ad*/ and /*be*/ and /*cf*/ in Fig. 36 are 260 themselves familiar from past experience. It simply is not true that as much experience has been had with /*be*/ as with the *b* in *abc* and the *e* in *def*.

IX. When an object appears upon a homogeneous 265 field there must be stimulus differentiation (inhomogeneity) in order that the object may be perceived. A perfectly homogeneous field appears as a total field [*Ganzfeld*] opposing subdivision, disintegration, etc. To effect a segregation within this 270 field requires relatively strong differentiation between the object and its background. And this holds not only for ideally homogeneous fields but

also for fields in which, e.g., a symmetrical brightness distribution obtains, or in which the "homogeneity" consists in a uniform dappled effect. The
best case for the resulting of a figure in such a field
is when in the total field a closed surface of simple
form is different in colour from the remaining field.
Such a surface figure is not one member of a duo
(of which the total field or "ground" would be the
other member); its contours serve as boundary lines only for *this* figure. The background is not
limited by the figure, but usually seems to continue unbroken beneath that figure.

    Within this figure there may be then further sub-
division resulting in subsidiary wholes. The procedure here as before is in the direction "from above
downward" and it will be found that the Factors discussed in §VII are crucial for these subdivisions.[3] As
regards attention, fixation, etc., it follows that they are
secondarily determined relative to the natural relations already given by whole constellations as such.
Consider, e.g., the difference between some artificially determined concentration of attention and that
spontaneously resulting from the pro-structural
emphasis given by a figure itself. For an approach
"from above downward," i.e. from whole-properties
downward towards subsidiary wholes and parts,
individual parts ("elements") are not primary, not
pieces to be combined in and-summations, but are
parts of wholes.

FIGURE 36

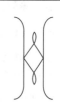

procedure: the order of processes by which the mind grasps the figures—the *wholes*—in the perceptual scene

artificially determined concentration: for example, trying to see Figure 1 as a/bc/de

FIGURE 37

Wertheimer's *from below* and *from above* have become today's familiar *bottom-up* and *top-down*.

[3] Epistemologically this distinction between "above" and "below" is of great importance. The mind and the psychophysiological reception of stimuli do *not* respond after the manner of a mirror or photographic apparatus receiving individual "stimuli" *qua* individual units and working them up "from below" into the objects of experience. Instead response is made to articulation as a whole—and this after the manner suggested by the Factors of § VII. It follows that the apparatus of reception cannot be described as a piecewise sort of mechanism. It must be of such a nature as to be able *to grasp the inner necessity* of articulated wholes. When we consider the problem in this light it becomes apparent that pieces are not even experienced as such but that apprehension itself is characteristically "from above."

FOR DISCUSSION

1. What point is Wertheimer making in the first sentence of this reading?

2. What are some auditory examples (e.g., from music and speech) of some of Wertheimer's gestalt principles?

3. Wertheimer remarks that "even a very 'complicated' addition may promote unity of the resultant whole" (p. 435, lines 161–163). Try to find or devise a figure that illustrates this point.

Ivan Petrovich Pavlov (1849–1936)

Conditioned Reflexes: An Investigation of the Physiological Activity of the Cerebral Cortex (1927)

Lecture I

It is ironic that Pavlov and his famous salivating dogs are so strongly associated in the popular imagination with psychology, for Pavlov was not a psychologist and had no wish to be thought of or remembered as one. Pavlov was a physiologist, and he always saw his work as belonging to that field. Early in his career Pavlov studied the nervous mechanisms responsible for regulating blood pressure. Around 1879 he began his studies of the physiology of digestion, for which he was awarded the Nobel Prize in 1904.

It is important to keep in mind that Pavlov's work on learning was not at first motivated by an interest in animal learning, but rather followed directly from his work on digestion. In the course of that work, which focused on the digestive glands, Pavlov noticed what he called "psychic secretions" in his dogs: If a stimulus (e.g., footsteps) regularly occurred just before feeding, the dog would soon begin to respond to that stimulus by salivating, even before the food arrived. This discovery was the nucleus of what would soon become one of the most widely familiar psychological phenomena of all time: the conditioned reflex. In the terminology traditionally used to describe conditioning, the original reflex is one in which food in the mouth (the *unconditioned*

Source: Pavlov, I. P. (1927). *Conditioned reflexes: An investigation of the physiological activity of the cerebral cortex* (G. V. Anrep, Trans.). London: Oxford University Press. Reprinted with permisssion. [Russian original published 1923.]

stimulus [US]) automatically elicits salivation (the *unconditioned response* [UR]). Pavlov's discovery was that when a neutral stimulus such as the sound of his assistant's footsteps was repeatedly paired with food, the neutral stimulus became a *conditioned stimulus* (CS) that elicited salivation (the *conditioned response* [CR]); thus

unconditioned (built-in) reflex: food (US)   →   salivation (UR)

conditioned (learned) reflex: footsteps (CS)   →   salivation (CR)

In 1902 Pavlov turned his full attention to psychic secretions, beginning a vast and systematic investigation of conditioned reflexes that occupied him for the rest of his life and earned him a prominent place in the history of psychology. In the reading below, Pavlov argues that physiology must be involved in understanding not just sensation and motor activity but also more complex activity.

The cerebral hemispheres stand out as the crowning achievement in the nervous development of the animal kingdom. These structures in the higher animals are of considerable dimensions and exceedingly complex, being made up in man of millions upon millions of cells—centres or foci of nervous activity—varying in size, shape and arrangement, and con-

5 nected with each other by countless branchings from their individual processes. Such complexity of structure naturally suggests a like complexity of function, which in fact is obvious in the higher animal and in man. Consider the dog, which has been

10 for so many countless ages the servant of man. Think how he may be trained to perform various

processes: In biology, a process is a projecting part of a tissue. Here Pavlov refers to the branching of the axon and dendrites of a nerve cell.

duties, watching, hunting, etc. We know that this complex behaviour of the animal, undoubtedly involving the highest nervous activity, is mainly associated with the cerebral hemispheres. If we remove the hemispheres in the dog (Goltz, 1892; Rothmann, 1909), the animal becomes

15 not only incapable of performing these duties but also incapable even of looking after itself. It becomes in fact a helpless invalid, and cannot long survive unless it be carefully tended.

In man also the highest nervous activity is dependent upon the structural and functional integrity of the cerebral hemispheres. As soon as these structures become damaged and their functions impaired in any way, so man also becomes an invalid. He can no longer proceed with

20 his normal duties, but has to be kept out of the working world of his fellow men. In astounding contrast with the unbounded activity of the cerebral hemispheres stands the meagre content of present-day physiological knowledge concerning them. Up to the year 1870, in fact, there was no

25 physiology of the hemispheres; they seemed to be out of reach of the physiologist. In that year the common physiological methods of stimulation and extirpation were first applied to them (Fritsch and Hitzig, 1870). It was found by these workers

30 that stimulation of certain parts of the cortex of the hemispheres (motor cortex) regularly evoked contractions in definite groups of skeletal muscles: extirpation of these parts of the cortex led to disturbances in the normal functioning of the same

35 groups of muscles.

stimulation and extirpation: These were the first methods for directly studying the function of nervous tissue in vivo. In one case the relevant part of the brain is exposed, an electrical stimulus is applied, and the resulting behavior (if any) is noted. In the other case the animal is carefully observed to establish a behavioral baseline. Then a specific part of the brain is surgically destroyed, and the animal's subsequent behavior (after recovering from the surgery) is compared to the baseline; any missing behavior is presumed to be a function of the area that has been destroyed.

Shortly afterwards it was demonstrated (Ferrier, 1876; Munk, 1890/1909) that other areas of the cortex which do not evoke any motor activity in response to stimulation are also functionally dif-

40 ferentiated. Extirpation of these areas leads to definite defects in the nervous activity associated

David Ferrier, using electrical stimulation, produced a fairly detailed map of the monkey's sensory cortex. Hermann Munk showed that each occipital lobe was responsible for vision in the opposite visual field.

organ of Corti: The part of the basilar membrane, in the cochlea (inner ear), containing the hair cells that turn acoustic vibrations into nerve impulses. The organ of Corti is thus to hearing exactly what the retina is to seeing.

with certain receptor organs, such as the retina of the eye, the organ of Corti, and the sensory nerve-endings in the skin. Searching investigations have been made, and still are being made, by numerous workers on this question of localization of function in the cortex. Our knowledge has been increased in precision and filled out in detail, especially as regards the motor area, and has even found useful application in medicine. These investigations, however, did not proceed fundamentally beyond the position established by Fritsch and Hitzig. The important question of the physiological mechanism of the whole higher and complex behaviour of the animal which is—as Goltz showed—dependent upon the cerebral hemispheres, was not touched in any of these investigations and formed no part of the current physiological knowledge.

Although it is not central to Pavlov's argument, the early study of localization of psychological function in the brain is a fascinating and important chapter in the history of modern psychology. Some of the landmarks are Broca (1861/1960), Ferrier (1876), Flourens (1824/1960), Fritsch & Hitzig (1870/1960), and Hughlings Jackson (1873). For comprehensive historical treatments, see Brazier (1988), Clarke & Dewhurst (1972), Finger (1994, 2000), and Martensen (2004).

When therefore we ask the questions: What do those facts which have up to the present been at the disposal of the physiologist explain with regard to the behaviour of the higher animals? What general scheme of the highest nervous activity can they give? Or what general rules governing this activity can they help us to formulate?—the modern physiologist finds himself at a loss and can give no satisfactory reply. The problem of the mechanism of this complex structure which is so rich in function has got hidden away in a corner, and this unlimited field, so fertile in possibilities for research, has never been adequately explored.

The reason for this is quite simple and clear. These nervous activities have never been regarded from the same point of view as those of other organs, or even other parts of the central nervous system. The activities of the hemispheres have been talked about as some kind of special psychical activity, whose working we feel and apprehend in ourselves, and by analogy suppose to exist in animals. This is an anomaly which has placed the physiologist in an extremely difficult position. On the one hand it would seem that the study of the activities of the cerebral hemispheres, as of the activities of any other part of the organism, should be within the compass of physiology, but on the other hand it happens to have been annexed to the special field of another science—psychology.

What attitude then should the physiologist adopt? Perhaps he should first of all study the methods of this science of psychology, and only afterwards hope to study the physiological mechanism of the hemispheres? This involves a serious difficulty. It is logical that in its

analysis of the various activities of living matter physiology should base itself on the more
75   advanced and more exact sciences—physics and chemistry. But if we attempt an approach
from this science of psychology to the problem confronting us we shall be building our super-
structure on a science which has no claim to exactness as compared even with physiology. In
fact it is still open to discussion whether psychology is a natural science, or whether it can be
regarded as a science at all.

80   It is not possible here for me to enter deeply into this question, but I will stay to give one fact
which strikes me very forcibly, viz. that even the advocates of psychology do not look upon
their science as being in any sense exact. The eminent American psychologist, William James,
has in recent years referred to psychology not as a
science but as a *hope* of science. Another striking
85   illustration is provided by Wundt, the celebrated
philosopher and psychologist, founder of the so-
called experimental method in psychology and
himself formerly a physiologist. Just before the
War (1913), on the occasion of a discussion in

> *hope of science:* This comes from the last
> page of James's (1892) *Psychology.* In its
> original context the phrase does not seem
> to mean quite what Pavlov implies.

90   Germany as to the advisability of making separate Chairs of Philosophy and Psychology,
Wundt opposed the separation, one of his arguments being the impossibility of fixing a common examination schedule in psychology, since every professor had his own special ideas as
to what psychology really was. Such testimony seems to show clearly that psychology cannot
yet claim the status of an exact science.

95   If this be the case there is no need for the physiologist to have recourse to psychology. It
would be more natural that experimental investigation of the physiological activities of the
hemispheres should lay a solid foundation for a future true science of psychology; such a course
is more likely to lead to the advancement of this branch of natural science.

        The physiologist must thus take his own path, where a trail has already been blazed for him.
100 Three hundred years ago Descartes evolved the idea of the reflex. Starting from the assumption that animals behaved simply as machines, he regarded every activity of the organism as a
necessary reaction to some external stimulus,
the connection between the stimulus and the
response being made through a definite nervous

> Descartes describes the reflex (though he
> doesn't use that word) in the *Treatise on
> Man* (1629–1633/1972). The word *reflex*
> was not used in the present sense until
> the 18th century.

105 path: and this connection, he stated, was the fundamental purpose of the nervous structures in the
animal body. This was the basis on which the study
of the nervous system was firmly established. In
the eighteenth, nineteenth and twentieth cen-
110 turies the conception of the reflex was used to the
full by physiologists. Working at first only on the
lower parts of the central nervous system, they came
gradually to study more highly developed parts,
until quite recently Magnus (1924), continuing the

> *necessary reaction:* not in the sense of
> *needed* but in the sense of *determined*
> or *fixed*

Charles Sherrington (1857–1952) was one of the founders of modern neurophysiology. Much of his research on reflexes was done with decorticated animals. With the higher brain centers disconnected from the spinal cord, these animals' reflexes are mediated by the spinal cord alone, allowing a clearer view of nervous function.

classical investigations of Sherrington (1906) upon the spinal reflexes, has succeeded in demonstrating the reflex nature of all the elementary motor activities of the animal organism. Descartes' conception of the reflex was constantly and fruitfully applied in these studies, but its application has stopped short of the cerebral cortex.

It may be hoped that some of the more complex activities of the body, which are made up by a grouping together of the elementary locomotor activities and which enter into the states referred to in psychological phraseology as "playfulness," "fear," "anger," and so forth, will soon be demonstrated as reflex activities of the subcortical parts of the brain. A bold attempt to apply the idea of the reflex to the activities of the hemispheres was made by the Russian physiologist, I. M. Sechenov, on the basis of the knowledge available in his day of the physiology of the central nervous system. In a pamphlet entitled "Reflexes of the Brain," published in Russian in 1863, he attempted to represent the activities of the cerebral hemispheres as reflex—that is to say, as *determined*. Thoughts he regarded as reflexes in which the effector path was inhibited, while great outbursts of passion he regarded as exaggerated reflexes with a wide irradiation of excitation. A similar attempt was made more recently by Richet (1925), who introduced the conception of the psychic reflex, in which the response following on a given stimulus is supposed to be determined by the association of this stimulus with the traces left in the hemispheres by past stimuli. And generally speaking, recent physiology shows a tendency to regard the highest activities of the hemispheres as an association of the new excitations at any given time with traces left by old ones (associative memory, training, education by experience).

Pavlov refers to Ivan Mikhailovich Sechenov (1829–1905) as the "father of Russian physiology," and it is not hard to see Pavlov's intellectual debt. Here is Sechenov's summary of *Reflexes of the Brain:*

[I]n his everyday conscious and semi-conscious life man is never free from the sensory influences exerted by the environment through his sense organs, as well as from sensations ensuing from his own organism (his own feelings); it is these factors which maintain his entire psychical life with all of its motor manifestations, because psychical life is inconceivable when the senses are lost (this supposition was confirmed twenty years later by observations on very rare cases of patients who had lost almost all their senses). Just as man's movements are determined by the indications of the sense organs, his mode of behaviour in psychical life is determined by desires and wishes. Both the reflexes and psychical processes resulting in action, are of an expedient character. The beginning of the reflex is always caused by a certain external sensory influence; the same thing takes place—often imperceptibly—in the whole of our psychical life (since in the absence of sensory influences psychical life is impossible). In most cases the reflexes end in movements; but there are reflexes which end in the suppression of movement; the same thing can be observed in psychical acts; most of them are manifested in facial expressions and actions, but in very many cases their ending is suppressed, with the result that instead of three members the act consists only of two; the meditative mental side of life takes on this form. Emotions are rooted, directly or indirectly, in the so-called systemic senses which can develop into strong desires (sensation of hunger, instinct of self-preservation, sexual desire, etc.) and which are expressed in impetuous actions; for this reason they can be included in the category of reflexes with an intensified ending. (Sechenov, 1863/1965, p. 112)

140 All this, however, was mere conjecture. The time was ripe for a transition to the experimental analysis of the subject—an analysis which must be as objective as the analysis in any other branch of natural science. An impetus was given to this transition by the rapidly developing science of comparative physiology, which itself sprang up as a direct result of the Theory of Evolution. In dealing with the lower members of the animal kingdom physiologists were, of

145 necessity, compelled to reject anthropomorphic preconceptions, and to direct all their effort towards the elucidation of the connections between the external stimulus and the resulting response, whether locomotor or other reaction. . . .

Under the influence of these new tendencies in biology, which appealed to the practical bent of the American mind, the American School of Psychologists—already interested in the

150 comparative study of psychology—evinced a disposition to subject the highest nervous activities of *animals* to experimental analysis under various specially devised conditions. We may fairly regard the treatise by Thorndike, *The Animal Intelligence* (1898), as the starting point for systematic investigations of this kind. In these investigations the animal was kept in a box, and food was placed outside the box so that it was visible to the animal. In order to get the food the

155 animal had to open a door, which was fastened by various suitable contrivances in the different experiments. Tables and charts were made showing how quickly and in what manner the animal solved the problems set it. The whole process was understood as being the formation of an association between the visual and tactile stimuli on the one hand and the locomotor apparatus on the other. This method, with its modifications, was subsequently applied by

160 numerous authors to the study of questions relating to the associative ability of various animals.

Edward L. Thorndike (1874–1949) was one of the first to conceive of learning in strictly objective terms, independent of any consideration of an animal's (unobservable) representation of what it knows. The investigations Pavlov refers to here, the famous "puzzle box" studies, led Thorndike to his law of effect:

Of several responses made to the same situation, those which are accompanied or closely followed by satisfaction to the animal will, other things being equal, be more firmly

(Continued)

(Continued)

connected with the situation, so that, when it recurs, they will be more likely to recur; those which are accompanied or closely followed by discomfort to the animal will, other things being equal, have their connections with that situation weakened, so that, when it recurs, they will be less likely to occur. The greater the satisfaction or discomfort, the greater the strengthening or weakening of the bond. (Thorndike, 1911, p. 244)

The law of effect and Pavlov's conditioned reflex became two of the cornerstones of American behaviorism.

At about the same time as Thorndike was engaged on this work, I myself (being then quite ignorant of his researches) was also led to the *objective* study of the hemispheres, by the following circumstance: In the course of a detailed investigation into the activities of the digestive glands I had to inquire into the so-called psychic secretion of some of the glands, a task which I attempted in conjunction with a collaborator. As a result of this investigation an unqualified conviction of the futility of subjective methods of inquiry was firmly stamped upon my mind. It became clear that the only satisfactory solution of the problem lay in an experimental investigation by strictly objective methods. For this purpose I started to record all the external stimuli falling on the animal at the time its reflex reaction was manifested (in this particular case the secretion of saliva), at the same time recording all changes in the reaction of the animal.

> *psychic secretion:* See introduction to this reading.

165

170

. . .

I shall now turn to the description of our material, first giving as a preliminary an account of the general conception of the reflex, of specific physiological reflexes, and of the so-called "instincts." Our starting point has been Descartes' idea of the nervous reflex. This is a genuine scientific conception, since it implies necessity. It may be summed up as follows: An external or internal stimulus falls on some one or other nervous receptor and gives rise to a nervous impulse; this nervous impulse is transmitted along nerve fibres to the central nervous system, and here, on account of existing nervous connections, it gives rise to a fresh impulse which passes along outgoing nerve fibres to the active organ, where it excites a special activity of the cellular structures. Thus a stimulus appears to be connected of necessity with a definite response, as cause with effect. It seems obvious that the whole activity of the organism should conform to definite laws. If the

> *existing nervous connections:* the innate "hard wiring" of the nervous system

175

180

> *special activity:* a *specific* activity, most likely secretion (if the organ is a gland) or contraction (if a muscle)

185

animal were not in exact correspondence with its environment it would, sooner or later, cease
190   to exist. To give a biological example: if, instead of being attracted to food, the animal were
repelled by it, or if instead of running from fire the animal threw itself into the fire, then it would
quickly perish. The animal must respond to changes in the environment in such a manner that
its responsive activity is directed towards the preservation of its existence. This conclusion
holds also if we consider the living organism in terms of physical and chemical science. Every
195   material system can exist as an entity only so long as its internal forces, attraction, cohesion,
etc., balance the external forces acting upon it. This is true for an ordinary stone just as much
as for the most complex chemical substances; and its truth should be recognized also for the
animal organism. Being a definite circumscribed
material system, it can only continue to exist so
200   long as it is in continuous equilibrium with the   *circumscribed:* self-contained
forces external to it: so soon as this equilibrium is
seriously disturbed the organism will cease to exist as the entity it was. Reflexes are the elemental units in the mechanism of perpetual equilibration. Physiologists have studied and are
studying at the present time these numerous machine-like, inevitable reactions of the organ-
205   ism—reflexes existing from the very birth of the animal, and due therefore to the inherent organization of the nervous system.

Reflexes, like the driving-belts of machines of human design, may be of two kinds—positive
and negative, excitatory and inhibitory. Although the investigation of these reflexes by physiologists has been going on now for a long time,
210   it is as yet not nearly finished. Fresh reflexes are
continually being discovered. We are ignorant of   *those receptor organs:* Here Pavlov refers to
the properties of those receptor organs for which   mechanisms by which the body regulates
the effective stimulus arises inside the organism,   internal states such as blood pressure and
and the internal reflexes themselves remain a   temperature.
215   field unexplored. The paths by which nervous
impulses are conducted in the central nervous
system are for the most part little known, or not
ascertained at all. The mechanism of inhibitions
confined within the central nervous system   *inhibitory reflexes:* In Lecture 18 Pavlov
220   remains quite obscure: we know something only   mentions a dog that "had among others an
of those inhibitory reflexes which manifest them-   inhibitory alimentary conditioned reflex to a
selves along the inhibitory efferent nerves.   metronome rate of 60 beats per minute,
Furthermore, the combination and interaction of   while a rate of 120 beats per minute served
different reflexes are as yet insufficiently under-   as a positive stimulus."
225   stood. Nevertheless physiologists are succeeding
more and more in unravelling the mechanism of
these machine-like activities of the organism, and   *Efferent nerves* are motor nerves, as distinct
may reasonably be expected to elucidate and   from *afferent,* or sensory, nerves.
control it in the end.

To those reflexes which have long been the subject of physiological investigation, and which concern chiefly the activities of separate organs and tissues, there should be added another group of inborn reflexes. These also take place in the nervous system, and they are the inevitable reactions to perfectly definite stimuli. They have to do with reactions of the organism as a whole, and comprise that general behaviour of the animal which has been termed "instinctive." Since complete agreement as regards the essential affinity of these reactions to the reflex has not yet been attained, we must discuss this question more fully. We owe to the English philosopher, Herbert Spencer, the suggestion that instinctive reactions are reflexes. Ample evidence was later advanced by zoologists, physiologists, and students of comparative psychology in support of this. I propose here to bring together the various arguments in favour of this view. Between the simplest reflex and the instinct we can find numerous stages of transition, and among these we are puzzled to find any line of demarcation. To exemplify this we may take the newly hatched chick. This little creature reacts by pecking to any stimulus that catches the eye, whether it be a real object or only a stain in the surface it is walking upon. In what way shall we say that this differs from the inclining of the head, the closing of the lids, when something flicks past its eyes? We should call this last a defensive reflex, but the first has been termed a feeding instinct: although in pecking nothing but an inclination of the head and a movement of the beak occurs.

Spencer (1820–1903) was neither scholar nor scientist and yet was, in his day, one of the most influential and celebrated writers on philosophical and scientific matters.

It has also been maintained that instincts are more complex than reflexes. There are, however, exceedingly complex reflexes which nobody would term instincts. We may take vomiting as an example. This is very complex and involves the co-ordination of a large number of muscles (both striped and plain) spread over a large area and usually employed in quite different functions of the organism. It involves also a secretory activity on the part of certain glands which is usually evoked for a quite different purpose.

Again, it has been assumed that the long train of actions involved in certain instinctive activities affords a distinctive point of contrast with the reflex, which is regarded as always being built on a simple scale. By way of example we may take the building of a nest, or of dwellings in general, by animals. A chain of incidents is linked together: material is gathered and carried to the site chosen; there it is built up and strengthened. To look upon this as reflex we must assume that one reflex initiates the next following—or, in other words, we must regard it as a chain-reflex. But this linking up of activities is not peculiar to instincts alone. We are familiar with numerous reflexes which most certainly fuse into chains. Thus, for example, if we stimulate an afferent nerve, *e.g.* the sciatic nerve, a reflex rise of blood pressure occurs; the high pressure in the left ventricle of the heart, and first part of the aorta, serves as the effective stimulus to a second reflex, this time a depressor reflex which has a moderating influence on the first. Again, we may take one of the chain reflexes recently established by Magnus. A cat, even when deprived of its cerebral hemispheres, will in most cases land on its feet when thrown from a

Rudolf Magnus (1873–1927), German physiologist.

230

235

240

245

250

255

260

265

270

height. How is this managed? When the position of the otolithic organ in space is altered a definite reflex is evoked which brings about a contraction of the muscles in the neck, restoring the animal's head to the normal position. This is the first reflex. With the righting of the head a fresh reflex is evoked, and certain muscles of the trunk and limbs are brought into play, restoring the animal to the standing posture. This is the second reflex.

> *otolithic organ:* a part of the inner ear, roughly between the cochlea and the semicircular canals, in which the inertial and gravitational movements of tiny calcium carbonate crystals (the otoliths, from *oto-*, ear, and *lith,* stone) are sensed by hair cells. The brain uses input from the otolithic organ to determine the head's orientation in space, and hence to maintain balance.

Some, again, object to the identification of instincts with reflexes on this ground: instincts, they say, frequently depend upon the internal state of an organism. For instance, a bird only builds its nest in the mating season. Or, to take a simpler case, when an animal is satiated with eating, then food has no longer any attraction and the animal leaves off eating. Again, the same is true of the sexual impulse. This depends on the age of the organism, and on the state of the reproductive glands; and a considerable influence is exerted by hormones (the products of the glands of internal secretion). But this dependence cannot be claimed as a peculiar property of "instincts." The intensity of any reflex, indeed its very presence, is dependent on the irritability of the centres, which in turn depends constantly on the physical and chemical properties of the blood (automatic stimulation of centres) and on the interaction of reflexes.

> *irritability:* in this context, the capability of responding to a given kind of stimulus; sensitivity

Last of all, it is sometimes held that whereas reflexes determine only the activities of single organs and tissues, instincts involve the activity of the organism as a whole. We now know, however, from the recent investigations of Magnus and de Kleijn, that

> Adriaan de Kleijn (1883–1949), Dutch otorhinolaryngologist

standing, walking and the maintenance of postural balance in general, are all nothing but reflexes.

It follows from all this that instincts and reflexes are alike the inevitable responses of the organism to internal and external stimuli, and therefore we have no need to call them by two different terms. Reflex has the better claim of the two, in that it has been used from the very beginning with a strictly scientific connotation.

The aggregate of reflexes constitutes the foundation of the nervous activities both of men and of animals. It is therefore of great importance to study in detail all the fundamental reflexes of the organism. Up to the present, unfortunately, this is far from being accomplished, especially, as I have mentioned before, in the case of those reflexes which have been known vaguely as "instincts." Our knowledge of these latter is very limited and fragmentary. Their classification under such headings as "alimentary," "defensive," "sexual," "parental" and "social" instincts, is thoroughly inadequate. Under each of these heads is assembled often a large number of individual reflexes. Some of these are quite unidentified; some are confused with others; and many are still only partially appreciated. . . .

As another example of a reflex which is very much neglected we may refer to what may be called the *investigatory reflex*. I call it the "What-is-it?" reflex. It is this reflex which brings about the immediate response in man and animals to the slightest changes in the world around them, so that they immediately orientate their appropriate receptor organ in accordance with the perceptible quality in the agent bringing about the change, making full investigation of it. The biological significance of this reflex is obvious. If the animal were not provided with such a reflex its life would hang at every moment by a thread. In man this reflex has been greatly developed with far-reaching results, being represented in its highest form by inquisitiveness—the parent of that scientific method through which we may hope one day to come to a true orientation in knowledge of the world around us.

. . .

As the fundamental nervous reactions both of men and of animals are inborn in the form of definite reflexes, I must again emphasize how important it is to compile a complete list comprising all these reflexes with their adequate classification. For, as will be shown later on, all the remaining nervous functions of the animal organism are based upon these reflexes. . . .

Let us return now to the simplest reflex from which our investigations started. If food or some rejectable substance finds its way into the mouth, a secretion of saliva is produced. The purpose of this secretion is in the case of food to alter it chemically, in the case of a rejectable substance to dilute and wash it out of the mouth. This is an example of a reflex due to the physical and chemical properties of a substance when it comes into contact with the mucous membrane of the mouth and tongue. But, in addition to this, a similar reflex secretion is evoked when these substances are placed at a distance from the dog and the receptor organs affected are only those of smell and sight. Even the vessel from which the food has been given is sufficient to evoke an alimentary reflex complete in all its details; and, further, the secretion may be provoked even by the sight of the person who brought the vessel, or by the sound of his footsteps. All these innumerable stimuli falling upon the several finely discriminating distance receptors lose their power for ever as soon as the hemispheres are taken from the animal, and those only which have a direct effect on mouth and tongue still retain their power. The great advantage to the organism of a capacity to react to the former stimuli is evident, for it is in virtue of their action that food finding its way into the mouth immediately encounters plenty of moistening saliva, and rejectable substances, often nocuous to the mucous membrane, find a layer of protective saliva already in the mouth which rapidly dilutes and washes them out. Even

nocuous: noxious, harmful

greater is their importance when they evoke the motor component of the complex reflex of nutrition, *i.e.* when they act as stimuli to the reflex of seeking food.

Here is another example—the reflex of self-defence. The strong carnivorous animal preys on weaker animals, and these if they waited to defend themselves until the teeth of the foe were in their flesh would speedily be exterminated. The case takes on a different aspect when the defence reflex is called into play by the sights and sounds of the enemy's approach. Then the prey has a chance to save itself by hiding or by flight.

How can we describe, in general, this difference in the dynamic balance of life between the
355   normal and the decorticated animal? What is the general mechanism and law of this distinction? It is pretty evident that under natural conditions the normal animal must respond not only
to stimuli which themselves bring immediate benefit or harm, but also to other physical or
chemical agencies—waves of sound, light, and the like—which in themselves only signal the
approach of these stimuli; though it is not the sight and sound of the beast of prey which is in
360   itself harmful to the smaller animal, but its teeth and claws.

Now although the *signalling stimuli* do play a part in those comparatively simple reflexes we
have given as examples, yet this is not the most important point. The essential feature of the
highest activity of the central nervous system, with which we are concerned and which in the
higher animals most probably belongs entirely to the hemispheres, consists not in the fact that
365   innumerable signalling stimuli do initiate reflex reactions in the animal, but in the fact that
under different conditions these same stimuli may initiate quite different reflex reactions; and
conversely the same reaction may be initiated by different stimuli.

In the above-mentioned example of the salivary reflex, the signal at one time is one particular vessel, at another time another; under certain conditions one man, under different conditions
370   another—strictly depending upon which vessel had been used in feeding and which man had
brought the vessel and given food to the dog. This evidently makes the machine-like responsive
activities of the organism still more precise, and adds to it qualities of yet higher perfection. So
infinitely complex, so continuously in flux, are the
conditions in the world around, that that complex
375   animal system which is itself in living flux, and that
system only, has a chance to establish dynamic
equilibrium with the environment. Thus we see that
the fundamental and the most general function of
the hemispheres is that of reacting to signals pre-
380   sented by innumerable stimuli of interchangeable
signification.

> *dynamic equilibrium:* a term with wide
> application in physics and chemistry. In its
> broadest sense it describes a system in
> which opposing forces or processes are
> balanced such that a specific variable of
> interest—e.g., motion, concentration—is
> held constant.

For Discussion

1. According to Pavlov, Sechenov describes thoughts as "reflexes in which the effector path
   [is] inhibited" (p. 446, line 132). What are the implications of this idea for psychology?

2. Compare Pavlov's notion of "perpetual equilibration" (p. 449, line 203) with Freud's of
   "mastering stimuli" (4.5, pp. 356–357, lines 77–88).

3. Would Darwin's account of instincts (4.3) apply likewise to reflexes? How?

4. Why is Pavlov eager to construe innate behavior in terms of reflexes rather than
   instincts? Why does it matter whether we call something a reflex or an instinct?

5. How much of an organism's behavior does Pavlov think can be explained in terms of
   reflexes, both conditioned and otherwise?

Kurt Lewin (1890–1947)
Experiments in Social Space (1939)

Lewin insisted that human social behavior cannot be understood by just looking at individuals; it is necessary, instead, to consider both the individual and the environment in which he exists. In its simplest form, Lewin proposed that behavior (B) is a function of an interaction between a person (P) and that person's environment (E). Thus, $B = f$ (P, E). Lewin also referred to P and E as the individual's "life space," and so $B = f$ (life space).

This seems like a simple idea, and a reasonable one, but it was a radical approach to studying social behavior in Lewin's time. When Lewin began studying "group dynamics," a term that he created, "only the individual was considered to be 'real' and, thus, a proper subject for psychological study. The study of groups was taboo" (Berscheid, 2003, p. 114). Floyd Allport (in Berscheid, 2003, p. 114) wrote in 1924 that groups are simply "sets of ideals, thoughts, and habits repeated in each individual mind and existing only in those minds," and "Psychology in all its branches is a science of the individual. To extend its principles to larger units is to destroy their meaning."

Influenced by philosopher Ernst Cassirer and the Gestalt psychologists but motivated primarily by his own desire to understand social behavior, Lewin consistently did exactly what Allport said should not be done—he studied groups. He frequently defended this activity and questioned the notion that groups lack "reality" and so cannot be studied in a meaningful way. In one of his clearest defenses, Lewin wrote: "Like social taboos, a scientific taboo is kept up not so much by a rational argument as by a common attitude among scientists" (Lewin, 1951, p. 190) and "The taboo against believing in the existence of a social entity is probably most effectively broken by handling this entity experimentally" (p. 193). This is exactly what Lewin did.

Lewin developed field theory, a theory that postulated concepts and allowed for the development of hypotheses about these concepts that could be tested empirically. The basic idea, that $B = f$ (life space) becomes much more complicated when one begins to think seriously

Source: Lewin, K. (1939a). Experiments in social space. *Harvard Educational Review*, 9, 21–32. Copyright by the President and Fellows of Harvard College. Reprinted with permission. [Reprinted in Lewin (1948).]

about the nature of a person's life space. For example, Lewin argued that our behavior is not caused by the past or the future, but by the present. Of course, if you bring the past or future into the present by thinking about them, they become part of your life space.

Lewin used diagrams to describe the life space. There are regions, physical, social or psychological; there are valences, positive or negative feelings one has toward another person, a thing, or an idea; there are barriers, obstacles that prevent people from achieving their goals; there is locomotion, an individual's movement, physically or psychologically within the life space; there is tension, unmet needs and unfulfilled goals; and all aspects of the life space are constantly changing.

Field Theory provides a system with which it is possible to increase our understanding of group dynamics. It is rich in hypotheses that can be studied empirically. It also provides something more—a way to think about and create social change—something in which Lewin was always very interested (Lewin, 1947). Some of Lewin's "action" research was done during World War II. Along with a number of other social psychologists, Lewin did research on how to get Americans to make some changes in their attitudes and behaviors, necessary because some things were in very short supply (e.g., gasoline, meat, and sugar) and helped to develop programs to create these changes. Lewin's primary interest in social change, though, was the reduction of prejudice, especially anti-Semitism. He pursued this interest in his writing and in his work to increase tolerance and understanding.

Lewin was not only the person who brought the study of group dynamics into social psychology, he was also the person who took psychologists out into the world to study social behavior and to use what they had studied and learned for social good. These contributions were exemplified in his establishment of the Research Center for Group Dynamics at MIT in 1945 (the center moved to the University of Michigan after Lewin's death).

It is likely that Lewin's interest in social change was, in part, a result of his own experiences. He was born in Mogilno, a small village in what was then Prussia but is now Poland (as it was years before as well) (Lewin, 1998). Anti-Semitism existed throughout Germany, but it was particularly virulent in Prussia (Gold, 1999), and the Lewins were Jewish. When Hitler became chancellor of Germany, Lewin knew that he and his wife and children had to leave. He came to the United States in 1933 and taught for 2 years at Cornell University and then moved to the University of Iowa, where he stayed until his death in 1947.

Lewin is praised for developing a theory, a system, that allows us to think about social behavior in a broad context, for demonstrating that concepts related to group behavior can be studied empirically, and for urging psychologists to use theory and research to understand (and sometimes to change) things of importance in the world. As his wife, Gertrud Weiss Lewin, wrote (in her introduction to Lewin, 1948),

> I recall the intense joy, almost ecstasy, that my husband used to feel when he drove his car across the great American bridges. . . . No doubt he conceived of his particular field of research as equally capable of joining what seemed such widely separated stretches of territory. The connection of theory and the profoundly disturbing social issues of our reality especially led him to experience this intense, persistent "tension." (p. xvi)

The study we've included here is an excellent example of Lewin's ability to find a way to study concepts that most didn't believe could be studied in more than a subjective manner. In this study, he manipulated "group atmosphere" and "leadership style" and looked at the effects of the manipulations on a number of measurable behaviors.

I

I am persuaded that it is possible to undertake experiments in sociology which have as much right to be called scientific experiments as those in physics and chemistry. I am persuaded that there exists a social space which has all the essential properties of a real empirical space and deserves as much attention by students of geometry and mathematics as the physical space, although it is *not* a physical one. The perception of social space and the experimental and conceptual investigation of the dynamics and laws of the processes in social space are of fundamental theoretical and practical importance.

Being officially a psychologist I should perhaps apologize to the sociologists for crossing the boundaries of my field. My justification for doing so is that necessity forces the move, and for this the sociologists themselves are partially to blame. For they have stressed that the view which holds a human being to be a biological, physiological entity is utterly wrong. They have fought against the belief that only physical or biological facts are real, and that social facts are merely an abstraction. Some of the sociologists have said that only the social group has reality and that the individual person is nothing more than an abstraction—a being who properly should be described as a cross section of the groups to which he belongs.

Whichever of these statements one might consider correct, one certainly will have to admit that psychology has learned, particularly in the last decade, to realize the overwhelming importance of social factors for practically every kind and type of behavior. It is true that the child from the first day of his life is a member of a group and would die without being cared for by the group. The experiments on success and failure, level of aspiration, intelligence, frustration, and all the others, have shown more and more convincingly that the goal a person sets for himself is deeply influenced by the social standards of the group to which he belongs or wishes to belong. The psychologist of today recognizes that there are few problems more important for the development of the child and the problem of adolescence than a study of the processes by which a child takes over or becomes opposed to the ideology and the style of living predominant in his social climate, the forces which make him belong to certain groups, or which determine his social status and his security within those groups.

> *level of aspiration:* the performance goals you set for yourself (e.g., How many pounds can you lift? How many math problems can you do?). A person's level of aspiration depends on personality, past successes and failures, and the performance of others (e.g., If my peers can do 10 of the math problems, I want to do at least that many. If a 3rd grader can do 10 problems, I want to do more than that.) (Lewin, Dembo, Festinger, & Sears, 1944).

A genuine attempt to approach these problems—for instance, that of social status or leadership—experimentally implies technically that one has to create different types of groups and to set up experimentally a variety of social factors which might shift this status. The experimental social psychologist will have to acquaint himself with the task of experimentally creating groups, creating a social climate or style of living. The sociologist I hope will therefore forgive him when he cannot avoid handling also the so-called sociological problems of groups

40   and group life. Perhaps the social psychologist might prove to be even of considerable help to the sociologist. Frequently the investigation on the border line between two sciences has proved to be particularly fruitful for the progress of both of them.

Take, for instance, the concept "social group." There has been much discussion about how to define a group. The group often has been considered as something more than the sum of

45   the individuals, something better and higher. One has attributed to it a "group mind." The opponents of this opinion have declared the concept of "group mind" to be mere metaphysics and that in reality the group is nothing other than the sum of the individuals.

Questions about the existence of the "group mind" derive, in part, from Sherif's studies on the formation of social norms (1936, pp. 89–112). Sherif's research on norms used the autokinetic effect, the fact that everyone will see a stationary point of light in a completely dark environment as moving. He asked participants to tell him how much the light was moving and found that different participants saw different amounts of movement, but each participant established a small range of responses over a series of trials. Sherif then put people with different typical responses together and found that the group came to agreement about how much the light was moving—they established a group norm. The existence of these group norms raised questions about whether groups have personalities, or minds, of their own. The issue became more interesting when Jacobs and Campbell (1951) replicated Sherif's experiment but added a new feature. After the group norm was established, they replaced one member of the original group with a new person and then replaced each of the other original members in turn. The social norm persisted over these changes and, as Jacobs & Campbell continued to rotate individuals in and out of the group, the original norm continued for at least four or five generations after the last of the original members was replaced. Group mind?

An aside: Some think the autokinetic effect is responsible for some UFO sightings (Sofka, 1999).

To one who has watched the development of the concept of organism, whole, or Gestalt, in psy-

50   chology this argumentation sounds strangely familiar. In the beginning of Gestalt theory, at the time of Ehrenfels, one attributed to a psychological whole, such as melody, a so-called Gestalt quality—that is, an additional entity like a group mind, which the

55   whole was supposed to have in addition to the sum of its parts. Today we know that we do not need to assume a mystical Gestalt quality, but that any dynamical whole has properties of its own. The whole might be symmetric in spite of its parts

60   being asymmetric, a whole might be unstable in spite of its parts being stable in themselves.

Christian von Ehrenfels (1859–1932) introduced the term *Gestalt* (form or whole) to psychology. He argued that perceptions have qualities not contained in isolated sensations and that perceptions emerge from these sensations. He was a teacher of Max Wertheimer, the founder of the Gestalt school of psychology, who took the next step and suggested that we do not first apprehend sensations and then create perceptions from them but instead directly apprehend the perception. Lewin, as this paragraph makes clear, shared Wertheimer's view (see 5.1).

As far as I can see, the discussion regarding group versus individual in sociology follows a similar trend. Groups are sociological wholes; the unity of these sociological wholes can be defined operationally in the same way as a unity of any other dynamic whole, namely, by the interdependence of its parts. Such a definition takes mysticism out of the group conception and brings the problem down to a thoroughly empirical and testable basis. At the same time it means a full recognition of the fact that properties of a social group, such as its organization, its stability, its goals, are something different from the organization, the stability, and the goals of the individuals in it.

How, then, should one describe a group? Let us discuss the effect of democratic, autocratic and laissez faire atmospheres on clubs which have been experimentally created by R. Lippitt (Lewin & Lippitt, 1938; Lippitt, 1939) and by R. Lippitt and R. K. White (Lewin, Lippitt, & White, 1939) at the Iowa Child Welfare Research Station. Let us assume the club had five members and five observers were available. It might seem the simplest way always to assign one observer to one member of the club. However, the result at best would be five parallel micro-biographies of five individuals. This procedure would not yield a satisfactory record even of such simple facts of the group life as its organization, its subgroups, and its leader-member relationship, not to speak of such important facts as the general atmosphere. Therefore, instead of assigning every observer to one individual, one observer was assigned to record from minute to minute the organization of

More detailed descriptions of the coding systems used to observe and record data can be found in Barker, Dembo, and Lewin (1941/1976), Lewin and Lippitt (1938), and in Lewin, Lippitt, and White (1939).

the group into subgroups, another the social interactions, etc. In other words, instead of observing the properties of individuals, the properties of the group as such were observed.

In one additional point sociology may well profit from psychology. It is a commonplace that the behavior of individuals as well as groups depends upon their situation and their peculiar position in it. In my mind the last decade of psychology has shown that it is possible to give a clearly detailed description of the peculiar structure of a concrete situation and its dynamics in scientific terms. It can even be done in exact mathematical terms. The youngest discipline of geometry called "topology" is an excellent tool with which to determine the pattern of the life space of an individual, and to determine within this life space the relative positions which the different regions of activity or persons, or groups of persons bear to each other.

topology: a branch of geometry that studies what properties of objects are preserved when the object is stretched or pulled or twisted. A circle can become an ellipse by stretching it, but it can be pushed back into a circle. If you cut a circle, however, it cannot be made into a circle again. This is a very simple example. As you get involved in it, topology is not so simple.

It has become possible to transform into mathematical terms such everyday statements as: "He is now closer to his goal of being a first-rate physician," "He has changed the direction of his actions," or "He has joined a group." In other words, it is possible to determine, in a geometrically precise

manner, the position, direction, and distance within the life space, even in such cases where the position of the person and the direction of his actions are not physical but social in nature
105   (Lewin, 1938; Lewin, 1939b; Lippitt, 1939). With this in mind let us return to the social experiment which was undertaken at the Iowa Child Welfare Research Station.

II

It is well known that the amount of success a teacher has in the classroom depends not only on her *skill* but to a great extent on the *atmosphere* she creates. This atmosphere is something intangible; it is a property of the social situation as a whole, and might be measured scientifi-
110   cally if approached from this angle. As a beginning, therefore, Mr. Lippitt selected a comparison between a democratic and an autocratic atmosphere for his study (Lippitt, 1939). The purpose of his experiment was not to duplicate any given autocracy or democracy or to study an "ideal" autocracy or democracy, but to create setups which would give insight into the underlying group dynamics. Two groups of boys and girls, ten and eleven years of age, were
115   chosen for a mask-making club from a group of eager volunteers of two different school classes. With the help of the Moreno test both groups were equated as much as possible on such qualities as leadership and interpersonal relations.

> More information on how the groups were formed can be found in Lewin, Lippitt, and White (1939) and in Lippitt (1939).
>
> The "Moreno test" mentioned here refers to an assessment technique developed by J. L. Moreno (1941; Moreno, Jennings, Criswell, Katz, Blake, et al., 1960)—sociometry—that allowed Lippitt to put together the two groups based on the relationships among the children. The children would have been asked, for example, to indicate which of the other volunteers they liked the most and which they liked the least. This technique allowed Lippitt to match the groups in terms of the nature of the social relationships among the children in each group.

There were eleven meetings of the groups, the democratic group meeting always two days ahead of the autocratic one. The democratic group chose its activities freely. Whatever they
120   chose the autocratic group was then ordered to do. In this way the activities of the group were equated. On the whole, then, everything was kept constant except the group atmosphere.

The leader in both groups was an adult student. He tried to create the different atmospheres by using the technique [detailed in the chart on p. 460].

During the meetings of the two groups, the observers noted the number of incidents and
125   actions per unit of time. It was observed that the autocratic leader put forth about twice as much action towards the members as the democratic leader, namely, 8.4 actions as against 4.5. This difference is even greater if one takes into account only the initiated social approach,

Democratic	Authoritarian
1. All policies a matter of group determination, encouraged and drawn out by leader.	1. All determination of policy by the strongest person (leader).
2. Activity perspective given by an explanation of the general steps of the process during discussion at first meeting (clay mould, plaster of Paris, papier-mâché, etc). Where technical advice was needed, the leader tried to point out two or three alternative procedures from which choice could be made.	2. Techniques and steps of attaining the goal (completed mask) dictated by the authority, one at a time, so that future direction was always uncertain to a large degree.
3. The members were free to work with whomever they chose and the division of tasks was left up to the group.	3. The authority usually determined autocratically what each member should do and with whom he should work.
4. The leader attempted to be a group member in spirit and in discussion but not to perform much of the actual work. He gave objective praise and criticism.	4. The dominator criticized and praised individual's activities *without giving objective reasons,* and remained aloof from active group participation. He was always impersonal rather than outwardly hostile or friendly (a necessary concession in method).

ascendant: the state of being in power; here, setting the tone for an interaction or activity

Lippitt (1939) described the three categories used to code behavior as ascendant behaviors (including dominating, friendly, and objective behaviors), submissive behaviors, and objective behaviors (including general conversation, objective criticism, and asking for information).

R. F. Bales (1950) would later develop interaction process analysis (IPA), a 12-category system for coding small group interactions and behavior that shows some interesting similarities to the system created by Lippitt and Lewin.

namely, 5.2 as against 2.1. Still greater is this difference in relation to ascendant or initiated ascendant behavior: the ascendant actions of the autocratic leader were nearly three times as frequent as those of the democratic leader. 130

In regard to submissive actions, the proportion was opposite, namely, more frequent by the democratic leader, although in both groups submissive actions of the leader were relatively rare. A similar relation held for the objective, matter-of-fact actions. Here too the democratic leader showed a higher frequency. 135

On the whole, then, there existed a much greater impact on the members of the group by the leader in autocracy than in democracy, and the approach was much more ascendant and less matter-of-fact. 140

When we attempt to answer the question "How does the leader compare with the ordinary member in an autocracy and a democracy?" we must refer to an ideal average member who 145 is a statistical representation of what would happen if all activities were distributed equally among the members of the group, including the leader. In Mr. Lippitt's experiment (1939) the figures showed two facts clearly: first, in both groups the leader was really leading. The autocratic leader showed 118 per cent more initiated ascendant acts than the average ideal

150   member, and the democratic leader 41 per cent more. Both leaders were less submissive than the average member, namely, the autocrat 78 per cent, the democrat 53 per cent. It was interesting to note that both showed also more matter-of-fact action than the average ideal member.

However, the difference between the ordinary member and the leader was much less pro-

155   nounced in democracy than in autocracy, both in ascendant and submissive action. The democratic leader distinguished himself, also relatively, more by his greater matter-of-factness.

What do these figures indicate about the situation in which the autocratic and democratic group members find themselves? I can only mention a few aspects: In the autocratic group it is the leader who sets the policy. For instance, a

160   child says: "I thought we decided to do the other mask." The leader answers: "No, *this* is the one *I* decided last time would be the best one." In dynamical terms such an incident means that the child would have been able to reach his own goal

165   but the leader puts up a barrier against this locomotion. Instead he induces another goal for the child and a force in this direction. We are calling such goals, set up by the power of another person, an *induced* goal.

> *locomotion:* Lewin used *locomotion* to describe both bodily movement within one's current life space (e.g., approaching or moving away from something) and also psychological movement (e.g., graduating from college or getting "closer" to someone). Psychological locomotion may involve a change in the individual's life space (Lewin, 1936).

170   A parallel example in the democratic group might be this: A child asks, "How big will we make the mask? Are they out of clay or what?" The leader answers: "Would you like me to give you a little idea of how people generally make masks?" In other words, the leader in the democratic group, instead of hindering the children in getting to their own goal, bridges over whatever regions of difficulty might

175   exist. For the democratic group, many paths are open; for the autocratic only one, namely, that determined by the leader. In an autocracy the leader determines not only the kind of activity but also who should work with whom. In our experimental democracy all work cooperation was the result of spontaneous sub-grouping of the children. In the autocracy 32 per cent of the work groups were initiated by the leader, as against 0 per

180   cent in the democracy.

On the whole, then, the autocratic atmosphere gives a much greater and more aggressive dominance of the leader, and a narrowing down of the free movement of the members, together with a

185   weakening of their power fields.

> *power field:* the "sphere of influence of a person"; the physical or psychological space one controls and can move freely in (Lewin, 1936)

III

What is the effect of this atmosphere on the group life of the children? As measured by the observers the child-to-child relationship was rather different in the two atmospheres. There was about thirty times as much hostile domination in the autocracy as in the democracy, more demands for attention and much more hostile criticism; whereas in the democratic atmosphere cooperation and praise of the other fellow was much more frequent. In the democracy more   190
constructive suggestions were made and a matter-of-fact or submissive behavior of member to member was more frequent.

In interpreting these data, we might say that the "style of living and thinking" initiated by the leader dominated the relations between the children. Instead of a cooperative attitude, a hostile and highly personal attitude became prevalent. This was strikingly brought out by the   195
amount of group or "we" feeling as against "I" feeling. Statements which were "we-centered" occurred twice as often in the democracy as in the autocracy, whereas far more statements in the autocracy were "I-centered" than in the democracy.

So far as the relation of the children toward the leader was concerned, the statistical analysis revealed that the children in the autocratic group who were *less submissive* to each other   200
were about *twice* as submissive to their leader, as the children in the democratic group. Initiated approaches to the leader in the democratic group were less frequent than in the autocratic group. In autocracy the action by the member toward the leader had more the character of a *response* to an approach of the leader. The approach to the leader in the autocracy was more submissive, or kept at least on a matter-of-fact basis.   205

On the whole, then, the style of living in both atmospheres governed the child-child relation as well as the child-leader relation. In the autocratic group the children were less matter-of-fact, less cooperative, and submissive toward their equals, but more submissive to their superior than in the democracy.

Behind this difference of behavior lie a number of factors. The tension is greater in the auto-   210
cratic atmosphere, and the dynamic structure of both groups is rather different. In an autocratic group there are two clearly distinguished levels of social status: the leader is the only one having higher status, the others being on an equally low level. A strong barrier kept up by the leader prevents any one from increasing his status by acquiring leadership. In a democratic atmosphere the difference in social status is slight and there exists no barrier against acquir-   215
ing leadership.

This has a rather clear effect on the amount of individuality. In our experiment every individual in the democracy showed a relatively greater individuality, having some field of his own in spite of the greater "we" feeling among them, or perhaps because of it. In the autocratic group on the contrary the children all had a low status without much individuality. The type   220
of sub-grouping showed this difference even more clearly. In the autocracy, there was little "we" feeling and relatively little spontaneous sub-grouping among the children. If the work required the cooperation of four or five members, it was the leader who had to order the

225 members to get together. In the democracy those groups came together spontaneously and they kept together about twice as long as in the autocracy. In the autocracy these larger units disintegrated much faster when left to themselves.

These group structures, in combination with the high tension in the autocracy, led in Lippitt's experiments to a *scapegoat* situation. The children in the autocratic group ganged together not against their leader, but against one

230 of the children and treated him so badly that he ceased coming to the club. This happened twice during twelve sessions. Under autocratic rule any increase in status through leadership was blocked and the attempt to dominate was dic-

235 tated by the style of living. In other words, every child became a potential enemy of every other

> *scapegoat:* If you are frustrated or otherwise made angry by a person or situation and cannot show aggression toward that person or situation, you may direct your anger at another person or group, the scapegoat.

one and the power fields of the children weakened each other, instead of strengthening each other by cooperation. Through combining in an attack against one individual the members who otherwise could not gain higher status were able to do so by violent suppression of one

240 of their fellows.

One may ask whether these results are not due merely to individual differences. A number of facts rule out this explanation, although of course individual differences always play a role. Of particular interest was the transfer of one of the children from the autocratic to the democratic group, and of another from the democratic to the autocratic one. Before the transfer the

245 difference between the two children was the same as between the two groups they belonged to, namely, the autocratic child was more dominating and less friendly and objective than the democratic one. However, after the transfer the behavior changed so that the previously autocratic child now became the less dominating and more friendly and objective child. In other words, the behavior of the children mirrored very quickly the atmosphere of the group in which

250 they moved.

Recently R. Lippitt and R. K. White (Lewin, Lippitt, & White, 1939) have studied four new clubs with other leaders. They have included a third atmosphere, namely that of laissez faire, and have exposed the same children successively to a number of atmospheres. On the whole, the results bear out those of Lippitt (1939). They show a striking difference between laissez faire

255 and democracy very much in favor of democracy. They show further two types of reaction in the autocratic groups, one characterized by aggression, the second by apathy.

On the whole, I think there is ample proof that the difference in behavior in autocratic, democratic, and laissez faire situations is not a result of individual differences. There have been few experiences for me as impressive as seeing the expression in children's faces change dur-

260 ing the first day of autocracy. The friendly, open, and cooperative group, full of life, became within a short half hour a rather apathetic-looking gathering without initiative. The change from autocracy to democracy seemed to take somewhat more time than from democracy to autocracy. Autocracy is imposed upon the individual. Democracy he has to learn.

FIGURE 1   After the eighth meeting Sue was transferred from the democratic to the autocratic group, Sarah from the autocratic to the democratic group. The overt characteristics of both children changed according to the atmosphere (from Lippitt, 1939).

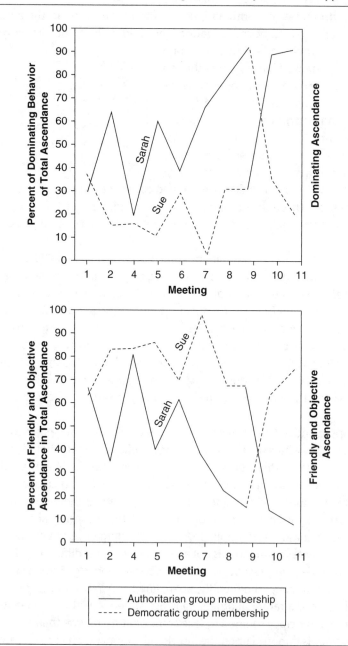

IV

These experiments as a whole, then, bear out the observations of cultural anthropology and are well in line with other experiments on the effect of the situation as a whole, such as those of *Wellman* and Skeels (Wellman,1938).

The social climate in which a child lives is for the child as important as the air it breathes. The group to which a child belongs is the ground on which he stands. His relation to this group and his status in it are the most important factors for his feeling of security or insecurity. No wonder that the group the person is a part of, and the culture in which he lives, determine to a very high degree his behavior and character. These social factors determine what space of free movement he has, and how far he can look ahead with some clarity into the future. In other words, they determine to a large degree his personal style of living and the direction and productivity of his planning.

It is a commonplace of today to blame the deplorable world situation on the discrepancy between the great ability of man to rule physical matter and his inability to handle social forces. This discrepancy in turn is said to be due to the fact that the development of the natural sciences has by far superseded the development of the social sciences.

No doubt this difference exists and it has been and is of great practical significance. Nevertheless, I feel this commonplace to be only half true, and it might be worth while to point to the other half of the story. Let us assume that it would be possible suddenly to raise the level of the social sciences to that of the natural sciences. Unfortunately this would hardly suffice to make the world a safe and friendly place to live in. Because the findings of the physical and the social

Wellman pulled together data from a number of studies that demonstrated that children's intelligence test scores are influenced positively by being in a favorable environment and negatively by being in an unfavorable one.

In a more recent series of studies, Steele and Aronson (1995) found that a seemingly subtle factor—how a particular test is described—can enter a person's life space and change the person's behavior. When black and white college students were given a difficult test that was described simply as a laboratory problem-solving task, the two groups performed at the same level. When the same test was described as diagnostic of intellectual ability, however, the white students performed substantially better than the black students. Steele (1997) relates this result to the presence of stereotype threat, the introduction of a culturally familiar racial stereotype that causes members of a stereotyped group to fear that they will be seen "through the lens of diminishing stereotypes and low expectations" (Steele, 1999, p. 45). This fear can then interfere with their performance. Other studies have found the same sort of threat to affect women's performance on math tests (Fredrickson, Roberts, Noll, Quinn, & Twenge, 1998) as well as white males' performance on a golf task said to require natural athletic ability and black males' performance on the same golf task said to require sports intelligence (Stone, Lynch, Sjomeling, & Darley, 1999). These studies not only are compatible with Lewin's conception of how we can think about behavior, but they also provide useful ideas about how we might bring about something that Lewin greatly valued, the reduction of prejudice and discrimination.

sciences alike can be used by the gangster as well as by the physician, for war as well as for peace, for one political system as well as for another.

Internationally we still live essentially in a state of anarchy similar to that of the rule of the sword during medieval times. As long as no international agency exists which is able and willing to enforce international laws, national groups will always have to choose between bowing to international gangsterism and defending themselves. 305

It seems to be "natural" for people living in a thoroughly democratic tradition like that of the United States to believe that what is scientifically reasonable should finally become accepted everywhere. However, history shows and experiments like the one I have described will, I think, prove anew that the belief in reason as a social value is by no means universal, but is itself a result of a definite social atmosphere. To believe in reason means to believe in democracy, because it grants to the reasoning partners a status of equality. It is therefore not an accident that not until the rise of democracy at the time of the American and French Revolutions was the goddess of "reason" enthroned in modern society. And again, it is not [an] accident that the first act of modern fascism in every country has been officially and vigorously to dethrone this goddess and instead to make emotions and obedience the all-ruling principles in education and life from kindergarten to death. 310 / 315

I am persuaded that scientific sociology and social psychology based on an intimate combination of experiments and empirical theory can do as much, or more, for human betterment as the natural sciences have done. However, the development of such a realistic, non-mystical social science and the possibility of its fruitful application presuppose the existence of a society which believes in reason. 320

Kariel (1956) raised some questions about the ideological and practical basis for this study and Lewin's general attempt to unite theory, empiricism, and social activism. Kariel pointed out that Lewin assumed that there is agreement about the right ways to function and about the nature and destructive potential of tension. He notes that from a Lewinian point of view, "Those groups are scientifically the best which maximize the individual's opportunity to belong." (p. 283) In Lewin's democratic atmosphere, "Thanks to sound leadership, individual members are induced, never commanded, to play their role . . . voluntarily. They will share a homogeneous outlook and act in accordance with their interests—provided always that they are rightly led." (p. 284). Thus, in Kariel's analysis, the kind of democracy that Lewin is praising and the kind of democracy that he later attempted to facilitate in his social activism has more to do with morale than with democratic processes. The members of the democratic mask-making group were happy. They got along well. They functioned well together. Their "leader" led but did not command. If one of the children had challenged the value of making masks, they would be jollied back into the group. Groups that are cohesive—groups that the members are attracted to—usually function better than do groups lacking cohesion. Cohesive groups can, however, fall into irrationality when no one wants to destroy the harmony by questioning an activity or assumption (see, e.g., Janis, 1982).

Lewin had clear ideas about what is best in a society, and he encouraged scientific work that would both demonstrate these values and help to implement them. Kariel argues that Lewin's framework "seeks the final good of social harmony by activating what appears sluggish and integrating what appears random.... When scientists are prepared to act consistently on the basis of these beliefs . . . they cannot respect the procedures which liberal democratic theory has traditionally valued" (p. 289).

There is no question about the honesty of Lewin's social concerns, and many agree with and admire his assumptions as well as his methods. Kariel asks us to think a bit about some possible implications and to think about what democracy is.

FOR DISCUSSION

1. In the Lewin, Lippitt, and White (1939) study in which children moved from one atmosphere to another, how do you think the children moving from an autocratic group to a laissez-faire group would behave? How about children moving from a democratic group to a laissez-faire group?

2. How do you think the children's behavior in the laissez-faire group would be compared to the behavior in autocratic and democratic groups in terms of "we-ness" and leadership?

3. Why were the members of the autocratic group more hostile to one another and more critical of one another than were the members of the democratic group?

4. What was there about the democratic atmosphere that produced more constructive suggestions?

5. This study used children as group members and an adult as the leader. How would the results change if the designated leader in the groups does not differ in obvious status from the group members? If the designated leader is a female? If no leader is designated?

6. Can you think of another social situation in which you could use Lewin's field theory (valences, barriers, locomotion, tension) to learn more about group processes?

7. How might you use Lewin's field theory to help in making a personal choice among a set of options?

Edward Chace Tolman (1886–1959)
Cognitive Maps in Rats and Men (1948)

Edward Chace Tolman was born in Newton, Massachusetts. He received a bachelor of science degree in electrochemistry from MIT in 1911 and a PhD in philosophy and psychology from Harvard in 1915 (at the time philosophy and psychology were in the same department). After completing his graduate work, Tolman took a faculty position at Northwestern University and stayed there until 1918, at which time he was urged to move on, probably because he had given his name to a student publication that had a "pacifist tinge." After leaving Northwestern, Tolman joined the faculty at the University of California, Berkeley. He remained there until his retirement in 1954.[1]

Tolman was a behaviorist. In his early writing, he was critical of the introspective techniques of Wundt (1.3) and Titchener (3.2), arguing that "the inadequacy of the merely introspective method as such has been becoming more and more obvious" (Tolman, 1951). Tolman believed that only by studying behavior would it be possible to make progress toward an understanding of mental processes such as learning and memory.

Although he was a behaviorist, Tolman took issue with Watson's (4.6) view that behavior could be reduced to simple stimuli and responses and also to the idea that stimuli and responses could be usefully reduced to physiological terms. Many describe Tolman as a "cognitive behaviorist" because his interest was not in the behavior itself but in what the behavior could tell us about the cognitive processes that produced it. He is also given credit for bringing together Gestalt principles and a behaviorist perspective. Tolman had studied with Kurt

---

Source: Tolman, E. C. (1948). Cognitive maps in rats and men. *Psychological Review, 55*, 189–208. [This paper was presented as the 34th Annual Faculty Research Lecture at the University of California, Berkeley, March 17, 1947. It was also presented on March 26, 1947, as one in a series of lectures in dynamic psychology sponsored by the division of psychology of Western Reserve University, Cleveland, Ohio. It is also reprinted in Tolman (1951).]

[1] Biographical information is from Tolman (1952) and Gleitman (1991).

Koffka for a summer while a graduate student and later had frequent interactions with other Gestalt theorists, especially Kurt Lewin (5.3). Like the Gestalt theorists, Tolman believed in taking a molar view (big picture, goal-directed, purposive) not a molecular view (pieces of the picture, muscle movements, etc.) of behavior.

Tolman was at Berkeley during the McCarthy era, a time when Senator Joseph McCarthy led a national campaign to identify and punish all communist sympathizers ("pinkos," "fellow travelers") within the United States. As part of the hunt for sympathizers, academics at state colleges and universities in California, including UC Berkeley, were asked to sign loyalty oaths, swearing allegiance to the United States and denying ever having had a connection to the Communist party. Because he was passionate about the search for truth and about the importance of academic freedom in this search, Tolman refused to sign and was a leader of the faculty in the fight against the loyalty oath.

Probably the best description of Tolman's empirical and theoretical work can be found in his book, *Purposive Behavior in Animals and Men,* first published in 1932 and reissued in 1967. In the preface, Tolman says, "This book has grown out of an experimental interest in animal learning grafted upon an arm-chair urge toward speculation" (p. xvii). This suggests a kind of cozy discussion of the research he had done and some of the rather informal ideas he had along the way. In fact, the book contains a thorough and elegant discussion of his research and a tight discussion of the psychology and philosophy underlying his assumptions and his interpretations. The article included here is, of course, discussed in the book. It is certainly one of the most influential of his studies. The distinction made between learning and behavior is an important one. Finding a way to investigate cognitive processes from a behaviorist standpoint was a significant contribution. For many, Tolman's work—his "arm-chair" speculation and his empirical work—established the field of cognitive psychology.

. . .

In the typical experiment a hungry rat is put at the entrance of the maze . . . and wanders about through the various true path segments and blind alleys until he finally comes to the food box and eats. This is repeated . . . one trial every 24 hours and the animal tends to make fewer and fewer errors (that is, blind-alley entrances) and to take less and less time between start and goal-box until finally he is entering no blinds at all and running in a very few seconds   5
from start to goal. . . .

All students agree as to the facts. They disagree, however, on theory and explanation.

> *students:* those interested in the psychology of learning

(1) First, there is a school of animal psychologists which believes that the maze behavior of rats is a matter of mere simple stimulus-response con-   10
nections. Learning, according to them, consists in the strengthening of some of these connections and in the weakening of others. According to this 'stimulus-response' school the rat in progressing down the maze is helplessly responding to a succession of external stimuli—sights, sounds, smells, pressures, etc. impinging upon his external sense organs—plus internal stimuli   15
coming from the viscera and from the skeletal muscles. These external and internal stimuli call out the walkings, runnings, turnings, retracings, smellings, rearings, and the like which appear. The rat's central nervous system, according to this view, may be likened to a complicated telephone switchboard. There are the incoming calls from sense-organs and there are the outgo-

> *synapse:* the junction between the axon of one neuron and the dendrite or cell body of another. The two neurons do not physically touch but communicate through an electrochemical process.

ing messages to muscles. Before the learning of a   20
specific maze, the connecting switches (synapses according to the physiologist) are closed in one set of ways and produce the primarily exploratory responses which appear in the early trials. *Learning,* according to this view, consists in the respective   25
strengthening and weakening of various of these connections; those connections which result in the animal's going down the true path become relatively more open to the passage of nervous impulses, whereas those which lead him into the blinds become relatively less open.

It must be noted in addition, however, that this stimulus-response school divides further into   30
two subgroups.

(a) There is a subgroup which holds that the mere mechanics involved in the running of a maze is such that the crucial stimuli from the maze get presented simultaneously with the correct responses more frequently than they do with any of the incorrect responses. Hence, just on a basis of this greater frequency, the neural connections between the   35
crucial stimuli and the correct responses will tend, it is said, to get strengthened at the expense of the incorrect connections.

(b) There is a second subgroup in this stimulus-response school which holds that the reason the appropriate connections get strengthened relatively to the inappropriate

40   ones is, rather, the fact that the responses resulting from the correct connections are followed *more* closely in time by need-reductions. Thus a hungry rat in a maze tends to get to food and have his hunger reduced *sooner* as a result of the true path responses than as a result of the blind alley responses. And such immediately following need-reductions or, to use another term, such 'positive reinforcements' tend somehow, it is

45   said, to strengthen the connections which have most closely preceded them. Thus it is as if—although this is certainly not the way this subgroup would themselves state it—

the satisfaction-receiving part of the rat telephoned back to Central and said to the girl: "Hold that connection: it was good;

50   and see to it that you blankety-blank well use it again the next time these same stimuli come in." These theorists also assume (at least some of them do some of the time) that, if bad results—'annoyances,'

55   'negative reinforcements'—follow, then this same satisfaction-and-annoyance-receiving part of the rat will telephone back and say, "Break that connection and don't you dare use it next time either."

> The term *negative reinforcement* is usually used to describe a situation in which a response is reinforced because it eliminates an aversive stimulus. For example, if I take an aspirin and my headache goes away, I am more likely to take an aspirin the next time I have a headache. Tolman seems to be equating negative reinforcement with annoying, although typically the term refers to the removal of annoying things.

. . .

60   (2) Let us turn now to the second main school. This group (and I belong to them) may be called the field theorists. We believe that in the course of learning something like a field map of

the environment gets established in the rat's brain. We agree with the other school that the rat in running a maze is exposed to stimuli and is finally led

65   as a result of these stimuli to the responses which actually occur. We feel, however, that the intervening brain processes are more complicated, more patterned and often, pragmatically speaking, more autonomous than do the stimulus-

70   response psychologists. Although we admit that the rat is bombarded by stimuli, we hold that his nervous system is surprisingly selective as to which of these stimuli it will let in at any given time.

> *more autonomous:* As Tolman describes in the next paragraph, from his point of view, the learning that the rat does is not based on individual stimulus-response connections. It is based on learning about the relationships among the stimuli—a sense of the "field." The brain processes, similarly, involve connections that are not dependent on particular stimulus-response connections.

Secondly, we assert that the central office itself is far more like a map control room than it is like

75   an old-fashioned telephone exchange. The stimuli, which are allowed in, are not connected by just simple one-to-one switches to the outgoing responses. Rather, the incoming impulses are usually worked over and elaborated in the central control room into a tentative, cognitive-like map of the environment. And it is this tentative map, indicating routes and paths and environmental relationships, which finally determines what responses, if any, the animal will finally release.

Finally, I, personally, would hold further that it is also important to discover in how far these maps are relatively narrow and strip-like or relatively broad and comprehensive. Both strip-maps and comprehensive-maps may be either correct or incorrect in the sense that they may (or may not), when acted upon, lead successfully to the animal's goal. The differences between such strip maps and such comprehensive maps will appear only when the rat is later presented with some change within the given environment. Then, the narrower and more strip-like the original map, the less will it carry over successfully to the new problem; whereas, the wider and the more comprehensive it was, the more adequately it will serve in the new set-up. In a strip-map the given position of the animal is connected by only a relatively simple and single path to the position of the goal. In a comprehensive-map a wider arc of the environment is represented, so that, if the starting position of the animal be changed or variations in the specific routes be introduced, this wider map will allow the animal still to behave relatively correctly and to choose the appropriate new route.

> Tolman is often described as an S-S (stimulus-stimulus) theorist rather than an S-R (stimulus-response) theorist because his interest is in how and what rats learn about the nature of the situation in which they find themselves.

But let us turn, now, to the actual experiments. . . .

> Hugh Carlton Blodgett was a graduate student at Berkeley (E. Hafter, personal communication, March 7, 2008), and his work on the relation among learning, behavior, and reward was part of his 1925 doctoral thesis. Although Tolman brought the issue of latent learning to our attention, Blodgett's work certainly led the way.

"Latent Learning" Experiments. The first of the latent learning experiments was performed at Berkeley by Blodgett. It was published in 1929. Blodgett not only performed the experiments, he also originated the concept. He ran three groups of rats through a six-unit alley maze, shown in Fig. 1.

He had a control group and two experimental groups. The error curves for these groups appear in Fig. 2. The solid line shows the error curve for Group I, the control group. These animals were run in orthodox fashion. That is, they were run one trial a day and found food in the goal-box at the end of each trial. Groups II and III were the experimental groups. The animals of Group II, the dash line, were not fed in the maze for the first six days but only in their home cages some two hours later. On the seventh day (indicated by the small cross) the rats found food at the end of the maze for the first time and continued to find it on subsequent days. The animals of Group III were treated similarly except that they first found food at the end of the maze on the third day and continued to find it there on subsequent days. It will be observed that the experimental groups as long as they were not finding food did not appear to learn much. (Their error curves did not drop.) But on the days immediately succeeding their first finding of the food their error curves did drop astoundingly. It appeared, in short, that during the non-rewarded trials these animals had been learning much more than they had exhibited. This learning, which did not manifest itself until after the food had been introduced, Blodgett called "latent learning." Interpreting these results anthropomorphically, we would say

FIGURE 1 6-unit alley T-maze (from Blodgett, 1929, p. 117).

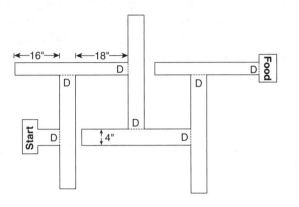

FIGURE 2 Control group and experimental groups error curves (from Blodgett, 1929, p. 120)

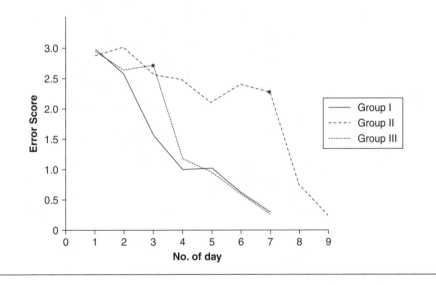

that as long as the animals were not getting any food at the end of the maze they continued to take their time in going through it—they continued to enter many blinds. Once, however, they knew they were to get food, they demonstrated that during these preceding non-rewarded trials they had learned where many of the blinds were. They had been building up a 'map,' and could utilize the latter as soon as they were motivated to do so.

Honzik and myself [Tolman & Honzik, 1930] repeated the experiments . . . with the 14-unit T-mazes shown in Fig. 3, and with larger groups of animals, and got similar results. The resulting curves are shown in Fig. 4. We used two control groups—one that never found food in the maze (HNR) and one that found it throughout (HR). The experimental group (HNR-R) found food at the end of the maze from the 11th day on and showed the same sort of a sudden drop.

FIGURE 3   Plan of maze: 14-unit T-Alley maze (from Elliott, 1928, p. 20)

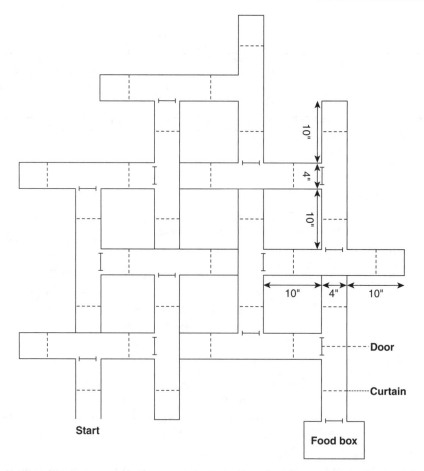

FIGURE 4   Error curves for HR, HNR, and HNR-R (from Tolman & Honzik, 1930, p. 267)

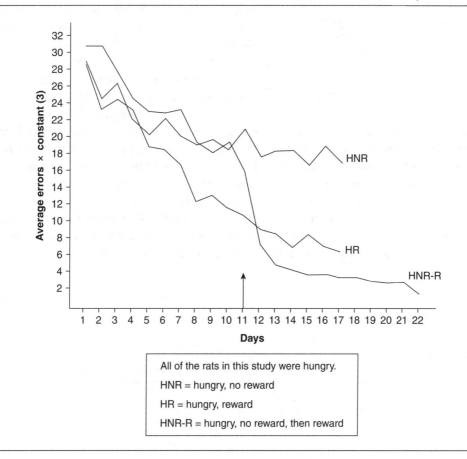

But probably the best experiment demonstrating latent learning was . . . done . . . at the University of Iowa, by Spence and Lippitt. Only an abstract of this experiment has as yet been published. However, Spence has sent a preliminary manuscript from which the following account is summarized. A simple Y-maze (see Fig. 5) with two goal-boxes was used. Water was at the end of the right arm of the Y and food at the end of the left arm. During the training period the rats were run neither hungry nor thirsty. They were satiated for both food and water before each day's trials. However, they were willing to run because after each run they

The rats chose which side to go to on the 1st and 3rd trials. They were forced to go to the other side on the 2nd and 4th trials because the side chosen on the trial before was blocked.

were taken out of whichever end box they had got to and put into a living cage, with other animals in it. They were given four trials a day in this fashion for seven days, two trials to the right and two to the left.   140

In the crucial test the animals were divided into two subgroups one made solely hungry and one solely thirsty. It was then found that on the first   145 trial the hungry group went at once to the left, where the food had been, statistically more frequently than to the right; and the thirsty group went to the right, where the water had been, statistically more frequently than to the left. These results indicated that under the previous non-differential and very mild rewarding conditions of merely being returned to the home   150 cages the animals had nevertheless been learning where the water was and where the food was. In short, they had acquired a cognitive map to the effect that food was to the left and water to the right, although during the acquisition of this map they had not exhibited any stimulus-response propensities to go more to the side which became later the side of the appropriate goal.   155

. . .

FIGURE 5   Ground plan of the apparatus (from Spence & Lippitt, 1946, p. 494). [In this article they were describing another experiment but used the same maze.]

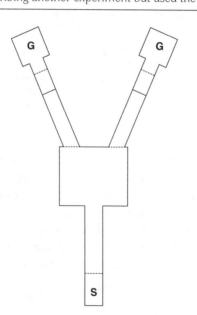

The results of the study Tolman attributes to Spence and Lippitt were later published by Spence, Bergman, and Lippitt (1950), and when all the data from the study were in, the results were not as favorable to Tolman's theory as they had looked when he wrote this article. It was true, as Tolman says, that on the first trial "the hungry group went at once to the left, where the food had been, statistically more frequently than to the right, and the thirsty group went to the right, where the water had been, statistically more frequently than to the left." But on the second set of trials (the next day), when the rats who had been hungry were thirsty, and the rats who had been thirsty were hungry, things did not work so well. The rate of choosing the correct side in the second test trial was no different from the rate they had shown when they made a choice with no deprivation. Why did this happen? Why didn't more of the hungry (or thirsty) rats go to the side where they would find food (or water). Spence et al. suggest that they may have "learned" to go to the side they had gone to on the first test trial because it had provided reinforcement—a very un-Tolmanian explanation and one that strengthens the notion that learning and reinforcement are necessarily linked.

Spence et al. also reviewed several studies similar to their own, the results of which were often contradictory. The factor underlying the contradictions seemed to be the presence or absence of motivation to run the maze when a state of deprivation does not exist. In their own study, Spence et al. had originally tried to allow the rats to explore the maze (and learn the locations of food and water) with no particular reinforcement for doing so. Under these conditions, the rats simply didn't do anything. They finally had to put the rats into a social cage after each run (an "irrelevant motivation") in order to get them to complete the run.

In the end, Spence et al. were unable to explain their results with any certainty, although they made suggestions based on Clark Hull's principle of the fractional anticipatory goal response. They were certain about one thing, however, that "Tolman's theory is as yet totally inadequate to account for these [Spence et al.'s] experimental results."

Based on his own reading of similar studies and more complete knowledge of Spence et al.'s findings, Tolman (1949) offered some possible explanations for the findings, but basically was uncertain, as were Spence et al., about what to make of them.

"Searching for the Stimulus." I refer to a recent, and it seems to me extremely important experiment, done for a Ph.D. dissertation by Hudson [1947]. Hudson was first interested in the question of whether or not rats could learn an avoidance reaction in one trial. His animals were tested one at a time in a living cage . . . with a small striped visual pattern at the end, on which was mounted a food cup. The hungry rat approached this food cup and ate. An electrical arrangement was provided so that when the rat touched the cup he could be given an electric shock. And one such shock did appear to be enough. For when the rat was replaced in this same cage days or even weeks afterwards, he usually demonstrated immediately strong avoidance reactions to the visual pattern. The animal withdrew from that end of the cage, or piled up sawdust and covered the pattern, or showed various other amusing responses all of which were in the nature of withdrawing from the pattern or making it disappear.

But the particular finding which I am interested in now appeared as a result of a modification of this standard procedure. Hudson noticed that the animals, anthropomorphically speaking, often seemed to look around *after* the shock to see what it was that had hit them. Hence it occurred to him that, if the pattern were made to disappear the instant the shock occurred, the rats might not establish the association. And this indeed is what happened in the case of many individuals. Hudson added further electrical connections so that when the shock was received during the eating, the lights went out, the pattern and the food cup dropped out of sight, and the lights came on again all within the matter of a second. When such animals were again put in the cage 24 hours later, a large percentage showed no avoidance of the pattern. Or to quote Hudson's own words:

Learning what object to avoid ... may occur exclusively during the period *after* the shock. For if the object from which the shock was actually received is removed at the moment of the shock, a significant number of animals fail to learn to avoid it, some selecting other features in the environment for avoidance, and others avoiding nothing.

FIGURE 6 Apparatus used in preliminary training (from Tolman, Ritchie, & Kalish, 1946, p. 16).

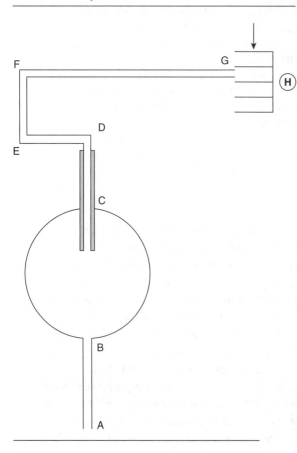

In other words, I feel that this experiment reinforces the notion of the largely active selective character in the rat's building up of his cognitive map. He often has to look actively for the significant stimuli in order to form his map and does not merely passively receive and react to all the stimuli which are physically present.

. . .

"Spatial Orientation" Experiments. As early as 1929, Lashley reported incidentally the case of a couple of his rats who, after having learned an alley maze, pushed back the cover near the starting box, climbed out and ran directly across the top to the goal-box where they climbed down in again and ate. Other investigators have reported related findings. All such observations suggest that rats really develop wider spatial maps which include more than the mere trained-on specific paths. In the experiments now to be reported this possibility has been subjected to further examination.

In the first experiment, Tolman, Ritchie and Kalish [1946] ... used the set-up shown in Fig. 6.

This was an elevated maze. The animals ran from A across the open circular table through CD (which had alley walls) and finally to G, the food box. H was a light which shone directly down the path from G to F. After four nights, three trials per night, in which the rats learned to run directly and without hesitation from A to G, the apparatus was changed to the sun-
210   burst shown in Fig. 7. The starting path and the table remained the same but a series of radiating paths was added.

The animals were again started at A and ran across the circular table into the alley and found themselves blocked. They then returned onto the table and began exploring practically all the radiating paths. After going out a few inches only on any one path, each rat
215   finally chose to run all the way out on one. The percentages of rats finally choosing each of the long paths from 1 to 12 are shown in Fig. 8. It appears that there was a preponderant tendency to choose path No. 6 which ran to a point some four inches in front of where the entrance to the food-box had been. The only other path chosen with any appreciable frequency was No. 1—that is, the path which pointed perpendicularly to the food-side of
220   the room. These results seem to indicate that the rats in this experiment had learned not only to run rapidly down the original roundabout route but also, when this was blocked and radiating paths presented, to select one pointing rather directly towards the point where the food had been or else at least to select a path running perpendicularly to the food-side of the room.

Tolman suggests that several rats chose path 1 because it was the first path on the right side (i.e., the side that the food had been on during training) or because during training the last turn they made before reaching the food was a 90-degree right turn onto the F-G path and, coming out of A during the test trial, path 1 offered a 90-degree turn.

During training (Fig. 6) there was a light at H that the rat could see as it ran from F to G. This light was in the same location during the test trials, and it was turned on. This raises the possibility that most of the rats chose path 6 because they could see the light, and it served as a conditioned stimulus, associated with the presence of food.

Tolman, Ritchie, and Kalish (1946) offer two arguments against this possibility. First, if the visible light was a conditioned stimulus, then a number of rats should also have chosen path 5 because the light was visible at the end of that path as well. In fact, only 4% of the rats chose path 5, about the same percentage of rats choosing each of the paths other than 6 and 1. Second, during training the first turn that the rats made from the round table was a left-hand turn taking them from D to E. This was a turn away from the light (and away from the food side of the room). If the rats were responding to the test trial in terms of conditioned responses, it seems more likely that they would chose a path on the left and not the path with the light.

FIGURE 7   Apparatus used in the test trial (from Tolman, Ritchie, & Kalish, 1946, p. 17).

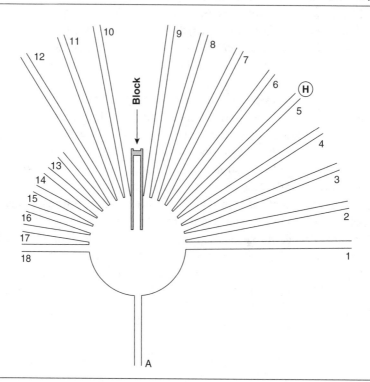

Tolman et al. also noted that if the rats' behavior was a result of S-R connections, the most likely choices on the test trial would have been paths 9 or 10—the paths closest to their original (now blocked) route.

The authors also asked why only 36% of the rats chose path 6—the path that led most directly to the location of the food during training. After considering several possibilities, they concluded that many of the rats did not have enough training time and had not been able to develop an accurate cognitive map. In any case, significantly more rats chose path 6 than chose any of the other possibilities.

As a result of their original training, the rats had, it would seem, acquired not merely a strip-map to the effect that the original specifically trained-on path led to food but, rather, a wider comprehensive map to the effect that food was located in such and such a direction in the room.

. . .

225

FIGURE 8   Numbers of rats which chose each of the paths (from Tolman, Ritchie, & Kalish, 1946, p. 19).

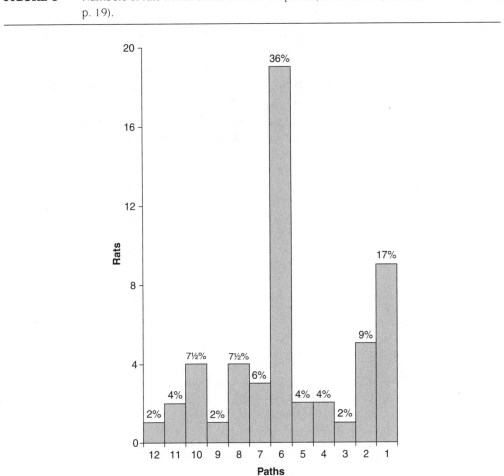

FOR DISCUSSION

1. Tolman calls himself a "field theorist." How is Tolman's field theory like and unlike Lewin's (5.3)?

2. What is a cognitive map? What sorts of information does it contain?

3. Do you have cognitive maps? Are all the maps in your head cognitive maps?

4. What do Blodgett's and Tolman and Honzik's studies (pp. 472–475) tell us about the role of reinforcement in learning?

5. Why is Tolman considered a cognitivist? a behaviorist? a cognitive behaviorist? a purposive behaviorist? a gestalt behaviorist?

6. Do we have cognitive maps not just about physical locations but also about other situations in which we want to get from "here" to "there," for example, getting into college, planning a big wedding, or seeking a promotion.

7. Do you think that this reading might be included in Part III of this book (Opening the Black Box) as appropriately as in this part (Levels of Explanation)? Why or why not?

Donald O. Hebb (1904–1985)
Organization of Behavior: A Neuropsychological Theory (1949)

From the Introduction

Our species has (almost) always seen, however dimly, that there is a relation between the mind and the lumpy gray stuff inside our heads. A long and important thread in the history of science is the journey from this vague conviction of a psycho-physiological connection to the beginnings of a detailed understanding of how that connection works. Most of this journey has happened quite recently. The 19th century scientific explosion gave a tremendous boost to our understanding of basic mechanisms of the nervous system, but it is one thing to understand the mechanisms and quite another to see how they collectively accomplish the mind. It wasn't until the 20th century that the mechanisms and characteristics of neural conduction and communication were clear enough to permit the next step.

In 1943 McCulloch and Pitts published a short, nearly impenetrable, and extremely influential paper titled "A logical calculus of the ideas immanent in nervous activity," showing how small numbers of neurons might be connected with one another to compute the basic functions of propositional logic (e.g., "A and B," "A or B but not both"). McCulloch and Pitts's suggestion that the brain accomplishes the mind by computing logic functions was unconvincing (the authors themselves soon abandoned it; see Pitts & McCulloch, 1947), but this did not diminish the paper's importance one bit, for it showed that we now knew enough (maybe) about the pieces to begin thinking about how the whole thing worked.

Source: Hebb, D. O. (1949). *Organization of behavior: A neuropsychological theory.* New York: Wiley. Reissued by Lawrence Erlbaum, 2002. Reprinted with permission of Mary Ellen Hebb.

Hebb's 1949 book *Organization of Behavior* is a less rigorous but far more ambitious and comprehensive attempt to show how the brain might be organized in order to do the sorts of things (perceive, think, remember) it does. The central idea is the *cell assembly,* a self-organizing group of neurons whose connections with one another are modified by experience and activity. Hebb's idea was not entirely new, but his articulation of it was persuasive and influential—and apparently on the right track. The book was widely read and is still cited in the neuroscience literature, no small feat in such a fast-moving field.

Donald Olding Hebb was born in Chester, Nova Scotia, and majored in English at Dalhousie University. He was attracted to psychology by reading William James (1.2), Sigmund Freud (3.3 & 4.5), and John Watson (4.6), and while earning his living as a school principal he took graduate courses at McGill University. He became interested in Karl Lashley's work and went to Chicago to study with him. Hebb then followed Lashley to Harvard and completed his PhD there in 1936 with a dissertation on perceptual effects of early visual deprivation in the rat. Wilder Penfield, a neurosurgeon, offered Hebb a postdoctoral fellowship at the Montreal Neurological Institute (at McGill), where he explored the effects of brain injury on intelligence and behavior in humans. In 1942 Hebb rejoined Lashley at the Yerkes Laboratory of Primate Biology at Harvard and began the work that became the *Organization of Behavior.* (Lashley was not only Hebb's mentor but an importance influence on his thought; see Lashley, 1929, 1950.) In 1947 Hebb returned permanently to McGill. For more about Hebb's life and work, see his autobiography (Hebb, 1980) and his *Essay on Mind* (Hebb, 1980); see also the portraits by Glickman (1996) and Milner (1986) and the festschrift by Jusczyk and Klein (1980). In the half century since Hebb's book there has been a great deal of attention to the question of how simple mechanisms (such as Hebb's cell assemblies) can give rise to complex behavior. A quirky but very readable and stimulating introduction to the problem is Valentino Braitenberg's (1984) *Vehicles.* See also Hubel and Wiesel (1962), Kandel and Hawkins (1992), and McClelland, Rumelhart, and Hinton (1986).

In the present selection Hebb leads up to a brief description of his theory by considering what a psychological theory needs to explain (and how), and anticipates criticism from all sides.

I t might be argued that the task of the psychologist, the task of understanding behavior and reducing the vagaries of human thought to a mechanical process of cause and effect, is a more difficult one than that of any other scientist. Certainly the problem is enormously complex; and though it could also be argued that the progress made by psychology in the century following the death of James Mill, with his crude theory of association, is an achievement scarcely less than that of the physical sciences in the same period, it is nevertheless true that psychological theory is still in its

> James Mill (1773–1836), Scottish associationist philosopher; father of John Stuart Mill (1806–1873)

infancy. There is a long way to go before we can speak of understanding the principles of behavior to the degree that we understand the principles of chemical reaction.

. . .

However, psychology has an intimate relation with the other biological sciences, and may also look for help there. There is a considerable overlap between the problems of psychology and those of neurophysiology, hence the possibility (or necessity) of reciprocal assistance. The first object of this book is to present a theory of behavior for the consideration of psychologists; but another is to seek a common ground with the anatomist, physiologist, and neurologist, to show them how psychological theory relates to their problems and at the same time to make it more possible for them to contribute to that theory.

Psychology is no more static than any other science. Physiologists and clinicians who wish to get a theoretical orientation cannot depend only on the writings of Pavlov [5.2] or Freud [3.3 and 4.5]. These were great men, and they have contributed greatly to psychological thought. But their contribution was rather in formulating and developing problems than in providing final answers. Pavlov himself seems to have thought of his theory of conditioned reflexes as something in continual need of revision, and experimental results have continued to make revisions necessary: the theory, that is, is still developing. Again, if one were to regard Freud's theory as needing change only in its details, the main value of his work would be stultified. Theorizing at this stage is like skating on thin ice—keep moving, or drown. Ego, Id, and Superego are conceptions that help one to see and state important facts of behavior, but they are also dangerously easy to treat as ghostly realities: as anthropomorphic agents that *want* this or *disapprove* of that, *overcoming* one another by force or guile, and *punishing* or *being punished*. Freud has left us the task of developing these provisional formulations of his to the point where such a danger no longer exists. When theory becomes static it is apt to become dogma; and psychological theory has the further danger, as long as so many of its problems are unresolved, of inviting a relapse into the vitalism and indeterminism of traditional thought.

> *stultify:* Latin, "to make foolish"; here used in its modern sense to mean that Freud's work would be made ineffectual or beside the point

> *vitalism and indeterminism:* Hebb is referring generally to theories in which mind is a substance distinct from matter, with its own causal efficacy, and its operations not constrained by physical laws.

It is only too easy, no matter what formal theory of behavior one espouses, to entertain a concealed mysticism in one's thinking about that large segment of behavior which theory does not handle adequately. To deal with behavior at present, one must oversimplify. The risk, on the one hand, is of forgetting that one has oversimplified the problem; one may forget or even deny those inconvenient facts that one's theory does not subsume. On the other hand is the   45
risk of accepting the weak-kneed discouragement of the vitalist, of being content to show that existing theories are imperfect without seeking to improve them. We can take for granted that any theory of behavior at present must be inadequate and incomplete. But it is never enough to say, because *we* have not yet found out how to reduce behavior to the control of the brain, that no one in the future will be able to do so.   50

Modern psychology takes completely for granted that behavior and neural function are perfectly correlated, that one is completely caused by the other. There is no separate soul or life-force to stick a finger into the brain now and then and make neural cells do what they would not otherwise. Actually, of course, this is a working assumption only—as long as there are unexplained aspects of behavior. It is quite conceivable that some day   55
the assumption will have to be rejected. But it is important also to see that we have not reached that day yet: the working assumption is a necessary one, and there is no real evidence opposed to it. Our failure to solve a problem so far does not make it insoluble. One cannot logically be a determinist in physics and chemistry and biology, and a mystic in psychology.   60

All one can know about another's feelings and awarenesses is an inference from what he *does*—from his muscular contractions and glandular secretions. These observable events are determined by electrical and chemical events in nerve cells. If one is to be consistent, there is no room here for a mysterious agent that is defined as not physical and yet has physical effects (especially since many of the entities of physics are known only through   65
their effects). "Mind" can only be regarded, for scientific purposes, as the activity of the brain, and this should be mystery enough for anyone: besides the appalling number of cells (some nine billion, according to Herrick) and even more appalling number of possible con-   70
nections between them, the matter out of which cells are made is being itself reduced by the physicist to something quite unlike the inert stick or stone with which mind is traditionally contrasted. After all, it is that contrast that is at   75
the bottom of the vitalist's objection to a mechanistic biology, and the contrast has lost its force (Herrick, 1929). The mystic might well concentrate

C. J. Herrick (1868–1960), American neurologist

something quite unlike: Sticks and stones are not inert: modern physics has established that in fact all matter is dynamic and complexly structured.

on the electron and let behavior alone. A philosophical parallelism or idealism, whatever one
may think of such conceptions on other
grounds, is quite consistent with the scientific
method, but interactionism seems not to be.

Psychologist and neurophysiologist thus chart
the same bay—working perhaps from opposite
shores, sometimes overlapping and duplicating
one another, but using some of the same fixed
points and continually with the opportunity of
contributing to each other's results. The problem
of understanding behavior is the problem of
understanding the total action of the nervous system, and *vice versa*. This has not always been a
welcome proposition, either to psychologist or to
physiologist.

A vigorous movement has appeared both in
psychology and psychiatry to be rid of "physiologizing," that is, to stop using physiological
hypotheses. This point of view has been clearly
and effectively put by Skinner (1938), and it does not by any means represent a relapse into
vitalism. The argument is related to modern positivism, emphasizes a method of correlating
observable stimuli with observable response, and, recognizing that "explanation" is ultimately a statement of relationships between observed phenomena, proposes to go to the
heart of the matter and have psychology confine itself to such statements *now*. This point of
view has been criticized by Pratt (1939) and Köhler (1940). The present book is written in profound disagreement with such a program for
psychology. Disagreement is on the grounds that
this arises from a misconception of the scientific
method as it operates in the earlier stages. Those
apparently naive features of older scientific
thought may have had more to do with hitting
on fertile assumptions and hypotheses than seems necessary in retrospect. The anti-physiological position, thus, in urging that psychology proceed now as it may be able to proceed
when it is more highly developed, seems to be in short a counsel of perfection, disregarding
the limitations of the human intellect. However, it is logically defensible and may yet show
by its fertility of results that it is indeed the proper approach to achieving prediction and
control of behavior.

parallelism: A dualist theory of mind in
which mind and body are two causally
unconnected systems that work in parallel.
For instance, the mind may decide it wants
to wiggle its toes, and at that moment the
body will wiggle its toes. However, the
body's wiggling was not caused by the
mind's wish, and the wish was not caused
by the wiggling.

idealism: A monist theory of mind in which
only mind exists. In such a theory the "outside
world" does not exist, but our perception of
an apparent outside world is real.

vice versa: This is an important and
nonreductionist addition.

such a program: that is, Skinner's. It is
Skinner's (3.5) anti-physiological stance,
not his positivism, that Hebb objects to.

jib at: object to

If some psychologists jib at the physiologist for a bedfellow, many physiologists agree with them heartily. One must sympathize with those who want nothing of the psychologist's hairsplitting or 120 the indefiniteness of psychological theory. There is much more certainty in the study of the electrical activity of a well-defined tract in the brain. The only question is whether a physiology of the human brain as a whole can be achieved by such studies alone. One can discover the properties of its various parts more or less in isolation; but it is a truism by now that the part may have properties that are not evident in isolation, and these are to be discovered only by study 125 of the whole intact brain. The method then calls for learning as much as one can about what the parts of the brain do (primarily the physiologist's field), and relating behavior as far as possible to this knowledge (primarily for the psychologist); then seeing what further information is to be had about how the total brain works, from the discrepancy between (1) actual behavior and (2) the behavior that would be predicted from adding up what is known about the 130 action of the various parts.

This does not make the psychologist a physiologist, for precisely the same reason that the physiologist need not become a cytologist or biochemist, though he is intimately concerned with the information that cytology and biochemistry provide. The difficulties of finding order in behavior are great enough to require all one's attention, and the psychologist is interested 135 in physiology to the extent that it contributes to his own task.

The great argument of the positivists who object to "physiologizing" is that physiology has not helped psychological theory. But, even if this is true (there is some basis for denying it), one has to add the words *so far*. There has been a great access of knowledge in neurophysiology since the twenties. The work of Berger, Dusser de 140 Barenne, and Lorente de Nó (as examples) has a profound effect on the physiological conceptions utilized by psychology, and psychology has not yet assimilated these results fully.

Hans Berger (1873–1941), psychiatrist and pioneering electrophysiologist, developed the human electroencephalogram (EEG), a record of change in the brain's electrical activity over time, in the 1920s.

Joannes Gregarius Dusser de Barenne (1885–1940), a neurophysiologist, investigated the functions and interactions of cortical and subcortical regions of the brain.

Rafael Lorente de Nó (1902–1990), a neurophysiologist, studied the conduction of nerve impulses, among many other things.

The central problem with which we must find a 145 way to deal can be put in two different ways. Psychologically, it is the problem of thought: some sort of process that is not fully controlled by environmental stimulation and yet cooperates closely with that stimulation. From another point of view, 150 physiologically, the problem is that of the transmission of excitation from sensory to motor cortex. This statement may not be as much oversimplified as it seems, especially when one recognizes that the "transmission" may be a very complex process indeed, with a considerable time 155 lag between sensory stimulation and the final motor response. The failure of psychology to handle thought adequately (or the failure of neurophysiology to tell us how to conceive of cortical transmission) has been the essential weakness of modern psychological theory and the reason for persistent difficulties in dealing with a wide range of experimental and clinical data, as the following chapters will try to show, from the data of perception and learning to those of hunger, sleep, and neurosis.

In mammals even as low as the rat it has turned out to be impossible to describe behavior as an interaction directly between sensory and motor processes. Something like *thinking,* that is, intervenes. "Thought" undoubtedly has the connotation of a human degree of complexity in cerebral function and may mean too much to be applied to lower animals. But even in the rat there is evidence that behavior is not completely controlled by immediate sensory events: there are central processes operating also.

What is the nature of such relatively autonomous activities in the cerebrum? Not even a tentative answer is available. We know a good deal about the afferent pathways to the cortex, about the efferent pathways from it, and about many structures linking the two. But the links are complex, and we know practically nothing about what goes on between the arrival of an excitation at a sensory projection area and its later departure from the motor area of the cortex. Psychology has had to find, in hypothesis, a way of bridging this gap in its physiological foundation. In general the bridge can be described as some comparatively simple formula of cortical transmission.[1] The particular formula chosen mainly determines the nature of the psychological theory that results, and the need of choosing is the major source of theoretical schism.

Two kinds of formula have been used, leading at two extremes to (1) switchboard theory, and sensori-motor connections; and (2) field theory. (Either of these terms may be regarded as opprobrium; they are not so used here.) (1) In the first type of theory, at one extreme, cells in the sensory system acquire connections with cells in the motor system; the function of the cortex is that of a telephone exchange. Connections rigidly determine what animal or human being does, and their acquisition constitutes learning. Current forms of the theory tend to be vaguer than formerly, because of effective criticism of the theory in its earlier and simpler forms, but the fundamental idea is still maintained. (2) Theory at the opposite extreme denies that learning depends on connections at all, and attempts to utilize instead the field conception that physics has found so useful. The cortex is regarded as made up of so many cells that it can be treated as a statistically homogeneous medium. The sensory control of motor centers depends, accordingly, on the distribution of the sensory excitation and on ratios of excitation, not on locus or the action of any specific cells.

> *opprobrium:* term of contempt or condemnation

Despite their differences, however, both theoretical approaches seem to imply a prompt transmission of sensory excitation to the motor side, if only by failing to specify that this is not so. No one, at any rate, has made any serious attempt to elaborate ideas of a central neural mechanism to account for the delay, between stimulation and response, that seems so characteristic of

---

[1] The simplicity possibly accounts for the opinion expressed by an anatomist who claimed that psychologists think of the brain as having all the finer structure of a bowlful of porridge.

proprioception: literally, self perception; the perception of the positions and movements of the parts of one's body

The best-known motor theory of thought comes from J. B. Watson (4.6), who asserted that what we call thought is in fact nothing more than our proprioception of sub-vocal activity ("minimal muscular action") in the larynx and other parts of the speech apparatus. Hebb's treatment of this idea is more diplomatic than most; the philosopher Herbert Feigl is famously quoted as saying that Watson had "made up his windpipe that he had no mind." Watson later retracted this view, only to learn the hard way that this is more easily said than done.

interactionist philosophy: Cartesian dualism, in which mind and brain are different but interacting substances; see 1.1

long stretches: the blank spaces on the map, those areas of anatomy and physiology of which we are still ignorant

desideratum: Latin, "that which is wanted"

thought. There have indeed been neural theories of "motor" thought, but they amount essentially to a continual interplay of proprioception and minimal muscular action, and do not provide for any prolonged sequence of intracerebral events as such. 200

But the recalcitrant data of animal behavior have been drawing attention more and more insistently to the need of some better account of central processes. This is what Morgan (1943) has recognized in saying that "mental" variables, 205 repeatedly thrown out because there was no place for them in a stimulus-response psychology, repeatedly find their way back in again in one form or another. The image has been a forbidden notion for twenty years, particularly in animal psy- 210 chology; but the fiend was hardly exorcised before "expectancy" had appeared instead. What is the neural basis of expectancy, or of attention, or interest? Older theory could use these words freely, for it made no serious attempt to avoid an inter- 215 actionist philosophy. In modern psychology such terms are an embarrassment; they cannot be escaped if one is to give a full account of behavior, but they still have the smell of animism: and must have, until a theory of thought is developed to 220 show how "expectancy" or the like can be a physiologically intelligible process.

In the chapters that follow this introduction I have tried to lay a foundation for such a theory. It is, on the one hand and from the physiologist's point of view, quite speculative. On the other hand, it achieves some synthesis of psychological 225 knowledge, and it attempts to hold as strictly as possible to the psychological evidence in those long stretches where the guidance of anatomy and physiology is lacking. The desideratum is a conceptual tool for dealing with expectancy, 230 attention, and so on, and with a temporally organized intracerebral process. But this would have little value if it did not also comprise the main facts of perception, and of learning. . . . In outline, the conceptual structure is as follows: 235

Any frequently repeated, particular stimulation will lead to the slow development of a "cell-assembly," a diffuse structure comprising cells in the cortex and diencephalon (and also, perhaps, in the basal ganglia of the cerebrum), capable of acting briefly as a closed system, delivering facilitation to other such systems and usually having a specific motor facilitation. A series of such events constitutes a "phase sequence"—the thought process. Each assembly action may be aroused by a preceding assembly, by a sensory event, or—normally—by both. The central facilitation from one of these activities on the next is the prototype of "attention." The theory proposes that in this central facilitation, and its varied relationship to sensory processes, lies the answer to an issue that is made inescapable by Humphrey's (1940) penetrating review of the problem of the direction of thought.

The kind of cortical organization discussed in the preceding paragraph is what is regarded as essential to adult waking behavior. It is proposed also that there is an alternate, "intrinsic" organization, occurring in sleep and in infancy, which consists of hypersynchrony in the firing of cortical cells. But besides these two forms of cortical organization there may be disorganization. It is assumed that the assembly depends completely on a very delicate timing which might be disturbed by metabolic changes as well as by sensory events that do not accord with the pre-existent central process. When this is transient, it is called emotional disturbance; when chronic, neurosis or psychosis.

The theory is evidently a form of connectionism, one of the switchboard variety, though it does not deal in direct connections between afferent and efferent pathways: not an "S-R" psychology, if R means a *muscular* response. The connections serve rather to establish autonomous central activities, which then are the basis of further learning. In accordance with modern physiological ideas, the theory also utilizes local field processes and gradients, following the lead particularly of Marshall and Talbot (1942). It does not, further, make any single nerve cell or pathway essential to any habit or perception. Modern physiology has presented psychology with new opportunities for the synthesis of divergent theories and previously unrelated data, and it is my intent to take such advantage of these opportunities as I can.

For Discussion

1. Hebb says, "Freud has left us the task of developing these provisional formulations of his" (p. 485, line 37). What is it about Freud's formulations that Hebb considers provisional? What does a *non*provisional formulation look like?

2. What does Hebb mean when he says, "Psychologist and neurophysiologist thus chart the same bay" (p. 487, line 84)?

3. Why does Hebb refer to the data of animal behavior as "recalcitrant" (p. 490, line 201)? Does he think we need "mental" variables? If so, why?

Brenda Milner (b. 1918)
Larry R. Squire (b. 1941)
Eric R. Kandel (b. 1929)
Cognitive Neuroscience and the Study of Memory (1998)

In 1989 the U.S. Congress passed a joint resolution declaring the decade of the 1990s the "Decade of the Brain," and President George H. W. Bush signed a proclamation to that effect on July 17, 1990. Among the many *whereases* in the resolution (Joint Res. 174, 1989), Congress noted that there is "a technological revolution occurring in the brain sciences" (p. 13946); that "fundamental discoveries at the molecular and cellular levels of the organization of the brain are clarifying the role of the brain in translating neurophysiologic events into behavior, thought and emotion" (pp. 13946–13947); and that scientists now had "the capacity to map the biochemical circuitry of neurotransmitters and neuromodulators" (p. 13947). The resolution also pointed out that "the Nobel Prize for Medicine or Physiology has been awarded to 15 neuroscientists within the past 25 years, an achievement that underscores the excitement and productivity of the study of the brain and central nervous system and its potential for contributing to the health of humanity" (p. 13947). That excitement and productivity has taken the form of, among other things, a vast outpouring of papers detailing the results of thousands of experiments. To select any one such paper as somehow representative would be absurd, particularly as the significance of research is best seen in retrospect. Accordingly, we have selected not a research report but a review, written for the tenth anniversary issue of the journal *Neuron,* by three distinguished neuroscientists.

Brenda Milner was born in Manchester, England, and was a graduate student at Cambridge when World War II broke out. She began her psychological career in the British war effort,

Source: Milner, B., Squire, L. R., & Kandel, E. R. (1998). Cognitive neuroscience and the study of memory. *Neuron, 20,* 445–468. Reprinted with permission.

designing selection tests for air crews and evaluating radar displays. Toward the end of the war she left England for Canada, where she taught psychology at the University of Montreal while doing graduate work at McGill in physiological psychology. Against the advice of her supervisor, D. O. Hebb (5.5), she began studying the relations between brain (and brain damage) and psychological function in Wilder Penfield's patients at the Montreal Neurological Institute. Beginning with the important studies of "H. M." (described below) in the 1950s, Milner has been a leader in the effort to explore and understand the brain's memory systems. She is currently Dorothy J. Killam Professor at the Montreal Neurological Institute and professor in the Department of Neurology and Neurosurgery at McGill University.

Larry Squire, born in Cherokee, Iowa, uses clinical studies of humans with brain injuries and experimental studies of brain lesions in nonhuman primates to explore the anatomy and structure of memory. He is currently professor of psychiatry and neurosciences at the University of California School of Medicine, San Diego, and Research Career Scientist at the Veterans Affairs Medical Center, San Diego.

Eric Kandel left his native Vienna in April 1939, only months before Hitler went to war. After studying history at Harvard, he went to medical school at NYU, with the intention of becoming a psychoanalyst. (In Vienna he had lived a few blocks from Freud.) Along the way, he became increasingly interested in the idea of studying the mind from a biological point of view, and he has devoted most of his career to painstakingly working out the cellular and molecular basis of neural plasticity, for which he was awarded the Nobel Prize in 2000. Since 1974 Kandel has been at Columbia University, where he created the Center for Neurobiology and Behavior.

The present selection is more than a review of recent achievements in neuroscience. It is appropriate to include in this book because it takes a longer historical view than is typically found in research reports and appropriate for this section because it shows, in some detail, the interaction among levels of explanation within the study of a given set of phenomena—in this case those that we refer to as memory.

. . .

This review focuses on the topic of memory, but one aspect of cognitive neuroscience. We have not attempted to document fully the remarkable progress that has been achieved in our understanding of how the nervous system learns and remembers. Rather, we focus on two key components in the study of memory, as viewed through the work that the three of us have carried out with our colleagues during the past several decades. The first component is concerned with analyzing what memory is, where it is stored, and what brain systems are involved. This is the *systems problem* of memory. The second component of memory is concerned with analyzing *how* memory is stored. This is the *molecular problem* of memory.

WHERE ARE MEMORIES STORED?

The question of where memory is stored emerged at the beginning of the 19th century as part of the larger question—to what degree can *any* mental process be localized within the brain?

The first person to address this question was Franz Joseph Gall, who made two major conceptual contributions. First, Gall attempted to abolish mind–brain dualism. He argued, based on his anatomical studies, that the brain is the organ of the mind. Second, he appreciated that the cerebral cortex is not homogeneous but contains distinctive centers that control specific mental functions. Gall therefore proposed the idea of cortical *localization*. Gall asserted that the brain does not act as a unitary organ but is divided into at least 27 faculties (others were added later), each corresponding to a specific mental faculty. He thought that even the most abstract and complex of human traits, such as generosity and secretiveness, are localized to discrete areas of the brain.

> Gall (1758–1828) was born in Germany but spent most of his adult life , as a physician, in Vienna. An accomplished anatomist, Gall first distinguished between the brain's white matter, which we now understand to contain mostly myelinated nerve fibers, and the grey matter, which contains mostly nerve cell bodies.

Gall was not an experimentalist. He rejected the study of neurological lesions and the surgical manipulation of experimental animals and instead attempted to locate mental faculties by examining the surface of the skulls of individuals well endowed with particular functions. Perhaps not surprisingly, with this approach he misidentified the function of most parts of the cortex. This anatomically oriented approach to personality Gall called *organology*. Later, Gall's associate, Gaspard Spurzheim, adopted the better-known term *phrenology* to describe this approach.

Gall's ideas were subjected to experimental analysis by Pierre Flourens in France in the late 1820s. Flourens attempted to isolate the contributions of different parts of the nervous system to behavior by removing from the brains of experimental animals the functional centers identified

> Flourens (1794–1867) was among the first physiologists to use experimental ablation effectively to study brain function.

by Gall. From these experiments, Flourens concluded that individual sites in the brain are not sufficient for specific behaviors such as sexual behavior and romantic love and that all regions of the brain—especially the cerebral hemispheres of the forebrain—participate in every men-
40 tal function. He proposed that any part of the cerebral hemisphere is able to perform all the functions of the hemisphere. Injury to a specific area of the cerebral hemisphere should there-fore affect all higher functions equally.

Despite the findings of Broca and Wernicke on the localization of language, the ensuing debate
45 between cortical localization and equipotentiality in cognitive function dominated thinking about mental processes, including memory, well into the first half of the twentieth century. For example, in the period from 1920 to 1950, this dispute could be
50 followed in the work of Karl Lashley, perhaps the dominant figure in American neuropsychology in the first half of this century. Lashley explored the surface of the cerebral cortex in the rat, systemati-cally removing different cortical areas. In so doing,
55 he failed repeatedly to identify any particular brain region that was special to or necessary for the stor-age of memory. Based on these experiments, Lashley formulated the law of *mass action,* accord-ing to which the extent of the memory defect
60 was correlated with the size of the cortical area removed, not with its specific location (Lashley, 1929). Many years later, with additional experi-mental work, it was possible to arrive at a different understanding of Lashley's famous conclusion.

> Paul Pierre Broca (1824–1880), a French surgeon, established clinically in 1861 that spoken and written expression depend on an area toward the rear of the left frontal lobe. Broca's discovery was substantially responsible for renewed interest in Gall's discredited idea of localization of function.
>
> Carl Wernicke (1848–1905), a German neurologist and psychiatrist, established clinically in 1874 that lesions in a region of the left temporal lobe result in diminished ability to understand speech.

> *equipotentiality:* the view, associated with Lashley, that all mental activities are distributed throughout the cortex, and that if one region is damaged or destroyed, other parts will pick up the slack

65 Perhaps the first effective answer to Lashley came from Donald Hebb. In his book *The Organization of Behavior,* Hebb (1949) [see 5.5] convinced many that it was possible to think seriously about the brain processes underlying memory. He developed concrete proposals based on biological facts, taking into consideration the neuronal circuitry that might contribute to memory storage. To explain Lashley's result that learning could not be localized to a single
70 brain region, Hebb suggested that assemblies of cells work together to represent information and that these assemblies are distributed over large areas of cortex. Sufficient numbers of inter-connected cells will survive most lesions to ensure that information can still be represented. The idea of a distributed memory store was far sighted. With the accumulation of additional evidence, it has become apparent that no single memory center exists, and many parts of the
75 nervous system participate in the representation of any single event.

Hebb influenced many students and colleagues—in particular, Brenda Milner, who in 1957 described the remarkable patient H. M. (Scoville and Milner, 1957). H. M. had sustained a bilateral resection of the medial structures of the temporal lobe in 1953 to relieve severe epilepsy. It was immediately evident following the surgery that H. M. had a very profound impairment of recent memory in the apparent absence of other intellectual loss (Scoville, 1954). He could not remember what he had for breakfast, and he could not find his way around the hospital or recognize members of the hospital staff (except Scoville, whom he had known for many years). It seemed as though his life from the surgery onwards was not contributing to his store of knowledge. He was able to hold immediate impressions in his mind, but as soon as his attention was diverted they were lost. In contrast, old memories from his childhood seemed to be intact.

... [T]here had been no intellectual loss; in fact, H. M.'s IQ had risen postoperatively, from 104 to 117, presumably because he was having far fewer seizures. His capacity for sustained attention was also remarkable. Thus, Milner showed that he could retain the number 584 for at least 15 minutes by continuous rehearsal, combining and recombining the digits according to an elaborate mnemonic scheme, but the moment his attention was diverted by a new topic, the whole event was forgotten.

H. M.'s success in remembering a three-digit number for 15 minutes in the absence of distraction was at first sight consistent with Drachman's view that amnesics can hold a simple memorandum indefinitely provided that no interfering activity claims their attention (Drachman and Arbit, 1966). Yet it was already clear that for H. M. verbal rehearsal played a key role in this holding process. In contrast, certain simple nonverbal stimuli were forgotten by him within less than a minute. The evidence for this comes from delayed paired comparison and delayed matching studies.

In 1959, Konorski described a method for testing memory of single events, which was later adapted for work with human subjects by Stepien and Sierpinski (1960). This technique, called by Milner "delayed paired comparison," consists of presenting two stimuli in succession, separated by a short time interval. The subject must then indicate whether the second stimulus is the same as or different from the first. This means that subjects must retain an impression of the first stimulus in order to compare the second one with it. Task difficulty may be increased by lengthening the intratrial interval or by introducing an intratrial distraction. Prisko (1963; cited by Milner, 1972) used the Konorski method to demonstrate H. M.'s rapid forgetting of simple perceptual material. She sampled five different sets of stimuli (three visual and two auditory), each set constituting a separate task. The stimuli used were clicks, tones, shades of red, light flashes, and nonsense patterns. At least five values were assigned to each variable, to prevent as far as possible the use of verbal mediation to bridge the retention interval. All paired stimuli were easily discriminable at zero intratrial delay. These proved to be extremely easy tasks for normal subjects, who rarely made errors even with a 60-second delay and an interpolated distraction. In contrast, H. M. performed all tasks well at zero delay, but with

> *intratrial interval:* the period between the first stimulus and the second

> *verbal mediation:* creating covert verbal cues (descriptions, mnemonics, etc.) as an aid to memory

increasing intratrial intervals his performance deteriorated sharply, so that at the 60-second
delay scores were approaching the chance level and were not further impaired by distraction.

Subsequently, Sidman, Stoddard, and Mohr (1968) confirmed Prisko's findings, using a delayed matching-to-sample technique that allowed the plotting of discrimination gradients to show how far the subject's choice of a matching stimulus deviates from the sample stimulus as the intratrial interval lengthens. In the nonverbal form of their task, H. M. was required to indicate which one of eight ellipses matched the sample stimulus. With zero delay he chose correctly most of the time, showing a normal discrimination of axis-ratios, but with increasing delays his performance deteriorated until, at 32 seconds, the sample no longer exerted any control over his choice. In contrast,

> In *delayed matching to sample,* on each trial a stimulus (the sample) is presented and then removed. After a delay, a set of stimuli, one of which matches the sample in some respect, is presented, and the subject must pick the matching one. In the study described, the delay was an independent variable, allowing a quantitative description (the discrimination gradient) of the effect of delay on memory, as measured by the proportion of trials the subject answers correctly.

H. M. had no difficulty with a verbal version of the task, which required the matching of consonant trigrams. However, as with other short-term verbal memory tasks, he succeeded only by constant rehearsal; his lips could be seen moving throughout the delay period.

These and other related studies (Milner and Taylor, 1972) concur in showing that H. M. can register perceptual information normally, but that the information ceases to be available to him within about 30–40 seconds. Milner (1972) suggested that such results support the distinction between a primary memory process with a rapid decay and an overlapping secondary process (impaired in H. M.) by which the long-term storage of information is achieved.

THERE ARE MULTIPLE MEMORY SYSTEMS IN THE BRAIN

H. M.'s failure on delayed matching and delayed comparison tasks, which assess memory after a single presentation, did not rule out the possibility that he might be capable of some learning with intensive practice, or indeed that certain kinds of learning might take place at a normal rate. Accordingly, Milner and her students embarked on a variety of learning studies with H. M., including stylus maze tasks, both visual (Milner, 1965) and tactual (Corkin, 1965). With one notable exception, these studies merely served to demonstrate H. M.'s extreme difficulties with new learning, as evident also in his daily life. The exception was in the domain of motor skills, where, in 1962, Milner showed that H. M. could learn a mirror-drawing task efficiently with stable retention from day to day (Figure 1A).

> *stylus maze:* A maze in which the usual space between lines is replaced by a groove in a surface; the subject follows the grooves of the maze with a stylus. In the tactual version of this task the subject is blindfolded.

FIGURE 1   H. M. Showed Improvement in a Task Involving Learning Skilled Movements

In this test, he was taught to trace a line between the two outlines of a star, starting from the point S (Figure 1A), while viewing his hand and the star in a mirror. He showed steady improvement over the 3 days of testing, although he had no idea that he had ever done the task before. (The graph in Figure 1B plots the number of times, in each trial, that he strayed outside the boundaries as he drew the star.) Adapted from Milner (1962)

A

B

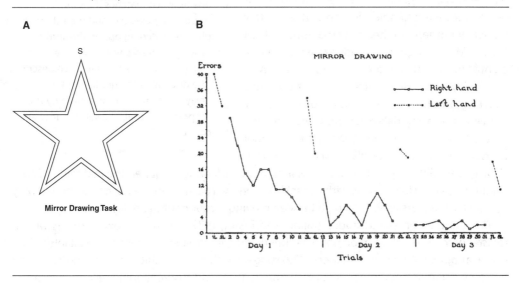

. . . Yet at the end he had no idea he had ever done the mirror drawing task before: this was learning without any sense of familiarity. Nowadays, we are well aware that such dissociations are possible following a discrete brain lesion, but for Milner, looking at it for the first time, it was quite astonishing. Her finding contributed some of the early evidence that there is more than one memory system in the brain.   160

. . .

The demonstration of intact motor skill learning in patient H. M. marked the beginning of a period of experimental work that eventually established the biological reality of multiple memory systems. This later work made it clear that the spared memory capacities of H. M. and other amnesic patients with bilateral medial temporal-lobe lesions are not limited to motor skills.   165

biological reality: as distinct from the behavioral reality

Motor skills are a subset of a large collection of learning and memory abilities, all of which are spared in amnesia and independent of the medial temporal lobe. . . .

THE DECLARATIVE AND NONDECLARATIVE MEMORY SYSTEMS

170　In 1980, Neal Cohen and Larry Squire showed that amnesic patients could learn the task of reading mirror-reversed print as well as normal subjects. These findings broadened further the scope of what amnesic patients could do and suggested a fundamental distinction in the way all of us process and store information about the world. The major distinction is between declarative memory and a collection of nondeclarative, nonconscious forms of memory.

175　Declarative memory (Figure 2) is what is ordinarily meant by the term memory. It depends on the integrity of the medial temporal lobe and affords the capacity for conscious recollections about facts and events. Declarative memory is propositional—it can be either true or false. It is involved in modelling the external world and storing representations about facts and episodes. Non-declarative memory is neither true nor false. It underlies changes in skilled

180　behavior and the ability to respond appropriately to stimuli through practice, as the result of conditioning or habit learning. It also includes changes in the ability to detect or identify objects as the result of recent encounters, a phenomenon known as *priming*. In the case of non-declarative memory, performance changes as the result of experience, which justifies the term memory, but performance changes without providing conscious access to any prior episodes

185　(Squire, Knowlton, & Musen, 1993; Schacter and Tulving, 1994). Many forms of nondeclarative memory, such as habituation, sensitization, and classical conditioning, are phylogenetically ancient and well developed in invertebrate animals that do not have a medial temporal lobe or hippocampus.

Habituation is defined behaviorally as a temporary reduction in the strength or frequency of an unconditioned response (e.g., startle) resulting from repetition of a relevant stimulus (loud noise). It is important to distinguish between habituation and *adaptation,* the gradual fatiguing of a sensory system due to frequent or constant stimulation over an extended period. Habituation is a form of learning, and adaptation is not.

Dishabituation is the recovery of the full strength of an unconditioned response when it is caused by something (e.g., a brilliant flash of light) other than the habituating stimulus.

Sensitization is the sudden increase in responsiveness to stimuli in general, following presentation of a particularly intense or unpleasant stimulus.

Classical conditioning is the process by which a reflexive behavior (the unconditioned response) comes to be elicited by an otherwise unrelated stimulus (the conditioned stimulus) that has been paired repeatedly with the stimulus (the unconditioned stimulus) that naturally elicits that response. Also known as *Pavlovian* or *respondent conditioning;* see 5.2.

Operant conditioning is the process by which the frequency of a specific behavior (the operant) is increased (or diminished) when some or all instances of that behavior are followed by a consequence that is in some way rewarding (or not rewarding or punishing) to the organism; see 3.5.

(Continued)

(Continued)

Note that classical and operant conditioning are both forms of *associative* learning, as the change in the organism's behavior corresponds to an association between two things (conditioned and unconditioned stimuli, operant and consequence) in the organism's environment. Habituation, dishabituation, and sensitization are forms of *nonassociative* learning.

Finally, to say that the above forms of learning are *phylogenetically ancient* refers to the fact that these capacities are found in organisms (such as snails) that appeared relatively early in evolutionary history.

A number of nondeclarative forms of memory have been subjected to intensive study. In humans, perhaps the best studied example of nondeclarative memory is priming, first explored   190 by Warrington and Weiskrantz (1968) and by Milner, Corkin, & Teuber (1968). Endel Tulving, Daniel Schacter, Larry Squire, and others have explored several paradigms in which subjects see lists of words, pictures of objects, or nonverbal material such as novel objects or designs (Weiskrantz, 1990; Tulving and Schacter, 1990). Subsequently, subjects are tested with both old and new items and asked to name words or objects as quickly as possible, to complete frag-   195 ments to form whole items, or to make rapid decisions about items.

FIGURE 2   A Taxonomy of Mammalian Memory Systems

This taxonomy lists the brain structures and connections thought to be especially important for each kind of declarative and nondeclarative memory.

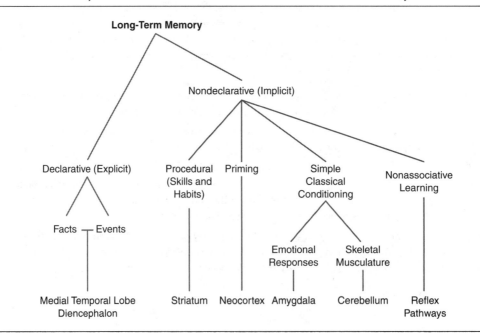

For example, when the first few letters (MOT__) of a recently studied word (MOTEL) are presented, priming is evidenced in the tendency to complete the word fragment to form the study word instead of other possible words. Severely amnesic patients exhibit fully intact priming, despite being unable to recognize as familiar the items that had been presented previously.

. . .

Perhaps the best studied example of nondeclarative memory in mammals is classical *Pavlovian* conditioning of discrete behavioral responses. A body of work initiated in the early 1980s by Richard Thompson and his colleagues has focused on basic delay conditioning of the rabbit eyeblink response (conditioned stimulus = tone; unconditioned stimulus = airpuff; conditioned response = eyeblink). Based on anatomical findings, electrical stimulation, and reversible lesion techniques, the results provide strong evidence that the essential memory trace circuit includes the cerebellum and related brain stem circuitry and that the memory traces themselves are formed and stored in the cerebellum (Thompson and Krupa, 1994). To date, eyeblink conditioning provides the clearest information about the localization of a memory within the mammalian brain.

> *delay conditioning:* a form of classical conditioning in which the interval between the presentation of the conditioned stimulus and the presentation of the unconditioned stimulus is gradually increased. Animals not only learn to respond to the conditioned stimulus but learn to delay the response until just before the unconditioned stimulus is presented.

In humans, several kinds of nondeclarative memory have been studied, which are likely based on perceptual learning. These include adaptation-level effects, the ability to resolve random-dot stereograms, the ability to learn the regularities of "artificial grammars" by studying lawfully ordered letter strings, and the ability to acquire knowledge about categories. In category learning, one extracts and stores information about the prototype (or representative instance) of a series of items by studying many different items that, when averaged together, describe the prototype. All these forms of memory are intact in amnesic patients (Squire, Knowlton & Musen, 1993; Squire and Zola-Morgan, 1996). These kinds of memory likely involve changes within the same cortical areas responsible for perceiving and analyzing the materials that are studied.

. . .

> *Adaptation-level effects* are ubiquitous. For example, we say that a 40 W light bulb is "dim" and that Venus is "very bright" despite the fact that the bulb provides far more illumination than does Venus. The point of adaptation-level theory (Helson, 1947, 1948, 1964) is that in our experience of light bulbs, and compared to other light bulbs, the 40 W specimen is on the "dim" side of our scale of brightness; Venus, on the other hand, sheds more light than most celestial objects and is therefore at the "bright" end of the scale.
>
> *(Continued)*

(Continued)

A *random-dot stereogram* consists of two images, each a random pattern of dots. Although the viewer cannot easily discover this by inspection, one dot pattern is a copy of the other except that the dots in a particular region have been moved slightly, either all to the left or all to the right. When viewed stereoscopically (i.e., such that the left eye sees only the left dot pattern, the right eye only the right pattern), the dot patterns fuse, producing a single image in which the displaced region of dots is seen to be either above or below the surrounding field of un-moved dots. The phenomenon is striking, and easier to experience than it is to describe; see Julesz (1964) or any introductory text in perception.

An *artificial grammar* is a set of rules governing the order in which members of a given set of symbols may appear. Such a grammar can be used to generate an arbitrarily large set of "grammatical" symbol strings (i.e., strings that follow the rules of the grammar), and the experimenter can likewise create any number of ungrammatical symbol strings. The two sets of strings are randomly mixed and shown, one at a time, to the subject, who does not know the grammar but must decide whether each string is grammatical or ungrammatical. The subject is given feedback (right/wrong) after each response. The subject's performance begins at chance, but over many trials improves to the point where the subject can reliably discriminate between grammatical and non-grammatical strings. Except when the grammar is trivially simple, however, the subject is typically unable to articulate ("declare") the rules of the grammar. The general significance, as well as the specific nature, of artificial-grammar learning are matters of considerable dispute and have generated a formidable literature. See Reber (1967, 1993).

THE MOLECULAR BIOLOGICAL APPROACH TO MEMORY STORAGE

How are we to think about the cellular and molecular mechanisms of memory storage? By the end of the nineteenth century, biologists had come to appreciate that mature nerve cells have lost their capacity to divide. This fact prompted Santiago Ramón y Cajal to propose that learning does not result in the proliferation of new nerve cells but instead causes existing nerve cells to grow more branches and to strengthen their connections with other nerve cells so as to be able to communicate with them more effectively (Ramón y Cajal, 1894). This prescient idea raised three sets of questions. 230 235

> Ramon y Cajal (1852–1934): Spanish neuroanatomist. His work on the anatomy of nerve cells, for which he won the 1906 Nobel Prize, played an essential part in the discovery of the synapse.

First, does memory involve persistent changes in synaptic strength? If so, what are the molecular underpinnings of these synaptic changes?

Second, how do short-term synaptic changes differ from the changes that support long-term storage? Do they occur at different loci, or can the same neuron store information for both short- and long-term memory? 240

Third, if memory storage results from changes in specific synaptic connections, do declarative memory and the various nondeclarative forms of memory use different molecular mechanisms for storage, or are the storage mechanisms used by these two memory systems fundamentally similar?

245 To explore these ideas, neurobiologists developed a number of model systems for the specific purpose of optimizing the ability to study synaptic change in the context of behavioral memory storage, with the ultimate goal of identifying the cellular and molecular basis of the synaptic changes responsible for the storage (see, for example, Kandel and Tauc, 1964; Thompson and Spencer, 1966; Kandel and Spencer, 1968). The reductionist approach to nondeclarative memory storage began with the cell biological studies of the

250 marine snail *Aplysia* by Kandel (Kandel and Tauc, 1964) and with the genetic studies of *Drosophila* by Benzer (Benzer, 1967).

> *Drosophila* ("dew-lover") is a genus of fruit flies used extensively in genetic research.

CELL BIOLOGICAL AND MOLECULAR INSIGHTS INTO NONDECLARATIVE MEMORY STORAGE

The cell biological studies in *Aplysia* (Kandel and Tauc, 1964; Kupfermann and Kandel, 1969; Castellucci, Pinsker, Kupfermann & Kandel, 1970) were soon joined by studies of other inver-

255 tebrates including other opisthobranch snails, specifically *Hermissenda* (Alkon, 1974) and *Pleurobranchaea* (Davis and Gillette, 1978), the land snail *Umax* (Gelperin, 1975), crayfish (Krasne, 1969), and honey bees (Menzel and Erber, 1978). The idea underlying these cell biological studies

260 was that the simple brains of certain experimentally tractable invertebrates combined the advantages of having a relatively small number of nerve cells in the brain with cells that (with the exception

> *Opisthobranchiata* ("rear-gills") is a subclass of gastropod mollusks in which the gills are behind the heart. Opisthobranchs are generally referred to as sea-slugs, and most have little or no shell.

of the honey bee) are unusually large and readily identifiable. These features made their

265 behavior and their ability to modify behavior by learning accessible to cellular and molecular analysis. Analogous reductionist approaches were also applied to the mammalian brain, in particular to the isolated spinal cord (Spencer, Thompson & Nielson, 1966), to brain slices of the hippocampus (Schwartzkroin and Wester, 1975), and to learned behavior dependent on the cerebellum (McCormick and Thompson, 1984) and the amygdala (LeDoux, 1995).

270 The first insight to emerge from this *simple systems approach* to nondeclarative memory was purely behavioral. Studies of invertebrates revealed that even animals with limited numbers of nerve cells—approximately 20,000 to 100,000 central neurons in the nervous systems of *Aplysia, Hermissenda, Pleurobranchaea,* and *Umax* and approximately 300,000 in *Drosophila*—had rather remarkable behavioral and learning capabilities (reviewed by Carew and Sahley, 1986). In fact,

275 even the gill withdrawal reflex, perhaps the simplest behavioral reflex of *Aplysia,* could be modified by several different forms of learning—habituation, dishabituation, sensitization, classical

FIGURE 3   Long-Term Habituation of the Withdrawal Reflex in *Aplysia* Is Represented on the Cellular Level by a Dramatic Depression of Synaptic Effectiveness Between the Sensory and Motor Neurons

(A) Behavior

(A) Time course of behavioral habituation. T1 to T4 represent the average of 10 trials a day for 4 days of training. R1, R7, and R21 are retention tests 1 day, 1 week, and 3 weeks after training. (From Carew et al., 1972. Reprinted with permisssion.)

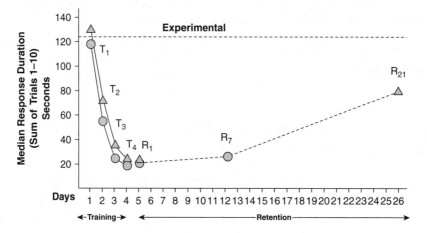

(B) Physiology

(B[A]) Comparison of the synaptic potentials in a sensory neuron and a motor neuron in a control (untrained) animal and in an animal that has been subjected to long-term habituation. In the habituated animal, the synaptic potential in the motor neuron is still undetectable 1 week after training. (From Castellucci et al., 1978. Reprinted with permisssion.)

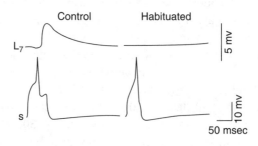

(B) Physiology [Continued]

(B[B]) The mean percentage of physiologically detectable connections in habituated animals at several points in time after long-term habituation training. (From Castellucci et al., 1978. Reprinted with permisssion.)

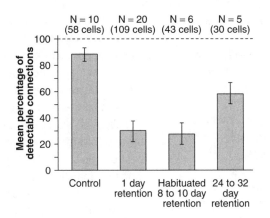

(C) Structure

(C) Long-term habituation and sensitization involve structural changes in the presynaptic terminals of sensory neurons. (Adapted from Bailey and Chen, 1983.) This histogram compares the number of presynaptic terminals in control animals with those in long-term habituated and sensitized animals. The number is highest in the sensitized animals.

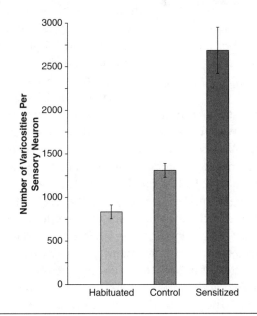

conditioning, and operant conditioning (reviewed by Carew and Sahley, 1986). Moreover, each of these forms of learning could give rise to both short- and long-term forms of nondeclarative memory as a function of the amount of repeated training. These studies suggested that an animal does not need a large brain or even many thousands of nerve cells for perfectly good long-term storage of a variety of different memories.

280

These early behavioral studies in invertebrates led to the delineation of a family of psychological concepts that paralleled those first described in vertebrates by both the classical behaviorists—Pavlov [see 5.2] and Thorndike—and their modern counterparts—Kamin, Rescorla, and Wagner. These concepts included the distinction between various forms of associative and nonassociative learning, the role of contingency as opposed to mere contiguity, short-term memory consolidation, storage, retrieval of long-term memory, and forgetting. Subsequent cellular studies of these simple forms of learning illustrated that these concepts, initially inferred from purely behavioral studies, could now be approached directly in terms of their underlying cellular and molecular mechanisms (reviewed by Kandel, 1976; Hawkins and Kandel, 1984; Carew and Sahley, 1986). Thus, the ability to analyze learning-related synaptic mechanisms brought to light not only a new set of mechanistic insights into the plastic properties of individual synaptic connections, but in so doing these studies brought concreteness and clarity to the psychological concepts themselves. For example, by identifying significant components of the neural circuits underlying simple behaviors such as the gill-withdrawal reflex in *Aplysia*, the tail flick in the crayfish, feeding in *Umax* or *Aplysia*, and

285

290

295

300

305

Edward Thorndike (1874–1949), American psychologist. See note in 5.2 (pp. 447–448).

Leon Kamin (b. 1927), Robert Rescorla (b. 1940), and Allan Wagner (b. 1934), among others, have made many important contributions to our understanding of what is learned in Pavlovian conditioning; see, for example, Kamin (1957) and Rescorla & Wagner (1972). Their work was with vertebrate animals (rats), but has been found to apply equally to invertebrates.

Plastic is here used in its pre-petroleum sense of "capable of being molded," from the Greek word meaning "to shape."

phototaxis in *Hermissenda,* studies in invertebrates delineated how elements in the behavioral circuits themselves changed when behavior was modified by various forms of learning (reviewed by Carew and Sahley, 1986). These findings illustrate that nondeclarative memory storage does not depend on specialized memory neurons or systems of neurons whose only function is to store rather than process information. Rather, simple nondeclarative memory storage results from changes in neurons that are themselves *components* of the reflex pathway. The storage of nondeclarative memory is embedded in the neural circuit that produces the behavior. These studies therefore provided the first clear insight that the organization and implementation of nondeclarative memory is different from declarative memory where a whole neural system, the medial temporal-lobe memory system, is needed to ensure the remembrance of things past.

310

315

Moreover, these cell biological studies illustrated several general principles about memory-related synaptic plasticity. To begin with, the studies provided the first direct evidence for two of Cajal's prescient suggestions: that the synaptic connections between neurons mediating

behavior are not fixed but can become modified by learning, and that these modifications
persist and can serve as elementary components of memory storage (Figure 3; Castellucci et
al., 1970, 1978; Zucker, Kennedy, and Selverston 1971; Castellucci and Kandel, 1974). In addition, these studies showed that the same set of synaptic connections was found to be able to
participate in several different learning processes and to be modified by them in opposite directions. For example, the synaptic strength of a single synaptic connection could be increased
with sensitization and classical conditioning, and it could be decreased with habituation
(Castellucci et al., 1978; Carew et al., 1979; Hawkins et al., 1983; Frost et al., 1985; Murphy and
Glanzman, 1997; Bao et al., 1997, 1998).

Furthermore, in the gill-withdrawal and tail-withdrawal reflex *of Aplysia* (Hawkins et al.,
1981a, 1981b; Frost et al., 1988; Cleary et al., 1995), and in the escape reflex of *Tritonia* (Katz
and Frost, 1995), there were changes in synaptic
strength with habituation and sensitization not
only in the connections between the sensory neurons and their motoneuron target cells, but also in

> *Tritonia* is another genus of opisthobranchs.

the connections made by interneurons onto the target cells. Thus, within the neural pathways
controlling the reflex, the storage of even a simple nondeclarative memory is distributed and
involves multiple storage.

Finally, just as behavioral studies of memory in the gill-withdrawal reflex had found that memory storage has stages—a short-term form lasting minutes and a long-term form lasting days to
weeks—so did the cellular studies find that the synaptic changes contributing to memory storage
also have stages (Castellucci et al., 1978; Carew et al.,
1979; Frost et al., 1988). Thus, both the acquisition of
learning and its retention as short- and long-term
memory were found to have a representation at
the level of individual synaptic connections.

The initial analyses in the 1970s focused on short-
term changes. These showed that one mechanism
for the synaptic plasticity induced in both the gill-
withdrawal reflex of *Aplysia* and in the tail flick
response of crayfish was through the modulation of
transmitter release. A depression of transmitter
release occurred with short-term habituation and an
enhancement with short-term sensitization (Zucker
et al., 1971; Castellucci et al., 1970, 1974, 1976).

A variety of cell biological studies on the
monosynaptic connections between the sensory neurons and motor neurons of the gill- and tail-withdrawal reflexes in *Aplysia* outlined one class of
molecular mechanisms for the short-term enhancement of transmitter release produced by sensitization
(Figure 4; Brunelli et al., 1976; Kandel and Schwartz,

> The *G protein* is the basis of a widespread
> system of signaling within cells. When a
> receptor in the cell membrane binds to its
> target molecule (in this case serotonin), a G
> protein molecule coupled to the receptor is
> transformed in such a way that it in turn
> binds to and activates a molecule of the
> enzyme adenylyl cyclase. The enzyme then
> produces cyclic adenosine monophosphate
> (cAMP), which diffuses through the cell.
>
> K^+ *channels* are portals in the cell
> membrane that, when open, allow
> potassium ions (K^+) to pass into the cell. This
> reduces the voltage across the membrane,
> inhibiting the action potential.
>
> Calcium ions (*Ca2+*) enter the cell
> through a different set of channels, causing
> the vesicles containing neurotransmitter to
> fuse with the cell membrane and release
> their contents into the synapse.

1982; Byrne and Kandel, 1995). A single sensitizing stimulus to the tail led to the activation of three classes of modulatory neurons, the most important of which uses serotonin (5-HT) as its transmitter. Serotonin acts on a G protein-coupled receptor to activate adenylyl cyclase and increase the level of cAMP in the sensory neurons. The increase in cAMP activates the cAMP-dependent protein kinases (PKA), which then enhance transmitter release in two ways: (1) by closure of K^+ channels leading to a broadening of the action potential, thereby enhancing Ca^{2+} influx necessary for vesicle exocytosis; and (2) by acting directly in ways that are not yet understood, on one or more steps in vesicle mobilization and exocytotic release (Castellucci et al., 1980, 1982; Byrne and Kandel, 1995). A similar second messenger signaling pathway for learning and short-term memory was identified in *Drosophila* using genetic approaches (Byers et al., 1981; Aceves-Piña et al., 1983; Davis, 1996).

365

370

FIGURE 4   Schematic Outline of Changes in the Sensory Neurons of the Gill-Withdrawal Reflex That Accompany Short- and Long-term Memory for Sensitization in *Aplysia*.

Sensitization is produced by applying a noxious stimulus to another part of the body, such as the tail. Stimuli to the tail activate sensory neurons that excite facilitating interneurons, which form synapses on the terminals of the sensory neurons innervating the siphon skin. At these axo-axonic synapses, the interneurons are able to enhance transmitter release from the sensory neurons (presynaptic facilitation). Serotonin (5-HT), a transmitter released by facilitatory neurons, acts on a sensory neuron to initiate both the short-term and the long-term facilitation that contribute to the memory processes. *Short-term facilitation* (lasting minutes) involves covalent modification of preexisting proteins (pathways 1 and 2). Serotonin acts on a transmembrane receptor to activate a GTP-binding protein that stimulates the enzyme adenylyl cyclase to convert ATP to the second messenger cAMP. In turn, cAMP activates protein kinase A, which phosphorylates and covalently modifies a number of target proteins. These include closing of K^+ channels, which prolongs the action potential and increases the influx of Ca^{2+}, thus augmenting transmitter release (pathway 1) as well as steps involved in transmitter availability and release (pathway 2). Can involve the joint action of PKA and protein kinase C (PKC). The duration of these modifications represents the retention or storage of a component of the short-term memory. *Long-term facilitation* (lasting one or more days) involves the synthesis of new proteins. The switch for this inductive mechanism is initiated by the protein kinase A. This kinase translocates to the nucleus (long-term pathway) where it phosphorylates the cyclic AMP response element-binding (CREB) protein. The transcriptional activators bind to cyclic AMP regulatory elements (CRE) located in the upstream region of two types of cAMP-inducible genes. To activate CREB-1, protein kinase A needs also to remove the repressive action of CREB-2, which is capable of inhibiting the activation capability of CREB-1. Protein kinase A is thought to mediate the derepression of CREB-2 by means of another protein kinase, MAP kinase. One gene (closed square) activated by CREB encodes a ubiquitin hydrolase, a component of a specific ubiquitin protease that leads to the regulated proteolysis of the regulatory subunit of PKA. This cleave of the (inhibitory) regulatory subunit results in persistent activity of protein kinase A, leading to persistent phosphorylation of the substrate proteins of PKA, including both CREB-1 and the protein involved in the short-term process. The second set of proteins (closed triangles) is important for the growth of new synaptic connections. (From Kandel, Schwartz, and Jessell, 1991)

(Continued)

FIGURE 4 (Continued)

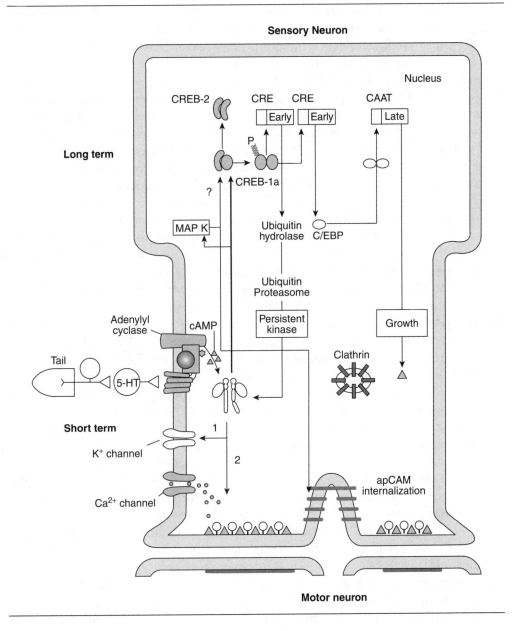

Behavioral studies in vertebrates had shown earlier that long-term memory differed from short-term memory not only in time course but also mechanistically (reviewed by Davis and Squire, 1984). Long-term memory requires synthesis of new proteins, whereas short-term memory does not. These behavioral studies raised a number of questions that could now be

explored on the cellular level. Can the same set of synaptic connections mediate both short-   375
term and long-term synaptic plasticity? Can PKA induce the long-term as well as the transient
changes, or does the long-term process recruit a new signaling system? Finally, is this requirement for protein synthesis evident at the level of single cells involved in memory storage? If so,
how is protein synthesis activated for long-term memory?

Studies in *Aplysia* during the last decade have found that the same set of connections that   380
undergo the short-term changes also undergo long-term changes, and the long-term changes
in synaptic plasticity parallel behavioral memory in also requiring new protein synthesis
(Goelet et al., 1986; Montarolo et al., 1986). Thus, a single synaptic connection can not only be
modified in opposite ways by different forms of learning, but it can be modified for periods
ranging from minutes to weeks by the different stages of a memory process. Whereas one train-   385
ing trial to the tail in the intact animal or one pulse of 5-HT to the sensory neurons initiates the
short-term process through covalent modification of preexisting proteins, five repeated training trials or five pulses of 5-HT initiate the protein synthesis-dependent long-term process. With
repeated training, the cAMP-dependent protein kinase recruits another kinase, a mitogen-
activated protein kinase (MAP kinase), and both of these kinases translocate into the cell's   390
nucleus where they activate the transcriptional activator CREB-1 (the cAMP response element-
binding protein) (see Bacskai et al., 1993; Kaang et al., 1993; Martin et al., 1997).

In *Aplysia* and *Drosophila,* both PKA and CREB-1 are not only necessary but are also sufficient
for the long-term enhancement of synaptic strength (Schacher et al., 1988; Yin et al., 1994, 1995;
Davis et al., 1996; reviewed by Martin and Kandel, 1996). In *Aplysia,* CREB-1 leads to the activa-   395
tion of a cascade of immediate-early genes. One of these, the gene for ubiquitin hydrolase, is
the first neuron-specific step in this signaling cascade (Hedge et al., 1997). This enzyme is a rate-
limiting step in the activation of the ubiquitin proteosome. The proteosome in turn cleaves the
regulatory subunit of PKA. This frees the catalytic subunit and establishes a persistently active
PKA, which can continue to phosphorylate substrate proteins necessary for the maintenance   400
of facilitation but *now* without requiring either 5-HT or cAMP.

This neuron-specific memory mechanism is active for about 10 hours (Hedge et al., 1997).
What gives the long-term facilitation self-maintained properties is the action of a second immediate-early gene, the transcriptional factor C/EBP. This factor acts on downstream genes,
which leads to the synthesis of proteins and the growth of new synaptic connections (Alberini   405
et al., 1994; Hedge et al., 1997). This growth of new synaptic contacts appears to be the stable,
anatomically self-maintained reflection of stable long-term memory (Bailey and Chen, 1988;
Glanzman et al., 1989; Bailey et al., 1992). Thus, synapses not only express plasticity by modu-
lating transmitter function; synapses also express plasticity in terms of their structural morphology and by increasing or decreasing the number of release sites.   410

The initial studies of the switch from short-term to long-term memory focused on positive
regulators that favor memory storage. Recent studies in *Drosophila* and *Aplysia* have revealed
the surprising finding that the switch to the long-term synaptic change and to the growth of
new synaptic connections are normally constrained by inhibitory factors—*memory suppressor
genes*—that oppose long-term memory storage and determine the ease with which short-term   415
memory can be converted to long-term memory (reviewed by Abel et al., 1998). One important

constraint is an inhibitory transcription factor, the repressor CREB-2 (Bartsch et al., 1995). Over-expression of the repressor selectively blocks long-term facilitation in *Aplysia*. Removal of the repression allows a single exposure of serotonin, which normally produces short-term facilitation lasting only minutes, to produce long-term facilitation lasting days and to induce the growth of new synaptic connections.

These several findings on the cell biology of nondeclarative memory storage in invertebrates carry with them the important implications that the cellular representation of short-term memory involves covalent modifications of pre-existing proteins and the strengthening of pre-existing connections. By contrast, the cellular representation of long-term memory involves CREB-mediated expression of genes, new protein synthesis, and the formation of new synaptic connections.

. . .

In *retrospect,* what we are seeing in memory storage illustrates a key principle in biological regulations. The dominant idea to emerge from the molecular study of cellular regulation—the cell cycle, signal transduction, apoptosis, cell growth, and oncogenesis—is that biological processes are remarkably conserved. Perhaps the most remarkable example has emerged from studies of development. The genes involved in the formation of the body plan of vertebrates derive from genes and genetic pathways evident in *Drosophila* and *C. elegans*—even though the vertebrate body plan bears little resemblance to that of the fly and even less to that of the worm. Indeed, these same genes are utilized again in the formation of the vertebrate brain.

apoptosis: cell disintegration

oncogenesis: tumor formation

Caenorhabditis elegans is a small (1 mm) nematode, or worm.

. . .

This finding (the conservation of biological processes) is an important vindication of an early decision of Kandel's, as he describes in his Nobel Prize autobiography (2001):

Influenced by Kuffler, Grundfest, and Crain, I yearned for a more radically reductionist approach to the biology of learning and memory. I wanted a system that would serve the cellular study of learning as well as the squid giant axon had served for studies of the action potential, or the nerve-muscle synapse of the frog had served for the study of synaptic transmission. I wanted to examine learning in an experimental animal in which a simple behavior was modifiable by learning. Ideally that behavior should be controlled by only a small number of large and accessible nerve cells, so that the animal's overt behavior could be related to events occurring in the cells that control that behavior.

(Continued)

(Continued)

Such a reductionist approach has been traditional in biology. In neurobiology it is exemplified by the work on the squid giant axon by Hodgkin and Huxley, the nerve-muscle synapse of the frog by Bernard Katz, and the eye of *Limulus* by Keefer Hartline. When it came to the study of behavior, however, most investigators were reluctant to apply a strict reductionist strategy. In the 1950s and 1960s it was often said that behavior was the area in biology in which simple animal models, particularly invertebrate ones, were least likely to produce fruitful results because the brain that really learns, the mammalian brain, especially the human brain, is so complex that inferences from studies of invertebrates would not stand up. It was thought that humans, because of higher-order capabilities not found in simpler animals, must have types of neuronal organization that are qualitatively different from those found in invertebrates. Although these arguments held some truth, they overlooked certain critical issues. Work by students of comparative behavior, such as Konrad Lorenz, Niko Tinbergen, and Karl von Frisch, had already shown that certain behavior patterns, including elementary forms of learning, were common to humans and simple animals. From the outset I therefore believed that the mechanisms of memory storage were likely to be conserved in phylogeny, and that a cellular analysis of learning in a simple animal would reveal universal mechanisms that are also employed in more complex organisms.

Not surprisingly, I was strongly discouraged in the early days from pursuing this strategy by some senior researchers in neurobiology, particularly John Eccles. His concern reflected, in part, the existing hierarchy of acceptable research questions in neurobiology. Few self-respecting neurophysiologists, I was told, would leave the study of learning in mammals to work on an invertebrate. Was I compromising my career? Of an even greater concern to me were the doubts expressed by some very knowledgeable psychologists I knew, who were sincerely skeptical that anything interesting about learning and memory could be found in a simple invertebrate animal. I had made up my mind, however. Since we knew nothing about the cell biology of learning and memory, I believed that any insight into the modification of behavior by experience, no matter how simple the animal or the task, would prove to be highly informative.

FOR DISCUSSION

1. Given what H.M. can and can't do, what other learning tasks would you predict he could do?

2. What are the different uses and values of the two kinds (systems and molecular) of memory research described in this paper?

Part VI

Normal and Abnormal

In every culture there are those who stand out as very different. At one time it was assumed that these people were possessed by demons. If the demons were good, the individual would be protected and cared for by others. They might even be revered as people who could see the future or cure illness. If the demons were bad, however, either the individual would be banished or the demons would have to be removed. Some early treatments involved making the person's body so uncomfortable that the demons would leave. The person might be beaten or put in icy water. In some societies, exorcism was used to roust the demons.

In Western cultures, the Renaissance brought a change in people's attitudes about science, and with that came a change in attitudes about abnormal behavior. By the 16th century, the idea that abnormality was an illness began to gain acceptance. At first the mad were sent to hospitals, but because there were no agreed-upon methods of treatment, asylums were created to provide sanctuary for them. Probably these asylums were originally intended to provide care if not cure, but they became crowded and their clientele typically could not pay for any care they received. With time, they received none. Inmates lived in filthy conditions; they were treated cruelly by their keepers and were often chained and poorly fed. One of the earliest asylums was the notorious St. Mary's of Bethlehem—known as Bedlam—in London. For a fee, the public could observe and marvel at the crazy behaviors of the inmates at Bedlam (the depressed inmates had no entertainment value, and so they either weren't displayed or they simply sat quietly with a cup and begged for money).

When any treatment was provided, it was based on the assumption that the causes of mental illness were physical, and the treatments had a physical nature as well (e.g., bloodletting, twirling, ice baths). It was all guesswork, and every form of treatment, however ridiculous it now seems, had some success—much as the treatments in the days of demonology had. No one really knew much about mental illness or what to do with these abnormal people.

In the late 1700s, things changed. Philippe Pinel was the director of a men's asylum in Paris. He began removing the chains and treating the inmates with kindness. He then made the same reforms at a women's asylum. His approach, called moral treatment, involved treating inmates with respect and encouraging fresh air, exercise, conversation, quiet time, and interesting activity. What had happened in the old asylums, however, began to happen in the new ones. They got crowded and people on the outside began to wonder why these mad people who weren't productive members of society were getting such good treatment.

In the late 1800s Richard von Krafft-Ebing demonstrated a link between a particular form of madness (general paresis) and syphilis. General paresis was an incurable disorder that included delusional behavior as well as organic symptoms. Krafft-Ebing injected a number of paretic patients with material from the syphilitic sores of people with early-stage syphilis, but the paretic patients didn't get syphilis. They were immune because they already had it. Syphilis, after its early stages, is dormant for a while, and general paresis is one of the ways in which it can later show up. Krafft-Ebing's finding lent strong support to the belief that all abnormal behavior is based on physical dysfunction—the somatogenic view of abnormality.

A competing view, the psychogenic view, began with work that Jean Charcot was doing at about the same time. Charcot was interested in hysteria—a disorder in which someone shows physical symptoms that have no physical basis. Charcot found that he could induce a range of physical and psychological symptoms in normal people using hypnosis. He originally believed that this suggestibility had a physiological basis, but he eventually came to believe that it was psychological. The work of Sigmund Freud and Josef Breuer supported this view, for they were able to remove hysterical symptoms by "talk therapy." (In other sections of this book, two readings by Freud [3.3 and 4.6] provide insight into his view of the nature and source of psychopathology.)

We have, of course, moved on a bit, but not necessarily advanced. Are we doing better? Do we know more?

The readings in this section illustrate a range of perspectives on the basic issue of exactly what it means to be normal or abnormal and the related issue of how we decide that a given person is one or the other. Because those issues are tied to questions about causes and treatments, these questions will inevitably enter the picture as well. In fact, you can learn a lot about a society's assumptions about normality and abnormality by looking at who is considered abnormal and how they are treated.

The reading by Benjamin Rush, a physician, provides a picture of who was classified as abnormal and how they were treated in the late 1700s and early 1800s. Henry Wegrocki's article deals with the issue of how cultural differences in behavior relate to judgments of normality. Karen Horney writes about how the sense of self in the neurotic person differs qualitatively from that in the normal person. Evelyn Hooker's study raises questions about the influence of social values and traditions on judgments of abnormality. Thomas Szasz asks us to think about whether there is such a thing as mental illness. Samuel Guze assures us that there is and makes clear that psychiatry can deal with it. Finally, Corey Keyes reminds us that we should think about mental health as much as we think about mental illness.

ADDITIONAL READING

Hippocrates   *Hippocratic writings* (ca 430–330 BCE): The sacred disease

Hippocrates, the Father of Medicine, rejected the idea that the so-called "sacred disease" (epilepsy) is the result of divine or supernatural punishment. Rather, he maintained that it had natural causes and could be treated by natural means.

Phillippe Pinel *Treatise on insanity* (1806)

A description of various kinds of derangement and of the appropriate treatment for each kind. Pinel argues for humane treatment for all those hospitalized for derangement.

Richard von Krafft-Ebing *Psychopathia sexualis: A medico-forensic study* (1886)

A scandalous book in its time. Krafft-Ebing described various forms of sexual deviance and added words such as fetishism, sadism, and masochism to our vocabulary. Krafft-Ebing's medical and moral views on sexual deviance were somewhat confused, but he did argue against the legal action taken against such behaviors.

Josef Breuer & Sigmund Freud *Studies on hysteria* (1895)

Freud's first book related to psychoanalysis. Breuer and Freud describe a number of cases of hysteria, including Breuer's famous work with Anna O.

Clifford Beers *A mind that found itself* (1908)

Beers wrote an autobiographical account of his own mental illness and of the inhumane treatment he received in several mental hospitals. His book brought attention to the problem, although change did not occur quickly.

Sigmund Freud *Introductory lectures on psycho-analysis* (1917)

A series of 28 lectures that Freud delivered in Germany, explaining and developing his theory. A shorter introduction (five lectures delivered at Clark University in 1909) is also available as *Five Lectures on Psycho-Analysis.*

Emil Kraepelin *Lectures on clinical psychology* (1913)

Kraepelin devised the first generally accepted system for the classification of psychiatric disorders. His system was based on a biomedical model of mental illness, and it described symptoms, syndromes, prognoses, and responses to various treatments.

August B. Hollingshead & Frederick C. Redlich *Social class and mental illness* (1958)

More up-to-date data are available on this topic, but Hollingshead and Redlich did an exceptionally careful and important description and analysis of the relationship between social class and mental illness.

Erving Goffman *Asylums* (1961)

A frightening description of what living in a "total institution" is like and what it does to the individuals who live there—with special attention to mental hospitals and prisons.

Joseph Schildkraut *The catecholamine hypothesis of affective disorders: A review of supporting evidence* (1965)

A classic and important article dealing with the efficacy of psychopharmalogical treatment for the mood disorders.

Hans Eysenck *The effects of psychotherapy* (1966)

Eysenck had serious doubts about how well traditional talk therapy or medical treatment actually works to improve a patient's condition. He analyzed the published results on various treatments and argued that the treatments did no better than time alone would have done.

George Rosen   *Madness in society: Chapters in the historical sociology of mental illness* (1969)

A collection of essays on mental illness in a variety of times and places. A serious and scholarly look at changing views of mental illness, its treatment, and related fads and fallacies.

Aaron Beck   *Depression: Clinical, experimental, and theoretical aspects* (1967); *Cognitive therapy of depression* (1979)

Two of Beck's earlier books on cognitive behavior therapy (usually referred to as CBT although Beck himself calls it CT). Beck is largely responsible for the development and success of CBT methods. CBT combines cognitive (how we think about things) with behavioral (how we behave in response to things) approaches in therapeutic settings. It is an empirically supported method that is increasingly used in therapy.

Joseph Wolpe   *The practice of behavior therapy* (1969)

Wolpe devised a number of ways in which operant and classical conditioning techniques such as systematic desensitization and operant learning can be used to bring about desired behavior change.

Henri Ellenberger   *The discovery of the unconscious: The history and evolution of dynamic psychiatry* (1970).

Ellenberger provides a detailed account of the origins of the psychogenic theory in the work of Janet, Charcot, and Freud.

Elliot Valenstein   *Blaming the brain: The truth about drugs and mental health* (1998)

A critical history of psychopharmacology. Valenstein traces the history of the use of drugs to treat mental illness, critiques some of the research on these drugs, and questions the assumption that mental illness has a biochemical basis.

American Psychiatric Association   *Diagnostic and Statistical Manual of Mental Disorders, fourth edition, text revision (DSM-IV-TR)* (2000)

A categorical classification of mental disorders.

C. R. Snyder & Shane J. Lopez (Eds.)   *Handbook of positive psychology* (2002)

An excellent and wide-ranging set of readings that look at the possibilities for studying and exploring the positive aspects of the human experience—cognitive, behavioral, social, and emotional.

Benjamin Rush (1746–1813)
Medical Inquiries and Observations Upon the Diseases of the Mind (1812)

Chapter 2. *Of the* Remote *and* Exciting Causes *of Intellectual Derangement*

Benjamin Rush was born near Philadelphia in 1746. Five years after his birth, his father died. His mother opened a grocery store in Philadelphia to support the family and in 1753 sent Rush to the West Nottingham Academy in Maryland, a school that had been opened by her brother-in-law, Reverend Samuel Finley. After completing his studies there, Rush went on to the College of New Jersey (now Princeton University), where Finley had just been named president. After graduating, Rush apprenticed to a Philadelphia physician and took some medical courses at the College of Philadelphia (the first American medical school, now the University of Pennsylvania) and then attended medical school at the University of Edinburgh, doing additional studies in London and Paris. He returned to America in 1769, having completed his medical training, and was named professor of chemistry in the College of Philadelphia, where he published the first American textbook on chemistry.

Rush strongly supported colonial rights and became involved in pre-Revolutionary political movements in Pennsylvania. Rush was one of the signers of the Declaration of

Source: Rush, B. (1967). *Medical inquiries and observations upon the diseases of the mind* (facsimile edition). New York: Hafner. [Original work published in 1812 by Kimber & Richardson, Philadelphia.]

Independence in 1776, and in 1777 he was named a surgeon general in the Continental Army. When he returned to Philadelphia at the end of the Revolutionary War, he continued his academic duties and joined the staff of the Pennsylvania Hospital (the first hospital in the American colonies, established in 1752), where he remained until his death in 1813.

In keeping with the spirit of the revolutionary times in which he lived, Rush had faith in the potential of all people and in the possibility of social progress. He was an advocate of better education for those who were typically denied educational opportunities: slaves, the poor, Native Americans, and women. He crusaded actively against slavery. He opened the first free medical dispensary in the United States. He argued for penal reform and urged the creation of hospitals for alcoholics and higher education facilities for women. Rush proposed establishing a cabinet position for a Secretary of Peace in the United States government.[1]

Rush was also an advocate for the humane treatment of the mentally ill. When his career in medicine began, Rush's views on the treatment of mental illness were quite traditional. This treatment, if it is fair to call it that, consisted mostly of very basic physical care and the use of methods that punished a person for inappropriate behavior or ideas, in the hope of jolting the patient into sanity. Occasionally, it seemed to do so. As Rush learned more about the treatment methods being used in Europe, however, he was persuaded that humane treatment was not only more moral, but also more effective. He put some of Pinel's (1806/1977) practices in place at Philadelphia Hospital and developed additional humane methods of treatment of his own.

In describing treatments for various mental disorders, Rush (1812) emphasized things that are considered good for everyone. This was the heart of the "moral treatment" that was gaining favor at the time. Good food, opportunities for exercise, interesting activities or amusements to engage in, and opportunities to socialize and to have privacy were parts of many of the regimes he described. Rush also had a certain cleverness, some say trickiness, in his treatment methods. He describes a patient who believed that he had a living animal inside his body. This man, like others with similar symptoms, was perfectly rational and reasonable in all other beliefs. In treating such a patient, Rush suggested that one should give the patient a medicine said to have the power to destroy the animal. Then, a dead animal of the species he believes to be inhabiting his body should be "secretly conveyed into his close stool" (his chamber pot) (Rush, 1812, p. 109). Problem solved. In discussing the prevention of suicide, Rush tells the following story. A gentleman went into a tavern with a loaded pistol and the intention to destroy himself. To conceal this intention he ordered a decanter of wine. He then locked the room and cocked his pistol. He decided to try the wine before discharging the pistol, and liked it so much that he had a second, then a third glass, and finally finished the whole decanter. He felt much better and abandoned thoughts of suicide (Rush, 1812, p. 128–129). Distraction is sometimes useful, and alternatives can be helpful. Rush very rarely advocated the use of intoxication in treatment, however.

Although Rush introduced more humane care into the Philadelphia Hospital's treatments of the insane, he retained some old-fashioned methods of treatment as well, especially blood-letting. Even those who praise Rush's work in reforming the treatments offered at the hospital question why he continued to use blood-letting when most other physicians considered it

---

[1] Biographical information is from Alexander and Selesnick (1966) and Carlson (1972).

ineffectual. One reason may just be habit; another that, because Rush believed that mental illness is related to the blood vessels in the brain, he couldn't help but believe that blood-letting would be therapeutic. Rush also advocated the use of some other old-fashioned or harsh treatments when nothing else seemed to be working or when the patient could not be brought under control by ordinary medical or psychological means. He devised a strait chair (kinder than a straitjacket), poured cold water down patients' sleeves, rotated them in his gyrator, or, in extreme cases of violence or abuse by patients, threatened them with being put in chains. He emphasized that these methods were rarely needed, and when they were needed, they were usually needed only once.

Rush believed that an understanding and appreciation of the "intellectual faculties of man" (i.e., the mind) was a necessity for all physicians, not just for those working with the mentally disordered.

[Knowledge of the mind] should be the *vade mecum* of every physician. It opens to him many new duties. It is calculated to teach him, that in feeling the pulse, inspecting the eyes and tongue, examining the state of the excre-

> *vade mecum:* a manual or guidebook that can be carried around

tions, he performs but half his duty in a sick room. To render his prescriptions successful, he should pry into the state of his patient's mind, and so regulate his conduct and conversation as to aid the operation of his physical remedies. (Rush [1792], quoted in Carlson, 1972, p. viii)

He took a particular interest in understanding the role of the mind in the development and treatment of mental illness. In the reading below Rush describes the causes of intellectual derangement. He divides the causes into those that are completely physical, those that involve the body's influence on the mind, and those that seem to be the result of the mind's influence on the body. He also describes demographic and situational factors that relate to the development of mental disorders. Although Rush describes many causes that seem purely psychological, he believed that the brain is always involved in madness, for in these cases the mind is influencing the activity of the brain. Rush's descriptions are very readable, and he is skilled in presenting case histories in an interesting and compelling way. In spite of a difference of two centuries, most of the people and the problems he describes make sense and seem at least slightly familiar.

Benjamin Rush did much to increase and shape the interest in insanity within the medical community in the United States. His approach is accessible, and he was able to deal with difficult issues with skill and sensitivity. He is considered the first American psychiatrist.

. . .

They [the causes of intellectual derangement] have been divided . . . into such as act, *directly* upon the body; and . . . such as act *indirectly* upon the body, through the medium of the mind.

I. [There are] causes which act *directly* upon the brain. These are,

læsions: lesions

Malconformation and læsions of the brain. . . . 5

Certain local disorders, induced by enlargement of bone, tumors, abscesses, and water in the brain.

Certain diseases of the brain, particularly apoplexy, palsy, epilepsy, vertigo, and headache. It occurs but rarely from the last of those causes.

insolation: exposure to the sun's rays

Insolation. Two cases of madness from this cause 10 occurred under my care between July 1807, and February 1808.

Certain odours. There is a place in Scotland where madness is sometimes induced by the fumes of lead. Patients who are affected with it bite their hands, and tear their flesh upon the other parts of their bodies. . . . An ingenious dyer, in this city, informed me 15 that he often observed the men who were employed in dying blue, of which colour indigo is the basis, to become peevish, and low spirited, and never even to hum a tune, while engaged at their work. 20

Indigo is both the name of a shade of blue (as in blue jeans) and the name of the dye that produces this color.

II. There are certain causes which induce madness, by acting upon the brain in common with the whole body. These are,

Gout, dropsy, consumption, pregnancy, and fevers of all kinds.

Inanition from profuse evacuations, or from a 25 defect of nourishment. . . .

inanition: empty; specifically, the condition resulting from an insufficiency of nourishment

When madness follows parturition, it is most commonly derived from this cause.

parturition: childbirth

The excessive use of ardent spirits. During the time Dr. Nicholas Waters acted as resident 30 physician and apothecary of the Pennsylvania Hospital, he instituted an inquiry at my request, into the proportion of maniacs from

ardent spirits: strong, alcoholic beverages

35 this cause, who were confined in the Hospital. They amounted to one-third of the whole number.

Inordinate sexual desires and gratifications. Several cases of madness from this cause have come under my notice.

40 Onanism. Four cases of madness occurred, in my practice, from this cause, between the years 1804 and 1807. It is induced more frequently by this cause in young men, than is commonly supposed by parents and physicians. The morbid effects of intemperance in a sexual intercourse with women are feeble, and of a transient nature, compared with the strain of physical and moral evils which this solitary vice fixes upon the body and 45 mind. . . .

onanism: masturbation

Great pain. . . .

Extremely hot and cold weather.

III. . . . Madness is induced by corporeal causes, which act sympathetically upon the brain. These are,

50 Certain narcotic substances, particularly opium, hemlock, night-shade, hen-bane, and acconitum, taken into the stomach.

hemlock, night-shade, hen-bane, acconitum: poisonous or narcotic plants

The suppression of any usual evacuation, such as the menses, lochia, milk, semen, or blood 55 from the hæmorrhoidal vessels.

lochia: the discharge from the uterus following childbirth

Worms in the alimentary canal.

Irritation from certain foreign matters retained in irritable parts of the body. . . . It has been brought on in one instance by decayed teeth, which were not accompanied with pain.

60 Madness is sometimes induced by what is called a metastasis of some other disease to the brain. These diseases are, dropsy . . . , consumption . . . . , St. Vitus's dance . . . , hysteria, . . . certain cutaneous eruptions . . . , 65 the measles. . . .

metastasis: transmission of pathogens from their original body site to a site or sites elsewhere

IV. . . . The causes which induce intellectual derangement, by acting upon the body through the medium of the mind, are of a direct and indirect nature.

the *understanding:* the intellectual faculty; the mind

antediluvian: old; literally, before the flood

faculty: Faculty psychology is an approach to the study of the mind that assumes that the mind has a fixed number of capacities or faculties such as will, intellect, reason, and memory. Its development is associated with Christian Wolff (1679–1754), a German philosopher. The most extreme version of the faculty approach was phrenology, a field developed by Franz Josef Gall (1758–1828) that was based on the idea that different faculties are located in different parts of the brain, and that by feeling the bumps on a person's head one can determine which of the person's abilities and characteristics are most developed. Gall's ideas were tested, and discredited, by Pierre Flourens (1794–1867) who removed parts of the brains of experimental animals and then looked for behavioral changes. Flourens's negative results led him to conclude that the localization Gall had described did not exist.

Rush relates madness to four particular faculties: imagination, memory, emotionality, and morality.

A. The causes which act directly upon the understanding are,

1. Intense study, whether of the sciences or of the mechanical arts, and whether of real or imaginary objects of knowledge. The latter more frequently produce madness than the former. They are, chiefly, the means of discovering perpetual motion; of converting the base metals into gold; of prolonging life to the antediluvian age; of producing perfect order and happiness in morals and government, by the operations of human reason; and, lastly, researches into the meaning of certain prophesies in the Old and New Testaments. . . . 70 75

2. The frequent and rapid transition of the mind from one subject to another. It is said booksellers have sometimes become deranged from this cause. . . . The brain in these cases is deprived of the benefit of habit, which prevents fatigue to a certain extent. . . . 80

B. [Cases in which] . . . the understanding is affected chiefly in an indirect manner.

1. Through the medium of the imagination. It is conveyed into the understanding from this faculty, in all those people who become deranged from inordinate schemes of ambition or avarice. Mad-houses, in every part of the world, exhibit instances of persons who have become insane from this cause. The great extent and constant exercises of the imagination in poets, accounts for their being occasionally affected with this disease. 85 90

2. The understanding is sometimes affected with madness through the medium of the memory. Dr. Zimmerman relates the case of a Swiss clergyman, in whom derangement was induced by undue labour in committing his sermons to memory. 95

3. But madness is excited in the understanding most frequently by impressions that act primarily upon the heart. I shall enumerate some of these impressions, and afterwards mention such instances of their morbid effects as I have met with in the course of my reading and observations. 100 105

They are joy, terror, love, fear, grief, distress, shame from offended delicacy, defamation, calumny, ridicule, absence from native country, the loss of liberty, property, and beauty, gaming, and inordinate love of praise, domestic tyranny, and, lastly, the complete gratification of every wish of the heart.

> *calumny:* false charge, intended to damage another's reputation; a slanderous report

- Extravagant joy produced madness in many of the successful adventurers in the South-Sea speculation in England, in the year 1720. . . .
- Terror has often induced madness in persons who have escaped from fire, earthquakes, and shipwreck. . . .
- Where is the mad-house that does not contain patients from neglected or disappointed love?
- Fear often produces madness, Dr. Brambilla tells us, in new recruits in the Austrian army.
- Grief induced madness which continued fifty years, in . . . Hannah Lewis, formerly a patient in the Pennsylvania Hospital. . . .
- An exquisite sense of delicacy, Dr. Burton says, produced madness in a school-master, who was accidentally discovered upon a close-stool by one of his scholars.

> Giovanni Alessandro Brambilla (1728–1800) was the chief surgeon of the Imperial Austrian Army and the first director of the surgical academy in Vienna. He is known for his innovative surgical techniques.

- . . . history informs us of ministers of state and generals of armies having often languished away their lives in a state of partial derangement, in consequence of being unjustly dismissed by their sovereigns.

> *close-stool:* a chamber pot in a stool or box

- A player destroyed himself in Philadelphia, in the year 1803, soon after being hissed off the stage.
- The Swiss soldiers sometimes languish and die from that form of madness which is brought on by absence from their native country. . . .

It is remarkable, this disease is most commonly among the natives of countries that are the least desirable for beauty, fertility, climate, or the luxuries of life. They resemble in this respect, in their influence upon the human heart, the artificial objects of taste which are at first disagreeable, but which from habit take a stronger hold upon the appetite than such as are natural and agreeable.

- The Africans become insane, we are told, in some instances, soon after they enter upon the toils of perpetual slavery in the West Indies.
- Hundreds have become insane in consequence of unexpected losses of money. It is remarkable this disease occurs oftener among the rich who lose only a part of their property, than among persons in moderate circumstances, who lose their all. . . .
- The son of a late celebrated author in England became deranged in consequence of the severe treatment he received from his father in the course of his education. Several

instances of madness, induced by the cruel or unjust conduct of school masters and guardians to the persons who were the subjects of their power and care, are to be met with in the records of medicine. . . .

- Two instances are upon record, of persons who destroyed themselves immediately after drawing high prizes in a lottery. In all these cases death was the effect of derangement. 150

4. The understanding is sometimes deranged through the medium of the moral faculties. A conscience burdened with guilt, whether real or imaginary, is a frequent cause of madness. The latter produces it much oftener than the former.

An instance of insanity occurred in a married woman in this city some years ago, of the most exemplary character, from a belief that she had been unfaithful to the marriage bed. . . . There is further a morbid sensibility in the conscience in some people, that predisposes to madness from the most trifling causes. . . . 155

The most distressing grade of derangement under this head is, where real guilt, and a diseased imagination, concur in producing it. The occasional acts of self-mutilation which deranged patients sometimes inflict upon themselves, and the painful and protracted austerities voluntarily imposed upon the body in Catholic countries, appear to be the effects of the combined operation of these two causes upon the understanding. 160

But we sometimes observe intellectual derangement to occur from the moral faculties being unduly excited by supposed visions and revelations . . . 165

Let not religion be blamed for these cases of insanity. The tendency of all its doctrines and precepts is to prevent it from most of its mental causes. . . .

Philippe Pinel (1745–1826), like Rush, was a reformer. When he took over the Bicêtre and, later, the Salpêtrière hospitals in Paris, he removed the inmates' chains, closed the dungeons, and provided good food and opportunities for exercise. Pinel wrote about the etiology of insanity, the nature of different forms of madness, and the efficacy of various kinds of treatments (Pinel, 1806/1977).

Rush and Pinel had both been involved in national revolutions, and both the French and the American Revolutions were based on freedom and equality. The spirit of egalitarianism after the revolutions surely facilitated humane treatment of the mentally ill.

V. Intellectual derangement is more common from mental, than corporeal causes. Of 113 patients in the Bicêtre Hospital, in France, at one time, Mr. Pinel tells us 34 were from domestic misfortunes, 24 from disappointments in love, 30 from the distressing events of the French Revolution, and 25 from what he calls fanaticism, making in all the original number. I have taken pains to ascertain the proportion of mental and corporeal causes which have operated in producing madness in the Pennsylvania Hospital, but I am sorry to add, my success in this inquiry was less satisfactory than I wished. Its causes were concealed in some instances, and forgotten in others. Of 50 maniacs, the causes of whose disease were discovered by Dr. Moore and his assistant Mr. Jenney, in the month of April 1812, 7 were from disappointments, 170 175 180 185

chiefly in love; 7 from grief; 7 from the loss of property; 5 from erroneous opinions in religion; 2 from jealousy; 1 from terror; 1 from insolation; 1 from an injury to the head; 2 from repelled eruptions; 5 from intemperance; 3 from onanism; 2 from pregnancy; and 1 from fever; making in all 34 from mental, and 16 from corporeal causes. A predisposition to the disease was hereditary in but five of them.

> Rush says he is describing the causes of 50 cases of mania, but his numbers add up to only 44.

VI. I shall now mention all those circumstances in birth, certain peculiarities of the body, age, sex, condition and rank in life, intellect, occupation, climate, state of society, forms of government, revolutions, and religion, which predispose the body and mind to be acted upon by the remote and exciting causes that have been mentioned, so as to favour the production of madness.

A. A peculiar and hereditary sameness of organization of the nerves, brain, and blood-vessels, on which I said formerly the predisposition to madness depended, sometimes pervades whole families, and renders them liable to this disease from a transient or feeble operation of its causes. . . .

There are several peculiarities which attend this disease, where the predisposition to it is hereditary, which deserve our notice.

- It is excited by more feeble causes than in persons in whom this predisposition has been acquired.
- It generally attacks in those stages of life in which it has appeared in the patient's ancestors. . . .
- Children born previously to the attack of madness in their parents are less liable to inherit it than those who are born after it.
- Dr. Burton, in his Anatomy of Melancholy, remarks, that children born of parents who are in the decline of life, are more predisposed to one of the forms of partial insanity than children born under contrary circumstances.

> Robert Burton (1577–1640) was an English cleric. His *Anatomy of Melancholy* (Burton, 1621/2001) is much more than a book about depression and is still widely read.

- A predisposition to certain diseases seated in parts contiguous to the seat of madness, often descends from parents to their children. Thus we sometimes see madness in a son whose father or mother had been afflicted only with . . . habitual head-ache. . . .
- . . . I have wished to discover whether there be any peculiarity of shape in the skulls of mad people that predisposed to derangement, for which purpose I requested Dr. Vandyke, in the year 1810, to examine the dimensions of the heads of all the insane patients in our hospital in several different directions, and afterwards to measure in the same way the heads of a number of patients, belonging to the Hospital, with other diseases. The result of this inquiry was a discovery that there was no departure but in one instance from the ordinary and natural shape of the head, in between sixty and seventy mad people.

B. A predisposition to madness is said to be connected with dark coloured hair. Mr. Haslam 225
informs us that this was the case in two hundred and five out of two hundred and sixty-five
patients in the Bethlehem Hospital. He intimates that it was possibly from their consisting
chiefly of the natives of England, in whom that colour of the hair is very general; but the same
connection between madness and dark coloured hair has been discovered in the maniacs in
the Pennsylvania Hospital, who consist of persons from three or four different countries, or of 230
descendants who inherit their various physical characters. Of nearly seventy patients, who were
examined at my request, by Dr. Vandyke, in our Hospital, in the year 1810 . . . all except one, had
dark coloured hair. . . .

There is a greater predisposition to madness between twenty and fifty, than in any of the
previous or subsequent years of human life. Of the correctness of this remark, Mr. Pinel has
furnished us with the following proof. Of 1201 persons who were admitted into the Bicêtre 235
Hospital, in France, between the years 1784 and 1794, 955 were between the two ages that
have been mentioned. 65 were between fifteen and twenty, 131 were between fifty and sixty,
and 51 between sixty and seventy-one. . . . From the state of the body and mind within those
periods, it is easy to account for this being the case. The blood-vessels and the nerves are
then in a highly excitable state, and the former readily assume morbid or inflammatory action 240
from the remote and exciting causes of disease. The mind too, within those years, possesses
more sensibility, and of course is more easily acted upon by mental irritants, the sources of
which from family afflictions, and disappointments in the pursuits of business, pleasure and
ambition, are more numerous in those years, than in any of the previous or subsequent
stages of life. 245

Madness, it has been said, seldom occurs under puberty. . . . The reason why children and
persons under puberty are so rarely affected with madness must be ascribed to mental impressions . . . being too transient in their effects, from the instability of their minds, to excite their
brains into permanently diseased actions. It is true, children are often affected with delirium,
but this is a symptom of general fever, which is always induced . . . by corporeal causes. 250

From the records of the Bicêtre Hospital, in France, it appears that madness rarely occurs in
old age. . . . It has been said that maniacs seldom live to be old. . . . There are two reasons why
this disease so rarely attacks old people. Their blood-vessels lose their vibratility from age . . .
and . . . the diminution of sensibility in their nerves and brains. . . . [T]hey revert to that state
which takes place in children, and which I have said protects them from the frequent occur- 255
rence of this disease.

Women, in consequence of the greater predisposition imparted to their bodies by men-
struation, pregnancy, and parturition, and to their minds, by living so much alone in their
families, are more predisposed to madness than men. . . . . Of 8874 patients admitted into the
Bethlehem Hospital in London, between the years 1748 and 1794, four thousand eight hun- 260
dred and thirty-two were women; nearly a fifth more than men. In St. Luke's Hospital in
London, the proportion of women to men who have been admitted in a given number of
years is in the ratio of three to two. But this disproportion of women to men, who are affected
with madness, is by no means universal. In a Hospital for mad people in Vienna, one hundred
and seventeen men were admitted in a given number of years, and but ninety-four women. 265

In a Hospital of the same kind at Berlin, twice as many males were admitted in a given time as females. More of the former than of the latter have been admitted into the Pennsylvania Hospital. In all these cases accidental circumstances, such as the want of accommodations suited to female delicacy, or deep rooted prejudices against public mad-houses, and a pref-
270 erence of such as are private, may have lessened the proportion of women in the above instances, while the evils of war, bankruptcy, and habits of drinking, which affect men more than women, and which vary in their influence upon the mind in different countries, may have produced more instances of madness in the former than in the latter sex. Perhaps it would be correct to say, women are more subject to madness from natural causes, and men from such
275 as are artificial.

... The distressing impressions made upon the minds of women frequently vent themselves in tears, or in hysterical commotions in the nervous system, and bowels, while the same impressions upon the minds of men pass by their more compact nervous and muscular fibres, and descend into the brain, and thus more fre-
280 quently bring on hypochondriac insanity. If this remark be correct, it will confirm Dr. Heberden's assertion, that men are more disposed to suicide than women, for it necessarily follows their being most subject to that state of madness. ...

> Heberden is probably William Heberden the elder (1710–1801), an English physician renowned for his clinical acumen.

285 Single persons are more predisposed to madness than married people. Of seventy-two insane patients in the Pennsylvania Hospital, whose condition ... was ascertained by my young friends Dr. Moore and Mr. Jenny, in the month of April 1812, forty-two had never been married, and five were widows and widowers, at the time they became deranged.

The absence of real and present care, which gives the mind leisure to look back upon past,
290 and to anticipate future and imaginary evils, and the inverted operation of all the affections of the heart upon itself, together with the want of relief in conjugal sympathy from the inevitable distresses and vexations of life, and for which friendship is a cold and feeble substitute, are probably the reasons why madness occurs more frequently in single than in married people. Celibacy it has been said is a pleasant breakfast, a tolerable dinner, but a very bad supper. The
295 last comparison will appear to be an appropriate one, when we consider further, that the supper is not only of a bad quality, but eaten alone. No wonder it sometimes becomes a pre-disposing cause of madness.

The rich are more predisposed to madness than the poor, from their exposing a larger sur-face of sensibility to all its remote and exciting causes. Even where mental sensibility is the same
300 in both those classes of people, the disease is prevented in the latter, by the constant pressure of bodily suffering, from labour, cold, and hunger. These present evils defend their minds from such as are past and anticipated; and these are the principal causes of madness. When it occurs in poor people, it is generally the effect of corporeal causes.

"Great wit, and madness" are said by Dryden "to be nearly allied." If he meant by this affin-
305 ity between wit and madness, the rapid exercises of the mind in associating similar and dis-similar ideas or words which are peculiar to both, the remark is a correct one; but if he meant that great Wits are more predisposed to madness than other people, the remark is opposed by

all that is known of the solidity of understanding, and correctness of conversation and conduct of Butler, Chesterfield, Franklin, Johnson, and many other distinguished men, who possessed the talent of wit in an eminent degree. Nor is the remark true if the term wit be intended to des- 310 ignate men of great understandings. Their minds are sometimes worn away by intense and protracted study, but they are rarely perverted by madness.... Where madness has been induced by intense and protracted application to books, it has generally been in persons of weak intellects who were unable to comprehend the subjects of their studies.

Certain occupations predispose to madness more than others. Pinel says, poets, painters, 315 sculptors and musicians, are most subject to it, and that he never knew an instance of it in a chemist, a naturalist, a mathematician, or a natural philosopher. The reason of this will be understood by recollecting what was said under the preceding head. The studies of the former exercise the imagi- 320

natural philosopher: natural scientist

nation, and the passions, while the studies of the latter interest the understanding only. Dr. Arnold tells us, he has observed mechanics to be more affected with madness than merchants and members of the learned professions. This may arise from the vague and distracting exertions of genius, unassisted by education; or from corporeal causes, to which their employments expose them more than the classes of men that have been mentioned.... More farmers it has been said 325 become deranged than persons of the same grade of intellect and independence in cities. If this be the case, it must be ascribed to the greater solitude of their lives, more especially in the winter season, and to their being more exposed from labour and accidents, to its corporeal causes.

Certain climates predispose to madness. It is very uncommon in such as are uniformly warm. Dr. Gordon informed me in his visit to Philadelphia in the year 1807, that he had never seen, nor 330 heard of a single case of madness during a resi-dence of six years in the province of Berbice. It is a rare disease in the West Indies. While great and con-stant heat increase the irritability of the muscles, it gradually lessens the sensibility of the nerves and 335

Berbice: former Dutch colony in Guyana, South America

mind, and the irritability of the blood-vessels, and in these I formerly supposed the predisposition to madness to be seated. It is more common in climates alternately warm and cold, but most so, in such as are generally moist and cold, and accompanied at the same time with a cloudy sky. Instances of it are said to be most frequent in England in the month of November, at which time the weather is unusually gloomy from the above causes. Even the transient occurrence of that kind 340 of weather in the United States has had an influence upon this disease. In the month of May in the year 1806 it prevailed to a great degree, during which time three patients in the Pennsylvania Hospital made unsuccessful attempts upon their lives, and a fourth destroyed himself....

Certain states of society, and certain opinions, pursuits, amusements, and forms of government, have a considerable influence in predisposing to 345 derangement. It is a rare disease among savages. Baron Hombolt informed me, that he did not hear of a single instance of it among the uncivilized Indians

Alexander von Humboldt (1769–1859) was a Prussian naturalist and explorer.

in South America. Infidelity and atheism are frequent causes of it in Christian countries. In commercial countries, where large fortunes are suddenly acquired and lost, madness is a common disease. It is most prevalent at those times when speculation is substituted to regular commerce. . . . In the United States, madness has increased since the year 1790. This must be ascribed chiefly to an increase in the number and magnitude of the objects of ambition and avarice, and to the greater joy or distress, which is produced by gratification or disappointments in the pursuit of each of them. . . . Sixteen persons perished from suicide in the city of New York, in the year 1804, in most of whom it was supposed to be the effect of madness, from the different and contrary events of speculation.

. . . Gaming is an occasional cause of madness in some countries. At Penang in the East Indies, where men often stake their wives upon the issue of a game, this disease is very common. The unfortunate gambler often rises from his seat in a fit of derangement, and sallies out into the street with instruments of murder in his hands. A bell is rung at this time, which drives people into their houses, to avoid being killed. . . . I have heard the greater frequency of madness in England, than in some other countries, ascribed in part to its inhabitants preferring tragedy to comedy, in their stage entertainments. . . .

. . . In a government in which all the power of a country is representative, and elective, a day of general suffrage, and free presses, serve, like chimnies in a house, to conduct from the individual and public mind, all the discontent, vexation, and resentment, which have been generated in the passions . . .

In despotic countries where the public passions are torpid, . . . madness is a rare disease. Of the truth of this remark I have been satisfied by Mr. Stewart, the pedestrian traveller, who spent some time in Turkey: also by Dr. Scott, who accompanied lord M'Cartney in his embassy to China . . . Dr. Scott informed me that he heard of but a single instance of madness in China . . .

> *torpid:* sluggish, inactive, apathetic

> John Stewart (d. 1822), was an English traveler and writer. Lord M'Cartney, was an Irish peer. George III sent M'Cartney to China to open trade, but his mission was a failure.

Mr. Carr, in his Northern Summer [1805], tells us, that madness is an uncommon disease in Russia. It is a rare thing, says this professional traveller, to see a Russian peasant angry. He even persuades and reasons with his horse, when he wishes him to quicken his gait. It is to the long protracted civil and ecclesiastical tyranny of the late government of Spain, that we must ascribe the small number of maniacs in all the hospitals in that country. They amounted, according to Mr. Townsend, in the year 1786, to but 664, in a population which produces in Great Britain between 4,000 and 5,000; 2,600 of whom are in the city and neighbourhood of London. Habits of oppression in all those cases expend the excitability of the passions, and prevent their reacting upon the brain. But in some instances the understanding decays with the passions, in despotic countries. This state of the mind has been called fatuity. . . .

> John Carr (1772–1832) was an English traveler and writer.

fatuity: utter foolishness, inanity

Constantin François Chasseboeuf, Comte de Volney (1757–1820), French philosopher and historian

Revolutions in governments which are often accompanied with injustice, cruelty, and the loss of property and friends; and where this is not the case, with an inroad upon ancient and deep-seated principles and habits, frequently multiply instances of insanity. Mr. Volney informed me, in his visit to this city in the year 1799, that there were three times as many cases of madness in Paris in the year 1795, as there were before the commencement of the French Revolution. It was induced, I shall say hereafter, in several instances, by the events of the American Revolution. 390 395 400

Different religions, and different tenets of the same religion are more or less calculated to induce a predisposition to madness. Dr. Shebbeare says there are fewer instances of suicide (which is generally the effect of madness) in catholic, than in protestant countries. He ascribes it to the facility with which the catholics relieve their minds from the pressure of guilt, by means of confession and absolution. This assertion and the reasoning founded upon it are rendered doubtful by 150 suicides having taken place in the catholic city of Paris in the year 1782, and but 32 in the same year in the protestant city of London. It is probable however the greater proportion of infidels in the former, than in the latter city at 405

infidel: an unbeliever, one with no religious beliefs

that time, may have occasioned the difference in the number of deaths in the two places, for suicide will naturally follow small degrees of insanity, where there are no habits of moral order from religion, and no belief in a future state. Dr. Shebbeare's assertion 410

is rendered still less probable, by considering the usual effects of solitude upon the human mind, and this we know acts with peculiar force in the cells of monks and nuns. . . . Of between 240 and 250 deranged people, who were confined at one time in a mad-house in the city of Mexico, Mr. Roxas informed me, in a great majority of them the disease had been contracted in those recluse and gloomy situations. . . . 415

I shall conclude the history of the remote exciting and predisposing causes of madness by the following remarks. 420

Rush's descriptions here anticipate the diathesis-stress model now used in discussions of mental illness. Diathesis refers to inherited predisposition, and a psychological disorder is seen as the result of the interaction between stress and this predisposition.

1. Its remote causes generally induce predisposing debility. Its exciting causes more commonly induce that morbid excitement in the blood-vessels of the brain in which madness is seated, but the sudden and violent action of a remote cause is often sufficient for that purpose without the aid of an existing cause. 425

Both the remote and exciting causes of madness produce their morbid effects more certainly, promptly, or slowly, according as the system is more or less predisposed to the disease by the causes formerly mentioned. 430

The predisposing causes of madness sometimes act with so much force, as to induce it without the perceptible co-operation of either a remote or an exciting cause. The remote causes of madness likewise act with so much force in some instances as to induce it without the perceptible cooperation of a predisposing or exciting cause.

435   The predisposing causes of madness in like manner sometimes act with so much force as to induce it without the perceptible co-operation of a remote or an exciting cause.

> The following is from a later chapter of the book (pp. 243–244).
> Rush is writing about humane care.

In reviewing the slender and inadequate means that have been employed for ameliorating the condition of mad people, we are led . . . to lament the slower progress of humanity in its efforts to relieve them, than any other class of the afflicted children of men. For many centuries

440   they have been treated like criminals, or shunned like beasts of prey; or, if visited, it has been only for the purposes of inhuman curiosity and amusement. Even the ties of consanguinity have been dissolved by the walls of a mad house, and sons and brothers have sometimes languished . . . away

> *consanguinity:* relation by blood, family

445   their lives within them, without once hearing the accents of a kindred voice. Happily these times of cruelty to this class of our fellow-creatures, and insensibility to their sufferings, are now passing away. . . . A . . . change has taken place in the Pennsylvania Hospital, under the direction of its present managers, in the condition of the deranged subjects of their care. The clanking of chains, and the noise of the whip, are no longer heard in their cells. They now taste of the bless-

450   ings of air, and light and motion, in pleasant and shaded walks in summer, and in spacious entries, warmed by stoves in winter, in both of which the sexes are separated, and alike protected from the eye of the visitors of the hospital. In consequence of these advantages they have recovered the human figure, and, with it, their long forgotten relationship to their friends and the public. Much, however, remains yet to be done for their comfort and relief. To animate us

455   in filling up the measure of kindness which has been solicited for them, let us recollect the greatness of its object. It is not to feed nor clothe the body, nor yet to cure one of its common diseases; it is to restore the disjointed or debilitated faculties of the mind of a fellow-creature . . .

> And, finally, from another chapter, Rush describes the joy
> he feels in the progress he has seen (p. 97).

After the history that has been given of the distress, despair, and voluntary death, which are induced by that partial derangement which has been described, I should lay down my pen, and

460   bedew my paper with my tears, did I not know that the science of medicine has furnished a remedy for it, and that hundreds are now alive, and happy, who were once afflicted with it.

Blessed science! which thus extends its friendly empire, not only over the evils of the bodies, but over those of the minds, of the children of men!

FOR DISCUSSION

1. Rush speaks of madness where his 21st-century counterparts speak of mental illness. To what extent is this merely a change in terminology, and to what extent does it reflect a substantive change in our understanding of the sources and meaning of abnormal behavior?

2. What do you think Rush might have said in response to Samuel Guze's (6.6) remarks on biological psychiatry?

3. What kinds of evidence does Rush use to support his views on the causes of madness? In what ways is his analysis scientific, and in what ways is it not?

Henry J. Wegrocki (1909–1967)
A Critique of Cultural and Statistical Concepts of Abnormality (1939)

A great deal of anthropological data became available to researchers in the late 19th and early 20th centuries, and some of the behaviors in other cultures looked very strange and even maladaptive to those who observed them. Western psychologists and anthropologists were unsure when to consider these behaviors pathological and when to consider them normal for that culture. There were many opinions, and passionate debates filled the professional literature for decades.

In the reading below Henry Wegrocki takes up the question of how we can know when behavior is the result of psychopathology. Using anthropological data and good sense, Wegrocki does away with some views that were common in the early 20th century, and he leaves us with a very reasonable way to begin to think about the concept of abnormality and abnormal behavior. Wegrocki's article lays to rest certain possibilities, ties up loose ends, and makes sense of seemingly contradictory findings. He does a masterly job of working adroitly through a great deal of data and theory to make sense of a difficult issue.

Wegrocki received his PhD in psychology from Columbia University in 1940. Much of his professional writing dealt with issues in psychoanalysis, but in this classic article he tackles a more general question and provides some valuable answers.

Source: Wegrocki, H. J. (1939). A critique of cultural and statistical concepts of abnormality. *Journal of Abnormal and Social Psychology, 34,* 166–178.

envisagement: image or conceptualization of something

ethnology: scientific study of human cultures

salutary: improving, remedial

plastic: capable of being shaped or changed

depth psychology: This usually refers to psychoanalysis but can also refer to other therapeutic approaches that emphasize the role of the unconscious.

One of the most significant contributions to a proper orientation and envisagement of human behavior has been the body of data coming in the past few decades from the field of ethnological research. Human behavior had so long been seen in terms of the categories of Western civilization that a critical evaluation of cultures other than our own could not help exercising a salutary effect on the ever-present tendency to view a situation in terms of familiar classifications. The achievement of a realization that the categories of social structure and function are ever plastic and dynamic, that they differ with varying cultures and that one culture cannot be interpreted or evaluated in terms of the categories of another, represents as tremendous an advance in the study of social behavior as did the brilliant insight of Freud [3.3, 4.5] in the field of depth psychology.

Wundt (1900–1920) [1.3] to some extent, but especially Boas (1919), have emphasized this approach continuously. One may say that most of the "mistakes" of earlier anthropologists have been due to the tendency of seeing the features of other cultures simply in terms of the categories of Western civilization and forming, consequently, a distorted impression of those features, whether they relate to religion, marriage, or some other aspect of social life.

In connection with this modern ethnological conception of the relativity of interpretations and standards, there has arisen the problem of whether the standard of what constitutes abnormality is a relative or an absolute one. Foley (1935) infers from the ethnological material at hand that abnormality is a relative concept and criticizes Benedict (1934a), who seems to present evidence for the "statistical or relativity theory" yet "at times appears inconsistent in seeking for an absolute and universal criterion of abnormality." Briefly, the evidence from Benedict can be subsumed under three headings: (a) behavior considered abnormal in our culture but normal in other societal configurations; (b) types of abnormalities not occurring in Western civilization; and (c) behavior considered normal in our society but abnormal in others.

(a) Of "our" type of abnormal behavior considered normal in other cultures, Benedict gives, as an example, that of the Northwest Coast Indians whom Boas has studied at first hand. "All existence is seen in this culture in terms of an insult-complex." This complex is not only condoned but culturally reënforced. When the self-esteem and prestige of the chief is injured, he either arranges a "potlatch" ceremony or goes headhunting. The injury to his prestige is a

Indians whom Boas has studied: the Kwakiutl

function of the prevalent insult-complex. Almost anything is an insult. It may be the victory of a rival chief in a potlatch competition; it may be the accidental death of a wife, or a score of other situations, all of which are interpreted as having a reference to the individual.

45   If, on the other hand, he has been bested in competition with a rival chief, he will arrange a potlatch ceremony in which he gives away property to his rival, at the same time declaiming a recitative in which there is "an uncensored self-
50 glorification and ridicule of the opponent that is hard to equal outside of the monologue of the abnormal." . . .

    Among other "abnormal" traits which are an integral part of some culture patterns, ethno-
55 logical literature mentions the Dobuans (Fortune, 1932), who exhibit an "unnatural" degree of fear and suspicion; the Polynesians, who regard their chief as tabu to touch, allegedly because of a prevalent "défense de
60 toucher" neurosis; the Plains Indians with their religiously colored visual and auditory hallucinations; the Yogis with their trance states; and the frequent institutionalizations of homosexuality, whether in the religions of different cul-
65 tures (e.g., shamans of North Siberia or Borneo) or in their social structures (e.g., the berdache of American Indian tribes or the homosexual youth of Grecian-Spartan antiquity).

> *declaiming:* speaking loudly and vehemently
>
> *recitative:* a style used in opera in which text is declaimed in the rhythm of natural speech with slight melodic variation

> *Dobuans:* those living on the island of Dobu in eastern New Guinea

> *hallucination:* experience of an imagined sensory experience as if it were real

> *shaman:* one who can enter a trance (cataleptic) state and has the ability to heal and to foretell the future
>
> *berdache:* a Native American (usually male) who assumes the identity and social status of the opposite sex

70   (b) The second argument in favor of the cultural envisagement of abnormality is the existence of "styles" of abnormalities which presumably do not occur in our Western type of cultures. The "arctic hysteria" noted by Czaplicka (1914) and its tropical correlative "lâttah" (Clifford; 1897, 1898) with their picture of echolalia, echopraxia and uncontrolled expression of obscenities, as well as the "amok" seizure of the Malayan world, are given as examples.

> *arctic hysteria:* a form of disordered behavior observed in aboriginal Siberia. It takes somewhat different forms in different tribes and is observed most frequently in women and in the dark season. The most common form is ämürakh, similar to lâttah (Czaplicka, 1914).

(Continued)

(Continued)

lâttah (or *latah*): "Hypersensitivity to sudden fright, often with echolalia, echopraxia, command obedience, and dissociative or trancelike behavior" (American Psychiatric Association, *DSM-IV-TR*, 2000). It is observed mostly among middle-aged women.

   echolalia: compulsive repetition of words or phrases spoken by another

   echopraxia: compulsive repetition of gestures or movements made by another

amok: "A dissociative episode characterized by a period of brooding followed by an outburst of violent, aggressive, or homicidal behavior . . . [that] seems to be prevalent only among males." (American Psychiatric Association, *DSM-IV-TR*, 2000)

(c) Of normal behavior in our culture considered abnormal in others Benedict mentions as most conspicuous the role of personal initiative and drive in our own as compared with the Zuni culture. Among the Zuni Indians, for example, "the individual with undisguised initiative and greater drive than his fellows is apt to be branded a witch and hung up by his thumbs." Similarly, what seems to us a perfectly normal pattern of behavior—acquisitiveness, for example—would be looked upon by the potlatch celebrants as just a little "queer." For them, possession of property is secondary to the prestige they acquire when they distribute it.

These are then, briefly, the bases for the assertion that abnormality is a relative concept, differing from culture to culture; . . . it gains meaning only in terms of the social milieu in which it is considered.

The question of what are the differentia of normality and abnormality is of course the crux of the problem. Is the concept of abnormality culturally defined? Is that which is *regarded* as abnormal or normal in a particular culture the *only* criterion for calling a behavior pattern such? Foley, for whom abnormality is a purely statistical concept, would answer in a positive manner and points to Benedict's example of the Northwest

> *paranoia*: delusions (false beliefs), especially of persecution, reference, and grandeur

Coast Indians who institutionalize "paranoia." Let us, however, consider this "institutionalization of paranoia," as well as some of the other bits of evidence, critically.

Is it not stretching the point to call the Indians' megalomaniac activities and beliefs delusions in the sense that the paranoiac in the psychopathic institution has his beliefs called delusions? Macfie Campbell (1926) states that "the delusions of the ill-balanced and the beliefs of the orthodox are more closely akin than is usually recognized," and we cannot separate the two as sharply as we would wish to do. The abnormal delusion proper is, however, an attempt of the personality to deal with a conflict-producing situation, and the delusion "like fever, becomes an attempt by nature at cure." The patient's delusion is an internal resolution of a problem; it is his way of meeting the intolerable situation. That is why it is abnormal. It represents a spontaneous protective device of the personality,

something which is not learned. It is a crystallization of something which hitherto had been
prepotent. The individual's personality thereafter refracts and reflects in terms of a distorted
slant.

> *prepotent:* here, latent
> *refract:* deflect or alter
> *reflect:* throw or bend back

The Haida chief, upon the death of a member
of his family, also experiences a certain tension.
He resolves this tension, however, in a way
which is not only socially sanctioned but socially
determined. His reaction is not something spon-

> *Haida:* Northwest Coast Indians, similar in
> social organization to the Kwakiutl

taneous arising out of the nuclear substrate of his instinctive life. It is not a crystallization
in a certain direction of some previously unrealized protective potentialities of the psyche.
His reaction is pre-determined socially. Since his milieu expects that reaction of him, he
acts upon that expectation when the situation arises. Of course it is possible that historically the behavior may have had and must have had some spontaneous protective significance—most likely imbedded deeply in a web of primitive beliefs about magic practices.
Yet the modern Alaskan chief, unlike his distant prototype, has no conflicts of doubt about
the likelihood that malignant forces have caused the death of some member of his family;
he *knows,* and he acts upon that knowledge by venting his emotions. There is no permanent change in his personality when a tension-producing situation arises. Emotions are
aroused and appeased with no change in the personality profile.

In the personality of one who is labelled "abnormal" this change is, however, to be found.
There is always "the way he was before" and "the way he is now," regardless of the fact that a
present symptomatological picture had its roots in a prepotent substrate which would make
for a particular personality outline. This is not true
of the Haida Chief, in whom the "delusions" of reference and grandeur are externally imposed patterns. A Northwest Coast Indian, if given the
opportunity for a naturalistic investigation of the
situations that provoke his "paranoid" reactions—
as, for example, through an education—could
unlearn his previous emotional habits or at the
least modify them. He is capable of insight; the

> *delusion of reference:* false belief that
> others—other people, television characters,
> etc.—are speaking to or about you
>
> *delusion of grandeur:* false belief that you are
> a person of enormous power, influence, or
> importance

true paranoiac is usually beyond it. The latter, if he
kills the person who he thinks is persecuting him,
only temporarily resolves his difficulty; the Indian
chief who kills another family "to avenge the insult

> *affective:* related to the emotions

of his wife's death" achieves a permanent affective equilibration with regard to that incident.
His prestige restored, he once more enjoys his self-respect. The Haida defends imagined
assaults against his personal integrity only when some violent extra-personal event occurs. The
paranoid psychotic defends himself against imagined assaults even though there is no objective evidence of any.

The point that the writer would then emphasize is that the delusions of the psychotic and 145
the delusions of the Northwest Coast Indian cannot by any means be equated. Mechanisms like the conviction of grandeur are abnormal not by virtue of unique, abnormal qualia but by virtue of their *function in the total economy of the personality*. The true paranoiac reaction represents a *choice* 150
of the abnormal; the reaction of the Haida chief represents no such choice—there is but one path for him to follow. If one of the chief's men showed paranoid symptoms by proclaiming that *he* really was the chief of the tribe and that his lawful place was being usurped, the institutionalization of paranoid symptoms within that culture would not, I am sure, prevent the rest of the tribe from thinking him abnormal. 155

> qualia: subjective, experiential qualities

Fundamentally the same criticism might be applied to the "défense de toucher" neurosis supposedly exemplified by the Polynesian tabu on touching the chief. Here, as in paranoia, we must consider whether the mechanism is a cultural habit reënforced by emotional associations or whether it is a true morbid reaction. Obviously it is the former. Thus by reason of that fact it *is not* abnormal. As in the paranoia of the Haida, there is no choice here and consequently no conflict. If 160
a person is brought up with the idea that to touch the chief means death, his acting upon that idea in adulthood is not a neurosis but simply a habit. There is, in other words, the genetic aspect to true abnormality which cannot be evaded but which is overlooked when we speak of "abnormal" symptoms. The explanation of the *delusion of persecution* of the Dobu is of course subject to the same criticism, 165
which would hold likewise for trances, visions, the hearing of voices and hysterical seizures. When these are simply culturally reënforced pattern-suggestions, they are not abnormal in the true sense of the word. When the Plains Indian by a rigid physical regimen of 170
exhaustion and fatigue plus a liberal dose of suggestion achieves a vision, that achievement is not an abnormal reaction in the same sense that the visual hallucination of the *psychotic* is.

> delusion of persecution: the false belief that others are trying to harm you

> psychotic: someone who has lost touch with reality and is suffering from a serious mental disorder (psychosis)

A similar example presented as an argument for the cultural definition of abnormality is the 175
supposed institutionalization of homosexuality among different cultures. The difficulty with all discussions of this enormously complex topic is the lack of agreement among investigators as to the sense in which the homosexual is abnormal. Obviously, homosexuality is not the same type of morbid mental reaction as paranoia; in fact, it is not a morbid mental reaction at all. The abnormality of homosexuality exists at a different level; it is social and biological rather than 180
psychological.[1] Homosexuality as an abnormal form of behavior cannot be spoken of in the

---

[1] By this it is meant that homosexuality is not a compromise symptom due to a conflict, as is the case with paranoid manifestations. Whatever abnormality attaches to it is a secondary function due to the conflicts it creates in a social milieu. In short, it creates conflicts, it is not created by them. Only in those cases where it is used as an escape mechanism can it truly be called abnormal.

same sense in which one speaks of visual and auditory hallucinations or grandiose delusions. Sex inversion is rather a statistical type of abnor-

> *sex inversion:* homosexuality

185 mality. It represents extreme deviations from the norm and makes for the non-conformity which engenders social antagonism and ostracism in certain societies. We are not justified, then, in saying that certain cultures institutionalize this abnormality; because when we call homosexuality an abnormality in the same sense in which we speak of a delusion as abnormal, we are misusing the term and being inconsistent about its application.

190   The second point of view from which the cultural definition is sometimes argued is that there occur among different cultures abnormalities which are peculiar to them, as, for example, "arctic hysteria," "amok," "lâttah" *et al.* The untenability of this hypothesis becomes evident when a little analytic insight is applied to the phenomena considered. In his masterly analysis of the lâttah reaction, Van Loon (1927) has also,

195 the writer thinks, given a good explanation of "arctic hysteria." "Lâttah," he writes, "is chiefly a woman's complaint. The symptoms appear in consequence of a fright or some other sudden emotion; the startled patient screams" and exhibits

> Van Loon's description of the symptoms and psychic structure of lâttah is very similar to the description of arctic hysteria.

200 echolalia, echopraxia, shouting of obscenities and a strong feeling of fear and timidity. "The immediate cause of becoming lâttah the patients report to be a dream of a highly sexual nature which ends in the waking up of the dreamer with a start. The waking up is here a substitute for the dream activity, protecting the dreamer's consciousness against the repressed complex." The same analysis might be applied to "arctic hysteria," which seems to show all the lâttah

205 symptoms, although the occurrence of a sudden waking from sleep as the beginning of the complaint is nowhere reported.

       The amok type of seizure, Van Loon explains, is due to hallucinations of being attacked by men or animals and seems to be confined to men. Clifford (1897), on the other hand, considers amok from a genetic standpoint as having a

210 background of anger, grudge, excitement and mental irritation, what the Malay calls "sâkit hâti" (sickness of the liver). "A Malay loses something he values, his father dies, he has a quarrel—any of

> *Genetic* here refers to the cause or origin of the behavior, not to heredity

these things cause him 'sickness of the liver.' The state of feeling which drives the European to

215 suicide makes the Malay go amok." In the heat of the moment "he may strike his father, and the hatred of self which results, causes him to long for death and to seek it in the only way which occurs to a Malay, viz. by running amok." ...

       From the above discussion it is evident that the various "unique types of mental disorder" probably would yield readily to an analysis in terms of the categories of psychopathology. The

220 mental disturbance can, to be sure, be understood only in terms of the cultural and social pattern within which it occurs, but the form that it does take is a secondary function of the abnormality. Only in this sense does culture condition abnormality. The paranoid reaction can occur in almost any culture, but the form that it takes is culturally modifiable. Although the psychotic

can feel himself persecuted in almost any culture, in the one the persecutor may be the sorcerer, in another a usurping chief, and in still another the President of the United States. 225

The third argument for the cultural definition of abnormality is one which infers that inasmuch as traits considered normal in our society are considered abnormal in other cultures, abnormality can be looked upon as simply that form of behavior which a group considers aberrant.

As previously mentioned with reference to homosexuality, the term "abnormality" cannot with exactitude be applied to *all* those forms of behavior which fail to meet with social sanc- 230
tion. That would be making the term meaningless. The same criticism might be applied to this third argument. There is no element of internal conflict in the Zuni, for instance, who, feeling full of energy, gives vent to that energy. His behavior is aberrant because it conflicts with the prevailing pattern. That, however, *does not* constitute abnormality. Such a Zuni is not abnormal; he is delinquent (Mead, 1928). He is maladjusted to the demands of his culture and comes 235
into conflict with his group, not because he adheres to a different standard but because he violates the group standards which are also his own (to paraphrase Mead). . . .

From the above criticisms we can readily see that a relativity or statistical theory of abnormality which argues from the ethnological material at hand cannot stand a close analysis. From Benedict's writings one might get the impression that she also, like Foley, believes that what 240
is abnormal depends simply on whether or not it is regarded as such by the greater majority of individuals in a specific culture. In various parts of her book (1934b) though, as well as in her articles, there are statements which run counter to any such belief. That is what Foley had in mind when he stated that Benedict seemed "inconsistent in seeking for an absolute and universal criterion of abnormality." In a private communication, Benedict explains this seeming 245
paradox as follows. "In 1930–1931 when I wrote the article you refer to and the bulk of the book, writers in abnormal psychology constantly confused adequate personal adjustment and certain fixed symptoms. I wanted to break down the confusion, to show that interculturally adequate functioning and fixed symptoms could not be equated." When Benedict showed that the Northwest Coast Indians exhibited paranoid-like symptoms, she did not wish to prove that 250
what the psychopathologist would call abnormal has no universal validity, but rather that, in spite of the fact the Northwest Coast Indians acted *like* paranoids, they were actually well-adjusted and "adult" individuals. What she was really arguing against was the confusion between fixed symptoms and adequate personal adjustment.

There is, of course, one way in which culture *does* determine abnormality and that is in the 255
number of possible conflicts it can present to its component individuals. (In this sense "determine" has, however, a different meaning from that used above.) . . .

Benedict speculates that possibly the aberrant may represent "that arc of human capacities that is not capitalized in his culture" and that "the misfit is one whose disposition is not capitalized in his culture." She concludes that "the problem of understanding abnormal human 260
behavior in any absolute sense independent of causal factors is still far in the future." "When data are available in psychiatry, this minimum definition of abnormal human tendencies will be probably quite unlike our culturally conditioned, highly elaborated psychoses such as those described, e.g., under the terms schizophrenic and manic-depressive." Keeping away

265   from any committal to a relativity theory of abnormality, she is criticized therefore by Foley (1935).... For Foley ... deviation from normative mean and abnormality are synonymous. In that sense, then, abnormality is for him a statistical concept.

There are, however, many objections to this aspect of the statistico-relative formulation. The most important one is probably the fact that a statistical theory considers only the actual
270   observable behavior of an individual without delving into its meaning. Thus an erroneous identification is established between behavior patterns which are similar but do not have the same causal background. For example, the paranoid behavior of the schizophrenic and the "paranoid" behavior of the Northwest Coast Indian are equated; because the latter does not represent a deviation from the norm of that culture's behavior pattern while the former does, they
275   are accepted as substantiating the statistical relativity theory. Of course we may arbitrarily define *abnormality* in such a way that it will mean the same as *deviation* ...

A statistical norm implies a graduated scale in which the items can be ranged on the basis of the possession of "more" or "less" of a certain property.... It would, however, have only a qualitative significance if we spoke of one person's being "more" deluded than another or "less"
280   paranoid. In this sense, therefore, we are not justified in speaking of abnormality as a statistical concept. There are ... certain abnormalities which, because of their nature, can be ranged on graduated scales and others which, because of a different substrate, cannot be similarly measured. A ... scale similar to one used in attitude testing can of course be utilized, but its use is bound up with all the prejudice that subjective judgments embody when topics of wide per-
285   sonal opinion-variance are considered. Besides, there is no real basis for comparative evaluation. Should, for example, a paranoid trait such as the conviction of persecution, be measured by judges with respect to the degree in which it inhibits the satisfactory functioning of the total personality and causes personal unhappiness, or with respect to the degree in which it interferes with an adequate adjustment to the social group and creates opposition within the envi-
290   ronment? Should the frequency with which it manifests itself in life situations be the determining criterion, or the intensity with which it is adhered to? Finally, should the degree of insight a person has into it be the standard? The bases for judging the "more" or "less" of a paranoid trait are, as is obvious, very divergent. No single criterion is any more justifiable than any other. A "paranoid scale" would, therefore, be of slight operational significance.
295   Skaggs (1933) was aware of this difficulty when he said: "It is the writer's view that abnormality is, of necessity, a qualitative and not a quantitative concept at the present time. While definitions of abnormality which involve statistical norms are

> Karen Horney (6.3) shares Skaggs's view.

300   commendable in their aim, the soundness of such definitions appears to be questionable."

Realizing further that only confusion results when we try to generalize about different abnormalities, he even suggests that "the terms sub-normal and super-normal be kept strictly apart from the term 'abnormality.'" Bridges (1930) places all abnormalities not of a sub-normal or super-normal type in the category of the "para-normal," a group which,
305   for Skaggs, is really the only one deserving of the name "abnormal." Because this group

cannot be quantitatively ranged it is small surprise that, for Skaggs, the normative definition of abnormality as a lack of integration and balance of the total personality seems the
most logical one.

. . .

Obviously abnormal behavior is *called* abnormal because it deviates from the behavior of
the general group. It is not, however, the *fact* of deviation which makes it abnormal but its   310
causal background. That is why the hallucinations of the Plains Indians are not abnormal, while
those of the schizophrenic are. It is not the *fact* of social sanction in Plains Indian society which
makes that bit of behavior normal, but the fact
that it does not have the background of a symp-

analogous: similar in some ways but not in
origin or structure

homologous: similar in structure and origin
but not in function

tomatic resolution of an inner conflict such as pro-   315
duces that phenomenon in the schizophrenic. The
"abnormal" behavior of the Indian is analogous to
the behavior of the psychotic *but not homologous.*
Just because it is analogous, the confusion has
arisen of identifying the two.   320

If, therefore, behavior anomalies which are at bottom constitutionally or pathologically conditioned be excluded or subsumed as a different group under the category of the non-normal,
we could state the quintessence of abnormality (Bridges' "para-normality") as *the tendency to
choose a type of reaction which represents an escape from a conflict-producing situation instead of
a facing of the problem.* . . . An essential element in this type of problem-resolution is that the con-   325
flict does not seem to be on a conscious level, so that the strange bit of behavior resulting is
looked upon as an abnormal intruder and, at least in its incipient stage, is felt as something which
is not ego-determined. . . . Inasmuch as pathologi-
cal and, above all, constitutional factors cannot be

aetiology: (etiology) study of causes

partialled out in the aetiology of a behavior anom-   330
aly, however, the above definition has only an ideal
value of slight practical significance. . . .

It does clarify though, to some extent, the confusion which arises from labelling any bit
of behavior "abnormal." It is obvious, for example, that masturbation *per se* is not abnormal and represents a quite normal, i.e., usual, growing-up phenomenon. In certain   335
instances, however, its great frequency or its inappropriateness point to the use of it as an
escape mechanism. What holds true for masturbation is true of all "abnormal mechanisms."
It is not the mechanism that is abnormal; it is its function which determines its abnormality. It
is precisely for this reason that the institutionalized "abnormal" traits in various cultures are
not properly called "abnormal" entities. Because this distinction is not kept in mind and   340
because a primarily statistico-relative conception of abnormality is adhered to, the unwar-
ranted conclusion is drawn that standards of "abnormality" differ with cultures and are
culturally determined.

FOR DISCUSSION

1. What, according to Wegrocki, are the causes of mental illness? Is his argument consistent with a biological view of mental illness (e.g., Guze 6.6)? With a psychological view (e.g., Horney 6.3)?

2. Wegrocki quotes Campbell as saying, "the delusions of the ill-balanced and the beliefs of the orthodox are more closely akin than is usually recognized" (p. 536, line 96). Does Wegrocki agree? Do you?

3. Is a behavior always normal when it is accepted in the culture in which it appears? Is a behavior always pathological when it is not accepted in the culture in which it appears?

4. Can a culture prevent or facilitate the development of normal behavior? Can it prevent or facilitate the development of pathological behavior?

5. How does Wegrocki distinguish between abnormality and delinquency?

6. On what grounds does Wegrocki reject the statistico-relative formulation of abnormality?

7. Wegrocki describes two paranoid people, one whose behavior is "socially determined" and "socially sanctioned" and another whose behavior is the product of an internal personal conflict. According to Wegrocki, the first has no choice, but the second does (pp. 536–538, lines 98–155). Does one really have more choice than the other?

8. Wegrocki tells us that the Haida chief, upon the death of his wife, believes that malignant forces caused her death and he may kill another family "to avenge the . . . death" (p. 537, lines 108–123). Could a Haida non-chief or a Haida woman do the same thing? Why or why not?

Karen Horney (1885–1952)
Neurosis and Human Growth (1950)

Chapter 3: The Tyranny of the Should

Karen Clementina Theodora Danielsen was born near Hamburg, Germany in 1885.[1] She entered medical school in Freiburg in 1906 and continued her medical studies in Göttingen in 1908. In 1910 she began psychoanalysis with Karl Abraham and developed a fascination for Freudian theory that would be the center of her work. In 1920 Horney was one of the founding members of the Berlin Psychoanalytic Institute. In the early 1930s Hitler's influence in Germany began to increase, and the Nazis were opposed to psychoanalysis from the start. Horney sailed to the United States in 1932 and settled in Chicago, where she was active in the Chicago Institute for Psychoanalysis. In 1934 Horney moved to New York and joined the New York Psychoanalytic Institute as a lecturer and clinical supervisor.

Horney was not an orthodox psychoanalyst; it was not in her nature to accept any theory without asking questions and pursuing implications. Her early writing had involved a critical analysis of Freud's views on women's psychology. Her essays on this topic are published in *Feminine Psychology* (Horney, 1967). Among other ideas, Horney suggested that the penis envy Freud suggested women experience is relatively trivial, except for the fact that it is symbolic of women's envy of men's status. With time, Horney's analysis of Freudian theory extended beyond gender issues. She questioned the biological and deterministic nature of psychoanalysis and argued that it failed to acknowledge the powerful influence of social and cultural factors.

Source: Horney, K. (1950). *Neurosis and human growth*. New York: Norton. Copyright renewed 1978 Renate Patterson, Brigitte Swarzenski, and Marianne VonEckardt. Reprinted with permission from W. W. Norton & Company, Inc.

[1] Horney's personal life was intriguing and her contribution to the understanding of human behavior was significant. There have been several excellent biographies written about her personal and professional life (e.g., Quinn, 1988, and Rubins, 1978).

When Horney published *New Ways in Psychoanalysis* in 1939, she still considered herself to be an analyst, but to be one involved in the evolution and development of the theory. Some members of the New York Psychoanalytic Institute did not agree. They considered her a heretic and in 1941 stripped her of some of her roles at the institute. Horney, along with Clara Thompson and several others, immediately resigned. Horney established a new organization—the Association for the Advancement of Psychoanalysis (AAP)—and was joined there by Thompson, Erich Fromm, Harry Stack Sullivan, and other supporters.

Horney's independence, her insistence on questioning everything, and her willingness to speak her mind often led her into controversy. These same qualities allowed her to produce a set of writings that include the seeds of feminist psychology, ego psychology, and object relations theory. Two of Horney's last books—*Our Inner Conflicts* (1945) and *Neurosis and Human Growth* (1950)—do not deal extensively with her questions about orthodox psychoanalysis but instead describe her own views.

In these books Horney discusses the development and actualization of the real self. She also describes the neurotic's sense of self. We all have idealized images of what we should or would like to be, how we should feel, and how we would like to act. These images usually serve to direct and energize the development of our real self. In the neurotic, however, Horney believes that such idealized images become the idealized self, and the neurotic becomes alienated from his real self. He will "shift the major part of his energies to the task of molding himself, by a rigid system of inner dictates, into a being of absolute perfection"(1950, p. 13). "The energies driving toward self-realization are shifted to the aim of actualizing the idealized self" (1950, p. 24). Although everyone can relate to Horney's discussion of idealized images, she argues that the role they play in neurosis is qualitatively different from that which they play in normal human development.

neurosis: (or psychoneurosis). Freud used the word *neurosis* to describe disorders in which a person is unable to control the anxiety caused by unconscious conflicts by using only ego defense mechanisms. The anxiety, then, appears as symptoms. It can be directly expressed (general anxiety neurosis) or displaced or converted (e.g., phobias, obsessive-compulsion, hysteria, dissociation).

The *Diagnostic and Statistical Manual* (*DSM*), a publication of the American Psychiatric Association, defines and categorizes all mental disorders. Originally the *DSM* included the neuroses, defining them in the way that Freud had. In the 1980 edition of the *DSM*, however, the APA defined disorders in terms of symptoms, not causes, and stopped using the word "neurosis." The disorders that had been categorized as neurotic are now included with the anxiety disorders, mood disorders, somatoform disorders, or dissociative disorders.

We have discussed so far chiefly how the neurotic tries to actualize his idealized self with regard to the *outside world:* in achievements, in the glory of success or power or triumph. . . . And whenever he falls palpably short of being his idealized self, his claims enable him to make factors outside himself responsible for such "failures." 5

We shall now discuss that aspect of self-actualization, briefly mentioned in the first chapter, in which the focus is *within himself.* Unlike Pygmalion, who tried to make another person into a creature fulfilling his concept of beauty, the neurotic sets to work to mold himself into a supreme being of his own making. He holds before his soul his image of perfection and unconsciously tells himself: "Forget about the disgraceful creature you actually *are;* this is how you *should* be; and to be this idealized self is all that matters. You should be able to endure everything, to understand everything, to like everybody, to be always productive"—to mention only a few of these inner dictates. Since they are inexorable, I call them "the tyranny of the should." 10 15 20

The inner dictates comprise all that the neurotic should be able to do, to be, to feel, to know—and taboos on how and what he should not be. . . . 25

. . .

What strikes us first is the same *disregard for feasibility* which pervades the entire drive for actualization. Many of these demands are of a kind which no human being could fulfill. They are plainly fantastic, although the person himself is not aware of it. He cannot help recognizing it, however, as soon as his expectations are exposed to the clear light of critical thinking. Such an intellectual realization, however, usually does not change much, if anything. . . . 30

. . .

Other demands on self may not be fantastic in themselves yet show a complete *disregard for the conditions* under which they could be fulfilled. Thus many patients expect to finish their analysis in no time because they are so intelligent. But the progress in analysis has little to do with intelligence. The reasoning power which these people have may, in fact, be used to obstruct progress. . . . 35

This expectation of easy success operates not only in reference to the length of the whole analysis, but equally so in regard to an individual insight gained. For instance, recognizing some of their neurotic claims seems to them the equivalent of having outgrown them altogether.

That it requires patient work; that the claims will persist as long as the emotional necessities for having them are not changed—all of this they ignore. They believe that their intelligence should be a supreme moving power. Naturally, then, subsequent disappointment and discouragement are unavoidable. . . .

The inner dictates, exactly like political tyranny in a police state, operate with a supreme *disregard for the person's own psychic condition*—for what he can feel or do as he is at present. One of the frequent shoulds, for instance, is that one should never feel hurt. As an absolute (which is implied in the "never") anyone would find this extremely hard to achieve. How many people have been, or are, so secure in themselves, so serene, as never to feel hurt? This could at best be an ideal toward which we might strive. To take such a project seriously must mean intense and patient work at our unconscious claims for defense, at our false pride—or, in short, at every factor in our personality that makes us vulnerable. But the person who feels that he should never feel hurt does not have so concrete a program in mind. He simply issues an absolute order to himself, denying or overriding the fact of his existing vulnerability.

. . .

In trying to account for the amazing blindness of the shoulds, we again have to leave many loose ends. This much, however, is understandable from their origin in the search for glory and their function to make oneself over into one's idealized self: *the premise on which they operate is that nothing should be, or is, impossible for oneself.* . . .

This trend is most apparent in the application of demands directed toward the past. Concerning the neurotic's childhood, it is not only important to elucidate the influences which set his neurosis going, but also to recognize his present attitudes toward the adversities of the past. These are determined less by the good or the bad done to him than by his present needs. If he has developed, for instance, a general need to be all sweetness and light, he will spread a golden haze over his childhood. If he has forced his feelings into a strait jacket, he may feel that he does love his parents because he should love them. If he generally refuses to assume responsibility for his life, he may put all the blame for all his difficulties on his parents. The vindictiveness accompanying this latter attitude, in turn, may be out in the open or repressed.

He may finally go to the opposite extreme, and seemingly assume an absurd amount of responsibility for himself. In this case he may have become aware of the full impact of intimidating and cramping early influences. His conscious attitude is quite objective and plausible. He may point out, for instance, that his parents could not help behaving the way they did. The patient sometimes wonders himself why he does not feel any resentment. One of the reasons for the absence of conscious resentment is a retrospective *should* that interests us here. Though he is aware that what has been perpetrated on him was quite sufficient to crush anybody else, *he* should have come out of it unscathed. He should have had the inner strength and fortitude not to let these factors affect him. So, since they did, it proved that he was no good from the beginning. In other words, he is realistic up to a point; he would say: "Sure, that was a cesspool of hypocrisy and cruelty." But then his vision becomes blurred: "Although I was helplessly exposed to this atmosphere, I should have come out of it like a lily out of a swamp."

Like other psychoanalysts, Horney believed that the roots of neurosis are in childhood. Unlike Freud, Horney believed that neuroses develop when adverse influences such as domination, overprotection, intimidation, irritability, or erratic behavior on the part of those in the child's environment prevent his or her growth and sense of inner security. She referred to a child's resulting feelings of insecurity, isolation, and helplessness as "basic anxiety."

If he could assume a matter-of-fact responsibility for his life instead of such a spurious one, he would think differently. He would admit that the early influences could not fail to mold him in an unfavorable way. And he would see that, no matter what the origin of his difficulties, they do disturb his present and future life. For this reason he had better muster his energies to outgrow them. Instead, he leaves the whole matter at the completely fantastic and futile level of his demand that he should not have been affected. It is a sign of progress when the same patient at a later period reverses his position and rather gives himself credit for not having been entirely crushed by the early circumstances.

. . . Naturally we all regret having failed in this or that regard. But we can examine why we failed, and learn from it. We must also recognize that in view of the neurotic difficulties existing at the time of the "failures," we may actually have done the best we could at that time. But, for the neurotic, to have done his best is not good enough. In some miraculous way he should have done better.

Similarly, the realization of any present shortcoming is unbearable for anybody harassed by dictatorial shoulds. Whatever the difficulty, it must be removed quickly. How this removal is effected varies. The more a person lives in imagination, the more likely it is that he will simply spirit away the difficulty. Thus a patient who discovered in herself a colossal drive for being the power behind the throne, and who saw how this drive had operated in her life, was convinced by the next day that this drive was now entirely a matter of the past. She should not be power ridden; so she was not. . . .

Others try to remove by dint of sheer will power the difficulty of which they have become aware. People can go to an extraordinary length in this regard. I am thinking, for instance, of two young girls who felt that they should never be afraid of anything. One of them was scared of burglars and forced herself to sleep in an empty house until her fear was gone. The other was afraid of swimming when the water was not transparent because she felt she might be bitten by a snake or a fish. She forced herself to swim across a shark-infested bay. Both girls managed in this way to crush their fears. Thus the incidents seem to be grist for the mills of those who regard psychoanalysis as newfangled nonsense. Do they not show that all that is necessary is to pull oneself together? But actually the fears of burglars or snakes were but the most obvious, manifest expression of a general, more hidden apprehensiveness. And this pervasive undercurrent of anxiety remained untouched by the acceptance of the particular "challenge." It was merely covered up, driven deeper by disposing of a symptom without touching the real disorder.

This argument would later become a common—and often reasonable—critique of therapeutic techniques based only upon behavior change.

120   In analysis we can observe how the will-power machinery is switched on in certain types as soon as they become aware of foibles. They resolve, and try, to keep a budget, to mix with people, to be more assertive or more lenient. This would be fine if they showed an equal interest in understanding the implications and sources of their troubles. Unfortunately, this interest is sadly lacking. The very first step, which is to see the whole extent of the particular

125   disturbance, would go against their grain. It would indeed be the exact opposite to their frantic drive to make the disturbance *disappear*. Also, since they feel they should be strong enough to conquer it by conscious control, the process of careful disentangling would be an admission of weakness and defeat. . . .

    Most neurotic disturbances resist even the most strenuous efforts at control. Conscious

130   efforts simply do not avail against a depression, against a deeply ingrained inhibition to work, or against consuming daydreams. One would think that this would be clear to any person who has gained some psychological understanding during analysis. But again the clarity of thinking does not penetrate to the "I should be able to master it." The result is that he suffers more intensely under depressions, etc., because, in addition to its being painful anyhow,

135   it becomes a visible sign of his lack of omnipotence. Sometimes the analyst can catch this process at the beginning and nip it in the bud. Thus a patient who had revealed the extent of her daydreaming, while exposing in detail how subtly it pervaded most of her activities, came to realize its harmfulness—at least to the extent of understanding how it sapped her energies. The next time she was somewhat guilty and apologetic because the daydreams

140   persisted. Knowing her demands on herself, I injected my belief that it would be neither possible nor even wise to stop them artificially, because we could be sure that they fulfilled . . . important functions in her life—which we would have to come to understand gradually. She felt very much relieved . . .

    . . .

    The more we get a feeling for the nature of the shoulds, the more clearly do we see that

145   the difference between them and real moral standards or ideals is not a quantitative but a qualitative one. It was one of Freud's gravest errors to regard the inner dictates (some of the features of which he had seen and described as superego), as constituting morality in general. To begin with, their connection with moral questions is not too close. True enough, the commands for moral perfection do assume a prominent place among the shoulds, for the simple

150   reason that moral questions are important in all our lives. But we cannot separate these particular shoulds from others, just as insistent, which are plainly determined by unconscious arrogance, such as "I should be able to get out of a Sunday-afternoon traffic jam" or "I should be able to paint without laborious training and working." We must also remember that many demands conspicuously lack even a moral pretense, among them "I should be able to get

155   away with anything," "I should always get the better of others," and "I should always be able to get back at others." Only by focusing on the totality of the picture are we able to get the proper perspective on the demands for moral perfection. Like the other shoulds, they are permeated by the spirit of arrogance and aim at enhancing the neurotic's glory and at making him godlike. They are, in this sense, the neurotic counterfeit of normal moral strivings. When

one adds to all this the unconscious dishonesty necessarily involved in making blemishes   160
disappear, one recognizes them as an immoral rather than a moral phenomenon. It is necessary to be clear about these differences for the sake of the patient's eventual reorientation
from a make-believe world into the development of genuine ideals.

> Within Freudian theory, the superego develops at about age 5 to resolve or reduce boys'
> castration anxiety. (Needless to say, girls are already castrated and so do not have the same
> incentive. As a result, their superegos may be less well developed.) Freud's superego is made up
> of a conscience and an ego-ideal. As Horney says, however, Freud tends to discuss the superego
> mostly in terms of conscience and morality, and she is describing something broader in the
> "shoulds."
>
> Freud and Horney agreed that the superego and the shoulds have their roots early in life, and
> thus are immature and often irrational. Horney believed that early experiences inevitably influence
> later behaviors, feelings, and expectations but that later experiences can, in turn, modify the effect
> of the early ones. Freud, however, believed that early experiences remain intact and can affect us
> in unchanging ways throughout life.
>
> Horney writes more about the relationship between her theoretical approach and Freud's in
> Chapter 15. She sums it up as follows: "Freud's philosophy, in this deep sense, is a pessimistic one.
> Ours, with all its cognizance of the tragic element in neurosis, is a positive one" (p. 378).
>
> As Quinn (1988) points out, Horney's insistence on the positive aspects of her approach can be
> seen as "falsely optimistic," and that this may make her work seem shallow and superficial, which,
> according to Quinn, it is not (pp. 388–389).

There is one further quality of the shoulds that distinguishes them from genuine standards.
It is implied in the previous comments but carries too much weight of its own not to be stated   165
separately and explicitly. That is their *coercive character*. Ideals, too, have an obligating power
over our lives. For instance, if among them is the belief in fulfilling responsibilities which we ourselves recognize as such, we try our best to do so even though it may be difficult. To fulfill them
is what we ourselves ultimately want, or what we deem right. The wish, the judgment, the decision is ours. And because we are thus at one with ourselves, efforts of this kind give us freedom   170
and strength. In obeying the shoulds, on the other hand, there is just about as much freedom
as there is in a "voluntary" contribution or ovation within a dictatorship. In both instances there
are quick retributions if we do not measure up to expectations. In the case of the inner dictates,
this means violent emotional reactions to nonfulfillment—reactions which traverse the whole
range of anxiety, despair, self-condemnation, and self-destructive impulses. To the outsider   175
they appear entirely out of proportion to the provocation. But they are entirely in proportion
to what it means to the individual.

. . .

… A person may function fairly well as long as he lives in accordance with his inner dictates. But he may be thrown out of gear if he is caught between two contradictory shoulds. For instance, one man felt that he should be the ideal physician and give all his time to his patients. But he should also be the ideal husband and give his wife as much time as she needed to be happy. When realizing he could not do both to the full, mild anxiety ensued. It remained mild because he immediately tried to solve the Gordian knot by cutting it with a sword: by determining to settle down in the country. This implied giving up his hopes for further training and thus jeopardizing his whole professional future.

> *Gordian knot:* a problem that seems to defy solution. According to legend, Gordius of Phrygia (in what is now Turkey) tied up his ox cart with an intricate knot. It was said that whoever could untie the knot would rule Asia. Many tried and failed, but in 333 BCE, Alexander the Great cut through the knot with his sword and went on to rule Asia. Did he cheat by cutting the knot or was he the first to realize that this was the only solution?

. . .

Naturally such contradictory shoulds render it difficult, if not indeed impossible, to make a rational decision between them because the opposing demands are equally coercive. One patient had sleepless nights because he could not decide whether he should go with his wife on a short vacation or stay in his office and work. Should he measure up to his wife's expectations or to the alleged expectations of his employer? The question as to what *he* wanted most did not enter his mind at all. And, on the basis of the shoulds, the matter simply could not be decided.

A person is never aware either of the full impact of the inner tyranny or of its nature. But there are *great individual differences* in the *attitudes toward this tyranny and the ways of experiencing it.* They range between the opposite poles of compliance and rebellion. While elements of such different attitudes operate in each individual, usually one or the other prevails. To anticipate later distinctions, the attitudes toward and ways of experiencing inner dictates are primarily determined by the greatest appeal life holds for the individual: mastery, love, or freedom. Since such differences will be discussed later, I shall here indicate only briefly how they operate with regard to the shoulds and taboos.

The expansive type, for whom mastery of life is crucial, tends to identify himself with his inner dictates and, whether consciously or unconsciously, to be proud of his standards. He does not question their validity and tries to actualize them in one way or other. He may try to measure up to them in his actual behavior. He should be all things to all people; he should know everything better than anybody else; he should never err; he should never fail in anything he attempts to do—in short, fulfill whatever his particular shoulds are. And, in his mind, he does measure up to his supreme standards. His arrogance may be so great that he does not even consider the possibility of failure, and discards it if it occurs. His arbitrary rightness is so rigid that in his own mind he simply never errs.

The more he is engulfed in his imagination, the less necessary it is for him to make actual efforts. It is sufficient, then, that in his mind he is supremely fearless or honest, no matter how beset he is by fears or how dishonest he actually is. The border line between these two ways of "I should" and "I am" is vague for him—for that matter, probably not too sharp for any of us. . . . The more a person's imagination prevails over his reasoning, the more the border line disappears and he *is* the model husband, father, citizen, or whatever he should be.

The self-effacing type, for whom love seems to solve all problems, likewise feels that his shoulds constitute a law not to be questioned. But when trying—anxiously—to measure up to them, he feels most of the time that he falls pitiably short of fulfilling them. The foremost element in his conscious experience is therefore self-criticism, a feeling of guilt for *not* being the supreme being.

When carried to the extreme, both these attitudes toward the inner dictates render it difficult for a person to analyze himself. Tending toward the extreme of self-righteousness may prevent him from seeing any flaws in himself. And tending toward the other extreme—that of too readily feeling guilty—entails the danger of insights into shortcomings having a crushing rather than a liberating effect.

The resigned type, finally, to whom the idea of "freedom" appeals more than anything else, is, of the three, most prone to rebel against his inner tyranny. Because of the very importance which freedom—or his version of it—has for him, he is hypersensitive to any coercion. He may rebel in a somewhat passive way. Then everything that he feels he should do, whether it concerns a piece of work or reading a book or having sexual relations with his wife, turns—in his mind—into a coercion, arouses conscious or unconscious resentment, and in consequence makes him listless. If what is to be done is done at all, it is done under the strain produced by the inner resistance.

He may rebel against his shoulds in a more active way. He may try to throw them all overboard, and sometimes go to the opposite extreme by insisting upon doing only what he pleases when he pleases. The rebellion may take violent forms, and then often is a rebellion of despair. If he can't be the ultimate of piety, chastity, sincerity, then he will be thoroughly "bad," be promiscuous, tell lies, affront others.

Sometimes a person who usually complies with the shoulds may go through a phase of rebellion. It is usually then directed against external restrictions. J. P. Marquand has described such temporary rebellions in a masterly way. He has shown us how easily they can be put down, for the very reason that the restricting external standards have a mighty ally in the internal dictates. And then afterward the individual is left dull and listless.

> J. P. Marquand wrote about the changing lives of the American middle and upper classes in the early part of the 20th century. Among the books Horney may be thinking of here are *H. M. Pulham* (1951) and *So Little Time* (1943).

Finally, others may go through alternating phases of self-castigating "goodness" and a wild protest against any standards. To the observant friend such people may present an insoluble puzzle. At times they are offensively irresponsible in sexual or financial matters, and at others they show highly developed moral sensibilities. . . . In others there may be a constant shuttling between an "I should" and "no, I won't." "I should pay a debt. No, why should I?" "I should keep to a diet. No, I won't." Often these people give the impression of spontaneity and mistake their contradictory attitudes toward their shoulds for "freedom."

Whatever the prevailing attitude, a great deal of the process is always externalized; it is experienced as going on between self and others. . . . [A] person may primarily impose his standards upon others and make relentless demands as to *their* perfection. The more he feels himself to be the measure of all things, the more he insists—not upon general perfection but upon his particular norms being measured up to. The failure of others to do so arouses his contempt or anger. Still more irrational is the fact that his own irritation with himself for not being, at any moment and under all conditions, what he should be may be turned outward. Thus, for instance, when he is not the perfect lover, or is caught in a lie, he may turn angrily against those he failed and build up a case against them.

Again he may primarily experience his expectations of himself as coming from others. And whether these others actually do expect something or whether he merely thinks they do, their expectations then turn into demands to be fulfilled. In analysis he feels that the analyst expects the impossible from him. He attributes to the analyst his own feelings that he should always be productive, should always have a dream to report, should always talk about what he thinks the analyst wants him to discuss, should always be appreciative of help and show it by getting better.

If he believes in this way that others are expecting or demanding things of him, he may, again, respond in two different ways. He may try to anticipate or guess at their expectations and be eager to live up to them. In that case he usually also anticipates that they would condemn him or drop him at a moment's notice if he fails. Or, if he is hypersensitive to coercion, he feels that they are imposing upon him, meddling in his affairs, pushing him or coercing him. He then minds it bitterly, or even openly rebels against them. He may object to giving Christmas presents, because they are expected. He will be at his office or at any appointment just a little later than expected. He will forget anniversaries, letters, or any favor for which he has been asked. He may forget a visit to relatives just because his mother had asked him to make it, although he liked them and meant to see them. He will overreact to any request made. He will then be less afraid of the criticism of others than resentful of it. His vivid and unfair self-criticism also becomes tenaciously externalized. He then feels that others are unfair in their judgment of him or that they always suspect ulterior motives. Or, if his rebellion is more aggressive, he will flaunt his defiance and believe that he does not in the least care what they think of him.

The overreaction to requests made is a good lead to recognizing the inner demands. Reactions which strike us ourselves as being out of proportion may be particularly helpful in self-analysis. The following illustration, in part self-analysis, may be useful in showing also certain faulty conclusions we may draw from self-observations. It concerns a busy executive whom I saw occasionally. He was asked by phone whether he could go to the pier

As a therapist, Horney not only helped her patients to understand and transform themselves, she also taught them how to engage in the process on their own. In 1942 she wrote what is probably the first self-help book on psychotherapy, *Self-Analysis*.

Paris (2000), Quinn (1988), and Rubins (1978) all suggest that Horney herself engaged in self-analysis throughout her life and that many of the ideas and clinical examples she used in her writing come from this activity. They mention particularly that the case of Clare in *Self-Analysis* is strongly autobiographical.

and meet a refugee writer coming from Europe. He had always admired this writer and had met him socially on a visit to Europe. Since his time was jammed with conferences and other work, it would actually have been unfeasible to comply with this request, particularly since it might have involved waiting on the pier for hours. As he realized later on, he could have reacted in two ways, both of them sensible. He could either have said that he would think it over and see whether he could make it, or he could have declined with regret and asked whether there was anything else he could do for the writer. Instead he reacted with immediate irritation and said abruptly that he was too busy and never would call for anybody at the pier.

Soon after this he regretted his response, and later went to some length to find out where the writer was located so that he could help him if necessary. He not only regretted the incident; he also felt puzzled. Did he not think as highly of the writer as he had thought he did? He felt sure that he did. Was he not as friendly and helpful as he believed himself to be? If so, was he irritated because he was put on the spot in being asked to prove his friendliness and helpfulness?

Here he was on a good track. The mere fact of his being able to question the genuineness of his generosity was for him quite a step to take—for, in his idealized image, he was the bene-factor of mankind. It was, however, more than he could digest at this juncture. He rejected this possibility by remembering that afterward he was eager to offer and give help. But while clos-ing one avenue in his thought he suddenly hit upon another clue. When he *offered* help the ini-tiative was his, but the first time he had been *asked* to do something. He then realized that he had felt the request as an unfair imposition. Provided he had known about the writer's arrival, he would certainly have considered on his own the possibility of meeting him at the boat. He now thought of many similar incidents in which he had reacted irritably to a favor asked and realized that apparently he felt as imposition or coercion many things which in actual fact were mere requests or suggestions. . . . [A]ny request plunged him into an inner conflict: he should accede to it and be very generous and also he should not allow anybody to coerce him. The irri-tability was an expression of feeling caught in a dilemma which at that time was insoluble.

. . .

. . . the shoulds always contribute to *disturbances in human relations* in one way or another. The most general disturbance on this score is hyper-sensitivity to criticism. Being merciless toward himself, he cannot help experiencing any criticism on the part of others—whether actual or merely anticipated, whether friendly or unfriendly—as being just as condemnatory as his own. We shall understand the intensity of this sensitivity better when we realize how much he hates himself for any lagging behind his self-imposed standards. . . .

Most important of all, the shoulds further *impair the spontaneity* of feelings, wishes, thoughts, and beliefs—i.e., the ability to feel his own feelings, etc., and to express them. The person, then, can at best be "spontaneously compulsive" (to quote a patient) and express "freely" what he *should* feel, wish, think, or believe. We are accustomed to think that we cannot control feelings but only behavior. In dealing with others we can enforce labor but we cannot force anybody to love his work. Just so, we are accustomed to think that we can force ourselves to act as if we were not suspicious but we cannot enforce a feeling of confidence. This remains essentially true. And, if we needed a new proof, analysis could supply it. But if the shoulds issue an order as to

305

310

315

320

325

330

335

340

feelings, imagination waves its magic wand and the border line between what we *should* feel and what we do feel evaporates. We consciously believe or feel then as we should believe or feel.

This appears in analysis when the spurious certainty of pseudofeelings is shaken, and the patient

345   then goes through a period of bewildering uncertainty which is painful but constructive. A person for instance who believed she liked everybody because she should do so may then ask: Do I really like my husband, my pupils, my patients? Or anybody at that? And at that point the questions are unanswerable because only now can all the fears, suspicions, and resentments that have always

350   prevented a free flow of positive feelings, and yet were covered up by the shoulds, be tackled. I call this period constructive because it represents a beginning search for the genuine.

> spurious: false

. . .

The creation of make-believe feelings is most striking in those whose idealized image lies in the direction of goodness, love, and saintliness. They should be considerate, grateful, sympathetic, generous, loving, and so in their minds they *have* all these qualities. They talk and go

355   through the motions *as if* they simply were that good and loving. And, since they are convinced of it, they even can be temporarily convincing to others. But of course these make-believe feelings have no depth and no sustaining power. . . .

More often the shallowness of the made-to-order feelings shows in other ways. They may disappear easily. Love readily makes way for indifference, or for resentment and contempt,

360   when pride or vanity is hurt. In these instances people usually do not ask themselves: "How does it happen that my feelings or opinions change so easily?" They simply feel that here is another person who has disappointed their faith in humanity, or that they never "really" trusted him. All of this does not mean that they may not have slumbering capacities for strong and alive feelings, but what appears on more conscious levels often is a massive pretense with

365   very little that is genuine in it. In the long run they give the impression of something unsubstantial, elusive, or—to use a good slang word—of being phonies. . . .

At the other extreme, feelings of callousness and ruthlessness can also be exaggerated. The taboos on feelings of tenderness, sympathy, and confidence can be just as great in some neurotics as the taboos on hostility and vindictiveness are in others. These people feel that they

370   should be able to live without any close personal relations, so they believe that they do not need them. They should not enjoy anything; so they believe they do not care. Their emotional life then is less distorted than plainly impoverished.

. . .

We are less aware of the harm done our feelings by these pervasive shoulds than of other damage inflicted by them. Yet it is actually the heaviest price we pay for trying to mold ourselves into perfection. Feelings are the most alive part of ourselves; if they are put under a dic-

375   tatorial regime, a profound uncertainty is created in our essential being which must affect adversely our relations to everything inside and outside ourselves.

We can hardly overrate the *intensity* of the impact of the inner dictates. The more the drive to actualize his idealized self prevails in a person, the more the shoulds become the sole motor

force moving him, driving him, whipping him into action. When a patient who is still far   380
removed from his real self discovers some of the cramping effects of his shoulds, he may nevertheless be entirely unable to consider relinquishing them because without them—so he
feels—he would or could not do anything. . . .

When we realize the enormous coercive power of the shoulds we must raise one question,
the answer to which we shall discuss in the fifth chapter: what does it do to a person when he   385
recognizes that he cannot measure up to his inner dictates? To anticipate the answer briefly:
then he starts to hate and despise himself. We cannot in fact understand the full impact of the
shoulds unless we see the extent to which they are interwoven with self-hate. It is the threat
of a punitive self-hate that lurks behind them, that truly makes them a regime of terror.

But there is hope. In *Our Inner Conflicts* (1945) Horney described the role that therapy can play:

> The task of therapy, therefore, is to make the patient aware of his idealized image in all its
> detail, to assist him in gradually understanding all its functions and subjective values, and
> to show him the suffering that it inevitably entails. He will then start to wonder whether the
> price is not too high. But he can relinquish the image only when the needs that have created
> it are considerably diminished. (p. 114)

Carl Rogers, the developer of Client-Centered Therapy, used the Q-technique (Stephenson, 1953)
to study the therapeutic process. He measured the relationship between a client's self-concept and
ideal-self concept over the course of therapy. His clients sorted a large number of personality
characteristics into those most like themselves and those least like themselves and then did the
same for the characteristics most and least like their ideal selves. Looking at changes in the self-
sorts, the ideal-sorts, and the relationship between the self and ideal-self concepts, Rogers was able
to measure the amount and kind of change that occurred during therapy. Although the results of
Rogers's work with the Q-technique were quite complex, they seem to have supported Horney's
notion that the outcome of therapy was either to bring the self and ideal-self closer together or,
for neurotics, to allow the client to abandon an unrealistic sense of his or her real self. (Rogers, 1951,
1961; Rogers & Dymond, 1954; Rogers & Russell, 2002)

FOR DISCUSSION

1. In what ways does a neurotic person's ego ideal differ from that of a normal person?

2. Does Horney seem to believe that all neurotics are driven by "shoulds" in order to escape
   an unconscious sense of their own worthlessness?

3. What happens to a person's "real" (or inner) self when the neurotic ideal self takes over?

4. How much progress do I make in therapy if I acknowledge my "shoulds"?

5. Horney argues that there is a qualitative difference between the ego ideals of the neurotic and normal ego ideals. Is a mixture possible? Could a person treat some parts of their ego ideal as absolute (neurotic) shoulds and other parts as (normal) aspirations?

6. Why does Horney argue that a neurotic who makes a conscious decision to change his or her undesirable or unwanted behavior (e.g., I will stop trying to be perfect; I will listen to others with more care and sensitivity) will inevitably not reduce their neuroticism?

7. Why does Horney describe the neurotic's world as a make-believe world? (p. 550, line 163)

8. When Horney wrote this paper, neurosis was considered a form of mental illness. Horney regards neurotic thinking as qualitatively different from normal thinking. How can we reconcile this with the fact that many of the neurotic behaviors that Horney describes are behaviors we all see regularly in ourselves and in others?

9. What sort of evidence does Horney's theory rest on?

Evelyn Hooker (1907–1996)
The Adjustment of the Male Overt Homosexual (1957)

On November 22, 1996, the *New York Times* reported that

> Dr. Evelyn Hooker, a psychologist who defied conventional wisdom and greatly embold-
> ened the fledgling homosexual rights movement in the 1950s by finding there was no
> measurable psychological difference between homosexual and heterosexual men, died
> on Monday at her home in Santa Monica, Calif. She was 89. (Dunlap, 1996)

Evelyn Gentry Hooker received a baccalaureate and a master's degree in psychology from the
University of Colorado, Boulder, having done her thesis with Karl Muenzinger on vicarious trial-
and-error learning in rats (Gentry, 1930). She wanted to go on to Yale to work with Robert Yerkes,
but the department chair at Colorado, a Yale PhD, thought it inappropriate to recommend a
woman to the Yale doctoral program. So Hooker went to Johns Hopkins University. She continued to do behaviorist research on discrimination learning in rats and earned a PhD in 1932.

In the late 1930s Hooker became interested in clinical psychology, and a fellowship permitted her to study at the Institute for Psychotherapy in Berlin. While in Germany, Hooker lived
with a Jewish family who were later killed in the concentration camps. Through their eyes she
experienced the horrors of Hitler's Germany.

Source: Hooker, E. (1957). The adjustment of the male overt homosexual. *Journal of Projective Techniques, 21,*
18–31. [Paper read at the American Psychological Association Convention. Chicago, August 30, 1956.]

Editorial Note: It is an uncommon event in these days of compulsive publication to discover an author who has
worked diligently and with great detail and who hesitates to publish well-substantiated findings until proof is virtually incontrovertible. A study such as Dr. Hooker's challenges several widespread and emotional convictions. In view
of the importance of her findings it seemed desirable to the editors that they be made public, even in their preliminary form. If some of Dr. Hooker's comments, as cautiously presented as they are, seem premature or incompletely
documented, the blame must fall on the editors who exercised considerable pressure on her to publish now.—BRF

In 1939 Hooker applied for a full-time faculty position in the psychology department at UCLA. Knight Dunlap, the chair of the department, told her that there were already too many women in the department. He offered her a position as a research associate and the opportunity to teach in the extension division. Except for one year spent at Bryn Mawr, Hooker would stay at UCLA until 1970.

In her early years at UCLA Hooker continued to do laboratory work with white rats (e.g., Gentry, 1943; Gentry & Dunlap, 1942). But her area of research changed when Sam From, an ex-student of hers, became her friend. He was homosexual, and over time he introduced Hooker to a number of his homosexual friends and to the "gay world." From urged her to use her research skills to study the underground network of people and places that made up the gay community.

The 1940s and early 1950s were a time when a great deal of social and political attention was given to homosexuality (D'Emilio, 1983, 2002). In World War II homosexuality became grounds for exclusion from the military, and psychiatrists began studying ways to distinguish homosexuals from malingerers (those feigning homosexuality to avoid service) (Bérubé, 1990; Hegarty, 2003). At the same time, "the war had ironically allowed many men and women opportunities for the discovery and recognition of gay and lesbian desires, identities and subcultures, through . . . a form of institutional life that did not take the nuclear family as its basic unit" (Hegarty, 2003, p. 110). In 1948 Kinsey, Pomeroy, and Martin published *Sexual Behavior in the Human Male,* a book that made clear that male homosexual behavior and fantasy are not as unusual as many believed. In 1952 the American Psychiatric Association identified homosexuality as a mental disorder. In 1953 the employment of homosexuals was prohibited in all government jobs by executive order (D'Emilio, 2001). The McCarthy hearings in the early 1950s insisted that there was a link between homosexuality and communism (Hay, in Cusac, 1999).

In 1953 Hooker submitted a proposal to the National Institute of Mental Health (NIMH) for a grant to do a study comparing homosexual and heterosexual males. Her proposal was funded, rather a surprise, considering the negative attitudes toward homosexuality prevalent at the time, and the grant continued to be renewed until 1961, when Hooker received an NIMH Research Career Award to continue her work indefinitely.[1]

Hooker's first paper on the gay community (Hooker, 1956) began with a discussion of the factors that lead to a general acceptance or rejection of homosexuality in society. She then looked at the personal characteristics associated with male homosexuals in American culture and argued that these characteristics are related, not to their homosexuality itself, but to the status of homosexuals as minority group members in American society. Using Gordon Allport's (1954) description of the typical responses to victimization that minority group members often show, Hooker related the stereotypes about gay men, and certain aspects of the behavior of gay men, to their minority status. These themes and a more detailed description of the "gay community" continued to be important parts of Hooker's thinking (e.g., Hooker, 1965).

Her next paper, reprinted here, was a direct attack on the idea that homosexuals are mentally ill—an idea that had been formalized in the first edition of the *Diagnostic and Statistical Manual*

---

[1] The biographical information on Evelyn Hooker is from Boxer & Carrier (1998), Kimmel & Garnets (2000), Marcus (1992), and Shneidman (1998). There is also an award-winning documentary film, *Changing Our Minds: The Story of Dr. Evelyn Hooker* (Haugland & Schmiechen, 1991).

of Mental Disorders (DSM) in 1952. The *DSM*, published by the American Psychiatric Association, is the most influential system of classification of mental illnesses in the United States and is used by clinicians—psychiatrists, social workers, psychologists, clergy, and others—to diagnose the "illnesses" from which their clients suffer. The *DSM* provides a common vocabulary for all clinicians and also provides information about prognosis and treatment possibilities. Hooker challenged the inclusion of homosexuality as a mental disorder, and she provided empirical evidence in her 1957 article that demonstrated that homosexuality is not pathological and homosexuals are not mentally ill.

It would take the American Psychiatric Association 16 years to change the *DSM*. In the 1973 edition (*DSM-II*) homosexuality was finally removed as a diagnostic category, although it was replaced with "Sexual Orientation Disturbance," a diagnosis meant to apply only to homosexuals. This latter diagnosis was replaced in the *DSM-III* in 1980 with "ego-dystonic homosexuality," a diagnosis reserved for individuals who are distressed either because they experience unwanted homosexual arousal or because they do not experience the heterosexual arousal necessary for a desired heterosexual relationship. In 1987 this diagnosis was removed and replaced by "Sexual Disorders Not Otherwise Specified."

This history makes clear that diagnostic categories, at least those related to "mental disorders," are influenced by social factors. Since its first edition in 1952, the *DSM* has undergone many changes. In 1980 the psychodynamic organization was changed to a more biomedical system of categorization, and over the years particular diagnoses have been added or removed. There is continued debate over whether such a formalized system of diagnosis is useful, about whether its disadvantages outweigh its advantages, and about whether it will ever be possible to have a valid system (e.g., Cooper, 2004; Haglin, 2005; Kirk & Kutchins, 1992).

The elimination of homosexuality as a form of mental illness was probably the most dramatic and public change made to the *DSM*. Bayer (1981) describes the events, politics, and people that finally led the American Psychiatric Association to change its views in 1973. In discussing Evelyn Hooker's role, he says,

> Hooker's work in the mid-1950s was of critical importance for the evolution of the homophile movement. Her findings provided "facts" that could buttress the position of homosexuals who rejected the pathological view of their condition. She had met the psychiatrists on their own terms and provided their critics with clinical data with which to do battle. . . . She became not only a source of ideological support, but an active participant in the homosexual struggle. (p. 53)

Current psychiatric and psychological opinion about the adjustment of the homosexual may be illustrated by a quotation from a report on homosexuality recently issued by the Group for the Advancement of Psychiatry (1955, p. 2): "When such homosexual behavior persists in an adult, it is then a symptom of a severe emotional disorder." If one wishes to subject this opinion to experimental investigation, one is immediately confronted by problems of considerable magnitude. One problem is the attitude and theoretical position of the clinician who may be asked to examine the data. I quote again from the Group for the Advancement of Psychiatry in the same report (p. 4): "It is well known that many people, including physicians, react in an exaggerated way to sexual deviations and particularly to homosexuality with disgust, anger, and hostility. Such feelings often arise from the individual's own conflict centering about his unconscious homosexual impulses. These attitudes may interfere with an intelligent and objective handling of the problem." One hopes that the clinician does not react with "disgust, anger, and hostility." It is not realistic to hope that he will avoid theoretical preconceptions when looking at psychological material which he knows was obtained from a homosexual.

From a survey of the literature it seemed highly probable that few clinicians have ever had the opportunity to examine homosexual subjects who neither came for psychological help nor were found in mental hospitals, disciplinary barracks in the Armed Services, or in prison populations. It therefore seemed important, when I set out to investigate the adjustment of the homosexual, to obtain a sample of overt homosexuals who did not come from these sources; that is, who had a chance of being individuals who, on the surface at least, seemed to have an average adjustment, provided that (for the purpose of the investigation) homosexuality is not considered to be a symptom of maladjustment. It also seemed important to obtain a comparable control group of heterosexuals. This group would not only provide a standard of comparison but might also make it possible to avoid labels and thus assist the clinician in suspending theoretical preconceptions. This, I recognized, would be fraught with extreme difficulties. And so it was. Without relating in detail the—in many ways—fascinating, frustrating, and gratifying aspects of the attempts to secure both of these groups, I shall describe the homosexual and heterosexual samples of thirty individuals each finally obtained.

Each homosexual man is matched for age, education, and IQ with a heterosexual man. It would have been desirable to match for other variables, also, including occupation, but this was manifestly impossible. It should also be stated at the outset that no assumptions are made about the random selection of either group. No one knows what a random sample of the homosexual population would be like; and even if one knew, it would be extremely difficult, if not impossible, to obtain one. The project would not have been possible without the invaluable assistance of the Mattachine Society, an organization which has as its stated purpose the development of a homosexual ethic in

Henry Hay established the Mattachine Society in Los Angeles in 1950. According to Hay (in Cusac, 1999), the society was named for a dance (*les Mattachines*) that unmarried men performed in France during the Renaissance. The society had two goals: to eliminate anti-gay discrimination and to build a strong homosexual community.

order to better integrate the homosexual into society. The members of the Mattachine Society not only made themselves available as subjects but also persuaded their friends to become subjects. Because the heterosexuals were, for the most part, obtained from community organizations which must remain anonymous, I cannot describe further the way in which they were obtained.

Considerable effort was devoted to securing the 30 matched pairs of subjects, and the data in Table 1 indicate that in most instances the matching was unusually close.

> Table 1 indicates that the age range was 26–57.

> 91–135 according to Table 1.

The homosexuals, and thus the heterosexuals, ranged in age from 25 to 50, with an average age of 34.5 for the homosexual group and 36.6 for the heterosexual group. The IQ range, as measured by the Otis Self-Administering Tests of Mental Ability, was from 90 to 135, with an average for the homosexual group of 115.4 and for the heterosexual group of 116.2. In education the range was from completion of grammar school to the equivalent of a master's degree, with an average for the homosexual group of 13.9 years and for the heterosexual group of 14.3.

In both groups subjects were eliminated who were in therapy at the time. If, in the preliminary screening, evidence of considerable disturbance appeared, the individual was eliminated (5 heterosexuals; 5 homosexuals). I attempted to secure homosexuals who would be pure for homosexuality; that is, without heterosexual experience. With three exceptions this is so. These three subjects had not had more than three heterosexual experiences, and they identified themselves as homosexual in their patterns of desire and behavior. The heterosexual group is exclusively heterosexual beyond the adolescent period, with three exceptions; these three had had a single homosexual experience each. In the effort to control the presence of homosexuality, latent or otherwise, in the heterosexual group, each potential subject was referred by a responsible leader of a community group, who described him as being a thorough-going heterosexual and well adjusted. This was an attempt to take precautions to eliminate as many men as possible with homosexual patterns of behavior. It did not do so, and some individuals came who had to be eliminated because, though married and functioning in the community as married men, they had had extensive homosexual experience (four subjects).

The heterosexual subjects came because they were told that this was an opportunity to contribute to our understanding of the way in which the average individual in the community functions, since we had little data on normal men. They were told nothing beforehand about the homosexual aspects of the project. When an individual came to me, after describing to him the nature of the testing and the interview and securing his willingness to participate in the project, I then described very briefly the purpose of the study, including the homosexual group. It was impossible to avoid this explanation. The community leaders who referred these men

TABLE 1

Number	Homosexual			Heterosexual		
Matched Pairs	Age	IQ	Education	Age	IQ	Education
1	42	105	12	41	105	12
2	29	104	12	28	104	12
3	29	109	9	31	109	12
4	31	120	16	30	123	16
5	44	127	18	45	126	17
6	33	127	16	32	129	16
7	40	124	16	42	123	16
8	33	124	16	36	122	16
9	40	98	12	42	100	12
10	33	101	14	32	105	15
11	30	127	14	29	127	16
12	42	91	12	39	94	14
13	41	98	9	44	100	12
14	36	114	16	36	117	16
15	33	120	14	34	120	16
16	40	106	12	44	107	12
17	37	116	12	34	113	14
18	36	127	16	36	127	16
19	35	103	12	37	101	11
20	26	133	18	27	133	18
21	33	124	13	36	122	16
22	32	123	12	39	120	12
23	26	123	16	29	133	16
24	26	123	16	29	133	16
25	41	135	16	39	119	16
26	28	114	16	35	112	13
27	27	118	13	48	119	13
28	27	110	14	48	113	16
29	57	95	14	46	100	12
30	26	124	14	30	129	12

Because confidentiality was extremely important during a time when homosexuality was considered to be a sin, a crime, and a disease, Hooker conducted all her research at her home; she erased the tapes after they had been transcribed; she removed all identification from the records (Hooker, 1993); and in the last years of her life, she shredded all of them (Boxer & Carrier, 1998).

There were several methods used to analyze the Rorschach in the 1950s. Bruno Klopfer had popularized the Rorschach in America and was one of its principal advocates and interpreters. Because of that and because Hooker was a colleague and friend of his (Hooker, 1960; Kimmel & Garnets, 2000; Marcus, 1992), it is likely that she used his method (Klopfer, Ainsworth, Klopfer, & Holt, 1954). The most common method of analysis used now, at least by psychologists, was developed by Exner (1974). It combines several previous approaches and includes extensive empirical data on frequent responses.

were concerned about possible repercussions of a "sex study." They required that each man be informed that the total project involved a comparison of homosexual and heterosexual men. I had, therefore, to risk the effect of this information upon my subjects. So, having very briefly described the project to him, I then asked whether he had had any homosexual inclinations or experience. This question was put in a matter-of-fact way and only after a good relationship of cooperation had been established. If the individual seemed to be severely disturbed by the question, or responded in a bland way, or denied it vehemently, I did not include him in the sample of 30. It is possible, though I doubt it, that there are some heterosexuals in my group who have strong latent or concealed overt homosexuality.

The materials used for the comparative study of personality structure and adjustment of these two groups of men consisted of a battery of projective techniques, attitude scales, and intensive life history interviews. The material I am reporting on here is largely from an analysis of the Rorschach, TAT, and MAPS, with some references to life histories, the detailed analysis of which has not yet been completed.

Projective tests: tests in which it is assumed that you project your personality, needs, anxieties, defenses, etc., into the responses you give to an ambiguous stimulus.

Rorschach: A test developed by Hermann Rorschach in 1921 (Rorschach, 1942). The test consists of 10 cards, each with a symmetrical ink blot on it. Those taking the test are asked to describe what they see when they look at each of the ink blots.

TAT (Thematic Apperception Test): The TAT was created in the late 1930s by Henry Murray and Christiana Morgan. If you take the TAT, you are usually shown a series of 10 pictures, most including one or more people, and asked to "make up as dramatic a story as you can for each. Tell what has led up to the event shown in the picture, describe what is happening at the moment, what the characters are feeling and thinking; and then give the outcome" (Murray, 1943). Another set of 10 pictures can be shown on another day with the same instructions. Some of the cards contain photographs; some contain drawings; one is blank.

MAPS (Make-A-Picture Story): This is a test created by Edwin Shneidman in 1952. Like the TAT, the MAPS asks the person taking the test to make up a story, but the MAPS asks the person to choose his or her own characters and sometimes his or her own background scenes.

The Rorschach is still very frequently used in clinical work. The TAT is used in personality and clinical research and is used in clinical practice as well, although probably less frequently than the Rorschach. MAPS is referred to very infrequently in the current psychometric or clinical literature.

I used the Rorschach because many clinicians believe it to be the best method of assessing total personality structure and, also, because it is one of the test instruments currently used for the diagnosis of homosexuality. The 60 Rorschach protocols were scored by me, the usual tab-ulations made, and the profiles constructed. With all identifying information except age elim-
110 inated, they were then arranged in random order. Two clinicians, who are also experts in Rorschach, analyzed each of the 60 protocols separately in this order. Because of the impor-tance of knowing how, by what process, using what evidence in the Rorschach, a judge arrived at his rating or judgment in each of the categories, each judge was urged to describe as much as he could of the procedure he was using, the conclusions arrived at, and the evi-
115 dence used; and the whole process was recorded by Audograph. . . . My success in persuading Dr. Klopfer and Dr. Mortimer Meyer, for the Rorschach, and Dr. Shneidman, for the TAT and MAPS, to give so generously of themselves in this project was primarily due to their belief in its importance and to their eagerness to see a unique body of material and to engage in what they anticipated to be a rewarding learning experience.
120 The purpose of the Rorschach analysis was two-fold: (1) to obtain an unbiased judgment (that is, without knowledge of homosexual or heterosexual identification of subjects and without life-history materials) of personality structure and overall adjustment of the subjects in both groups; (2) to determine the accuracy with which expert clinicians who are Rorschach workers can differentiate homosexual from heterosexual records. . . . The adjustment rating
125 was on a five-point scale: from 1, superior, to 5, maladjusted; with 3 representing average adjustment. . . . The meanings of the five points of the rating scale were defined as follows: (1) superior, or top adjustment; better than the average person in the total population, evi-dence of superior integration of capacities, both intellectual and emotional; ease and com-fort in relation to the self and in functioning effectively in relation to the social environment;
130 (3) as well-adjusted as the average person in the total population; nothing conspicuously good or bad; (5) bottom limit of normal group and/or maladjusted, with signs of pathology. Ratings 2 and 4 are self-evident, 2 being better-than-average but not quite superior, and 4 being worse-than-average, or the bottom limit of the average group. These ratings are very difficult to objectify, and it is very difficult to be sure that they were used in the same way by
135 the two judges.

One further comment about procedure, before discussing the results of the judging on adjustment: each judge, before he began, knew that some records were homosexual and some were heterosexual. Most clinicians in the Los Angeles area are familiar with the project, and it would have been impossible to secure experts without some knowledge of it. The judge was told that the opportunity to distinguish homosexual from heterosexual records would come 140 later and that the present task was that of telling me as much as he could about what he thought the subject to be like in personality structure and adjustment. If anything impressed him about the pattern of sexual adjustment, he should say it, but this was not the primary purpose of this stage of the analysis. The task of the judges was broken down into two steps: (1) The protocols were analyzed, with overall adjustment ratings given and summary judg- 145 ments made, in the categories already described; and (2) each judge was then presented with 30 pairs of protocols, matched for age, education, and IQ, the task being to distinguish the homosexual record in each pair.

The results of the judging of adjustment from the Rorschach protocols are presented in Table 2.

It will be noted that there are no significant differences between the number of homosex- 150 uals and heterosexuals having a rating of 3 and better for each judge; two-thirds of each group are assigned an adjustment rating of 3 or better. There are apparent differences between judges. For Judge "B" there is a greater unwillingness to assign a top rating. In fact, for Judge "B," there is a slight but insignificant trend in the direction of superior adjustment for the homosexual group. By the method of "grand medians," chi square for Judge "A" is zero for the dif- 155 ferences in adjustment between heterosexuals and homosexuals and for Judge "B" the difference is 2.31, which is insignificant.

. . .

TABLE 2   Ratings of overall adjustment—Rorschach

	Ratings				
	(Top)				*(Bottom)*
	1	2	3	4	5
Group					
Judge "A" Homosexual	9	9	4	3	5
Heterosexual	6	12	5	3	4
Total	15	21	9	6	9
Judge "B" Homosexual	2	15	5	4	4
Heterosexual	2	8	9	8	3
Total	4	23	14	12	7

TABLE 3

Differences	Number of Subjects		
	Total	Homosexual	Heterosexual
0 (exact agreement)	19	8	11
1 rating step	23	12	11
2 rating steps	14	7	7
3 rating steps	4	3	1
	60	30	30

Table 3 shows that the two judges agreed exactly in 19 of the 60 cases, 8 being homosexual and 11 heterosexual. In 23 cases they disagreed by one rating step, 12 of these being
160   homosexual and 11 heterosexual. This *means that in 42 out of the 60 cases there was either exact agreement or disagreement by only one step.* So it is safe to say that in two-thirds of the total distribution there is high agreement. . . .

How is one to interpret this finding? Is one to take it at face value and assume that the Rorschach is a valid instrument for determining adjustment in the way in which
165   we have defined it? If so, then clearly there is no inherent connection between pathology and homosexuality. But caution is needed. As clinicians, we are well aware, in daily practice, of the limitations of projective material ana-
170   lyzed "blind." Nevertheless, the quantitative results are striking, and they are confirmed in part by observations of the judges, as well as—and I say this with great caution—by life-history data.

> Typically a clinician has additional information about a person—age, background, occupation, and so on—to aid in the interpretation and analysis of projective test results.

175   But let us look at the results in the second task given the judges, that of distinguishing between matched pairs of homosexual and heterosexual records. This is a much easier task than that which the clinician ordinarily faces, of identifying homosexuality in one record out of many; and yet it proved to be a very difficult one. As a judge compared the matched protocols, he would frequently comment, "There are no
180   clues"; or, "These are so similar that you are out to skin us alive"; or, "It is a forced choice"; or, "I just have to guess." The difficulty of the task was reflected not only in the comments of the judges but also in the results. Judge "A" correctly identified 17 of the 30 pairs, and Judge "B" 18 of the 30. Thus neither judge was able to do better than

chance. In seven pairs both judges were incorrect, that is, identifying the homosexual as the heterosexual, and vice versa; in twelve pairs, correct; and in the remaining eleven they disagreed.   185

> As Hooker points out in a later article (1958), although the accuracy of each of the judges was at the chance level, the fact that the judges agreed on 12 correct judgments exceeds chance expectations. However, the judges knew that one member of each pair was homosexual and one heterosexual, making this a simpler task than that usually facing a clinician.
>
> In the earlier part of the study, the judges were asked to look individually at all 60 protocols and to make a number of ratings, including one dealing with the men's sexual adjustment. In that part of the study Judge "A" correctly identified the sexual orientation of 28 of the 60 men, and Judge "B" of 23 men. The judges agreed with one another on only six correct judgments of homosexuality and six correct judgments of heterosexuality. In these ratings, the individual judgments were at the chance level, and their combined judgments were as well.

Let us look at the problems the judges faced. In some pairs of records none of the clues usually considered to be signs of homosexuality occurred. In some pairs the "homosexual clues" appeared in both records. These "homosexual clues" were primarily anality, open or dis-   190
guised; avoidance of areas usually designated as vaginal areas; articles of feminine clothing, especially under-clothing, and/or art objects elaborated with unusual detail; responses giving evidence of considerable sexual confusion,   195
with castration anxiety, and/or hostile or fearful attitudes toward women; evidence of feminine cultural identification, and/or emotional involvement between males. When these clues

> In the 1940s a number of clinicians were trying to identify the "clues" in Rorschach responses that would discriminate between heterosexuals and homosexuals. The system developed by Wheeler (1949) seems to have been the most accepted, and most of the clues mentioned by Hooker are included in his list of 20 signs.

appeared in neither or in both records, the judge was forced to look for other evidence,   200
and most frequently depended upon peculiar verbalization, or responses with idiosyncratic meaning, or the "flavor" of the total record. When careful examination failed to reveal anything distinctive, the judge assumed that the more banal or typical record was that of the heterosexual, an assumption which was sometimes false.

After the judging was completed, and, indeed, even while it was in process, both judges   205
commented on the fact that the records which they thought to be homosexual were unlike the ones they were familiar with in the clinic. They were not the disturbed records ordinarily seen. One judge, in the process of choosing, said, "It begins to look as if the homosexuals have

210 all the good things: for example, M's and Fc." It may be pertinent to reiterate that I had made an effort to secure records of homosexuals who ordinarily would not be seen in a clinic. A discussion of the validity and reliability of homosexual signs is tangential to this symposium,[2] but I would point

215 out in passing that my data indicate the need for a thorough-going reconsideration of this problem. At a minimum, healthy skepticism about many (but not all) so-called homosexual-content signs in the Rorschach is, I think, called for. The

220 inability of the judges to distinguish the homosexual from the heterosexual records better than would be expected by chance fits, I think, the

> *M:* Movement. In the Klopfer system, *M* refers to human movement, both active and passive.
>
> *Fc:* Form with shading or texture. In the Klopfer system, *F* refers to a response that identifies a form, a thing, and *c* to the description of surface or texture associated with that form.
>
> Klopfer et al. (1954) mention that "Both *Fc* and *M* may have implications that the person is capable of empathy in his relationships with other people" (p. 274).

finding on adjustment of the two groups. Some of the records can be easily distinguished; the fact that the judges agreed in their identification of twelve pairs indicates this. These were

225 records of individuals with strong emphasis on "femininity" and/or anality. But apart from these, which constitute about a third of the group, the remaining two thirds cannot be easily distinguished. If the homosexual records had been similar to those frequently seen in the clinic, that is, severely disturbed, there might have been greater probability that they could have been correctly identified, although this cannot be said with certainty. I have now seen

230 about two hundred homosexual records and would be skeptical about my ability to identify correctly records similar to many in this group.

---

[2] A paper on "Homosexuality in the Rorschach" is in process of preparation. It will contain a full discussion of homosexual signs as well as other aspects of homosexuality in the Rorschach.

The paper referred to is Hooker (1958). In this paper Hooker reviews a number of studies that looked for differences between the Rorschach responses of heterosexual and homosexual men. She concludes that, across all these studies, the only factors that seem consistently to differentiate the groups are "anal orientation" and "feminine emphasis," factors that are more likely to appear in homosexual than in heterosexual protocols. Because they do not appear often, however, this is not terribly useful.

In a later article (Hooker, 1959), she looked at similar research using the TAT. There was less work done with the TAT, but, except for men who consistently tell overtly homosexual stories, there seemed to be no pattern of responses consistently associated with sexual orientation. Hooker suggests that projective test results do not contain "clues" that will allow clinicians to identify homosexual men with adequate accuracy, and she is more explicit about a point she included in her 1958 paper—that the search for such "clues" is fruitless because it assumes that there is such a thing as "the" homosexual male. She wrote, "I am not greatly disturbed by the fact that projective techniques are not demonstrably valid means for diagnosing homosexuality. In fact I am rather encouraged by this, because I hope it will force us to re-examine the much over-simplified picture we have had" (pp. 280–281).

. . .

Let us turn now to the TAT and MAPS. These were administered as a single test, the selected MAPS items following the TAT. Altogether, 12 pictures were used: 3BM, 6BM, 7BM, 12M, 13MF, 16, and 18GF of the TAT; and from the MAPS, the Living Room, the Street Scene, the Bathroom, the Bedroom, and the Dream. It was hoped that the TAT and MAPS would be helpful in revealing current conflicts. The MAPS was used in addition to the TAT because of the opportunity it gives the subject for the selection of figures together with backgrounds with different situational pulls of particular importance in this study. Very fortunately, Dr. Shneidman agreed to analyze the MAPS and TAT protocols of the 60 subjects, using the same categories for analysis and overall adjustment as did the Rorschach judges. . . . The problem of identifying the homosexual protocol from this material was essentially a much easier one than that encountered with the Rorschach, since few homosexuals failed to give open homosexual stories on at least one picture. The second task given the Rorschach judges, of distinguishing the homosexual from the heterosexual records when they were presented in matched pairs, was therefore omitted. In every other respect, however, both with respect to task and procedure and including the recording, the TAT-MAPS judge proceeded as had the Rorschach judges. In the first 30 records the TAT and MAPS protocols for each man were analyzed together, with judgments given about overall adjustment rating and the other categories, such as methods of handling aggression, etc. In the second 30 records, the TAT protocols were analyzed in succession, with judgments given, and then the MAPS—the judge not knowing which MAPS protocol corresponded with which TAT. This was done in an effort to prevent a "halo" effect, since homosexuality was openly revealed in some TAT records and not in the MAPS (for the same man), and vice versa. Some very interesting results were obtained, to which I shall refer later.

> Because the TAT is a projective test, it is important to have at least one character in each picture who is the same gender and age as the person taking the test. As a result, there are some different cards for men, women, and adolescents. Pictures labeled BM are intended for boys and men; those labeled GF are for girls and women.

235

240

245

250

255

Table 4 shows the data on the adjustment ratings. The results are essentially the same as for the Rorschach. *The homosexuals and heterosexuals do not differ significantly in their ratings.* Chi square = 2.72, df = 4, p = > .70. This judge does not place a single subject in Rating 1, and he places only one in Rating 5 (a heterosexual). . . .

260

TABLE 4   Adjustment ratings on MAPS-TAT

| | Ratings | | | | |
| | (Top) | | | | (Bottom) |
Group	1	2	3	4	5
Homosexual	0	9	15	6	0
Heterosexual	0	7	19	3	1
Total	0	16	34	9	1

Freedman (1971) did a study to determine whether there were any differences in the mental health of homosexual and heterosexual women. Unlike Hooker, he used two self-report questionnaires—the Personal Orientation Inventory (Shostrom, 1963) and the Eysenck Personality Inventory (Eysenck & Eysenck, 1963) to measure mental health. Like Hooker, he found no difference between the two groups.

Let me turn now to some qualitative descriptions of the homosexuals from the projective material. Perhaps even better than do the quantitative results, these will convey the problem. Man #16 is described by one judge in summary fashion as "an individual who has
265 the most superb and smooth mastery of intellectual processes we have seen. Intellectualization is his major defense, although there is no compulsive flavor. On one side there is isolation of aggression. But essentially he is submissive, and since he is so sensitive and responsive, he cannot give in to the submissive seduction. His dependency needs are filtered and sublimated. He is the ethical type. Intellectual introspection must be his major
270 preoccupation. He is really balanced on a razor's edge. An extremely clever person." He was correctly identified by this judge, who gave him a rating of 1, and incorrectly by the other judge, who placed him in Rating 2. The latter describes him in the following terms. "He gives an original twist to ordinary things. For him it is very important not to be conventional. He avoids it like the plague. He tries to keep it cool. I get the feeling that he wants to deny
275 dependency. He has passive longings, but these would not fit in with his ego-ideal of being strong, superior, and wise. He would be able to be very rewarding emotionally. He does not wish to expose his aggression ordinarily, but would in relation to manly intellectual pursuits. I think he is heterosexual."

This man is described on the MAPS and TAT as being "the most heterosexual-looking
280 homosexual I have ever seen. Up to the last two stories on the MAPS, I would say confidently, 'This is a heterosexual record.' His attitudes to sexuality are fairly moral. He has refined, quiet relationships to people. I would give him a rating of 2. The unconscious conflicts are very deep, but they are not disturbing clinically. No idea of clinical label. I would not have known he is a homosexual except for a 'give away' on two of the MAPS stories."

285 This man is in his early 40's and holds two master's degrees in different artistic fields from one of the major educational institutions of this country. He had a long career as a college teacher—long, and apparently successful. He was caught in what was, to the police, suspicious circumstances with another man, and in the space of a few minutes his entire professional career was destroyed. He now is the manager of a magazine. Although in his early life
290 he passed through the "cruising" stage, he now has highly stable personal relationships, including a "homosexual marriage." If one brackets the fact that he is a homosexual, one would think of him as being a highly cultured, intelligent man who, though unconventional in his manner of living, exhibits no particular signs of pathology. He has never sought psychological or psychiatric help. He has been a homosexual from adolescence, with no hetero-
295 sexual experience or inclination.

channelization: The words *channelization* and *canalization* are considered synonymous by many. Bischof (1970), however, makes a distinction. Gardner Murphy (1966) used the term *canalization* to refer to the fact that we tend to seek the same satisfiers that we have sought in the past. George Kelly (1955), on the other hand, used the word *channelized* to describe the fact that our behavior is guided by a network of pathways that provide means to ends. Murphy, then, looked only to the past to understand why drives are satisfied in particular ways; Kelly looked to the future as well. Whichever meaning the judge was using, it certainly had to do with the fact that an individual's behavior tends to flow through existing canals or channels.

Let me describe another (Subject #50) of these individuals who was placed in adjustment categories 1 or 2 by both Rorschach judges and misidentified as being a heterosexual. One judge described this man "as being so ordinary that it's hard to say anything specific about him. His impulse control is very smooth. He uses channelization rather than repression. Except for a little too much emphasis on conquest in heterosexual relations, he is well adjusted and smooth. His aggressive impulses are expressed in phallic gratification. Good fusion of tenderness and aggression, though he subjugates tenderness to phallic gratification. He must be a heterosexual. I would really have to force myself, to think of him as not heterosexual." By the second judge this man is described in the following terms: "He must be a very interesting guy. He must convey comfort to people. He takes essentials and doesn't get lost in details. A solid citizen, neatly and solidly integrated, with no specific defenses. Neither aggression nor dependency is a problem. I think that this man is heterosexual."

Man #50 is twenty-seven. He works in the electronics industry, in a very large firm in which he has a supervisory job. He lives alone in an apartment, though in an apartment house in which other homosexuals reside. His homosexual pattern involves rather a large number of homosexual partners. He is thoroughly immersed in the homosexual way of life, but apart from this I see no particular evidence of disturbance.

The TAT was analyzed first, and on the TAT he talks about homosexuality, thus revealing that he is a homosexual. The judgments to which the clinician comes are essentially that he is a promiscuous, driven person; that there are compulsive elements; that he goes from one relationship to another, not even aware of what he is seeking, a fairly lonely man, although with an adjustment slightly below 3. The first four stories of the MAPS were described by the judge as being definitely heterosexual. On the last story, the Dream, I should like to quote the judge directly: "I am surprised, because what this means is that this is the record of a homosexual; and it means that I had not seen this at all up to this point. It means, also, that he doesn't show it except over the jealousy and rivalry of homosexual partners. The record is clean psychiatrically up to this point. It wasn't especially rich, but it would certainly pass. I don't want to do fancy equivocation and say I see it all now, because I don't see a damn thing now. The Living Room is fine; it is as heterosexual as any story we have read in the entire series. The Street Scene simply shows the derogatory and disdainful attitudes that many heterosexual men have toward female sexuality. It is not the exclusive approach of the homosexual, though it is consistent with it. It has a heterosexual flavor. In the Bath, the privacy of the father is interrupted, but this, if anything would be heterosexual. The Bedroom is as normal a heterosexual story as I have ever read." The judge re-reads the story: "This is almost an encapsulated homosexual. I don't know if I am just being fancy, but we talk about a guy sometimes who functions fairly well until you mention 'Republican' or 'Communist,' then you plug in a whole series of paranoid and delusory material; at this point the guy is just crazy. *This* guy has an encapsulated homosexual system. If I had not been shown the Dream story, I would have bet 85 to 15 that he was heterosexual, and maybe even more. I also feel that this guy is a male homosexual. He plays the aggressive, masculine role. But I am puzzled. I can hardly speak intelligently of the dynamics of the homosexuality when, until the last moment, I thought of him as heterosexual. I would give him a rating of slightly better than 3. Not a rich record; not creative and imaginative. It's a rather perfunctorily heterosexual record. I am amazed at this record. He has intense involvement with people. He is not a promiscuous homosexual. There is strong affect. He practically acts like a husband and father. One of the statements about him is that he is a normal homosexual. . . . This record is schizophrenic like I am an aviator. If you want proof that a homosexual can be normal, this record does it."

Man #49 is described by Judge "A" as follows (Rating 1): "This record presents less problems of any sort than any other we have seen. The mental type is very clear-cut, calling a spade a spade. Looks like a well-integrated person. Impulse control really smooth, because he permits all impulses to express themselves in a context—both dependent and aggressive. Of all the cases, the best balance of aggression and dependency we have seen. No problem, clinical or otherwise. Relations with others skilful and comfortable." Judge "B" (Rating 2; if not 2, a 1): "Able to integrate well with all stimuli. Effective functioning. Heterosexual adjustment. Defense used: some repression. Not an 'acter outer.' Avoids intense emotional stimuli because they are disorganizing to him."

The TAT and MAPS were analyzed separately. In the first four stories of the TAT, the subject was described as being a thorough-going heterosexual. In 13MF the judge comments, "Here we have a fairly straightforward heterosexual story." In the blank card in the TAT, the judge says, "Here this guy opens up more than on the others. He is a sleeper. This is one of the best-adjusted and, in a sense, one of the most paradoxical records I have seen. What is here is indecision and a schizoid feeling. So this is not in any sense a superior personality. There is some withdrawal and some aridity. This is not an outgoing, warm, decisive person. It is a constricted, somewhat egocentric, somewhat schizoid, perturbed, a little guilty fellow. Even so, it is not a tormented record and is not necessarily a homosexual record. He talks about this quite casually and has a fairly good adjustment to his homosexuality. This guy is a very interesting person and quite a complicated guy. In many ways he is both well adjusted to his homosexuality and the kind of guy who could almost be heterosexual in a way that other homosexuals could not be. I don't think he would be swishy or over-masculine. He would pass. I find him very difficult to rate. I can't rate him as 1 or 2. To call him average is innocuous. He doesn't merit 3 or 4. I don't know. I will call him 3, but it doesn't give the flavor. I don't know what to do."

At another time the same judge analyzed the MAPS protocol, in which no homosexual stories are given. The judge comments: "I want to comment on his insistence on the normal situation and his freedom to use the nude. I think this is a very healthy guy, in a somewhat barren way. I have a feeling that this is a kind of emancipated person who has not made an issue of being independent but is able to stand on his own two feet. The fact that he doesn't have rich dynamics robs him of being interesting, creative, and unusual. I rate him as a 2 for sure. I don't know what a 1 would be. He handles hostility and sexuality easily. One shortcoming in the record—not pathological—is the conventionality; and I imply by that a touch of emptiness. He is able to love and to dislike. He is a good father and husband and would be a steady employee. I could see him as having a better-than-average job. He would not be a creative or imaginative person. I don't mean a Babbitt, but he would not take the risk of loving deeply. He is a middle-of-the-roader. This is as clean a record as I think I have seen. I don't think he has strong dependency needs. He is comfortable, and in that sense he is strong. I imply that this is a heterosexual record specifically."

> Babbitt was an outwardly successful but inwardly unhappy real-estate salesman in Sinclair Lewis's 1922 novel of the same name. Babbitt is caught between the desire to conform and the urge to do more. For a very brief time he breaks loose, but then returns to the fold. In *Babbitt,* as in much of his other work, Lewis takes a satiric look at American middle-class life and conformity.

This man is 37, and he works in a ceramics factory doing fairly routine work. He has a "homosexual marriage" of some six years' duration. He tried very hard to change his sexual pattern but was unsuccessful and has now accepted the homosexual "life." He has not had heterosexual experience.

Out of the 30 homosexual men, there were seven who were placed by one or the other judge in rating categories 4 or 5. Since these individuals have what is probably the more expected personality picture, I should like to describe several. One of these is #6. He was rated by one judge at a 5 level and by the other judge at 2. By the judge who places him at 5, he is described as a "pseudo-normal, near-psychotic, with brittle personality organization which is fairly stabilized. His reality testing is uncannily sharp,

> reality testing: the ability to test one's subjective perceptions against reality

but he is almost autistic. His chief defenses are projection and intellectual control. There are strong castration fears, strong orality, and the aggression is projected or transformed into irony. The emotional needs are withered away."

Man #52 is described by one judge who places him in the 4 category, as "a personality which is basically pathological. An anal character, with a strongly destructive flavor. Anal-sadistic. A past-master of intellectualization, though superficially socializes it. Just enough reality testing to be clinically normal. Impossible to separate the hysterical and paranoid elements. Dependency needs are repressed or crippled. Very narcissistic and incapable of guilt. A cloak of righteousness over it all." The second judge describes him in the following terms: "There is too much unconscious breaking through. Some ideational leakage. A chronic situation to which he has made an adjustment. He is not paranoid, but obsessive in a paranoid structure. On the surface he operates smoothly. Emotional relationships will

lack in depth and warmth. Uses over-ideation as a defense. His primary method is intel-
420   lectualization. His dependency needs will make him appear demanding. Essentially a
character picture."

Of a somewhat different nature is #28, who is placed by both judges at the bottom level of
adjustment. Described by one judge as "very defensive; every impulse ego-alien. Uses denial,
intellectualization, and repression. High level of narcissism. Regresses easily into the infantile.
425   The most unbalanced record one could find." By the other judge: "This looks like a clinic record.
An anxiety state, pre-psychotic. Is more scared of his own fantasies than the world. People present too many problems; he tries to preserve distant relations. Doesn't want to see sex in
people. Sex is very repulsive."

Thus, there is no single pattern of homosexual adjustment. This had been anticipated. The
430   richness and variety of ways in which the homosexual adjusts are as difficult to summarize as
to summarize 30 full, qualitative pictures of 30 individuals. If I were to read pictures of heterosexuals with the same level of adjustment, the pictures would be essentially the same, with the
exception of the bottom range, where one does not find the marked anal-destructive charac-
ter-structure or the emphasis on "femininity" (which may occur at other levels, also).

435   That homosexuality is determined by a multiplicity of factors would not now, I think, be seriously
questioned. That the personality structure and adjustment may also vary within a wide range now
seems quite clear. It comes as no surprise that some homosexuals are severely disturbed, and,
indeed, so much so that the hypothesis might be entertained that the homosexuality is the defense
against open psychosis. But what is difficult to accept (for most clinicians) is that some homosex-
440   uals *may* be very ordinary individuals, indistinguishable, except in sexual pattern, from ordinary
individuals who are heterosexual. Or—and I do not know whether this would be more or less difficult to accept—that some *may* be quite superior individuals, not only devoid of pathology (unless
one insists that homosexuality itself is a sign of pathology) but also functioning at a superior level.

. . . Another way of looking at the data from the projective tests may be that the homosex-
445   ual "pathology" occurs only in an erotic situation and that the homosexual can function well
in non-erotic situations such as the Rorschach, TAT, and MAPS. Thus, one could defend the
hypothesis that homosexuality is symptomatic of pathology, but that the pathology is confined
to one sector of behavior, namely the sexual.

. . .

A question . . . arises about the size of the sample used. It is possible that much larger
450   samples—for example, 100 in each group—would show differences. But would we not, in this
case, be dealing with a different question, namely, "How many homosexuals, as compared with
heterosexuals, are average or better in adjustment and how many are worse than average?" It
seems to me that for the present investigation the question is whether homosexuality is necessarily a symptom of pathology. All we need is a single case in which the answer is negative.
455   What are the psychological implications of the hypothesis that homosexuality is not necessarily a symptom of pathology? I would *very tentatively* suggest the following:

1. Homosexuality as a clinical entity does not exist. Its forms are as varied as are those of
   heterosexuality.

2. Homosexuality may be a deviation in sexual pattern which is within the normal range, psychologically. This has been suggested, on a biological level, by Ford and Beach (1951).   460

Ford (an anthropologist) and Beach (a psychologist) wrote *Patterns of Sexual Behavior* in which they included a chapter on homosexual behavior. They begin their discussion of attitudes toward homosexuality by saying, "Our own society disapproves of any form of homosexual behavior . . . In this it differs from the majority of human societies" (p. 125). They looked at anthropological data from 76 other cultures and found that homosexuality was accepted in 49 of these cultures, sometimes only for certain people or certain situations; sometimes more generally. The cross-cultural variations in attitudes and behaviors led them to believe that homosexuality can not be completely understood in physiological terms. They point out that, although homosexuality is not accepted behavior in the United States, there are data that suggest it occurs. They cite a number of studies indicating that a substantial number of adolescent males engage in manipulation of a same-sex partner's genitals and other studies describing the same-sex "crushes" that are common in adolescent females. This research is compatible with Sullivan's idea that in preadolescence we go through the same-sex "chum" stage that marks the first intimate attachment outside of the family (1953).

Ford and Beach point out that among non-human primates both males and females engage in homosexual activity, and they discuss the idea that the choice of a sexual partner, at least for males, may be more related to social dominance than to biological sex.

3. The role of particular forms of sexual desire and expression in personality structure and development may be less important than has frequently been assumed. Even if one assumes that homosexuality represents a severe form of maladjustment to society in the sexual sector of behavior, this does not necessarily mean that the homosexual must be severely maladjusted in other sectors of his behavior. Or, if one assumes that homosex-   465
uality is a form of severe maladjustment internally, it may be that the disturbance is limited to the sexual sector alone.

For Discussion

1. What kinds of influence could their knowledge of the purpose of this study have had on the responses the homosexual and heterosexual participants gave on the projective tests?

2. Hooker, who knew which men were homosexual and which were heterosexual, administered, scored, and tabulated the Rorschach responses, and wrote the profiles for the judges to use. Could her knowledge of the participants' sexuality have influenced her scoring?

3. Why did it have to be a female heterosexual who did this study?

4. Which of Hooker's three conclusions is most compelling and important?

5. What do you make of the fact that two respected psychiatrists made such different judgments from one another—not just about sexual orientation, but also about the men's levels of adjustment and other psychological characteristics?

Thomas S. Szasz (b. 1920)
The Myth of Mental Illness (1960)

Thomas Szasz was raised in Budapest, and as a youth he hoped to be a poet. As fascism spread across Europe in the 1930s, the Szasz family, like many others, emigrated to the United States. Szasz got his baccalaureate degree in physics and his medical degree from the University of Cincinnati. He then trained in psychiatry at the University of Chicago and in psychoanalysis at the Chicago Institute for Psychoanalysis. From 1956 until he retired in 1990, Szasz was on the faculty in the Department of Psychiatry at the SUNY Upstate Medical Center in Syracuse and maintained a small private practice.[1]

Szasz is a prolific writer. He has written more than 30 books and hundreds of articles. He is almost guaranteed to take an iconoclastic view on any of the controversial issues in psychiatry, and he has written on a wide range of topics: the validity of the categories that psychiatrists and psychologists use to diagnose patients, the use of drugs in the treatment of psychological disorders, the decisions about which recreational drugs are illegal, how addicts are treated in our courts and hospitals, the insanity defense, the involuntary commitment of those with "mental illnesses," and patient-assisted suicide.

Szasz is considered by some to be a gadfly or a troublemaker. This is unfair. The positions he takes on the issues he discusses are consistent with one another and rest on his libertarian beliefs as well as his knowledge of psychiatry. Szasz believes that individual development involves learning to master oneself and society. Anything that interferes with this process and prevents the individual from taking control of his or her own life is a mistake. Psychiatry's goals should involve preserving and protecting individual rights and liberties as well as providing the situations and support that can help those who are struggling to take responsibility for and control of their lives.

Szasz's most dramatic influence on the field of psychiatry probably had to do with involuntary commitment. At one time, it was relatively easy for families, with the aid of a physician,

---

Source: Szasz, T. S. (1960b). The myth of mental illness. *American Psychologist, 15,* 113–118.

[1] Biographical data are from Luft, E. v. d. (2001).

to get a relative committed to a mental hospital against his or her will. Once committed, patients lost their right to vote, to make financial decisions, or to leave the hospital at a time of their choosing. Szasz campaigned vigorously against involuntary commitment during the 1960s (e.g., Szasz, 1963). His campaign was aided by others who had their own disagreements with the way mental institutions were being run. Erving Goffman, a sociologist, wrote *Asylums* (1961), a book that revealed the abysmal, dehumanizing conditions in many mental hospitals. R. D. Laing, a psychiatrist and psychoanalyst, wrote *The Divided Self* in 1960 and argued for more humane and appropriate treatment of those who were institutionalized and against the assumptions and practices in place in hospitals at the time. Although the three—Szasz, Goffman, and Laing—probably would not have agreed on many issues, they did agree that what was happening in mental hospitals in the 1960s was not right, and they all made their concerns known. Since then there have been substantial legal changes in the requirements for involuntary commitment.

Szasz has not been so persuasive in his other campaigns, but he continues to voice his concerns and to argue for his point of view. In the article included here, Szasz makes his case against the label "mental illness." He argues that there are neither scientific nor moral grounds for diagnosing someone with "problems in living" as "mentally ill." It is an important article, and whether you agree with his position or not, Szasz raises issues and possibilities that cannot be ignored.

My aim in this essay is to raise the question "Is there such a thing as mental illness?" and to argue that there is not. Since the notion of mental illness is extremely widely used nowadays, inquiry into the ways in which this term is employed would seem to be especially indicated. Mental illness, of course, is not literally a "thing"—or physical object—and hence it can "exist"
5   only in the same sort of way in which other theoretical concepts exist. Yet, familiar theories are in the habit of posing, sooner or later—at least to those who come to believe in them—as "objective truths" (or "facts"). During certain historical periods, explanatory conceptions such as deities, witches, and microorganisms appeared not only as theories but as self-evident *causes* of a vast number of events. I submit that today mental illness is widely regarded in a somewhat
10   similar fashion; that is, as the cause of innumerable diverse happenings. As an antidote to the complacent use of the notion of mental illness—whether as a self-evident phenomenon, theory, or cause—let us ask this question: What is meant when it is asserted that someone is mentally ill?

In what follows I shall describe briefly the main
15   uses to which the concept of mental illness has been put. I shall argue that this notion has outlived whatever usefulness it might have had and that it now functions merely as a convenient myth.

MENTAL ILLNESS AS A SIGN OF BRAIN DISEASE

The notion of mental illness derives its main
20   support from such phenomena as syphilis of the brain or delirious conditions—intoxications, for instance—in which persons are known to manifest various peculiarities or disorders of thinking and behavior. Correctly speaking, however, these
25   are diseases of the brain, not of the mind. According to one school of thought, *all* so-called mental illness is of this type. The assumption is made that some neurological defect, perhaps a very subtle one, will ultimately be found for all the
30   disorders of thinking and behavior. Many contemporary psychiatrists, physicians, and other scientists hold this view. This position implies that people *cannot* have troubles—expressed in what are *now called* "mental illnesses"—because of dif-
35   ferences in personal needs, opinions, social aspirations, values, and so on. *All problems in living* are

syphilis: a sexually transmitted disease caused by a bacterium that attacks the nervous system; it can now be treated with antibiotics. Before the use of antibiotics (i.e., before the 1940s), syphilis was a devastating disease. If untreated, the early symptoms could disappear, often for years, and then much more serious symptoms would appear. These later symptoms could take a number of forms, one of which was "general paresis," a disorder characterized by both physical symptoms (e.g., paralyses, strange gaits) and psychological symptoms (e.g., delusions of grandeur, depression). In the 1800s patients suffering from general paresis were typically assumed to be mentally ill.

In 1897 Richard von Krafft-Ebbing, a neurologist, demonstrated that general paresis was probably related to syphilis. He injected paretic patients with material from the sores of syphilis patients. None of them contracted syphilis, suggesting that all of them already had the disease. Krafft-Ebbing's finding lent strong support to the idea that all forms of mental illness have physical causes (the somatogenic hypothesis).

attributed to physicochemical processes which in due time will be discovered by medical research.

"Mental illnesses" are thus regarded as basically no different than all other diseases (that is, of the body). The only difference, in this view, between mental and bodily diseases is that the former, affecting the brain, manifest themselves by means of mental symptoms; whereas the latter, affecting other organ systems (for example, the skin, liver, etc.), manifest themselves by means of symptoms referable to those parts of the body. This view rests on and expresses what are, in my opinion, two fundamental errors.

In the first place, what central nervous system symptoms would correspond to a skin eruption or a fracture? It would *not* be some emotion or complex bit of behavior. Rather, it would be blindness or a paralysis of some part of the body. The crux of the matter is that a disease of the brain, analogous to a disease of the skin or bone, is a neurological defect, and not a problem in living. For example, a *defect* in a person's visual field maybe satisfactorily explained by correlating it with certain definite lesions in the nervous system. On the other hand, a person's *belief*—whether this be a belief in Christianity, in Communism, or in the idea that his internal organs are "rotting" and that his body is, in fact, already "dead"—cannot be explained by a defect or disease of the nervous system. Explanations of this sort of occurrence—assuming that one is interested in the belief itself and does not regard it simply as a "symptom" or expression of something else that is *more interesting*—must be sought along different lines.

The second error in regarding complex psychosocial behavior, consisting of communications about ourselves and the world about us, as mere symptoms of neurological functioning is *epistemological*. In other words, it is an error pertaining not to any mistakes in observation or reasoning, as such, but rather to the way in which we organize and express our knowledge. In the present case, the error lies in making a symmetrical dualism between mental and physical (or bodily) symptoms, a dualism which is merely a habit of speech and to which no known observations can be found to correspond. Let us see if this is so. In medical practice, when we speak of physical disturbances, we mean either signs (for example, a fever) or symptoms (for example, pain). We speak of mental symptoms, on the other hand, when we refer to a patient's *communications about himself, others, and the world about him.* He might state that he is Napoleon or that he is being persecuted by the Communists. These would be considered mental symptoms *only* if the observer believed that the patient was *not* Napoleon or that he was *not* being persecuted by the Communists. This makes it apparent that the statement that "*X* is a mental symptom" involves rendering a judgment. The judgment entails, moreover, a covert comparison or matching of the patient's ideas, concepts, or beliefs with those of the observer and the society in which they live. The notion of mental symptom is therefore inextricably tied to the *social* (including *ethical*) *context* in which it is made in much the same way as the notion of bodily symptom is tied to an *anatomical* and *genetic context* (Szasz, 1957b, 1957c).

To sum up what has been said thus far: I have tried to show that for those who regard mental symptoms as signs of brain disease, the concept of mental illness is unnecessary and misleading. For what they mean is that people so labeled suffer from diseases of the brain; and, if that is what they mean, it would seem better for the sake of clarity to say that and not something else.

MENTAL ILLNESS AS A NAME FOR PROBLEMS IN LIVING

The term "mental illness" is widely used to describe something which is very different than a disease of the brain. Many people today take it for granted that living is an arduous process. Its hardship for modern man, moreover, derives not so much from a struggle for biological survival as from the stresses and strains inherent in the social intercourse of complex human personalities. In this context, the notion of mental illness is used to identify or describe some feature of an individual's so-called personality. Mental illness—as a deformity of the personality, so to speak—is then regarded as the *cause* of the human disharmony. It is implicit in this view that social intercourse between people is regarded as something *inherently harmonious,* its disturbance being due solely to the presence of "mental illness" in many people. This is obviously fallacious reasoning, for it makes the abstraction "mental illness" into a cause, even though this abstraction was created in the first place to serve only as a shorthand expression for certain types of human behavior. It now becomes necessary to ask: "What kinds of behavior are regarded as indicative of mental illness, and by whom?"

The concept of illness, whether bodily or mental, implies *deviation from some clearly defined norm.* In the case of physical illness, the norm is the structural and functional integrity of the human body. Thus, although the desirability of physical health, as such, is an ethical value, what health *is* can be stated in anatomical and physiological terms. What is the norm deviation from which is regarded as mental illness? This question cannot be easily answered. But whatever this norm might be, we can be certain of only one thing: namely, that it is a norm that must be stated in terms of *psychosocial, ethical,* and *legal* concepts. For example, notions such as "excessive repression" or "acting out an unconscious impulse" illustrate the use of psychological concepts for judging (so-called) mental health and illness. The idea that chronic hostility, vengefulness, or divorce are indicative of mental illness would be illustrations of the use of ethical norms (that is, the desirability of love, kindness, and a stable marriage relationship). Finally, the widespread psychiatric opinion that only a mentally ill person would commit homicide illustrates the use of a legal concept as a norm of mental health. The norm from which deviation is measured whenever one speaks of a mental illness is a *psychosocial and ethical one.* Yet, the remedy is sought in terms of medical measures which—it is hoped and assumed—are free from wide differences of ethical value. The definition of the disorder and the terms in which its remedy are sought are therefore at serious odds with one another. The practical significance of this covert conflict between the alleged nature of the defect and the remedy can hardly be exaggerated.

Having identified the norms used to measure deviations in cases of mental illness, we will now turn to the question: "Who defines the norms and hence the deviation?" Two basic answers may be offered: *(a)* It may be the person himself (that is, the patient) who decides that he deviates from a norm. For example, an artist may believe that he suffers from a work inhibition; and he may implement this conclusion by seeking help *for* himself from a psychotherapist. *(b)* It may be someone other than the patient who decides that the latter is deviant (for example, relatives, physicians, legal authorities, society generally, etc.). In such a case a psychiatrist may be hired by others to do something *to* the patient in order to correct the deviation.

These considerations underscore the importance of asking the question "Whose agent is the psychiatrist?" and of giving a candid answer to it (Szasz, 1956, 1958). The psychiatrist (psychologist or nonmedical psychotherapist), it now develops, may be the agent of the patient, of the relatives, of the school, of the military services, of a business organization, of a court of law, and so forth. In speaking of the psychiatrist as the agent of these persons or organizations, it is not implied that his values concerning norms, or his ideas and aims concerning the proper nature of remedial action, need to coincide exactly with those of his employer. For example, a patient in individual psychotherapy may believe that his salvation lies in a new marriage; his psychotherapist need not share this hypothesis. As the patient's agent, however, he must abstain from bringing social or legal force to bear on the patient which would prevent him from putting his beliefs into action. If his *contract* is with the patient, the psychiatrist (psychotherapist) may disagree with him or stop his treatment; but he cannot engage others to obstruct the patient's aspirations. Similarly, if a psychiatrist is engaged by a court to determine the sanity of a criminal, he need not fully share the legal authorities' values and intentions in regard to the criminal and the means available for dealing with him. But the psychiatrist is expressly barred from stating, for example, that it is not the criminal who is "insane" but the men who wrote the law on the basis of which the very actions that are being judged are regarded as "criminal." Such an opinion could be voiced, of course, but not in a courtroom, and not by a psychiatrist who makes it his practice to assist the court in performing its daily work.

To recapitulate: In actual contemporary social usage, the finding of a mental illness is made by establishing a deviance in behavior from certain psychosocial, ethical, or legal norms. The judgment may be made, as in medicine, by the patient, the physician (psychiatrist), or others. Remedial action, finally, tends to be sought in a therapeutic—or covertly medical—framework, thus creating a situation in which *psychosocial, ethical,* and/or *legal deviations* are claimed to be correctible by (so-called) *medical action.* Since medical action is designed to correct only medical deviations, it seems logically absurd to expect that it will help solve problems whose very existence had been defined and established on nonmedical grounds. I think that these considerations may be fruitfully applied to the present use of tranquilizers and, more generally, to what might be expected of drugs of whatever type in regard to the amelioration or solution of problems in human living.

THE ROLE OF ETHICS IN PSYCHIATRY

. . . Lest there be any vagueness, however, about how or where ethics and medicine meet, let me remind the reader of such issues as birth control, abortion, suicide, and euthanasia as only a few of the major areas of current ethicomedical controversy.

Psychiatry, I submit, is very much more intimately tied to problems of ethics than is medicine. I use the word "psychiatry" here to refer to that contemporary discipline which is concerned with *problems in living* (and not with diseases of the brain, which are problems for neurology). Problems in human relations can be analyzed, interpreted, and given meaning only within given social and ethical contexts. Accordingly, it *does* make a difference—arguments to the contrary notwithstanding—what the psychiatrist's socio-ethical orientations happen to be; for these will influence his ideas on what is wrong with the patient, what deserves comment or interpretation, in what possible directions change might be desirable, and so forth. Even in medicine proper, these factors play a role, as for instance, in the divergent orientations which physicians, depending on their religious affiliations, have toward such things as birth control and therapeutic abortion. Can anyone really believe that a psychotherapist's ideas concerning religious belief, slavery, or other similar issues play no role in his practical work? If they do make a difference, what are we to infer from it? Does it not seem reasonable that we ought to have different psychiatric therapies—each expressly recognized for the ethical positions which they embody—for, say, Catholics and Jews, religious persons and agnostics, democrats and communists, white supremacists and Negroes, and so on? Indeed, if we look at how psychiatry is actually practiced today (especially in the United States), we find that people do seek psychiatric help in accordance with their social status and ethical beliefs (Hollingshead & Redlich, 1958). This should really not surprise us more than being told that practicing Catholics rarely frequent birth control clinics.

> Oliver Sacks, a neurologist, has written a number of fascinating books describing the relation between diseases of the brain and cognitive or behavioral functioning (e.g., *The Man Who Mistook His Wife for a Hat and Other Clinical Tales*, 1985).

> Hollingshead and Redlich looked at the relation between social class and the incidence of various mental illnesses. More recent data on the same issue are available (e.g., Brim, Ryff, & Kessler, 2004).

The foregoing position which holds that contemporary psychotherapists deal with problems in living, rather than with mental illnesses and their cures, stands in opposition to a currently prevalent claim, according to which mental illness is just as "real" and "objective" as bodily illness. This is a confusing claim since it is never known exactly what is meant by such words as "real" and "objective." I suspect, however, that what is intended by the proponents of this view is to create the idea in the popular mind that mental illness is some sort of disease entity, like an infection or a malignancy. If this were true, one could *catch* or *get* a "mental illness," one might *have* or *harbor* it, one might *transmit* it to others, and finally one could get *rid* of it. In my opinion, there is not a shred of evidence to support this idea. To the contrary, all the evidence is the other way and supports the view that what people now call mental illnesses are for the most part *communications* expressing unacceptable ideas, often framed, moreover, in an unusual idiom. The scope of this essay allows me to do no more than mention this alternative theoretical approach to this problem (Szasz, 1957a).

This is not the place to consider in detail the similarities and differences between bodily and mental illnesses. It shall suffice for us here to emphasize only one important difference between them: namely, that whereas bodily disease refers to public, physicochemical occurrences, the notion of mental illness is used to codify relatively more private, socio-psychological happenings of which the observer (diagnostician) forms a part. In other words, the psychiatrist does not stand *apart* from what he observes, but is, in Harry Stack Sullivan's apt words, a "participant observer." This means that he is *committed* to some picture of what he considers reality—and to what he thinks society considers reality—and he observes and judges the patient's behavior in the light of these considerations. This touches on our earlier observation that the notion of mental symptom itself implies a comparison between observer and observed, psychiatrist and patient.

> Harry Stack Sullivan (1892–1949) was a psychiatrist and psychoanalyst whose approach to therapy, like Horney's (6.3) and Adler's, placed more emphasis on social factors than had Freud's. Among his other contributions to the field, Sullivan (1954) wrote about the social role of the psychiatrist in therapeutic interactions.

This is so obvious that I may be charged with belaboring trivialities. Let me therefore say once more that my aim in presenting this argument was expressly to criticize and counter a prevailing contemporary tendency to deny the moral aspects of psychiatry (and psychotherapy) and to substitute for them allegedly value-free medical considerations. Psychotherapy, for example, is being widely practiced as though it entailed nothing other than restoring the patient from a state of mental sickness to one of mental health. While it is generally accepted that mental illness has something to do with man's social (or interpersonal) relations, it is paradoxically maintained that problems of values (that is, of ethics) do not arise in this process.[2] Yet, in one sense, much of psychotherapy may revolve around nothing other than the elucidation and weighing of goals and values—many of which may be mutually contradictory—and the means whereby they might best be harmonized, realized, or relinquished.

The diversity of human values and the methods by means of which they may be realized is so vast, and many of them remain so unacknowledged, that they cannot fail but lead to conflicts in human relations. Indeed, to say that human relations at all levels—from mother to child, through husband and wife, to nation and nation—are fraught with stress, strain, and disharmony is, once again, making the obvious explicit. Yet, what may be obvious may be also poorly understood. This I think is the case here. For it seems to me that—at least in our scientific theories of behavior—we have failed to *accept* the simple fact that human relations are inherently fraught with difficulties and that to make them even relatively harmonious requires much patience and hard work. I submit that the idea of mental illness is now being put to work to obscure certain difficulties which at present may be inherent—not that they need be unmodifiable—in the social intercourse of persons. If this is true, the concept functions as a disguise;

195

200

205

210

215

220

225

---

[2] Freud went so far as to say that: "I consider ethics to be taken for granted: Actually I have never done a mean thing" (Jones, 1957, p. 247). This surely is a strange thing to say for someone who has studied man as a social being as closely as did Freud. I mention it here to show how the notion of "illness" (in the case of psychoanalysis, "psychopathology," or "mental illness") was used by Freud—and by most of his followers—as a means for classifying certain forms of human behavior as falling within the scope of medicine, and hence (by *fiat*) outside that of ethics!

230 for instead of calling attention to conflicting human needs, aspirations, and values, the notion of mental illness provides an amoral and impersonal "thing" (an "illness") as an explanation for *problems in living* (Szasz, 1960a). We may recall in this connection that not so long ago it was devils and witches who were held responsible for men's problems in social living. The belief in mental illness, as something other than man's trouble in getting along with his fellow man, is the proper heir to the belief in demonology and witchcraft. Mental illness exists or is "real" in

235 exactly the same sense in which witches existed or were "real."

CHOICE, RESPONSIBILITY, AND PSYCHIATRY

While I have argued that mental illnesses do not exist, I obviously did not imply that the social and psychological occurrences to which this label is currently being attached also do not exist. Like the personal and social troubles which people had in the Middle Ages, they are real enough. It is the

240 labels we give them that concerns us and, having labelled them, what we do about them. While I cannot go into the ramified implications of this prob-

> *therapy along theological lines*: e.g., exorcism

lem here, it is worth noting that a demonologic conception of problems in living gave rise to therapy along theological lines. Today, a belief in mental illness implies—nay, requires—therapy

245 along medical or psychotherapeutic lines.

What is implied in the line of thought set forth here is something quite different. I do not intend to offer a new conception of "psychiatric illness" nor a new form of "therapy." My aim is more modest and yet also more ambitious. It is to suggest that the phenomena now called mental illnesses be looked at afresh and more simply, that they be removed from the category

250 of illnesses, and that they be regarded as the expressions of man's struggle with the problem of *how* he should live. The last mentioned problem is obviously a vast one, its enormity reflecting not only man's inability to cope with his environment, but even more his increasing self-reflectiveness.

By problems in living, then, I refer to that truly explosive chain reaction which began with

255 man's fall from divine grace by partaking of the fruit of the tree of knowledge. Man's awareness of himself and of the world about him seems to be a steadily expanding one, bringing in its wake an ever larger *burden of understanding* (an expression borrowed from Susanne Langer, 1953). *This burden,* then, *is to be expected and must not be misinterpreted.* Our only *rational* means for lightening it is *more understanding,* and appropriate *action* based on such under-

260 standing. The main alternative lies in acting as though the burden were not what in fact we perceive it to be and taking refuge in an outmoded theological view of man. In the latter view, man does not fashion his life and much of his world about him, but merely lives out his fate in a world created by superior beings. This may logically lead to pleading nonresponsibility in the face of seemingly unfathomable problems and difficulties. Yet, if man fails to take increasing

265 responsibility for his actions, individually as well as collectively, it seems unlikely that some

higher power or being would assume this task and carry this burden for him. Moreover, this seems hardly the proper time in human history for obscuring the issue of man's responsibility for his actions by hiding it behind the skirt of an all-explaining conception of mental illness.

CONCLUSIONS

I have tried to show that the notion of mental illness has outlived whatever usefulness it might have had and that it now functions merely as a convenient myth. As such, it is a true heir to religious myths in general, and to the belief in witchcraft in particular; the role of all these belief-systems was to act as *social tranquilizers,* thus encouraging the hope that mastery of certain specific problems may be achieved by means of substitutive (symbolic-magical) operations. 270

Thus, by labeling certain behaviors as "mental illnesses" we can ignore the societal ills that may play a significant role in creating them.

So, for Szasz mental health is more than the absence of mental illness.

The notion of mental illness thus serves mainly to obscure the everyday fact that life for most people is a continuous struggle, not for biological survival, but for a "place in the sun," "peace of mind," or some other human value. For man aware of himself and of the world about him, once the needs for preserving the body (and perhaps the race) are more or less satisfied, the problem arises as to what he should do with himself. Sustained adherence to the myth of mental illness allows people to avoid facing this problem, believing that mental health, conceived as the absence of mental illness, automatically insures the making of right and safe choices in one's conduct of life. But the facts are all the other way. It is the making of good choices in life that others regard, retrospectively, as good mental health! 275 280 285

The myth of mental illness encourages us, more-over, to believe in its logical corollary: that social intercourse would be harmonious, satisfying, and the secure basis of a "good life" were it not for the disrupting influences of mental illness or "psychopathology." The potentiality for universal human happiness, in this form at least, seems to me but another example of the I-wish-it-were-true type of fantasy. I [do believe][3] that human happiness or well-being on a hitherto unimaginably large scale, and not just for a select few, is possible. This goal could be achieved, however, only at the cost of many men, and not just a few being willing and able to tackle their personal, social, and ethical conflicts. This means having the courage and integrity to forego waging battles on false fronts, finding solutions for substitute problems—for instance, fighting the battle of stomach acid and chronic fatigue instead of facing up to a marital conflict. 290 295

---

[3] The original article reads "I do not believe." In a footnote to the Psych Classics online text of Szasz's paper (http://psychclassics.yorku.ca/Szasz/myth.htm), Christopher Green, the site's editor, reports that "Dr. Szasz has informed me, however, that it was a typo, which [he] corrected when [he] reprinted the piece, e.g., in *Ideology and Insanity* (personal communication, 2002)." (Eds.)

300

Our adversaries are not demons, witches, fate, or mental illness. We have no enemy whom we can fight, exorcise, or dispel by "cure." What we do have are *problems in living*—whether these be biologic, economic, political, or sociopsychological. In this essay I was concerned only with problems belonging in the last mentioned category, and within this group mainly with those pertaining to moral values. The field to which modern psychiatry addresses itself is vast, and I made no effort to encompass it all. My argument was limited to the proposition that men-

305

tal illness is a myth, whose function it is to disguise and thus render more palatable the bitter pill of moral conflicts in human relations.

Szasz's ideas have gotten attention in psychiatry and psychology, and probably most of the attention has been critical because he is challenging the way things are. Some of the criticism is defensive or off the point. Much of it, however, is both useful and thoughtfully presented. Ausubel (1961) wrote a classic and very reasonable criticism of the ideas Szasz expresses in the present reading. Dammann (1997) categorized and summarized much of the criticism and added his own informative discussion of each kind of criticism.

The debate between Szasz and his critics is often conducted in terms of the mind-body issue. Szasz is discussing the mental (mind) and the physical (body) as they relate to disease and illness, and the question of how the mental and the physical relate to one another is a contentious one (see Part I). His critics often argue that Szasz's position assumes that everything must be categorized absolutely as mental or physical, and then they give examples of physical diseases that are related to life choices (e.g., high blood pressure, lung cancer) and mental illnesses in which bodily or genetic factors play a major role (e.g., schizophrenia). Their examples are compelling, but this doesn't mean that Szasz is wrong.

The real issue may not involve the mind-body dilemma, although solving that would be a very welcome accomplishment. It may have more to do with how we think about people who are "different" or who seem to be in great distress. On one side, many people who work to help those with "mental illnesses" see that term as useful for a number of reasons: They see the degree to which many are suffering and believe that the medical model provides the best context for the kinds of help that are currently available; they see psychological and social value in removing responsibility from the person for his or her illness; they recognize that "treatment" and "cure" are often possible only when health insurance permits it (hence, "disease" status is necessary); they believe that the direct and indirect costs of "mental illness" affect all of society and cannot be ignored; they believe that research—both physiological and behavioral—has taught us much about how to help individuals who are suffering or ostracized; or they believe that psychological problems have a physical basis—they are illnesses.

Szasz and Szaszians, on the other hand, believe that the "mental illness" label serves to rob people of responsibility for their lives; it can deprive them of their human rights and civil liberties; it labels them as "invalid"; it leaves them feeling helpless and doesn't encourage them to take control of what is happening; it covers up a host of societal problems that affect many and puts the blame on the individuals who are suffering; it continues to provide the field of medicine with the opportunity to extend its control over and expertise in "mental" matters; it sometimes has the effect of not holding individuals legally responsible for immoral or criminal behavior. And many of them believe that the problems categorized as mental illness do not have a physical basis.

FOR DISCUSSION

1. What are some of the societal and personal problems that Szasz believes result from viewing problems in living as mental illnesses?

2. What are Szasz's main arguments for rejecting the concept of mental illness?

3. Is Szasz a dualist, a monist, or an epiphenomenalist?

4. As a practicing psychiatrist, how would Szasz work with his "patients"? What style or kind of "therapy" do you think he would use?

5. Is constantly eating a vast number of fatty burgers and greasy fries and as a result developing high cholesterol levels and a propensity for heart problems a medical problem or a "problem in living" (or a problem in lifestyle)? Should the treatment be only medical (e.g., drugs) or should one also urge behavior change (e.g., in eating habits)?

6. Pain is considered a physical symptom, although it is known to others only through our communication about it. Suicide attempts are considered mental symptoms, although the acts themselves are physical. Where does Szasz draw the line between the mental and the physical?

Samuel B. Guze (1923–2000)
Biological Psychiatry: Is There Any Other Kind? (1989)

There has always been controversy within psychiatry about how to understand and treat mental disorders. Did Freud (3.3, 4.5) place too much emphasis on sex? Was Jung too mystical? Did Adler and Horney (6.3) pay too much attention to social factors? In the 1960s some psychiatrists, as well as others outside the profession, went a step farther and began questioning psychiatry itself. R. D. Laing openly criticized psychiatry's assumptions about the nature of mental disorders. He questioned the belief that the speech and behavior of schizophrenics defied understanding and argued that psychiatrists need to pay more attention to family dynamics (Laing, 1960, 1967, 1972). Thomas Szasz (6.5) vigorously denied that psychological disorders are "illnesses" or "diseases," arguing that they should instead be thought of as "problems in living." Szasz also campaigned for the civil rights of those judged to be "mentally ill" (Szasz, 1961, 1963, 1965, 1970). Erving Goffman, a sociologist, described the ways in which people institutionalized because of psychological problems were treated and the dehumanizing effects of institutionalization itself (Goffman, 1961). This questioning of traditional psychiatry has been referred to as the "anti-psychiatry" movement, and it received a great deal of attention, not just in psychiatry.

Because of the controversy the movement generated, the field of psychiatry moved away from its commitment to a medical model, one using terms such as *illness, treatment, cure, symptom, diagnosis,* and *patient.* As Kandel (1998) describes it,

> In the years following World War II . . . psychiatry was transformed from a medical discipline into a practicing therapeutic art. In the 1950s and . . . into the 1960s, academic

Source: Guze, S. B. (1989). Biological psychiatry: Is there any other kind? *Psychological Medicine, 19,* 315–323. Presented as the Mapother Lecture at the Institute for Psychiatry and the Maudsley Hospital, London, on 17 November 1988. Reprinted with permission of Cambridge University Press.

psychiatry transiently abandoned its roots in biology and experimental medicine and evolved into a psychoanalytically based and socially oriented discipline that was surprisingly unconcerned with the brain as an organ of mental activity. (p. 457)

In the 1970s several things happened that began to reverse this and reestablish psychiatry's roots in biology and medicine. Those who supported the traditional biomedical approach argued persuasively and energetically against the changes that had occurred within the field in response to the anti-psychiatry movement. The development of neuroimaging technologies (e.g., positron emission tomography [PET scans]; functional magnetic resonance imaging [fMRI]) gave researchers a way to link psychological disorders to brain functioning. The development of psychoactive drugs to treat or control psychological disorders increased dramatically and achieved substantial success, providing evidence of a link between brain biochemistry and psychological disorders. In spite of its growing acceptance, the biomedical model still had its critics. In the present reading, written in 1989, Samuel Guze makes a strong, eloquent, and convincing argument for the idea that all mental disorders are biological and that the discipline of psychiatry should continue to function within the biomedical, or medical, model of mental illness.

Guze began his medical career as an internist but later switched to psychiatry. He received his medical degree from Washington University in St. Louis and stayed on at the university, serving during his tenure there as the Spencer T. Olin Professor of Psychiatry, the head of psychiatry, vice chancellor for medical affairs, and the psychiatrist-in-chief at Barnes-Jewish Hospital and St. Louis Children's Hospital. His career was a distinguished one, and his reputation and influence in the field of psychiatry were substantial (Dryden, 1998; Westerhouse, 2000).

Guze played a significant role in the development of the third edition of the American Psychiatric Association's *Diagnostic and Statistical Manual of Mental Disorders* published in 1980 (the *DSM-III*), which was organized in a way very different from the first (American Psychiatric Association, 1952) and second (American Psychiatric Association, 1973) editions. The earlier editions took a psychodynamic approach, describing disorders in terms of their causes as well as their symptoms and using terminology associated with psychoanalysis. For example, hysteria was seen as based on anxiety. This anxiety was defended against by the development of physical symptoms (that were not based on organic dysfunction) or by dissociation (amnesia, fugue, multiple personalities). The third edition abandoned much of the psychoanalytic vocabulary (e.g., "neurosis" and "hysteria") and described disorders only in terms of symptoms (Compton & Guze, 1995). The organization introduced in the *DSM-III* was based on empirical data, not on theory, and the *DSM-III* was more compatible with a biomedical approach to psychological and behavioral disorders.

Guze's research on the genetic underpinnings of disorders such as alcoholism, schizophrenia, and affective disorders; his contributions to the modifications introduced in the *DSM-III*; and his ability to argue persuasively for the appropriateness of the medical model were all important in establishing the biomedical approach as the dominant approach within psychiatry in the late 20th and early 21st centuries.

It is important in reading Guze's article to remember that psychiatrists are medical doctors who specialize in psychiatry. Guze is writing for and about those who practice psychiatry. He is not writing for or about those who practice clinical psychology, counseling, or social work. Because he argues that psychopathology is first and foremost biological, however, it isn't clear exactly what role he sees for these other clinicians.

It has been my custom as Head of the Department of Psychiatry at Washington University to interview as many as possible of the medical students applying for positions in our residency training programme. I typically ask the candidates how they decided to apply to us, what they know about our programme, and what they have heard from others about our department. The answers to these questions have been interesting and informative to me and have characteristically provided a good basis for the discussions that followed, designed to help us decide about the applicants and, equally important, to help the applicants decide about us.

Needless to say, I am more favourably disposed to candidates who know most about us, who have read about some of the work reported from our department, and have some sense of its possible significance. I appreciate a student who can offer comparisons between competing programmes and has a viewpoint about his or her goals and priorities. I have learned a good deal from these discussions about the perceptions and expectations of medical students concerning psychiatry, as a discipline and as a career.

There is one subject I have selected from these discussions to talk about on this occasion, because it is an issue that has come up often and touches on a very important subject for psychiatry. Sometimes sheepishly, sometimes challengingly, students report that they have been cautioned about our department's 'strong biological orientation.' When such experiences are reported, I try to get the student to elaborate upon the reported evaluation, to say what the comment might signify to him or her. All too often I find that the student is unable to go very far with this. A favourite response of mine is to raise the question about how can one think about psychiatry and psychiatric disorders except in terms and concepts strongly rooted in biology. Naturally, and unsurprisingly given the situation, nearly all students smile at this point and nod their heads to signify that they agree with me or at least that they are sufficiently skilled in such encounters not to disagree directly.

... What can psychiatrists mean who worry about colleagues being too biological? What definition of biology governs their thinking and concerns? I could speculate about possible answers that others might give to these questions but I prefer to try to give my own thoughts and ideas about psychiatry that lead me to assert that *there is no such thing as a psychiatry that is too biological.* I say this even though I believe that we still know all too little about the physiology of the brain in most psychiatric conditions.

I start my argument with evolution, the bedrock of modern biology. Of central interest to psychiatry is the fact that evolution has shaped the development of the brain—the organ of mental functions or what we call the mind. The process of biological evolution has involved selection—from among existing and varied possible permutations and combinations. Out of these choices viable new forms and functions have arisen (Mayr, 1982). All brain functions including perception, learning, thought, memory, emotions, communication, language, etc. reflect the results of such evolution. The capacity to feel, to be aware, to recognize, to remember, to learn, to talk, to think—all depend upon this wonderfully evolved brain with its still mysterious complexity, made possible by what we must take to be a finite genotype.

genotype: the genetic makeup of a specific individual

nucleotide: building block of RNA and DNA molecules, consisting of a nitrogen base, a phosphate molecule, and a sugar molecule

human genome: the complete set of genes needed to create a human being

For example, many insects can see ultraviolet markings on flowers. We can't. For humans, ultraviolet is not part of the visible spectrum.

A major portion of the approximately three billion nucleotides constituting the human genome is devoted to programming the brain. These nucleotides determine our sensitivity to all sorts of external stimuli and shape the way we learn to respond to these stimuli. To some of these stimuli we seem to be unresponsive; to others we react by perceiving sounds, sights, taste, changes in temperature, etc. These appropriately arranged nucleotides shape the growth and development of the brain and provide a basis for individual differences and for the powerful forces of cultural evolution. The nucleotides provide the code that guides and sets limits to the ways the cells of the brain mature and survive and establish synapses in response to all sorts of external and internal stimuli. . . . By making possible richly developed language and memory, coupled with the capacity for abstract thinking, the genes coding for the brain facilitate the development of art, music, science, religion, philosophy, politics, and all the other elaborations of human culture and civilization.

Our knowledge and understanding of how the brain works is progressing rapidly, but is still very limited. We have learned much about the way individual cells work and communicate but we are just beginning to develop concepts and theories that can be applied to studying the coordination and integration of large assemblies of brain cells (Edelman & Mountcastle, 1978; Young, 1978; Changeaux, 1985; Kandel & Schwartz, 1985; Edelman, 1987). We have only the most rudimentary ideas about how complex memories can be stored and retained for decades, how language can be coded and translated, and how abstract ideas can be formed and developed. But we know that the brain must be involved in all of this.

At the same time we understand that no two genotypes are the same (except for monozygotic twins) and we have strong reasons to believe that the . . . development of the brain (the result of the genotype–environment interaction) varies greatly among individuals so that vast numbers of possibilities are available for individual differences in many brain functions (Edelman, 1987; Edelman & Mountcastle, 1978). It does not require great speculative leaps to hypothesize that people learn differently, perceive differently, and think differently, because their brains develop differently as the result of different genotypes interacting with different and constantly varying environments (both internal and external to the organism).

The mutually reciprocal interaction between the genotype and culture are only beginning to be conceptualized and studied. We know little yet about how child-rearing practices, patterns of familial interaction, living arrangements, educational programmes, and many other features of culture interact with the genetic blueprint to produce the many varied patterns of mental functioning. But biology has long provided an important place for environmental forces that shape development and learning, temperament and personality. Ethology and ecology are important scientific disciplines that explicitly recognize the central fact that all forms of life are shaped by and in turn shape their environments and that behaviour is part of this interaction. In medicine, the discipline of epidemiology has historically reflected the same understanding. We have learned that all sorts of factors influence growth and development, behaviour, and health and illness, including geography, climate, social and economic status, sex, race, age, exposure to a wide range of environmental substances (in food, water, and air), and many more. We do not know yet how all of these interactions operate at the physiological level, but beginnings have been made in many areas (Changeaux, 1985; Purves & Lichtman, 1985).

> *ethology:* the study of behavior in its natural environment
>
> *ecology:* the study of the relationship between animals and the environment
>
> *epidemiology:* the study of the distribution, causes, and control of disease

Against this very broadly painted background, there remains only one way in which psychiatry and psychiatrists could reasonably be considered too biological. If it could be asserted that few if any of the states or conditions that constitute the focus of psychiatry are the result of differences in the development or physiology of the brain, biology would seem to be of only marginal interest. If it could be argued that all or most of our patients develop their disorders primarily, if not exclusively, through normal learning processes that are independent of brain variability, the emphasis on biology might justifiably be seen as excessive and unjustifiable. If it could be argued, in addition, that most individuals exposed to a certain pattern of child-rearing or other cultural conditioning would develop the same disorder, psychiatry would have much less need for neuroscience and much more need for cultural anthropology, sociology, and social psychology.

Having specified the conditions for arguing that a biological view of psychiatry might be overblown or unjustified, I hasten to note what we all know, that such conditions have not been demonstrated for *any* psychiatric disorder. No one has presented convincing evidence that most individuals exposed to a particular psychologically meaningful experience develop a particular disorder. In fact, only a minority of individuals do so in any study and various vulnerabilities or diatheses are hypothesized to explain the findings. Often, if not usually, these predispositions are suggested to be the result of various biological factors.

> *diatheses:* inherited predispositions to disease. The "diathesis-stress hypothesis" says that a disorder is the result of the interaction between a biological predisposition and precipitating environmental stress.

The point I am making is not that psychologically meaningful experiences are irrelevant to the development of psychiatric disorders. I remain agnostic about their ultimate importance because, in the great majority of instances, these putative causes of psychiatric disorders seem to reflect only the usual range of human troubles that most people experience without becoming

> *putative:* generally regarded as such

ill (Guze & Helzer, 1985). But even if ultimately it can be shown convincingly that these experiences play causal roles in illness, it is to the specific vulnerability that we must direct our attention if we are to hope for essential scientific understanding and effective therapeutic intervention. It appears highly unlikely that an intervention strategy designed to reduce or eliminate the troubles, disappointments, frustrations, and pressures of daily living will prove feasible or powerful enough.

The argument may be clearer if one were to consider a general medical disorder, coronary artery disease, to illustrate these same points. Certain symptoms of coronary atherosclerosis, those of myocardial ischaemia, are frequently and regularly precipitated by physical activity and emotion. But no one therefore challenges the belief that coronary artery disease is a biological phenomenon and that trying to understand the genetic and epigenetic factors that lead to differential vulnerability to coronary atherosclerosis is the most promising strategy for research and hope for truly effective intervention. And no one is likely to suggest that intervening to reduce physical activity or emotion-provoking experiences is likely to be of more than marginal importance. The question concerning the possible role of personality or coping style as a risk factor for coronary atherosclerosis is another matter, but in no way inconsistent with the biological view. That personality is intimately correlated with neural systems is increasingly evident. In fact, it appears highly likely that personality is itself an important manifestation of the epigenetic development of such neural systems (Cloninger, 1989).

> *coronary atherosclerosis:* buildup of plaque in the interior of the coronary artery. The condition can cause coronary heart disease.
>
> *myocardial ischaemia:* reduction of blood supply to the myocardium (muscle tissue of the heart)

> *epigenetic:* gene–environment interaction

It seems highly likely that the same overall conceptual strategies will prove to be appropriate for conditions such as schizophrenia, obsessional disorders, depression, mania, etc. For example, the notion of the schizophrenigenic mother is by now largely discredited, as it should be. But even if it were still credible, however, it would require us to ask why only a minority of children raised by these same mothers develop schizophrenia and whether most cases of schizophrenia arise in children of such mothers. Furthermore, the question would be raised as to whether the mothers were not themselves suffering from a partial form of the illness, suggesting then that the familial association might reflect a genetic cause rather than a social-psychological one or that both kinds of factors might be involved.

> *schizophrenigenic mother:* a mother who is cold but dominating and thus puts her child in double-bind situations (e.g., saying, "Come here, dearest" but grimacing while saying it). It is now considered unlikely that this form of mothering is necessary or sufficient to cause schizophrenia.

The conclusion appears inescapable to me that what is called psychopathology is the manifestation of disordered processes in various brain systems that mediate psychological functions.

165 Psychopathology thus involves biology. Biology's scientific strategies are directed at understanding how organisms have evolved and how they develop and function within a genotype-environment interaction framework. The genotype establishes a range of possibilities and limits. Development (including learning) selects from these possibilities and shapes the way they ultimately turn out (Mayr, 1982; Purves & Lichtman, 1985; Ruse, 1986).

170 The *tabula rasa* assumption is no longer tenable for any living organism, let alone for humans (Mayr, 1982; Changeaux, 1985; Young, 1987). We are all born with powerful predispositions that determine what we respond to, whether we respond, and how we respond. At the same time,

> *tabula rasa* (Latin for "blank slate"): the idea associated primarily with John Locke (4.2) that no ideas are built into the brain

175 there appears to be a very large range of possible responses, thus accounting for the great variability among individuals even within a species. Biological theory can thus simultaneously begin accounting for uniformity as well as variability in all forms of life, including humans. By taking into consideration genetic codes and epigenetic development, guided and shaped by broad-ranging environmental influences, only some of which are now recognized and under-
180 stood, biology clearly offers the only comprehensive scientific basis for psychiatry, just as it does for the rest of medicine. It has even been argued that Freud, himself, sensed this, at least early in his career, though of course his ideas were constrained by the more primitive state of biological knowledge at the time (Sulloway, 1983).

Resistance to the fundamental biological basis of psychiatry has much in common with and
185 extensively overlaps the resistance to the role of genetic factors in the aetiology of psychiatric disorders. This pattern of resistance derives from a number of important, interrelated assumptions that lead its adherents to their position. Some believe that accepting a genetic or other biological

> *aetiology:* (etiology) study of causes

190 predisposition to psychopathology is tantamount to accepting a hopelessness about treating or preventing the disorder. Some of these same individuals as well as others, because of their adherence to certain political or social ideologies, give primacy to political, cultural, and economic systems in explaining human behaviour (including attitudes, perceptions, and emotions). They fear that any focus or emphasis on genetic or other biological predisposition will result in
195 ignoring the role of organized political and economic systems and may even lead to 'blaming the victims' for their disabilities and disorders. Finally, some who resist the importance of genetic and other biological contributions to psychopathology and psychiatric disorders do so because of philosophical and/or religious beliefs. These individuals fear that recognition of the biological basis for behaviour and mental function in humans will destroy the basis for 'free will'
200 and undermine religious faith because mankind's 'special place' in nature will be questioned.

It seems obvious to me that all three of these concerns are not well founded and are mistaken. Modern medical advances in understanding the aetiology and pathogenesis of many genetically conditioned illnesses (such as diabetes,

> *pathogenesis:* the development of pathology

gout, and epilepsy, as examples) and the development of effective intervention from these   205
advances indicate clearly that the more we learn about aetiology and pathogenesis, the more
likely are we to be able to intervene somewhere in the process that leads to pathology, illness,
and disability.

Similarly, there is nothing in modern biological thought that denies important places for cultural practices, political systems, and economic states in the development of humans, includ-   210
ing their patterns of health and illness. Quite the contrary, as epidemiological research
progresses and as biological factors will be taken into consideration in the design of studies,
our understanding of the role of cultural evolution in health and disease will become specific
and will point the way for more effective interventions, both preventive and therapeutic.

Lastly, with regard to the concerns stemming from philosophical and religious perspectives,   215
it is apparent that modern biology and modern philosophy are reaching out to each other,
struggling to understand the other's questions, methods, and conclusions (Churchland, 1986;
Young, 1987). We are beginning to see that issues concerning free will may need to be sharp-
ened to become more specific so that answers satisfactory to both biologists and philosophers
become possible (Dennett, 1984)....   220

Psychiatrists, including those who accept the fundamental biological basis of psychiatry,
cannot ignore culture philosophy, ethics, and religion as they try to understand psychiatric disorders. But psychiatrists, like all other physicians, start with living, reacting, thinking individuals who are suffering from a variety of disorders. To understand and help them, psychiatry must
turn increasingly to biological science. Cultural anthropology, sociology, philosophy, and reli-   225
gion may all have important contributions to make to the understanding of psychopathology
and its treatment, but these disciplines too will have to take into account human biology if they
are to be of maximum use. The nature and development of mental functions is the centre of
psychiatric interest, just as the nature and development of bodily functions generally are the
centre of medical interest. Psychiatry is a branch of medicine, which in turn is a form of applied   230
biology. It follows, therefore, that biological science, broadly defined, is the foundation of medical science and hence of medical practice. The other disciplines can and must make their
contributions, but they cannot displace biology from its critical role.

I have tried, very briefly of course, to sketch the outline of a conceptual approach to psychiatry that is rooted explicitly in biology. I have elsewhere characterized this approach as the   235
Medical Model emphasizing thereby that psychiatry, as a medical discipline, should be based,
like the rest of medicine, on modern biological science, including genetics, neurobiology, and
epidemiology (Guze & Helzer, 1985). I have argued explicitly that the science of biology comprises a very broad view of human life, including mental experiences, within an evolutionary
framework that places appropriate emphasis on the individual's social, cultural, and physical   240
environment. It is within such a context that I have concluded that there can be no psychiatry
that is not biological.

. . .

At this point, I want to return to the matter of the source of resistance to the emphasis on
biology in psychiatric thinking. I want to consider the resistance that is derived from the belief

245   or fear that biological psychiatry fails to give appropriate emphasis to the individual's mental
life, which properly is of central concern to psychiatrists. I have already tried to indicate, very
generally of course, that modern biology is, on the contrary, very much interested in such matters, but that they are viewed within a certain theoretical framework (Guze & Helzer, 1985).
I believe further that this resistance and fear often stem from a particular view about the place
250   of psychotherapy in psychiatric theory and practice (Guze, 1988).

Good medicine and good psychiatry involve
much more than simply prescribing medicine. Any
physician or any psychiatrist who believes that
such prescribing is all that is required is failing his
255   or her patients. Medicine, including psychiatry,
involves much more than clinical pharmacology.
There need be no inherent conflict between biological psychiatry and the practice of psychotherapy. That psychologically meaningful experiences
260   affect the body's physiology is beyond dispute.

> Drugs are now commonly used to treat
> psychological disorders, and there is a
> substantial and growing literature on their
> value. Many criticize what they see as a
> tendency to use drugs as the first or only
> method of treatment (e.g., Metzl, 2003;
> Valenstein, 1998).

That discussions about one's problems, concerns, and life circumstances can often be helpful
is also beyond dispute. That many, if not nearly all, sick persons need and want such discussions
appears to me to be self-evident. . . .

An important activity in psychotherapy is the offering of 'meaning' to the patient's experi-
265   ences, including the patient's illnesses. Thus, one can try to interpret the meaning or significance
of a patient's cancer, tuberculosis, AIDS, mania, or
panic attacks. Such hermeneutic efforts can be
helpful—both to the patient and to the therapist,
because of our near universal need for under-

> *hermeneutic:* interpretive, explanatory

270   standing and explaining—*but they may have nothing to do with the aetiology of the condition.* For
example, one possible interpretation could be that the particular disorder reflects the patient's
unconscious guilt and need to suffer. There may, in fact, be evidence from the patient's communications that a strong tendency to feel guilty characterizes the patient's approaches to life
in general and to human relationships especially, but this would not be significant evidence that
275   the guilt contributed to either the cancer or the depression. In fact, it might even be more plausible that the illness with its suffering, disability, and associated fears, like other significant experiences for the patient, exacerbated or intensified the tendency to guilt.

The powerful role of suggestion in the offering and accepting of interpretations during psychotherapy has thus far been beyond serious scientific control. No one has provided even mod-
280   erately convincing evidence that suggestion can be eliminated as a major factor—if not *the*
principal factor—in the development of what some psychotherapists refer to as 'insight' (Spence,
1982). But equally important, and probably more significant, the psychotherapeutic process is
inherently incapable of distinguishing between two possibilities: (1) that the mental event
hypothesized or described through the insight process is the cause of the overt clinical prob-
285   lem (the depression, the mania, the panic attacks, the obsessional personality) and (2) that

also Guze, 1992; Guze and Helzer, 1985

these mental events (whether conscious or unconscious) are the result or the manifestation of the clinical problem (Guze, 1988).

During psychotherapy many causal hypotheses may be generated. Sometimes a given hypothesis may be accepted by the patient as 'making sense' and seems to be associated with clinical improvement, though I am unaware of any systematic data bearing on this. It would be very interesting, though obviously very difficult, to test systematically the response of patients to a variety of different hypotheses offered as interpretations. But it clearly is necessary to test any such hypotheses outside of the therapeutic situation (Grunbaum, 1984; Guze, 1988).

290

George Kelly (1955) developed a cognitive theory of personality and psychotherapy called the psychology of personal constructs. His approach to psychotherapy is based on the idea that most people seeking help for psychological problems need to find a new way to think about life and the challenges it presents. He encouraged clients to develop new interpretations (constructs) of people and events and to abandon or revise old interpretations that paint them into a corner from which they cannot escape.

Kelly shared Guze's doubts that the specific content of an interpretation is the source of improvement in the clinical setting, but, unlike Guze, Kelly believed that offering or soliciting interpretation is often a central part of the clinical enterprise. Although Kelly did not supply any systematic data on this issue, he did provide some anecdotal information supporting Guze's suspicion:

> I became a "Freudian," if not by training, at least by persuasion. The Freudian language of explanation provided me with a way of understanding the difficulties of those who came to me for aid. . . . Through my Freudian interpretations . . . a good many unfortunate persons seemed to be profoundly helped.
>
> . . . I began to be uncomfortable with my Freudian "insights." . . . So I began fabricating "insights." I . . . offered "preposterous interpretations" to my clients. Some of them were about as un-Freudian as I could make them. . . . What happened? Well, many of my preposterous explanations worked, some of them surprisingly well. (Kelly, 1969, pp. 51–52)

From Kelly's point of view, the therapeutic value of interpretation lies in its ability to create options and possibilities, new interpretations of oneself and the world. Even "preposterous interpretations" can help someone to see things in a new way and to realize that we each can play an active role in deciding how we see and judge what is in our environments.

It appears to me, therefore, that at the heart of the point of view that psychiatry is becoming too biological, in addition to the points made earlier, is the assumption that we already know much about aetiology and that psychotherapy is the path through which such knowledge is obtained.

295

300   I accept that there is an important place for psychotherapy in the practice of psychiatry as in all of medicine, and that its role in no way presents a conflict or challenge to the biological view (Guze, 1988). Psychotherapy from this perspective is not based on any unfounded conviction concerning the aetiology of psycho-pathological reactions, though any practitioner may speculate about these matters and most do. Such psychotherapy has been defined as rehabilitative (Guze & Murphy, 1963; Guze, 1988) because, like other practices in rehabilitation

305   medicine, it focuses on the patient's problems, strengths, weaknesses, and circumstances, regardless of aetiology. The patient's personality, life style, vulnerabilities and propensities, relationships, resources, and goals are the focus of review and discussion, with the aim of improved understanding of self and situation in the service of handling symptoms, disabilities, responsibilities, and opportunities more effectively.

310   Helping the patient identify and understand his or her perceptions, needs, concerns, and adjustment patterns can also be helpful. Sometimes, the relationship between the patient and the therapist provides an unusually useful set of circumstances in which the patient's characteristic patterns of adjustment and coping

315   become more obvious (transference). But there is no way to rise above speculation when it comes to suggesting within the psychotherapeutic process how the patient's personality developed or why the patient became sick.

> *transference:* in psychoanalysis, the patient's displacement of emotions or attitudes toward other individuals (usually the parents) onto the therapist

320   To restate the essence of my argument, psychotherapy can provide emotional support, an opportunity to understand one's self better, a chance to consider the meaning of one's experiences, a setting in which to consider future options and possibilities in terms of one's attributes and circumstances, and a protective situation in which to express one's frustrations and disappointments. Psychotherapy can also generate hypotheses concerning causal connections

325   but it cannot test these hypotheses at the same time. The process of psychotherapy provides no opportunities to control for the therapist's preexisting assumptions, the patient's preexisting assumptions, and the impact of the therapist's interpretations and suggestions on the patient's communications. But, most importantly, the process of psychotherapy cannot distinguish the causal direction between phenomena of interest. It cannot tell whether a partic-

330   ular phenomenon is the cause of the illness or the result of the illness (Guze, 1988). . . .

It seems clear that continued debate about the place of biology in psychiatric thinking, like parallel discussions about genetics, is not likely to prove useful unless it is appreciated that modern biological and genetic science includes the recognition of the powerful roles of the environment, learning, and even culture in the growth and development of all forms of life,

335   including human life. If some would like to make this more explicit by referring to the 'biopsychosocial' model, I have no quarrel, though I do not consider it necessary. But I do take issue with anyone who worries about psychiatry being 'too biological.'

To conclude: I believe that continuing debate about the biological basis of psychiatry is derived much more from philosophical, ideological and political concerns than from scientific

ones. Modern biology encompasses sufficiently broad perspectives to accommodate all valid   340
and pertinent observations. At the same time, however, it focuses appropriately on the fundamental elements of all forms of life: evolution, development, structure, and function. Modern
psychiatry is inescapably biological because it shares this focus as applied to psychopathology.
I truly believe that most psychiatrists will lose interest in the debate as new understanding
evolves from advances in genetics, neurobiology, and epidemiology. We will increasingly be   345
thinking about and discussing specific questions of fact and their interpretation rather than
argue about ideological matters as substitutes for scientific discourse.

   Obviously, a biological concept of psychiatry is in no way incompatible with recognizing and
being concerned about the powerful impact of economic, political, and organizational factors
on the availability of clinical services; the extent, quality, and cost of such services; and the out-   350
come of various interventions. No thoughtful and knowledgeable individual advocates an
approach to psychiatry (or to the rest of medicine for that matter) that isolates it from its social
and cultural context. But to the extent that the central concern of both clinicians and patients
focuses on the nature of the patient's disorder—including its aetiology, pathogenesis, and
response to treatment—biological concepts and approaches remain central and indispensable.   355

For Discussion

1. On what kinds of evidence might Guze have based his claim that the environmental or
   experiential factors that accompany mental illness "reflect only the usual range of human
   troubles that most people experience without becoming ill" (p. 593, lines 122–123)? If one
   accepts his view, does that mean that mental illness is biologically caused?

2. Guze says that opponents of the focus on biological factors in mental illness fear that
   this focus will lead to "blaming the victims" (p. 595, lines 184–200). Why would a
   medical approach to mental illness lead people to blame the patient?

3. Feldman (2007) reviewed a number of studies that demonstrate that drug treatment and
   cognitive behavioral therapy are equally effective in relieving symptoms of depression.
   How would Guze explain this?

4. Guze says that, even if environmental or experiential factors can be shown to play an
   important role in the development of mental illness, "it is to the specific [biological]
   vulnerability that we must direct our attention" (p. 594, line 124). How does he support
   this view?

5. That psychopathology involves biology is inescapably true, for all behavior does, but
   does that necessarily mean that "what is called psychopathology is the manifestation of
   disordered processes in various brain systems" (p. 594, lines 162–163, our emphasis)?

6. Most of Guze's own research dealt with psychoses (schizophrenia and mood disorders).
   Is it possible that milder forms of pathology are less likely to have the same
   overwhelmingly biological basis?

Corey L. M. Keyes (b. 1962)
The Mental Health Continuum: From Languishing to Flourishing in Life (2002)

Think about how we describe someone who is mentally ill or who seems a bit "odd." They are crazy, insane, mad as a hatter, psycho, mental, off his rocker, loony, abnormal, *non compos mentis,* nutty as a fruitcake, cuckoo, daft, unhinged, bananas, loco, whacko, out of her mind, or deranged. He has bats in his belfry. A screw loose. She's lost her marbles. The list is endless.

Now think about how we describe someone who is mentally healthy. The list is a lot shorter. He or she might be described as mature or self-actualized or well-adjusted. There aren't a lot of options, and they lack the pizzazz of the first list. Maybe that is why we devote much less attention to mental health than to mental illness. Maybe because so little attention has been devoted to mental health, we don't have a rich vocabulary to talk about it. It is probably a little of both, and it is probably also a result of the general acceptance of the medical model of mental illness.

The medical model holds that when something is wrong with an individual the clinician's role is to fix the problem, to cure the person, to eliminate the symptoms. Then the person is normal again. Normal means that there is nothing wrong. The fact that we call it mental "illness" and talk about "cure" and "symptoms" suggests that madness is analogous to if not identical with physical disorder. In applying the medical model to mental illness, a clinician's goal is to remove a problematic behavior or set of ideas that is interfering with a person's ability to live "normally." When this is done, the person is okay, they are normal. Is this as good as it gets? Some psychologists have given attention to thinking about what it means to be something beyond "okay."

Source: Keyes, C. L. M. (2002). The mental health continuum: From languishing to flourishing in life. *Journal of Health and Behavior Research, 43,* 207–222. Reprinted with permission of the American Sociological Association and the author.

Gordon Allport (1937) devoted a chapter of his textbook on personality to the "mature personality." In his view, the mature, or fully developed, individual has three qualities: a variety of interests and a willingness to set goals and to pursue them; insight and a sense of humor about the self; and a "unifying philosophy of life." He urged psychologists to devote more attention to the study of positive human functioning:

> It is especially in relation to the formation and development of human *personality* that we need to open doors. For it is precisely here that our ignorance and uncertainty are greatest. Our methods, however well suited to the study of sensory processes, animal research, and pathology, are not fully adequate; and interpretations arising from the exclusive use of these methods are stultifying. Some theories . . . are based largely upon the behavior of sick and anxious people or upon the antics of captive and desperate rats. Fewer theories have derived from the study of healthy beings, those who strive not so much to preserve life as to make it worth living. (1955, p.18)

In 1958 Marie Jahoda wrote *Current Concepts of Positive Mental Health,* a book usually considered to be the first on positive mental health. In the Introduction she writes:

> Knowledge about deviations, illness, and malfunctioning far exceeds knowledge of healthy functioning. . . . [S]cience requires that the previous concentration on the study of inappropriate functioning be corrected by greater emphasis on appropriate functioning, if for no other reason than to test such assumptions as that health and illness are different only in degree.
>
> Other members of the scientific community oppose . . . concern with mental health. In part such opposition is based on an unwillingness to work with a notion so vague. . . . In part it is rooted in the conviction that the science of behavior advances best by studying behavior, without reference to whether it is "good" or "bad." Only in this manner . . . can science remain free from "contamination by values." (p. 6)

In spite of the risk of getting values involved, Jahoda identifies six concepts associated with positive mental health: attitudes toward the self, development of self-actualization, integration of psychological functions, autonomy, accurate perception of reality, and environmental mastery.

Several other psychologists have contributed significantly to positive psychology. Abraham Maslow (e.g., 1954, 1968, 1970) wrote extensively about how and why psychology had gone wrong by studying only normative or negative behaviors and avoiding the issue of what the human experience could be:

> If one is preoccupied with the insane, the neurotic, the psychopath, the criminal, the delinquent, the feeble-minded, one's hopes for the human species become perforce more and more modest, more and more realistic, more and more scaled down. One expects less and less from people. From dreams of peace, affection, and brotherhood, we retreat. . . . (1954, p. 360)

Maslow's theory was an influential attempt to right this wrong. His theory of motivation assumes that human needs and motivations are "organized into a hierarchy of relative prepotency"

(1954, p. 83; 1970, p. 38). At each need level, a person must achieve reasonable satisfaction before moving on. The first needs that must be met are the physiological needs; for example, hunger and thirst. If these are not satisfied, the person does not move on to higher order needs: safety, belongingness and love, esteem, and finally the self-actualization need. The first four of the needs are considered deficiency needs; they motivate us to fulfill a deficit state. The need for self-actualization, however, is not based on deficiency. It is a positive desire to fulfill one's potential, and seeking self-actualization may increase, not decrease, tension. Those who are self-actualized share a number of qualities, such as accurate perception of reality, acceptance of self, autonomy, freshness of appreciation, mystic experiences, humor, and democratic character (Maslow, 1954, Chapter 12; Maslow, 1970, Chapter 11). In a later book, Maslow (1976) wrote more about the mystical experiences that self-actualized people have and referred to these as peak experiences, strong experiences of awe, selflessness, and wholeness.

Mihaly Csikszentmihalyi (1990, 1993, 1997) introduced the term "flow," a concept similar to Maslow's concept of peak experience. Csikszentmihalyi had begun his research on creativity and first introduced "flow" to refer to the total involvement that artists have when painting. He soon realized that this experience is not confined to artists but occurs in many kinds of people and in many kinds of settings. He extended the notion of flow to activities in which a person is totally absorbed. As did Maslow, Csikszentmihalyi believes that people who experience flow frequently are much more likely to be psychologically healthy and that social pressures often constrict us and limit our psychological health. We are taught to follow the rules. As a result, many of us are conventional, rather dull, and not terribly happy. We need to be more independent of social constraints and to find goals and activities that reward and satisfy us. Csikszentmihalyi writes about the nature of the flow experience itself, the discipline necessary to experience flow, the child rearing practices that are most likely to facilitate the experience, and the personality characteristics associated with individuals who experience flow most frequently.

Interest in positive psychology seems to have increased significantly in the 1990s, and there are now new concepts and much more research on mental health. One of the difficulties faced by those studying positive psychology is, as Marie Jahoda warned in 1958, defining "mental health." Another possible problem is that of avoiding "contamination by values" (Jahoda, 1958, p. 6). But, these same issues of vagueness and values exist when we try to define "abnormality."

Corey Keyes is one of the most active contributors to positive psychology. Keyes describes the mentally healthy as "flourishing," and he has done a substantial amount of research to identify the characteristics associated with flourishing. Keyes also introduced a new concept to positive psychology—languishing. In the present reading, about 17.2% of adults are flourishing. Another 56.6% are moderately mentally healthy (they're "okay"), 12.1% are languishing, and 14.1% are depressed. Those who are languishing are not mentally ill, but they show few signs of mental health. Because his conceptual approach goes far beyond simply looking at the super-healthy and because his ideas are grounded in empirical work, Keyes has created a framework for thinking about mental health—its presence and its absence—that makes it possible for him to ask a range of new questions.

Keyes's article provides new ways to think about mental health. He argues skillfully for the importance of facilitating flourishing and for paying attention to the problems associated with languishing, and he provides a conceptual framework that will allow us to learn more about what flourishing is, who the people are who are languishing, and what the consequences are of being at different points along the mental health continuum.

> *etiology:* the study of causes

There are grave reasons for concern about the prevalence and etiology of mental illness. Unipolar depression, for example, strikes many individuals annually and recurrently throughout life (Angst, 1988; Gonzales, Lewinsohn, and Clarke, 1985). Upwards of one-half of adults may experience [5] a serious mental illness in their lifetime; between 10 percent and 14 percent of adults experience an episode of major depression annually (Cross-National Collaborative Group, 1992; Kessler et al., 1994; Robins and Regier, 1991; U.S. Department of Health and Human Services, 1999). As a persistent and substantial deviation from normal functioning, mental illness impairs the execution of social roles (e.g., employee) and it is associated with emotional suffering [10] (Keyes, 2001; Spitzer and Wilson, 1975). Depression costs billions each year due to work absenteeism, diminished productivity, healthcare costs (Greenberg et al., 1993; Keyes and Lopez, 2002; Murray and Lopez, 1996; Mrazek and Haggerty, 1994), and it accounts for at least one-third of completed suicides (Rebellon, Brown, and Keyes, 2001; U.S. Department of Health and Human Services, 1998). [15]

Yet about one-half of the adult population should remain free of serious mental illnesses over its lifespan, and as much as 90 percent should remain free of major depression annually.

> In this paper, when Keyes says "mental illness" he is referring exclusively to depression.

Are adults who remain free of mental illness annually and over a lifetime mentally healthy and productive? This is a pivotal question for proponents [20] of the study of mental health (Keyes and Shapiro, 2004), and it is the guiding question to this study. Mental health is, according to the Surgeon General (U.S. Department of Health and Human Services, 1999), " . . . a state of successful performance of mental function, resulting in productive activities, fulfilling relationships with [25] people, and the ability to adapt to change and to cope with adversity" (p. 4). Social scientists have lobbied over 40 years for a definition of mental health as more than the absence of mental illness (Jahoda, 1958). M. Brewster Smith (1959) lamented that "positive" mental health is a "slogan" and a "rallying call" rather than the empirical concept and variable it deserves to be. Despite the Surgeon General's definition 41 years later, mental health remains the antonym of [30] mental illness and a catchword of inert good intentions.

> *syndrome:* a set of symptoms that occur together. In traditional clinical language, a syndrome is a particular disorder. Here Keyes is forcing us out of this traditional usage.

This paper introduces and applies an operationalization of mental health as a syndrome of symptoms of positive feelings and positive functioning in life. It summarizes the scales and [35] dimensions of subjective well-being, which are symptoms of mental health. Whereas the presence of mental health is described as flourishing, the absence of mental health is characterized as languishing in life. Subsequently, this study addresses four research questions. First, what is the [40] prevalence of flourishing, languishing, and moderate mental health in the United States?

Second, what is the burden of languishing relative to major depression episode and to flourishing in life? Third, is mental health (flourishing) associated with better psychosocial functioning relative to major depression and languishing in life? Fourth, is mental health, like most mental illnesses, unequally distributed in the population; who, in other words, is mentally healthy?

45

> More on these questions can be found in Keyes (2007).

MENTAL HEALTH AND ITS SYMPTOMS

Like mental illness, mental health is defined here as an emergent condition based on the concept of a syndrome. A state of health, like illness, is indicated when a set of symptoms at a specific level are present for a specified duration and this constellation of symptoms coincides with distinctive cognitive and social functioning (cf. Keyes, 2001; Mechanic, 1999). Mental health may be operationalized as a syndrome of symptoms of an individual's subjective well-being. During the last 40 years, social scientists have conceptualized, measured, and studied the measurement structure of mental health through the investigation of subjective well-being (e.g., Headey, Kelley, and Wearing, 1993; Keyes, Shmotkin, and Ryff, 2002). Subjective well-being is individuals' perceptions and evaluations of their own lives in terms of their affective states and their psychological and social functioning (Keyes and Waterman, 2003).

50

55

Emotional well-being is a cluster of symptoms reflecting the presence or absence of positive feelings about life. Symptoms of emotional well-being are ascertained from individuals' responses to structured scales measuring the presence of positive affect (e.g., individuals is in good spirits), the absence of negative affect (e.g., individual is not hopeless), and perceived satisfaction with life. Measures of the expression of emotional well-being in terms of positive affect and negative affect are related but distinct dimensions (e.g., Bradburn, 1969; Watson and Tellegen, 1985). Last, measures of avowed (e.g., "I am satisfied with life") and expressed (i.e., positive and negative affect) emotional well-being are related but distinct dimensions (Andrews and Withey, 1976; Bryant and Veroff, 1982; Diener, 1984; Diener, Sandvik, and Pavot, 1991; Diener et al., 1999).

60

65

Like mental illness (viz. depression), mental health is more than the presence and absence of emotional states. In addition, subjective well-being includes measures of the presence and absence of positive functioning in life. Since Ryff's (1989) operationalization of clinical and personality theorists' conceptions of positive functioning (Jahoda, 1958), the field has moved toward a broader set of measures of well-being. Positive functioning consists of six dimensions of psychological well-being: self-acceptance, positive relations with others, personal growth, purpose in life, environmental mastery, and autonomy (see Keyes and Ryff's 1999 review). That is, individuals are functioning well when they like most parts of themselves, have warm and trusting relationships, see themselves developing into better people, have a direction in life, are able to shape their environments to satisfy their needs, and have a degree of self-determination. The psychological well-being scales are well-validated and reliable (Ryff, 1989), and the

70

75

validity: the extent to which a test measures what it is intended to measure

reliability: consistency measurement over time or within a test

six-factor structure has been confirmed in a large and representative sample of U.S. adults (Ryff and Keyes, 1995). 80

However, there is more to functioning well in life than psychological well-being. Elsewhere (Keyes, 1998) I have argued that positive functioning includes social challenges and tasks, and 85 I proposed five dimensions of social well-being. Whereas psychological well-being represents more private and personal criteria for evaluation of one's functioning, social well-being epitomizes the more public and social criteria whereby people evaluate their functioning in life. These social dimensions consist of social coherence, social actualization, social integration, social acceptance, and social contribution. Individuals are functioning well when they see 90 society as meaningful and understandable, when they see society as possessing potential for growth, when they feel they belong to and are accepted by their communities, when they accept most parts of society, and when they see

construct validity: the extent to which the results of a test agree with other measures of the same quality or predict particular outcomes in expected ways

themselves contributing to society. The social well-being scales have shown good construct 95 validity and internal consistency, and the five-factor structure has been confirmed in two studies based on data from a nationally representative sample of adults (Keyes, 1998).

It is probably less evident that the dimensions of social well-being, compared with emotional and psychological well-being, are indicative of an individual's mental health. However, 100 the Surgeon General's definition of mental health included particular reference to criteria such as "productive activities," "fulfilling relationships," and "the ability to adapt to change," all of which imply the quality of an individual's complete engagement in society and life. Measures of emotional well-being often identify an individual's satisfaction or positive affect with "life 105 overall," but rarely with facets of their social lives. The dimensions of psychological well-being are intra-personal reflections of an individual's adjustment to and outlook on their life. Only one of the six scales of psychological well-being—positive relations with others—reflects the ability to build and maintain intimate and trusting interpersonal relationships. I have argued

factor analysis: a statistical procedure in which correlations among a large number of variables are used to identify higher-level groups (factors) of variables

elsewhere and have shown empirically (Keyes, 110 1998) that an individual's adjustment to life includes the aforementioned facets of social well-being. That is, factor analyses showed that the mental health measures formed three correlated but distinct factors: emotional, psychological, and 115 social well-being.

Last, some dimensions of social well-being (viz. social integration) are identical with theoretical explanations of interpersonal and societal level causes of mental health (e.g., social support and social networks). We have argued elsewhere (Keyes and Shapiro, 2004) that constructs

120 such as social integration exist at multiple levels of analysis (i.e., societal, interpersonal, and individual). However, I concur with Larson (1996), who said that "The key to deciding whether a measure of social well-being is part of an individual's health is whether the measure reflects *internal* responses to stimuli—feelings, thoughts and behaviors reflecting satisfaction or lack of satisfaction with the social environment" (p. 186). From this perspective, the measures of
125 social well-being, like the measures of psychological and emotional well-being, should be viewed as indicators of an individual's mental health status.

TOWARD A DIAGNOSIS OF MENTAL HEALTH

Empirically, mental health and mental illness are not opposite ends of a single measurement continuum. Measures of symptoms of mental illness (viz. depression) correlate negatively and modestly with measures of subjective well-being. In two separate studies reviewed by Ryff and
130 Keyes (1995), the measures of psychological well-being correlated, on average, –.51 with the Zung depression inventory and –.55 with the Center for Epidemiological Studies depression (CESD) scale. Indicators and scales of life satisfaction and happiness (i.e., emotional well-being) also tend to correlate around –.40 to –.50 with scales of depression symptoms (see Frisch et al., 1992).
135 Confirmatory factor analyses of the sub-scales of the CESD and the scales of psychological well-being scales in a sample of U.S. adults supported the two-factor theory (Keyes, Ryff, and Lee, 2001). That is, the best-fitting model was one where the CESD subscales were indicators of . . . the presence and absence of mental illness (see also Headey et al., 1993). The psychological well-being scales were indicators of . . . the presence and absence of mental
140 health. In short, mental health is not merely the absence of mental illness; it is not simply the presence of high levels of subjective well-being. Mental health is best viewed as a complete state consisting of the presence and the absence of mental illness and mental health symptoms.
The mental health continuum consists of complete and incomplete mental health.
145 Adults with complete mental health are *flourishing* in life with high levels of well-being. To be flourishing, then, is to be filled with positive emotion and to be functioning well psychologically and socially. Adults with incomplete mental health are *languishing* in life with low well-being. Thus, languishing may be conceived of as emptiness and stagnation, constituting a life of quiet despair that parallels accounts of individuals who describe them-
150 selves and life as "hollow," "empty," "a shell," and "a void" (see Cushman, 1990; Keyes, 2003; Levy, 1984; Singer, 1977).
Conceptually and empirically, measures of subjective well-being fall into two clusters of symptoms: emotional and functional well-being. The measures of emotional well-being comprise a cluster that reflects emotional vitality. In turn, the measures of psychological well-being
155 and social well-being reflect a multifaceted cluster of symptoms of positive functioning. These two clusters of mental health symptoms mirror the symptom clusters used in the *DSM-III-R*

DSM: *Diagnostic and Statistical Manual*, a manual published by the American Psychiatric Association that classifies mental disorders

(American Psychiatric Association, 1987) to diagnose major depression episode. Major depression consists of symptoms of depressed mood or anhedonia (e.g., loss of pleasure derived from activities) and a multifaceted cluster of symptoms (i.e., vegetative and hyperactive) of malfunctioning (e.g., insomnia or hypersomnia). Of the nine symptoms of major depression, a diagnosis of depression is warranted when a respondent reports five or more symptoms, with at least one symptom coming from the affective cluster.

160

Five or more of the following symptoms most days during a two week period are sufficient for the diagnosis of a major depressive episode (*DSM-IV-TR*, 2000):

1. Depressed mood most of the day
2. Markedly diminished interest or pleasure in almost all activities
3. Significant weight gain or loss, or decrease or increase in appetite
4. Insomnia (trouble sleeping) or hypersomnia (excessive sleeping)
5. Psychomotor agitation or retardation
6. Fatigue or loss of energy
7. Feelings of worthlessness or excessive guilt
8. Decreased ability to think or concentrate, or indecisiveness
9. Thoughts of death or suicide, a suicide attempt, or creating a specific plan for committing suicide

The first two are affective (emotional) indicators of depression.

The *DSM* approach to the diagnosis of major depression is employed as a theoretical guide for the diagnosis of mental health, whose symptom clusters mirror theoretically and empirically the symptom clusters for depression. That is, mental health is best operationalized as [a] syndrome that combines symptoms of emotional well-being with symptoms of psychological and social well-being. In the present study, respondents completed a structured scale of positive affect and a question about life satisfaction (i.e., emotional well-being). Respondents also completed the six scales of psychological well-being and the five scales of social well-being. Altogether, this study included two symptom scales of emotional vitality, and 11 symptom scales of positive functioning (i.e., six psychological and five social).

165

170

The diagnostic scheme for mental health parallels the scheme employed to diagnose major depression disorder wherein individuals must exhibit just over half of the total symptoms (i.e., at least five of nine). To be *languishing* in life, individuals must exhibit a low level (low = lower tertile) on one of the two measures of emotional well-being, and low levels on six of the 11 scales of positive functioning. To be *flourishing* in life,

175

lower tertile: lower third of the distribution

180   individuals must exhibit a high level (high = upper tertile) on one of the two measures of emotional well-being and high levels on six of the 11 scales of positive functioning. Adults who are *moderately mentally healthy* are neither flourishing nor languishing in life. . . .

METHODS

Sample

Data are from the MacArthur Foundation's Midlife in the United States survey. This survey was a random-digit-dialing sample of non-institutionalized English-speaking adults age 25 to
185   74 living in the 48 contiguous states, whose household included at least one telephone. In the first stage of the multistage sampling design, investigators selected households with equal probability via telephone numbers. At the second stage, they used disproportionate stratified sampling to select respondents. The sample was stratified by age and sex, and males between ages 65 and 74 were over-sampled.

190   Field procedures were initiated in January of 1995 and lasted 13 months. Respondents were contacted and interviewed by trained personnel, and those who agreed to participate in the entire study took part in a computer-assisted telephone interview lasting 30 minutes, on average. Respondents then were mailed two questionnaire booklets requiring 1.5 hours, on average, to complete. Respondents were offered $20, a commemorative pen, periodic reports of
195   study findings, and a copy of a monograph on the study.

The sample consists of 3,032 adults. With a 70 percent response rate for the telephone phase and an 87 percent response rate for the self-administered questionnaire phase, the combined response is 61 percent ($.70 \times .87 = .61$). Descriptive analyses are based on the weighted sample to correct for unequal probabilities of household and within household respondent selection. The sample
200   weight post-stratifies the sample to match the proportions of adults according to age, gender, education, marital status, race, residence (i.e., metropolitan and non-metropolitan), and region (Northeast, Midwest, South, and West) based on the October 1995 Current Population Survey.

Measures

The measures that Keyes used in this study were

Mental illness, measured by the CIDI-SF (Composite International Diagnostic Interview Short Form) scales (Kessler et al., 1998)

Mental health, measured by a total of 13 scales:

Two scales measured emotional well-being:

Positive Affect Scale

Life Satisfaction Scale

(Continued)

(Continued)

Six scales measured psychological well-being:

Self-acceptance Scale

Positive Relations with Others Scale

Personal Growth Scale

Purpose in Life Scale

Environmental Mastery Scale

Autonomy Scale

Five scales measured social well-being:

Social Acceptance Scale

Social Actualization Scale

Social Contribution Scale

Social Coherence Scale

Social Integration Scale

Psychological functioning and impairment, measured by three scales:

Rating of their own emotional, mental health

Rating of the degree to which their health limited them in the activities of daily life

Estimate of the number of workdays they had lost or shortened

Sociodemographic variables included here were age, sex, race, marital status, and education.

RESULTS

Prevalence

From the frequencies reported in Table 1, the percentages in this paragraph should be as follows: Of adults who did not have depression 20.0% were flourishing, 14.1% were languishing, and 65.9% were moderately mentally healthy. Of adults who did have depression 6.3% were flourishing, 60.4% had moderate mental health, and 33.3% were languishing.

Table 1 presents the prevalence estimates of major depression episode and mental health status, as well as the cross-classification of mental health status with major depression. Most adults, 85.9 percent, did not have a depressive episode. Only 17.2 percent of adults who did not have depression were flourishing in life, 12.1 percent were languishing in life, and just over one-half were moderately mentally healthy. Of the 14.1 percent of adults who had a depressive episode during the past year, only

0.9 percent were flourishing, 8.5 percent had moderate mental health, and 4.7 percent
215   were also languishing.

Exactly 28 percent of languishing adults had major depression, while 13.1 percent of adults
with moderate mental health, and 4.9 percent of flourishing adults, had a major depressive
episode during the past year. Thus, compared with flourishing adults, moderately well adults
were about 2.1 times more likely to have had major depression during the past year, while lan-
220   guishing adults were 5.7 times more likely. These findings, though cross-sectional, suggest that
the absence of mental health (languishing) may be a risk factor for episodes of major depression.

TABLE 1   The Prevalence of Mental Health and Major Depression among Adults between the
Ages of 25 and 74 in the 1995 Midlife in the United States Study

| | Mental Health Status | | | |
	Languishing N %	*Moderately Mentally Healthy* N %	*Flourishing* N %	*Total* N %
Major Depressive Episode				
NO	368	1,715	520	2,603
	12.1	56.6	17.2	85.9
	Pure Languishing	Moderately Mentally Healthy	Flourishing	
YES	143	259	27	429
	4.7	8.5	0.9	14.1
	Depressed and Languishing	Pure Depression	Pure Depression	
TOTAL	511	1,974	547	3,032
	16.8	65.1	18.1	100

Note: $\chi^2 = 120.5, p < .001$ (two-tailed)

Is pure languishing confounded with subthreshold depression? Studies have consistently
shown that depressive symptoms that do not meet the criteria for major depression are associated with physical disease and functional impairments at levels sometimes comparable to that
225   of major depression (see Pincus, Davis, and McQueen, 1999). Thus, it would be unclear whether
any association of languishing with functional impairment is due to the absence of mental health
or the presence of some symptoms of depression. However, the mean number of symptoms of
depression (range = 0–9) among adults with pure languishing (i.e., not depressed) was .13 (SD =
.58). Thus, nearly all adults with pure languishing
230   had no symptom of depression and therefore did
not fit the criteria for any form of subthreshold
depression (e.g., minor depression or dysthymia).

dysthymia: a chronic depressive mood state

Psychosocial Functioning and Impairment

Table 2 presents the bivariate association of the prevalence of indicators of levels of impairment with the combined diagnosis of major depression episode and mental health. About 18 percent of languishing adults, and 22 percent of adults with depression, said their emotional health was poor or fair; over twice as many, 55 percent, of languishing adults who had depression during the past year said their emotional health was poor or fair. Only 6 percent of moderately well and 1 percent of flourishing adults said their emotional health was poor or fair. In contrast, about 61 percent of moderately well and 81 percent of flourishing adults said their emotional health was very good or excellent. About 34 percent of languishing adults, 35 percent of adults with pure depression, and only 15 percent of languishing adults with major depression said their emotional health was very good or excellent.

TABLE 2 Prevalence of Psychosocial Impairment by Mental Illness and Mental Health Status

| | Mental Illness and Mental Health Status | | | | | |
Impairment Indicator	Languishing and Depression	Pure Depression	Pure Languishing	Moderately Mentally Healthy	Flourishing	χ^2
Emotional Health						660.1*** df = 8
Poor or Fair	55.2	22.2	17.7	5.7	0.6	
Good	29.4	43.3	48.2	33.9	18.1	
Very Good or Excellent	15.4	34.5	34.1	60.5	81.3	
One or More Severe[a] Limitation of Daily Activities of Living	69.4	54.7	64.0	54.7	42.0	59.1*** df = 4
Six or More Work Days Lost[b]	11.9	2.5	2.2	0.5	0	144.1*** df = 4
Six or More Work Days Cut Back[c]	16.8	7.0	1.6	0.4	0	243.0*** df = 4

Note: *p < .05 **p < .01 ***p < .001 (two-tailed)

a. Defined as any activity in which respondent perceived "a lot" of limitation.

b. Number days of past 30 in which respondent was completely unable to work due to reasons of mental health or to combination of mental and physical health.

c. Number days of past 30 in which respondent had to reduce or cut back on amount of work completed due to reasons of mental health or to combination of mental and physical health.

245 Next, the analysis focused on severe activity limitation, operationalized as the report of "a lot" of limitation in one or more activities of daily living. About 64 percent of languishers, 55 percent of depressed only adults, and 69 percent of the languishing adults who also had major depression, reported a severe activity limitation. Moreover, 55 percent of moderately mentally healthy adults, compared with 42 percent of flourishing adults, reported a severe limitation of daily living in at least one activity. Last, the analysis focused on severe loss of workdays and

250 severe cutbacks, where severe was operationalized as a loss or cutback of six or more days during the past 30 days. About 2 percent of languishing, 2.5 percent of depressed, and 12 percent of the languishing adults with an episode of major depression had a severe level of workdays lost due to mental health. Only .5 percent of moderately mentally healthy, and none of the flourishing adults, had a severe level of workdays lost due to mental health. In terms of work

255 cutback, 1.6 percent of languishing, 7 percent of depressed only, and 17 percent of languishing adults with an episode of major depression had a severe level of work cutback due to mental health. Only .4 percent of the moderately mentally healthy and none of the flourishing adults had a severe level of workdays cut back due to mental health.

. . .

260 Who is mentally healthy? Table 3 presents the descriptive epidemiology of the mental health diagnosis by gender, age, education, and marital status. Consistent with prior research, this study finds a higher prevalence of poor mental health

Epidemiology is the study of the prevalence and distribution of illness (and health).

among females, younger adults, less educated individuals, and unmarried adults. Pure depres-

265 sion is more prevalent among females, among adults between the ages of 25 to 54, and among separated and divorced individuals. Pure depression is about equally prevalent across the educational categories. The most dysfunctional category of languishing with an episode of depression is more prevalent among females, among adults between the ages of 25 and 54, among individuals with 11 or fewer years of education, and among divorced individuals. Pure lan-

270 guishing is more prevalent among younger adults between the ages of 25 and 64, among adults with a high school degree (or equivalent) or less, and among adults who are separated from their spouse; pure languishing is about equally prevalent for males and females. Mental health, or flourishing in particular, is more prevalent among males, older adults between the ages of 45 and 74, individuals with 16 or more years of education, and among married adults.

275 The findings are therefore consistent with and extend past research. . . .

DISCUSSION

Many individuals remain free of mental illness each year and over their lifetimes. However, is the absence of mental illness reflective of genuine mental health? The Midlife in the United States study provides a rare opportunity to investigate the costs and benefits associated with the absence (i.e., languishing) and the presence (i.e., flourishing) of mental health as well as mental illnesses such as major depression. The results of this paper suggest there are two grave reasons to be as concerned about pure languishing in life (i.e., the absence of mental health and mental illness) as the presence [of] major depression. First, pure languishing is associated with substantial psychosocial impairment at levels comparable to an episode of pure depression. Second, pure languishing is as prevalent as pure episodes of major depression in this study.

Languishing is associated with poor emotional health, with high limitations of daily living, and with a high likelihood of a severe number (i.e., 6 or more) of lost days of work . . . that respondents attribute to their mental health. . . . Pure depression, too, was a burden. A major depressive episode was associated with poor emotional health, high limitations of activities of daily living, and a high likelihood of severe work cutback. . . .

Functioning is considerably worse when languishing and major depressive episode are comorbid during the past year. Languishing adults who had a major depressive episode in the past year reported the worst emotional health, the most limitation of activities of daily living, the most days of work lost and cut back, and the highest probability of having severe levels of workdays lost and workdays cut back by half. In contrast, functioning is markedly improved among mentally healthy adults. That is, moderately mentally healthy and flourishing adults reported the best emotional health, the fewest days of work loss, and the fewest days of work cutbacks. Moreover, flourishing adults reported even fewer limitations of activities of daily living than adults who were moderately mentally healthy.

> *comorbid:* a disorder that appears in conjunction with another disorder

Languishing was as prevalent as having an episode of major depression. Nearly 5 percent of the sample had the most debilitating condition of languishing combined with an episode of major depression. Less than one-quarter of adults were flourishing; one-half of adults had a moderate level of mental health. When extrapolated to the target population,[1] the prevalence estimates suggest that a combined total of 45 million adults were either languishing, depressed, or both (which constituted 29 percent of the sample). By comparison, about 32 million adults were mentally healthy based on the prevalence of flourishing in life. The bulk of the population is neither mentally ill nor mentally healthy. . . .

> *45 million:* according to Table 1, 26.2% of the sample were languishing, depressed, or both, and so the population prevalence would be about 40.5 million. From the same data, about 28 million would be flourishing.

> The second limitation, not included here, is a technical issue having to do with the nature of the scales used in this study.

There are two important study limitations that suggest directions for future research. First, the

---

[1] Data from the Census Bureau suggested that the target population of adults between the ages of 25 and 74 in 1995 was approximately 154 million.

data are cross-sectional. The ability to collect data from the Midlife in the United States survey respondents in successive waves would permit investigation of whether languishing causes work impairments and physical disability or whether work cutbacks and the onset
320   of physical disability cause languishing. That said, cross-sectional studies of the burden of depression have been followed up with longitudinal studies showing that depression caused physical disability and diminished work productivity (Broadhead et al., 1990; Bruce et al. 1994). Languishing, too, may precede many forms of psychosocial impairment. Moreover, flourishing in life, and perhaps moderate mental health, could be a source of resilience,
325   acting as a stress buffer against stressful live events and life transitions.

. . .

Despite this study's limitation, its findings have implications for the conception of mental health and the treatment and prevention of mental illness. The National Institute of Mental Health (NIMH) periodically convenes scholars to identify research priorities. The first sentence in the 1995 report (U.S. Department of Health and Human Services, 1995) states that the mis-
330   sion of the NIMH is "To improve this nation's mental health . . ." by supporting " . . . a wide range of research related to the etiology, diagnosis, treatment, and prevention of mental *disorders*" (p. 1) (emphasis added). Based on the present study, the question is whether the NIMH can "get there (i.e., to mental health) from here (i.e., mental disorders)."

Proponents of the study of mental health, and the implications of this study, would suggest
335   that the mission of the NIMH is incomplete. Mental illness and mental health are highly correlated but belong to separate continua, and therefore the prevention and treatment of mental illnesses will not necessarily result in more mentally healthy individuals. Moreover, there appears to be a Pandora's box of economic and social burdens associated with the absence (i.e., languishing) of mental health, which is completely ignored by current programs in the
340   NIMH and elsewhere (e.g., World Health Organization). The promotion of this nation's mental health will require programmatic infrastructure and funding for a wide range of research related to the etiology, diagnosis, treatment, prevention, and promotion of the absence and presence of mental health.

Moreover, treatment objectives for mental illness are symptom reduction and prevention
345   of relapse (Gladis et al., 1999; U.S. Department of Health and Human Services, 1999). However, findings from this study suggest mental health promotion should be the preeminent treatment objective. Moreover, interventions to prevent mental illness are based on findings of the study of risk and protective factors for mental illness. Future research should also investigate whether and how languishing adults are at risk for depression. Another
350   source of prevention knowledge may be gleaned from the study of the life course and social contexts of mentally healthy youth and adults. Understanding the nature and etiology of the strengths and competencies of flourishing individuals may provide therapeutic insights for promoting strengths and competencies in mentally ill patients (see e.g., Fava, 1999). It is time, in short, to retire the slogan of mental health and to invigorate the study and promotion of
355   mental health.

TABLE 3   The Prevalence of Mental Health and Illness by Select Sociodemographic Characteristics (Sample Weighted).

	Mental Illness and Mental Health Status					
Sociodemographics	Languishing and Depression N %	Pure Depression N %	Pure Languishing N %	Moderately Mentally Healthy N %	Flourishing N %	χ^2
Gender						
Males	40	93	158	763	264	40.4***
	3.0	7.1	12.0	57.9	20.0	df = 4
Females	104	193	210	952	256	
	6.1	11.3	12.2	55.5	14.9	
Age						
25 to 34	44	93	85	44	115	72.2***
	5.6	11.9	10.8	57.0	14.7	df = 16
35 to 44	53	92	129	437	123	
	6.4	11.0	15.5	52.4	14.7	
45 to 54	26	52	66	307	123	
	4.5	9.1	11.5	53.5	21.4	
55 to 64	11	29	49	273	95	
	2.4	6.3	10.7	59.7	20.8	
65 to 74	8	19	33	237	58	
	2.3	5.4	9.3	66.8	16.3	
Education						
0 to 11 years	38	36	53	227	45	122.4***
	9.5	9.0	13.3	56.9	11.3	df = 16
12 years or GED	51	100	178	659	173	
	4.4	8.6	15.3	56.8	14.9	
13 to 15 years	39	82	989	440	114	
	5.0	10.6	12.7	56.9		
16 years or more	15	67	37	390	188	
	2.2	9.6	5.3	56.0		
Marital Status						
Married	74	167	234	1,187	404	84.1***
	3.6	8.1	11.3	57.5	19.6	df = 16
Separated	5	15	17	36	10	
	6.0	18.1	20.5	43.4	12.0	
Divorced	38	53	59	204	41	
	9.6	13.4	14.9	51.6	10.4	
Widowed	5	14	12	88	21	
	3.6	10.0	8.6	62.9	15.0	
Never Married	21	37	46	201	45	
	6.0	10.6	13.1	57.4	12.9	

Note: *p < .05 **p < .01 ***p < .001 (two-tailed)

FOR DISCUSSION

1. Keyes reports that about 1% of the population is flourishing and severely depressed (or, to put it another way, about 5% of those who are flourishing are severely depressed). What can we make of this?

2. Keyes reports that people who are more mentally healthy miss fewer days of work, cut back on work on fewer days, and have fewer limitations in their daily lives. What are the possible reasons for these relationships?

3. As Keyes points out, the data from this study indicate that languishing may be as debilitating as major depression (although the combination of the two is considerably more debilitating than either alone). Because about 12% of the population is languishing but not depressed (and presumably not in treatment) how might we, as a society, reach out to languishers?

4. How, as a society, could we help people to flourish?

5. The Midlife in the U.S. (MIDUS; Brim, Ryff, & Kessler, 2004) study has information about a wide range of demographic characteristics, attitudes, feelings, mental health, and experience. If you had access to the data, what additional questions would you like to ask?

References

Abel, T., Martin, K. C., Bartsch, D., & Kandel, E. R. (1998). Memory suppressor genes: inhibitory constraints on the storage of long-term memory. *Science, 279,* 338–341.

Aceves-Piña, E. O., Booker, R., Duerr, J. S., Livingstone, M. S., Quinn, W. G., Smith, R. F., et al. (1983). Learning and memory in *Drosophila,* studied with mutants. *Cold Spring Harbor Symposia on Quantitative Biology, 48,* 831–840.

Adler, A. (1908). Der Aggressionstrieb im Leben und in der Neurose. [The aggressive instinct in life and in neurosis.] *Fortschritte der Medizin, 26,* 577–584.

Agin, G. J. (1972). *Representation and description of curved objects.* Stanford Artificial Intelligence Project Memo AIM-173, Stanford University, Stanford, CA.

Alberini, C. M., Ghirardi, M., Mertz, R., & Kandel, E. R. (1994). C/EBP is an immediate-early gene required for the consolidation of long-term facilitation in *Aplysia. Cell, 76,*1099–1114.

Alexander, F. G., & Selesnick, S. T. (1966). *The history of psychiatry: An evaluation of psychiatric thought and practice from prehistoric times to the present.* New York: Harper & Row.

Alhacen (2001). *Alhacen's theory of visual perception: A critical edition, with English translation and commentary, of the first three books of Alhacen's* De Aspectibus, *the medieval Latin version of Ibn al-Haytham's* Kitâb al-Manâzir (A. M. Smith, Trans., Ed.). Philadelphia: American Philosophical Society. (Original work published in 11th century.)

Alkon, O. L. (1974). Associative training in *Hermissenda. Journal of General Physiology, 64,* 70–84.

Allport, D. A. (1980). Developing the concept of working memory. In G. Claxton (Ed.), *Cognitive Psychology: New Directions* (pp. 112–153). Boston: Routledge & Kegan Paul.

Allport, G. W. (1937). *Personality: A psychological interpretation.* New York: Henry Holt.

Allport, G. W. (1954). *The nature of prejudice.* Cambridge, MA: Addison-Wesley.

Allport, G. W. (1955). *Becoming: Basic considerations for a psychology of personality.* New Haven, CT: Yale University Press.

American Psychiatric Association. (1952). *Diagnostic and statistical manual of mental disorders.* Washington, DC: Author.

American Psychiatric Association. (1973). *Diagnostic and statistical manual of mental disorders* (2nd ed.). Washington, DC: Author.

American Psychiatric Association. (1980). *Diagnostic and statistical manual of mental disorders* (3rd ed.). Washington, DC: Author.

American Psychiatric Association. (1987). *Diagnostic and statistical manual of mental disorders* (3rd ed., rev.). Washington, DC: Author.

American Psychiatric Association. (2000). *Diagnostic and statistical manual of mental disorders* (4th ed., text rev.). Washington, DC: Author.

Anderson, J. R. (1980). *Cognitive psychology and its implications.* San Francisco: Freeman.

Andrews, F. M., & Withey, S. B. (1976). *Social indicators of well-being: Americans' perceptions of life quality.* New York: Plenum Press.

Angst, J. (1988). Clinical course of affective disorders. In T. Helgason & R. J. Daly (Eds.), *Depressive illness: Prediction of course and outcome* (pp. 1–47). Berlin, Germany: Springer-Verlag.

Aristotle (1907). *De anima* [On the soul] (R. D. Hicks, Trans.). Cambridge, England: Cambridge University Press. (Original work written in 4th century BCE.)

Aristotle (1984). *Sense and sensibilia* [De Sensu] (J. I. Beare, Trans.). In J. Barnes (Ed.), *The complete works of Aristotle: The revised Oxford translation* (pp. 693–713). Princeton, NJ: Princeton University Press.

Ausubel, D. P. (1961). Mental illness is a disease. *American Psychologist, 16,* 69–74.

Baars, B. J. (1988). *A cognitive theory of consciousness.* New York: Cambridge University Press.

Baars, B. J., Banks, W. P., & Newman, J. B. (Eds.). (2003). *Essential sources in the scientific study of consciousness.* Cambridge, MA: MIT Press.

Bacskai, B. J., Hochner, B., Mahoaut-Smith, M., Adams, S. R., Kaang, B-K., Kandel, E. R., et al. (1993). Spatially resolved dynamics of cAMP and protein kinase A subunits in *Aplysia* sensory neurons. *Science, 260,* 222–226.

Bailey, C. H., & Chen, M. (1983). Morphological basis of long-term habituation and sensitization in *Aplysia. Science, 220,* 91–93.

Bailey, C. H., & Chen, M. (1988). Long-term memory in *Aplysia* modulates the total number of varicosities of single identified sensory neurons. *Proceedings of the National Academy of Sciences USA, 85,* 2372–2377.

Bailey, C. H., Chen, M., Keller, F., & Kandel, E. R. (1992). Serotonin-mediated endocytosis of apCAM: An early step of learning-related synaptic growth in *Aplysia. Science, 256,* 645–649.

Bailey, M. B., & Bailey, R. E. (1993). "Misbehavior": A case history. *American Psychologist, 48,* 1157–1158.

Bailey, R. E. (2003). A gentle woman for all seasons. *Division 25 Recorder, 36,* 3–5. Retrieved June 21, 2005, from www.behavior.org/animals/animals_bailey

Baldwin, J. M. (1894). The origin of right-handedness. *Popular Science Monthly, 44,* 606–615.

Baldwin, J. M. (1903). *The story of the mind.* New York: D. Appleton.

Bales, R. F. (1950). *Interaction process analysis: A method for the study of small groups.* Cambridge, MA: Addison-Wesley.

Bao, J.-X., Kandel, E. R., & Hawkins, R. D. (1997). Involvement of pre- and postsynaptic mechanisms in posttetanic potentiation in *Aplysia* synapses. *Science, 275,* 969–973.

Bao, J.-X., Kandel, E. R., & Hawkins, R. D. (1998). Involvement of pre- and postsynaptic mechanisms in pairing-specific facilitation by serotonin at *Aplysia* sensory-motor neuron synapses in isolated cell culture. *Journal of Neuroscience, 18,* 458–466.

Barker, R., Dembo, T., & Lewin, K. (1976). *Frustration and regression: An experiment with young children.* New York: Arno Press. (Original work published in 1941.)

Bartley, S. H. (1941). *Vision, a study of its basis.* New York: Van Nostrand.

Bartsch, D., Ghirardi, M., Skehel, P. A., Karl, K. A., Herder, S. P., Chen, M., et al. (1995). *Aplysia* CREB2 represses long-term facilitation: Relief of repression converts transient facilitation into long-term functional and structural change. *Cell, 83,* 979–992.

Bayer, R. (1981). *Homosexuality and American psychiatry.* New York: Basic Books.

Beach, F. A. (1950). The snark was a boojum. *American Psychologist, 5,* 115–124.

Beare, J. I. (1906). *Greek theories of elementary cognition: From Alcmaeon to Aristotle.* Oxford: Clarendon.

Bekhterev, V. M. (1932). General principles of human reflexology: An introduction to the objective study of personality. (E. Murphy & W. Murphy, Trans.). New York: International. (Original work published in 1928.)

Beck, A. T. (1967). *Depression: Clinical, experimental, and theoretical aspects.* New York: Harper & Row.

Beck, A. T. (1979). *Cognitive therapy of depression.* New York: Guilford Press.

Beers, C. W. (1908). *A mind that found itself: An autobiography.* New York: Longmans, Green.

Benedict, R. (1934a). Anthropology and the abnormal. *Journal of General Psychology, 10,* 59–82.

Benedict, R. (1934b). *Patterns of culture.* Boston: Houghton Mifflin.

Benton, A. L. (1968). Differential behavioral effects in frontal lobe disease. *Neuropsychologia, 6*(1), 53–60.

Benzer, S. (1967). Behavioral mutants of *Drosophila* isolated by counter-current distribution. *Proceedings of the National Academy of Sciences USA, 58,* 1112–1119.

Berkeley, G. (1948). An essay towards a new theory of vision. In A. A. Luce & T. E. Jessop (Eds.), *The works of George Berkeley, Bishop of Cloyne* (Vol. 1, pp. 141–239). London: Nelson. (Original work published in 1709.)

Berkeley, G. (1949a). A treatise concerning the principles of human knowledge. In A. A. Luce & T. E. Jessop (Eds.), *The works of George Berkeley, Bishop of Cloyne* (Vol. 2, pp. 1–113). London: Nelson. (Original work published in 1710.)

Berkeley, G. (1949b). Three dialogues between Hylas and Philonous. In A. A. Luce & T. E. Jessop (Eds.), *The works of George Berkeley, Bishop of Cloyne* (Vol. 2, pp. 163–263). London: Nelson. (Original work published in 1713.)

Berkeley, G. (1950). Alciphron or the minute philosopher. In A. A. Luce & T. E. Jessop (Eds.), *The works of George Berkeley, Bishop of Cloyne* (Vol. 3, pp. 25–337). London: Nelson. (Original work published in 1732.)

Berkeley, G. (1963). *Works on vision.* (C. M. Turbayne, Ed.). Indianapolis, IN: Bobbs-Merrill.

Berscheid, E. (2003). Lessons in "greatness" from Kurt Lewin's life and works. In R. J. Sternberg (Ed.), *The anatomy of impact: What makes the great works of psychology great* (pp. 109–123). Washington, DC: American Psychological Association.

Bérubé, A. (1990). *Coming out under fire: The history of gay men and women in World War Two.* New York: Free Press.

Binford, T. O. (1971, December). Visual perception by computer. Paper presented at the I.E.E.E. Conference on Systems and Control, Miami, FL.

Bischof, L. J. (1970). *Interpreting personality theories* (2nd ed.). New York: Harper & Row.

Bisiach, E., & Luzzatti, C. (1978). Unilateral neglect of representational space. *Cortex, 14,* 129–133.

Bjork, D. W. (1993). *B. F. Skinner: A life.* New York: Basic Books.

Blanton, M. G. (1917). The behavior of the human infant during the first thirty days of life. *Psychological Review, 24,* 456–483.

Bleuler, E. (1970). *Autistic undisciplined thinking in medicine and how to overcome it* (E. Harms, Trans.). Darien, CT: Hafner. (Original work published in 1919.)

Block, N. (1995). On a confusion about a function of consciousness. *Behavioral and Brain Sciences, 18,* 227–287.

Blodgett, H. C. (1929). The effect of the introduction of reward upon the maze performance of rats. *University of California Publications in Psychology, 4,* 113–134.

Blum, H. (1973). Biological shape and visual science. Part 1. *Journal of Theoretical Biology, 38,* 205–287.

Boas, F. (1919). *Mind of primitive man.* New York: Macmillan.

Boles, D. B., & Eveland, D. C. (1983). Visual and phonetic codes and the process of generation in letter matching. *Journal of Experimental Psychology, 9,* 657–674.

Boring, E. G. (1933). *The physical dimensions of consciousness.* New York: Century.

Boring, E. G. (1935). The relation of the attributes of sensation to the dimensions of the stimulus. *Philosophy of Science, 2,* 236–245.

Boring, E. G. (1950). *A history of experimental psychology* (2nd ed.). New York: Appleton-Century-Crofts.

Boxer, A. M., & Carrier, J. M. (1998). Evelyn Hooker: A life remembered. *Journal of Homosexuality, 36,* 1–17.

Bradburn, N. M. (1969). *The structure of psychological well-being.* Chicago: Aldine.

Braitenberg, V. (1984). *Vehicles: Experiments in synthetic psychology.* Cambridge, MA: MIT Press.

Brazier, M. A. B. (1961). *A history of the electrical activity of the brain: The first half-century.* New York: Macmillan.

Brazier, M. A. B. (1988). *A history of neurophysiology in the 19th century.* New York: Raven Press.

Breland, K. (1961). Letter from Breland to B. F. Skinner. Retrieved June 8, 2005, from www.mnsu.edu/psych/KBreland_to_Skinner/kbreland_letters

Breland, K., & Breland, M. (1951). A field of applied animal psychology. *American Psychologist, 6,* 202–204.

Breland, K., & Breland, M. (1961). The misbehavior of organisms. *American Psychologist, 16,* 681–684.

Breland, K., & Breland, M. (1966). *Animal behavior.* New York: Macmillan.

Breuer, J., & Freud, S. (1973). Studies on hysteria. In J. Strachey (Ed. & Trans.), *The standard edition of the complete psychological works of Sigmund Freud* (Vol. 2). London: Hogarth. (Original work published in 1895.)

Bridges, J. W. (1930). *Psychology—Normal and abnormal.* New York: Appleton, Century.

Brim, O. G., Ryff, C. D., & Kessler, R. C. (Eds.) (2004). *How healthy are we? A national study of well-being at midlife.* Chicago: University of Chicago Press.

Broadhead, W. E., Blazer, D. G., George, L. K., & Tee, C. (1990). Depression, disability days, and days lost from work in a prospective epidemiologic survey. *Journal of the American Medical Association, 264,* 2524–2528.

Broca, P. P. (1960). Remarks on the seat of the faculty of articulate language, followed by an observation of aphemia. In G. von Bonin (Ed. & Trans.), *Some papers on the cerebral cortex* (pp. 49–72). Springfield, IL: Charles C Thomas. (Original work published in 1861.)

Bruce, M. L., Seeman, T. E., Merrill, S. S., & Blazer D. G. (1994). The impact of depressive symptomatology on physical disability: MacArthur studies of successful aging. *American Journal of Public Health, 84,* 1796–1799.

Brunelli, M., Castellucci, V. F., & Kandel, E. R. (1976). Synaptic facilitation and behavioral sensitization in *Aplysia:* Possible role of serotonin and cAMP. *Science, 194,* 1178–1181.

Bryant, F. B., & Veroff, J. (1982). The structure of psychological well-being: A sociohistorical analysis. *Journal of Personality and Social Psychology, 43,* 653–673.

Burton, R. (2001). The anatomy of melancholy (H. Jackson, Ed.). New York: New York Review of Books. (Original work published in 1621.)

Byers, D., Davis, R. L., & Kiger, J. A. (1981). Defect in cyclic AMP phosphodiesterase due to the dunce mutation of learning in *Drosophila melanogaster. Nature, 289,* 79–81.

Byrne, J. H., & Kandel, E. R. (1995). Presynaptic facilitation revisited: State and time dependence. *Journal of Neuroscience, 16,* 425–435.

Campbell, C. M. (1926). *Delusion and belief.* Cambridge, MA: Harvard University Press.

Capshew, J. H. (1997). Engineering behavior: Project Pigeon, World War II, and the conditioning of B. F. Skinner. In L. T. Benjamin, Jr. (Ed.), *A history of psychology: Original sources and contemporary research* (2nd ed.). New York: McGraw-Hill. (Original work published in 1993.)

Carew, T. J., Castellucci, V. F., & Kandel, E. R. (1979). Sensitization in *Aplysia:* Restoration of transmission in synapses inactivated by long-term habituation. *Science, 205,* 417–419.

Carew, T. J., Pinsker, H. M., and Kandel, E. R. (1972). Long-term habituation of a defensive withdrawal reflex in *Aplysia. Science, 175,* 451–454.

Carew, T. J., & Sahley, C. J. (1986). Invertebrate learning and memory: From behavior to molecules. *Annual Review of Neuroscience, 9,* 435–487.

Carlson, E. T. (1972). Preface. In B. Rush, *Two essays on the mind* (pp. v–xii). New York: Brunner/Mazel.

Carr, J. (1805). *A northern summer; or, Travels round the Baltic.* Philadelphia: Samuel F. Bradford.

Carr, T. H., & Pollatsek, A. (1985) *Recognizing printed words: A look at current models.* In D. Besner, T. G. Walker, & G. E. MacKinnon (Eds.) *Reading research: Advances in theory and practice* (Vol. 5, pp. 1–82). San Diego, CA: Academic Press.

Castellucci, V. F., Carew, T. J., & Kandel, E. R. (1978). Cellular analysis of long-term habituation of the gill-withdrawal reflex of *Aplysia californica. Science, 202,* 1306–1308.

Castellucci, V. F., & Kandel, E. R. (1974). A quantal analysis of the synaptic depression underlying habituation of the gill-withdrawal reflex in *Aplysia. Proceedings of the National Academy of Sciences USA, 71,* 5004–5008.

Castellucci, V. F., & Kandel, E. R. (1976). Presynaptic facilitation as a mechanism for behavioral sensitization in *Aplysia. Science, 194,* 1176–1178.

Castellucci, V. F., Kandel, E. R., Schwartz, J. H., Wilson, F. D., Nairn, A. C., & Greengard, P. (1980). Intracellular injection of the catalytic subunit of cyclic AMP-dependent protein kinase simulates facilitation of transmitter release underlying behavioral sensitization in *Aplysia. Proceedings of the National Academy of Sciences USA, 77,* 7492–7496.

Castellucci, V. F., Nairn, A., Greengard, P., Schwartz, J. H., & Kandel, E. R. (1982). Inhibitor of adenosine 3':5'-monophosphate-dependent protein kinase blocks presynaptic facilitation in *Aplysia. Journal of Neuroscience, 2,* 1673–1681.

Castellucci, V. F., Pinsker, H., Kupfermann, I., & Kandel, E. R. (1970). Neuronal mechanisms of habituation and dishabituation of the gill-withdrawal reflex in *Aplysia. Science, 167,* 1745–1748.

Cattell, J. M. (1886a). The time taken up by cerebral operations, Parts 1 & 2. *Mind, 11,* 220–242.

Cattell, J. M. (1886b). The time taken up by cerebral operations, Part 3. *Mind, 11,* 377–392.

Cattell, J. M. (1887). The time taken up by cerebral operations, Part 4. *Mind, 11,* 524–538.

Changeaux, J.-P. (1985). *Neuronal man: The biology of mind.* New York: Pantheon Books.

Chess, S., & Thomas, A. (1996). *Temperament: Theory and practice.* New York: Brunner/Mazel.

Chomsky, N. (1959). Review of the book *Verbal behavior,* by B. F. Skinner. *Language, 35,* 26–58.

Chomsky, N. (1966). *Cartesian linguistics.* New York: Harper & Row.

Chomsky, N. (1969). Some empirical assumptions in modern philosophy of language. In S. Morgenbesser, P. Suppes, and M. White (Eds.), *Essays in honor of Ernest Nagel* (pp. 260–285). New York: St. Martin's.

Chomsky, N. (1970). Phonology and reading. In H. Levin and J. P. Williams (Eds.), *Basic studies in reading* (pp. 3–18). New York: Basic Books.

Chomsky, N. (1971, December 30). The case against B. F. Skinner [Review of the book *Beyond freedom and dignity*]. *New York Review of Books, 17,* 18–24.

Chomsky, N. (1972). *Language and mind* (enl. ed.). New York: Harcourt Brace Jovanovich.

Chomsky, N. (1996). Silent children, new language: Noam Chomsky interviewed by anonymous interviewer (BBC, Fall 1996). Retrieved June 20, 2007, from http://www.chomsky.info/interviews/1996----.htm

Church, A. (1936). An unsolvable problem of elementary number theory. *American Journal of Mathematics, 58,* 345–363.

Churchland, P. S. (1986). *Neurophilosophy: Toward a unified science of the mind/brain.* Cambridge, MA: MIT Press.

Clarke, E., & Dewhurst, K. (1972). *An illustrated history of brain function.* Berkeley: University of California Press.

Classen, A. (1862). *Das Schlussverfahren des Sehaktes.* Rostock: E. Kuhn.

Cleary, L. J., Byrne, J., & Frost, W. (1995). Role of interneurons in defensive withdrawal reflexes in *Aplysia. Learning and Memory, 2,* 133–151.

Clifford, H. (1897). *In court and kampong.* London: G. Richards.

Clifford, H. (1898). *Studies in brown humanity.* London: G. Richards.

Cloninger, C. R. (1989). Epidemiology and genetics of alcoholism. New York: Oxford University Press.

Cohen, N. J., & Squire, L. R. (1980). Preserved learning and retention of pattern analyzing skill in amnesia: Dissociation of knowing how and knowing that. *Science, 210,* 207–209.

Colapinto, J. (2007, April 16). The interpreter. *New Yorker,* 118–137.

Collins, A. M., & Quillian, M. R. (1969). Retrieval time from semantic memory. *Journal of Verbal Learning and Verbal Behavior, 8,* 240–247.

Colman, A. M. (2003). *Oxford dictionary of psychology.* Oxford: Oxford University Press.

Coltheart, M. (1985). Cognitive neuropsychology and the study of reading. In M. I. Posner & O. S. M. Marin (Eds.), *Attention and performance XI* (pp. 3–37). Hillsdale, NJ: Lawrence Erlbaum.

Compton, W. M., & Guze, S. B. (1995). The neo-Kraepelinian revolution in psychiatric diagnosis. *European Archives of Psychiatry and Clinical Neuroscience, 245,* 196–201.

Condillac, E. B. de, (1930). *Condillac's treatise on the sensations* (G. Carr, Trans.). Los Angeles: School of Philosophy, University of Southern California. [Original work published in 1754 as *Traité des sensations.*]

Coon, D. J. (2000). Salvaging the self in a world without soul: William James's *The principles of psychology. History of Psychology, 3,* 83–103.

Cooper, L. A. (1976). Demonstration of a mental analog of an external rotation. *Perception and Psychophysics, 19,* 296–302.

Cooper, R. (2004). What is wrong with the DSM? *History of Psychiatry, 15,* 5–25.

Corkin, S. (1965). Tactually guided maze learning in man: Effects of unilateral cortical excisions and bilateral hippocampal lesions. *Neuropsychologia, 3,* 339–351.

Cornelius, C. S. (1861). *Die Theorie des Sehens und räumlichen Vorstellens: von physikalischen, physiologischen und psychologischen Standpunkte.* [The theory of vision and spatial concept, from a physical, physiological, and psychological point of view.] Halle, Germany: H. W. Schmidt.

Cornelius, C. S. (1864). *Zur Theorie des Sehens, mit Rücksicht auf die neuesten Arbeiten in diesem Gebiete.* [On the theory of vision, including the newest studies in this field.] Halle, Germany: H. W. Schmidt.

Cramer, C. (2000). A pioneer in humane methods for training animals. *Main Connection, 8,* 8.

Cranefield, P. F. (1970). On the origin of the phrase *Nihil est in intellectu quod non prius fuerit in sensu. Journal of the History of Medicine, 25,* 77–80.

Crick, F. (1994). *The astonishing hypothesis.* New York: Scribner's.

Cross-National Collaborative Group (1992). The changing rate of major depression: Cross-national comparisons. *Journal of the American Medical Association, 268,* 3098–3105.

Csikszentmihalyi, M. (1990). *Flow: The psychology of optimal experience.* New York: Harper & Row.

Csikszentmihalyi, M. (1993). *The evolving self: A psychology for the third millennium.* New York: HarperCollins.

Csikszentmihalyi, M. (1997). *Finding flow: The psychology of engagement with everyday life.* New York: Basic Books.

Cusac, A.-M. (1999, September). Harry Hay interview. [Electronic version]. *The Progressive*. Retrieved October 14, 2005, from progressive.org/mag_cusachay

Cushman, P. (1990). Why the self is empty: Toward a historically situated psychology. *American Psychologist, 45,* 599–611.

Czaplicka, M. A. (1914). *Aboriginal Siberia: A study in social anthropology.* Oxford: Clarendon Press.

Damasio, A. R. (1994). *Descartes' error: Emotion, reason, and the human brain.* New York: Putnam.

Damasio A. R., & Damasio, H. (1983). The anatomic basis of pure alexia. *Neurology, 33,* 1573–1583.

Damasio, A. R., & Van Hoesen, G. W. (1983). Emotional disturbances associated with focal lesions of the limbic frontal lobe. In K. Heilman and P. Satz (Eds.), *The neuropsychology of human emotion: Recent advances* (pp. 85–110). New York: Guilford Press.

Dammann, E. J. (1997). "The myth of mental illness": Continuing controversies and their implications for mental health professionals. *Clinical Psychology Review, 17,* 733–776.

Darwin, C. (1859). *On the origin of species by means of natural selection.* London: John Murray.

Davis, G. W., Schuster, C. M., & Goodman, C. S. (1996). Genetic dissection of structural and functional components of synaptic plasticity: Part 3. CREB is necessary for presynaptic functional plasticity. *Neuron, 17,* 669–679.

Davis, H. P., & Squire, L. R. (1984). Protein synthesis and memory: A review. *Psychological Bulletin, 96,* 518–559.

Davis, R. L. (1996). Physiology and biochemistry of *Drosophila* learning mutants. *Physiological Reviews, 76,* 299–317.

Davis, W. J., & Gillette, R. (1978). Neural correlate of behavioral plasticity in command neurons of *Pleurobranchaea. Science, 799,* 801–804.

Degenaar, M. J. L. (1996). *Molyneux's problem: Three centuries of discussion on the perception of forms.* Dordrecht, Netherlands: Kluwer Academic.

D'Emilio, J. (1983). *Sexual politics, sexual communities: The making of a homosexual minority in the United States, 1940–1970.* Chicago: University of Chicago Press.

D'Emilio, J. (2001, July 17). 50 years of gay and lesbian activism. *The Progressive.* Retrieved October 14, 2005, from progressive.org/media_1811.

D'Emilio, J. (2002). *The world turned: Essays on gay history, politics, and culture.* Durham, NC: Duke University Press.

Dennett, D. C. (1978). Skinner skinned. In D. C. Dennett, *Brainstorms* (pp. 53–70). Cambridge, MA: MIT Press.

Dennett, D. C. (1984). *Elbow room: The varieties of free will worth wanting.* Cambridge, MA: MIT Press.

Dennett, D. C. (1991). *Consciousness explained.* Boston: Little, Brown.

Dennett, D. C. (2001). Are we explaining consciousness yet? *Cognition, 79,* 221–237.

DeRenzi, E. (1982). *Disorders of space exploration and cognition.* New York: Wiley.

Descartes, R. (1931). Notes directed against a certain programme. In E. S. Haldane & G. R. T. Ross (Trans.), *The philosophical works of Descartes* (Vol. 1, pp. 431–450). London: Cambridge University Press. (Original work published in 1648.)

Descartes, R. (1931). *Passions of the soul.* In E. S. Haldane & G. R. T. Ross (Trans.), *The philosophical works of Descartes* (Vol. 1, pp. 331–427). London: Cambridge University Press. (Original work published in 1649.)

Descartes, R. (1954). *Discourse on method.* In E. Anscombe & P. T. Geach (Eds. & Trans.), *Descartes: Philosophical writings.* London: Thomas Nelson. (Original work published in 1637.)

Descartes, R. (1958). Letter from Descartes to Princess Elizabeth, May 31, 1643. In N. Kemp Smith (Trans. & Ed.), *Descartes: Philosophical writings* (p. 251). New York: Random House.

Descartes, R. (1972). *Treatise of man* (T. S. Hall, Trans.). Cambridge, MA: Harvard University Press. (Original work published in 1629–1633.)

Descartes, R. (1984). *Meditations on first philosophy* (J. Cottingham, Trans.). In J. Cottingham, R. Stoothoff, & D. Murdoch (Trans.), *The philosophical writings of Descartes* (Vol. 2, pp. 3-62). Cambridge, England: Cambridge University Press. (Original work published in 1641.)

Descartes, R. (1985). *Principles of philosophy* (J. Cottingham, Trans.). In J. Cottingham, R. Stoothoff, & D. Murdoch (Trans.), *The philosophical writings of Descartes* (Vol. 1, pp. 179-291). Cambridge, England: Cambridge University Press. (Original work published in 1644.)

Descartes, R. (1991). Letter to More, February 5, 1649. In J. Cottingham, R. Stoothoff, D. Murdoch, & A. Kenny (Trans.), *The philosophical writings of Descartes* (Vol. 3, pp. 360–367). Cambridge, England: Cambridge University Press.

Descartes, R. (2001). *Discourse on method, optics, geometry, and meteorology* (P. J. Olscamp, Trans.). Indianapolis, IN:Hackett. (Original work published in 1637.)

Dewey, J. (1896). The reflex arc concept in psychology. *Psychological Review, 3,* 357–370.

Diener, E. (1984). Subjective well-being. *Psychological Bulletin, 95,* 542–575.

Diener, E., Sandvik, E., & Pavot, W. (1991). Happiness is the frequency, not the intensity, of positive versus negative affect. In F. Strack, M. Argyle, & N. Schwarz (Eds.), *Subjective well-being: An interdisciplinary perspective* (pp. 119–139). Oxford: Pergamon Press.

Diener, E., Suh, E. M., Lucas, R. E., &. Smith, H. L. (1999). Subjective well-being: Three decades of progress. *Psychological Bulletin, 125,* 276–302.

Donders, F. C. (1969). On the speed of mental processes (W. G. Koster, Trans.). *Acta Psychologica, 30,* 412–431. (Original work published in 1868–1869.)

Drachman, D. A., & Arbit, J. (1966). Memory and the hippocampal complex: Part 2. Is memory a multiple process? *Archives of Neurology, 15,* 52–61.

Dryden, J. (1998). Charles Zorumski named Guze Professor of Psychology. Retrieved March 6, 2006, from http://record.wustl.edu/archive/1998/04-16-98/articles/zorumski.html

Duncan, J. (1980). The locus of interference in the perception of simultaneous stimuli. *Psychological Review, 87,* 272–300.

Duncker, K. (1945). On problem solving. *Psychological Monographs, 58* (270).

Dunlap, D. W. (1996, November 22). Evelyn Hooker [Obituary.]. *New York Times,* p. D-19.

Ebbinghaus, H. (1964). *Memory: A contribution to experimental psychology* (H. A. Ruger & C. E. Bussenius, Trans.). New York: Dover. (Original work published in 1885.)

Ebbinghaus, H. (1973). *Psychology: An elementary text-book* (M. Meyer, Trans.). New York: Arno Press. (Original work published in 1908.)

Eccles, J. C. (1994). *How the self controls its brain.* New York: Springer-Verlag.

Edelman, G. M. (1987). *Neural Darwinism: The theory of neuronal group selection.* New York: Basic Books.

Edelman, G. M., & Mountcastle, V. B. (1978). *The mindful brain: Cortical organization and the group-selection theory of higher brain function.* Cambridge, MA: MIT Press.

Eden, M. (1967). Inadequacies of neo-Darwinian evolution as a scientific theory. In P. S. Moorhead & M. M. Kaplan (Eds.), *Mathematical challenges to the neo-Darwinian interpretation of evolution* (pp. 5–20). Philadelphia: Wistar Institute Press.

Ehrenfels, C. von (1890). Über Gestaltqualitäten. [On gestalt qualities.] *Vierteljahresschrift für wissenschaftliche Philosophie, 14,* 249–292.

Elizabeth of Bohemia (1958). Letter from Princess Elizabeth to Descartes, May 16, 1643. In N. Kemp Smith (Trans. & Ed.), *Descartes: Philosophical writings* (pp. 250–251). New York: Random House.

Ellenberger, H. F. (1970). *The discovery of the unconscious: The history and evolution of dynamic psychiatry.* New York: Basic Books.

Elliott, M. H. (1928). The effect of change of reward on the maze performance of rats. *University of California Publications in Psychology, 4,* 19–30.

Enroth-Cugell, C., & Robson, J. G. (1966). The contrast sensitivity of retinal ganglion cells of the cat. *Journal of Physiology, 187,* 517–552.

Epicurus (1940). Letter to Herodotus (C. Bailey, Trans.). In W. J. Oates (Ed.), *The Stoic and Epicurean philosophers* (pp. 3–15). New York: Random House. (Original work written in 4th–3rd century BCE.)

Evans, C. O. (1970). *The subject of consciousness.* London: Allen & Unwin.

Everett, D. L. (2005). Cultural constraints on grammar and cognition in Pirahã: Another look at the design features of human language. *Current Anthropology, 46,* 621–646.

Exner, J. E. (1974). *The Rorschach: A comprehensive system* (Vol. 1). New York: John Wiley & Sons.

Eysenck, H., & Eysenck, S. (1963). *The Eysenck personality inventory.* San Diego, CA: Education and Industrial Testing Service.

Eysenck, H. J. (1966). *The effects of psychotherapy.* New York: International Science Press.

Fancher, R. E. (1996). *Pioneers of Psychology* (3rd ed.). New York: Norton.

Fantz, R. L. (1961). The origin of form perception. *Scientific American, 204,* 66-72.

Fantz, R. L. (1963). Pattern vision in newborn infants. *Science, 140,* 296-297.

Fava, G. A. (1999). Well-being therapy: Conceptual and technical issues. *Psychotherapy and Psychosomatics, 68,* 171-179.

Fechner, G. T. (1966). *Elements of psychophysics* (Vol. 1) (H. E. Adler, Trans.; D. H. Howes & E. G. Boring, Eds.). New York: Holt, Rinehart and Winston. (Original work published in 1860.)

Feigenbaum, E. A. (1961). The simulation of verbal learning behavior. *Proceedings of the Western Joint Computer Conference, 19,* 121-132.

Feigenbaum, E. A. (2001). Herbert A. Simon, 1916-2001. *Science, 291,* 2107.

Feldman, G. (2007). Cognitive and behavioral therapies for depression: Overview, new directions, and practical recommendations for dissemination. *Psychiatric Clinics of North America, 30,* 39-50.

Feldman, J., Tonge, F. M., Jr., & Kanter, H. (1961, December 19). Empirical explorations of a hypothesis-testing model of binary choice behavior. Report No. SP-546. Santa Monica, CA: System Development Corporation.

Ferenczi, S. (1950). Introjection and transference. In S. Ferenczi, *Sex in Psychoanalysis* (E. Jones, Trans. pp. 35-57). New York: Basic Books. (Original work published in 1909.)

Ferrier, D. (1876). *The functions of the brain.* London: Smith, Elder.

Ferster, C. B. (1964). Arithmetic behavior in chimpanzees. *Scientific American, 210,* 98-106.

Finger, S. (1994). *Origins of neuroscience: A history of explorations into brain function.* New York: Oxford University Press.

Finger, S. (2000). *Minds behind the brain: A history of the pioneers and their discoveries.* New York: Oxford University Press.

Flourens, M.-J. P. (1960). Investigations of the properties and the functions of the various parts which compose the cerebral mass (G. von Bonin, Trans.), in *Some papers on the cerebral cortex* (pp. 3-21). Springfield, IL: Charles C. Thomas, 1960. (Original work published in 1824.)

Fodor, J. A. (1981, January). The mind-body problem. *Scientific American, 244,* 114-123.

Foley, J. P., Jr. (1935). The criterion of abnormality. *Journal of Abnormal and Social Psychology, 30,* 279-290.

Ford, C. S., & Beach, F. A. (1951). *Patterns of sexual behavior.* New York: Harper & Brothers.

Fortune, R. F. (1932). *Sorcerers of Dobu.* New York: Routledge.

Fox, P. T., Miezin, F. M., Allman, J. M., Van Essen, D. C., & Raichle, M. E. (1987). Retinotopic organization of human visual cortex mapped with positron-emission tomography. *Journal of Neuroscience, 7,* 913-922.

Fox, P. T., Mintun, M. A., Raichle, M. E., Miezin, F. M., Allman, J. M., & Van Essen, D. C. (1986). Mapping human visual cortex with positron emission tomography. *Nature, 323,* 806-809.

Fox, P. T., Mintun, M. A., Reiman, E. M., & Raichle, M. E. (1988). Enhanced detection of focal brain responses using intersubject averaging and change-distribution analysis of subtracted PET images. *Journal of Cerebral Blood Flow and Metabolism, 8,* 642-653.

Fredrickson, B. L., Roberts, T. A., Noll, S. M., Quinn, D. M., & Twenge, J. M. (1998). The swimsuit becomes you: Sex differences in self-objectification, restrained eating, and math performance. *Journal of Personality. & Social Psychology, 75,* 269-284.

Freedman, M. (1971). *Homosexuality and psychological functioning.* Belmont, CA: Brooks/Cole.

Freeman, K. (1957). *Ancilla to the pre-Socratic philosophers.* Cambridge, MA: Harvard University Press.

Freud, S. (1954). Project for a scientific psychology. (Trans. E. Mosbacher & J. Strachey). In M. Bonaparte, A. Freud, & E. Kris (Eds.), *The origins of psycho-analysis: Letters to Wilhelm Fliess, drafts and notes: 1887-1902* (pp. 347-445). New York: Basic Books. (Original work written in 1895.)

Freud, S. (1955). Beyond the pleasure principle. In J. Strachey (Ed. & Trans.), *The standard edition of the complete psychological works of Sigmund Freud* (Vol. 18, pp. 7-66). London: Hogarth. (Original work published in 1920.)

Freud, S. (1957). Instincts and their vicissitudes. In J. Strachey (Ed. & Trans.), *The standard edition of the complete psychological works of Sigmund Freud* (Vol. 14, pp. 111-140). London: Hogarth. (Original work published in 1915.)

Freud, S. (1958a). Formulations on the two principles of mental functioning. In J. Strachey (Ed. & Trans.), *The standard edition of the complete psychological works of Sigmund Freud* (Vol. 12, pp. 213–226). London: Hogarth. (Original work published in 1911.)

Freud, S. (1958b). The interpretation of dreams. In J. Strachey (Ed. & Trans.), *The standard edition of the complete psychological works of Sigmund Freud* (corr. ed., Vols. 4 & 5). London: Hogarth. (Original work published in 1900.)

Freud, S. (1961). The economic problem of masochism. In J. Strachey (Ed. & Trans.), *The standard edition of the complete psychological works of Sigmund Freud* (Vol. 19, pp. 157–162). London: Hogarth. (Original work published in 1924.)

Freud, S. (1963a). Instincts and their vicissitudes (Trans. Cecil M. Baines). In P. Rieff (Ed.), *Freud: General psychological theory* (pp. 83–103). New York: Macmillan. (Original work published in 1915.)

Freud, S. (1963b). Introductory lectures on psychoanalysis. In J. Strachey (Ed. & Trans.), *The standard edition of the complete psychological works of Sigmund Freud* (Vols. 15 & 16). London: Hogarth. (Original work published in 1915–1916.)

Freud, S. (1963c). Repression (Trans. Cecil M. Baines). In R. Rieff (Ed.), *Freud: General psychological theory.* New York: Macmillan. (Original work published in 1915.)

Freud, S. (1964). An outline of psychoanalysis. In J. Strachey (Ed. & Trans.), *The standard edition of the complete psychological works of Sigmund Freud* (Vol. 23, pp. 144–208). London: Hogarth. (Original work published in 1940.)

Freud, S. (1965). *The psychopathology of everyday life* (A. Tyson, Trans.), New York: Norton. (Original work published in 1901.)

Freuder, E. C. (1975). A computer vision system for visual recognition using active knowledge. (Technical Report No. 345). Cambridge, MA: MIT Artificial Intelligence Laboratory.

Friedrich, F. J., Walker, J. A., & Posner, M. I. (1985). Effects of parietal lesions on visual matching: Implications for reading errors. *Cognitive Neuropsychology, 2*(3), 253–264.

Frisch, M. B., Cornell, J., Villanueva, M., & Retzlaff, P. J. (1992). Clinical validation of the Quality of Life Inventory: A measure of life satisfaction for use in treatment planning and outcome assessment. *Psychological Assessment, 4,* 92–101.

Fritsch, G. T. & Hitzig, E. (1960). On the electrical excitability of the cerebrum (G. von Bonin, Ed. & Trans.), in *Some papers on the cerebral cortex* (pp. 73–96). Springfield, IL: Charles C Thomas, 1960. (Original work published in 1870.)

Frost, W. N., Castellucci, V. F., Hawkins, R. D., & Kandel, E. R. (1985). Monosynaptic connections made by the sensory neurons of the gill- and siphon-withdrawal reflex in *Aplysia* participate in the storage of long-term memory for sensitization. *Proceedings of the National Academy of Sciences USA, 82,* 8266–8269.

Frost, W. N., Clark, G. A., & Kandel, E. R. (1988). Parallel processing of short-term memory for sensitization in *Aplysia. Journal of Neurobiology, 19,* 297–334.

Galilei, Galileo. (1957). *The assayer* (S. Drake, Trans.). New York: Anchor. (Original work published in 1623.

Galton, F. (1869). *Hereditary genius: An inquiry into its laws and consequences.* London: Macmillan.

Garcia, J., & Koelling, R. A. (1966). Relation of cue to consequence in avoidance learning. *Psychonomic Science, 4,* 123–124.

Gavaudan, P. (1967). L'évolution considérée par un botaniste-cytologiste [Evolution as seen by a botanist-cytologist] (Aletheia Services, Trans.). In P. S. Moorhead & M. M. Kaplan (Eds.), *Mathematical challenges to the neo-Darwinian interpretation of evolution.* Philadelphia: Wistar Institute Press.

Gelperin, A. (1975). Rapid food-aversion learning by a terrestrial mollusk. *Science, 189,* 567–570.

Gentry, E. (1930). A substitution for trial and error in the white rat. Unpublished master's thesis, University of Colorado, Boulder.

Gentry, E. (1943). Disorganization in the white rat. *Journal of Comparative Psychology, 37,* 3–16.

Gentry, E., & Dunlap, K. (1942). An attempt to produce neurotic behavior in rats. *Journal of Comparative Psychology, 33,* 107–112.

Geschwind, N. (1965). Disconnexion syndromes in animals and man: Part 1. *Brain, 88,* 237–294.

Gibson, E. J. (1969). *Principles of perceptual learning and development*. New York: Appleton-Century-Crofts.

Gibson, E. J., & Pick, A. (2000). *An ecological approach to perceptual learning and development*. New York: Oxford University Press.

Gibson, E. J., & Walk, R. D. (1960). The visual cliff. *Scientific American, 202*, 64–71.

Gibson, J. J. (1937). Adaptation with negative after-effect. *Psychological Review, 44*, 222–244.

Gibson, J. J. (1948). Studying perceptual phenomena. In T. Andrews (Ed.), *Methods of Psychology* (pp. 158–188). New York: Wiley.

Gibson, J. J. (1950). *The perception of the visual world*. Boston: Houghton Mifflin.

Gibson, J. J. (1979). *The ecological approach to visual perception*. Boston: Houghton Mifflin.

Gillaspy, J. A., & Bihm, E. M. (2002). Marian Breland Bailey (1920–2001). *American Psychologist, 57*, 292–293.

Gladis, M. M., Gosch, E. A., Dishuk, N. M., & Crits-Christoph, P. (1999). Quality of life: Expanding the scope of clinical significance. *Journal of Consulting and Clinical Psychology, 67*, 320–331.

Glanzman, D. L., Mackey, S. L., Hawkins, R. D., Dyke, A. M., Lloyd, P. E., & Kandel, E. R. (1989). Depletion of serotonin in the nervous system of *Aplysia* reduces the behavioral enhancement of gill withdrawal as well as the heterosynaptic facilitation produced by tail shock. *Journal of Neuroscience, 9*, 4200–4213.

Gleitman, H. (1991). Edward Chace Tolman: A life of scientific and social purpose. In G. A. Kimble, M. Wertheimer, & C. White (Eds.), *Portraits of pioneers in psychology* (pp. 227–242). Hillsdale, NJ: Lawrence Erlbaum.

Glickman, S. (1996). Donald Olding Hebb: Returning the nervous system to psychology. In G. Kimble, C. Boneau, & M. Wertheimer (Eds.), *Portraits of pioneers in psychology* (Vol. 2, pp. 227–244). Mahwah, NJ: Lawrence Erlbaum.

Glines, C. V. (2005, May). Bat and bird bombers. *Aviation History, 15*(5), 38–44.

Goelet, P., Castellucci, V. F., Schacher, S., & Kandel, E. R. (1986). The long and short of long-term memory—A molecular framework. *Nature, 322*, 419–422.

Goffman, E. (1961). *Asylums: Essays on the social situation of mental patients and other inmates*. Garden City, NY: Anchor.

Gold, M. (1999). *The complete social scientist*. Washington, DC: APA.

Goldman-Rakic, P. S. (1988). Topography of cognition: Parallel distributed networks in primate association cortex. *Annual Review of Neuroscience, 11*, 137–156.

Goltz, F. (1892). Der Hund ohne Grosshirn: Siebente Abhandlung über die Verrichtungen des Grosshirns. [The decorticate dog: Seventh treatise on the functions of the cerebrum.] *Archiv für die gesammte Physiologie des Menschen und der Thiere, 51*, 570–614.

Gonzales, L., Lewinsohn, P. M., & Clarke, G. (1985). Longitudinal follow-up of unipolar depressives: An investigation of predictors of relapse. *Journal of Consulting and Clinical Psychology, 53*, 461–469.

Gould, S. J. (1996). *The mismeasure of man* (2nd ed.). New York: W.W. Norton.

Gray, J. (2004). *Consciousness: Creeping up on the hard problem*. New York: Oxford University Press.

Green, C. (Ed.) (n.d.). Thomas Szasz: The myth of mental illness. Retrieved June 3, 2003, from http://psychclassics.yorku.ca/Szasz/myth.htm

Greenberg, P. E., Stiglin, L. E., Finkelstein, S. N., & Berndt, E. R. (1993). The economic burden of depression in 1990. *Journal of Clinical Psychiatry, 54*, 405–418.

Gregory, R. L., & Wallace, J. G. (1963). *Recovery from early blindness: A case study*. Experimental Psychology Society Monograph No. 2. Cambridge, England: Heffers.

Grimson, W. E. L., & Marr, D. C. (1979). A computer implementation of a theory of human stereo vision. In L. S. Baumann (Ed.), *Image understanding: Proceedings of a workshop held at Palo Alto, California, April 24–25, 1979* (pp. 41–45). Arlington, VA: Science Applications.

Group for the Advancement of Psychiatry, Committee on Cooperation with Governmental (Federal) Agencies. (1955, January). Report on homosexuality with particular emphasis on this problem in governmental agencies. (Report No. 30). White Plains, NY: Author.

Grunbaum, A. (1984). *The foundations of psychoanalysis*. Berkeley, CA: University of California Press.

Guze, S. B. (1988). Psychotherapy and the etiology of psychiatric disorders. *Psychiatric Developments, 6*, 183–194.

Guze, S. B. (1989). Biological psychiatry: Is there any other kind? *Psychological Medicine, 19*, 315–323.

Guze, S. B. (1992). *Why psychiatry is a branch of medicine.* New York: Oxford University Press.

Guze, S. B., & Helzer, J. E. (1985). The medical model and psychiatric disorders. In J. O. Cavenar (Ed.), *Psychiatry* (Vol. 1, pp. 1-8). Philadelphia: J. B. Lippincott.

Guze, S. B., & Murphy, G. E. (1963). An empirical approach to psychotherapy: The agnostic position. *American Journal of Psychiatry, 120*, 53–57.

Haglin, R. P. (2005). *Taking sides: Clashing views on controversial issues in abnormal psychology.* Dubuque, IA: McGraw-Hill/Dushkin.

Halpern, D. (1997). Sex differences in intelligence. *American Psychologist, 52*, 1091–1102.

Harris, B. (1979). Whatever happened to Little Albert? *American Psychologist, 34*, 151–160.

Harris, J. (1751). *Hermes, or a philosophical inquiry concerning universal grammar.* London: J. Nourse.

Hartline, H. & Ratliff, F. (1957). Inhibitory interaction of receptor units in the eye of *Limulus. Journal of General Physiology, 40*, 357–376.

Hartree, D. R. (1949). *Calculating instruments and machines.* Urbana: University of Illinois Press.

Haugland, D. (Producer), & Schmiechen, R. (Director). (1991). *Changing our minds: The story of Dr. Evelyn Hooker* [Film/Video]. San Francisco, CA: Frameline.

Hawkins, R. D., Abrams, T. W., Carew, T. J., & Kandel, E. R. (1983). A cellular mechanism of classical conditioning in *Aplysia:* Activity-dependent amplification of presynaptic facilitation. *Science, 219*, 400–405.

Hawkins, R. D., Castellucci, V. F., & Kandel, E. R. (1981a). Interneurons involved in mediation and modulation of the gill-withdrawal reflex in *Aplysia*: Part 1. Identification and characterization. *Journal of Neurophysiology, 45*, 304–314.

Hawkins, R. D., Castellucci, V. F., & Kandel, E. R. (1981b). Interneurons involved in mediation and modulation of the gill-withdrawal reflex in *Aplysia*: Part 2. Identified neurons produce heterosynaptic facilitation contributing to behavioral sensitization. *Journal of Neurophysiology, 45*, 315–326.

Hawkins, R. D., & Kandel, E. R. (1984). Is there a cell biological alphabet for simple forms of learning? *Psychological Review, 91*, 375–391.

Headey, B. W., Kelley, J., & Wearing, A. J. (1993). Dimensions of mental health: Life satisfaction, positive affect, anxiety, and depression. *Social Indicators Research, 29*, 63–82.

Hebb, D. O. (1949). *The organization of behavior: A neuropsychological theory.* New York: Wiley.

Hebb, D. O. (1960). The American revolution. *American Psychologist, 15*, 735–745.

Hebb, D. O. (1980). Autobiography. In G. Lindzey (Ed.), *A history of psychology in autobiography* (Vol. 7, pp. 273–303). San Francisco: Freeman.

Hebb, D. O. (1980). *Essay on mind.* Hillsdale, NJ: Lawrence Erlbaum.

Hedge. A. N., Inokuchi, K., Pel, W., Casadio, A., Ghirardi, M., Chain, D. G., et al. (1997). Ubiquitin C-terminal hydrolase is an immediate-early gene essential for long-term facilitation in *Aplysia. Cell, 89*, 115–126.

Hegarty, P. (2003). *Interpreting the Rorschach test: Poststructuralist histories of psychology and the production of knowledge about sexuality.* Paper presented at the 35th Annual Meeting of the Cheiron Society, Durham, NH, June 19–22.

Heider, F. (1926). Ding und Medium [Thing and medium]. *Symposion, 1*, 109–157.

Held, R., & Hein, A. (1963). Movement-produced stimulation in the development of visually guided behavior. *Journal of Comparative and Physiological Psychology, 56*, 872–876.

Helmholtz, H. von. (1847). *Über die Erhaltung der Kraft: Eine physikalische Abhandlung, Vorgetragen in der Sitzung der physikalischen Gesellschaft zu Berlin am 23. Juli 1847.* [On the conservation of energy (or force): A physical treatise, read before the meeting of the Physical Society in Berlin on July 23, 1847.] Berlin: G. Reimer.

Helmholtz, H. von. (1850). Über die Fortpflanzungsgeschwindigkeit der Nervenreizung. [On the propagation speed of the nerve impulse.] *Archiv für Anatomie, Physiologie und wissenschaftliche Medicin,* 71–73.

Helmholtz, H. von (1875). *On the sensations of tone as a physiological basis for the theory of music* (A. J. Ellis, Trans.). London: Longmans, Green. (Original work published in 1863)

Helmholtz, H. von (1962). *Helmholtz's treatise on physiological optics.* (J. P. C. Southall, Trans). New York: Dover. (Original work published in 1867.)

Helmholtz, H. von (1971). The facts of perception. In R. Kahl (Ed.), *Selected writings of Hermann von Helmholtz* (pp. 366–408). Middletown, CT: Wesleyan University Press. (Original work published in 1878.)

Helson, H. (1947). Adaptation level as frame of reference for prediction of psychological data. *American Journal of Psychology, 60,* 1–29.

Helson, H. (1948). Adaptation level as a basis for a quantitative theory of frames of reference. *Psychological Review, 55,* 297–313.

Helson, H. (1964). *Adaptation level theory: An experimental and systematic approach to behavior.* New York: Harper & Row.

Henik, A., Friedrich, F. J., & Kellogg, W. A. (1983). The dependence of semantic relatedness effects upon prime processing. *Memory and Cognition, 11,* 366–373.

Herbart, J. F. (1816). *Lehrbuch zur Psychologie.* [Textbook in psychology.] Königsberg : A. W. Unzer.

Herbart, J. F. (1825). *Psychologie als Wissenschaft.* [Psychology as science.] Königsberg: A. W. Unzer.

Hering, E. (1861–1864). *Beiträge zur Physiologie.* [Contributions to physiology.] Leipzig: W. Engelmann.

Herrick, C. J. (1929). *The thinking machine.* Chicago: University of Chicago Press.

Hippocrates. (1983). The sacred disease (J. Chadwick & W. N. Mann, Trans.). In G. E. R. Lloyd (Ed.), *Hippocratic writings* (pp. 237–251). London: Penguin. (Original work written in 5th–4th century BCE.)

Hobbes, T. (1839). On body (Anonymous, Trans.). In W. Molesworth (Ed.), The English works of Thomas Hobbes of Malmesbury, v. 1. London: J. Bohn. (Original work published in 1655; translation first published in 1656.)

Hobbes, T. (1998). Leviathan. New York: Oxford University Press. (Original work published in 1651.)

Hobson, J. A. (1988). *The dreaming brain.* New York: Basic Books.

Hoffman, J. E., & Macmillan, F. W. (1985). Is semantic priming automatic? In M. I. Posner, & O. S. M. Marin (Eds.), *Attention and performance XI* (pp. 585–599). Hillsdale, NJ: Lawrence Erlbaum.

Hollingshead, A. B., & Redlich, F. C. (1958). *Social class and mental illness.* New York: Wiley.

Hooker, E. (1956). A preliminary analysis of group behavior of homosexuals. *Journal of Psychology, 41,* 217–225.

Hooker, E. (1957). The adjustment of the male overt homosexual. *Journal of Projective Techniques, 21,* 18–31.

Hooker, E. (1958). Male homosexuality in the Rorschach. *Journal of Projective Techniques, 22,* 33–54.

Hooker, E. (1959). Symposium on current aspects of the problems of validity: What is a criterion? *Journal of Projective Techniques, 23,* 278–281.

Hooker, E. (1960). The fable. *Journal of Projective Techniques, 24,* 240–245.

Hooker, E. (1965). Male homosexuals and their "worlds." In J. Marmor (Ed.), *Sexual inversion: The multiple roots of homosexuality.* New York: Basic Books.

Hooker, E. (1993). Reflections of a 40-year exploration. *American Psychologist, 48,* 450–453.

Horn, B. K. P. (1975). Obtaining shape from shading information. In P. H. Winston (Ed.), *The psychology of computer vision* (pp. 115–155). New York: McGraw-Hill.

Horney, K. (1939). *New ways in psychoanalysis.* New York: W. W. Norton.

Horney, K. (1942). *Self-Analysis.* New York: W. W. Norton.

Horney, K. (1945). *Our inner conflicts.* New York: W. W. Norton.

Horney, K. (1950). *Neurosis and human growth.* New York: W. W. Norton.

Horney, K. (1967). *Feminine psychology.* New York: W. W. Norton.

Hubel, D. H. (1982). Exploration of the primary visual cortex, 1955–78. *Nature, 299,* 515–524.

Hubel, D. H., & Wiesel, T. N. (1959). Receptive fields of single neurones in the cat's striate cortex. *Journal of Physiology, 148,* 574–591.

Hubel, D. H., & Wiesel, T. N. (1962). Receptive fields, binocular interaction and functional architecture in the cat's visual cortex. *Journal of Physiology, 160,* 106–154.

Hubel, D. H., & Wiesel, T. N. (1968). Receptive fields and functional architecture of monkey striate cortex. *Journal of Physiology, 195,* 215–243.

Hubel, D. H., & Wiesel, T. N. (1979). Brain mechanisms of vision. *Scientific American, 241,* 150–162.

Hudson, B. (1947). One trial learning: A study of the avoidance behavior of the rat. Unpublished doctoral dissertation, University of California, Berkeley, CA.

Hughlings, Jackson, J. (1873). *On the localisation of movements in the brain* (Clinical and Physiological Researches on the Nervous System Reprint No. 1). London: J. and A. Churchill.

Humboldt, W. von (1999). *On language: On the diversity of human language construction and its influence on the mental development of the human species* (M. Losonsky, Ed.; P. Heath, Trans.). New York: Cambridge University Press, 1999. (Original work published in 1836.)

Hume, D. (1999). *An enquiry concerning human understanding.* New York: Oxford University Press. (Original work published in 1748.)

Humphrey, G. (1940). The problem of the direction of thought. *British Journal of Psychology, 30,* 183–196.

Huxley, T. H. (1874). On the hypothesis that animals are automata, and its history. *Nature, 10,* 362–366.

Ibn al-Haytham. [See Alhacen].

Ivry, R. B., Keele, S. W., & Diener, H. C. (1988). Dissociation of the lateral and medial cerebellum in movement timing and movement execution. *Experimental Brain Research, 73,* 167–180.

J. Res. 174, 101st Cong.,135 Cong. Rec. 13946–13947 (1989) (enacted).

Jaager, J. J. de (1970). *Origins of psychometry: Johan Jacob de Jaager, student of F. C. Donders on reaction time and mental processes* (J. Brožek & M. S. Sibinga, Trans.). Nieuwkoop, Netherlands: B. de Graaf. (Original work published in 1865.)

Jacobs, R. C., & Campbell, D. T. (1951). The perpetuation of an arbitrary tradition through several generations of a laboratory microculture. *Journal of Abnormal and Social Psychology, 62,* 649–658.

Jahoda, M. (1958). *Current concepts of positive mental health.* New York: Basic Books.

James, W. (1879). Are we automata? *Mind, 4,* 1–22.

James, W. (1890). *Principles of psychology.* New York: Holt.

James, W. (1892). *Psychology.* New York: Holt.

Janis, I. L. (1982). *Groupthink* (2nd ed.). Boston: Houghton Mifflin.

Jefferson, G. (1949). The mind of mechanical man. Lister Oration for 1949. *British Medical Journal, 1,* 1105–1121.

Jensen, A. R. (1969). How much can we boost IQ and scholastic achievement? *Harvard Educational Review, 39,* 1–124.

Jones, E. (1957). *The life and work of Sigmund Freud.* (Vols. 1–3). New York: Basic Books.

Jones, M. C. (1924). The elimination of children's fears. *Journal of Experimental Psychology, 7,* 382–390.

Jones, M. C. (1974). Albert, Peter, and John B. Watson. *American Psychologist, 29,* 581–583.

Joos, M. (Ed.) (1966). *Readings in linguistics* (4th ed.). Chicago: University of Chicago Press.

Julesz, B. (1964). Binocular depth perception without familiarity cues. *Science, 145,* 356–362.

Julesz, B. (1971). *Foundations of cyclopean perception.* Chicago: University of Chicago Press.

Jung, C. G. (1968). The concept of the collective unconscious. In C. G. Jung, *The archetypes and the collective unconscious* (2nd ed., pp. 42–53) (R. F. C. Hull, Trans.). Princeton, NJ: Princeton University Press. (Original work published in 1936.)

Jusczyk, P. W., & Klein, R. M. (Eds.) (1980). *The nature of thought: Essays in honour of D. O. Hebb.* Hillsdale, NJ: Lawrence Erlbaum.

Kaang, B.-K., Kandel, E. R., & Grant, S. G. N. (1993). Activation of cAMP-responsive genes by stimuli that produce long-term facilitation in *Aplysia* sensory neurons. *Neuron, 10,* 427–435.

Kagan, J. (1994). *Galen's prophecy: Temperament in human nature.* New York: Basic Books.

Kagan, J. (1997). Temperament and the reactions to unfamiliarity. *Child Development, 68,* 139–143.

Kagan, J. (2003). Biology, context, and developmental inquiry. *Annual Review of Psychology, 54,* 1–23.

Kagan, J., Reznick, J. S., & Snidman, N. (1988). Biological bases of childhood shyness. *Science, 240,* 167–171.

Kagan, J., & Snidman, N. (2004). *The long shadow of temperament.* Cambridge, MA: The Belknap Press.

Kamin L. J. (1957). The retention of an incompletely learned avoidance response. *Journal of Comparative and Physiological Psychology, 50,* 457–460.

Kandel, E. R. (1976). *Cellular basis of behavior.* San Francisco: Freeman.

Kandel, E. R. (1998). A new intellectual framework for psychiatry. *American Journal of Psychiatry, 155,* 457–469.

Kandel, E. R. (2001). Autobiography. In T. Frängsmyr (Ed.), *Les Prix Nobel. The Nobel Prizes 2000.* Stockholm, Sweden: Nobel Foundation.

Kandel, E. R., & Hawkins, R. D. (1992, September). The biological basis of learning and individuality. *Scientific American, 267,* 78–86.

Kandel, E. R., & Schwartz, J. H. (1982). Molecular biology of learning: Modulation of transmitter release. *Science, 218,* 433–443.

Kandel, E. R., & Schwartz, J. H. (Eds.) (1985). *Principles of neural science* (2nd ed.). New York: Elsevier.

Kandel, E. R., Schwartz, J. H., & Jessell, T. M. (Eds.) (1991). *Principles of neural science* (3rd ed.). New York: Elsevier.

Kandel, E. R., & Spencer, W. A. (1968). Cellular neurophysiological approaches in the study of learning. *Physiological Reviews, 48,* 65–134.

Kandel, E. R., & Tauc, L. (1964). Mechanism of prolonged heterosynaptic facilitation. *Nature, 202,* 145–147.

Kant, I. (1787/1934). *Critique of pure reason* (J. M. D. Meiklejohn, Trans.). London: J. M. Dent & Sons. [Originally published as *Kritik der reinen Vernunft* in 1781, revised in 1787.]

Kariel, H. S. (1956). Democracy unlimited: Kurt Lewin's field theory. *American Journal of Sociology, 62,* 280–289.

Katz, P. S., & Frost, W. N. (1995). Intrinsic neuromodulation in the *Tritonia* swim CPG: Serotonin mediates both neuromodulation and neurotransmission by the dorsal swim interneurons. *Journal of Neurophysiology, 74,* 2281–2294.

Kelly, G. A. (1955). *The psychology of personal constructs: Vol. 1. A theory of personality.* New York: Norton.

Kelly, G. A. (1969). Clinical psychology and personality: The selected papers of George Kelly (B. Maher, Ed.). New York: Wiley.

Kepler, J. (2000). Optics (W. H. Donahue, Trans.). Santa Fe: Green Lion Press. (Original work published in 1604.)

Kessler, R. C., Andrews, G., Mroczek, D., Ustun, B., & Wittchen, H.-U. (1998). The World Health Organization composite international diagnostic interview short form (CIDI-SF). *International Journal of Methods in Psychiatric Research, 7,* 171–185.

Kessler, R. C., McGonagle, K. A., Zhao, S., Nelson, C. B., Hughes, M., Eshleman, S., et al. (1994). Lifetime and 12 month prevalence of *DSM-III-R* psychiatric disorders in the United States: Results from the National Comorbidity Survey. *Archives of General Psychiatry, 51,* 8–19.

Keyes, C. L. M. (1998). Social well-being. *Social Psychology Quarterly, 61,* 121–140.

Keyes, C. L. M., (2001). Definition of mental disorders. In C. E. Faupel and P. M. Roman (Eds.), *The encyclopedia of criminology and deviant behavior* (Vol. 4, pp. 373–376). London: Taylor and Francis.

Keyes, C. L. M. (2002). The mental health continuum: From languishing to flourishing in life. *Journal of Health and Social Behavior, 43,* 207–222.

Keyes, C. L. M. (2003). Complete mental health: An agenda for the 21st century. In C. L. M. Keyes and J. Haidt (Eds.), *Flourishing: Positive psychology and the life well-lived* (pp. 293–312). Washington, DC: American Psychological Association.

Keyes, C. L. M. (2007). Promoting and protecting mental health as flourishing: A complementary strategy for improving national mental health. *American Psychologist, 62,* 95–108.

Keyes, C. L. M., & Lopez, S. J. (2002). Toward a science of mental health: Positive directions in diagnosis and interventions. In C. R. Snyder &. S. J. Lopez (Eds.), *The handbook of positive psychology* (pp. 45–59). New York: Oxford University Press.

Keyes, C. L. M., & Ryff, C. D. (1999). Psychological well-being in midlife. In S. L. Willis & J. D. Reid (Eds.), *Middle aging: Development in the third quarter of life* (pp. 161–180). Orlando, FL: Academic Press.

Keyes, C. L. M., Ryff, C. D., & Lee, Y.-H. (2001). Somatization and mental health: A comparative study of South Korean and U.S. adults. Unpublished manuscript.

Keyes, C. L. M., & Shapiro, A. (2004). Social well-being in the United States: A descriptive epidemiology. In O. G. Brim, C. D. Ryff, & R. C. Kessler (Eds.), *How healthy are we? A national study of well-being at midlife.* Chicago: University of Chicago Press.

Keyes, C. L. M., Shmotkin, D., & Ryff, C. D. (2002). Optimizing well-being: The empirical encounter of two traditions. *Journal of Personality and Social Psychology, 82,* 1007–1022.

Keyes, C. L. M., & Waterman, M. B. (2003). Dimensions of well-being and mental health in adulthood. In M. Bornstein, L. Davidson, C. L. M. Keyes, & K. A. Moore (Eds.), *Well-being: Positive development throughout the life course* (pp. 481–501). Mahwah, NJ: Lawrence Erlbaum.

Kimmel, D. C., & Garnets, L. D. (2000). What a light it shed: The life of Evelyn Hooker. In G. A. Kimble & M. Wertheimer (Eds.), *Portraits of pioneers in psychology* (Vol. 4, pp. 253–267). Mahwah, NJ: Lawrence Erlbaum.

Kinsey, A. C., Pomeroy, W. B., & Martin, C. E. (1948). *Sexual behavior in the human male.* Philadelphia: W. B. Saunders.

Kirk, S. A. & Kutchins, H. (1992). *The selling of DSM: The rhetoric of science in psychiatry.* New York: Aldine de Gruyter.

Kleene, S. C. (1935). General recursive functions of natural numbers. *American Journal of Mathematics, 57,* 153–173; 219–244.

Kleiman, G. M. (1975). Speech recoding in reading. *Journal of Verbal Learning and Verbal Behavior, 14,* 323–339.

Kleinpaul, R. (1892). *Menschenopfer und Ritualmorde.* [Human sacrifice and ritual murder.] Leipzig: Schmidt & Günther.

Klopfer, B., Ainsworth, M. D., Klopfer, W. G., & Holt, R. R. (1954). *Developments in the Rorschach technique* (Vol. 1). Yonkers-on-Hudson, New York: World Book.

Koffka, K. (1935). *Principles of gestalt psychology.* New York: Harcourt-Brace.

Köhler, W. (1929). *Gestalt psychology.* New York: Liveright.

Köhler, W. (1940). *Dynamics in psychology.* New York: Liveright.

Konorski, J. (1959). A new method of physiological investigation of recent memory in animals. *Bulletin de l'Académie Polonaise des Sciences: Série des Sciences Biologiques, 7,* 115–117.

Kosslyn, S. M. (1980). *Image and mind.* Cambridge, MA: Harvard University Press.

Kosslyn, S. M., Holtzman, J. D., Farah, M. J., & Gazzaniga, M. S. (1985). A computational analysis of mental image generation: Evidence from functional dissociations in split-brain patients. *Journal of Experimental Psychology, 114,* 311–341.

Kotovsky, K., & Simon, H. A. (1973). Empirical tests of a theory of human acquisition of concepts for sequential events. *Cognitive Psychology, 4,* 399–424.

Kraepelin, E. (1913). *Lectures on clinical psychiatry* (3rd English ed. trans. from 2nd [1905] German ed.; T. Johnstone, Trans.). New York: W. Wood. (Original German work published as *Einführung in die Psychiatrische Klinik,* 1901.)

Krafft-Ebing, R. von (1965). *Psychopathia sexualis: A medico-forensic study* (H. E. Wedeck, Trans.). New York: Putnam. (Original work published in 1886.)

Krasne, F. B. (1969). Excitation and habituation of the crayfish escape reflex: The depolarization response in lateral giant fibers of the isolated abdomen. *Journal of Experimental Biology, 50,* 29–46.

Kuffler, S. W. (1953). Discharge patterns and functional organization of mammalian retina. *Journal of Neurophysiology, 16,* 37–68.

Külpe, O. (1895). *Outlines of psychology* (E. B. Titchener, Trans.). London: Sonnenschein. [Original work published 1893.]

Kupfermann, I., & Kandel, E. R. (1969). Neuronal controls of a behavioral response mediated by the abdominal ganglion of *Aplysia. Science, 164,* 847–850.

LaBerge, D., & Samuels, S. J. (1974). Toward a theory of automatic information processing in reading. *Cognitive Psychology, 6,* 293–323.

Laing, R. D. (1960). *The divided self: An existential study in sanity and madness.* New York: Pantheon.

Laing, R. D. (1967). *The politics of experience.* New York: Ballantine.

Laing, R. D. (1972). *The politics of the family and other essays.* New York: Vintage.

La Mettrie, J. O. de (1996). *Machine man* (A. Thomson, Trans.). Cambridge, England: Cambridge University Press. (Original work published in 1747.)

Langer, S. K. (1953). *Philosophy in a new key.* New York: Mentor Books.

Larson, J. S. (1996). The World Health Organization's definition of health: Social versus spiritual health. *Social Indicators Research, 38,* 181–192.

Lashley, K. S. (1929). *Brain mechanisms and intelligence: A quantitative study of injuries to the brain.* Chicago: University of Chicago Press.

Lashley, K. S. (1950). In search of the engram. *Symposia of the Society for Experimental Biology, 4,* 454–482.

Lashley, K. S. (1951). The problem of serial order in behavior. In L. A. Jeffress (Ed.), *Cerebral mechanisms in behavior* (pp. 112–136). New York: Wiley.

Laughery, K. R., & Gregg, L. W. (1962). Simulation of human problem-solving behavior. *Psychometrika, 27,* 265–282.

Le Bon, G. (1960). *The crowd: A study of the popular mind.* New York: Viking Press. (Original work published in 1895.)

LeDoux, J. E. (1995). Emotion: Clues from the brain. *Annual Review of Psychology, 46,* 209–264.

Leibniz, G. W. (1951a). *Discourse on metaphysics.* In P. P. Wiener (Ed.), *Leibniz: Selections* (pp. 290–345). New York: Charles Scribner's Sons. (Original work published in 1686.)

Leibniz, G. W. (1951b). *New essays on the human understanding.* In P. P. Wiener (Ed.), *Leibniz: Selections* (pp. 367–480). New York: Charles Scribner's Sons. (Original work published in 1704.)

Leibniz, G. W. (1951c). *New system of nature.* In P. P. Wiener (Ed.), *Leibniz: Selections* (pp. 106–117). New York: Charles Scribner's Sons. (Original work published in 1695.)

Lenneberg, E. H. (1967). *Biological foundations of language.* New York: Wiley.

Lettvin, J. Y., Maturana, H. R., McCulloch, W. S., & Pitts, W. H. (1959). What the frog's eye tells the frog's brain. *Proceedings of the Institute of Radio Engineers, 47,* 1940–1951. (Reprinted in W. S. McCulloch (Ed.), *Embodiments of mind.* MIT Press, 1965.)

Lévesque de Pouilly, L.-J. (1749). *The theory of agreeable sensations.* London: W. Owen. (Original work published in French in 1747.

Levy, S. T. (1984). Psychoanalytic perspectives on emptiness. *Journal of the American Psychoanalytic Association, 32,* 387–404.

Lewin, K. (1936). *Principles of topological psychology* New York: McGraw-Hill.

Lewin, K. (1938). *The conceptual representation and the measurement of psychological forces.* Durham, NC: Duke University Press.

Lewin, K. (1939a). Experiments in social space, *Harvard Educational Review, 9,* 21–32. (Reprinted in Lewin, 1948.)

Lewin, K. (1939b). Field theory and experiment in social psychology. *American Journal of Sociology, 44,* 868–896.

Lewin, K. (1947). Group decision and social change. In T. M. Newcomb & Eugene L. Hartley (Eds.), *Readings in social psychology* (pp. 340–344). New York: Henry Holt.

Lewin, K. (1948). *Resolving social conflicts: Selected papers on group dynamics.* New York: Harper & Brothers.

Lewin, K. (1951). *Field theory in social science: Selected theoretical papers* (D. Cartwright, Ed.). New York: Harper & Brothers.

Lewin, K., Dembo, T., Festinger, L., & Sears, P. (1944). Level of aspiration. In J. M. Hunt (Ed.), *Personality and the behavior disorders* (pp. 333–378). Oxford: Ronald Press. [Reprinted in Gold, 1999.]

Lewin, K., & Lippitt, R. (1938). An experimental approach to the study of autocracy and democracy: A preliminary note. *Sociometry, 1,* 292–300.

Lewin, K., Lippitt, R., & White, R. K. (1939). Patterns of aggressive behavior in experimentally created "social climates." *Journal of Social Psychology, S.P.S.S.I. Bulletin, 10,* 271–299. [Reprinted in Gold, 1999.]

Lewin, M. A. (1998). Kurt Lewin: His psychology and a daughter's recollections. In G. A. Kimble & M. Wertheimer (Eds.), *Portraits of pioneers in psychology* (Vol. 3, pp. 105–120). Mahwah, NJ: Lawrence Erlbaum.

Lewontin, R. C. (1970, March). Race and intelligence. *Bulletin of the Atomic Scientists, 26,* 2–8.

Lindberg, D. C. (1976). *Theories of vision from Al-Kindi to Kepler.* Chicago: University of Chicago Press.

Lippitt, R. (1939). Field theory and experiment in social psychology: Autocratic and democratic group atmospheres. *American Journal of Sociology, 45,* 26–49.

Locke, J. (1690). *An essay concerning human understanding.* London: Routledge.

Lorenz, K. (1941). Kants Lehre vom Apriorischen in Lichte gegenwärtiger Biologie. [Kant's doctrine of the a priori in the light of modern biology.] *Blätter für Deutsche Philosophie, 15,* 94–125.

Lorenz, K. (1950). Innate behaviour patterns. In *Symposia of the Society for Experimental Biology:* No. 4. *Physiological mechanisms in animal behaviour.* New York: Academic Press.

Lotze, R. H. (1852). *Medizinische Psychologie: oder Physiologie der Seele.* [Medical psychology, or physiology of the soul.] Leipzig, Germany: Weidmann.

Lotze, R. H. (1856). Mikrokosmus; Ideen zur Naturgeschichte und Geschichte der Menschheit; Versuch einer Anthropologie. [Microcosmus: an essay concerning man and his relation to the world]. Leipzig, Germany: Hirzel.

Luce, R. D. (1986). *Response times: Their role in inferring elementary mental organization.* New York: Oxford University Press.

Lucretius. (55 BCE). *On the nature of the universe* (R. E. Latham, Trans.). London: Penguin.

Luft, E. v. d. (2001, Summer). Thomas Szasz, MD: Philosopher, psychiatrist, libertarian. *SUNY Upstate Medical University Alumni Journal*.

Lyell, C. (1830). *Principles of geology.* London: John Murray.

MacLeod, R. B. (1947). The effects of artificial penumbrae on the brightness of included areas. In Université catholique de Louvain (Ed.), *Miscellanea Psychologica Albert Michotte: études de psychologie offertes à M. Albert Michotte à l'occasion de son jubilé professoral* (pp. 138–154). Louvain, Belgium: Institut Supérieur de Philosophie.

Magnus, R. (1924). *Körperstellung.* [Posture.] Berlin: Springer-Verlag.

Marcel, A. J. (1983). Conscious and unconscious perception: Experiments on visual masking and word recognition. *Cognitive Psychology, 15,* 197–237.

Marcus, E. (1992). *Making history.* New York: HarperCollins.

Marquand, J. P. (1943). *So little time.* Boston: Little, Brown.

Marquand, J. P. (1951). *H. M. Pulham.* Boston: Little, Brown.

Marr, D. (1969). A theory of cerebellar cortex. *Journal of Physiology, 202*(2), 437–470.

Marr, D. (1970). A theory for cerebral neocortex. *Proceedings of the Royal Society of London B, 176,* 161–234.

Marr, D. (1971). Simple memory: A theory for archicortex. *Philosophical Transactions of the Royal Society of London B, 262,* 23–81.

Marr, D. (1976). Early processing of visual information. *Philosophical Transactions of the Royal Society of London B, 275,* 483–519.

Marr, D. (1977a). Analysis of occluding contour. *Proceedings of the Royal Society of London B, 197,* 441–476.

Marr, D. (1977b). Artificial intelligence–A personal view. *Artificial Intelligence, 9,* 37–48.

Marr, D. (1978). Representing visual information. In S. A. Levin (Ed.), *Lectures on mathematics in the life sciences:* Vol. 10. *Some mathematical questions in biology* (pp. 101–180). Providence: American Mathematical Society. [Also published as MIT Artificial Intelligence Laboratory Memo 415 (1977) and has appeared more than once in various anthologies.]

Marr, D. (1980). Visual information processing: The structure and creation of visual representations. *Philosophical Transactions of the Royal Society of London B, 290,* 199–218.

Marr, D. (1982). *Vision: A computational investigation into the human representation and processing of visual information.* San Francisco: W. H. Freeman.

Marr, D., & Hildreth, E. (1980). Theory of edge detection. *Proceedings of the Royal Society of London B, 207,* 187–217.

Marr, D., & Nishihara, H. K. (1978). Representation and recognition of the spatial organization of three-dimensional shapes. *Proceedings of the Royal Society of London B, 200,* 269–294.

Marr, D., & Poggio, T. (1977). From understanding computation to understanding neural circuitry. *Neurosciences Research Program Bulletin, 15,* 470–488.

Marr, D., & Poggio, T. (1979). A computational theory of human stereo vision. *Proceedings of the Royal Society of London B, 204,* 301–328.

Marr, D., Poggio, T., & Ullman, S. (1979). Bandpass channels, zero-crossings and early visual information processing. *Journal of the Optical Society of America, 69,* 914–916.

Marr, D., & Ullman, S. (1981). Directional selectivity and its use in early visual processing. *Proceedings of the Royal Society of London B, 211,* 151–180.

Marshall, J. C., & Newcombe, F. (1973). Patterns of paralexia: A psycholinguistic approach. *Journal of Psycholinguistic Research, 2,* 175–199.

Marshall, W. H., & Talbot, S. A. (1942). Recent evidence for neural mechanisms in vision leading to a general theory of sensory acuity. In Klüver, H. (Ed.), *Visual Mechanisms* (pp. 117–164). Oxford: Jacques Cattell.

Martensen, R. L. (2004). *The brain takes shape: An early history.* New York: Oxford University Press.

Martin, K. C., & Kandel, E. R. (1996). Cell adhesion molecules, CREB, and the formation of new synaptic connections. *Neuron, 17,* 567–570.

Martin, K. C., Michael, D., Rose, J. C., Barad, M., Casadio, A., Zhu, H., et al. (1997). MAP kinase translocates into the nucleus of the presynaptic cell and is required for long-term facilitation in *Aplysia. Neuron, 18,* 899–912.

Maslow, A. H. (1954). *Motivation and personality.* New York: Harper & Brothers.

Maslow, A. H. (1968). *Toward a psychology of being* (2nd ed.). New York: Van Nostrand Rinehold.

Maslow, A. H. (1970). *Motivation and personality* (2nd ed.). New York: Harper & Row.

Maslow, A. H. (1976). *Religions, values, and peak experiences.* New York: Penguin.

Mautner, T. (2000). *The Penguin dictionary of philosophy.* London: Penguin.

Mayr, E. (1982). *The growth of biological thought: Diversity, evolution, and inheritance.* Cambridge, MA: Harvard University Press.

McClelland, J. L., & Rumelhart, D. E. (1981). An interactive activation model of context effects in letter perception: Part 1. An account of basic findings. *Psychological Review, 88,* 375–407.

McClelland, J. L., & Rumelhart, D. E. (1986). A distributed model of human learning and memory. In J. L. McClelland & D. E. Rumelhart (Eds.), *Parallel distributed processing: Explorations in the microstructure of cognition* (Vol. 2, pp. 170–215). Cambridge, MA: MIT Press.

McClelland, J. L., Rumelhart, D. E., & Hinton, G. E. (1986). The appeal of PDP. In D. E. Rumelhart & J. L. McClelland (Eds.), *Parallel distributed processing: Explorations in the microstructure of cognition* (Vol. 1, pp. 3–44). Cambridge, MA: MIT Press.

McCormick, D. A., & Thompson, R. F. (1984). Cerebellum: Essential involvement in the classically conditioned eyelid response. *Science, 223,* 296–299.

McCulloch, W., & Pitts, W. (1943). A logical calculus of the ideas immanent in nervous activity. *Bulletin of Mathematical Biophysics, 5,* 115–133.

Mead, M. (1928). *Coming of age in Samoa.* New York: Morrow.

Mechanic, D. (1999). *Mental health and mental illness: Definitions and perspectives.* In A. V. Horwitz & T. L. Scheid (Eds.), A *handbook for the study of mental health: Social contexts, theories, and systems* (pp. 12–28). New York: Cambridge University Press.

Menzel, R., & Erber, J. (1978). Learning and memory in bees. *Scientific American, 239,* 102–110.

Mesulam, M. M. (1981). A cortical network for directed attention and unilateral neglect. *Annals of Neurology, 10,* 309–325.

Metzinger, T. (Ed.) (2000). *Neural correlates of consciousness: Empirical and conceptual questions.* Cambridge, MA: MIT Press.

Metzl, J. M. (2003). *Prozac on the couch.* Durham, NC: Duke University Press.

Mill, J. S. (1872). *A system of logic ratiocinative and inductive* (8th ed.). London: Longmans, Green, Reader and Dyer. (Original work published in 1843.)

Miller, G. A., Galanter, E., & Pribram, K. H. (1960). *Plans and the structure of behavior.* New York: Holt.

Milner, B. (1965). Memory impairments associated with bilateral hippocampal lesions. In P. M. Milner & S. Glickman (Eds.), *Cognitive processes and the brain* (pp. 97–111). Princeton, NJ: Van Nostrand. (Original work published in 1962.)

Milner, B. (1965). Visually guided maze learning in man: Effects of bilateral hippocampal, bilateral frontal, and unilateral cerebral lesions. *Neuropsychologia, 3,* 317–338.

Milner, B. (1972). Disorders of learning and memory after temporal-lobe lesions in man. *Clinical Neurosurgery, 19,* 421–446.

Milner, B., Corkin, S., & Teuber, H.-L. (1968). Further analysis of the hippocampal amnesic syndrome. *Neuropsychologia, 6,* 215–234.

Milner, B., Squire, L. R., & Kandel, E. R. (1998). Cognitive neuroscience and the study of memory. *Neuron, 20,* 445–468.

Milner, B., & Taylor, L. (1972). Right hemisphere superiority in tactile pattern recognition after cerebral commissurotomy: Evidence for nonverbal memory. *Neuropsychologia, 10,* 1–15.

Milner, P. M. (1986). The mind and Donald O. Hebb. *Scientific American, 268,* 124–129.

Minkowski, E. (1911). Zur Müllerschen Lehre von spezifischen Sinnesenergien. [On Müller's doctrine of specific sensory energies.] *Zeitschrift für Sinnesphysiologie, 45,* 129–152.

Minsky, M., & Papert, S. (1967, September). Perceptrons and pattern recognition. *Artificial Intelligence Memo No. 140, MAC-M-358, Project MAC, Cambridge, MA, September 1967.*

Montarolo, P., Schacher, S., Castellucci, V. F., Hawkins, R. D., Abrams, T. W., Goelet, P., et al. (1986). Interrelationships of cellular mechanisms for different forms of learning and memory. In R. L. Montalcini, P. Calissano, E. R. Kandel, & A. Maggi (Eds.), *Molecular aspects of neurobiology* (pp. 1–14). Berlin: Springer-Verlag.

Moravec, H. (1986). Dualism from reductionism. *Proceedings of the International Symposium on AI and the Human Mind, Yale University, New Haven, CT, March 1–3, 1986.*

Moravec, H. (1988). *Mind children: The future of robot and human intelligence.* Cambridge, MA: Harvard University Press.

Moreno, J. L. (1941). Foundations of sociometry: An introduction. *Sociometry, 4,* 15–35.

Moreno, J. L., Jennings, H. H., Criswell, J. H., Katz, L., Blake, R. R., Mouton, J. S., et al. (1960). *The Sociometry Reader.* Glencoe, IL: Free Press.

Morgan, C. T. (1943). *Physiological psychology.* New York: McGraw-Hill.

Mosso, A. (1881). *Über den Kreislauf des Blutes im menschlichen Gehirn.* [On the circulation of blood in the human brain: Sphygmographic research.] Leipzig: Viet. (Originally published as *Sulla circolazione del sangue nel cervello dell'uomo; ricerche sfigmografiche.* Rome: Salviucci, 1880.)

Mountcastle, V. B. (1978). Brain mechanisms for directed attention. *Journal of the Royal Society of Medicine, 71,* 14–28.

Mrazek, P. J., & Haggerty, R. J. (Eds.) (1994). *Reducing risks for mental disorders.* Washington, DC: National Academy Press.

Müller, J. (1826). *Zur vergleichenden Physiologie des Gesichtssinnes des Menschen und der Thiere: nebst einem Versuch über Bewegungen der Augen und über den menschlichen Blick.* [On the comparative physiology of vision in humans and animals: Including an essay on eye movement and human sight.] Leipzig: C. Cnobloch.

Müller, J. (1842). Elements of physiology (Vols. 1–2) (W. Baly, Trans.). London: Taylor and Walton. (Originally published as *Handbuch der Physiologie des Menschen* (Vols. 1–2). Coblenz, Germany: Hölscher, 1838.)

Munk, H. (1909). *Über die Functionen der Grosskirnrinde.* [On the functions of the cerebral cortex] Berlin: Hirschwald. (Original work published in 1890.)

Murphy, G. (1966). *Personality: A biosocial approach to origins and structure.* New York: Basic Books.

Murphy, G. G., & Glanzman, D. L (1997). Mediation of classical conditioning in *Aplysia californica* by long-term potentiation of sensorimotor synapses. *Science, 278,* 467–470.

Murray, C. J. L., & Lopez, A. D. (Eds.) (1996). *The global burden of disease: A comprehensive assessment of mortality and disability from diseases, injuries, and risk factors in 1990 and projected to 2020.* Cambridge, MA: Harvard School of Public Health.

Murray, H. A. (1943). *Thematic apperception test manual.* Cambridge, MA: Harvard University Press.

Nagel, A. (1861). *Das Sehen mit zwei Augen und die Lehre von den identischen Netzhautstellen.* [Binocular vision and the doctrine of identical retinal locations.] Leipzig: Winter.

Nagel, T. (1974). What is it like to be a bat? *Philosophical Review, 83,* 435–450.

Neely, J. H. (1977). Semantic priming and retrieval from lexical memory: Roles of inhibitionless spreading activation and limited-capacity attention. *Journal of Experimental Psychology: General, 106,* 226–254.

Nevatia, R. (1974). Structured descriptions of complex curved objects for recognition and visual memory. Stanford Artificial Intelligence Project Memo AIM-250. Stanford University, Stanford, CA.

Newell, A. (Ed.) (1961). *Information processing language—V manual.* Englewood Cliffs, NJ: Prentice Hall.

Newell, A., & Simon, H. A. (1961). GPS: A program that simulates human thought. In H. Billings, *Lernende automaten* (pp. 109–124). Munich, Germany: R. Oldenbourg. [Reprinted in E. A. Feigenbaum & J. Feldman (Eds.), *Computers and thought* (pp. 279–293). New York, McGraw-Hill, 1963.]

Newell, A., & Simon, H. A. (1962). Computer simulation of human thinking. *Science, 134,* 2011–2017.

Nickell, J., & Fischer, J. F. (1992). *Mysterious realms: Probing paranormal, historical, and forensic enigmas.* Buffalo, NY: Prometheus.

Nye, R. D. (1992). *The legacy of B. F. Skinner: Concepts and perspectives, controversies and misunderstandings.* Pacific Grove, CA: Brooks/Cole.

Online etymology dictionary. (n.d.). Lounge. Retrieved January 7, 2006, from www.etymonline.com

Paris, B. J. (2000). Karen Horney: The three phases of her thought. In G. A. Kimble & M. Wertheimer (Eds.), *Portraits of pioneers in psychology* (Vol. 4, pp. 163–179). Mahwah, NJ: Lawrence Erlbaum.

Pavlov, I. P. (1927). *Conditioned reflexes: An investigation of the physiological activity of the cerebral cortex* (G. V. Anrep, Trans.). London: Oxford University Press. (Russian original published 1923.)

Peirce, C. S. (1957). The logic of abduction. In V. Tomas (Ed.), *Peirce's essays in the philosophy of science* (pp. 235–255). New York: Liberal Arts Press.

Penfield, W. (1975). *The mystery of the mind.* Princeton, NJ: Princeton University Press.

Petersen, S. E., Fox, P. T., Miezin, F. M., & Raichle, M. E. (1988). Modulation of cortical visual responses by direction of spatial attention measured by PET. *Investigative Ophthalmology and Visual Science, 29*(Supp.), 22.

Petersen, S. E., Fox, P. T., Posner, M. I., Mintun, M., & Raichle, M. E. (1988). Positron emission tomographic studies of the cortical anatomy of single-word processing. *Nature, 331,* 585–589.

Petersen, S. E., Robinson, D. L., & Keys, W. (1985). Pulvinar nuclei of the behaving rhesus monkey: Visual responses and their modulation. *Journal of Neurophysiology, 54,* 867–886.

Piaget, J. (1954). *The construction of reality in the child* (M. Cook, Trans.). London: Routledge & Kegan Paul. (Original work published in 1937.)

Pincus, H. A., Davis, W. W., & McQueen, L. (1999). "Subthreshold" mental disorders: A review and synthesis of studies on minor depression and other "brand names." *British Journal of Psychiatry, 174,* 288–296.

Pinel, P. (1977). A treatise on insanity. London: Cadell and Davies. (Original work published in 1806.)

Pinker, S. (1994). *The language instinct.* New York: Morrow.

Pinker, S. (1997). *How the mind works.* New York: Norton.

Pinker, S. (1999). *Words and rules: The ingredients of language.* New York: Basic Books.

Pinker, S. (2002). *The blank slate: The modern denial of human nature.* New York: Viking.

Pitts, W., & McCulloch, W. (1947). How we know universals: The perception of auditory and visual forms. *Bulletin of Mathematical Biophysics, 9,* 127–147.

Plato. (1961). *Meno* (W. K. C. Guthrie, Trans.). In E. Hamilton & H. Cairns (Eds.), *The collected dialogues of Plato* (pp. 353–384). Princeton, NJ: Princeton University Press. (Original work written 4th c. BCE.)

Plato. (1961). *Phaedo.* (H. Tredennick, Trans.). In E. Hamilton & H. Cairns (Eds.), *The collected dialogues of Plato* (pp. 40–98). Princeton, NJ: Princeton University Press. (Original work written 4th c. BCE.)

Polya, G. (1945). *How to solve it.* Princeton, NJ: Princeton University Press.

Popper, K. R. (1966). Of clouds and clocks: An approach to the problem of rationality and the freedom of man. St. Louis: Washington University Press. [*The second Arthur Holly Compton Memorial Lecture, delivered April 21, 1965;* reprinted in Popper, K. R. (1979), *Objective knowledge: An evolutionary approach* (pp. 206–255). New York: Oxford University Press.]

Popper, K. R., & Eccles, J. C. (1977). *The self and its brain: An argument for interactionism.* New York: Springer International.

Posner, M. I. (1986). *Chronometric explorations of mind.* New York: Oxford University Press.

Posner, M. I., Cohen, Y., & Rafal, R. D. (1982). Neural systems control of spatial orienting. *Philosophical Transactions of the Royal Society of London B, 298,* 187–198.

Posner, M. I., Early, T. S., & Reiman, E. (1988). Asymmetries in hemispheric control of attention in schizophrenia. *Archives of General Psychiatry, 45,* 814–821.

Posner, M. I., Inhoff, A. W., Friedrich, F. J., & Cohen, A. (1987). Isolating attentional systems: A cognitive-anatomical analysis. *Psychobiology, 15,* 107–121.

Posner, M. I., Lewis, J., & Conrad, C. (1972). Some problems of classification. In J. F. Kavanaugh & I. G. Mattingly (Eds.), *Language by ear and by eye.* (pp. 159–192). Cambridge, MA: MIT Press.

Posner, M. I., Petersen, S. E., Fox, P. T., & Raichle, M. E. (1988). Localization of cognitive operations in the human brain. *Science, 240,* 1627–1631.

Posner, M. I., Rafal, R. D., Choate, L. S., & Vaughan, J. (1985). Inhibition of return: Neural basis and function. *Cognitive Neuropsychology, 2,* 211–228.

Posner, M. I., Walker, J. A., Friedrich, F. J., & Rafal, R. D. (1984). Effects of parietal injury on covert orienting of attention. *Journal of Neuroscience, 4,* 1863–1874.

Pratt, C. C. (1939). *The logic of modern psychology.* New York: Macmillan.

Preston, J., & Bishop, M. (Eds.). (2002). *Views into the Chinese room: New essays on Searle and artificial intelligence.* New York: Oxford University Press.

Proctor, R. W. (1981). A unified theory for matching-task phenomena. *Psychological Review, 88,* 291–326.

Purves, D., & Lichtman, J. W. (1985). *Principles of neural development.* Sunderland, MA: Sinauer Associates.

Quinn, S. (1988). A *mind of her own: The life of Karen Horney.* New York: Addison-Wesley.

Rafal, R. D., & Posner, M. I. (1987). Deficits in human visual spatial attention following thalamic lesions. *Proceedings of the National Academy of Sciences USA, 84,* 7349–7353.

Raichle, M. E. (1983). Positron emission tomography. *Annual Review of Neuroscience, 6,* 249–267.

Raichle, M. E. (1998). Behind the scenes of functional brain imaging: A historical and physiological perspective. *Proceedings of the National Academy of Sciences USA, 95,* 765–772.

Ramón y Cajal, S. (1894). La fine structure des centres nerveux. [The fine structure of the nerve centers.] *Proceedings of the Royal Society of London, 55,* 444–468.

Rebellon, C., Brown, J., & Keyes, C. L. M. (2001). Suicide and mental illness. In C. E. Faupel & P. M. Roman (Eds.), *The encyclopedia of criminology and deviant behavior:* Vol. 4. *Self destructive behavior and disvalued identity* (pp. 426–429). London: Taylor and Francis.

Reber, A. S. (1967). Implicit learning of artificial grammars. *Journal of Verbal Learning and Verbal Behavior, 6,* 855–863.

Reber, A. S. (1993). *Implicit learning and tacit knowledge.* New York: Oxford University Press.

Reber, A. S., & Reber, E. S. (2001). *The Penguin dictionary of psychology* (3rd ed.). New York: Penguin Putnam.

Reicher, G. M. (1969). Perceptual recognition as a function of meaningfulness of stimulus material. *Journal of Experimental Psychology, 81,* 275–280.

Reid, T. (1969). *Essays on the intellectual powers of man.* Cambridge, MA: MIT Press. (Original work published in 1814–1815.)

Rescorla, R. A., & Wagner, A. R. (1972). A theory of Pavlovian conditioning: Variations in the effectiveness of reinforcement and nonreinforcement. In A. H. Black & W. F. Prokasy (Eds.), *Classical conditioning II: Current research and theory* (pp. 64–99). New York: Appleton-Century-Crofts.

Restle, F. (1970). Theory of serial pattern learning: Structural trees. *Psychological Review, 77,* 481–495.

Rhine, J. B. (1934). Extra-sensory perception. Boston: Boston Society for Psychic Research.

Rhine, J. B. (1947). The reach of the mind. New York: W. Sloane Associates.

Richet, C. (1925). Réflexes psychiques. Réflexes conditionels. Automatisme mental. [Psychic reflexes. Conditional reflexes. Mental automatism.] *Pavlov's Jubilee Volume.* Petrograd.

Riddoch, M. J., & Humphreys, G. W. (1987). Perceptual and action systems in unilateral visual neglect. In M. Jeannerod (Ed.), *Neurophysiological and neuropsychological aspects of spatial neglect* (pp. 151–181). Amsterdam and New York: North-Holland.

Rilling, M. (2000). John Watson's paradoxical struggle to explain Freud. *American Psychologist, 55,* 301–312.

Robins, L. N., & Regier, D. A. (Eds.) (1991). *Psychiatric disorders in America: The epidemiological catchment area study.* New York: Free Press.

Rogers, C. R. (1951). *Client-centered therapy: Its current practice, implications, and theory.* Boston: Houghton Mifflin.

Rogers, C. R. (1961). *On becoming a person: A therapist's view of psychotherapy.* Boston: Houghton Mifflin.

Rogers, C. R. & Dymond, R. F. (1954). *Psychotherapy and personality change.* Chicago: University of Chicago Press.

Rogers, C. R., & Russell, D. E. (2002). *Carl Rogers, the quiet revolutionary: An oral history.* Roseville, CA: Penmarin.

Rood, O. N. (1861). On the relation between our perception of distance and color. *American Journal of Science and Arts ("Silliman's Journal"), 32,* 184–185.

Rorschach, H. (1942). *Psychodiagnostics: A diagnostic test based on perception.* (P. Lemkau & B. Kronenberg, Trans.) (2nd ed.). Berne, Switzerland: Hans Huber.

Rosen, G. (1969). *Madness in society: Chapters in the historical sociology of mental illness.* New York: Harper & Row.

Rothmann, M. (1909). Der Hund ohne Grosshirn. [The decorticate dog.] *Neurologisches Centralblatt, 28,* 1045–1046.

Rozycki, E. G. (1995). A critical review of B. F. Skinner's philosophy. *Educational Studies, 26,* 12–22.

Rubins, J. L. (1978). *Karen Horney: Gentle rebel of psychoanalysis.* New York: Dial Press.

Ruse, M. (1986) *Taking Darwin seriously.* Oxford: Basil Blackwell.

Rush, B. (1967). *Medical inquiries and observations upon the diseases of the mind* (Facsimile edition). New York: Hafner. (Original work published in 1812.)

Russell, B. (1908). Mathematical logic as based on the theory of types. *American Journal of Mathematics, 30,* 222–262.

Russell, B. (1945). *History of western philosophy.* New York: Simon & Schuster.

Rutherford, A. (2000). Mary Cover Jones (1896–1987). Retrieved July 3, 2006, from www .psych.yorku.ca/femhop/Cover%20Jones.htm

Ryff, C. D. (1989). Happiness is everything, or is it? Explorations on the meaning of psychological well-being. *Journal of Personality and Social Psychology, 57,* 1069–1081.

Ryff, C. D., & Keyes, C. L. M. (1995). The structure of psychological well-being revisited. *Journal of Personality and Social Psychology, 69,* 719–727.

Ryle, G. (1949). *The concept of mind.* New York: Barnes & Noble.

Sacks, O. (1985). *The man who mistook his wife for a hat and other clinical tales.* New York: Summit.

Sacks, O. (1990, November 22). Neurology and the soul. *New York Review of Books,* 44–50.

Schacher, S., Castellucci, V. F., & Kandel, E. R. (1988). CAMP evokes long-term facilitation in *Aplysia* sensory neurons that requires new protein synthesis. *Science, 240,* 1667–1669.

Schacter, D. L., & Tulving, E. (1994). What are the memory systems of 1994? In D. L. Schacter & E. Tulving (Eds.), *Memory systems 1994* (pp. 1–38). Cambridge, MA: MIT Press.

Schildkraut, J. J. (1965). The catecholamine hypothesis of affective disorders: A review of supporting evidence. *American Journal of Psychiatry, 122,* 509–522.

Schützenberger, M.-P. (1967). Algorithms and the neo-Darwinian theory of evolution. In P. S. Moorhead & M. M. Kaplan (Eds.), *Mathematical challenges to the neo-Darwinian interpretation of evolution* (pp. 73–80). Philadelphia: Wistar Institute Press.

Schwartzkroin, P. A., & Wester, K. (1975). Long-lasting facilitation of a synaptic potential following tetanization in the *in vitro* hippocampal slice. *Brain Research, 89,* 107–119.

Scott, J. P. (1972). *Animal behavior* (2nd ed.). Chicago: University of Chicago Press.

Scott, J. P., & Fuller, J. L. (1965). *Genetics and the social behavior of the dog.* Chicago: University of Chicago Press.

Scoville, W. B. (1954). The limbic lobe in man. *Journal of Neurosurgery, 77,* 64–66.

Scoville, W. B., & Milner, B. (1957). Loss of recent memory after bilateral hippocampal lesions. *Journal of Neurology, Neurosurgery, and Psychiatry, 20,* 11–21.

Searle, J. R. (1980). Minds, brains, and programs. *Behavioral and Brain Sciences, 3,* 417–457.

Searle, J. R. (1984). *Minds, brains, and science.* Cambridge, MA: Harvard University Press.

Searle, J. R. (1992). *The rediscovery of the mind.* Cambridge, MA: MIT Press.

Sechenov, I. (1965). *Reflexes of the brain* (S. Belsky, Trans.). Cambridge, MA: MIT Press. (Original work published in 1863.)

Senden, M. von (1960). *Space and sight: The perception of space and shape in the congenitally blind before and after operation* (P. Heath, Trans.). London: Methuen. (Original work published in 1932.)

Shepard, R. N., & Metzler, J. (1971). Mental rotation of three-dimensional objects. *Science, 171,* 701–703.

Sherif, M. (1936). *The psychology of social norms.* New York: Harper & Brothers.

Sherrington, C. S. (1906). *The integrative action of the nervous system,* New Haven, CT: Yale University Press.

Shneidman, E. S. (1952). *Projective techniques monographs: Manual for the Make a Picture Story method.* New York: Society for Projective Techniques and Rorschach Institute.

Shneidman, E. S. (1998). Evelyn Hooker (1907–1996). *American Psychologist, 53,* 480–481.

Shostrom, E. (1963). *The personal orientation inventory.* San Diego, CA: Educational and Industrial Testing Service.

Sidman, M., Stoddard, L. T., & Mohr, J. P. (1968). Some additional quantitative observations of immediate memory in a patient with bilateral hippocampal lesions. *Neuropsychologia, 6,* 245–254.

Sieroff, E., Pollatsek, A., & Posner, M. I. (1988). Recognition of visual letter strings following injury to the posterior visual spatial attention system. *Cognitive Neuropsychology, 5,* 427–449.

Sieroff, E., & Posner, M. I. (1988). Cueing spatial attention during processing of words and letter strings in normals. *Cognitive Neuropsychology, 5,* 451–472.

Simon, H. A., & Greeno, J. G. (1974). Processes for sequence production. *Psychological Review, 81,* 187–198.

Simon, H. A., & Kotovsky, K. (1963). Human acquisition of concepts for sequential patterns. *Psychological Review, 70,* 534–546.

Simon, H. A., & Sumner, R. (1968). Pattern in music. In B. Kleinmuntz (Ed.). *Formal representation of human judgment* (pp. 219–250). New York: Wiley.

Singer, M. (1977). The experience of emptiness in narcissistic and borderline states: Part 2. The struggle for a sense of self and the potential for suicide. *International Review of Psycho-Analysis, 4,* 47–79.

Skaggs, E. B. (1933). The meaning of the term "abnormality" in psychology. *Journal of Abnormal and Social Psychology, 28,* 113–118.

Skinner, B. F. (1938). *The behavior of organisms; an experimental analysis.* New York: Appleton-Century.

Skinner, B. F. (1948). Superstition in the pigeon. *Journal of Experimental Psychology, 38,* 168–172.

Skinner, B. F. (1948). *Walden two.* New York: Macmillan.

Skinner, B. F. (1957). *Verbal behavior.* New York: Appleton-Century-Crofts.

Skinner, B. F. (1958). Reinforcement today. *American Psychologist, 13,* 94–99.

Skinner, B. F. (1959). *Cumulative record.* New York: Appleton-Century-Crofts.

Skinner, B. F. (1960). Pigeons in a pelican. *American Psychologist, 15,* 28–37.

Skinner, B. F. (1967). B. F. Skinner. In E. G. Boring & G. Lindzey (Eds.), *A history of psychology in autobiography* (Vol. 5, pp. 387–413). New York: Appleton-Century-Crofts.

Skinner, B. F. (1971). *Beyond freedom and dignity.* New York: Knopf.

Skinner, B. F. (1974). *About behaviorism.* New York: Random House.

Skinner, B. F. (1976). *Particulars of my life.* New York: Knopf.

Skinner, B. F. (1979). *The shaping of a behaviorist: Part two of an autobiography.* New York: Knopf.

Skinner, B. F. (1983). *A matter of consequences: Part three of an autobiography.* New York: Knopf.

Skinner, B. F., & Ferster, C. B. (1957). *Schedules of reinforcement.* New York: Appleton-Century-Crofts.

Smith, M. B. (1959). Research strategies toward a conception of positive mental health. *American Psychologist, 14,* 673–681.

Snyder, C. R., & Lopez, S. (2002). *Handbook of positive psychology.* New York: Oxford University Press.

Sofka, M. D. (1999). The UFOs of October. Retrieved July 11, 2004, from www.rpi.edu/~sofkam/papers/ufo talk.html

Spence, D. P. (1982). *Narrative truth and historical truth.* New York: W. W. Norton.

Spence, K. W., Bergmann, G., & Lippitt, R. (1950). A study of simple learning under irrelevant motivational-reward conditions. *Journal of Experimental Psychology, 40,* 539–551.

Spence, K. W., & Lippitt, R. (1946). An experimental test of the sign-gestalt theory of trial and error learning. *Journal of Experimental Psychology, 36,* 491–502.

Spencer, W. A., Thompson, R. F., & Nielson, D. R., Jr. (1966). Decrement of ventral root electrotonus and intracellularly recorded PSPs produced by iterated cutaneous afferent volleys. *Journal of Neurophysiology, 29,* 253–273.

Spinoza, B. (1955). *Ethics.* (R. H. M. Elwes, Trans.). New York: Dover. (Original work published in 1677.)

Spitzer, R. L., & Wilson, P. T (1975). Nosology and the official psychiatric nomenclature. In A. Freedman, H. Kaplan, & B. Sadock (Eds.), *Comprehensive textbook of psychiatry* (pp. 826–845). Baltimore: Williams and Wilkins.

Squire, L. R. (1986). Mechanisms of memory. *Science, 232,* 1612–1619.

Squire, L. R., Knowlton, B., & Musen, G. (1993). The structure and organization of memory. *Annual Review of Psychology, 44,* 453–495.

Squire, L. R., & Zola-Morgan, S. (1996). Structure and function of declarative and nondeclarative memory systems. *Proceedings of the National Academy of Sciences USA, 93,* 13515–13522.

Steele, C. M. (1997). A threat in the air: How stereotypes shape intellectual identity and performance. *American Psychologist, 52,* 613–629.

Steele, C. M. (1999). Thin ice: "Stereotype threat" and black college students. *Atlantic Monthly, 284,* 44–47, 50–54.

Steele, C. M. & Aronson, J. (1995). Stereotype vulnerability and intellectual test performance of African Americans. *Journal of Personality. & Social Psychology, 69,* 797–811.

Steinbuch, J. G. (1811). *Beiträge zur Physiologie der Sinne.* [Contributions to the physiology of the senses.] Nürnberg, Germany: J. L. Schrag.

Stephenson, W. (1953). *The study of behavior: Q-technique and its methodology.* Chicago: University of Chicago Press.

Stepien, L., & Sierpinski, S. (1960). The effect of focal lesions of the brain upon auditory and visual recent memory in man. *Journal of Neurology, Neurosurgery and Psychiatry, 23,* 334–340.

Sternberg, S. (1966). High-speed scanning in human memory. *Science, 153,* 652–654.

Stevens, K. A. (1978). Computation of locally parallel structure. *Biological Cybernetics, 29,* 19–28.

Stevens, S. S. (1946). On the theory of scales of measurement. *Science, 103,* 677–680.

Stone, J., Lynch, C. I., Sjomeling, M., & Darley, J. M. (1999). Stereotype threat effects on black and white athletic performance. *Journal of Personality & Social Psychology, 77,* 1213–1227.

Sullivan, H. S. (1953). *The interpersonal theory of psychiatry.* New York: Norton.

Sullivan, H. S. (1954). *The psychiatric interview.* New York: Norton.

Sulloway, F. J. (1983). *Freud: Biologist of the mind.* New York: Basic Books.

Szasz, T. S. (1956). Malingering: "Diagnosis" or social condemnation? *AMA Archives of Neurology and Psychiatry, 76,* 432–443.

Szasz, T. S. (1957a). On the theory of psychoanalytic treatment. *International Journal of Psycho-Analysis, 38,* 166–182.

Szasz, T. S. (1957b). *Pain and pleasure: A study of bodily feelings.* New York: Basic Books.

Szasz, T. S. (1957c). The problem of psychiatric nosology: A contribution to a situational analysis of psychiatric operation. *American Journal of Psychiatry, 114,* 405–413.

Szasz, T. S. (1958). Psychiatry, ethics, and the criminal law. *Columbia Law Review, 58,* 183–198.

Szasz, T. S. (1960a). Moral conflict and psychiatry. *Yale Review, 49,* 555–556.

Szasz, T. S. (1960b). The myth of mental illness. *American Psychologist, 15,* 113–118.

Szasz, T. S. (1961). *The myth of mental illness: Foundations of a theory of personal conduct.* New York: Harper & Row.

Szasz, T. S. (1963). *Law, liberty, and psychiatry: An inquiry into the social uses of mental health practices.* New York: Macmillan.

Szasz, T. S. (1965). *Psychiatric justice.* New York: Macmillan.

Szasz, T. S. (1970). *Ideology and insanity: Essays on the psychiatric dehumanization of man.* Garden City, NY: Anchor.

Szasz, T. S. (1974, December). Against behaviorism. (A review of B. F. Skinner's *About Behaviorism*). *Libertarian Review, 111,* 6–7.

Tenenbaum, J. M., & Barrow, H. G. (1976). Experiments in interpretation-guided segmentation (Tech. Note No. 123). Stanford, CA: Stanford Research Institute.

Thompson, R. F., & Krupa, O. J. (1994). Organization of memory traces in the mammalian brain. *Annual Review of Neuroscience, 17,* 519–550.

Thompson, R. F., & Spencer, W. A. (1966). Habituation: A model phenomenon for the study of neuronal substrates of behavior. *Psychological Review, 173,* 16–43.

Thorndike, E. L. (1898). *Animal intelligence: an experimental study of the associative processes in animals.* New York: Columbia University.

Thorndike, E. L. (1911). *Animal intelligence: Experimental studies.* New York: Macmillan.

Thorpe, W. H. (1967). Animal vocalization and communication. In C. H. Millikan & F. L. Darley (Eds.), *Brain mechanisms underlying speech and language* (pp. 2–12). New York: Grune and Stratton.

Tinbergen, N. (1951). *The study of instinct.* Oxford: Oxford University Press.

Titchener, E. B. (1896). *An outline of psychology.* New York: Macmillan.

Tolman, E. C. (1948). Cognitive maps in rats and men. *Psychological Review, 55,* 189–208.

Tolman, E. C. (1949). There is more than one kind of learning. *Psychological Review, 56,* 144–156.

Tolman, E. C. (1951). *Collected papers in psychology.* Berkeley, CA: University of California Press.

Tolman, E. C. (1952). Edward Chace Tolman. In E. G. Boring, H. S. Langfeld, H. Werner, & R. M. Yerkes (Eds.), *A history of psychology in autobiography* (Vol. 4, pp. 323–339). Worcester, MA: Clark University Press.

Tolman, E. C. (1967). *Purposive behavior in animals and men.* New York: Appleton-Century-Crofts. (Original work published in 1932.)

Tolman, E. C., & Honzik, C. H. (1930). Introduction and removal of reward, and maze performance in rats. *University of California Publications in Psychology, 4,* 227–272.

Tolman, E. C., Ritchie, B. F., & Kalish, D. (1946). Studies in spatial learning: Part 1. Orientation and the short-cut. *Journal of Experimental Psychology, 36,* 13–24.

Troland, L. T., (1929–1932). *The principles of psychophysiology* (Vols. 1–3). New York: Van Nostrand.

Tulving, E., & Schacter, D. L. (1990). Priming and human memory systems. *Science, 247,* 301–306.

Turing, A. M. (1937). On computable numbers, with an application to the Entscheidungsproblem. *Proceedings of the London Mathematical Society, Series 2, 42,* 230–265.

Turing, A. M. (1950). Computing machinery and intelligence. *Mind, 59,* 433–460.

U. S. Department of Health and Human Services. (1995). *Basic behavioral science research for mental health: A report of the National Advisory Mental Health Council.* Rockville, MD: Author.

U. S. Department of Health and Human Services. (1998). *Suicide: A report of the surgeon general.* Rockville, MD: Author

U. S. Department of Health and Human Services (1999). *Mental health: A report of the surgeon general.* Rockville, MD: Author.

Ullman, S. (1979*a*). The interpretation of structure from motion. *Proceedings of the Royal Society of London B, 203,* 405–426.

Ullman, S. (1979*b*). *The interpretation of visual motion.* Cambridge, MA: MIT Press.

Valenstein, E. S. (1998). *Blaming the brain: The truth about drugs and mental health.* New York: Free Press.

Van Loon, F. H. G. (1927). Amok and lâttah. *Journal of Abnormal and Social Psychology, 21,* 434–444.

von Neumann, J. (1958). *The computer and the brain.* New Haven, CT: Yale University Press.

Waitz, T. (1849). *Lehrbuch der Psychologie als Naturwissenschaft.* Braunschweig, Germany: F. Vieweg.

Walk, R. D., Shepherd, J., & Miller, D. R. (1988). Attention and the depth perception of kittens. *Bulletin of the Psychonomic Society, 26,* 248–251.

Wallach, H., & O'Connell, D. N. (1953). The kinetic depth effect. *Journal of Experimental Psychology, 45,* 205–217.

Warrington, E., & Weiskrantz, L. (1968). New method of testing long-term retention with special reference to amnesic patients. *Nature, 217,* 972–974.

Watson, D., & Tellegen, A. (1985). Toward a consensual structure of mood. *Psychological Bulletin, 98,* 219–235.

Watson, J. B. (1913). Psychology as the behaviorist views it. *Psychological Review, 20,* 158–177.

Watson, J. B. (1919). *Psychology from the standpoint of a behaviorist.* Philadelphia: J. B. Lippincott.

Watson, J. B. (1925). *Behaviorism.* New York: People's Institute.

Watson, J. B. (1926). What the nursery has to say about instincts. In M. Bentley, K. Dunlap, W. S. Hunter, K. Koffka, W. Köhler, W. McDougall, et al. (Eds.), *Psychologies of 1925: Powell lectures in psychological theory* (pp. 1–35). Worcester, MA: Clark University.

Watson, J. B. (July, 1927). The behaviorist looks at instincts. *Harper's Monthly Magazine, 155,* 228–235.

Watson, J. B. (1928a, October). What about your child? *Cosmopolitan,* 76–77, 108, 110, 112.

Watson, J. B. (1928b). *Psychological care of infant and child.* New York: W. W. Norton.

Watson, J. B., & McDougall, W. (1928). *The battle of behaviorism: An exposition and an exposure.* London: Kegan Paul, Trench, Trubner.

Watson, J. B., & Rayner, R. (1920). Conditioned emotional reactions. *Journal of Experimental Psychology, 3,* 1–14.

Wegrocki, H. J. (1939). A critique of cultural and statistical concepts of abnormality. *Journal of Abnormal and Social Psychology, 34,* 166–178.

Weiskrantz, L. (1990). Some contributions of neuropsychology of vision and memory to the problem of consciousness. In A. Marcel & E. Bisiach (Eds.), *Consciousness and contemporary science* (pp. 183–197). New York: Oxford University Press.

Wellman, B. L. (1938). Our changing concept of intelligence. *Journal of Consulting Psychology, 2,* 97–107.

Wertheimer, M. (1961). Experimental studies of the seeing of motion (D. Runes & T. Shipley, Trans.). In T. Shipley (Ed.), *Classics in psychology* (pp. 1031–1089). New York: Philosophical Library. (Original work published in 1912.)

Wertheimer, M. (1938). Principles of perceptual organizations. In W. D. Ellis (Ed. and Trans.), *Source book of gestalt psychology* (pp. 71–88). New York: Routledge & Kegan Paul. (Original work published in 1923.)

Wertheimer, M. (1945). *Productive thinking.* New York: Harper.

Wertheimer, M. (1991). Max Wertheimer: Modern cognitive psychology and the gestalt problem. In G. A. Kimble, M. Wertheimer, & C. L. White (Eds.), *Portraits of pioneers in psychology* (pp. 189–208). Washington, DC: American Psychological Association; Mahwah, N.J.: Lawrence Erlbaum.

Westerhouse, J. (2000). Famed psychiatrist Samuel Guze dies. Retrieved November 7, 2005, from http://record.wustl.edu/archive/2000/08-10-00/articles/guze.html

Whalen, R. E. (1961). Comparative psychology. *American Psychologist, 16,* 84.

Wheeler, W. M. (1949). An analysis of Rorschach indices of male homosexuality. *Rorschach Research Exchange & Journal of Projective Techniques, 13,* 97–126.

Wiener, D. N. (1996). *B. F. Skinner: Benign anarchist.* Boston: Allyn and Bacon.

Wiest, W. M. (1967). Recent criticisms of behaviorism and learning. *Psychological Bulletin, 67,* 214–225.

Wilcoxon, H. C., Dragoin, W. B., & Kral, P. A. (1971). Illness-induced aversions in rats and quails: Relative salience of visual and gustatory cues. *Science, 17,* 826–828.

Wolfert, I. (1957, October). Keller Breland's amazing "I. Q. Zoo." *Reader's Digest,* 153–158.

Wolpe, J. (1969). *The practice of behavior therapy.* New York: Pergamon.

Wundt, W. (1862). *Beiträge zur Theorie der Sinneswahrnehmung.* [Contributions to the theory of sense perception.] Leipzig, Germany: C. F. Winter.

Wundt, W. (1897). *Outlines of psychology* (C. H. Judd, Trans.) Leipzig, Germany: Engelmann.

Wundt, W. (1900–1920). *Völkerpsychologie* (Vols. 1–10). [Folk-psychology] Leipzig, Germany: Engelmann.

Wurtz, R. H., Goldberg, M. E., and Robinson, D. L. (1980). Behavioral modulation of visual responses in the monkey: Stimulus selection for attention and movement. *Progress in Psychobiology and Physiological Psychology, 9,* 43–83.

Yin, J. C. P., Del Vecchio, M., Zhou, H., & Tully, T. (1995). CREB as a memory modulator: Induced expression of a dCREB2 activator isoform enhances long-term memory in *Drosophila. Cell, 81,* 107–115.

Yin, J. C. P., Wallach, J. S., Del Vecchio, M., Wilder, E. L., Zhuo, H., Quinn, W. G., et al. (1994). Induction of a dominant-negative CREB transgene specifically blocks long-term memory in *Drosophila. Cell, 79,* 49–58.

Young, J. Z. (1978). *Programs of the brain.* Oxford: Oxford University Press.

Young, J. Z. (1987). *Philosophy and the brain.* Oxford: Oxford University Press.

Zucker, R. S., Kennedy, D., & Selverston, A.I. (1971). Neuronal circuit mediating escape responses in crayfish. *Science, 173,* 645–650.

Index

Abduction, 416
Abel, T., 510
Abraham, Karl, 544
Abstract ideas, 351–352
Abstract space and aviation, 162–164
Aceves-Piña, E. O., 508
Action, attention for, 287
Actuality of mind, 40–41
Adaptation-level effects, 501
Adler, A., 589
Aether, 152
Affection, 27, 316
   as a conscious element, 232–235
   definition of, 232–233
   investigating, 234–235
   sensation and, 233–234
Afferent nerves, 449 (box)
After-images, visual, 142–143
Agassiz, Louis, 22
Aggregates, sensation, 343–344
Ainsworth, M. D., 564 (box)
Akinetic mutism, 292
Alberini, C. M., 510
Alexia, 290
Alhacen, 88, 92
Al-Haytham, Ibn, 88, 92
Alimentation, 27, 228, 230–231
Al-Kindi, 89
Alkon, O. L., 503
Allman, J. M., 289
Allport, D. A., 287, 292
Allport, Floyd, 454
Allport, Gordon, 559, 602
Amativeness, 27
American Psychiatric Association, 516, 536, 559, 560, 608
Amnesia, 499
Analogy, conclusions from, 140–141
Analytical Engine, 54–55

Analyzing mechanisms, 419
Anatomy of Melancholy, 525 (box)
Anderson, J. R., 283
Andrews, F. M., 605
Angell, Frank, 219–220
Angst, J., 604
Animal Behavior Enterprises, 392
Animal Intelligence, The, 447
Animals
   avoidance reactions, 477–478
   clicker training, 392
   diversity in birth equipment of, 383
   domesticated, 326–335
   experience and, 347–348
   latent learning experiments with, 472–476
   learning by, 447–448
   nondeclarative memory systems, 503–511
   operant conditioning of, 391–392
   reflexes, 452–453
   spatial orientation, 478–480, 481 (figure)
   stimulus-response connections, 470–471
   study of behavior in, 391–399
   See also Birds
Animal spirits, 9–10, 12–13, 18
Aplysia, 503–511
Apoptosis, 511
Appeal of PDP, The, 205
Apperception, 43, 145–147
Aquinas, Thomas, 399 (box)
Arbit, J., 496
Arctic hysteria, 535
"Are we automata?", 4
Aristotle, 3, 92, 127 (box), 129, 232 (box), 399 (box)
   on relation of mind and thoughts, 309
Aronson, J., 465 (box)
Articular sensations, 228, 230–231
Artificial grammar, 501, 502
Artificial horizons, 162

Artificial intelligence (AI), 65
  capabilities of, 180–181
  rules and symbols in, 76–78
  strong and weak, 75
  thought and, 75–84
  Turing test and, 77, 80
  various replies and, 78–79
  See also Computing machinery; Intelligence
Aspiration, level of, 456
Assayer, The, 92
Associationist theory, 418n8
Association of ideas, 43, 276–277
Astronomy, 157
Asylums, 515, 578
Atherosclerosis, coronary, 594
Atoms in the void, 68
Attention
  for action, 287
  direct, 286
  visual spatial, 286–287
Attributes of sensation, 223–224
Audobon, John James, 325
Ausubel, D. P., 587
Autocracy, 459–461
  children and, 462–464
Aversive control, 266
Aversive stimuli, 273–274
Aviation
  abstract space and, 162–164
  psychology, 162
Avoidance reactions, 477–478
Awareness, 241 (box)
Axioms, mathematics, 117–118

Babbage, Charles, 54 (box)
Babbitt, 574 (box)
Bacon, Francis, 5, 414
Bacskai, B. J., 510
Bailey, Bob, 392
Bailey, C. H., 505 (figure), 510
Baldwin, J. M., 387–388
Bales, R. F., 460 (box)
Bao, J.-X., 507
Barker, R., 458 (box)
Bayer, R., 560
Beach, F. A., 393, 576
Beare, J. I., 87–88
Beck, Aaron, 516
Beers, Clifford, 515

Behavior
  animal, 391–399
  aversive control and, 266
  brain organization and, 483–491
  culture and, 534–542
  deprivation and, 266–267
  early training and, 379–381
  heredity and environment in, 295–297,
    592–593
  idea and will in, 267–269
  informality of, 56–57
  instinct and human, 373–383
  laboratory studies on genesis of, 383–389
  law of effect and, 264–265
  life space and, 454–455
  mental illness and, 520–521, 527–530
  motivation theory of, 602–603
  the nervous system and, 494–495
  purpose and intention affecting, 269–270
  reinforcement, 263–265, 271–272
  slanting and, 374
  societal views of normal and abnormal,
    513–514, 534–542
  sociology and, 456–457
  wants, needs, desires and wishes and,
    265–267
  See also Operant conditioning; Social
    behavior
Behaviorism, 67, 204, 220, 261–262, 408
  (box), 468–469
Behaviorism, 372
Behavior of Organisms, The, 392
Bekhterev, V. M., 370
Benedict, R., 534, 540
Benzer, S., 503
Berger, Hans, 281, 488
Bergman, G., 477
Berkeley, George, 91, 124, 131, 138, 219, 296
  on blindness, 100–101, 106, 110
  clergy and philosophical work of, 95
  on color, 101, 105
  debate over, 94
  on language and perception, 103–104
  on touch and perception, 102, 103–105,
    106–107, 344 (box)
  on vision and distance of objects, 96–102
Bérubé, A., 559
Beyond Freedom and Dignity, 261
Binary digits, 59

Binocular cues for depth, 162
Biological Bases of Childhood Shyness, 298
Biological Basis of Learning and Individuality, The, 426
Biological evolution, 591
Biology
   memory and, 502–512
   psychiatry and, 591–600
Birds, 325–326, 327
   instincts of cuckoo, 329–331
   slave-making instinct, 331–334
   See also Animals
Birth equipment of human young, 384–388
Bischof, L. J., 572 (box)
Bisiach, E., 293
Bjork, D. W., 261
Black box, psychological, 203–205, 261
Blake, R. R., 459
Blaming the Brain, 516
Blank slate, The, 299
Blank slate theory, 106, 306, 337, 595
Bleuler, Eugen, 242 (box)
Blindness, 100–101, 106, 110, 142, 344–345
Blind spots, 142
Blodgett, Hugh Carlton, 472–473
Blood, 18
Blood letting, 518–519
Blum, H., 194
Boas, Franz, 534
Bodily self-seeking, 27
Boles, D. B., 284
Boring, E. G., 178, 219, 261
Boxer, A. M., 564 (box)
Bradburn, N. M., 605
Brain, the
   animal spirits and, 10
   blood flow in, 281
   causing minds, 70–72, 82
   of children, 59–62
   cognitive neuroscience and, 493, 494
   computer metaphors for, 204–205
   conservation of energy, 208–209
   cortical localization in, 494
   decade of, 492
   electrical activity in, 281
   function during sensation, 209–218
   genetics and development of, 591–592
   hemispheres, 443–444, 448
   imaging, 281, 283, 287–293, 590

   imitation by computing machines, 46, 59–60
   injury to, 495–498
   memory and, 19–20
   mental functions in, 279–280
   morphology, 208
   multiple memory systems in, 497–498
   neurophysiology and, 182, 446 (box), 488
   occipital area of, 289–290
   organization and behavior, 483–491
   organ of Corti, 444
   pain perception and, 69–70
   phrenology and, 279–280
   pineal gland in, 17–18, 20
   protein synthesis in, 507–511
   reflexes and, 446–447
   synapses, 470, 502–503, 506–507, 510–511
   thought processes and consciousness, 69–75
   ventricles of, 17
   See also Cognitive operations; Memory; Mental illness; Nervous system, the
Braitenberg, Valentino, 426, 484
Brambilla, Giovanni Alessandro, 523
Brazier, M. A. B., 282, 444
Breland, Keller, 296, 391–399
Breland, Marian, 391–399
Breuer, Josef, 237, 514, 515
Brightness of light, 228–229
Brim, O. G., 583 (box)
Broadhead, W. E., 615
Broca, Paul, 205, 280, 444, 495
Brown, J., 604
Bruce, M. L., 615
Brunelli, M., 507
Bryant, F. B., 605
Burton, Robert, 525
Bush, George H. W., 492
Byers, D., 508
Byrne, J. H., 508
Byron, Augusta Ada, 54–55

Caius, 154
Campbell, D. T., 457
Campbell, Macfie, 536
Canonical shapes, 194, 196, 197
Capshew, J. H., 392
Carew, T. J., 503, 504 (figure), 506, 507
Carlson, E. T., 519

Carr, J., 283, 284, 285, 285 (figure), 286, 290
Carr, John, 529
Carrier, J. M., 564 (box)
"Casabianca," 61
Cassirer, Ernst, 454
Castellucci, V. F., 503, 505 (figure), 507, 508
Catecholamine Hypothesis of Affective Disorders, The, 515
Caton, Richard, 281
Cattell, James McKeen, 207
Causal activity of matter, 38
Causation
  free will and, 268–269
  law of, 159, 351–352
  mental, 68–72, 82, 83–84
Cavendish, Henry, 157 (box)
Cervantes, Miguel de, 5
Change, embodiment of, 29
Changeaux, J.-P., 592, 593, 595
Channelization, 572
Charcot, Jean, 514
Charge-coupled device (CCD) technology, 201
Charles I, King of England, 305
Charles II, King of England, 305
Chasseboeuf, Constantin François, 530 (box)
Chen, M., 505 (figure), 510
Cheselden, William, 101 (box)
Chess, S., 374
Chess-playing programs, 63 (box)
Chickens, 394–398
Children
  birth equipment of, 384–388
  brains of, 59–63
  classical conditioning of, 371–372
  democracy versus autocracy and, 462–464
  early training and behavior of, 379–381
  innate ideas in, 303
  laboratory study of, 383–389
  mental illness in, 526
  neurotic, 547–548
  origin of ideas in, 311–312
  schizophrenigenic mothers and, 594
  social climate and, 462–465
  social groups and, 466–467
Choate, L. S., 287
Choice, responsibility, and psychiatry, 585–586

Chomsky, Noam, 268
  on acquisition of knowledge of language, 415–418
  on analyzing mechanisms, 418
  on comparative ethology, 418–421
  on diversity of language, 409–412
  on evolution of human language, 403–409
  on generative grammar, 406–409
  on origin of language, 412–413
  study of children and language, 401–402
Christina of Sweden, Queen, 7
Church, 50
Churchland, P. S., 283
Circles of presentabilia, 344, 348
Circles of quality, 340
Circulatory sensations, 230–231
Clarke, E., 444
Clarke, G., 604
Classical conditioning, 263 (box), 370–371, 499
Classification of sensations, 226–228
Cleary, L. J., 507
Clicker training, 392
Clifford, H., 539
Closure, factor of, 436
Codes, internal, 283–285
Coercion, 552–554
Cognitive neuroscience, 493, 494
Cognitive operations
  acquisition of language and, 414–415
  attention for action in, 287
  brain study and, 280–281
  elementary, 284
  internal codes and, 283–285
  PET imaging of words, 287–292
  phonology and, 284–285, 290–292
  phrenology and, 279–280
  reaction time in, 284
  visual identity in, 284
  visual spatial attention in, 286–287
  word superiority effect, 286
  See also Brain, the
Cognitive psychology, 469
Cohen, A., 287
Cohen, Neil, 499
Cohen, Y., 287
Colapinto, J., 411 (box)

Collins, A. M., 207
Collins, Allan, 205
Color, 101, 105, 130, 134, 151–152
   saturated, 144
   sensations of, 229, 230 (figure)
   vagueness of, 143–144
Coltheart, M., 283, 284, 285, 285
      (figure), 286, 290
Columbia Encyclopedia, 270
Combining medium, the soul as a, 31
Comparative ethology, 418–421
Comparative psychology, 447–448
Composite sense-symbols, 147
Compton, W. M., 590
Computational approach to vision, 183–184,
      200–201
   2 1/2-D sketch, 190–192, 201
   modules of early visual processing, 187–190
   primal sketch, 184–187
Computer and the Brain, The, 4
Computing machinery
   ability to think, 75–84
   algorithms, 182–183
   beliefs, 76
   charge-coupled device (CCD), 201
   compared to children's brains, 59–62
   consciousness and, 51–52
   Copernican theory and, 50
   disabilities of, 52–54
   expectations about, 180–181
   extra-sensory perception and, 57–58
   imitation game, 46, 59–60
   informality of behavior and, 56–57
   Lady Lovelace and, 54–55
   learning machines, 58–63
   mathematical objections and, 50–51
   metaphors for the brain, 204–205
   nervous system as, 56
   question and answer method and, 46–48
   rules and symbols, 76–78
   theology and, 49
   Turing test and, 77, 80
   universal digital, 45
   various replies, 78–79
   Very-Large-Scale Integration (VLSI), 201
   See also Artificial intelligence (AI)
Concept of Mind, The, 4
Concept of the Collective Unconscious, The, 298

Conclusions
   from analogy, 140–141
   inductive, 154–155
Condillac, Etienne Bonnot de, 297, 343 (box)
Conditioned reflexes, 441–442
Conditioning. *See* Classical conditioning;
      Operant conditioning; Pavlovian
      conditioning
Conduction velocity of motor-nerve, 209–210
Cone shapes, generalized, 195–197, 200
Conrad, C., 284, 285, 285 (figure)
Consciousness
   affection and, 232–235
   computing machines and, 51–52
   dimensions of, 178
   free association and, 240 (box)
   induction and, 154–157
   in the mind-body problem, 68–75
   natural, 158–159
   possibility of, 72–75
   psychology and, 221
   pulse of, 33–34
   scientific observation and, 157–158
   sensation as an element of, 223–228
   stream of, 31, 34–35
"Consciousness explained," 4
Conservation of energy, 137, 208–209
Constancy, perceptual, 418
Construction of Reality in the Child, The, 298
Construct validity, 606
Continuity of images, 189–190
Contour generator, 198
Control, aversive, 266
Coon, D. J., 34
Cooper, Anthony Ashley, 305
Cooper, L. A., 284, 560
Coordinate systems and shapes, 195–200
Copernican theory, 5, 50
Copernicus, Nicolas, 5
Corkin, S., 497, 500
Coronary atherosclerosis, 594
Corporeal movements, 301
Corporeal structure, 324–325
Correspondence, psychophysical, 177–178
Criswell, J. H., 459
Critique of Pure Reason, 138, 297, 337
Cromwell, Oliver, 305
Cross-National Collaborative Group, 604

Crowd, The, 425
Csikszentmihalyi, Mihaly, 603
Cuckoo birds, 329–331
Culture and behavior, 534–542
Current Concepts of Positive Mental Health, 602
Cusac, A.-M., 559, 561 (box)
Cushman, P., 607
Cutaneous sensations, 227
Cuvier, Frederick, 323
Czaplicka, M. A., 535

Damasio, A. R., 290, 292
Damasio, H., 290
Dammann, E. J., 587
Darley, J. M., 465 (box)
Darwin, Charles, 22, 296, 381
  on domesticated animals and heredity, 326–335
  on instinct, 323–326
  natural selection theory, 323–335
  objections to, 334–335
  study by, 320–322
Darwin, Erasmus, 320
Darwin, Robert, 320
Davis, G. W., 508, 509, 510
Davis, W. J., 503
Davis, W. W., 611
Death, 9
  instinct, 368
Declarative memory systems, 499–502
De corpore, 3
Degenaar, M. J. L., 101 (box)
De la Mettrie, Julien, 3
Delay conditioning, 501
Delayed matching to sample, 497
Delayed paired comparison, 496
Delusion of persecution, 538
Delusion of reference, 537
Delusions, 537–538
Dembo, T., 458 (box)
D'Emilio, J., 559
Democracy, 459–461, 466
  children and, 462–464
Democritus, 129
Dennett, D. C., 268
Depression: Clinical, Experimental, and Theoretical Aspects, 516

Depression, major
  absence of mental health and, 605–607
  diagnosis of, 607–609
  etiology of, 604–605
  languishing and, 614–615, 616 (table)
  methods of measuring, 609–610
  prevalence of, 610–611
  psychosocial functioning and impairment due to, 612–613
Deprivation, 266–267
Depth, binocular and monocular cues for, 162
Depth psychology, 534
DeRenzi, E., 286
Descartes, René, 2, 3, 5–6, 39 (box), 67, 124, 125, 126, 127
  on innate ideas, 300–303
  on the mind-body connection, 6–20, 130–131
  on reflex, 445
  on the soul, 12–20
  on speech, 403 (box)
  on vision, 90, 138
"Descartes' error," 4
Descending influence, 188
Destiny, factor of uniform, 434
Dewey, John, 425
Dewhurst, K., 444
Diagnostic and Statistical Manual of Mental Disorders, 516, 545 (box), 559–560, 590, 608
Diathesis, 530, 593
Dickens, Charles, 52
Dictates, inner, 546–547, 549–551
Diener, H. C., 293, 605
Digestion, 441–442
Dioptric: Optics, 11, 301, 302 (box)
Direct attention, 286
Discontinuity, surface, 198
Discourse on Metaphysics, 3, 42 (box)
Discourse on the Method of Rightly Conducting the Reason and Seeking for Truth in the Sciences, 6, 11
Discovery of the Unconscious, The, 516
Discrete-state machines, 55 (box), 56
Disease and sensations, 121
Dishabituation, 499
Disposition of the eyes, 98

Distance
   cues as stimulation gradients, 174–176
   texture in, 169–174
   visual perception and, 96–102, 115–116
Disturbance
   functional, 239
   in reproduction, 242
Divided Self, The, 578
Doctrine of past experience, 436–438
Domesticated animals, 326–335
Donders, F. C., 206–207, 281, 284
      (box), 289n1
   on brain function during sensation,
      209–218
   on morphology, 208
   on stimulation of the ear by sound, 212–218
Double images, 142
Drachman, D. A., 496
Drosophila, 503–511
Dualism, 1–2, 403, 490
Du Bois-Reymond, Émile, 36, 209
Duncan, J., 287, 292
Duncker, Karl, 428
Dunlap, Knight, 559
Dusser de Barenne, Joannes Gregarius, 488
Dymond, R. F., 556
Dyson, Freeman, 76
Dysthymia, 611

Early, T. S., 294
Ears
   hearing and, 102–103, 227
   otolithic organ, 451
   stimulation by sound, 212–218
   See also Sound
Ebbinghaus, Hermann, 36, 205
*Ecological Approach to Perceptual Learning
      and Development, An,* 93
*Ecological Approach to Visual Perception,
      The,* 93
Ecology, 593
Edelman, G. M., 592
Effect, law of, 264–265, 447–448
Effects of Psychotherapy, The, 515–516
Efferent nerves, 449
Ego
   Freud on, 363–367, 550
   pure, 24 (box), 29

Ehrenfels, Christian von, 427, 457
Einstein, Albert, 38 (box)
Élan vital, 72
Electroencephalography, 281
Elementary Perceiver and Memorizer
      (EPAM), 251
Elementary sensations, 231–232
Elements of Physiology, 92, 339
Elements of Psychophysics, 92
Elizabeth I, Queen of England, 304
Elizabeth II, Queen of England, 304
Elizabeth of Bohemia, Princess, 6
Ellenberger, Henri, 516
Embodiment of change, 29
Emotions
   affection, 27, 232–235, 316
   bodily changes and, 275–276
   guilt, 524
   hate, 366–367
   love, 362–368, 495
   malevolent, 121
   mental illness and, 522–524
   normal versus abnormal, 537
   self-appreciation, 26–27
   sensations and, 119–124
   spontaneity of, 554–555
   well-being and, 605–607
Empedocles, 1
Empirical self, 24–25
Empiricism, 295
Encyclopaedia Britannica, 59
Energy
   conservation of, 137, 208–209
   matter and, 38–39
England, 304–305
Enquiry Concerning Human Understanding, 297
Environment and behavior, 295–297,
      592–593
Epicurus, 3, 92
Epidemiology, 613
Erber, J., 503
Errors and computing machines, 53–54
Essay Concerning Human Understanding, 305
Essay on Mind, 484
*Essays on the Active Powers of the Human
      Mind,* 113
Essays on the Intellectual Powers of Man, 113
Essay Towards a New Theory of Vision, An, 94

Essen, D. C. van, 289
Estes, William, 391
Ether, 152, 222 (box)
Ethics, 3, 42 (box)
Ethics in psychiatry, 582–585
Ethology, 393, 404, 534, 593
   comparative, 418–421
Etiology of mental illness, 604–605
Eugenics, 375, 376, 378
Eveland, D. C., 284
Everett, D. L., 411 (box)
Evidence
   of existence, 6
   statistical, 57 (box)
Excitatory reflexes, 449
Exhibitionism, 362
Existence, evidence of, 6
Exner, J. E., 564 (box)
Experience
   doctrine of past, 436–438
   instinct and, 357–358
   intuition and, 343–345
   knowledge and, 337–338, 349–350
   memory and, 346
   mind-body relation and, 40–43
Experimentation, scientific, 157–158,
   223–224
   avoidance reactions, 477–478
   latent learning, 472–476
   memory, 495–497
   spatial orientation, 478–480, 481 (figure)
Extinction, behavior, 271–272
Extirpation, 443
Extra-sensory perception, 57–58
Eyes, 20
   disposition of, 98
   distance of objects and perception by,
     96–100
   examination, 137
   floaters in, 141
   fundus, 140
   impressions made on, 139–140
   luminous dust, 143
   luminous phenomenon and, 159
   physiology, 87–90, 139–143, 152–154,
     346–347
   retina, 89–90, 96
   stereopsis, 188–189
   See also Vision

Eysenck, Hans, 515–516, 571
Eysenck, S., 571
Eysenck Personality Inventory, 571

Factor analysis, 606
Factor of closure, 436
Factor of proximity, 432–434
Factor of similarity, 432–433
Factor of the "good curve," 436
Factor of uniform destiny, 434
Faculty psychology, 378, 522 (box)
Farah, M. J., 293
Fava, G. A., 615
Fechner, Gustav T., 29, 36, 92, 356 (box)
Feelings. *See* Emotions
Feigenbaum, Edward, 244, 251 (box)
Feigl, Herbert, 490 (box)
Feminine Psychology, 544
Ferenczi, S., 364
Ferrier, David, 281, 443, 444
Ferster, C. B., 271
Fichte, Johann Gottlieb, 138, 340,
   344, 350
Field theory, 454–455, 471–472, 489
Finger, S., 282, 444
Finley, Samuel, 517
Fischer, J. F., 241 (box)
Fizeau, Armand, 157
Flavius, 154
Floaters, 141
Flourens, Pierre, 205, 280, 444, 494–495,
   522 (box)
Focused light, 165
Fodor, J. A., 67
Foley, J. P., Jr., 534, 541
Ford, C. S., 576
Fortune, R. F., 535
Foucault, Jean, 157
Fox, Peter T., 204, 282
   on attention for action, 287
   on internal codes, 283–285
   on PET imaging of words, 287–292
   on visual spatial attention, 286–287
Fredrickson, B. L., 465 (box)
Free association, 240 (box)
Freedman, M., 571
Freedom and neuroses, 552–553
Free will, 23, 268–269
Fresco/mosaic metaphor, 225–226

Freud, Sigmund, 204, 296, 425, 484, 485, 514, 515, 544, 584 (box), 589
  on ego, 363–367, 550
  influence of, 237–238
  on instinct, 353–368, 368
  on neuroses, 545 (box), 549
  on objects of instinct, 358–359
  patients treated by, 353
  on physiology and instinct, 355–357
  psychoanalysis by, 239–243
  on repression, 367
  on satisfaction and instinct, 357–358
  on sexuality, 359–368
Friedrich, F. J., 286, 287, 293
Frisch, Karl von, 419 (box), 512, 607
Fritsch, Gustav, 281, 444
Fromm, Erich, 545
Frost, W. N., 507
Fruit flies, 503–511
Fuller, J. L., 374
Functional disturbance, 239
Functionalism, 67
Functional magnetic resonance imaging, 281
Fundamental laws of psychical phenomena, 44
Fundus, eye, 140
Fusion of distinct mental states, 30–31, 43

Galanter, E., 269
Galen, 89
Galileo Galilei, 5, 6, 38, 49, 91, 92
Gall, Franz Joseph, 279–280, 378 (box), 494, 522 (box)
Galton, Francis, 297
Gambling, 270, 272, 529
Ganzfeld, 167 (box)
Garcia, J., 399 (box)
Garnets, L. D., 564 (box)
Gazzaniga, M. S., 293
Gelperin, A., 503
Gender and mental illness, 526–527
Generalized cone shapes, 195–197, 200
General Problem Solver (GPS), 251
Generative grammar, 406–409
Generator, contour, 198
Genetics. See Heredity
Genome, human, 592
Genotypes, 592
Gentry, Evelyn. See Hooker, Evelyn

Geometry, 345–346
Germ plasm, 376–377
Gestalt psychology, 427–428, 454, 457, 468–469
Gestalt Psychology, 428
Gestural systems, 406
Gibson, Eleanor J., 92, 93, 298
Gibson, James J., 91, 93, 429 (box)
  on abstract space and aviation, 162–164
  compared to Helmholtz, 161
  on cues for distance, 174–176
  on ordinal stimulation, 165–168
  on psychophysical correspondence, 177–178
  on stimulus correlates, 164–165
  on texture, 169–174
Gillette, R., 503
Gladis, M. M., 615
Glanzman, D. L., 507, 510
Glines, C. V., 269
God, 118–119
  as Author of our being, 317
  existence of, 74
  innate ideas about, 302–303
Goelet, P., 510
Goethe, Johann Wolfgang von, 350
Goffman, Erving, 515, 578, 589
Goldberg, M. E., 286
Goldman-Rakic, P. S., 283, 286
Goltz, F., 444
Gonzales, L., 604
"Good curve," factor of the, 436
Gordian knot, 551
Gould, John, 330
Gould, Stephen Jay, 299
GPS, a Program That Simulates Human Thought, 205
Gradients
  concept of, 176
  cues for distance as stimulation, 174–176
  retinal, 169–174
Grammar, 406–412
Greenberg, P. E., 604
Greeno, J. G., 247 (box)
Gregory, R. L., 101 (box)
Grey-level intensity array, 184
Grimson, W. E. L., 201
Group for the Advancement of Psychiatry, 561
Grouping of facts, 38
Groups, social, 457–459, 466–467

Grunbaum, A., 598
Grundriss der Psychologie, 220
Grundzüge der physiologischen Psychologie, 220
Guilt, 524
Guttman, Norman, 391
Guze, Samuel, 514, 590
    on biology and psychiatry, 591–600
    on the blank slate theory, 595
    on psychopathology, 594–595
    on psychotherapy, 597–599

Habituation, 499, 504 (figure)
Hafter, E., 472 (box)
Haggerty, R. J., 604
Haglin, R. P., 560
Halpern, Diane, 298
Handbook of Positive Psychology, 516
Handedness, 387–389
Harris, B., 371
Harris, James, 407 (box)
Hartline, Haldan, 92
Hartline, Keefer, 512
Hartree, D. R., 54
Harvey, William (box), 18
Hate, 366–367
Hawkins, Robert, 426, 484, 506, 507
Hay, Henry, 561 (box)
Headey, B. W., 605, 607
Hearing. *See* Sound
Hebb, Donald O., 393, 425, 483–484, 493
    on memory, 495
    on science of modern psychology, 485–491
Heberden, William, 527
Hedge, A. N., 510
Hegarty, P., 559
Hegel, Georg, 138
Heider, F., 166
Hein, A., 344
Held, R., 344
Helmholtz, Hermann von, 91, 136–137,
    162, 206, 296
    on apperception, 145–147
    on color, 143–144, 151–152
    compared to Gibson, 161
    on compound sensations, 143–144
    on induction, 154–157
    on intuition, 340–345
    on Kant, 337–352
    on perception of light and sound, 340
    on physiology of the eye, 139–143, 346–347
    on properties of objects and perception,
        150–152
    research on nerves, 209
    on sensation of ideas and reality, 149–156
    on timbre of sound, 144–145
    on vision-perception, 138–139, 147–149,
        340–345
    on voluntary movement, 156–157
    on the will, 349–350
Helson, H., 501
Helzer, J. E., 595, 597, 598 (box)
Hemans, Felicia, 61 (box)
Hemispheres, brain, 443–444, 448
Henik, A., 287
Henslow, John Stevens, 320
Hereditary Genius, 297
Heredity
    behavior and, 295–297, 592–593
    brain development and, 591–592
    characteristics, 295–297
    instinct and, 356, 373–383
    mental illness and, 525–526
    natural selection and, 323–335
Hering, Ewald, 86
Hering illusion, 85 (figure), 86
Herrick, C. J., 486
Heuristic methods, 413–414, 418
Hildreth, E., 185
Hinton, Geoffrey, 205, 484
Hippocrates, 514
Hippocratic Writings, 514
Hitzig, Eduard, 281, 444
H. M. Pulham, 552
Hobbes, Thomas, 3, 5
Hoesen, G. W. van, 292
Hoffman, J. E., 287
Holism, 423–425
Hollingshead, August B., 515, 583 (box)
Holt, Henry, 23
Holt, R. R., 564 (box)
Holtzman, J. D., 293
Homogeneity of appearance, 438–439
Homogeneous total field, 167 (box)
Homosexuality
    advocacy groups, 561–562
    described as neurosis, 535, 538–539
    identification of, 565–571
    IQ and, 562–566

psychological implications of, 575–576
qualitative descriptions of, 571–575
Rorschach test of, 564–568
study of, 559–560, 561–571
TAT and MAPS tests of, 564–565, 570–575
Honzik, C. H., 474
Hooker, Evelyn, 514, 558–560
    Make-A-Picture Story test used by,
        565, 570–575
    on psychological implications of
        homosexuality, 575–576
    qualitative descriptions of homosexuals
        by, 571–575
    study methods, 561–564
    Thematic Apperception Test used by,
        564–565, 570–575
    use of the Rorschach test by, 564–568
Hope of science, 445
Horace, 352 (box)
Horn, B. K. P., 190
Horney, Karen, 514, 541, 544–545, 584
        (box), 589
    on control of neuroses, 548–549
    on freedom, 552–553
    on inner dictates, 546–547, 549–551,
        555–556
    on neuroses in children, 547–548
    on self-actualization, 546–547
    on spontaneity of feelings, 554–555
    on superego, 550
Howland, John, 384
*How Much Can We Boost IQ and Scholastic
    Achievement?,* 299
How the Mind Works, 298
How the Self Controls Its Brain, 4
How to Solve It, 428
Hubel, David H., 183, 298, 418, 484
Huber, Jean Pierre, 323, 325, 331–332
Hudson, B., 477, 478
Hull, Clark, 418 (box), 477
Human genome, 592
Human nature, instinctive, 373–383,
        381–383, 389
    See also Behavior
Humboldt, Alexander von, 528
Humboldt, Wilhelm von, 407, 410–411
Hume, David, 138, 297, 419
Humphrey, G. W., 293, 491
Hunger, 266

Huxley, Thomas Henry, 4
Hypothesis of ordinal stimulation, 165–168

Idealists, 2
Ideas
    abstract, 351–352
    association of, 43, 276–277
    blank slate theory, 106, 306
    in children, 311–312
    innate, 300–303
    methods of inquiry into, 307–308
    neither made nor destroyed by the
        mind, 313–314
    origin and source of, 308–313
    perception of, 104–105, 149–156
    of reflection, 312–313, 316–319
    of sensation, 314–315, 316–319
    simple, 313–314, 316–319
    of solidity, 315–316
    and will, 267–269
    See also Thought
Identity, personal, 32
Illuminants, 188
Illusions, visual, 85 (figure), 86
Imagination, 13–14, 15
    neuroses and, 551–552, 555
    sensations and, 123
Imaging, brain, 281, 283, 287–293, 590
Imitation game, 46, 59–60
Indeterminism, 485
Induction, 154–157, 246, 413–414, 416
    spark, 212
Infants. *See* Children
Inflection points, 198–199
Inflections, 410
Informality of behavior, 56–57
Information processing
    characterization of sequential patterns
        in, 247–250
    evidence of serial patterns and, 246–247
    examination of empirical data in, 255–258
    generating sequences in, 250–253
    human versus program performance,
        258–259
    internal codes and, 283–285
    pattern generators and, 253–255
*Inhibitory Interaction of Receptor Units in the
    Eye,* 92
Inhibitory reflexes, 449

Inhoff, A. W., 287
Injury, brain, 495–498
Innate ideas, 300–303
Innate releasing mechanism, 418
Inner dictates, 546–547, 549–551, 555–556
Instinct, 323–326
    animal behavior and, 398–399
    at birth, 383–389
    death, 368
    defining, 353–354
    in domesticated animals, 326–335
    human nature and, 373–383, 381–383, 389
    objections to theory of natural selection as
        applied to, 334–335
    objects of, 358–359
    physiology and, 355–357
    race and, 374–377
    reflexes versus, 450–453
    satisfaction and, 357–358
    sexuality and, 359–368
    slave-making, 331–334
    special, 328–334
    See also Behavior
Intelligence, 60
    acquisition of knowledge and, 415–418
    brain injury and, 495–498
    environment and, 465 (box)
    homosexuality and, 562–566
    See also Artificial intelligence (AI)
Intensity arrays, 184, 186, 188
Intentionality, 68, 69, 73, 269–270, 489
Interactionist philosophy, 490
Intermittent reinforcement, 272
Internal codes and cognition, 283–285
Interpretation of Dreams, The, 239
Introductory Lectures on Psycho-Analysis, 515
Introspection
    psychological, 223–224
    of sensation, 226
Intuition
    experience and, 343–345
    physiology and, 340–345
    theory, 139, 149
    transcendental forms of, 339, 351–352
*Investigations of the Properties and Functions
    of the Nervous System in Vertebrate
    Animals,* 205
Investigatory reflexes, 452
Ivry, R. B., 293

Jaager, J. J. de, 213
Jackson, Hughlings, 444
Jacobs, R. C., 457
Jahoda, Marie, 602, 604, 605
James, Henry, 22
James, William, 2, 4, 22–24, 36, 381 (box),
        415 (box), 445, 484
    on brain blood flow, 281
    on the mind-body connection, 161
    on the self as knower, 29–35
    on the self as known, 24–29, 32
    on stream of consciousness, 31, 34–35
    theory of emotion, 275–276
James I, King of England, 305
James II, King of England, 305
Janis, I. L., 466
Jefferson, Geoffrey, 51–52, 54
Jennings, H. H., 459
Jensen, Arthur, 299
Jones, Mary Cover, 385–386
Joos, Martin, 411
Julesz, B., 183, 502
Jung, Carl, 298, 589
Jusczyk, P. W., 484

Kaang, B.-K., 510
Kagan, Jerome, 298, 374
Kalish, D., 478–480, 481 (figure)
Kamin, Leon, 506
Kandel, Eric R., 425, 426, 484, 493, 592
    on cell biology and nondeclarative
        memory, 503, 506, 507, 508, 510
    on psychiatry, 589–590
    on reductionism, 511–512
Kant, Immanuel, 24 (box), 138, 297
    Helmholtz on, 337–352
    on intuition, 341, 352
Kariel, H. S., 466
Katz, Bernard, 512
Katz, L., 459
Katz, P. S., 507
Keele, S. W., 293
Kelley, J., 605
Kellogg, W. A., 287
Kelly, George, 572 (box), 598
Kennedy, D., 507
Kepler, Johannes, 5, 88, 89, 91, 92
Kessler, R. C., 583 (box), 604
Keyes, Corey, 514, 603

on diagnosis of mental health, 607–609
on etiology of mental illness, 604–605
on languishing, 614–615, 616 (table)
on mental health symptoms, 605–607
on methods of measuring mental
   health, 609–610
on prevalence of mental illness, 610–611
on psychosocial functioning and
   impairment due to depression,
   612–613
Keys, W., 286, 287
Kimmel, D. C., 564 (box)
Kinsey, A. C., 559
Kirchhoff, Gustav, 350–351
Kirk, S. A., 560
Kleene, 50
Kleijn, Adriaan de, 451
Kleiman, G. M., 284, 290
Klein, R. M., 484
Klopfer, Bruno, 564 (box), 565, 569 (box)
Klopfer, W. G., 564 (box)
Knight, Thomas Andrew, 326 (box)
Knower, the self as, 29–35
Knowledge
   experience and, 337–338, 349–350
   of language, 415–418
Knowlton, B., 499, 501
Known, the self as, 24–29, 32
Knox, Ronald, 94
Koelling, R. A., 399 (box)
Koffka, Kurt, 166, 427, 428, 469
Köhler, Wolfgang, 427, 428, 487
Konorski, J., 496
Kosslyn, S. M., 293
Kotovsky, Kenneth, 245
   on characterization of sequential
      patterns, 247–250
   on evidence of serial patterns, 246–247
   examination of empirical data, 255–258
   on generating sequences, 250–253
   on human versus program performance,
      258–259
   on pattern generators, 253–255
Kraepelin, Emil, 515
Krafft-Ebing, Richard von, 514, 515, 579 (box)
Krasne, F. B., 503
Krupa, O. J., 501
Kuffler, S. W., 183
Külpe, O., 220

Kupfermann, I., 503
Kutchins, H., 560

LaBerge, D., 283, 284, 285, 285 (figure), 286,
   290
Laing, R. D., 578, 589
Lamarck, Jean Baptiste, 321
Langer, Susanne, 585
Language
   children and, 401–402
   cognitive mechanism in, 414–415
   diversity of, 409–412
   evolution of human, 403–409
   general schema of, 413–415
   grammar and, 406–412
   inflections in, 410
   memory and, 239–240
   origin of, 412–413
   perception and, 103–104, 133–134
   uniqueness of human, 403 (box)
   See also Words
Languishing, 614–615, 616 (table)
Larson, J. S., 607
Lashley, Karl, 404, 425, 484
   law of mass action, 495
Latah, 536, 539
Latent learning, 472–476
Law of causation, 159, 351–352
Law of effect, 264–265, 447–448
Law of mass action, 495
Law of specific nerve energies, 209, 210, 339
Laws of organization in perceptual
   forms, 429–439
Learning
   by animals, 447–448
   by children, 60–61
   field theory and, 454–455, 471–472
   latent, 472–476
   law of effect and, 264–265, 447–448
   machines, 58–63
   nonassociative, 500, 506
   nondeclarative memory and, 503–511
   synapses and, 470
LeBon, Gustave, 425
Lectures on Clinical Psychology, 515
Lectures on the Human and Animal Mind, 36
LeDoux, J. E., 503
Lee, Y.-H., 607
Legacy of B. F. Skinner, 261

Leibniz, Gottfried Wilhelm, 3, 42 (box), 138, 297, 337
Lenneberg, Eric, 418
Letter to Herodotus, 3, 92
Lettvin, J. Y., 418
Lettvin, Jerome, 298
Level of aspiration, 456
Lévesque de Pouilly, Louis-Jean, 123 (box)
Levy, S. T., 607
Lewin, Gertrud Weiss, 455
Lewin, Kurt, 425, 454–455, 469
    on children, 462–465
    on democracy versus autocracy,
        459–464, 466
    on gestalt psychology, 457
    on levels of aspiration, 456
    on the Moreno test, 459–460
    on social groups, 457–459
    social science and society, 465–467
Lewinsohn, P. M., 604
Lewis, J., 284, 285, 285 (figure)
Lewis, Sinclair, 574 (box)
Lewontin, Richard, 299
Libido, 359–360
Licthman, J. W., 593, 595
Life space, 454–455
Light
    brightness of, 228–229
    focused, 165
    nerve reaction to, 340
Linear perspective, 176
Linguistic competence, 407
Lippitt, R., 458, 459–460, 461, 463, 475, 477
Local signs, 346
Locke, John, 124, 125, 127, 138, 219, 276
        (box), 337, 339, 399 (box)
    blank slate theory, 106, 306, 337
    on ideas of one sense, 314–315
    method of inquiry b y, 307–308
    on origin and source of ideas, 308–313
    political turmoil and, 305
    on reflection, 309, 311–313, 316–319
    on simple ideas, 313–314, 316–319
    on solidity, 315–316
Locomotion, 461
Logic, 50–51, 62
Lopez, A. D., 604
Lopez, Shane J., 516, 604
Lorente de Nó, Rafael, 488

Lorenz, Konrad, 393, 419, 512
Lotze, R. H., 215 (box), 346
Love, 362–368, 495
Lovelace, Lady, 54–55
Luce, R. D., 207
Lucius, 154
Lucretius, 3
Luminous dust, 143
Luminous phenomenon, 159
Luzzatti, C., 293
Lyell, Charles, 320–321
Lynch, C. I., 465 (box)

Machines. *See* Computing machinery
Macmillan, F. W., 287
Madness in Society, 516
Magnus, Rudolf, 445, 450
Make-A-Picture Story (MAPS), 565,
    570–575
Man a Machine, 3
*Man Who Mistook His Wife for a Hat and
    Other Clinical Tales, The,* 583 (box)
Marcel, A. J., 287
Marcus, E., 564 (box)
Marquand, J. P., 552
Marr, David, 91, 180–181
    computational approach to vision,
        183–192, 200–201
    on later processing problems, 192–200
    on modules of early visual processing,
        187–190
    on neurophysiology, 182
    on primal sketch, 184–187
    on 3-D model representation, 194–200
    2 1/2-D sketch, 190–192
Marshall, J. C., 283, 284, 285, 285 (figure),
    286, 290
Marshall, W. H., 491
Martensen, R. L., 444
Martin, C. E., 559
Martin, K. C., 510
Mary, Queen of England, 305
Maslow, Abraham, 602–603
Mass action, law of, 495
Materialists, 2
Material me, 25
Mathematics
    axioms, 117–118
    logic and computing machines, 50–51

Mattachine Society, 561 (box)
Matter and energy, 38–39
Maturana, Humberto, 298
Mature personality, 602
Mayr, E., 591, 595
McCarthy, John, 76
McCarthy, Joseph, 469
McClelland, James, 205, 283, 286, 287, 290, 484
McCormick, D. A., 503
McCulloch, Warren, 298, 483
McDougall, William, 373
McQueen, L., 611
Mead, Margaret, 540
Mechanic, D., 605
Mechanism, 72
Meditations, 3
Memory, 19–20, 138
  conditioning and, 499–500
  declarative and nondeclarative, 499–502, 503–512
  experience and, 346
  location of stored, 494–497
  molecular biological approach to storage of, 502–503
  multiple systems of, 497–498
  phonological coding and, 290–292
  psychoanalysis and, 239–243
  sensation and, 225–226
  short- and long-term, 506–511
  suppressor genes, 510–511
  See also Brain, the
Memory (Ebbinghaus), 205
Meno, 297
Mental health
  diagnosis of, 607–609
  languishing and, 614–615, 616 (table)
  methods of measuring, 609–610
  prevalence of, 610–611
  symptoms of, 605–607
Mental illness
  behavior and, 520–521, 527–530
  choice, responsibility, and, 585–586
  clinician's role in identifying and treating, 601
  culture and, 534–542
  diagnosis of, 607–609
  disease and, 521
  emotion and, 522–524

etiology of, 604–605
  gender and, 526–527
  heredity and, 525–526
  languishing and, 614–615, 616 (table)
  methods of measuring, 609–610
  myth of, 586–587
  as a name for problems in living, 581–582
  prevalence of, 610–611
  psychosocial functioning and impairment due to, 612–613
  psychotherapy and, 597–599
  and the role of ethics in psychiatry, 582–585
  as a sign of brain disease, 579–580
  societal definitions of, 513–514
  theories on causes of, 520–527
  treatment of, 518–519, 578, 585–586
Mental states
  brain functioning in, 69–72, 82
  causation in, 68–69, 82, 83–84
  fusion of distinct, 30–31, 43
  psychology and, 221
  See also Thought
Mental traits and inheritance, 377–378
Menzel, R., 503
Mesulam, M. M., 283, 286
Metzler, J., 183
Meyer, Mortimer, 565
Miezin, F. M., 291 (figure)
Mill, James, 29, 485
Mill, John Stuart, 3, 154, 485 (box)
Miller, D. R., 344
Miller, G. A., 269
Milner, Brenda, 425, 492–498, 500
"The mind-body problem," 4
Mind-body problem, the, 1–2
  actuality of mind and, 40–41
  animal spirits and, 9–10, 12–13
  artificial intelligence and, 66
  computing machinery and, 46–63
  concept of mind in, 38–44
  consciousness in, 68–75
  Descartes on, 6–20
  ego and, 363–364
  imaginations and, 13–14, 15
  innate ideas and, 300–303
  James on, 22–35
  learning machines and, 58–63

mind-substance and, 39–40
movement and, 6–12, 20, 74
in operant behavior, 274–277
perceptions and, 13, 14–15
physical and mental abilities of man
    and, 48–58
psychology and, 221–223
psycho-physical parallelism and, 42–44
Searle on, 66–75
the self as knower and, 29–35
the self as known and, 24–29, 32
self-cause in, 70–72
the soul and, 6–20
Wundt on, 36–44
See also Thought
"Mind children: The future of robot and
    human intelligence," 4
"Minds, brains, and programs," 4
Mind-substance, 39–40
Mind that Found Itself, A, 515
Minsky, Marvin, 76, 418n8
Mintun, F. M., 289, 292
Mismeasure of Man, The, 299
Modularity, 378 (box)
Mohr, J. P., 497
Molecular biology
    memory storage and, 502–503
    nondeclarative memory and, 503–512
Molière, 5
Molyneux, William, 106
Monarchs, 304–305
Monists, 2
Monocular cues for depth, 162
Montarolo, P., 510
Monteverdi, Claudio, 5
Moravec, Hans, 80
Moreno, J. L., 459
Moreno test, 459–460
Morgan, C. T., 490
Morgan, Christiana, 564
Morphology, 208
Mortality of men, 154
Mosso, Angelo, 281
Motion parallax, 176
Motivation, theory of, 602–603
Motor nerves, 449 (box)
Mouches volantes, 141, 142
Mountcastle, V. B., 286, 592

Movement and the mind-body connection,
    6–12, 20, 74, 156–157
    conduction velocity of motor-nerve,
        209–210
    intuition in, 342
Mrazek, P. J., 604
Muenzinger, Karl, 558
Muller, Adolf, 329
Müller, Johannes, 36, 90–91, 92, 137, 138,
    139, 340
    on conduction velocity in the nerves,
        209, 210, 339
Multiple memory systems, 497–498
Munk, Hermann, 443
Murphy, G. G., 507
Murphy, Gardner, 572 (box)
Murray, C. J. L., 604
Murray, Henry, 564
Muscles, 10–12
    nerve-muscle junction, 209–210
    sensations, 228, 230–231
    stimulation and extirpation, 443
Musen, G., 499, 501
Mutism, akinetic, 292
Mystery of the Mind, The, 205

Nagel, Thomas, 426
Narcissism, 363, 366–367
National Institute of Mental Health, 615
Nativism, 295, 347–348
Natural coordinate systems, 197–200
    among birds, 325–326
Natural selection, 263, 323–326
    in domesticated animals, 326–335
    objections of theory of, 334–335
    slave-making instinct and, 331–334
    special instincts and, 328–334
Nature, laws of, 159
Neely, J. H., 287
Negative reinforcement, 273–274, 471
Nervous reflexes, 448–449
Nervous system, the
    behavior and, 494–495
    as a discrete-state machine, the, 56
    efferent and afferent nerves in, 449 (box)
    intuition and, 342
    law of specific nerve energies, 209,
        210, 339

nerve-muscle junction, 209–210
    reflexes and, 264, 445–453
    sound and, 212–218
    vision and, 90–91, 340
    See also Brain, the
"Neurology and the soul," 4
Neurophysiology, 182, 446 (box), 488
Neuroscience, cognitive, 493, 494
Neuroses, 545
    in children, 547–548
    coercion and, 552–554
    control of, 548–549
    freedom and, 552–553
    imagination and, 551–552
    inner dictates and, 546–547, 549–551,
        555–556
    Q-technique and, 556
    self-actualization and, 546–547
    spontaneity of feelings and, 554–555
Neurosis and Human Growth, 545
Newcombe, F., 283, 284, 285, 285 (figure),
    286, 290
Newell, Alan, 76, 205, 244, 251 (box)
New Essays on the Human Understanding, 297
New System of Nature, 42 (box)
New Theory of Vision, 131 (box)
Newton, Isaac, 54 (box), 157
New Ways in Psychoanalysis, 545
Nickell, J., 241 (box)
Nielson, D. R., Jr., 503
Nishihara, H. K., 191, 192 (figure), 193 (figure)
Noll, S. M., 465 (box)
Nonassociative learning, 500, 506
Nondeclarative memory systems, 499–502,
    503–512
Non-substantival words, 239
*Notes Directed Against a Certain
    Programme,* 300
Nucleotides, 592
Nye, R. D., 261

Obloquy, 27
Observation, scientific, 157–158, 225
Occipital area of brain, 289–290
O'Connell, D. N., 189
Odor. *See* Smell, sense of
Oncogenesis, 511
"On Problem Solving," 428

"On the hypothesis that animals are
    automata, and its history," 4
On the Nature of the Universe, 3
*On the Sensations of Tone as a Physiological
    Basis for a Theory of Music,* 137
On the Soul, 3, 92
Operant conditioning, 499–500
    animals and, 391–399
    association of ideas in, 276–277
    aversive stimuli and punishment in,
        273–274
    idea and will in, 267–269
    law of effect and, 264–265
    the mind in, 274–277
    purpose and intention in, 269–270
    reinforcers, 263–265, 271–272
    wants, needs, desires and wishes and,
        265–267
Ophthalmology, 206
Optics (al-Haytham), 92
Optics (Descartes), 90
Optics (Helmholtz), 347 (box)
Optics (Kepler), 92
Ordinal stimulation, 165–168
Organic sensations, 228, 230–231
Organization in perceptual forms,
    429–439
Organization of Behavior, 483, 484, 495
Organ of Corti, 444
Origin of Species, The, 322
Otolithic organ, 451
Our Inner Conflicts, 545, 556
Outer experience, 40–41, 42
Outline of Psychology, An, 220
Owen, Richard, 331

Pain, 69–70, 132–135, 231, 317–318
Papert, S., 418n8
Paradoxes in perception, 132–134
Parallelepipeds, 146
Parallelism, psycho-physical, 42–43, 487
Parallelogram of forces, 30–31
Paranoia, 536, 541
Paresis, 378
Paris, B. J., 553 (box)
Parsimonious theory, 247
Passions of the Soul, The, 7
Past experience, doctrine of, 436–438

Patterns. *See* Sequential patterns
Patterns of Sexual Behavior, 576
Pavlov, Ivan Petrovich, 370, 425, 485
    on brain hemispheres, 443–444, 448
    on comparative psychology, 447–448
    digestion research, 441–442
    on instinct, 450–453
    on nervous reflexes, 448–449
    on reflexes, 445–453
    on stimulation and extirpation, 443
Pavlovian conditioning, 263 (box), 501
Pavot, W., 605
Peirce, Charles Sanders, 415–418, 419
Penfield, Wilder, 484, 493
Perception
    of color, 101, 134, 144, 151–152
    conclusions from analogy, 140–141
    distance and, 96–102, 115–116
    experience and, 348
    extra-sensory, 57–58
    of ideas, 104–105, 149–156
    language and, 103–104, 133–134
    laws of organization in, 429–439
    mathematics axioms and, 117–118
    pain, 69–70, 132–135
    paradoxes in, 132–134
    phenomenalism and, 94
    primary and secondary qualities of
        objects and, 103–104, 109–110,
        115–116, 125–132
    scientific observation and, 157–158
    sensation and, 119–124, 134–135
    the soul and, 13, 14–15
    sound and, 102–103, 144–145
    symbolism and, 149–150
    touch and, 102, 103–105, 106–107,
        128, 344–345
    the unconscious and, 348–350
    of the vulgar, 124, 128–129, 134
    See also Space perception; Vision and
        visual processing
Perceptual constancy, 418
Peripatetic system, 125
Personal identity, 32
Personality
    mature, 602
    psychology, 598
Personal Orientation Inventory, 571

Petersen, Steven E., 204, 282
    on attention for action, 287
    on internal codes, 283–285
    on PET imaging of words, 287–292
    on visual spatial attention, 286–287
Phaedo, 24 (box), 297
Phenomenalism, 94
Phi phenomenon, 427
Phonautograph, 213
Phonology, 284–285, 290–292
Phrenology, 279–280
Physicalism, 67
Physics, 136–137
Physiology
    affection and, 235
    comparative ethology and, 418–421
    eye, 87–89, 139–143, 152–154, 346–347
    instinct and, 355–357
    intuition and, 340–345
    neuro-, 182, 446 (box), 488
    psychology and, 444–445
Piaget, Jean, 298
Picasso, 197 (figure), 198
Pick, Anne, 93
Pickwick Papers, 52
Pincus, H. A., 611
Pineal gland, 17–18, 20
Pinel, Philippe, 513, 515, 518, 524, 526, 528
Pinker, Steven, 298, 299, 407
Pinsker, H., 503
Pitts, Walter, 298, 483
Plato, 2, 3, 24 (box), 232 (box), 297
Pleasure principle, 356–357
Plosives, 215 (box)
Poggio, T., 201
Pohl seesaw, 211–212
Points, inflection, 198–199
Pollatsek, A., 283, 284, 285, 285 (figure), 286,
    287, 290, 291 (figure)
Polya, George, 428
Pomeroy, W. B., 559
Popper, Karl, 403–404
Positive psychology, 603
Positron emission tomography, 281, 283
    of words, 287–292
Posner, Michael I., 204, 282
    on attention for action, 287
    on internal codes, 283–285

on PET imaging of words, 287–292
on visual spatial attention, 286–287
Power fields, 461
Practice of Behavior Therapy, The, 516
Pratt, C. C., 487
Presentabilia, circles of, 344, 348
Pretensions, 29
Pribram, K. H., 269
Primal sketch, computational approach to
    vision, 184–187
Primary and secondary qualities of
    objects, 103–104, 109–110,
    115–116, 125–132, 150–152
Principles of Geology, 320
Principles of Gestalt Psychology, 428
Principles of Human Knowledge, 131 (box)
*Principles of Perceptual Learning and
    Development,* 92
Principles of Physics, 300
Principles of Psychology, The, 23, 36
Prisons of clay, 24 (box)
Problem of Serial Order in Behavior, The, 425
Proctor, R. W., 284
Productive Thinking, 428
Project for a Scientific Psychology, 425
Projective tests, 564
Project Pigeon, 391–392
Protein synthesis in the brain, 507–511
Proximity
    factor of, 432–434
    spatial, 434–435
Psychiatry
    biology and, 591–600
    choice, responsibility, and, 585–586
    diagnosis of mental illness, 581–582
    ethics in, 582–585
    as a medical discipline, 589–590, 595–598
    psychopathology and, 594–595
    students, 591
    use of drugs in, 597
    See also Mental illness
Psychoanalysis, 204, 221–222, 237, 239–243,
    544–545, 599
Psychological Review, 370
Psychology
    affection, 234–235
    cognitive, 469
    comparative study of, 447–448

depth, 534
faculty, 378, 522 (box)
field theory in, 454–455, 471–472
gestalt, 427–428, 454, 457, 468–469
holism versus reductionism in, 423–425
information processing approach to,
    246–260
introspection, 223–224, 226
localization of function in the brain
    and, 444–445
meaning and problem of, 221–223
organization of behavior and, 484–491
parallelism in, 42–43, 487
personality, 598, 602
positive, 603
as a science, 445
social well-being and, 606
sociology and, 456–457
Psychology: Briefer Course, 23, 445
Psychopathia sexualis, 515
Psychopathology, 594–595
Psychophysical correspondence, 177–178
Psycho-physical parallelism, 42–44
Psychophysics, 182
Psychotherapy, 597–599
Pulse of consciousness, 33–34
Punishment, 273–274
Pure ego, 24 (box), 29
Purpose and intention, 269–270
Purposive Behavior in Animals and Men, 469
Purves, D., 593, 595

Q-technique, 556
Quality, circles of, 340
Question and answer method, 46–48
Quillian, M. Ross, 205, 207
Quinn, D. M., 465 (box)
Quinn, S., 550, 553 (box)

Raccoons, 395–396
Race and instinct, 374–377
Race and Intelligence, 299
Rafal, R. D., 286, 287
Raichle, Marcus E., 204, 281, 282
    on attention for action, 287
    on internal codes, 283–285
    on PET imaging of words, 287–292
    on visual spatial attention, 286–287

Ramón y Cajal, Santiago, 502
Random-dot stereograms, 502
Raw primal sketch, 185
Rayner, Rosalie, 371, 384 (box)
Reasoning, spatial, 295
Rebellon, C., 604
Reber, A. S., 378 (box), 502
Reber, E. S., 378 (box)
*Receptive Fields of Single Neurons in the Cat's
    Striate Cortex,* 298
Redlich, Frederick C., 515, 583 (box)
Reductionism, 423–425, 511–512
Reflection as source of ideas, 309, 311–313,
    316–319
Reflex Arc Concept in Psychology, The, 425
Reflexes, 264, 445–447
    animal, 452–453
    conditioned, 441–442
    excitatory and inhibitory, 449
    versus instinct, 450–453
    investigatory, 452
    nervous, 448–449
    salivary, 453
    self-defense, 452
Regier, D. A., 604
Regius, Henricus, 300
Reich, Ferdinand, 157, 219
Reicher, G. M., 286, 290
Reid, Thomas, 91, 113–114
    on the objects of perception, 125–132
    on pain, 132–135
    on perception, 115–119
    on sensation, 119–124
Reiman, E. M., 289, 292, 294
Reinforcement, 391–392
    negative, 273–274, 471
    operant conditioning, 263–265,
        271–272
*Remarks on the Seat of the Faculty of
    Articulate Language, Followed by an
    Observation of Aphemia,* 205
Replies, various, 78–79
Repression, 367
Rescorla, Robert, 506
Respiratory sensations, 230–231
Responsibility, choice, and psychiatry,
    585–586
Restle, F., 247 (box)

Retina, 89–90, 96, 141, 215
    gradients as variables of stimulation,
        169–174
    ordinal stimulation and, 165–168
Retrieval Time From Semantic Memory, 205
Reznick, J. Steven, 298, 374
Rhine, J. B., 57 (box)
Richet, C., 446
Riddoch, M. J., 293
Rilling, M., 371n1
Ritchie, B. F., 478–480, 481 (figure)
Rivalry and conflict, self, 28–29
Roberts, T. A., 465 (box)
Robins, L. N., 604
Robinson, D. L., 286, 287
Rogers, Carl, 556
Roman Catholic Church, 5–6
Rorschach test, 564–568
Rosen, George, 516
Rosser, 50
Rousseau, Jean-Jacques, 411 (box)
Roy, Henri de, 300
Rozycki, E. G., 268
Rubins, J. L., 553 (box)
Rumelhart, David, 205, 283, 286,
    287, 290, 484
Ruse, M., 595
Rush, Benjamin, 514, 517–519
    blood letting and, 518–519
    on causes of mental illness, 520–531
    on treatment of mental illness,
        518–519, 531–532
Russell, Bertrand, 61 (box)
Russell, D. E., 556
Ryff, C. D., 583 (box), 605, 606, 607

Sacks, Oliver, 583 (box)
Sadism-masochism, 360–361
Sahley, C. J., 503, 506
Salivary reflex, 453
Sameness in the self as known and
    knower, 32–33
Samuels, S. J., 283, 284, 285, 285 (figure),
    286, 290
Sandvik, E., 605
Satisfaction and instinct, 357–358
Saussure, Ferdinand de, 417 (box)
Scapegoating, 463

Schacher, S., 510

Schacter, Daniel L., 499

Schelling, Friedrich, 138

Schildkraut, Joseph, 515

Schizophrenigenic mothers, 594

Schwartz, J. H., 507, 592

Schwartzkroin, P. A., 503

Science, hope of, 445

Scientific observation, 157–158, 225

Scopophilia, 362

Scott, Édouard-Léon, 213 (box)

Scott, J. P., 374

Scoville, W. B., 495

Searle, John, 2, 65
  on the ability of computing machines to
      think, 75–84
  on the mind-body problem, 66–75

Sechenov, Ivan Mikhailovich, 446–447

Self, the
  as knower, 29–35
  as known, 24–29, 32
  material me and, 25
  rivalry and conflict and, 28–29
  self-seeking and, 27–28
  social me and, 26
  spiritual me and, 26

Self-actualization, 546–547

Self-Analysis, 553 (box)

Self and Its Brain, The, 4

Self-appreciation, 26–27

Self-defense reflex, 452

Self-seeking, 27–28

Selverston, A. I., 507

Semantics, 82
  operations, 290

Senden, M. Von, 101 (box)

Sensation, 119–124
  affection and, 233–234
  aggregates, 343–344
  articular, 228, 230–231
  attributes of, 223–224
  brain function during, 209–218
  of brightness, 228–229
  circulatory, 230–231
  classification of, 226–228
  of color, 151–152, 229, 230 (figure)
  composite sense-symbols and, 147
  compound, 143–144

  as a conscious element, 223–228
  definition of, 223
  electromotive process of, 210–218
  elementary, 231–232
  of ideas and reality, 149–156
  ideas of, 314–315, 316–319
  introspection of, 226
  investigating, 223–228
  movement and, 156–157
  nervous system and, 339
  objects of perception and, 125–132,
      134–135
  organic, 228, 230–231
  pain, 69–70, 132–135, 231, 317–318
  -perception, 138–140, 147, 155
  quality of, 228–232, 340
  respiratory, 230–231
  sexual, 230–231
  smell, 120, 129–130, 156, 227
  as source of ideas, 309–310
  static sense, 230–231
  stimulus and, 227–228
  taste, 120, 130, 156, 227
  tendinous, 228, 230–231
  unconscious conclusions from, 140

Sense and sensibilia, 92

Sensitization, 499

Sensory nerves, 449 (box)

Sequential patterns
  characterization of, 247–250
  evidence of, 246–247
  examination of empirical data in,
      255–258
  generating, 250–253
  human versus program performance
      with, 258–259
  programs for generating, 253–255

Serial patterns, 246–247

Sex Differences in Intelligence, 298

Sexual Behavior in the Human Male, 559

Sexuality
  homo-, 535, 538–539
  instinct and, 359–368
  libido and, 359–360
  love and, 362–368
  nervous system and, 495
  sadism-masochism and, 360–361
  sensations, 230–231

Shakespeare, William, 5, 233
Shapes
    admitting 3-D model descriptions,
        194–197, 201
    natural coordinate system, 197–200
Shapiro, A., 606
Shepard, R. N., 183
Shepherd, J., 344
Sherif, M., 457
Sherrington, Charles, 446
Shmotkin, D., 605
Shneidman, Edwin, 565
Shostrom, E., 571
Sidman, M., 497
Sieroff, E., 287, 290, 291 (figure)
Sierpinski, S., 496
Sight. *See* Vision
Signalling stimuli, 453
Silhouettes, 197–198
Similarity, factor of, 432–433
Simon, Herbert, 76, 205, 244–245
    on characterization of sequential
        patterns, 247–250
    on evidence of serial patterns, 246–247
    examination of empirical data, 255–258
    on generating sequences, 250–253
    on human versus program performance,
        258–259
    on pattern generators, 253–255
Simple ideas, 313–314, 316–319
Sin, 27
Singer, M., 607
Single mental sciences, 41
Sjomeling, M., 465 (box)
Skaggs, E. B., 541–542
Skinner, B. F., 204, 261–262, 297,
        408 (box), 487
    animal behavior studies and, 391–399
    on association of ideas, 276–277
    on aversive stimuli and punishment,
        273–274
    on feelings of reinforcers, 263–265, 271–272
    on idea and will, 267–269
    on language acquisition, 417n7
    on the mind in operant behavior, 274–277
    Project Pigeon and, 391–392
    on purpose and intention, 269–270
    on wants, needs, desires and wishes,
        265–267

Skin sensations, 227
Slanting, 374
Slave-making instinct, 331–334
Smell, sense of, 120, 129–130, 156, 227
Smith, Adam, 113
Smith, Frederick, 331
Smith, M. Brewster, 604
Snails, 503–511
Snidman, Nancy, 298, 374
Snyder, C. R., 516
Social behavior
    democracy versus autocracy and, 459–464
    groups and, 457–459
    level of aspiration and, 456–457
    life space and, 454–455
    power fields and, 461
    See also Behavior
Social Class and Mental Illness, 515
Social groups, 457–459, 466–467
Social me, 26
Social self-seeking, 28
Sociology, 456–457
Socrates, 24 (box)
Sofka, M. D., 457
Solidity, 315–316
So Little Time, 552
Solpsists, 51
Soul, the
    acting on the body, 18
    animal spirits and, 12–13, 18
    as a combining medium, 31
    functions of, 8, 12–13
    imaginations and, 13–14
    memory and, 19–20
    passions of, 15–16
    perceptions and, 14–15
    the pineal gland and, 17–18
    supplying movement and heat
        to the body, 8–9, 20
    theology on, 49
    thought proceeding from, 8–9, 13, 49–50
Sound
    hearing and, 102–103, 227
    language evolution and, 404–405
    plosive, 215 (box)
    stimulation of the ear by, 212–218
    timbre of, 144–145
    vowel, 216–218
Space-apperception, 139

Space perception
    abstract space and, 162–164
    ordinal stimulation in, 165–168
    stimulus correlates, 164–165
    texture in, 169–174
Space-relations, 152–153
Spatial attention, visual, 286–287
Spatial coincidence assumption, 185, 200
Spatial orientation experiments, 478–480,
        481 (figure)
Spatial proximity, 434–435
Spatial reasoning, 295
Special instinct, 328–334
Specific Energy of the Senses, 138
Specific nerve energies, law of, 209, 210, 339
Spence, K. W., 475, 477
Spencer, Herbert, 450
Spencer, W. A., 503
Sperry, Elmer, 162 (box)
Spinoza, Baruch, 3, 42 (box)
Spiritual me, 26
Spiritual self-seeking, 28
Spitzer, R. L., 604
Spontaneity, 554–555
Spurzheim, Johann Gaspar, 279
Square, tangible, 108–109
Squire, Larry R., 294, 425, 493, 499,
        500, 501, 509
Static sense sensations, 230–231
Statistical evidence, 57 (box)
Steele, C. M., 465 (box)
Stephenson, W., 556
Stepien, L., 496
Stereopsis, 188–189
Stereoscopic views, 146–147, 162
Sternberg, S., 207
Stevens, S. S., 178
Stewart, John, 529
Stick-figure models, 194
Stimulation, ordinal, 165–168
Stimuli
    aversive, 273–274
    correlates, 164–165
    extirpation and, 443
    innate releasing mechanism, 418
    instinct and, 355–357
    principles of arranging and dividing,
        429–439
    -response connections, 470–471

sensation and, 227–228
    signalling, 453
Stoddard, L. T., 497
Stone, J., 465 (box)
Storage of memories, 494–497
Stream of consciousness, 31, 34–35
Studies on Hysteria, 515
Study of Instinct, The, 298
Stylus mazes, 497
Subjectivity of mental states, 68, 69
Sublimation, 360
Successive thinkers, 33
Sullivan, Harry Stack, 545, 584
Sulloway, F. J., 595
Sumner, R., 247 (box)
Surface discontinuity, 198
Switchboard theory, 489
Symbolism and perception, 149–150
    artificial grammar, 501, 502
Synapses, 470, 502–503, 506–507, 510–511
Syntax, 82
Syphilis, 514, 579
*System of Logic Ratiocinative and Inductive,
    A,* 3, 154
Szasz, Thomas S., 268, 514, 577–578, 589
    on choice, responsibility, and psychiatry,
        585–586
    on mental illness as a name for problems
        in living, 581–582
    on mental illness as a sign of brain disease,
        579–580
    on the myth of mental illness, 586–587

Talbot, S. A., 491
Tangible square, 108–109
Taste, sense of, 120, 130, 156, 227
Tauc, L., 503
Taylor, L., 497
Tellegen, A., 605
Tendinous sensations, 228, 230–231
Tennyson, Alfred, 233
Teuber, H.-L., 500
Texture gradients, 169–174, 175
Thematic Apperception Test (TAT), 564–565,
        570–575
Theology, 49
Theory of Agreeable Sensations, The, 123 (box)
Thomas, A., 374
Thompson, Clara, 545

Thompson, R. F., 501, 503
Thorndike, Edward L., 264–265, 447–448, 506
Thorpe, W. H., 404
Thought
  ability of computers, 75–84
  consciousness of, 68, 69
  electromotive process of, 210–218
  fusion of distinct mental states and, 30–31
  induction and, 154–156
  innate ideas and, 300–303
  intentionality of, 68, 69, 73, 489
  by machines, 48–58
  memory and, 19–20, 138
  mental causation of, 68–72, 82
  passions of the soul and, 15–16
  perceptions and, 13, 14–15
  proceeding from the soul, 8–9, 13, 49–50
  pulse of consciousness and, 33–34
  sense of personal identity and, 32
  stream of consciousness and, 31, 34–35
  subjectivity of, 68, 69
  tran, 351–352
  transcendental forms of, 339
  unity of the passing, 29–30
  See also Ideas; Mental states; Mind-body
    problem, the
Three Dialogues Between Hylas and
  Philonous, 94
3-D model representation, 194–200, 201
Timbre of sounds, 144–145
Tinbergen, Nikolaas, 298, 393, 419 (box), 512
Titchener, E. B., 204, 219–220, 429 (box), 468
  on affection as a conscious element,
    232–235
  fresco/mosaic metaphor, 225–226
  on mental process, consciousness and
    mind, 221
  on the problem of psychology, 221–223
  on quality of sensation, 228–232
  on sensation as a conscious element,
    223–228
Tolman, Edward Chace, 425, 468–469
  on avoidance reactions, 477–478
  as a cognitive behaviorist, 468–469
  on field theory, 471–472
  on latent learning, 472–476
  on spatial orientation, 478–480, 481 (figure)
  on stimulus-response connections, 470–471

Topology, 458
Touch
  intuition and, 344–345
  perception and, 102, 103–105, 106–107,
    121, 128
Transcendental forms of intuition and
  thought, 339, 351–352
Transference, 599
Treatise Concerning the Principles of Human
  Knowledge, A, 94
Treatise on Insanity, 515
Treatise on Man, 445 (box)
Treatise on Physiological Optics, 137
Treatise on the Sensations, 297
Truth, 350–351
Tulving, Endel, 499, 500
Turing, 50
Turing, Alan, 65, 77
  ability of machines to think, 48–58
  imitation game, 46
  question and answer method, 46–48
  and the Turing machine, 45
Turing test, 77, 80
Twenge, J. M., 465 (box)
2 1/2-D sketch, 190–192, 201
2001: A Space Odyssey, 180
Two Treatises of Government, 305

Ullman, S., 187, 189, 190 (figure)
Ulterior questions, 26
Unconscious, the
  awareness and, 241 (box)
  free association and, 240 (box)
  language and, 239
  perception and, 348–350
Uniform destiny, factor of, 434
Uniqueness of images, 189
Unity of the passing thought, 29–30
Universal digital computer, 45
Universal grammar, 407–408, 409
Unpardonable sin, 27
U.S. Department of Health and Human
  Services, 604, 615

Valenstein, Elliot, 516
Van Loon, F. H. G., 539
Various replies, 78–79
Vaughan, J., 287

Vehicles: Experiments in Synthetic Psychology,
   426, 484
Ventricles, brain, 17
Verbal Behavior, 408 (box)
Verbal mediation, 496
Veroff, J., 605
Very-Large-Scale Integration (VLSI), 201
*Vision: A Computational Investigation
   into the Human Representation and
   Processing of Visual Information,* 181
Vision and visual processing
   abstract space, 162–164
   after-images, 142–143
   apperception and, 145–147
   aviation and, 162–164
   blindness and, 100–101, 106, 110,
      142, 344–345
   blind spots, 142
   classification of, 227
   color and, 101, 105
   computational approach to, 183–192,
      200–201
   conclusions from analogy and, 140–141
   continuity of images and, 189–190
   depth, 162
   as digital image processing, 185–186
   distance and, 96–102, 115–116, 174–176
   distinct, 100
   double images and, 142
   eye physiology and, 87–90
   focused light and, 165
   Greek theories on, 87–88
   illusions and, 85 (figure), 86
   impressions made on the eye in, 139–140
   later processing, 192–193
   local signs and, 346
   memory and, 138
   modules of early visual processing,
      187–190
   ordinal stimulation and, 165–168
   primary and secondary qualities of
      objects and, 103–104, 109–110,
      115–116, 150–152
   quality of sensations in, 228–229, 340
   retinal gradients and, 169–174
   of shapes, 195–200
   stereopsis, 188–189
   stereoscopic views, 146–147
   stimulus correlates and, 164–165
   tangible ideas and, 108–109
   texture and, 169–174
   3-D model representation,
      194–200, 201
   touch and, 102, 103–105, 106–107
   2 1/2-D sketch, 190–192, 201
   uniqueness of images and, 189
   See also Perception
Visual Cliff, The, 298
Visual identity, 284
Visual spatial attention, 286–287
Visual word forms, 289–290
Vitalism, 72, 137, 485, 486–487
Viva voce, 51–52
Vowel-sounds, 216–218
Vulgar, the, 124, 128–129, 134

Wagner, Allan, 506
Walden Two, 261
Walk, Richard, 298, 344
Walker, J. A., 286, 293
Wallace, Alfred Russel, 321–322
Wallace, J. G., 101 (box)
Wallach, H., 189
Wants, needs, desires, and wishes,
   265–267
Warrington, E., 500
Waterman, M. B., 605
Watson, D., 605
Watson, John B., 296, 370–372, 468,
   484, 490 (box)
   on early training and behavior, 379–380
   on inheritance of mental traits, 377–378
   on instinctive human nature, 373–383,
      381–383, 389
   laboratory studies on genesis of behavior,
      383–389
   on race and instinct, 374–377
Wearing, A. J., 605
Wegrocki, Henry, 514, 533
   on cultural views of behavior, 534–542
   on delusions, 537–538
   on homosexuality, 535, 538–539
   on paranoia, 536, 541
Weiskrantz, L., 500
Wellman, B. L., 465 (box)
Wernicke, Karl, 281, 495

Wertheimer, Max, 183, 425, 427–428,
    457 (box)
  on laws of organization in perceptual
    forms, 429–439
Wertheimer, Michael, 428
Wester, K., 503
Whalen, R. E., 393
What Is it Like to Be a Bat?, 426
What the Frog's Eye Tells the Frog's Brain, 298
Wheeler, W. M., 568 (box)
White, R. K., 458, 463
Whitney, William Dwight, 410, 411
Wiener, D. N., 261
Wiesel, Torsten, 183, 298, 484
Wiest, W. M., 408n2
Will, the, 13, 349–350
  idea and, 267–269
William of Orange, 305
Williams, J. Whitridge, 384
Wilson, P. T., 604

Wishful ideas, 243
Withey, S. B., 605
Wolfert, I., 392
Wolff, Christian, 378 (box), 522 (box)
Wolpe, Joseph, 516
Words
  positron emission tomography of,
    287–292
  superiority effect, 286
  visual forms, 289–290
  See also Language
Wundt, Wilhelm, 36–37, 207, 220,
    445, 468, 534
Wurtz, R. H., 286

Yin, J. C. P., 510
Young, J. Z., 592, 595

Zola-Morgan, S., 501
Zucker, R. S., 507

About the Editors

Barbara F. Gentile (PhD, Cornell) is a social psychologist. She is Associate Professor of psychology and Chairperson of the department at Simmons College, where she teaches courses in social psychology, social psychology research, and the history of psychology. Her research interests include non-verbal behavior, survey research methodology, and the teaching of psychology.

Benjamin O. Miller (PhD, City University of New York) is an experimental psychologist. He is Associate Professor of psychology at Salem State College, where he teaches courses in perception, memory, the history of psychology, and statistics and methods. He is author of *Beyond Statistics: A Practical Guide to Data Analysis* (Allyn & Bacon, 2001). His current research focus is on basic questions about false memories, such as the conditions in which they occur and our ability to distinguish them from true memories.